Politics

The Central Texts

Theory against Fate

Roberto Mangabeira Unger

Edited and introduced by Zhiyuan Cui

V

London • New York

This edition first published by Verso 1997

First published in *Social Theory: Its Situation and Its Task* (Cambridge University Press 1987), *False Necessity: Anti Necessitarian Social Theory in the Service of Radical Democracy* (Cambridge University Press 1987), *Plasticity into Power: Comparative-Historical Studies on the Institutional Conditions of Economic and Military Success* (Cambridge University Press 1987)

Verso
UK: 6 Meard Street, London W1F 0EG
USA: 20 Jay St, Suite 1010, Brooklyn, NY 11201

Verso is the imprint of New Left Books

ISBN: 978-1-85984-131-0

British Library Cataloguing in Publication Data
A catalogue record for this book is available from the British Library

Library of Congress Cataloging-in-Publication Data
Unger, Roberto Mangabeira.
Politics : theory against fate / Roberto Mangabeira Unger : edited and introduced by Zhiyuan Cui.
p. cm.
Includes index.
ISBN 1–85984–870–2 (hbk.). — ISBN 1–85984–131–7 (pbk.)
1. Sociology. 2. Political science. 3. Philosophy. I. Title.
HM24.U5356 1997
301—dc21 96–49384
CIP

Typeset by Keystroke, Jacaranda Lodge, Wolverhampton, UK
Printed by Biddles Ltd, Guildford and King's Lynn, UK

Contents

Introduction

Zhiyuan Cui

Roberto Mangabeira Unger's project of developing a "constructive social theory" is breathtaking. He defends the "radical democratic project." But his definition of this project is much broader and more inclusive than most others: "John Stuart Mill, Alexander Herzen, Karl Marx, P.J. Proudhon and Virginia Woolf were all champions of the cause." He is influenced by Marxism, especially those Marxist theories that emphasized the autonomy of politics. But he is not a Marxist, because he refuses to entangle transformative aspirations in determinist assumptions. He argues for "disentrenchment," "destabilization rights," and "negative capability." But he does not belong to the school of "deconstruction," because his own "constructive" theory recognizes that our freedom to resist, reimagine, and reconstruct the social worlds we inhabit is itself a variable up for grabs in history. He is not an antiliberal. But he calls his theory "superliberal," in the sense of realizing the highest aspirations of liberalism by transforming its conventional institutional commitments.

How does he reach such an unusual intellectual standpoint? What is the practical relevance of his "constructive social theory?" Without trying to do full justice to this most ambitious social-theoretical work of the late twentieth century, my introduction seeks to highlight some salient features of Unger's social theory in the hope that it will motivate readers to study the text on their own.

SOCIETY AS ARTIFACT

Unger's social theory can be understood as an effort to carry the idea of "society as artifact" to the extreme. He teaches that "society is made and imagined, that it is a human artifact rather than the expression of an underlying natural order."

The idea of "society as artifact" has its origin in the European Enlightenment. However, its full implications have been worked out only halfway: the effort to push the idea of "society as artifact" to its limits has been blocked by the countertendency within modern social theories to develop a "science of history."

The intellectual reason for this countertendency is too complicated to deal with fully here. For now, we need only remember that modern social thought was born in a post-Christian situation. The idea of "society as artifact" implies, at the minimum, that human history is not subject to divine providence. Rather, people can make and remake society at their will. There are many expressions of this idea of human agency in early modern social thought. One prominent example is the argument by Hobbes that "natural right" is not derived from "natural law." In this way, modern natural rights and social-contract theories started to strip away the theological content of the medieval conception of natural law and sought to develop social theory based on the idea of "society as artifact." Another famous example is Vico's argument that amid the "immense ocean of doubt" there is a "single tiny piece of earth" on which we can stand firmly: this world of civil society has been made by man.

However, modern social thought failed to take the idea of "society as artifact" to the hilt. Some people believe that the reason for this failure lies in an over-reaction to the demise of Christian eschatology. When modern thinkers abandoned Christian eschatology, they still wanted to develop a "philosophy or science of history," as if they desired to show that modern thought can answer any question raised by Christianity. In a sense, modern social thought began "reoccupying" the position of the medieval Christian schema of creation and eschatology. In this light, Tocqueville's view of the irresistible march of democracy as a divine decree may be more than a simple metaphor.

Whether this explanation is historically true is a controversial matter going beyond the reach of this introduction. However, we can be sure that the search for the "law of history" has led modern social theory astray. What Unger calls "deep-structure social theory" is the star example of the effort of modern social thought to develop a "science of history," rich in lawlike explanations. Although Unger chose Marx to exemplify "deep-structure social theory," he made it clear that Durkheim and Weber – the other members of the social-theoretical canon – also bear the stamp of this tradition.

According to Unger, deep-structure social analysis is defined by its devotion to three recurrent theoretical moves. The first move is the attempt to distinguish in every historical circumstance a formative context, structure, or framework from the routine activities this context helps reproduce; the second is the effort to represent the framework identified in a particular circumstance as an example of a repeatable and indivisible type of social organization such as capitalism; the third is the appeal to the deep-seated constraints and the developmental laws that can generate a closed list or a compulsive sequence of repeatable and indivisible frameworks.

Unger shows that deep-structure social theory has reached an advanced state of disintegration. Its commitment to the above-mentioned three moves is becoming increasingly discredited by historical and contemporary practical experience. One response to this discredited deep-structure social theory is "positivist social science," which denies altogether the distinction between a "formative context" and "routine activities" within the context. But Unger argues that positivist social science is no way out. For the rejection of the context–routine distinction leads social scientists to study routines of conflict and compromise within the existing institutional and imaginative context only. As long as a formative context is stable, its influence upon routine activities can be forgotten. The study of voting behavior of different groups in a stable social framework is an apt example. Thus positivist social scientists miss the conflict over the formative context – the fundamental institutional and imaginative structure of social life. They end up taking the existing formative context for granted and seeing society through the eyes of a "resigned insider." Caught between the pretense of "deep-structure social theory" to be "the science of history" on the one hand, and the uncritical approaches of positivist social science on the other, modern social thought worked out both "partial dissolutions and partial reinstatements of the naturalistic view of society." Unger's theoretical work, in a nutshell, is an effort to carry the idea of "society as artifact" all the way through, to develop a radically antinaturalistic, antinecessitarian social theory. In this sense, Unger's social theory stages a double rebellion against classical social theory, with its functionalist and determinist heritage, as well as against the positivist social sciences.

AGAINST STRUCTURE FETISHISM AND INSTITUTIONAL FETISHISM

Unger rejects "deep-structure social theory" and "positivist social science," but he is not a nihilist. He preserves the first move of deep-structure theory – the distinction between "formative contexts" and "formed routines" – while rejecting its two other moves – the subsumption of each formative context under an indivisible and repeatable type, and the search for general laws governing such types. This selective approach distinguishes Unger from conventional Marxists, who wholeheartedly embrace deep-structure social theory, as well as from positivist social scientists who deny the context–routine distinction. It also distances him from any nihilist practice of post-modern "deconstruction."[1]

The distinctive conceptual instrument for Unger's theoretical innovation is his insight into "formative contexts" and the *degree* of their revisability or disentrenchment vis-à-vis human freedom. As Perry Anderson well observed, the notion of "formative context" is "presented expressly as an alternative

[1] Richard Rorty nicely captures Unger's theoretical position in his discussion of Castoriadis and Unger: "Castoriadis and Unger are willing to work with, rather than deconstruct, the notions that already mean something to people presently alive – while nonetheless not giving the last word to the historical world they inhabit." See Richard Rorty, "Unger, Castoriadis, and the Romance of a National Future," in Robin W. Lovin and Michael J. Perry, eds, *Critique and Construction: A Symposium on Roberto Unger's Politics* (New York: Cambridge University Press, 1987).

to the mode of production in the Marxist tradition, cast aside as too rigid and replicable. A formative context is something looser and more singular – an accidental institutional and ideological cluster that regulates both normal expectations and routine conflicts over the distribution of key resources."[2] Although we can never escape completely the constraints of a "formative context," we can make it more open to challenge and revision. Unger argues that this degree of openness is itself variable. For example, hereditary castes in ancient India, corporately organized estates in feudal Europe, social classes today, and "parties of opinion" tomorrow mark the presence of groups characteristic of increasingly open or "plastic" formative contexts. Unger proposes the notion of "negative capability" to signify the relative degree of openness and disentrenchment of a formative context.

The term "negative capability" comes originally from a letter of John Keats, dated December 28, 1817. Unger's usage generalizes and transforms the poet's meaning. It denotes the active human will and its capacity to transcend every given formative context by negating it in thought and deed. To increase "negative capability" amounts to creating institutional contexts more open to their own revision – so diminishing the gap between structure and routine, revolution and piecemeal reform, and social movement and institutionalization. Unger values the strengthening of negative capability both as an end in itself – a dimension of human freedom – and as a means to the achievement of other goals. For he holds there to be a significant causal connection between the disentrenchment of formative contexts and their success at advancing along the path of possible overlap between the conditions of material progress and the conditions of individual emancipation.

Therefore, Unger's distinctive theoretical standpoint is characterized by a two-sided view of formative contexts: while recognizing their resilience and power, he deprives these contexts of their aura of higher necessity or authority. He emphasizes that "to understand society deeply" requires us to "see the settled from the angle of the unsettled." This perspective gives rise to the critique of structure fetishism and institutional fetishism.

According to Unger, structure fetishism denies that we can change the quality of formative contexts. Here, the quality of a formative context is characterized by its degree of openness to revision. Structure fetishism remains committed to the mistaken thesis that "a structure is a structure." A structure fetishist may be a skeptical post-modern relativist, who gives up on universal standards of value and insight. Alternatively, a structure fetishist may be a nihilist, whose concern is to deconstruct everything. However, both theoretical positions are pseudo-radical, because they end up subscribing to the view that, because everything is contextual, all we can

[2] Perry Anderson, "Roberto Unger and the Politics of Empowerment," in his *A Zone of Engagement* (London and New York: Verso, 1992), p. 135.

do is to choose a social context and play by its rules, rather than change its quality of entrenchment. Unger's thesis about the relative degree of revisability or disentrenchment of formative contexts provides a solution to this dilemma of postmodernism-turned-conservatism. The way out is to recognize that when we lose faith in an absolute standard of value, we need not surrender to the existing institutional and imaginative order. We can still struggle to make institutional and discursive contexts that better respect our spiritual nature, that is to say our nature as context-transcending agents.

You may wonder about the metric of this "degree of openness and revisability." It is measured by the distance between structure-reproducing routine activities and structure-challenging transformative activities. The less the distance, the more open and revisable a formative context becomes.

Here we touch upon a crucial point in Unger's social theory. Unger does not share with most other contemporary social theorists and liberal political philosophers the obsession with establishing the "neutrality" of our basic institutions among clashing ideals of human association. For him, the mirage of neutrality gets in the way of the more important objective of finding arrangements friendly to a practical experimentalism of initiatives and a real diversity of experiences. We cannot distinguish within human nature attributes that are permanent and universal from those that vary with social circumstance. It is futile to present an institutional order as an expression of a system of rights supposedly neutral among clashing interests and conflicting visions of the good.[3] What counts is to narrow the distance between the reproduction and the revision of our practices and arrangements. We thus help fulfill the requirements for those forms of material progress that can coexist with the liberation of individuals from rigid social divisions and hierarchies.

If the critique of "structure fetishism" attacks from one direction the fate allotted to us by our institutions, the critique of "institutional fetishism" attacks this fate from another direction. Institutional fetishism, for Unger, is the imagined identification of highly detailed and largely accidental institutional arrangements with abstract institutional concepts like representative democracy, a market economy, or a free civil society. The institutional fetishist may be the classical liberal who identifies representative democracy and the market economy with a makeshift set of governmental and economic arrangements that happen to have triumphed in the course of modern European history. He may also be the hard-core Marxist who treats these same arrangements as an indispensable stage toward a future, regenerate order whose content he sees as both preestablished and resistant

[3] In his comparative study of Rawls, Habermas and Unger, Geoffrey Hawthorn points out that the search for neutrality looms large in both Rawls and Habermas. See Geoffrey Hawthorn, "Practical Reason and Social Democracy: Reflections on Unger's Passion and Politics," in Lovin and Perry, eds, *Critique and Construction*.

to credible description. He may even be the positivist social scientist or the hard-nosed political or economic manager who accepts current practices as an uncontroversial framework for interest balancing and problem solving.[4]

One prominent example of institutional fetishism is what Unger describes as "the mythical history of democracy." According to this mythical viewpoint, "the trials and errors of modern political experience, and the undoubted failure of many proposed alternatives, have confirmed that the emergent institutional solutions were much more than flukes."[5] Contrary to this "mythical history," Unger insists that we recognize how accidental are the institutional arrangements of contemporary representative democracies and market economies. For example, the liberal constitutionalism of the eighteenth century sought to grant rule to a cadre of politically educated and financially secure notables, fully able to safeguard the polities they governed against mob rule and seduction by demagogues.

This early liberal constitutionalism was not the royal road to democracy. One of its legacies has been a style of constitutionalism combining the democratic fragmentation of power with an antidemocratic bias toward the deliberate slowing down of politics and the perpetuation of constitutional or electoral impasse. Both the American presidential regime of "checks and balances" and the need to base political power upon broad consensus within the political class in parliamentary regimes exemplify this legacy.

In contrast, Unger proposes a new constitutional program. This program accelerates democratic experimentalism and breaks away from eighteenth-century constitutionalism. It combines a strong plebiscitarian element with broad and multiple channels for the political representation of society. In fact, the "dualistic constitutions" of the interwar period (1918–39) and the Portuguese Constitution of 1978 hinted at the possibility of a constitutional regime more open to democratic experimentalism.

Another prominent example of institutional fetishism is what Unger describes as the "mythical history of private rights." According to this mythical history, the current Western legal system of property and contract embodies the inherent logic of a market economy. Contrary to this view, Unger insists that a market economy has no unique set of built-in legal–institutional arrangements. The current Western system of property and contract is less a reflection of a deep logic of social and economic necessity than a contingent outcome of political struggles. It could have assumed other institutional forms. The deviant cases and tendencies within the current law of property and contract, such as "reliance interests" not dependent upon the fully articulated will of contracting parties, already suggest

[4] Roberto Mangabeira Unger, *Social Theory: Its Situation and Its Task* (Cambridge: Cambridge University Press, 1987), pp. 200–201.

[5] Roberto Mangabeira Unger, *False Necessity: Anti Necessitarian Social Theory in the Service of Radical Democracy* (Cambridge: Cambridge University Press, 1987), p. 211.

elements of an alternative legal–institutional ordering of the market economy. Unger devotes a major part of his constructive social theory to the development of alternative systems of property and contract. He shows how we can achieve this goal by redirecting and restructuring the deviant tendencies within the current private-rights system.

Unger's critique of the "mythical history of democracy" and the "mythical history of private rights" is only a part of his institutional genealogy. He also presents an alternative, possibility-enhancing view of the genesis of contemporary institutions of government and labor. He outlines a parallel genealogy of Soviet and communist Chinese institutions. In each case, Unger "makes the familiar strange," that is he shows how accidentally these institutions were generated and evolved, and how they look "natural" in retrospect only to a mind under the spell of false necessity.

The overall theme of Unger's genealogy is the falsehood of institutional fetishism: existing institutional arrangements form a subset of broader possibilities. Unger emphasizes this fact in his treatment of "petty commodity production": the economy of small-scale, relatively equal producers, operating through a mix of cooperative organization and independent activity. Radicals and conservatives alike have usually considered "petty commodity production" doomed to failure, because it precludes the economies of scale in production and exchange vital to technological dynamism.

Unger sees "petty commodity production" differently. He neither accepts nor rejects it in its unreconstructed form. Rather, he tries to "rescue" it by inventing new economic and political institutions. For example, we can satisfy the imperative of economies of scale by finding a "method of market organization that makes it possible to pool capital, technologies, and manpower without distributing permanent and unqualified rights to their use." This solution amounts to the new regime of property rights in Unger's programmatic proposal, discussed below. We can invent new institutions rescuing from the old dream of yeoman democracy and small-scale independent property the kernel of a practical alternative, open to economic and technological progress as well as to democratic ideals.

Indeed, one of the most fascinating themes in Unger's discussion of the new forms of a market economy is the connection he establishes between these institutional problems and the emerging advanced practices of vanguardist production today. Here again, Unger helps us realize that inherited and established arrangements do not reflect the higher order of a "natural law of human history." We can transform them if we want. By so doing, we can remain faithful to the progressive impulse of democracy.

PROGRAMMATIC ALTERNATIVES TODAY

Unger's critique of structure fetishism and institutional fetishism is closely related to his programmatic arguments; a strong bond unites the explanatory and the programmatic sides of Unger's "constructive social theory." As Unger puts it, the programmatic arguments of his social theory reinterpret and generalize the liberal and leftist endeavor by freeing it from unjustifiably restrictive assumptions about the practical institutional forms that representative democracies, market economies, and the social control of economic accumulation can and should assume.

In today's world, Unger's programmatic arguments are urgently needed. The pseudo-scientific thesis of convergence has gained intellectual respectability worldwide. This convergence thesis stipulates that market economies and representative democracies in the world are converging to the single best set of institutions – some variation on the established arrangements of the North-Atlantic democracies. In the Third World and the former Soviet-bloc countries this same thesis, sometimes also called the "Washington consensus," takes the form of "neoliberalism." Carried to its hilt, this convergence thesis is "institutional fetishist" to its core. As it hails, for example, the fading of differences among American, German, and Japanese styles of corporate governance, it fails to identify, or sympathize with, other differences that are in the process of appearing.

In its most abstract and universal form, neoliberalism or the "Washington consensus" is the program committed to orthodox macroeconomic stabilization, especially through fiscal balance, achieved by the containment of public spending rather than by increases in the tax take; to liberalization, accomplished through free trade (free for goods and capital, not for labor); to privatization, understood both more narrowly as the withdrawal of government from production and more generally as the adoption of standard Western private law; and to the deployment of "social safety-nets" designed to counteract the unequalizing effects of the other planks in the orthodox platform.

What is striking about this dominant version of neoliberalism is that it incorporates the conventional social-democratic program of social insurance. This fact shows clearly that the social-democratic ideal has long lost its radical transformative inspiration. Instead of challenging and reforming the institutions of the existing forms of market economy and representative democracy, the social-democratic program merely seeks to moderate the social consequences of structural divisions and hierarchies it has come to accept. Conservative social democracy defends the relatively privileged position of the labor force working in the capital-intensive, mass-production industries, at the social cost of exclusion of large numbers of outsiders in the disfavored, disorganized "second economy." If the division between insiders and outsiders is already a formidable problem in European social democracies, its proportions and effects become far more daunting in countries like Brazil and Mexico. Compensatory social policy remains unable to make up for extreme inequalities, rooted in stark divisions between economic vanguards and economic rearguards.

Because neoliberalism incorporates the social-democratic program,

Unger's programmatic alternative to neoliberalism is at the same time an institutional alternative to social democracy. It seeks to overcome economic and social dualism in both rich and poor countries by making access to capital more open and decentralized, and by creating political institutions favorable to the repeated practice of structural reform. The main reason for the existence of economic and social dualism – the division between insiders and outsiders of the advanced industrial sectors in both rich and poor countries – is the privilege current arrangements afford to the insiders. However substantial the interests that pit workers in advanced sectors against their bosses, they nevertheless share common interests against those of the disorganized working people (the outsiders) at large.

Conservative social democracy defines itself today by contrast to a managerial program of industrial renovation. This program wants to strengthen the freedom of capital to move where it will and to encourage cooperation at the workplace. It manages the tensions between these two commitments by devices such as the segmentation of the labor force. Conservative social democracy responds by seeking to restrain the hypermobility of capital through something close to job tenure. It also wants to multiply the recognition of stakes and stakeholders (workers, consumers, and local communities as well as shareholders) in productive enterprises. The result, however, is to aggravate the complaints of paralysis and conflict that helped inspire managerial programs while accepting and reinforcing the established divisions between insiders and outsiders.

The intuitive core of Unger's proposal for economic reconstruction lies in the attempt to replace the demand for job tenure by an enhancement of the resources and capabilities of the individual worker–citizen and to substitute a radical diversification of forms of decentralized access to productive opportunity for the stakeholder democracy of conservative social democracy. The first plank in this platform leads to the generalization of social inheritance through social-endowment accounts available to everyone; the second, to the disaggregation of traditional private property and the recombination and reallocation of its constitutive elements. Both planks, in turn, need sustenance from institutions and practices favoring the acceleration of democratic politics and the independent self-organization of civil society. The traditional devices of liberal constitutionalism are inadequate to the former just as the familiar repertory of contract and corporate law is insufficient to the latter.

Unger draws out the affirmative democratizing potential in that most characteristic theme of modern legal analysis: the understanding of property as a "bundle of rights." He proposes to dismember the traditional property right and to vest its component faculties in different kinds of rightholders. Among these successors to the traditional owner will be firms, workers, national and local government, intermediate organizations, and social funds. He opposes the simple reversion of conventional private ownership to state ownership and workers' cooperatives, because this reversion merely redefines the identity of the owner without changing the nature of "consolidated" property. He argues for a three-tier property structure: the central capital fund, established by the national democratic government for ultimate decisions about social control of economic accumulation; the various investment funds, established by the government and by the central capital fund for capital allotment on a competitive basis; and the primary capital takers, made up of teams of workers, engineers and entrepreneurs. Underlying this scheme is a vision of the conditions of economic growth and of the terms on which economic growth can be reconciled with democratic experimentalism. In this vision, the central problem of material progress is the relation between cooperation and innovation. Each needs the other. Each threatens the other. Our work is to diminish their mutual interference.

We can appreciate Unger's ideas about "disaggregrated property" from the standpoints of both the radical-leftist tradition and the liberal tradition. From the perspective of radical-democratic thinking, Unger's program is related to Proudhon's petty-bourgeois radicalism. Proudhon was a forerunner of the theory of property as a "bundle of rights," and his classic work *What is Property?* provides a thorough critique of "consolidated property." It is important to realize that, in its economic aspects, Unger's program amounts, in a sense, to a synthesis of Proudhonian, Lassallean, and Marxist thinking. From the petty-bourgeois radicalism of Proudhon and Lassalle, he absorbs the importance of the idea of economic decentralization for both economic efficiency and political democracy; from the Marxist critique of petty-bourgeois socialism, he comes to realize the inherent dilemmas and instability of petty-commodity production. This realization stimulates Unger to reverse the traditional aversion of an emancipatory and decentralizing radicalism to national politics. He develops proposals for decentralized cooperation between government and business. He connects these proposals with reforms designed to accelerate democratic politics through the rapid resolution of impasses among branches of governments, to heighten and sustain the level of institutionalized political mobilization, and to deepen and generalize the independent self-organization of civil society.

From the perspective of the liberal tradition, Unger's program represents an effort to take both economic decentralization and individual freedom one step further. In today's organized, corporatist "capitalist" economies, economic decentralization and innovation have been sacrificed to the protection of the vested interests of capital and labor in advanced industrial sectors. Unger's program remains more true to the liberal spirit of decentralized coordination and innovation than does the current practice of neoliberalism and social democracy.

Conventional, institutionally conservative liberalism takes the absolute, unified property right as the model for all other rights. By replacing absolute, consolidated property rights with a scheme for reallocation of the disaggregated elements of property among different types of rightholders, Unger both rejects and enriches the liberal tradition. He argues that the left should reinterpret rather than abandon the language of rights. He goes beyond both Proudhon–Lassalle–Marx and the liberal tradition by reconstructing law to include four types of rights: immunity rights, market rights, destabilization rights, and solidarity rights.

In this sense, we can understand why Unger sometimes describes his program as "superliberal" rather than antiliberal. Any reader of John Stuart Mill's *Autobiography* would recognize that "superliberalism" – the realization of liberal aspirations by changing liberal institutional forms – recalls Mill's new thinking after his mental crisis. Unger forces us to confront the difference between a liberalism that, through its emphasis upon cumulative and motivated institutional tinkering, keeps democratic experimentalism alive, and one that remains satisfied with tax-and-transfer-style redistribution within an order it leaves unchallenged.

We can thus view Unger's programmatic alternative as a synthesis of the radical-democratic and liberal traditions. This synthesis bears in at least three ways on the future of the democratic project.

First, the synthesis of Proudhon–Lassalle–Marx and the liberal tradition nourishes a program of "empowered democracy."[6] It represents an economic and political alternative to neoliberalism and social democracy, with great appeal for a wide range of liberals, leftists and modernist visionaries. In our post-Cold War era, it reopens the horizons of alternative futures, and rescues us forcefully from the depressing sense that history has ended.

Second, this synthesis promises a reorientation of the strategy of social transformation of the left in rich and poor countries alike. One embarrassment of the Marxist-inspired left is the historical fact that the industrial working class has never become a majority of the population. Fear of the left and resentment at organized labor have often separated the "middle classes" from industrial and agrarian workers and turned them toward the right. Unger's synthesis of Proudhon–Lassalle–Marx and the liberal tradition may prove to be a useful mobilizational tool for a more inclusive alliance in the service of radical-democratic change.

Third, this synthesis gives new meaning to the idea of "society as artifact." Unger's social theory represents an effort to theorize "jumbled experience." He draws upon, and attempts to encourage, forms of practical and passionate human connection that recombine activities traditionally associated with different nations, classes, communities, and roles. Through this worldwide recombination and innovation, we broaden our collective sense of the possible. This enlarged sensibility in turn helps sustain the institutional arrangements in Unger's program of empowered democracy. Thus,

[6] Unger's forthcoming book *Democratic Experimentalism* (London and New York: Verso, 1998) develops in detail his programmatic vision, linking it with contemporary problems and opportunities.

Unger's institutional program and his vision of change in the way individuals associate reinforce each other.

This book is a selection from Unger's three-volume *Politics, A Work in Constructive Social Theory*. The first part of the selection draws from the first volume of *Politics*, which describes the starting points of Unger's "radically antinaturalist social theory" and shows how the criticism of classical social theories and contemporary social sciences generates materials for an alternative practice of social understanding. The second part of the selection is from the second and third volumes of *Politics*: the relation between the openness and flexibility of formative contexts and the development of our collective capacity to produce or to destroy. The third part of the selection takes material from the second volume of *Politics*, which presents Unger's programmatic proposals to reconstruct our economic and political institutions. The last part of the selection comes from the first and second volumes: texts showing how Unger's institutional program and "cultural-revolutionary" personalist program reinforce each other.

Several reviewers of Unger's work, Richard Rorty among them, have emphasized that Unger is a Brazilian citizen. In Rorty's words, "Remember that Unger – though he has put in many years of hard work here in North America, changing the curricula of many of our law schools and the self-image of many of our lawyers – is a man whose mind is elsewhere. For him, none of the rich North Atlantic democracies are home. Rather, they are places where he has gathered some lessons, warnings, and encouragements." Reading this sentence, I cannot help recalling Max Weber's remark that inspiration for many decisive cultural accomplishments has often come from the periphery of a civilization.

In Unger's description of Brazil in 1985, we find him saying, "Indefinition was the common denominator of all these features of the life of the state . . . All this indefinition could be taken as both the voice of transformative opportunity and the sign of a paralyzing confusion." These words could equally describe today's world as a whole. I view China now as Unger does Brazil. Is Perry Anderson right in seeing in Unger a "philosophical mind out of the Third World turning the tables, to become synoptist and seer of the First"? The hope of progress toward a more vibrant democratic experimentalism may reside today in the large but marginalized countries like Brazil, China, India, and Russia, countries that can still imagine themselves as alternative worlds. We are all living in a time when a great chance of democratic transformation of all aspects of social life coexists with great confusion in our explanatory and programmatic ideas. It was in this condition of need, confusion, and hope that I first came to read Unger's work three years ago, and found it so inspiring that I felt it had been written expressly for me. It is my hope now that this feeling will be shared by other readers of this volume of selections from Unger's *Politics*.

A Radically Antinaturalist Social Theory

1

Introduction

Society as Artifact

MODERN social thought was born proclaiming that society is made and imagined, that it is a human artifact rather than the expression of an underlying natural order. This insight inspired the great secular doctrines of emancipation: liberalism, socialism, and communism. In one way or another, all these doctrines held out the promise of building a society in which we may be individually and collectively empowered to disengage our practical and passionate relations from rigid roles and hierarchies. If society is indeed ours to reinvent, we can carry forward the liberal and leftist aim of cleansing from our forms of practical collaboration or passionate attachment the taint of dependence and domination. We can advance the modernist goal of freeing subjective experience more fully from a pre-written and imposed script. We may even be able to draw the left-liberal and modernist goals together in a larger ambition to construct social worlds whose stability does not depend on the surrender of our society-making powers or on their confiscation by privileged elites. The practical point of the view of society as made and imagined is to discover what is realistic and what illusory in these objectives and to find guidance for their execution.

No one has ever taken the idea of society as artifact to the hilt. On the contrary, the social theories that provided radical politics with its chief intellectual tools balanced the notion that society is made and imagined against the ambition to develop a science of history, rich in lawlike explanations. This science claimed to identify a small number of possible types of social organization, coexisting or succeeding one another under the influence of relentless developmental tendencies or of deep-seated economic, organizational, or psychological constraints. Marxism is the star example.

Such theories have become ever less credible. A mass of historical knowledge and practical experience has battered them. Inconvenient facts have discredited their characteristic beliefs in a short list of types of social organization and in laws that determine the identity of these types or govern their history.

But the most visible result of this battering has not been to extend the idea of society as artifact. On the contrary, it has been to abandon more and more of the field to a style of social science that seeks narrowly framed explanations for narrowly described phenomena. This social science – positivist or empiricist as it is sometimes called – rejects the search for comprehensive social or historical laws in favor of a more limited explanatory task. In so doing, it comes to see society as a vast, amorphous heap of conflicting individual or group interests and exercises in interest accommodation, of practical problems and episodes of problem solving. Such a social science lacks the means with which to address the institutional and imaginative assumptions on which routine problem solving and interest accommodation take place. Whatever the adepts of this social science may say, their practice has a built-in propensity to take the existing framework of social life for granted and thereby to lend it a semblance of necessity and authority. In this respect, positivist social science is even more dangerous than the ambitious social theories of the nineteenth and early twentieth centuries. These theories at least defined the present institutional and imaginative order of society as a transitory though necessary stage of social evolution or as only one of several possible types of social organization.

Meanwhile the radical project – the shared enterprise of liberal and leftist doctrines and of the political movements that embraced them – has also suffered a daunting series of setbacks. The communist revolutions, despite their economic and redistributive achievements, failed to establish social institutions that could credibly claim to carry the radical project beyond the point to which it has already been brought by the rich Western democracies and market economies. At the same time, party politics in these democracies has settled down to a series of routine struggles over marginal economic redistribution, within an institutional and imaginative ordering of social life that remains largely unchallenged. Third world countries continue to be the playing ground of predatory oligarchies that often can scarcely be distinguished from self-appointed revolutionary vanguards. It becomes hard to continue hoping that poorer and more fluid societies might stage promising experiments in the advancement of the radical project.

Such defeats have produced a sense of social life combining an awareness that nothing has to be the way it is with a conviction that nothing important can be changed by deliberate collective action. All revolutionary programs are made to seem utopian reveries, bound to end in despotism and disillusionment. This experience of faithless prostration, the stigma and shame of our time, provides an ironic commentary on the conception of society as artifact: while respecting the literal truth of this conception, it eviscerates the idea of its force.

The message of this book is that these disheartening intellectual and political events tell only half the story, the half that evokes intellectual entropy and social stagnation. *Social Theory: Its Situation and Its Task* deals chiefly with the other, hidden half. It shows how the criticism and self-criticism of received traditions of social theory have prepared the way for a practice of social and historical understanding that extends even further than the ambitious European social theories of the past the idea of society as artifact and enables us to broaden and refine our sense of the possible. The resulting insights inform efforts to carry both liberal and socialist commitments beyond the point to which contemporary societies have taken them. Thus, what seems to be a circumstance of theoretical exhaustion and political retrenchment can be redefined as a gathering of forces for a new and more powerful assault upon superstition and despotism.

The critical argument of this book leads directly into constructive explanatory and programmatic ideas. The character and concerns of the critical diagnosis may best be outlined by suggesting the orientation of the constructive view it prepares.

This constructive view includes both an explanatory approach to society and a program for social reconstruction. The explanatory proposals of *Politics* cuts the link between the possibility of social explanation and the denial or downplaying of our freedom to remake the social worlds we construct and inhabit. Like classic doctrines such as Marxism but unlike traditional, positivist social science, these explanations assign central importance to the distinction between routine deals or quarrels and the recalcitrant institutional and imaginative frameworks in which they ordinarily occur. Such frameworks comprise all the institutional arrangements and imaginative preconceptions that shape routine conflicts over the mastery and use of key resources. These resources enable the occupants of some social stations to set terms to what the occupants of other stations do. They include economic capital, governmental power, technical expertise, and even prestigious ideals. (The terms context, structure, and framework are employed synonymously throughout this book.)

In the contemporary Western democracies the social framework includes legal rules that use property rights as the instrument of economic decentralization, constitutional arrangements that provide for representation while discouraging militancy, and a style of business organization that starkly contrasts task-defining and task-executing activities. In the industrial democracies the formative structure of social life also incorporates a series of models of human association that are expected to be realized in different areas of social existence: a model of private community applying to the life of family and friendship, a model of democratic organization guiding the activities of governments and political parties, and a model of private contract combined with impersonal technical hierarchy addressing the prosaic realm of work and exchange.

The explanatory theory developed in *Politics* differs from positivist social science in its insistence that the distinction between formative structures and formed routines is central to our understanding of society and history. The institutional and imaginative frameworks of social life supply the basis on which people define and reconcile interests, identify and solve problems.

These frameworks cannot be adequately explained as mere crystallized outcomes of interest-accommodating or problem-solving activities. Until we make the underlying institutional and imaginative structure of a society explicit we are almost certain to mistake the regularities and routines that persist, so long as the structure is left undisturbed, for general laws of social organization. At the very least, we are likely to treat them as the laws of a particular type of society and to imagine that we can suspend them only by a revolutionary switch to another type. Superstition then encourages surrender.

If the explanatory theory of *Politics* is incompatible with positivist social science, it is also irreconcilable with some of the characteristic tenets of the classic social theories. Like the view for which *Politics* argues, these theories assigned a central explanatory role to the contrast between frameworks and routines. Thus, for example, the Marxist studies modes of production (his frameworks) and the distinctive laws of each mode (his routines). The approach anticipated in this book nevertheless repudiates two major assumptions with which the contrast between frameworks and routines, formative structures and formed routines, has traditionally been associated.

One of these assumptions is the belief in the existence of a limited number of types or stages of social organization, all of whose parts combine to form an indivisible package. The style of social analysis to which this work contributes dispenses with ideas about such types and stages. Each framework is unique rather than an example of a general type that can be repeated in different societies at different times. The components of such an institutional and imaginative order are only loosely and unevenly connected. They can be replaced piece by piece rather than only as an inseparable whole.

The other repudiated assumption with which the contrast between frameworks and routines has ordinarily been connected is the thesis that general explanations of the genesis, workings, and reinvention of these frameworks must take the form of appeals to deep-seated economic, organizational, and psychological constraints or to irresistible developmental forces supposedly underlying the chaos of historical life. The theory advocated and anticipated here shows how we can develop an account of context making whose generality does not depend upon laws that generate a closed list or a preordained sequence of forms of social life.

A third idea extends the two sets of necessitarian assumptions that have traditionally accompanied the distinction between frameworks and routines. This third assumption is less directly connected to the other two than they are to each other, and it represents more an unexamined prejudice than a considered belief. This prejudice is the belief that structures will be structures. They always have the same relation to the practical and discursive routines that they influence and to the constraints and tendencies that in turn shape them. The arguments of *Politics* claim, however, that we can diminish the power of these all-important structures to impose a script upon people's practical or passionate relations and weaken the contrast between structure-preserving routines and structure-transforming conflicts.

We have an important stake in changing our relation to the formative institutions and preconceptions of our societies. Less entrenched and more revisable sets of arrangements and beliefs help us empower ourselves individually and collectively. They encourage the development of productive capabilities by enabling us to experiment more freely with the practical forms of production and exchange. They free group life of some of its characteristic dangers of dependence and depersonalization by diminishing the hold of rigid hierarchies and roles over our dealings with one another. They allow us to engage in group life without becoming the victims of compulsions we do not master and hardly understand.

Nothing in the development of the effort to disengage the framework–routine distinction from its inherited associations requires a solution to the metaphysical problem of free will and determinism. The aim is not to show that we are free in any ultimate sense and somehow unrestrained by causal influences upon our conduct. It is to break loose from a style of social understanding that allows us to explain ourselves and our societies only to the extent we imagine ourselves helpless puppets of the social worlds we build and inhabit or of the lawlike forces that have supposedly brought these worlds into being. History really is surprising; it does not just seem that way. And social invention, deliberate or unintended, is not just an acting out of preestablished and narrowly defined possibilities.

A view of the institutional and imaginative contexts of social life, of how these contexts stick together, come apart, and get remade, lies at the center of the explanatory theory of *Politics*. From such a view we can hope to get critical distance on our societies. We can disrupt the implicit, often involuntary alliance between the apologetics of established order and the explanation of past or present societies. We can find an explanatory practice that, by providing us with a credible account of discontinuous change and social novelty, inspires rather than subverts the advancement of the radical project: the effort, shared by liberals and socialists, to lift the burden of rigid hierarchy and division that weighs on our practical and passionate relations with one another.

The approach to social and historical explanation for which this book argues has practical implications. Our beliefs about ideals and interests are shaped by the institutional and imaginative frameworks of social life. But they are not shaped completely. The formative contexts of social life never entirely control our practical dealings and passionate attachments. We regularly invest our recognized interests and ideals with ill-defined longings that we cannot satisfy within the limits imposed by current institutional and imaginative assumptions. But we just as regularly fail to grasp the conflict between longings and assumptions because of our failure to imagine alternative possibilities of social organization. This failure in turn prompts us to underestimate the wealth of materials available for context-transforming use: the surviving residues of past institutional arrangements and imaginative worlds, the stubborn anomalies of a social order, and the endless, petty practical and imaginative quarrels that may escalate at any time into structure-subverting fights. A believable social theory teaches the imagination how to take these deviations seriously and how to use them as starting points for the inauguration of new forms of social organization and personal experience.

The explanatory view of *Politics* goes hand in hand with a program for social reconstruction. Like the explanatory theory that informs it, the program is anticipated in this introductory book. The program takes sides with the cause that modernist and liberal or leftist radicals contentiously and half-consciously share. But in siding with this cause and in trying to justify, to develop, and to unify it, the argument also changes it. The change affects both the conception of what the cause is for and the view of its practical implications for the reordering of society.

The programmatic arguments of *Politics* reinterpret and generalize the liberal and leftist endeavor by freeing it from unjustifiably restrictive assumptions about the practical institutional forms that representative democracies, market economies, and the social control of economic accumulation can and should assume. At the heart of this vision of alternative institutional forms lies an appreciation of the link between the extent to which an institutional and imaginative framework of social life makes itself available to revision in the midst of ordinary social activity and the success with which this framework undermines rigid social roles and hierarchies. *Politics* argues for a particular way of reorganizing governments and economies that promises to realize more effectively both aspects of the radical commitment: the subversion of social division and hierarchy and the assertion of will over custom and compulsion. The traditional disputes between leftists and liberals are seen to be based on a misunderstanding, once we recognize that the present forms of decentralized economies and pluralistic democracies (markets based on absolute property rights, democracies predicated on the skeptical quiescence of the citizenry) are neither the necessary nor the best expressions of inherited ideals of liberty and equality. They frustrate the very goals for whose sake we uphold them.

The same ideas that change our view of the institutional message of radical politics also revise and clarify our conception of their purpose. We come to recognize the ideal of social equality, for example, as a partial, subsidiary aspect of our effort to free ourselves from a social script that both subordinates us unnecessarily to an over-powering scheme of class, communal, gender, and national divisions and denies us as individuals, as groups, and as whole societies a greater mastery over the institutional and imaginative contexts of our lives. This enlarged view of the radical cause in turn allows us to connect leftism and modernism, the radical politics of institutional reform and the radical politics of personal relations, a political vision obsessed with issues of dependence and domination and a moral vision concerned with the inability of the individual to gain practical, emotional, or even cognitive access to other people without forfeiting his independence.

The programmatic and explanatory arguments of *Politics* stand much more closely connected than our inherited preconceptions about facts and values suggest is possible. One of the many connections should be singled out here because it illuminates the direction of this introductory work. The explanatory ideas of *Politics* focus on what may at first seem a mere embarrassment to the pretensions of general social theory. We sometimes act as if our shared institutional and imaginative contexts did not in fact bind us. We hold on to deviant examples of human association, often the left-overs of past or rejected bids to establish a settled ordering of social life. We pass occasionally and often unexpectedly from context-respecting disputes to context-defying struggles. This endless, baffling experience of hidden or open defiance eludes the explanatory styles favored by both the classical social theories and the positivist social sciences. But the apparent obstacle to our explanatory capacities in fact points the way to a better strategy of explanation. The failure of our social contexts, or of the tendencies and constraints that help shape them, to prevent or to govern their own revision is the very fact that supplies the cornerstone for the approach of *Politics* to social and historical explanation.

What the explanatory argument takes as an opportunity for insight, the programmatic argument sees as a source of practical and ideal benefits. A central thesis of *Politics* is that all the major aspects of human empowerment or self-assertion depend on our success at diminishing the distance between context-preserving routine and context-transforming conflict. They rely on our ability to invent institutions and practices more fully respectful of the same context-revising freedom that provides the explanatory view of *Politics* with both its problem and its opportunity.

Why a critical assessment of the situation of social thought? Why not pass directly to the constructive explanatory and programmatic ideas?

The conception of intellectual history underlying this critical diagnosis is not the image of intellectual systems eventually collapsing under the weight of contrary evidence until a theoretical revolution replaces them with alternative theories. It is rather the picture of a twofold process of dissolution and construction: as the intellectual traditions dissolve, they also provide the materials and the methods for their own substitution. In this view of the situation of social thought, we need to explicate and to extend the fragments of an alternative social theory already implicit in the self-subverting activities of contemporary social thought. Thus, for example, the disintegration of Marxism is often misinterpreted by conservatives or antitheorists as the punishment due to overweening theoretical ambition. In fact, however, the internal controversies of the Marxist tradition have produced many of the insights needed to develop the idea that society is made and imagined and that it can therefore be remade and reimagined. The reluctance to push to extremes the criticism of an inherited tradition of social and historical analysis is habitually justified by the fear that its outcome will be nihilism. But this fear is misplaced not only because it makes us cling to confused and mistaken ideas but also because it deprives us of the constructive insights that help prevent the feared nihilistic result.

A great deal more than a hypothesis about intellectual history is at stake in this approach to the constructive implications of what may appear to be a purely disintegrative process. The practical issue is whether we must begin the reconstruction of social theory as nearly from scratch as possible. In the view that emphasizes the creation and overthrow of entire theoretical systems, we must not only formulate a brand new set of categories and methods but also laboriously develop a new empirical basis for our theories. Past observations will have been more or less contaminated by the flawed theoretical assumptions that partly shaped them. But in the conception of intellectual history employed here, the materials for an alternative vision – methods, insights, and interpreted observations – already lie at hand, though in undeveloped, fragmentary, and distorted form.

Another reason to preface the constructive explanatory and programmatic argument of *Politics* with a discussion of the contemporary situation of social and historical studies is to identify alternative though similarly motivated responses to the same intellectual and political circumstance. Though the critical discussion developed in this introductory book foreshadows the affirmative explanatory and programmatic ideas of the larger work, the relation between criticism and construction remains loose. The explanatory and programmatic argument of *Politics* is certainly not the sole promising response to the intellectual predicament described here. At least one rival line of development deserves attention. This alternative, which this book labels ultra-theory, also pushes to extremes the conception of society as artifact. But it does so by abandoning rather than by transforming the effort to formulate general explanations and comprehensive proposals for social reconstruction. It puts in place of such explanations and proposals not positivist social science but an array of critical and constructive practices, which range from the trashing of particular necessitarian explanations to the utopian evocation of forms of social life more responsive to the radical project. The argument of this book remains neutral between this skeptical, antinecessitarian approach and the equally antinecessitarian but aggressively theoretical tack pursued in *Politics*.

Social Theory: Its Situation and Its Task does not merely show intellectual and political opportunities arising from apparent theoretical disorientation and social blockage. It also seeks to convey a sense of the variety of constructive possibilities existing even within a field of thought defined by commitments to the view of society as artifact and to the radical project in politics.

A final aim of this introductory book is to enlist the reader's help in the theoretical campaign that this work initiates. *Politics* sets out to execute a program for which no ready-made mode of discourse exists. It changes the sense of terms and problems drawn from other bodies of thought, inspired by other intentions. It raids many disciplines and imposes on its inquiry an order no discipline acknowledges as its own. It develops, as it moves forward, a language for a vision. When the larger argument falls into confusion and obscurity, when I stagger and stumble, help me. Refer to the purpose described in this book and revise what I say in the light of what I want.

Social Theory: Its Situation and Its Task does not follow a single continuous argument. Instead, it proposes several points of departure from which to arrive, by convergent routes, at the same theoretical outcome. By far the most extensively considered of these points of departure is the internal situation of social thought, understood to include the whole field of social and historical studies. The discussion advances through a criticism of two intellectual traditions. One tradition, represented by positivist social science, disregards or downplays the contrast between the institutional and imaginative contexts, frameworks, or structures of social life and the routine activities, conflicts, and deals that these frameworks help shape. The other tradition accepts the distinction but subordinates it to unjustifiably restrictive assumptions about how frameworks change, what frameworks can exist, and what relations may hold between a framework and the freedom of the agents who move within it.

Marxism is the most cogent and elaborate example of this second class of theories. Yet both in Marx's own writings and in the later tradition of Marxist self-criticism we find the most uncompromising statements of the idea that society is made. We also discover many of the most powerful instruments with which to free this idea from the necessitarian assumptions about frameworks and their history that have played so large a role in Marxist thinking. Thus, the confrontation with Marxism remains a continuing concern – explicit in this preliminary book, largely implicit in the constructive work that follows.

The discussion of the internal situation of social theory suggests two parallel but distinct responses. One of these agendas, pursued in the main body of *Politics*, is intellectually ambitious. The other response is skeptical of the usefulness of general explanations and detailed proposals for reconstruction. But both carry to new extremes the conception of society as artifact. Both take sides with the people who, when faced with claims that current forms of social organization reflect inflexible economic, organizational, or psychological constraints, answer: No, they do not; they are just politics. Both show how the seemingly voluntaristic and nihilist claim that it is all politics permits a deeper insight into social life and even a better grasp of constraints upon transformative action.*

Preconceptions about scientific method have influenced practices of social description and explanation. The major traditions of social thought have modeled social explanation on their view of a scientific method most fully manifest in the natural sciences. The cruder versions of large-scale social theory and positivist social science have tried to come as close as possible to natural science. The subtler versions have seen in the historical, particularistic, and relatively contingent quality of social phenomena a reason to moderate the imitation of science. But they have then also moderated their explanatory and critical ambitions. Finally, those who have rebelled against the intimidating example of natural science have often done so by assimilating social theory to the humanities. The result has been to abandon the causal explanation of social facts and historical events to people who hold up the example of a single-minded view of science.

An antinecessitarian social theory must reject the choice between a scientistic social theory and a causally agnostic understanding. Thus, a discussion of the broader philosophical and scientific setting of social and historical studies caps my analysis of the internal situation of social theory. This discussion begins as an attempt to enlist certain discoveries of modern philosophy, psychology, and natural science in the endeavor to break the scientistic obsession. But it ends as an effort to use these same discoveries to make the constructive implications of the earlier criticism of social and historical studies clearer and more powerful.

The analysis of the internal situation of social thought and of its philosophical and scientific setting is preceded in this book by a discussion of three other themes. These themes deal with aspects of contemporary practical experience and ideology. Nevertheless, they too provide points of departure for the development of a social theory capable of carrying to extremes the view of social order as frozen politics. They highlight the practical importance of the effort to work out a body of ideas faithful to the insight that society is made and imagined. They suggest the diversity of paths for arriving at the same intellectual position.

*Throughout this book and its constructive sequel I use the term "politics" in both a narrower and a broader sense. The narrower sense is the conflict over the mastery and uses of governmental power. The broader sense is the conflict over the terms of our practical and passionate relations to one another and over all the resources and assumptions that may influence these terms. Preeminent among these assumptions are the institutional arrangements and imaginative preconceptions that compose a social framework, context, or structure. Governmental politics is only a special case of politics in this larger sense. In a theory that carries to extremes the view of society as artifact, this larger notion of politics merges into the conception of society making. The slogan "It's all politics" adds a further twist to this more inclusive idea. The additional twist is the notion that this society-making activity follows no preestablished plot and that its outcomes are not chiefly to be understood as the results of lawlike economic, organizational, and psychological constraints or overpowering developmental tendencies.

The first such starting point is the diffusion to ever broader numbers of people of an idea of work once restricted to tiny numbers of leaders, artists, and thinkers and not always and everywhere shared even by them. In this view of work, true satisfaction can be found only in an activity that enables people to fight back, individually or collectively, against the established settings of their lives – to resist these settings and even to remake them. The dominant institutional and imaginative structure of a society represents a major part of this constraining biographical circumstance, and it must therefore also be a central target of transformative resistance. Those who have been converted to the idea of a transformative vocation cannot easily return to the notion of work as an honorable calling within a fixed scheme of social roles and hierarchies, nor can they remain content with a purely instrumental view of labor as a source of material benefits with which to support themselves and their families.

The attraction of the ideal of a transformative vocation depends on the satisfaction of elementary material needs. Moreover, the distinctive traditions of particular nations and classes influence both the interpretation of this ideal and its persuasive force. Nevertheless, something in this conception of work represents the combination of a deeper insight with a more defensible aim of human striving, deeper and more defensible than the empirical and normative assumptions on which other available views of work depend. The social theory anticipated in this book is, among other things, an effort to develop the ideas that make sense of the transformative vocation and to justify its claim to allegiance.

A second starting point for my argument is the effort to develop ideas that elucidate and support what this book calls the radical project or the project of the modernist visionary. I do not claim that leftist liberals, or modernist radicals understand their cause in the precise terms by which it is described in these pages. On the contrary, the conception of the radical project already presupposes a criticism, a revision, and a reconciliation of separate and even antagonistic traditions: liberal and leftist proposals for social reconstruction and modernist attitudes toward rigid roles and conventions. The criticism of these loosely related traditions can lead us to rethink our ideas about society. This rethinking can converge with the intellectual agenda developed from the other points of departure discussed in this book. For in every instance the deficiencies of inherited leftist or liberal ideas turn out to be closely related to failures of our empirical understanding of society.

Institutional fetishism vitiates the most familiar liberal and leftist ideas.The classical liberal mistakenly identifies a particular group of makeshift compromises in the organization of representative democracies and market economies with the very nature of a free democratic and market order. The orthodox Marxist subsumes these same unique institutional arrangements under a general type of social organization that supposedly represents a well-defined stage of world history. He then excuses himself from the need to describe in detail the next, socialist stage of social evolution.

The modernist critic of roles and conventions often makes a different empirical mistake, at a higher level of abstraction. Human freedom, he is prone to believe, consists in the repeated defiance of all established institutions and conventions. We may not be able to purge social life of its structured and repetitious quality; but only so long as we continue trying can we hope to affirm our transcendence over the confining and belittling worlds in which we find ourselves.

This version of the modernist creed hopes for both too much and too little. It hopes for too much because it fails to see that we can never perform the act of defiance often enough or relentlessly enough to save ourselves from having to settle down in a particular social order. But it also hopes for too little. For all its negativism it fails to see that the relation of our context-revising freedom to the contexts we inhabit is itself up for grabs. The institutional and imaginative frameworks of social life differ in their quality as well as in their content, that is to say, in the extent to which they remain available for revision in the midst of ordinary social life. The adherent to the negativistic heresy within modernism believes that structures will be structures. But this belief imposes an unjustifiable restriction on the principle of historical variability that this same modernist ardently espouses.

The effort to correct and to unify the radical project by disengaging it from these errors holds an interest even for those who entertain little sympathy for any part of the radical commitment. The general insights and the concrete proposals that result from this exercise contribute to the solution of a dilemma that has increasingly over-shadowed our debates about social and personal ideals. We lose faith in the existence of a transcendent, secure place above particular collective traditions from which to evaluate these traditions. Yet we also rebel against the idea that we must merely choose a framework, or accept the framework we are in, and take for granted its preconceptions about the possible and desirable forms of human association. A social theory capable of informing a revised and unified version of the radical cause shows that this rebellion is justified and that it can be carried out without either promoting nihilism or perpetuating belief in an uncontroversial and definitive foundation for normative thought.

Here, as elsewhere, *Social Theory: Its Situation and Its Task* merely suggests a route that *Politics* actually clears and follows. The modest beginning serves as a reminder that we do not need a developed social theory to begin criticizing and correcting liberal, leftist, and modernist ideas. Instead, our attempts to combine, step by step, revised ideals and changed understandings can themselves help build such a theory.

A third point of departure for the intellectual enterprise launched in this book is the effort to rethink the implications of the setbacks and obstacles the radical project has encountered in recent history. (For the present purpose I have in mind the liberal and leftist rather than the modernist side of radicalism.) The disappointments of the communist revolutions and of third world experiments present the most dramatic admonitory fables. Wherever it has gained power the organized left has proved more successful at achieving economic growth, at redistributing wealth, and even at exciting nationalist fervor than at realizing the participatory self-government of which its leaders so often speak. We can glean more subtle and no less revealing lessons from the experience of leftist and liberal movements in the rich Western democracies.

In these countries the leftist and progressive liberal forces stand divided into two camps. One camp maintains the purity of its radical views at the cost of increasing difficulty in winning or maintaining electoral majorities. This left interprets radicalism from the vantage point of Marxist ideas that commit it to a rigid set of class alliances and to a narrow conception of transformative possibilities. It continues to present itself as the spokesman of an organized industrial working class, entrenched in mass-production industries that represent an ever weaker and smaller sector of the advanced economies. It remains committed to a contrast between a capitalist present whose place in world history it professes to understand and a socialist future to whose contours it can give little content other than redistribution and nationalization.

A second camp seeks to break into the mainstream and to become, or remain acceptable to, majorities. But it usually does so at the cost of abandoning its framework-transforming commitments. It settles down to a program of social democracy. This social-democratic program accepts the current institutional forms of representative democracies and regulated markets. It favors economic redistribution and grassroots participation in local government and in the workplace. And it argues that a more technical management of social problems has superseded great ideological conflicts over social life.

Social democrats regularly come face-to-face with the constraints that the existing institutional framework imposes on their redistributive and participatory aims. If they continue to take these institutional arrangements for granted they find their goals frustrated. If, on the other hand, they advocate and begin to realize alternative ways of institutionalizing representative democracies, market economies, and the social control of economic accumulation, their conception of their goals, and of their relation to familiar adversaries and allies, undergoes a drastic change.

For all its disappointments social democracy has become by default the most attractive political agenda in the world, the one with the broadest and most faithful following. Even parties whose orthodox leftist or classical-liberal rhetoric commits them to oppose the social-democratic program have, once in power, regularly contributed to its extension. The great political question of our day has become: Is social democracy the best that we can reasonably hope for?

The belief that social democracy is the best program we can expect to achieve rests on assumptions about what forms of governmental and economic organization are possible and how they change – the same assumptions criticized in other parts of this introductory book. If we are serious about assessing the claims of social democracy, we must subject these assumptions to criticism. When we do so, we discover that they do not hold up.

The explanatory and programmatic social theory into which this book leads formulates ideas that can help us push the radical project beyond the point to which social democracy has carried it. The explanatory ideas account for the failures of the radical project in ways that do not make current institutional arrangements appear to be the necessary outcomes of intractable organizational, economic, or psychological constraints. They help us find transformative opportunity in the midst of apparently insuperable constraint. They provide a credible view of social change and social invention, freeing us from the temptation to describe as realistic only those proposals that stick close to current practice. The programmatic ideas informed by these explanatory conjectures present a detailed alternative to social democracy and describe both the justifications that support this alternative and the style of transformative practice that can bring it into being. *Social Theory: Its Situation and Its Task* emphasizes the elements of the problem rather than the terms of the proposed solution. But the description of the problem anticipates the terms of the solution.

A clear connection links the three starting points that precede my discussion of the internal situation of social thought: the idea of the transformative vocation, the reinterpretation of the radical cause, and the discontent with social democracy. For the first represents the repercussion of the radical project on our expectations about work while the second shows the influence of this project on the imagination of possible social futures.

It is not surprising that a more credible social theory assists the modernist, liberal, and leftist radicals. We must be realists in order to become visionaries, and we need an understanding of social life (whether or not a theoretical understanding) to criticize and enlarge our view of social reality and social possibility. But the reverse claim that the radical perspective has a unique cognitive value, that it contributes to the development of a non-necessitarian social theory, seems far more controversial. Why, indeed, should the progress of our insight into social life be tied up with the concerns and fortunes of a particular program for the reconstruction of society? The main text of *Politics* argues that an explanatory social theory has a far closer connection to our normative commitments than modern philosophical preconceptions about facts and values allow. A fully developed social theory interprets our efforts at individual and collective self-assertion. This interpretation can prompt us to revise our preexisting beliefs about where to find self-assertion and how to achieve it. Given certain additional assumptions, which are themselves as factual as they are normative, it can even persuade us to change our ideals and commitments.

The case for the convergence of explanatory and prescriptive ideas is intricate and contentious. This argument plays no major role in this introductory work. But there is a looser and less doubtful link between the explanatory and the programmatic ideas prefigured in this book. As reinterpreted here, the radical project seeks to change the relation between formative structures and formed routines. It sees the disruption of the social mechanisms of dependence and domination as inseparable from the achievement of this objective. The basic puzzle of social explanation, the chief obstacle to generalization about society and history, the reason why social understanding remains so hard to square with scientific method, is that we are not governed fully by the established imaginative and institutional contexts of our societies and that such contexts are not interestingly determined by general laws or inflexible constraints. The radical is the person who can least afford to disregard this vocation for indiscipline. He wants to use it, to extend it, and even – by an apparent paradox – to embody it in a set of practices and institutions. He must therefore also comprehend it. Thus, to look at society and history from his standpoint (even though the onlooker may be a conservative) is to force yourself to confront the central explanatory scandal of social and historical studies in the hope of turning this embarrassment into a source of insight.

The discussion does not begin immediately with the points of departure enumerated in the preceding pages. Instead, it turns first to the description of a view of human activity – a picture of our relation to our contexts – that inspires all the programmatic and explanatory arguments of *Politics*. The social frameworks or structures with which these arguments deal are only a special case of the contexts addressed by this preliminary conception.

I do not mean this initial view of our relation to the mental or social contexts we construct and inhabit to be taken on faith. It is rather to be justified retrospectively by the relative success of the explanatory and programmatic ideas it informs. Its defense is what can be accomplished under its aegis. Nevertheless, the tentative statement of this picture of our relation to our contexts at the outset of the long, taxing, and implausible project that this book begins may help dispel ambiguities by clarifying intentions. It locates this theoretical venture in a speculative setting broader than any of the discrete points of departure for the argument.

This conception of our relation to our contexts gives a new twist to one of the oldest and most puzzling themes of our civilization: the idea that man is the infinite caught within the finite. His external circumstances belittle him. His ardors and devotions are misspent on unworthy objects. An adherent to this view of our basic circumstance is hopeful when he thinks that this disproportion between the quality of our longings and the nature of our circumstances can be diminished. He is doubly hopeful when he thinks that the methods for diminishing this disproportion are the same as the means for cleansing our relations to one another of their characteristic dangers of subjugation and of disrespect for the originality in each of us.

The social theory foreshadowed here gives a detailed social and historical content to this speculative conception and provides reasons for this double hope. Reconsidered from the perspective of this theory, the radical project has a moral significance that goes beyond the liberal or leftist aim of freeing society from structures of dependence and domination and beyond the modernist goal of rescuing subjectivity and intersubjectivity from rigid roles and unexamined conventions. This greater ambition is to make our societies more responsive to that within us which ultimately rejects these limited experiments in humanity and says that they are not enough.

2

The Conditional and the Unconditional

OUR thoughts and desires and our relations to one another never fit, completely or definitively, within the structures we impose upon belief and action. Sometimes we conduct ourselves as exiles from a world whose arrangements exclude no true insight and no worthwhile satisfaction. But more often we treat the plain, lusterless world in which we actually find ourselves, this world in which the limits of circumstance always remain preposterously disproportionate to the unlimited reach of striving, as if *its* structures of belief and action were here for keeps, as if *it* were the lost paradise where we could think all the thoughts and satisfy all the desires worth having. When we think and act in this way, we commit the sin the prophets called idolatry. As a basis for self-understanding, it is worse than a sin. It is a mistake.

Occasionally, however, we push the given contexts of thought, desire, and practical or passionate relations aside. We treat them as unreal and even as if our apparently unfounded devotion to them had been just a ploy. We think the thoughts and satisfy the desires and establish the relationships excluded, in the world we inhabit, by all the practical or conceptual structures to which we had seemed so thoroughly subjugated. We think and act, at such moments, as if we were not ultimately limited by anything. Our practical, theoretical, and spiritual progress is largely the record of these repeated limit breakings. The experience of freedom and achievement implied in such acts of defiance is iconoclastic: it works by doing things that cannot be dreamt of in the established mental or social world rather than by creating the world that could realize all dreams.

You can take the social theory anticipated in this book as the systematic development of this conception of human activity into a view of society and personality. The conception includes three elements.

The first element is the idea of the contextual or conditional quality of all human activity. To say that extended conceptual activity is conditional is to say that its practice depends on taking for granted, at least provisionally, many beliefs that define its nature and limits. These assumptions include criteria of validity, verification, or sense; a view of explanation, persuasion, or communication, and even an underlying ontology – a picture of what the world is really like. It may even include a set of premises about whether and in what sense thought and language have a structure.

Our representations cannot be both significant and open to complete revision within the framework of assumptions about sense, validity, or verification on which the significance of the representation depends. The impossibility of correcting our representations without having to change our frameworks is hardly self-evident. After all, people have often believed that they lived in a world where assumptions are never at risk. These people have not been confused They have, however, been mistaken. It just turns out that our world is really not like this. The contextual quality of thought is a brute fact. But it is not an isolated fact. It fits in with some of the other most important facts about ourselves.

All sustained practical activity takes for granted certain terms of the access that people have to one another: material, cognitive, emotional. These assumed terms appear most decisively as established powers and rights. Such rights and powers draw the outline within which people can make claims upon one another's help. Whatever its origins in conflict and coercion, a stable system of powers and rights must also work as the practical expression of a certain way of imagining society: of conceiving what the relations among people can and should be like in different areas of existence. Unless the rights and powers are read against such a background, they will not be respected and, in the end, they will not even be understood.

Society works and assumes a definite form because the fighting over all these terms of order is partly interrupted and contained. The ordinary modes of exchange and attachment, dependence and dominion, take the terms as given and derive from them both their basic shape and their accepted meaning. These facts constitute the contextual or conditional quality of social life.

There is no ordering of life in society of which we can say at the same time, first, that it can shape people's access to one another and second, that it can be compatible with all the forms of human association people might come to imagine and want. Again, this is no self-evident impossibility: you might imagine a natural form of society where the terms, though specific, were compatible with all the feasible and desirable forms of association. In such a view, the apparent departures from this natural form would turn out to be practically or morally disastrous and self-defeating. Throughout history many of the most influential social doctrines have taught some version of the belief in an authoritative model of society. Most of the modern thinkers who pretended to scorn this belief continued and continue faithful to embrace it in diluted and vestigial form.

The second element in this conception of human activity is the idea that we can always break through all contexts of practical or conceptual activity. At any moment people may think or associate with one another in ways that overstep the boundaries of the conditional worlds in which they had moved till then.

You can see or think in ways that conflict with the established context of thought even before you have deliberately and explicitly revised the context. A discovery of yours may be impossible to verify, validate, or even make sense of within the available forms of explanation and discourse; or it may conflict with the fundamental pictures of reality embodied in these forms. It may nevertheless be true. It may turn out to be a truth in the very fields that had no room for it. In the contest between the incongruous insight and the established context, the context may go under, and the proponents of the insight may discover retrospectively the terms that justify the forbidden idea.

What is true of different areas of thought, taken one by one, also holds for the work of the mind as a whole. Put together all the forms of discourse in science, philosophy, and art. Define their formative contexts however you like, so long as you define them with enough precision to save them from emptiness. The powers of the mind will never be exhaustively defined by this catalog. There will continue to be insights that do not fit any member of the list – and not just separate insights accommodated by casual adjustments here and there but whole lines of belief, explanation, or expression. No final balance can be achieved, either in the mind's life as a whole or in any segment of it, between possible insight and available discourse; the power of insight outreaches all the statable contexts of thought.

The same principle applies to the contexts of human association. People will always be able to order their relations to one another – from the most practical forms of collective labor to the most disinterested sorts of communal attachment – in ways that conflict with established terms of mutual access. Most of this deviation will be sufficiently fragmentary and truncated to seem a mere penumbra of distraction and uncertainty around the fundamentals of social order. But intensify the deviations far enough – either generalize or radicalize the local experiments – and the conflict becomes unmistakable.

What is true for any given society is true as well for all societies put together, no matter what our historical vantage point may be. There is no past, existent, or statable catalog of social orders that can accommodate all the practical or passionate relationships that people might reasonably and realistically and rightly want to establish. So the power to make society always goes beyond all the societies that exist or that have existed, just as the power to discover the truth about the world cannot keep within the forms of discourse that are its vehicles.

The second part of this view – the idea that all contexts can be broken – may seem incompatible with the first element – the idea that all activity is contextual. If, having broken the context they are in, people could simply remain outside any context, the thesis that all activity is contextual would be overturned. But the paradox is apparent. Context breaking remains both exceptional and transitory. Either it fails and leaves the preestablished context in place, or it generates another context that can sustain it together with the beliefs or relationships allied to it. An insight may enter into conflict with established criteria of validity, verification, and sense, or with a settled conception of fundamental reality. But if it tells a truth, then there will be criteria that can be retrospectively constructed with the aim of preserving it. A form of practical or passionate association may be incompatible with the established terms of mutual access. But unless it does irremediable violence to some demand of personal or collective existence, there must be a remade and reimagined social world in which it might figure. In the context of association, as in the context of representation, every act of limit breaking either fails or becomes an incident in a quick movement toward a reconstructed order.

We never overcome context dependence. But we may loosen it. For contexts of representation or relationship differ in the severity of the limits they impose on our activity. The acknowledgment of this difference is the third element in this picture of our relation to our contexts.

A conceptual or social context may remain relatively immunized against activities that bring it into question and that open it up to revision and conflict. To the extent of this immunity, a sharp contrast appears between two kinds of activities: the normal activities that move within the context and the extraordinary transformative acts that change the context itself. This contrast is both a truth and lie. Though it describes a reality, it also conceals the relativity of the distinction between context-preserving and context-breaking activities. Pushed far enough, the small-scale adjustments and revisions that accompany all our routines may turn into chances for subversion. Once you disregard this potential, the conditionality of the contexts becomes easy to forget. You can mistake the established modes of thought and human association for the natural forms of reason or relationship: that limitless plain where mind and desire and society making could wander freely without hitting against any obstacle to their further exertions.

But you can also imagine the setting of representation or relationship progressively opened up to opportunities of vision and revision. The context is constantly held up to light and treated for what it is: a context rather than a natural order. To each of its aspects there corresponds some activity that robs it of its immunity. The more a structure of thought or society incorporates the occasions and instruments of its own revision, the less you must choose between maintaining it and abandoning it for the sake of the things it excludes. You can just remake or reimagine it. Suppose, for example, a society whose formative system of powers and rights is continuously on the line, a system neither invisible nor protected against ordinary conflict; a society in which the collective experience of setting the terms of social life passes increasingly into the tenor of everyday experience; a society that therefore frees itself from the oscillation between modest, aimless bickering and extraordinary revolutionary outbursts; a society where, in some larger measure, people neither treat the conditional as unconditional nor fall to their knees as idolaters of the social world they inhabit. Imagine a scientific or artistic representation that extends the boundaries within which the mind can move without coming into conflict with the premises of the representation. Imagine, further, that this extension comes about by making the forms of representation themselves increasingly apparent, controversial, and revisable.

The cumulative change I describe in the conditions of reason or relationship neither hides nor abolishes context dependence. It recognizes it with a vengeance and, in so doing, changes its nature. To live and move in the conditional world is, then, constantly to be reminded of its conditionality. To gain a higher freedom from the context is to make the context more malleable rather than to bring it to a resting point of universal scope. Thus, the third element in the picture of human activity elucidates the coexistence of the other two elements – that everything is contextual and that all contexts can be broken.

The conception of human activity made up of these three elements confronts the mind with a central difficulty. It also helps shape an understanding of the ideal for the person and the society.

All our major problems in the understanding of society arise from the same source. They have to do with the difficulty of accounting for the actions of a being who, individually and collectively, in thought and relationship, might break through the contexts within which he ordinarily moves. The perennial temptation in the understanding of society and personality is to equate the very nature of explanation with an explanatory style that treats people's actions and thoughts as governed by a describable structure. When we make this mistake, we deny the power to discover truth and establish association beyond the limits of the available contexts. Or we treat these episodes of structure breaking as if they were themselves governed by metastructures. The metastructure may be a set of ultimate constraints upon possible social worlds accompanied by more specific accounts of why certain possible worlds become actual at given times. Or it may be the scheme of a lawlike evolution that controls the passage from one social order to the next. To disengage the idea of explanation from the exclusive hold of these styles of explanation is the beginning of insight in social thought. Indeed, for the theorist of society it is the most exacting and delicate of tasks.

The same picture of human activity transforms our vision of the ideal for society and personality if it does not generate an ideal by its own force. Because we do not move in a context of all contexts, there is the danger that our views of the social ideal will turn out to be a projection of the particular society into which we happen to have been thrown. The objectivity possible in the formulation of a social ideal must have something to do with its ability to incorporate the next best thing to absolute knowledge and fulfilled desire: not to be a prisoner of the context. The pursuit of this demand is intimately entangled with our desire not to be prisoners of one another. It is even bound up with the history of our practical capabilities.

The conception of human action I have outlined must be justified, in part, by its fruits. *Politics* turns it into a general view of society and personality. The spirit of this view is to understand reality from the perspective of transformation. The little, endless quarrels within contexts will be shown to contain the secret of the great struggles over contexts. The scheme of transformative variation that enables us to explain events must not be one that mythologizes society and history by treating the breaking of contexts either as if it were itself a context-governed activity or, to the extent it is not so governed, as if it were unintelligible, a gap in the powers of explanation and judgment. The truth of human freedom, of our strange freedom from any given finite structure, must count, count affirmatively, for the way we understand ourselves and our history.

The social theory that develops this view of our relation to our contexts is a theory that unrelentingly rejects what might be called the naturalistic premise about society. Because the discussion of this premise and of the consequences of its rejection plays a central role in the arguments of this introductory book, I now define it tentatively. The definition will be enriched, gathering both precision and richness of connotation, as the analysis moves forward.

The naturalistic premise represents a denial of the conditionality of social worlds. It takes a particular form of social life as the context of all contexts – the true and undistorted form of social existence. By repudiating the first element in the account of our relation to our contexts sketched earlier, the naturalistic thesis also rejects the other elements. The natural context of social life may pass through decay or renascence, but it cannot be remade. Nor is there, in this view, any sense in which the defining context of social life can become less contextual – less arbitrary and confining. It is already the real thing.

The naturalistic thesis may now be defined in slightly greater detail and more independently of this view of human activity. It holds up the picture of an ordering of human life that is not the mere product of force and fraud. This ordering, sustained by a system of powers and rights, includes a practical scheme of coordination, contrast, and ranking. It makes each individual's membership in the division of labor an occasion to reaffirm the general scheme of order. It constantly draws new life from the pursuit of ordinary interests within the terms it establishes. It claims to see into the innermost core of society and personality. This authentic pattern of social life can undergo corruption and regeneration. But it can never be rearranged. To uphold the natural social order is the basic social piety.

The canonical form of society is natural in the sense that the distinction between what it prescribes and what force and fraud conspire to establish is given: given in the truth about personality and society rather than merely chosen or brought about by fighting; changeless and only partly intelligible, like the great natural world around us. The reconstructive will and imagination can make only a modest dent on this natural order, when indeed they can exercise any influence on it at all.

Again, the canonical form of social life is natural in that it emerges when ravenous and fragmentary interests, and the partiality of viewpoint they favor, have been either effectively tamed or wisely combined. Natural society is society understood and established beyond the perspective of the will, always the perspective of one-sidedness and self-assertion.

Finally, the canonical form of social life is natural because it is seen as connecting fundamental truth about society to equally basic truth about personality. The import of this correspondence must be left deliberately loose: it bears different philosophical interpretations. All clear-cut versions of the naturalistic premise, however, attribute to the personality some proper order of emotions, or of virtues and vices. This order sustains, and is in turn renewed by, the arrangements of the larger society. A person's repeated willingness to meet the claims that the natural social order assigns to him exercises a shaping, incantatory, even redemptive influence upon the dark, labile force of his emotions.

The naturalistic premise has been the central element in most of the forms of social thought throughout history. Modern social theory rebelled against the naturalistic idea. It did so, however, incompletely. Many of its contradictions and inadequacies arise from the incompleteness of this rebellion. We must find a way to complete it.

3

The Circumstance of Social Theory

A Further Point of Departure

SOCIETY AS MADE AND IMAGINED

Each of the points of departure discussed in the previous chapters can carry us forward to the beginnings of a social theory that extends the conception of society as artifact. A criticism of the current situation of social and historical thought can reach similar results more directly. It can reach them quite apart from the effort to make sense of the idea of a transformative vocation, or to reimagine the social ideal, or to reflect on the constraints and opportunities of practical action.

I begin with a loose comparison of the history of our modern ideas about mind and society with the history of certain modern views of nature. This comparison lays the basis for the more detailed discussion that follows. It also connects the analysis of the internal problems of social theory with the picture of human activity presented at the start of the book.

The Broader Intellectual Context: The Rejection of Self-Evident and Unconditional Knowledge

The whole body of established ideas about nature was once viewed as a system of propositions ultimately deducible from axioms that were both true and self-evident. Self-evidence implies incorrigibility, truths that need never be revised. Incorrigibility and self-evidence together testify to truth. A particular theory of the physical world may have been discovered under the impulse of tortuous reasonings and carefully analyzed observations. Once formulated, however, its basis could be seen to lie in self-evident and incorrigible axioms.

This Euclidean view of science never recovered from the blow it suffered when Newton's mechanics turned out to be less than the last word on nature. The philosophical understanding of science sought refuge in a variety of fallback positions. People discovered that self-evidence was no touchstone of truth: no one picture of the physical world remained safe against rejection or demotion to the category of a special case. Neverthe-less, scientists and philosophers continued to hope that certain features of a way of doing science or certain ideas within the changing body of scientific theories might remain above the flux. Sometimes this device of immunity was found in certain privileged representations, like the concepts of space and time. These representations supposedly described a pre-theoretical experience whose core content remained stable as the substance of scientific theories changed. Sometimes the invariant guarantee of objectivity became a conception of the scientific method, including criteria of validity, verification, and sense. So long as claims could be justified by the appeal to a preestablished and unchanging canon of explanation, all was well. Thus, the idea of a theoretical system that gained self-evidence through its axioms was swept aside. It gave way to the chastened program of a science that based its hope of objectivity on the continuing deployment of a few immutable elements: its basic ideas or methods.

But the fallback positions from the Euclidean idea of science proved temporary reprieves. All candidates for the role of foundational conceptions, including the geometrical ideas that had originally supplied the model for absolute certainty in science, remained vulnerable to changes in the content of scientific theories. As the content of scientific theories changed, so, albeit more slowly, did fundamental scientific ideas and conceptions of scientific method.

The criteria for objectivity and progression in science had to be found elsewhere: in the self-correcting qualities of science or in the demonstrated bearing of this endless work of self-revision on the advancement of certain practical interests. Such interests defined a relation to the world more basic than knowledge. The major disputes about science became the controversies among ways – from the realist to the skeptical – to understand the intellectual situation resulting from the abandonment of views that tried to rescue part of the old ideal of incorrigibility.

To push the rejection of that ideal far enough, however, is to discover an alternative basis for objectivity. In its capacity to discover truth – to reason in new ways or to have incongruous perceptions – the mind is never entirely imprisoned by its current beliefs. It can achieve insights that it may not be able to verify, validate, or even make sense of within the established criteria of validity, verification, or sense. All past and present modes of discourse put together do not exhaust our faculties of understanding. If objectivity cannot consist in the attachment to unrevisable and self-authenticating elements in thought, then it may lie in the negative capability not to imprison insight in any particular structure of thought. It is even possible that science may progress through the development of ideas and practices that accelerate the process of self-correction. Thus, the wheel would come full circle: objectivity through maximum corrigibility.

The Failure to Rescue the Ideal of Unconditional Knowledge

The movement away from an ideal of incorrigible knowledge undermines belief in the quest for unconditional or absolute knowledge described at the start of this book. Unconditional knowledge is the knowledge whose basic structure of explanation and criteria of validity, verification, and sense are compatible with the discovery of any truth, or with the making of any defensible claim, about the world. Knowledge, in this view, can be incomplete and nevertheless unconditional so long as it can grow without subverting its own basic methods and assumptions. The decisive quality of unconditional claims is the definitive, all-inclusive character of the framework of standards of sense, validity, and verification on which these claims rely. For knowledge to be unconditional these assumptions must be both significant (that is, they must provide effective guidance) and sufficient (that is, they must accommodate all true or defensible claims). Once the ideal of unconditional knowledge is defined in this way, it no longer seems able to survive the repudiation of self-evidence as a criterion of truth. What is abandoned with the rejection of the Euclidean and Cartesian ideal of self-evidence is not simply a criterion of assent. It is also the ideal of unchallengeable assumptions.

Nor can we hope to rescue from the wreck of the idea of an absolute frame of reference, interpreted as a body of indisputable truths, the related notion of a type of knowledge whose guarantee of objectivity is its ability to account for all other more local representations of the world and for itself. Either we cannot tell a complete story about our experience, or about any part of our experience, or we can tell it only on terms that guarantee the availability of many different complete stories. The resulting need to choose among alternative complete stories severs the link between completeness and absolute knowledge. Moreover, the objectivity we are actually interested in has little to do with the completeness of the stories we can tell. A complete story would not stop with facts about non-human nature that lend themselves more or less successfully to explanation by reference to closed systems or random process. It would have to account for the mental and social activities that are not governed by any lawlike list of structures of thought or of social life. It would have to be a higher-order view capable of dealing with both the most structure-dependent and the most structure-breaking phenomena. But where are we to look for such a metaview? As it becomes more complete, it would probably also become more controversial and provisional. For that very reason, it would suggest alternative complete stories.

The same point can be restated more loosely and intuitively. Any complete story about nature and society lacks the compelling character of the most compelling local narratives. We cannot retell the interesting parts of such a story in the language of natural science: many if not all the things that matter most to us about society and consciousness slip through the net of natural-scientific explanation. Or they demand an immeasurably large and fine net: a theory that can never finish the statement of intermediate links between ultimate physical causes and immediate social or mental experiences in time to explain anything at all.

Many of the most influential modern thinkers tried to reestablish the idea of an absolute frame of reference. Yet in each instance their doctrines turn out to be compatible with the critique I have rehearsed. Consider the examples of two very different philosophers: Peirce and Hegel. For Peirce the basis of objectivity in science became the gradual convergence of scientific opinion toward a final opinion, "independent not indeed of thought but of all that is arbitrary and individual in thought." It hardly violates his central insight to interpret independence from what is arbitrary and individual as a heightened autonomy from confining presuppositions. This autonomy may in turn be seen less as an outcome, completed once and for all, within the history of thought, than as a continuing process and a regulative ideal governing this process. You can say the same, though with less assurance, of Hegel's idea of absolute insight. For, though we can interpret this idea as completed and unconditional knowledge, we can also read it as an ideal limit, never actually reached. It is the affirmative mirror image of the negative, cumulative practice of context smashing that plays so large a role in Hegel's detailed studies of mind and society.

So the history of our views of nature suggests that the ideal of unconditional knowledge cannot survive the rejection of self-evidence as a criterion of truth; that we can no more hope for unconditional knowledge as a complete story about all stories than for unconditional knowledge as incorrigible insight; that the abandonment of the search for an absolute frame of reference in either of these two senses does not prejudice the possibility of cumulative insight but supplies us instead with a more modest and realistic version of objectivity – the assurance of not being definitively and completely imprisoned by whatever basic assumptions we happen to have inherited; that objectivity so understood implies corrigibility rather than its opposite; and that this entire view, though leaving open all options in the philosophy of science short of extreme skepticism or dogmatism, can be reconciled with some of the famous philosophical doctrines that seem to antagonize it.

From the Rejection of the Ideal of Unconditional Knowledge to the Abandonment of the Naturalistic View of Society

The naturalistic premise dominated the most influential forms of social thought in much of world history. Whether or not the ruling doctrines invoked divine sanction, they portrayed a mode of social life meant to represent the natural form of civilization. The core form of society could undergo corruption or regeneration. But it could never be fundamentally remade or reimagined.

These doctrines had both a social and a personal message. Each transmuted a particular ordering of human life into a universal image of human possibility. In forming this image each treated a particular collective tradition as defining the universe of collective opportunities. But because each conceded that the social order might be corrupted it could also denounce contemporary social practices as departures from the canon of desirable human relations. The correct social order helped form the emotions in right and beneficial ways. These emotions, in turn, renewed the life of the canonical social scheme. When all went well, the just order of division and hierarchy in society would sustain, and be sustained by, a hierarchy of faculties in the soul.

These beliefs form a close counterpart to the Euclidean idea of science. They appeal to self-evidence as a test of truth. More generally, they provide an absolute frame of reference: the image of a social order that, though richly defined, provides an unconditional measure of human value and possibility. No wonder the gradual abandonment of the naturalistic premise in natural science offers so many parallels to the subversion of the naturalistic premise in social theory.

The history of all that is great and powerful in modern social thought is in large part the history of the rejection of this naturalistic view of society, each new movement of thought attacking its predecessor for the naturalistic residues it continued to harbor. Much in our modern ideas about society represents the relentless development of the principle contained in Vico's statement that man can understand the social world because he made it. But even today this idea has still not been carried to the extreme point. At the height of its struggle against the naturalistic view of society, the Vicoan principle came under the spell of alien conceptions and concerns. Thus, a series of compromises with the naturalistic theory emerged. In the character, and even in the motives, of their relation to earlier, more purely naturalistic doctrines, these compromises resembled the initial fallback positions from the Euclidean idea of science. They all made social and historical explanation depend upon a reference to deep-seated economic, organizational, or psychological constraints, often thought to generate a list of types or stages of social organization. To the extent that this concealed guiding plan failed to determine historical events or social facts, you had to resort to weaker, contextualized explanations.

The first example of this strategy of compromise with the naturalistic view had been the idea of a science of human nature or of morals that would lay bare the basic laws of mind and behavior (e. g., Mill's idea of a foundational science of ethology). Particular societies could then be portrayed as variations on the central themes described by this foundational science. For this idea to work, you had to believe that this science could explain the most important matters in history and society. The rest would be detail or development. The romantic movement in historiography, magnified by later anthropological and literary discoveries, posed the essential challenge to this project. There were just too many ways to be human. The differences among them went to the heart rather than to the details.

The second major compromise form of the naturalistic idea of society to appear in the history of modern Western social thought was the idea of a set of constraints rooted in practical social needs to produce, to organize, and to exchange. The convergence of this second compromise idea with the first one gave rise to classical political economy. The main objection to the second compromise was the looseness of the relation between the practical imperatives and the actual forms of society that these imperatives were alleged to shape. There always seemed to be too many social routes to the execution of the same practical tasks.

A third compromise appeared when people began to think that these transformative constraints had a certain cumulative direction of their own. Social worlds, in this view, fall into a natural sequence, each of them an indissoluble system of institutional traits. In the nineteenth-century heyday of Western world conquest, this belief found support in the impression that a mode of life and belief, originally championed by the conquering Western powers, lay on the verge of taking over the world.

The combination of this third compromise idea with the previous one inspired many of the great social theories of the late nineteenth and the early twentieth centuries. These are the views discussed in greater detail in the following sections of this book as deep-structure or deep-logic theories of society. Marxism is the most important example. History just did not happen as these deep-structure theories required. Events kept breaking out of the correct transformative sequence and producing social worlds that fitted none of the stages or alternatives through which mankind supposedly had to pass and from which it supposedly had to choose.

These compromises survive today in the form of an essentially simple intellectual predicament. The adherents to the deep-logic social theories oscillate between a reality-denying commitment to the hard-core versions of doctrines like Marxism and an attempt to absorb resistant fact by dissolving these doctrines into a morass of metaphor and suggestion. The mainstream of economics has abandoned the goal of combining a science of mind with a science of material and organizational constraints. Instead, it has taken refuge in a strategy of analytic neutrality toward substantive empirical or normative controversies about social life. The earlier, classical ambition survives only in the preconceptions and shibboleths of ruling elites (who nevertheless regard themselves as free from theoretical prejudice) and in the handy stratagems of macroeconomics. Finally, the idea of a foundational science of mind and morals reappears occasionally in the major traditions of individual psychology and psychiatry. In them, however, it connects only tenuously with the understanding of society. A multitude of self-contented researchers practice an empirical social science, confident of their freedom from the arbitrary and constraining assumptions made by the other, more high-flown brands of social theory. But their practice of explanation has proved to be less an alternative way of imagining personality or society than the more or less confused and unpremeditated combination of the fallback positions described later in this chapter.

Another way to understand the point of this book is to read it as an effort to take the antinaturalistic idea of society to the extreme. The argument anticipates a view that refuses to hedge on the conception of society as artifact. Such a theoretical project would just keep going from where all the incomplete realizations of the view of society as artifact – all the halfway departures from the naturalistic approach – leave off. Once the naturalistic premise had been conclusively rejected, the view of personality, the analysis of practical constraints, and the recognition of cumulative transformative influences might all be reintroduced, purged of the residues of the naturalistic idea. Social and historical explanations would no longer rely on lawlike conceptions claiming to define the limits of possible social worlds or to determine the necessary sequence of actual social orders.

To understand society in such a spirit represents the counterpart, in social thought, of the full-fledged abandonment of the Euclidean idea of science, with its appeal to incorrigibility as a test of truth and its search for an absolute frame of reference. People once feared that to abandon the Euclidean idea of science would be to lay down all defenses of skepticism. Only later did they discover that the rejection of objectivity as incorrigibility enabled them to recover objectivity as an extreme corrigibility. So, too, it may seem today that to sever all remaining connections with the naturalistic premise would leave us without a way to imagine society or to formulate the social ideal.

We ordinarily admit into our thoughts only that measure of seemingly disordered reality to which we can give an active response. To limit the perception of reality is the natural strategy of intellectual survival: the mind fears being overwhelmed by more than it can imaginatively order. But unless we occasionally move at the edge of our imaginative capabilities we cannot hope to extend our vision of reality and to refine our conception of how things may be ordered.

Social theory today must choose between two directions. It can stick to its compromises with the naturalistic premise, continuing to imagine society from the standpoint of a vision of compulsive sequence or of possible social worlds. When we choose this path we become entangled in an ever denser web of intellectual equivocation and aimlessness whose character the next few sections of this book describe. Alternatively, we can reject all compromise, pursue the initial, antinaturalistic route of modern social thought to its outermost limits, and see what happens.

The following pages set out in detail the circumstance of social theory at the close of the twentieth century. They then show how the effort to respond to this circumstance in different fields of thought about society suggests a point of departure for the remaking of social theory – a point of departure that is most constructive precisely where it seems most nihilistic. Just as you can reach similar concerns and ideas from other, more practical beginnings, so, within theory itself, you can also start from the internal problems of different disciplines and arrive at convergent conclusions.

DEEP-STRUCTURE SOCIAL THEORY

Two partial dissolutions and partial reinstatements of the naturalistic view of society dominate the history of modern social thought. One of them is the practice of deep-structure or deep-logic social theory, which has taken ever more diluted and equivocal forms. The other is conventional, empiricist, or positivist social science, whose theoretical agenda, methods, and self-conception have been shaped in large part by the perceived failures of the deep-logic tradition. The crucial difference between deep-structure social analysis and conventional social science turns on their respective attitudes toward the existence of institutional and imaginative frameworks that stand apart from the routines of social life and shape these routines.

In this section I examine the distinctive characteristics of deep-structure analysis. Marxism serves here as its most richly developed and influential example. But many other famous modern social theories also illustrate deep-logic methods and principles. Thus, Durkheim's theory of society, especially as stated in *The Division of Labor in Society*, might well replace Marxism as my primary example even though its distinctive explanations and political intentions differ strikingly from Marx's. Moreover, it should be clear from the outset that much in the writings of Marx and his followers not only resists assimilation to the tenets of deep-structure analysis but provides tools for attacking those tenets. The next section studies the lessons to be learned from the evolution of Marxism. For the moment the discussion focuses on an approach that no theorist has ever fully accepted but that many theorists have implicitly treated as the bedrock of generalization about society and history.

Deep-structure social analysis is defined by its devotion to three recurrent theoretical moves. These moves are not reducible to one another. Together, they represent a specific approach toward social and historical explanation. Despite the many difficulties to which it gives rise, this approach deserves study not only because of its remarkable influence but because of the continuing failure to construct an alternative at a comparable level of theoretical generality and ambition.

The Distinction Between Routines and Frameworks

The first distinctive mental operation of deep-structure social theory is the attempt to distinguish in every historical circumstance a formative context, structure, or framework from the routine activities this context helps reproduce. The most important of these routines are the repetitious practices of conflict and compromise that perpetually create the social future within the social present. These practices include the methods of normative controversy (legal, moral, or theological) as well as the methods for exchanging commodities and labor and for winning and using governmental power. To portray them is to describe the habitual disposition of the major resources of society making: economic capital, state power, practical knowledge, and accepted moral and social ideals.

The deep-structure analyst emphasizes the distinction between these routines and a framework of social life. This framework is distinctive, but, as we shall soon see, it is never unique. For deep-logic theory repudiates from the beginning the naturalistic commitment to a single, canonical ordering of human life. It prides itself on its ability to recognize the discontinuity among social worlds created in history, seeing in each of these worlds a genuinely unique solution to the problems of mankind.

Each of these formative contexts is defined by its ability to help generate and sustain a richly developed set of practical and imaginative routines and by its corresponding tendency to resist disturbance. The framework is not vulnerable to the effects of the low-level conflicts and compromises it shapes. A sharp contrast therefore exists between these everyday disputes or combinations and the revolutionary transformations that replace one basic structure with another. And a special theory is required to explain how such transformations come about.

A formative context may consist in imaginative assumptions about the possible and desirable forms of human association as well as in institutional arrangements or noninstitutionalized social practices. Each deep-logic theory pictures frameworks and the relative influence of the elements that compose them in its own way. This picture already implies an account of how such frameworks get made and remade.

In Marx's theory of history the formative contexts are the modes of production. The most important constituents of each mode of production, given Marx's theory of historical change, are the legally defined institutional arrangements that govern the regimes of labor and capital and, more specifically, the relation of each class to the productive resources of society. The most significant routines are the daily forms of production and exchange, especially the repeated transactions by which some classes (i.e., the occupants of standard positions in the social division of labor) gain control over the labor of other classes and over the product of that labor. But the mode of production exercises an influence over social life that goes far beyond the organization of production and influences even the most intimate and intangible aspects of social life.

It may seem strange to cite the distinction between the defining institutions and the resulting routines of a mode of production without immediately relating this distinction to the explanatory conjectures that loom so large in Marx's system: the ideas that a mode of production is eventually succeeded by another when it begins to hinder the maximum development of the productive forces of society and that it generates within itself a class with the interest and the ability to lead the transition to the next mode of production. But these ideas represent the specifically functionalist aspect of Marx's theory. They explain the emergence of a mode of production as a consequence of the contribution which that mode makes to the fullest development of the forces of production. They use class interest and class conflict to show how the consequence can operate as a cause. I want to show, however, that even within Marxism the deep-structure moves are more fundamental than the functionalist story.

Particular Frameworks as Instances of General Types

The second mental operation that distinguishes deep-structure theory is the effort to represent the framework identified in a particular circumstance as an example of a repeatable and indivisible type of social organization such as capitalism. There are two main variants of deep-structure social theory: one evolutionary, the other nonevolutionary. Each of them casts in a distinct light the types that particular frameworks exemplify. The nonevolutionary version sees a closed list of possible frameworks, not ordered in any necessary sequence. The evolutionary version believes in a compulsive, world-historical sequence of stages of social organization, with each stage a type.

In the nonevolutionary version the repeatable character of the type is unmistakable. In the right circumstances a form of social organization can recur. But repeatability also holds good in the evolutionary variant of this style of analysis. Even when the theory argues for an irreversible historical sequence it is likely to recognize that different countries may pass through the necessary stages at different times. This recognition represents more than a concession to historical plausibility; it also lends support to an explanatory approach that refuses to treat a framework as merely the singular outcome of a singular history.

Indivisibility is the other quality a framework must possess in order to play the explanatory role that deep-structure analysis demands of it. A formative context must stand or fall as a single piece. If it lacked this atomic quality the idea of a closed list of possible types of social organization or of a compulsive sequence of stages of social organization would be hard to maintain; there would simply be too many possible social worlds and evolutionary trajectories.

Much of Marx's theory of history can be understood as an evolutionary version of deep-structure analysis. The modes of production fall into a sequence, a sequence determined by the fit between sets of institutional arrangements and levels in the development of the productive forces of society. Capitalism is supposed to be capitalism in China as much as in England or Italy. Familiar controversies internal to Marxism, such as the debate about the "Asiatic mode of production," already suggest the difficulties that history places in the way of this theory; and the attempt to understand the worldwide hierarchical relations among supposedly capitalist national economies complicates matters further. The thesis that each mode of production represents a general and repeatable type is greatly strengthened if each such mode can be shown to arise by independent origin as well as by diffusion from a single source. But whatever importance may be given to independent origins, the deep-structure style of analysis requires that nothing vital about capitalism, for example, turn on its original European source.

A mode of production is also indivisible. Some of its elements may come under attack before others. But once the attack begins, either it must be temporarily suppressed or it must result in the replacement of one predefined stage or mode by another. One corollary is that there is a fundamental difference between the disputes and reforms that leave a system of relations of production intact and the revolutionary struggles and discoveries (discoveries rather than inventions) that usher in the next mode of production. Another corollary is that mixed modes of production turn out to be either unstable, transitional forms or satellites of another, dominant mode of production. An example that plays an important role later in *Politics* is petty commodity production: the would-be system of independent producers who neither work for others nor control (non-reciprocally) any considerable pool of dependent wage labor.

General Types as Subjects of Lawlike Explanations

The third characteristic move of deep-structure social analysis is the appeal to the deep-seated constraints and the developmental laws that can generate a closed list or a compulsive sequence of repeatable and indivisible frameworks. A view of the internal composition of these frameworks and a theory of their making and transformation complement each other.

The nonevolutionary deep-structure analyst must appeal to underlying constraints that set the limits to the list of possible social orders and that, by excluding many combined forms, determine the composition of the list. These constraints may be economic, organizational, or even psychological. The more interesting the theory, the tighter and more richly defined the mediating causal links that connect these ultimate constraints to observable features of particular social worlds and the more likely the theory is to define as possible certain forms of social life that have not yet been established while excluding as impossible others that people have vainly sought to inaugurate. If the theorist of possible social worlds is especially ambitious he may even explain why a possible form of organization becomes actual in a given circumstance. But these explanations may be particularistic or fragmentary, and they are in any event less important to this theoretical endeavor than the ideas that account for the configuration of the possible.

The evolutionary deep-structure analyst must deploy lawlike explanations that generate a particular sequence of particular frameworks. The purpose of the account must be to present what actually happened as a murky, unfinished procession of specific frameworks of social life and to credit this procession to a developmental logic of unfolding capabilities and insights or of cumulative causal influences. Marx provided such an account. There will be more to say about its character when the discussion turns to the relation between deep-structure analysis and functional explanation.

Both the evolutionary and nonevolutionary variants of deep-structure analysis must appeal to laws and constraints far removed from the intentions and understandings of historical agents. People may exceptionally will a new structure of social life into existence or grasp the relation between the invention of a new framework and the development of certain faculties or interests. But even then they are not conscious of standing on a single cumulative trajectory or do not agree on its definition. And the goals and consequences are likely to have at best a troubled relation to each other. When deep-logic theory is interesting, when it does more than lend a spurious semblance of necessity to established arrangements, it is also secret knowledge, and it requires a wrenching out from the perspective of commonsense experience.

The second and third moves of deep-structure social theory – the subsumption of a particular framework under a repeatable and indivisible type and the appeal to deep-seated laws and constraints – are closely linked. Without both of them the deep-structure theorist sees no way to combine explanatory generalization with respect for the distinction between the shaping structures and the shaped routines of social life. He would, he believes, be driven to a style of generalizing explanation that disregards, one way or another, the importance of the difference between change of a framework and change within a framework. He would therefore also lose the means with which to describe and understand the discontinuities among frameworks and among the whole forms of life, thought, and sensibility they help sustain. One outcome of this attempt to free generalizing explanation from the framework-routine distinction might be the return to the old project of a unified science of mind and behavior that can explain the diversity of customs. Another result might be to settle for much more modest explanations in the fashion of the positivist social science and the naive historiography discussed later in this book. Whatever its specified form, the abandonment of the contrast between the formative and the formed threatens our ability to acknowledge the radical differences among past frameworks of social life. It therefore also undermines our sense of our power radically to remake our own society. Without imagination of structural variety, the stakes go down in practical politics as well as in theoretical controversy.

The Limits of Deep-Structure Analysis

Much of the discussion in the following sections of this book is meant to show that deep-logic social theory purchases this conception of structural diversity at too high a cost. Part of the cost is a loss of descriptive and explanatory plausibility; the facts simply do not fit. Another part of the cost, however, has to do with the constraint that deep-structure analysis imposes on the imagination of structural diversity itself. It relies on the notion of a closed list of structures. It makes generalizing explanation depend on a script that towers over conscious actions and works through them. It fails to see that the character, as well as the content, of formative contexts is put up for grabs in history: there are major variations in the extent to which the institutional and imaginative orders of social life reduce us to passivity or, on the contrary, make themselves available to us for challenge and revision. In all these ways the deep-structure tradition hedges on the repudiation of the naturalistic premise and sacrifices to its scientistic apparatus much of its vision of social order as made and imagined rather than as given.

A major aim of *Politics* is to develop and illustrate an explanatory practice that preserves the first move of deep-structure social theory – the distinction between framework and routine – while replacing the other two moves with an alternative style of generalization. A great deal more than theoretical correctness depends on whether we can carry out such a reorientation. From its beginnings deep-logic social theory has been the chief theoretical instrument of what might be called the radical project or the enterprise of the modernist visionary: the effort to seek our individual and collective empowerment through the progressive dissolution of rigid social division and hierarchy and stereotyped social roles. The explanatory failures of deep-structure social theory jeopardize the advancement of that project. For, as my discussion of transformative practice has already suggested, these failures encourage prejudices and tactics that obstruct the realization of the leftist and modernist program.

The most serious dangers that deep-structure analysis poses to the endeavor of the modernist visionary are precisely the dangers that arise from its truncation of our insight into structural diversity: the closure imposed on the sense of historical possibility, the reliance on an explanatory script and, most importantly, the inability to grasp how and why the relation between the formative and the formed, between social structure and human agency, may change. Deep-structure social theory disorients political strategy and impoverishes programmatic thought by making both of them subsidiary to a ready-made list or sequence of social orders. Nowhere are these perils clearer than in the reliance of leftist movements, the major bearers of the radical project, on Marxism, the most developed version of deep-structure social theory.

Deep-Structure Analysis and Functional Explanation

The problem of functional explanation can now be related to the discussion of deep-logic social analysis. The tradition I have been calling deep-structural is often associated with functional explanation. The association is so constant and the difficulties of functional explanation so familiar that the criticism of functional accounts regularly overshadows the critique of the deep-structure moves.

Functional explanations account for the emergence or the perpetuation of a state of affairs by the consequences that the state of affairs produces. The consequence operates as a cause. When action is intentional the mechanism by which the consequence acquires causative power is straightforward: the consequence, intended by the agent, serves as a motive to action, and the agent's control over his environment enables him to carry out his intentions. But the further away we move in social and historical study from the paradigm instance of intentionality, the more controversial the use of functional explanation becomes: if there ceases to be a well-defined individual or collective agent, or if the agent's control over his environment weakens, or if the sheer length and complexity of the causal sequence disrupt the translation of intentions into consequences. Once any link with intentional action disappears, the justification for functional explanation in social or historical study may depend on the availability of a social counterpart to natural selection.

The form of functionalist explanation that fits most easily with deep-structure social analysis combines three ideas. Once again, Marx's theory of history provides the clearest illustration. The first idea is a test of reality or success. Read, in Marxism, the maximum development of the forces of production. The second key concept is that of a response: a state of affairs capable of ensuring that the test is met. Read the mode of production: the relations among people, centered on the organization of labor and the exchange of the products of labor, but implicating, in ever wider nets of influence, an entire way of life. The main weight of the system is borne by a third idea: a story that tells how over a period of time the states of affairs adjust so as to meet the test of reality or success.

A mode of production exhibits a given set of class relations. Eventually this set of class relations begins to hinder the further development of the productive forces of society. A new class emerges whose particular interest in the overthrow of the existing mode of production coincides with the universal human interest in the development of mankind's productive capabilities.

This story is functionalist because it is a consequence of contributing to the maximum expansion of the productive forces of society at a given level of their development that ultimately explains not only the rise and persistence of each mode of production but the world-historical sequence that all the modes follow. But in Marxism, as in many of the other most influential social theories, the functionalist story hinges on deep-structure assumptions. The deep-structure moves, not the functionalist quality of the explanation, are responsible for the thesis that only indivisible and repeatable frameworks – the modes of production – rather than, say, discrete institutional arrangements, can bring about the explanatory consequence – the fullest development of the productive forces. Many of the most familiar functionalist claims in Marx's theory depend on such implicit deep-structure premises.

Notice also that the most obvious and formidable objection to a functionalist narrative like the story about the productive forces and the modes of production has more to do with the deep-structural backdrop to the tale than with the functionalist's traditional conundrum of how the consequence serves as a cause. Any given set and level of practical capabilities can characteristically be realized by alternative sets of institutional arrangements, not just by a unique set. Many nonconvergent institutional pathways can therefore also lead to the development of similar practical abilities. The aspects of Marx's theory that stand in the way of recognizing such possibilities are the deep-structural tenets, not the functionalist style.

Suppose that we could successfully reform Marx's theory of history so as to make it consistent with the idea that alternative modes of production and alternative sequences of such modes can serve to realize a similar level of development of productive forces. Then, the traditional puzzle of functional explanation – the difficulty of explaining how the consequence acts as a cause – would be aggravated rather than solved. We would need to show why one trajectory prevails over another. We could not explain this prevalence functionally, for in our revised view the explanatory consequence (the development of the forces of production) can be achieved by more than one route. A nonfunctional explanation would be required. But once we had this explanation, functional explanation might well become superfluous. In explaining the triumph of one evolutionary route over another, we would also have explained the evolutionary route itself; no work would be left over for the functional account to do. The revisionist deep-structure analyst might well say of functional explanation what Laplace said of God: "I have no need of this hypothesis." Thus, when we try to expand deep-structure analysis to avoid the additional difficulties it creates for functional explanation we unwittingly intensify the functionalist's most traditional problem of linking final and efficient causes. We obscure rather than clarify the relevance of an analysis of the distant consequences of a state of affairs to an understanding of its occurrence. This problem, it seems, cannot be solved unless we sever the link between deep-structure analysis and functional explanation and abandon either one or the other.

A deep-structure social theory can dispense with functional explanations. Consider, for example, Durkheim's emphasis, in *The Division of Labor*, on sheer demographic pressure as a cause of the passage from mechanical to organic solidarity. Conversely, functionalist explanation may be deployed in theories that reject the deep-logic style of explanation. But deep structure without functionalism is likely to result in an aggressively mechanical and superdeterministic theory, portraying historical agents as caught in structures whose built-in tendencies dwarf conscious human interests and intentions. On the other hand, a theory that makes functional explanations independent of deep-structural assumptions must either reject the distinction between the formative context and the formed routines or find a way to make this distinction independent of the other two moves of deep-structure theory. These considerations go a long way toward explaining why deep-logic analysis and functional explanation appear so regularly conjoined despite the severability of their connection.

The criticism of the comprehensive social theories of the modern age has traditionally focused more on their functionalist aspects than on their deep-structure characteristics. The discussion here of the predicament of social thought reflects a belief that this emphasis is misplaced. For in these theories functional explanations characteristically achieve their power only when combined with deep-structure principles, and it is these tenets that bring us closest to the core intentions of the theories that are functionalist as well as deep-structural. More importantly, the primacy accorded to the critique of functionalism is misdirected because the substitution of the deep-structure moves can generate far more surprising and illuminating results than the abandonment or demotion of functionalist analysis. Once we do the right thing to the deep-structure tradition, the problems of functional explanation may very largely take care of themselves. As the argument of *Politics* passes from criticism to construction it makes good on these claims.

MARXISM AS AN EVOLUTIONARY DEEP-STRUCTURE SOCIAL THEORY

The Two-Sided Relation of Marxism to Deep-Structure Analysis

Marx's theory of history is the most richly developed and influential example of deep-structure social theory. As such, it has provided the radical project with its most important theoretical weapon. Yet in Marx's writings we may also find many ideas that not only resist assimilation to deep-structure views but also provide means with which to criticize and reconstruct those views. Three of these countervailing themes stand out. They are mentioned here less out of a desire to do justice to the historical Marx (who cares about that?) than because of the role that each, once revised, plays in the constructive social theory to which this critical diagnosis leads.

First and most important, consider the radically antinaturalistic animus that inspires much of Marx's work and that appears most unequivocally in his critique of English political economy. For Marx, the cardinal sin of political economy was its habitual mistaking of the constraints and regularities of a specific type of economy and society for the inherent laws of economic life – a confusion tempered only by the passing acknowledgment that these laws may not have fully applied to more primitive or despotic societies. The entirety of Marx's social theory can be understood as an attempt to criticize our commonsense or theoretical views of society in the spirit of his criticism of economics.

A second theme in Marx that stands in tension with deep-structure analysis relates to the idea that the sequence of modes of production advances toward the eventual breakdown of social division and hierarchy and the revelation or development of the unitary, creative, negating quality of human labor. This is certainly the aspect of Marx's ideas most closely connected with the project of the modernist visionary: the reach for individual and collective empowerment through the invention of institutions and ideas that dissolve the rankings and contrasts of society. The thesis of the unitary character of human labor suggests that organized frameworks of social life may differ in the extent to which they impose a predetermined structure upon our practical and passionate dealings. To be sure, Marx believed that only with the twofold end of scarcity and class conflict would mankind come out from under its domination by the reified and hierarchical social orders it had created; thus domination would have to increase (the loss of primitive communism and the succession of historical modes of production) before it could be overcome (the inauguration of true communism). But we can dispense with this simple contrast between acting under the compulsion of a framework before communism and acting freely from such compulsions, though not from other causal influences, after communism has been established. We can work toward a social theory that represents the structure-bound and structure-free situations Marx imagines to be radically discontinuous as in fact coexisting throughout history. We can go on to recognize that the institutional and imaginative frameworks of social life differ, among other things, in the extent to which they respect and develop the framework-transforming capabilities of the agents who inhabit them. And we can ask what style of social thought could turn these apparent obstacles to generalizing explanation into explanatory opportunities.

A third theme of Marx's theories that falls outside deep-structure analysis and provides a clue to its correction can be found chiefly in his more concrete political and historical writings. This theme contains the kernel of an entire theory of politics. The key idea here is the conception of a two-way connection between the place a community or class (say, the French peasantry under the Second Empire) occupies in society and its distinctive posture of prostration or resistance: the degree and the way in which the group either takes things for granted or treats them as up for grabs.

Given Marx's own ambivalence toward the deep-structure moves, it is not surprising to find that the tradition of Marxism, like much of the tradition of classical social theory as a whole, can be understood in two different ways. On the one hand, it can be seen as the entropic history of deep-structure theory: a gradual discovery of its deficiencies and consequences, limited only by the fear that a frank recognition of failure would result in theoretical nihilism and encourage political defeatism. On the other hand, however, the tradition of Marxism can also be studied as a series of loosely related critical and constructive explorations, one of which is the attempt to reform deep-structure analysis from within. The dimly perceived objective of this particular line of exploration is the attempt to preserve the first deep-structure move – the contrast between the formative framework and the formed routines – while replacing the other two moves with an alternative approach to the understanding of society. Though much in the following pages may seem responsive to the first of these two readings of the Marxist tradition, even this seemingly negative perspective is meant to contribute toward the reconstruction of deep-structure analysis.

Marxist Theory and Leftist Parties

The decision to single out Marxist deep structuralism for a relatively detailed discussion is justified not only by the hope of enlisting the critical results in a constructive effort but also by the extraordinary influence Marxist theory has exercised on the beliefs and the practice of leftist movements.

Popular movements in Europe in the late nineteenth and early twentieth centuries seized on the doctrines of Marx and his followers and made them an official creed. Their startling decision officially to commit themselves to the beliefs of a philosopher was then repeated on a larger scale and, with a greater show of success, in the non-European world. Power over mighty nations was there exercised in the name of these ideas, though the men who knew how to stay in power also knew how to take the theories at a heavy discount. In other places the doctrines vaporized into a haze of vague conceptions and catchwords. Sometimes, these fighting phrases served tightly organized parties, bent on capturing the state. Sometimes, they were just the favored slogans of large numbers of indignant and half-educated people, determined to side with the poor and the powerless.

In these latter-day apparitions the ideas lost their rigor. No longer able to work as living and critical thought, they nevertheless remained to confuse the commitment to political aims and movements with the belief in a dead man's doctrines. All over the world thousands of clever and bookish militants, who saw themselves as friends of the people, anguished and haggled over the limits of orthodoxy. Experiments in thought and action were stifled by the fear that they might be viewed as an apostasy from cherished beliefs and from the practical habits those beliefs justified.

The European parties pioneered in championing this theoretical system as a guide to political practice and a source of political vision. These parties had, on the whole, ended in failure. The political strategies of hopeless compromise they pursued, and the understandings of society they entertained, had helped get them into trouble. To the extent that they kept faith with their revolutionary transformative intentions, they became isolated from the majorities and excluded from power. When they broke out of this marginality, they did so by abandoning or diluting their transformative commitments.

The particular ideas and strategies adopted by the more radical European parties were not the only plausible ones to be derived from Marx's doctrines. Moreover, the same strategies and ideas might have been made to rest on entirely different theoretical traditions. But intellectuals and militants have regularly persuaded themselves that the theory and the practice are tightly connected; after all, the tightness of the connection was part of the theory itself. The adoption by the European left of this somewhat arbitrary mix of abstract conceptions and concrete beliefs gave the amalgam enormous influence. The influence extended to other parts of the world, where political movements of great promise anxiously emulated the language and the stratagems of a European failure.

Having radical transformative aims, believing in some reformed version of Karl Marx's doctrines, and even accepting some canonical interpretation of how these theories ought to be translated into a political movement – were all seriously taken as part of the same package. As a model for the kind of relation of theory to practice that democrats and revolutionaries should hope to achieve, this was a willful closure to the surprises of politics. Thus, it is, after all, important to show both that something is wrong with the ideas and that the ideas provide clues to their own correction.

The Core Problem of Indeterminacy

My discussion of Marxism focuses on an inclusive set of problems: problems that result from the difficulties of applying Marx's synthesis of deep-structure moves and functional explanation to the particulars of historical study and contemporary political experience. It is tempting to conclude that the difficulties arise merely from excessive theoretical ambition and that similar problems would plague any social theory of comparable generality. But there is something important to be learned from tracing whatever in these difficulties can be attributed to the specific features of Marx's synthesis of deep-structure argument and functionalism and then asking what a social theory would have to be like in order to solve these problems.

On the functionalist side, the crucial problem is the lack of a one-to-one correspondence between modes of production and levels of development of the productive forces of society. At any moment and in every circumstance there turn out to be alternative sets of institutional arrangements that can serve as a basis for the further development of any particular productive or destructive capability. There is no sure way to tell which of these alternatives has the best long-run potential. Though some alternatives are either more promising or more accessible than others, there is no good way to define the class of possible alternatives or evolutionary trajectories, even for a particular society at a particular moment in its history.

When we turn to the distinctively deep-structure elements of Marx's view, the major difficulties result from the attempt to carry through the second and third moves of deep-structure analysis. The sets of institutional arrangements that represent the most plausible candidates for the mode of production called capitalism do not in fact exhibit the qualities that a mode of production is supposed to have. They do not behave as a repeatable and indivisible type, marking a stage in a world-historical sequence. Nor can they be plausibly explained on the basis of the kinds of laws, tendencies, or constraints that would be capable of producing such a sequence. Moreover, the strategies of adjustment and revision that have been used to rescue the theory from these difficulties prove to be inadequate until they become points of departure for a more basic reform of deep-structure analysis along the lines I have already suggested and shall further develop.

The following argument moves forward in three steps. First, I discuss the difficulties of giving content to the key concept of capitalism. These difficulties anticipate, on the plane of mere description, the major objections to Marx's combination of deep-logic analysis and functional explanation. The second step of the argument shows how the most familiar stratagems for defending Marx's theory against these objections are tenable only as preliminaries to a more basic reconstruction of the approach they are employed to defend. The third step of the argument works out some implications of these theoretical controversies for transformative political practice.

The Troubles of the Concept of Capitalism

We can often infer the shortcomings of an explanatory theory from the difficulties we encounter in the use of its key concepts. For the explanatory view implies an interpreted description of its subject matter. The conundrums that beset the explanation can be counted on to reappear in the interpreted description. So it is in Marx's theory of history with the idea of capitalism.

The concept of capitalism in Marx's system is the paradigm for all other modes of production. In fact, the whole sequence of modes and the science that claims to account for this sequence were devised in large part as an effort to understand the realities to which the idea of capitalism refers. At the same time the concept of capitalism designates the framework within which the lawlike processes detailed in *Capital* hold good. The description of that framework implies, and is implied by, a view of these processes. To dilute the sense in which capitalism represents an indivisible type of social organization feasible in different societies at different times is to alter or diminish the sense in which the economies and societies we describe as capitalist do indeed operate according to laws.

When put to use, the concept of capitalism turned out to be both too universal and too particular. Whenever the concept was defined in a loose and general way, it proved to apply to a large range of historical situations. Many of the societies to which an inclusive concept of capitalism seemed to apply were not industrialized. In fact, many of these situations arose in societies utterly different – in their forms of state power, their types of social hierarchy and division, and their ruling beliefs – from the North Atlantic countries that led the worldwide industrial revolution. Even if, left to their own devices, these other "capitalisms" had eventually industrialized, it seems plausible to expect that they would have done so in social forms utterly different from the ones people had in mind when they spoke of capitalism.

To deal with these embarrassments of overinclusion, you were driven to make your definition of capitalism more concrete: to read into it a more particular set of institutional arrangements. These arrangements might define, for example, the rights and powers that governed the claims on other people's labor and the crucial savings-investments decisions that helped drive accumulation forward. In the setting of a particular theory such as Marxism, you might even define capitalism genetically and sequentially as well as structurally and descriptively. Capitalism then follows certain defined stages and precedes others. In this view, there *is* a sequence of types of social organization. If capitalism seems to occur out of order, look closer, and you will see that it is not really capitalism. Or else you must have the wrong theory.

As the concept of capitalism is made more concrete in the effort to escape overinclusion, it runs into a characteristic dilemma. On the one hand, until it has been totally locked into a stage-theoretical sequence and laden with all sorts of institutional details, it is still not exclusive enough. There are still too many examples of societies and circumstances that seem to meet the definition but are not really what you were thinking of nor anything that could have been counted on eventually to bring about what you had in mind. By the time you have finished parrying all the problems of overextension you seem to have ended up describing a very particular society and a very particular series of events. At the same time, you have passed your ad hoc descriptions off as a theoretical category ready to figure in general theoretical explanations.

On the other hand, long before the concept of capitalism has been compelled to play a set role within a foreordained historical description or taken on the characteristics of an ad hoc description, it has become too exclusive. There are too many examples of transition to an industrial economy even within the core North Atlantic zone, that seem to jar with the elements of your more detailed definition. Yet you would find it strange to say that these many deviant cases were not cases of capitalist industrialization. For capitalism would then have to describe a special, exemplary core case. And how would you choose this exemplary instance? Would it be the country that industrialized first? But what if its immediate successors and rivals followed a quite different route to industrialization? Or should the controlling case be the most common one? But what if no plausible candidate can be found to perform this role?

The point about this dilemma of abstraction and concreteness can be put another way. When you make the concept of capitalism more textured, you do so with the hope that the more concrete traits will reveal what is most significant about the more general and abstract traits you began with. You also expect them to single out the historically decisive cases of capitalist breakthrough. If deviations exist, they can be treated as variations on the central theme. It would weaken and even undermine the force of your argument if the more detailed definition turned out to describe situations and events that seemed no more faithful to the more abstract and general elements in the concept of capitalism than all the historical situations your more precise definition excluded. It would be equally disappointing if the excluded cases were at least as important historically as the included instances.

So far I have given only the disembodied analytic structure of a criticism of the concept of capitalism. Now let me give this structure content. The most promising basis for an abstract and general definition of capitalism lies in the combination of a structural trait with a dynamic orientation. The structural trait is the predominance of wage labor as opposed to all forms of coerced or communitarian work. The mass of ordinary people need to work. They lack, either individually or collectively, the means of production with which to produce on their own initiative or to sell the products of their labor for their own account. Another class, in control of the means of production, buys their labor. The dynamic orientation that complements this structural characteristic is the struggle for profit. The people in charge of the means of production compete with one another. They must try to move ahead in order not to fall behind, expanding and reinvesting their profits. Production must serve the accumulation of capital. The decisive majority of producers are free laborers dependent in fact on the resources supplied to them, in exchange for their labor, by the class that controls the chief means of production. (The technical refinements that these ideas gained in Marx's system may be put aside. My aim now is to explore the usefulness of the concept of capitalism even when you disengage it from the more detailed and distinctive segments of Marxist doctrine or indeed from any brand of Marxism at all).

In fact, however, economic orders with just these characteristics have existed at many moments in history. The North Atlantic countries seem to have been only a subset of the societies that meet this general definition. They stand apart by the fact that, for reasons not even hinted at by this definition of capitalism, they pioneered in the industrialization of society. In almost all the agrarian empires and in many city-state republics, there were long periods during which coercive or communitarian forms of labor played only a subsidiary role; a large class of legally free though economically dependent workers sold their labor in town and country, and rural and urban markets became thoroughly money-based.

Often the legal regime of free labor differed in its institutional details from the arrangements that emerged in late medieval and early modern Europe. But this difference is beside the point, unless the specific legal structure of European free labor is incorporated into the definition of capitalism. Often, in these non-European societies, free individual labor shaded into various sorts of communitarian work regimes. But the same could be said of Western Europe until quite late in the day and on the very eve of industrialization. Often the independent smallholder and the petty trader or manufacturer played just as prominent a role in the economy as the propertyless laborer. But so did they in several variants of the European experience. In the crucial area of agriculture, they continued to play this role even after manufacturing had moved toward mass-production industry and agriculture had passed through succeeding stages of mechanization (e. g., the development of North American agriculture).

Many of the non-European societies that met the structural criterion in this definition of capitalism – the prominence of free labor – also satisfied the dynamic criterion – the commitment to accumulation. Both outside or within Europe, the labor buyer's search for profit blended with his interest in prestige and power. Governments treated their concern with the enrichment of the country as an integral part of their struggle against domestic and foreign enemies. If there are finer distinctions to be made between the types of profit orientation that do and do not exemplify capitalism, the definition I have been discussing fails to suggest them.

Consider the example, such as China during the Sung Dynasty, of a society that seems to have gone far in meeting both the structural and dynamic elements of the definition of capitalism. It is possible to parry the disconcerting overextension of the concept of capitalism by two familiar techniques. One tactic is to say that the apparent example was really not capitalism at all because it lacked certain other essential traits of a capitalist order. On one variant of this tactic you claim that major aspects of society and culture altered the effect and changed the sense of what we are at first tempted to describe as capitalism. But this solution pushes the concept in the direction of increasing concreteness, with consequences that soon prove embarrassing. The other stratagem is to treat these troublesome analogies as cases of "seeds" of capitalism, developments that proved to be abortive because of independent supervening events. But, then, once all these cases of blocked development are cataloged, the concept of capitalism will be found to have been undermined. The case of successful capitalist development turns out to be an aberrational success story standing out against the background of a much longer list of relative failures. The first definition of capitalism, on its face, denotes the many instances of eventual failure as well as the few eventual successes. It seems unlikely to perform the decisive role in a theoretical explanation that distinguishes failures from successes.

So let us try again with a different though similarly abstract and general definition of capitalism. This second formulation can be viewed as either an alternative or a complement to the first. Like the first, it attempts to define capitalism with enough generality to keep the definition from being a label for a unique historical situation. In this second statement, the distinctive feature of capitalism becomes a shift in the relation between commercial–industrial capital and agriculture, with a corresponding transformation in the dealings between town and country. Capitalism, you might say, exists if, and only if, the accumulation of commercial and industrial capital, guided by the profit motive, gains a large measure of independence from the manipulations of the agrarian surplus and the exploitation of peasant labor. The town becomes a major center of commerce and production in its own right rather than just a place of residence for predatory officials and absentee landowners who, though served by a local urban population, remain primarily dependent upon the agrarian production and the cash flow it generates. These transformed cities witness the development of forms of technology and organization that end up revolutionizing agriculture itself.

Like its counterpart, however, this alternative approach to the definition of capitalism says both too much and too little. It says too much because, for all but the smallest countries with a highly specialized role within the world economy, agriculture has continued to impose an independent check on the pace and nature of urban industrialization. It imposes this check even in the economies that are held up as prime instances of capitalism by the historians and theorists most anxious to use the concept of capitalism as a major tool of analysis. At the same time, the alternative definition says too little. There are an indefinite number of ways in which commercial–industrial capital has in fact increased – or might one day increase – its margin of independence from the ups and downs of the agrarian economy: more or less state control; greater or smaller class disparities; and even more or less differentiation between town and country. Industry may, after all, be largely country-based. It may be dominated, for example, by a mixture of small-scale private or communal proprietorship and large-scale governmental initiative.

In fact, when you subject the second definition of capitalism to the same type of comparative application and analysis to which I earlier submitted the first definition, you come up with the same sorts of embarrassing results. Once again, you find many periods in the history of each of the major agrarian empires when commercial-industrial capital gained a certain measure of independence and the cities became centers of considerable trade and manufacturing. In some of these situations, there were even technical breakthroughs that raised the productivity of agriculture (per field size) to a level comparable to that of Western European agriculture before the industrial revolution. On the whole, these were the same periods in which small-scale proprietors and legally free but economically dependent laborers achieved a presence in the economy and its work force. Sung China is as spectacular an example of one set of changes as it is of the other. So were many periods in the history of other agrarian-bureaucratic societies.

These extended periods of commercialization, of flourishing independent wage labor and small-scale proprietorship, and of changed relations between agrarian surplus and commercial-manufacturing capital or between country and town did not lead into an industrial revolution. Instead, they were usually reversed. The typical reversal included the decommercialization and demonetization of the economy against a background of governmental decline or collapse, the rise of coerced, dependent labor and large-scale estates, and the waning of urban vitality. The non-European societies that stood the best chance of initiating an industrial revolution of their own before being overtaken by Europe were those that, for reasons examined in *Plasticity into Power*, had done best at postponing or imitating these periods of reversion.

The two abstract and general definitions of capitalism discussed in the preceding pages offer little help with these problems. Both definitions fail to mark out the exceptional successful case from all the analogous situations that nevertheless had utterly different outcomes. Either of them is therefore unsuited to play the key part in an explanation of the European breakthrough and of the spread of industrial techniques and organizations throughout the world. Neither of them marks out with adequate distinction what the devotees of the term really seem to have in mind when they talk of capitalism.

Now suppose that, in order to deal with the difficulties of these abstract definitions, you try to make the concept of capitalism more concrete. You may do this by simply adding further elements to the definition of capitalism. Or you may do it as well by specifying the sequence of social and economic orders of which you expect capitalism to be a stage. In either case, an explicit or tacit theory tells you why all these traits go together or why these stages follow upon one another as they do.

A more detailed definition of capitalism may, for example, focus on the initial stages of agricultural transformation. Capitalism, in this view, is the system that emerges from a process including the replacement of small-scale family farms, the triumph of the large, relatively non-labor-intensive estate, and a sequel of massive migration of the country population to the cities. But there were many Western European countries that underwent a very different kind of agrarian transformation and that preserved the small family farm as the basic agrarian unit throughout their experience of industrialization. It is hard to show that the European countries that preferred this alternative were backward *on that account* if they were backward at all.

For example, the Dutch failure to anticipate England in passing from "commercial capitalism" to industrialization had at best a complex and indirect relation to the Dutch pattern of family-size holdings. On the other hand, the beneficial effect of this agrarian style on the early economic success of the Dutch Republic was unmistakable. Even French fidelity to the family farm had ambiguous consequences. If agricultural productivity per man may have been lower in France than in England during much of the nineteenth century, English industrial productivity seems to have been correspondingly lower than its French counterpart in the same period. France was also helped by its agrarian option to avoid social dislocations that might have hindered its industrial progress at a later moment in its history and might have caused immense suffering.

So this addition to the concept of capitalism makes the concept too exclusive to describe the range of societies and situations to which it is traditionally applied by Marxists and non-Marxists alike. Yet, paradoxically, the addition also seems to leave the definition not exclusive enough. For throughout the history of agrarian empires, we find periods when the small agrarian property was squeezed out by the large estate. Though these estates might start out as active participants in a commercialized market economy, their rise was often an episode in, or a prelude to, a period of collapse. Markets and manufacturing would be set back. Surely the concept of capitalism is not meant to describe a step in a process of agrarian concentration that repeatedly led to economic regression and decommercialization – the reverse of the standard historical connotations of the concept.

Suppose you exclude the inconvenient analogies by making the definition even more textured. For example, you include the existence of a protective barrier between government and large-scale capital. For capitalism to exist, you say, the large property owners and investors must be protected from arbitrary governmental expropriation. The hands of the central government authorities must be tied enough to enable the crucial investing and innovating groups to act on their own. But everyone knows that German industrialization, for instance, was carried out with a degree of overtness and exuberance in the partnership of government with large-scale capital that, from an English vantage point, seems to border on capitalist heresy. Yet to say that this state-guided or state-led industrialization was simply a secondary distortion caused by the need to catch up quickly is to misconceive both its extent and its origin. For Wilhelmine Germany as for many of the countries that began to industrialize only in the twentieth century, the role assumed by the state had more to do with particular social conflicts, governmental opportunities, and authoritative ideas than with any inherent dynamic of the world economy and capital accumulation. Moreover, even in England itself, government undertook important preparatory, protective, and entrepreneurial tasks. It is not obvious from the more detailed definition how the "capitalist" forms of this governmental sponsorship differ from the noncapitalist ones.

Here, too, overinclusion is as troublesome as underinclusion. For there were many times in the history of the agrarian empires when the holders of central state power lost the capacity to intervene effectively in the control of resources or even to exact the minimum of taxes and recruits needed to uphold the state in foreign and domestic strife. Even at the zenith of their power, the rulers ran up against harsh factual if not legal constraints on their ability to intervene in the allocation of resources or the organization of work. The cause of decentralized economic decision making could rely on the recurrent weakness of governmental power even when it could not count on a fixed order of individual and collective entitlements.

We can go even further in tightening the comparison between the supposedly capitalist European situations and the periods of commercial and manufacturing vitality in many non-European societies before the industrial revolution. In these non-European societies, the legal structure of contract and property was sometimes utterly different from what it came to be in early modern Western Europe. But it was often just as effective in multiplying the sources of decision over the use and investment of resources and the control of labor and in circumscribing the reach of governmental power.

The effort at greater concreteness in the definition of capitalism can take yet a third route. This solution builds on the first abstract definition of a capitalist order: the prevalence of legally free but economically dependent wage labor, combined with the commitment to accumulation. In this view, for capitalism to exist, great numbers of independent earners must work side by side. Free labor and economic dependence must be combined with the disciplined organization of large pools of workers under the command of those who own the major means of production or who act as the owners' agents. These owners or agents must not be simply the direct rulers of the state even though the rulers may be drawn largely from their ranks or suffer their preponderant influence. It all adds up to something like the European factory and industrial system.

Once again, however, the more detailed conception remains both underinclusive and overinclusive. As applied to the West, it pushes the definition of capitalism to a relatively late stage of Western economic history, after industrialization was already in full swing. It disregards the fact that large-scale plants have never employed more than a minority of the active work force in any of the situations traditionally labeled capitalist. It fails to explain why the concentration of large numbers of workers in productive units as opposed to their dispersion in smaller but technologically advanced organizations should be singled out as indispensable or why this concentration is particularly connected to the features emphasized in the abstract definition of capitalism.

Moreover, outside Europe there were periods and societies in which hired labor, combined with different kinds of tenancy arrangements, often tilled large agricultural estates. The labor force did not work in mechanized factories because these societies had not yet been industrialized. It did not usually work in factories at all because the factory system pays off most in the setting of mechanization.

Every attempt to make the definition of capitalism more concrete comes up against the same hurdles. Every addition to the list of defining traits produces a category that seems to include both too much and too little and to have an arbitrary relationship to the more abstract conceptions of capitalism. If you go far enough, you no longer have a concept at all but the summary description of particular developments that took place in particular countries, with the particular outcomes that resulted from time to time.

The Sources of Difficulty

Why are attempts to deploy the concept of capitalism so troublesome? One source of trouble relates directly to the use of functional explanation. The idea of capitalism is meant to perform two different roles within Marx's theory. These roles cannot be reconciled because history just does not happen in the way required by the Marxist style of functional explanation.

On the one hand, the term capitalism is supposed to describe the necessary institutional basis (the relations of production) for a certain level in the development of the productive forces: the level at which machinery combined with the physical congregation of large numbers of workers multiplies the productivity of labor and at which surplus becomes enormous without vanquishing scarcity. To perform this role adequately the concept of capitalism can never be inclusive enough. The more we learn about history, the greater the variety we discover in the institutional contexts of any given measure of development of productive capabilities. Even in modern Western history the more familiar sets of institutional arrangements turn out to have coexisted with deviant and repressed alternatives. The containment of these alternatives can be credited more persuasively to a particular history of political victories and defeats, insights and illusions, than to their inherent practical limitations. The experience of institutional experimentation in an age of world history confirms and extends the conclusions of historical study. States constantly discover new ways to combine modern Western productive capability with forms of work organization without close Western counterparts, or Western modes of work organization with economic and governmental institutions more closely suited to the experiences, interests, and intentions of the indigenous elite. The ever widening range of variation that we encounter in our past and present suggests other variations that might have occurred or that might yet be introduced and that are not in any event precluded by deep-seated economic, organizational, or psychological constraints. The hunt for the institutional conditions that make possible a particular level of economic growth begins to seem futile.

In Marx's style of functional explanation, the concept of capitalism also performs another role. In this role it can never be exclusive enough. It describes a unique historical reality whose outward manifestations were familiar to Marx's readers: the realities of certain modern European institutions and ways of life. Like other classical social theories, Marxism saw global significance in the history and transformation of these institutions. In this second role, the concept of capitalism does not apply to the similar institutional arrangements of other societies or other epochs that failed to produce these revolutionary results.

A second source of trouble with the concept of capitalism has to do with the deep-structural rather than the functionalist aspects of Marxist theory. Here too the idea of capitalism performs two different roles. Here too the character of historical experience makes these roles irreconcilable.

On the one hand, the concept must describe an indivisible and repeatable type of social organization: indivisible in the sense that its elements cannot be disaggregated and recombined with other elements; repeatable in the sense that it does not merely designate, retrospectively, a unique state of affairs capable of being realized only once and in one place. To perform this role adequately the concept of capitalism can never be abstract enough. As soon as you begin to define it more richly and concretely, you see that its components have in fact been dissociated and rearranged in many ways. You lack good reasons to exclude the possibility of any number of analogous disaggregations and recombinations that never actually took place.

At the same time, however, the concept of capitalism must perform the role of designating a framework defined precisely enough to account for a complex set of repetitious, even lawlike economic and social processes. But once you define capitalism with the concreteness necessary to justify its formative role, you undermine the plausibility of its representation as an indivisible and repeatable type. You make it look, instead, like the name for a unique state of affairs, or a unique series of events, that must be understood as the outcome of a unique constellation of causes. The term capitalism then loses, together with its generality, its clarity and punch. It becomes a shorthand way of referring to a loosely connected series of events that happened in the North Atlantic world at a certain time. But which events exactly?

The two sets of difficulties – the functionalist and the deep-structural – overlap. Once again, the problems that result from the deep-structure assumptions are more basic than the difficulties that arise from the functionalist premises. You may be tempted to resolve the functionalist dilemma by affirming the existence of multiple institutional contexts for any given level of development of the productive forces and therefore also of multiple pathways of institutional change. But where a single type of organization and a single evolutionary sequence fail to do the job, it seems that several could not work either. For each type or sequence must still be defined richly enough to justify its shaping influence on a world of practical routines. To define a set of institutional arrangements with enough detail to show how they can exercise this formative influence is to undermine the plausibility of the attempt to represent such arrangements as examples of an indivisible and repeatable type or stage of social organization. There may indeed be constraints on the disaggregation and recombination of the elements that constitute such formative institutional orders. But it is a big step from recognizing such constraints to showing that they can generate a closed list or a compulsive sequence of institutional systems.

Concepts like capitalism continue to be used in historical and social-science writing and in ideological debates by people who would deny subscribing to functional or deep-structural assumptions but whose use of such concepts belies the denial. Without having found a substitute for deep-structure analysis they insist on speaking as if concepts like capitalism could be used as more than allusions to a historically unique and uniquely located state of affairs. They talk as if such concepts could designate indivisible and repeatable types of social organization, at once abstract and richly defined. They enact in their imagination and in their discourse a way of thinking they will not or cannot defend. Their equivocation is symptomatic of the troubled relation of current views of society and history to the deep-logic tradition. When we reach toward general explanation, we often lapse back into the deep-structure moves. But we do so fitfully and half-consciously because our discoveries and our experiences have deprived those moves of their legitimacy.

Two factors have brought to the surface these weaknesses in the use of the central categories of descriptive and explanatory social theory. One is an enlargement of the available knowledge about the past; the other, a change in the apparent lessons of contemporary history. Ignorance can protect against the former. Only obtuseness and indifference can conceal the latter.

In the mid- and late twentieth century, it has become possible to study the history of most past societies with what – by comparison to previous conditions of scholarship – is a fabulous glitter of secondary and primary sources. You can spend endless days and nights in a fever of exultant discovery learning the languages, studying the records, and reading the historians of these remote countries or epochs. The further you go, the more problems you find for the sequences of the Marxist theory and even for the attempt to analyze in its categories the experience of those societies it considered capitalist. The history of the great agrarian empires of antiquity or of the non-Western world, until recently the most numerous and productive societies of history, cannot be understood in its most astonishing and instructive aspects if forced into the straitjacket of its relation to the story about the rise of capitalism. To handle the historical material you have to loosen the theory until it vanishes into a cloud of words and intentions. Or else, following Marx's own example in some of his more historical writings, you have to open an ever larger gap between your theoretical professions and your actual explanations.

The other source of disturbance and enlightenment is the course of contemporary events. At the time Marx and the other great theorists of the late nineteenth and early twentieth century were developing their ideas, the intellectuals and thinkers of the pioneering countries lived their romance of practical reason. Much in the experience of the time suggested that a single pattern of social life was spreading out from Europe to the entire world. This pattern might be organized around the arrangements of production and power. But it also dragged along with it a whole system of hierarchy, habit, and belief. Other countries, in other parts of the globe, had to take it or leave it. If they wanted to survive in the worldwide contest, they needed to take it.

Social theories differed on how this practical convergence was connected with social conflict and the rise of the masses and on whether it prefigured a further, decisive transformation in society. Whatever the connection, the clash of nations, of spiritual visions, and of armed force – everything that was most unruly in history – seemed to have been revealed, once and for all, as a by-product of more prosaic and fundamental constraints.

Many among the rulers of the present world and their apologetic toadies or despondent subjects still seem to believe some version of this picture of things. A contemporary industrialized society, they say, is very complicated. It consists in large-sale organizations and delicate relationships. By the time you have done everything you have to do to keep these institutions running and to stop things from getting too bad, there is very little room left over for maneuver – which is to say, for politics and philosophizing. The rest is all daydreaming.

I have already referred to the aspects of contemporary history that have made it hard to believe in the romance of practical reason, in either its early, militant and theoretical, or its later, dumb and cringing, mode. The poorer, non-Western countries have long since begun to combine features of rich Western-style technology with non-Western varieties of work organization or Western types of work organization with different ways of organizing society. This practice of institutional invention has never gone as far as democrats and revolutionaries would have liked; but it has already gone far enough to make unclear the limits to this process of dissociation of advanced practical capabilities from their original institutional basis. In fact, neither the failure to dissociate more, nor the surprise of dissociating so much, seem to have any simple perspicuous relation to the Marxist account of the rise of capitalism or to any other account that combines functionalist and deep-structure tenets. Nor can either be easily explained by vague references to the requirements of industrialism.

A time has come in the world when hopeful democrats everywhere follow closely any sign of a social experiment, any place on earth, hoping that it may reveal something about the unexplored opportunities for the advancement of the radical project. To view these experiments, and these failures to experiment, as fumblings toward a vaguely foreordained conclusion or as sidelights upon an already disclosed truth is to miss the point. It is to trade citizenship of the age for membership in a sect.

Playing Up Politics: The Failure to Rescue the Theory from Within

The history of Marxist theory since Marx's own time is in large part the history of attempts to deal with the difficulties of functional and deep-structure argument that the troubles of the concept of capitalism illustrate. But these would-be rescue operations never seem to go far enough: the weaker, looser version of the theory remains open to a variant of the same objections leveled against the stronger, tighter version. These successive disappointments may be more than merely destructive in their results. They may help create the means for a more fundamental reconstruction of deep-logic theory.

One familiar defensive measure is to downplay the parts of the mature Marx's view that present a comprehensive theory of the evolution of modes of production and to place the emphasis instead on the internal analysis of capital, the subject of his major work. But this distinction cannot be maintained. The core of Marx's study of capitalism is an account of the characteristic laws of the capitalist modes of production. Some of these laws specify repetitious processes; others, developmental tendencies. The claim that such laws exist and the specification of the sense in which they are laws depend on assumptions about the existence, nature, and history of a mode of production. For the mode of production represents the framework within which those laws apply. The theory of modes of production does not merely trace the domains within which each set of laws operates; it shows why there can be laws and what kinds of laws they are.

Empirical observation may persuade us that the laws of motion Marx describes do not in fact hold. We may be tempted to reformulate them and to blame the inaccuracy of the original theory on unforeseeable developments or on disregarded factors. But the critique of the concept of capitalism, summarizing as it does a broader range of empirical studies, suggests that the search for laws of this kind is basically misguided. Even if we could correctly specify a set of repetitious processes and developmental tendencies, we would not be justified in interpreting them as the inherent laws of an indivisible and repeatable type of social organization. They might be merely the routines and trends encouraged by a unique and divisible complex of institutional arrangements. Their stability, rather than reflecting deeply rooted constraints or evolutionary laws, might be merely the expression of a redeemable failure to recommence practical and imaginative conflict over the basic terms of social life. The implications for theoretical understanding and political practice would be very different from a mere recognition that we had settled on the wrong laws of motion.

Of all efforts to save the initial theory, the most familiar and rewarding has been the attempt to emphasize the importance of traditions of belief, collective action, and governmental policy in determining the history and even the content of modes of production. Revisionists have shown how the evolution and variations of what they continue to call capitalism reflects the influence of varying degrees and varieties of grassroots collective organization, the multiple forms of class consciousness and class formation, the different possible ways in which governmental power can link up with social privilege, the ideas people have about themselves and society, and the many loose relations among all these subjects.

The effect this emphasis has on the peculiarly functionalist aspects of Marxist theory is to loosen the ties between the explanatory functional advantage (the development of the productive forces) and the institutional arrangements this advantage allegedly requires and helps explain (the mode of production). Thus, this revisionism goes in search of a theory of multiple evolutionary trajectories. Alongside the rigid functional account of the emergence of a mode of production it places nonfunctional explanations, mired in particularity, explanations that speak of the influence of distinct traditions of militancy and belief on the grand succession of social worlds.

The problems the detailed explanatory stories of the revisionist are meant to solve and the new problems they pose merely highlight insoluble difficulties in any social theory that deploys functional explanations against the background of deep-structure assumptions. The less detailed the story about how the functional advantage (in Marxism, the maximum development of the forces of production) becomes a cause of its own achievement, the harder it is to relate the story to historical learning and ordinary experience. On the other hand, the further the revisionist goes in providing an independent explanatory narrative of institutional, technological, or ideological change – a narrative concerned with the different circumstances of different groups in different societies – the less he finds himself referring to the functional advantage. The advantage begins to seem a by-product of independently caused events and independently intelligible processes. Thus, the overarching functional story (e.g., about forces of production driving changes in modes of production) starts to look superfluous. The revisionist turned skeptic can undermine functional explanation by leaving it without a job of its own. Particularistic, noncausal accounts take over.

Of course, this dilemma might be solved by positing complex and controversial connections between the operative functional consequence and the visible events of history or the conscious intentions of historical agents. After all, just such connections support functional explanation in natural science. But the question remains: Can we actually supply the missing links without either hedging on the largescale functional account or blinking many recalcitrant facts? Because there are never enough links available to close the gap, each dose of revision seems to require a further dose – or a lapse back into historical dogmatism.

The impact of this revisionist analysis on the deep-structural aspects of the theory is just as subversive as its effect on the properly functionalist parts of the doctrine. The revisionist tendency restricts the influence that a formative structure (i.e., a mode of production) exercises on the deeds and thoughts of historical agents. It appeals to particularistic or multiple explanations of their remaking, explanations that undermine confidence in the existence of evolutionary laws. And it plays up the causal importance of the differences among otherwise similar modes of production: the role that each mode allows to government, for example, or to the collective organization of peasants and workers.

Whether we look to the implications for deep-structure argument or to the effects on functional explanation, the problem remains the same: there is no good place to stop, no defensible line against further attacks on the distinctive explanatory style that arises from the combination of functionalist and deep-logic methods. If, for example, three alternative trajectories can be discovered where the hard-core version of Marxist theory required only one, why not say that thirteen were possible? If non-functional and particularistic explanations can account for many features of a mode of production, or of its genesis, who can be sure that more explanations of the same kind might not account for all its interesting characteristics? If factors left out of the initial definition of a mode of production are nevertheless crucial to the transformation of institutional arrangements and to the fate of social divisions and hierarchies, why not include them in the definition of the mode? And, having incorporated those factors into the definition, how can we hope to keep up the pretense that a mode of production is an indivisible and repeatable type?

Consider, for example, a characteristic disagreement in contemporary Marxist historiography: the role that collective peasant organization in Western Europe performed in opening the way to capitalism. Someone argues that a certain weakening of grassroots communal organization by the peasants is important to capitalism because it allows the formation of large capitalist-type estates by entrepreneurial landlords and tenants. This argument is meant to score points against historians who analyze developments in primarily demographic or technological terms and to underline the role of politics in the evolution of modes of production. At the same time, the argument is designed to uphold the idea of a sequence of steps toward capitalism. These steps necessarily pass, at a crucial stage, through the destruction of small-scale family farming and cooperative forms of peasant activity. Then someone claims that in Eastern Europe and Russia the defeat of the peasants was part of a tale of avoidance of capitalism. So further refinements have to be introduced about the role of the state (in Russia) or of a unified and unchecked landholding nobility (in Eastern Europe) in stamping out the early possibilities of capitalist development.

Then someone else shows that in many of the most enterprising centers of late medieval and early modern Western Europe the maintenance of customary rights by peasant collectives and the continued prosperity of small- and middle-scale farming turned out to favor transformations that might be also described as beginnings of successful capitalist development. There was no necessary passageway through the large-scale agrarian enterprise built up at the peasants' expense. So on and on it goes. The point is not just that historians disagree – even historians who believe that they are working within the same theoretical tradition. It is that the historiographic debates undermine confidence in the strength or necessity of the connections among the traits that define each mode of production or in the forces that lead from one mode to the next. They wreak havoc with the story the theory is supposed to tell.

As he discovers the inadequacies of prior revisionist efforts, the Marxist (or the adherent to any other deep-structure theory) can try to hold the line. But will he – even in his own eyes – succeed? He may even attempt an alliance of convenience with the prostrate social scientists or historians who attribute the embarrassments to the inherent inadequacies of theory. He may then console himself with the thought that his procrusteanism is the price of intellectual and political faith. Alternatively, he may carry the revisionist campaign further. Then he finds that each successive dilution of the inherited theory is never enough and always too much. It is never enough to prevent the same kind of objection from being raised again. It is always too much to preserve a coherent version of the theory, a version that does not play fast and loose with the deep-structure moves. In the end, the super-revisionist finds that he has turned the theory into a list of fighting words and obsessive concerns and embarked on Noah's ark without Noah.

If, however, you could work through and beyond the deep-logic approach by replacing its second and third moves while retaining its first move, these successive moments of disillusionment would appear in a different light. The seemingly negative insights they produced might be extended and generalized and shown to be compatible with an alternative style of generalizing explanation. Then, those cumulative acts of revision would no longer seem makeshift compromises along a line of retreat but approaches to another, stronger position.

The Practical Significance of Theoretical Error

The preceding discussion of Marxism as an instance of deep-structure analysis may seem to be of merely theoretical interest. Yet the implications are as relevant to the present as they are to the past and as important to political issues as to theoretical concerns. My earlier example of the confusions of engagement in Brazilian politics suggested, by anticipation, the perverse effect of deep-structure ideas on political practice. Now, that suggestion can be developed and exemplified in a North Atlantic setting.

To the extent that you pursued the revision of deep-structure theory to an ever more nihilistic conclusion, you jeopardized your ability to imagine past, present, or future frameworks, to contrast them with the routines they shape, and to talk about their history and transformation. You therefore lost the only readily available tool with which to resist the claim that existing routines were the inevitable products of organizational, economic, and psychological constraints or of the clash among numerous interests coexisting in tension with one another. If you acknowledged the influence of a formative institutional and imaginative context at all, you treated the components of this context as merely higher-order routines, time-tested collective rules of thumb. You slid into the shadowy, one-dimensional world of positivist social science and naive historiography described in a later section.

But suppose you tried to hold the line, as a Marxist or any other style of deep-structure analyst, against the extremes of revisionism. The results were damaging to both the programmatic inspiration and the strategic unity of transformative, leftist movements.

The chief consequence for programmatic ideas was to make it appear that no middle level existed between reformist tinkering, which helps a set of basic institutional arrangements and social preconceptions to survive in the face of changing circumstance, and all out revolution, which replaces an entire framework of social life. Thus, programmatic thinking turned away from the effort to imagine detailed institutional alternatives and transitional forms. Such proposals as were occasionally produced lacked support in any credible view of transformation.

Suppose, for example, that as a Marxist in a late twentieth century Western democracy you found yourself engaged in debates about efforts to reform the capitalist economy from within. The spirit of your theoretical system encouraged you to distinguish as sharply as possible reforms that were merely attempts to stave off crises predicted by the laws of motion from fundamental changes in the mode of production and the class system, with their corresponding or preparatory shifts in the control of the state. Take, for example, a governmental commitment to underwrite mass consumer demand during economic depressions as well as to make costly basic investments and difficult social accommodations. Such a commitment might be needed to keep the economy running and to stop the poor from disrupting it. But it would not necessarily alter the laws of motion (if they operated in the first place) nor redirect the basic aims of the workers' movement.

But what if the aim of the reforms was to alter the institutional structure of democracy and the market? It might be a matter of bringing the basic flows of investment decisions under political control. Or it might have to do with redesigning the constitutional organization of government so as to promote, rather than replace and avoid, repeated mass mobilization. Were these aims worth fighting for as an alternative to capitalism? Or were they just like those defensive reforms that contain crisis and conflict without transforming the basic reality that generated them? At what point would the implementation of such reforms render obsolete the concepts and laws of the analysis of capitalist economies?

The implications of a hardened version of deep-structure theory were no less dangerous to strategic thinking about social transformation. A formative structure of social life restricts and interrupts conflict over the basic terms of our availability to one another. It thereby produces and sustains a plan of division and hierarchy, held fast against the depredations of ordinary practical and imaginative fighting. (How much hierarchy, as opposed to division, this structure generates may depend on the extent to which groups are mobilizing economic or cultural resources on a society-wide basis when the moment of stabilization occurs.) The more indivisible and deeply rooted in general imperatives or in an evolutionary logic we believe such a structure of social roles and ranks to be, the greater the clarity we attribute to the system of class and communal interests each such structure generates. The person who sees society through the lens of deep-logic theory expects escalating conflict to make these interests more transparent. But in fact it muddies them by disturbing people's assumptions about social possibilities and group identities and by dissolving classes and communities into parties of opinion. The unreconstructed deep-structure theorist believes, for the same reasons, that certain class alliances or antagonisms are unavoidable and that each emergent type of social organization has its predetermined champions. But he is mistaken. The lines of alliance and antagonism are in fact fluid, both because the next step in context revision always remains uncertain and controversial and because fighting breaks down the very structure within which group interests seemed to be certain. The theoretical illusions exact their toll in practice, blinding people to many opportunities, providing them with alibis for inaction, and strengthening the animosities that they claimed faithfully to recognize.

Thus, many of the more ambitious labor and socialist parties of late twentieth century North Atlantic countries remained committed to ideas that represented the organized working class, headquartered in the declining mass-production industries, as the major force for social transformation. These parties continued to speak a language unresponsive to the concerns of the old petty bourgeoisie, of the independent professionals, of the new technical cadres, and even of the unorganized and suffering underclass. From this self-imposed isolation they escaped only into a program of marginal economic redistribution, welfare-statism, and administrative modernization. Sometimes they combined the worst of both worlds and continued to rehearse the language of proletarian challenge long after settling down to the routines of conflict management and redistributive compromise.

The preconceptions of Marxist deep-structuralist theory have contributed to the drastic understatement of the variety of institutional arrangements that accompanied European industrialization. In particular the biases of theory have obscured the leading role of artisans, skilled workers, and small-scale producers and professionals and of the advocates of small-scale and cooperative enterprises in challenging the emergent dominant order of the modern West. The aims of these publicists might have remained attached solely to a vision of petty proprietorship and decentralized authority. In this guise, their program would indeed have been fatally unstable and regressive in just the sense described by Marx's critique of petty commodity production: the transitional or subsidiary mode of production constituted by the existence of large numbers of independent, small-scale, and relatively equal producers. But their vision might also have served as a point of departure for the development of institutional proposals that met those criticisms.

Such proposals – a major theme in *Politics* – might have shown how access to capital and to governmental power could be made both more freely and equally available and more compatible with economies of scale and with effective governmental policy than it can be within the current institutional forms of markets and democracies. In these alternatives, the leftist parties might have found, and may yet find, a way to break out of their isolation without giving up their radical transformative ambitions. But Marxism and other deep-structure theories have come to stand in the way of this reformulation of vision and strategy. Vitiated by a retrospective sense of triumph – by an identification of dominant institutional systems with inevitable historical transitions – adherents of these theoretical traditions have turned a blind eye to less familiar historical transitions and anomalous institutional solutions. And they have failed to recognize that the most common form of social invention is the effort to turn deviations into models.

ECONOMICS AS A NONEVOLUTIONARY DEEP-STRUCTURE SOCIAL THEORY

In some of its early statements classical political economy offered a rudimentary version of an evolutionary deep-structure social theory. Adam Smith, for example, building on the work of his Scottish predecessors and contemporaries, distinguished stages of social evolution marked by turning points in economic development. Though he held a dynamic of self-interest and of productive opportunities responsible for the entire forward movement, the laws set out in *The Wealth of Nations* were meant to apply solely to the commercial economy, the final stage of evolution. That stage alone saw the final triumph of market institutions, by which Smith, like his predecessors, referred to a particular market order, complete with built-in rules of contract and property.

But economics soon turned aside from this style of theorizing. Instead, it took a direction that might have enabled it to serve as the model for a nonevolutionary version of deep-logic analysis. Such an account would have focused on the constraints that the satisfaction of material needs or ambitions imposes on social organization. In its most developed form it would have consisted in a theory of possible social worlds, specifying the alternative institutional systems that might satisfy those constraints. It might even have explained why any one of these alternatives became actual at a given time and place. For some time political economy bid fair to become just such a doctrine. Nevertheless, its work not only failed to produce this theory but demonstrated why any such theory would have to fail, just as the history of Marxism brought out the inadequacy of an evolutionary version of deep-logic theorizing.

The following discussion has a more general aim than to show the self-subversion of one more type of deep-structure analysis. This self-subversion was not followed by the development of an alternative way of thinking about the relation between economic activity and the institutional or imaginative framework within which this activity takes place. The undermining of the nonevolutionary form of deep-logic theory encouraged, instead, a dismissal of the very problem of the framework: the problem of understanding the relation of routine economic activity to the institutional and imaginative context within which it takes place.

If you were to give these events in intellectual history a clarity of purpose they in fact lacked, you might say that the rejection of the second and third moves of deep-structure argument led to a downplaying, if not a repudiation, of the first move: the basic contrast between a formative context and the routines it shapes. Thus, classical political economy shared its origins with the evolutionary variant of deep-structure theory. It went on to show by example the untenability of such a nonevolutionary view. But it ended up as the most rigorous model for a positivist social science distinguished by its indifference to the task of understanding the making and the influence of the institutional and imaginative contexts of social life. The next section discusses the momentous intellectual and political consequences of this indifference.

Classical political economy, as it developed in Western Europe from the seventeenth to the mid-nineteenth century, was a theory about the causal relations among the social activities most closely connected with the production and distribution of wealth. For good and ill, it lacked the special deep-logic structure of Marx's doctrine. Because the concerns that animated it were so explicitly tied to the statecraft of the day, it formulated some of its central problems in ways that more or less deliberately crossed the lines between an explanatory project and a political polemic. Hence, its favorite questions: What is the true basis of "value"? Which activities and classes contribute most to national wealth? Under what systems of rights and forms of government does a people grow richer?

The central tradition of political economy suffered the pressure of an effort to escape from the endless and largely sterile conundrums of value theory and to answer the old question of how use values could become prices. Through an analysis of the price system, free from all philosophizing about value, economists set out to discover universal coefficients of transformation in the economy: to show how exchange values, then consumer prices, and finally all aspects of a price system depended on one another. (Unlike their counterparts in physics, these coefficients were not natural constants.) The market economy, in which a large number of independent agents bargain on their own initiative and for their own account, could be represented as an ordered cosmos. A precise and narrow analytic meaning could be assigned to the idea of maximum efficiency in the allocation of a set of resources, given certain definitions of scarcity and wants. A large number of problems in economic analysis could be redefined in a way that made them amenable to mathematical formulation.

The other source of pressure for the transformation of classical economic theory was the desire to disengage the core of economics from contestable descriptive or normative commitments. Faced with socialist attacks on political economy and escalating social-theoretical debates about how society worked, the new marginalist market theory simply withdrew from the contested terrain. It relocated on what it believed to be a higher or, at least, a more general ground. The emerging analysis could do its limited work regardless of the positions people took on most of the disputed normative or empirical issues.

The marginalist general equilibrium theory, conclusively formulated by Walras, represented the influential answer to these two sources of pressure. The result was a theory that differed in its explanatory aims, as well as in its content and scope, from the tradition it displaced. The keynote of the new economics was the effort to achieve generality and certainty by putting to one side the explanatory and normative controversies that had beset political economy.

The new marginalist economics, however, failed to achieve complete immunity to factual or normative challenge. Even taking for granted the redefined explanatory aims of the theory, three closely related points of weakness remained. The effort to deal with them – an effort that has not yet been carried through to its final implications – kept up the pressure on economics. The pressure presented a choice: either to extend still further the break with classical political economy by making economics yet more general in scope and formal in purpose or to change course altogether.

The first point of weakness was the issue of whether equilibrium, in the marginalist sense, would in fact be spontaneously generated in a market economy. It was possible to argue that there was an inherent possibility, repeatedly realized, of persistent disequilibrium or of equilibrium at low levels of employment (it did not really matter much which description you preferred). Such an occurrence might be attributed to underinvestment and underconsumption: the hoarding of money. Or it might also be imputed to market failures: even in the absence of monopoly, wages and prices might prove systematically unresponsive to the signals that would clear markets and restore equilibrium at the highest level of resource employment. This stickiness of wages and prices might be ascribed to the differential organization of distinct segments of the work force, the infusion of wage or price relations by customary standards of fairness, the struggle of risk-averse managers to maintain relative financial autonomy and a stable relation to their core markets and labor force, or any number of other plausible factors. Finally, failure of self-correcting equilibrium might result from the distance that separated the marginalist picture of rational choice from the decision-making procedures used by managers, workers, and consumers, in conditions of ignorance and uncertainty. The distance was often great enough to take away much of the explanatory and prescriptive value of that picture. Everything interesting seemed to be in the behavioral and institutional facts that marginalist analysis had to take as givens rather than as topics for analysis and explanation.

The point about all these possible sources of constraint on spontaneous equilibrium is that they could not plausibly be disregarded by a market theory as either noneconomic or incidental. They seemed to be very deeply built into the market economies that in fact exist.

A second embarrassment to the marginalist theory has played a much smaller role in the development of mainstream economics, though its theoretical implications are just as important. It is the relation of the marginalist doctrine to the idea of a market rather than to the recurrence of disequilibrium. Analytically, the theory evoked the background image of a market as if that image were straightforward and determinate. The evocation of a seemingly uncontroversial view of what a market is in turn favored the polemical conception that markets – whatever they were – represented the naturally efficient framework for the allocation of resources. Here two problems arose.

For one thing the indeterminacy of the market concept becomes clear as soon as you begin to think of the concrete legal-institutional forms that markets can take. The rights and powers that make up the conventional categories of property and contract can be reshaped and reallocated in any number of ways. Each of these detailed institutional interpretations of the idea of a market has very different consequences for the social arrangements of power and production. Yet there is no way to tell, just by analyzing the market concept, which of these rival interpretations is most truly a market, even in the trivial sense of promoting the greatest amount of decentralized competition. Such questions are empirical and demand empirical answers. Any particular market picture already presupposes a prior commitment to one of the open-ended number of possible interpretations of the market idea. The commitment is justified by the claim that this is the right kind of market to have or that it is the peculiar kind that in fact exists in some economy that you are talking about.

For another thing, economists soon discovered that the analytic structure of marginalist theory – with all its rich connotations of effectiveness in getting things done – could easily be applied to a centralized command economy. Right-wing economists living at the first flush of marginalist triumph – von Wieser, Pareto, Barone – showed that there was no insuperable analytic obstacle. They demonstrated that a command economy could be described through a system of equations with a uniquely determined set of solutions, graced with all the properties that hold for the equations of the market economy. Decisions about distribution or other matters are simply made beforehand by the centralized socialist agency. To be sure, this planned economy might prove less productive. The nonmarket signals might function less effectively. The state administration of the production system might be inept. The command system might also undermine an independently justified program of civic freedom. But these arguments were hardly at the same level as those that attempt to justify the confinement of marginalist analysis to market economies.

The third point of weakness in marginalism had to do with the polemical uses of the concepts of efficiency or "Pareto optimality." Just as the new analysis had to be disentangled from the idea of self-sustaining equilibrium and from any determinate picture of the market, so it had to be separated out from all specific conceptions bout the economic arrangements that would either cause growth or guarantee a maximum satisfaction to the individual participants in the economy. Late nineteenth century economists like Alfred Marshall already understood the consequences. One consequence was the downplaying by marginalism of all considerations of distribution among individuals, classes, or generations; the distributive state of affairs was simply taken for granted. The other consequence was the lack of a dynamic perspective: the investments and innovations needed to generate repeated breakthroughs in productive capacity would not necessarily coincide with the relation of prices and quantities under any interpretation of equilibrium. Later argument, which showed the idea of aggregate satisfaction (the "collective welfare function") to be incoherent anyway, simply carried the point one step further. Marginalist efficiency could just not be taken as an effective guide to the making of collective wealth or welfare. What is still less widely recognized is that these limitations result directly from the lack of a way to deal with the relation between routine economic activity and the institutional and imaginative framework in which it takes place.

The three sources of trouble in marginalist theory share the same general character. There are two ways to deal with them. One tactic is to explicate and exaggerate still further the line of development that began with the marginalist break with classical political economy. Disengage the theory from self-adjusting equilibrium, determinate market institutions, or strongly defined efficiency. Make it into a general but narrowly defined theory of maximizing choice. Transform it, once and for all, into a pure analysis neither descriptive nor normative, although it may serve as a powerful tool in descriptive or normative theories built on other foundations. The alternative solution is to reverse direction and plunge back into all the contested empirical and normative issues that marginalist economics was partly designed to avoid.

By the close of the twentieth century, the leading economists in the mainstream marginalist tradition (so inaptly dubbed neoclassical) thought they were using both these strategies effectively. Actually, however, they had been much more successful at the first than at the second, partly because they failed to grasp the incongruity between this second aim and the explanatory methods that had emerged from the marginalist transformation of economics.

The two responses to the trouble are incompatible. The generalizing, agnostic solution amounts to an extension and clarification of what was most novel and coherent in early marginalism. To be successful, this textured empirical and normative approach would require a different kind of analysis rather than more and better of the same. It would demand a style of economic explanation focused on the interplay between production or exchange and the institutional and imaginative framework in which they occur. And it would therefore call for a solution to the very problems that deep-structure social analysis, in its evolutionary or nonevolutionary forms, have been unable to solve.

To understand the force of these last remarks, consider the relation between marginalism, in its final, most general development, and the causes that explain why self-adjusting equilibrium fails to occur. What these causes actually were or how they influenced one another and other forces was not something that pure economic analysis itself purported to describe and explain. They were conjectures and observations that had to be made outside the central explanatory structure rather than presented, and tested, as derivations from it. Sometimes you incorporated them by relaxing assumptions and sometimes you included them as values for the coefficients of variables in the equations. But you did not, within the core analysis itself, develop a theory of cause and effect relations between any extensive aspect of the material life of society.

Pure economic analysis and particular discoveries and conjectures about the actual workings of actual economies remained largely independent of one another. The former became little more than a language in which to formalize the latter. The latter never upset the former. As a result, the general parts of the analysis provided no pattern for such conjectures and discoveries. Either these empirical findings accumulated ad hoc, or they had to be ordered by a pattern derived from some other discipline.

For the same reasons, the uncovering of new facts need never lead to a change in the basic marginalist analysis of the economy. Once the theory was defined with sufficient care, and duly purged of unwarranted assumptions about self-adjusting equilibrium, about the determinacy and necessity of the market framework, and about the aggressive senses of the efficiency concept, it became neutral as between different empirical or normative positions on all these more concrete issues. If, however, it failed to achieve this neutrality, it lay itself open to all the objections that could be brought against the earlier, less general and coherent versions of marginalism. There had to be something wrong with any theory that was true by definition once you defined its terms carefully enough.

Mainstream economists shrugged their shoulders. With mock humility and sincere self-contentment they claimed to be doing science in the only way that it could be done: by piecemeal observation and gradual revision. They were mistaken in their understanding of both science and their own practice. This practice was not science in the sense of a strong account of possible worlds, with auxiliary hypotheses about the operation or genesis of an actual world, the manner of some branches of physics. Nor was it a science, like neo-Darwinian evolutionary theory, that presented a causal explanation of the workings and history of one particular world and of why and how a given state of affairs passed into some neighboring state of affairs. In this marginalist economics, mathematics, though extravagantly used, was less a storehouse of imaginative schemata that might or might not describe the world – which is what it had become in physics since Galileo – than a pure instrument of inference and calculation and the nearly empty analysis of a small number of simple ideas. Purists saw the core of this style of economics as an analytical apparatus, free of surprising and controversial hypotheses, except when coupled with observations whose accuracy and causes had to be determined outside the discipline. The intellectual consequences of this merely tangential connection between economic analysis and empirical discovery were far-reaching.

First, such an economics lacked the means for cumulative and continuous progression. It had no prospect of revolutionary pressure against its own assumptions and no organizing imagination with which to investigate relations in the world. When the theorist withdrew to the heartland of the analysis he had little to say about the surprising features of real economies. When he turned to these facts, his analysis left him more or less at sea. His surprises – a thinker's treasure – were wasted on ideas that nothing could surprise. The formal virtuosity of his general analysis was but the silver lining of its substantive sterility.

The second implication was that, driven by the desire to take a position on the empirical and normative disputes of the day, economists easily fell back into the assumptions of early marginalism, though not all of them played with the same double entendres at the same time. Sometimes, the trouble was the obscuring of the degree to which certain strong claims actually still depended on the hypothesis of self-adjusting, optimal equilibrium; sometimes the equivocal picture of the market as a more or less institutionally determinate idea, with the system of property and contract rights (though part of the definition of a market) taken for granted; and sometimes the unwarranted expansion of the efficiency idea to justify a particular distributive scheme or growth strategy. So the widely held belief that marginalist economics was apologetic by vocation – a belief so offensive to professional economists – had a large element of truth. The criticism was often confused, but not as much as the theory it indicted.

A third consequence for economics was the way in which the formulation of crucial debates in macroeconomics developed. A crisis in economic policy generated a response. The response reflected certain limited political aims and empirical conjectures peculiar to the intentions of its authors and the circumstances of its time. Later on, this relativity was forgotten, and the more or less successful stratagem was treated as a pattern for a general theory – given that general theories could not be derived from marginalist microeconomics. All this can be seen in the episode of Keynesianism, one of the strangest interludes in the history of economics.

The one organizing theoretical element in Keynes's mature doctrine was the development of the argument for the possibility of permanent disequilibrium or of equilibrium without the optimal properties of Walras's "special case." Faced with what he recognized as an underconsumption crisis and with the illusions of the doctrine of sound finance, Keynes offered a solution. His solution was keyed to an intention, a situation, and a narrow set of conjectures.

Keynes reckoned that it was politically easier to sustain aggregate demand by public spending than to socialize major investment decisions, though he recognized that either route might have provided a way out. He was dealing with circumstances in which the characteristic double limit of post-World War II economic policy had not yet become clear. Popularly elected governments were not yet faced with the contrasting impulse not to give in completely to either the investors (because underconsumption and unemployment would create social unrest and impoverish the nation) or to the working and consuming populace (because failure of investment confidence would produce economic crisis, with or without inflation). At the time of Keynes's campaigns, sound-finance doctrine still saw to it that the first pressure counted for more than the second. Finally, Keynes found himself in a situation in which the stimulus of economic activities could count on a large amount of unused capacity. The focus of concern was not yet on the ways in which a noninnovative, risk-averse managerial class, a segmented labor movement preoccupied with self-defense, and a paralyzed state worked to block continuous enlargements of output and productivity. When the last two sets of facts changed, Keynes's judgment about the first set of facts no longer held. Many of the crucial issues of redistribution and growth in the rich Western economies could be dealt with only by gaining political control over the basic flows of investment decisions.

Such controversies and positions never added up to a theory of any kind. To pretend they did and do is to depoliticize politics and to dehistoricize history. They have the same status, and many of the same themes, as the debates between the Soviet economic schools led by Bukharin and Preobrazhensky during the 1920s. When the American economists began to speak of microeconomics and macroeconomics as two mutually referring theoretical systems, they were doubly mistaken. Neither amounted to a theoretical system, though each fell short in its own way. One was a formal analytic of choice; the other, an exercise in statecraft, based on limited causal judgments whose validity could hardly outlast their occasions.

4

Making Sense of the Slogan "It's All Politics":

Toward a Radically Antinaturalistic Social Theory

Themes of a Theory

CONSIDER now a few of the central themes of a social theory that develops the ambitious speculative version rather than the armed skeptical interpretation of the claim that it's all politics. The worth of the view that elaborates these themes cannot be assessed until the theory has been worked out in detail. The thematic outline can nevertheless show what it takes to break loose, through the means of general theory, from the contemporary predicament of social thought. It can also strengthen our sense of intellectual possibility by suggesting an alternative that we have no reason to reject out of hand.

The Theme of the Distinction Between Formative Contexts and Formed Routines. In every social and historical situation we can identify a contrast between formative contexts and formed routines. An institutional or imaginative framework of social life arises through the containment and interruption of conflict. Defeated or exhausted, people stop fighting. They accept arrangements and preconceptions that define the terms of their practical and passionate relations to one another.

These terms are then continuously recast as an intelligible and defensible scheme of human association: a set of models of sociability to be realized in different areas of social life. This reconstruction is more than an imperative of justification. It is an aspect of what it means to settle down in a social world and to make out of it a home. People then no longer need to understand the organization of society as merely the truce lines and trophies of an ongoing social warfare. They can read one another's words and deeds against a subtext of shared assumptions.

A stabilized social framework, context, or structure sets the conditions of people's material, emotional, and even cognitive access to one another. It shapes the routines of conflict over mastery and use of the tangible and intangible resources that enable the occupants of some social stations to set terms to the activities of the occupants of other social stations. These resources include governmental power, economic capital, technical expertise, and prestigious ideals or the forms of argument that claim to show implications of these ideals. Once in place a formative institutional and imaginative context regenerates a system of social division and hierarchy, of roles and ranks. It also gives life to cycles of reform and retrenchment in governmental politics and to business cycles in the economy.

You can tell whether an institutional arrangement or a belief about the possible and desirable forms of human association deserves to be included in the definition of a society's formative context by applying two complementary criteria. First, the belief or arrangement must be taken for granted by the strategies with which people pursue their recognized individual or group interests. Second, its substitution must change the form and outcome of conflicts over the key resources of society making. (A complication in the use of this second standard is that some substitutions may be functional equivalents.)

In contemporary North Atlantic countries the institutions that satisfy these two criteria include a style of government that combines an eighteenth-century commitment to the fragmentation of governmental power with a nineteenth-century mode of partisan rivalry incongruously related to the persistent class and communal divisions of society; a form of regulated market economies that employs property rights nearly absolute in use and duration as its preferred device of economic decentralization while using regulation by professional bureaucrats and judges as its favored method of social control over decentralized economic activity; and an approach to the representation of labor and to the organization of industry that results in the differential unionization of the work force. The imaginative preconceptions that meet the two criteria are expressed clearly, though often tacitly, in the specialized discourses of party-political and legal controversy and more richly, interestingly, and contradictorily in popular expectation, argument, and sensibility. These premises include images of private community for family and friendship, of civic equality and official accountability for governmental politics, and of voluntary contract and technical hierarchy for work and exchange.

A formative context does not exist in the same sense as the atomic structure of a natural object, open to external observation. Nor does it exist as a mere set of illusions that insight can dispel. The primary sense of its existence is practical. It exists because (and in the sense that) it is hard to disturb and even to grasp in the course of ordinary activities. Its power to shape a world of routine deals and quarrels depends upon the extent to which it gains immunity – or rather immunizes itself against the possibility of challenge and revision.

The Theme of the Relativity of the Contrast Between Context-Preserving Routine and Context-Transforming Conflict. Formative contexts must be reproduced in the banal activities of daily life such as the forms of economic exchange, the habits of party-political competition, and the discourse of moral and legal controversy. These activities generate an endless series of petty conflicts – a Brownian motion of social life. These disputes are the small wars fought to save a social world from the wars that can pull this world apart. Yet the context-preserving disputes can always escalate into context-transforming struggles. For no ultimate difference divides them other than their relative scope and intensity. Some circumstances encourage escalation while others discourage it. But neither the actual occurrence of this escalation nor its outcome is governed by higher-order laws.

As practical or imaginative conflict widens and intensifies, different parts of the formative context are shaken. As a result, established assumptions about group interests, collective identities, and social possibilities also begin to come unstuck. For these assumptions are never more secure than the arrangements and preconceptions that supply the armature of a stabilized social world.

In a theory like Marxism, escalating conflict acts out the directional forces that lead from one preordained mode of production to another. It therefore also clarifies the logic of class interests embodied in each mode of production, or each transition between modes. But in a theory such as this one, the effect of escalation is just the opposite: to obscure and ultimately to dissolve the logic of class and communal interests. Nor is there any substitute system of interests waiting to take the place of the system that has been dissolved.

The more radically a formative context is disrupted, the more people find themselves thrown into a twofold circumstance of insecurity and openness. On the one hand, they descend into a Hobbesian war in which individuals and groups try to grab whatever apparent benefits they can seize and social life is consumed by a search for preemptive security. On the other hand, people divide into parties of opinion whose recruitment fails to map the preexisting lines of communal or class division and whose orientation fails to echo the interests and ideals that their members recognized at the earlier moment of stability. Instead of making the script fully explicit, escalation shows that there is no script.

Such a view recognizes that people will fight to retain the gross benefits and privileges of their acquired positions or to grab the privileges and benefits that, in the climate of expanded conflict, they no longer believe to be irretrievably beyond their reach. To account for this self-defensive or grasping activity, you need make no large assumptions about alternative systems of class interest: you need only acknowledge the impulse to seize the nearest and most tangible advantages in the midst of danger. Even this crude worldliness will be disturbed by the anxieties, animosities, and uncertainties of the moment.

The fierce struggle over material preferment will be accompanied by another series of events that the adherent to a theory like hardcore Marxism must try to dismiss as a temporary and self-correcting aberration. People whose class positions and material circumstances were similar when the fighting accelerated will find themselves disagreeing more often and more deeply than before. They will be divided by conflicting opinions and assumptions about what is good for them – or for the rest of society – and what they can reasonably expect or fear from the troubled situation. This fragmentation and regrouping will be all the more acute because the views of collective opportunity and of the social ideal on which they depend are incurably controversial. No simple historical sequence or list of alternative social orders exists to show each group its next best chance.

Thus, this view predicts that the experience of aggravated group struggle will regularly be a strange mixture of straightforward individual or collective self-aggrandizement and high conflicts of vision. Both the selfish and the ideal aspects of ordinary struggle will be exaggerated and, in their exaggerated form, they will taint each other ever more pervasively, until people can no longer tell them apart. Classes, rather than becoming more and more themselves, will, at least for the duration of the intensified conflict, become indistinguishable from parties of opinion. Indeed, in a very real way, parties of opinion will replace classes. Such predictions supply ways of testing the superiority of this view over its rivals. They will also be seen to have important practical implications.

The Theme of the Variability of Entrenchment. Formative contexts differ in the extent to which they are entrenched, that is to say, protected against being challenged and revised in the midst of ordinary conflicts and deals. The more entrenched a formative context, the greater the number of intermediate steps that must be traversed before context-preserving routines become context-transforming struggles. For example, before some of the society's formative institutional arrangements are seriously jeopardized, the habits of conflict over the mastery and uses of government that characterize a relatively more entrenched framework will have to undergo a longer and more easily interruptible process of escalation than the corresponding practices in a relatively less entrenched context. Similarly, the style of legal argument in a relatively more entrenched context will have to expose more concealed disharmonies among recognized principles or between pretense and practice before it turns into an attack on the dominant imaginative scheme of possible and desirable forms of human association.

Relative entrenchment and disentrenchment are not just things that happen to a formative context. They are consequences of particular ways of organizing and understanding social life. An advance toward disentrenchment should therefore not be mistaken for a move toward anarchy. A relatively more denaturalized or disentrenched context is at least as distinctive and detailed in its content as its relatively more disentrenched counterpart. In fact, if anything, it is richer in worked-out detail because the people who establish and reproduce it are more keenly aware of its artifactlike character. Compare, for example, the relatively more disentrenched frameworks of the contemporary North Atlantic countries to the relatively more entrenched contexts of the prerevolutionary monarchies. The former are no less richly defined than were the latter. Nor is there any reason to suppose that other, even more revisable orders would have any less detailed and distinctive substance.

The arrangements and preconceptions that compose a formative context shape social roles and hierarchies. The more entrenched are the preconceptions and arrangements, the more stable and rigidly defined become the hierarchies and roles that they support. For the privileged holds upon resources, or the discriminations of propriety and allegiance, implied by social division and ranking survive intact only so long as they remain hard to challenge and even hard to recognize. In fact, the relation between the revisability of a formative context and the force with which it imposes a system of division and hierarchy is so constant that the relative rigidity of roles or hierarchies may be considered part of the definition of entrenchment.

Thus, we can relate the spectrum of entrenchment to very distinct styles of social ranking. Hereditary castes or corporately organized estates, for example, occur in societies whose formative contexts are relatively entrenched. At the opposite extreme of disentrenchment, society would be divided only by freely formed parties of opinion whose membership bore no relation to any antecedent structure of social divisions or hierarchies. Somewhere toward the middle of this spectrum stand contemporary class societies, familiar with political parties that both speak and do not speak for particular classes and communities. The interplay between the weakened and fragmentary hierarchies of class and a practice of party politics that both reflects and transcends these hierarchies is a mark of societies partly, but only partly, emancipated from the constraints of false necessity.

Disentrenchment holds great practical interest for us because it can serve as the basis for a broad range of varieties of individual and collective empowerment. By opening social relations more fully to recombination and experiment it can contribute to the development of productive capabilities. By weakening roles and hierarchies it can help reconcile the enabling conditions of self-assertion: the need for engagement in group life and the countervailing need to avoid the dangers of dependence and depersonalization that attend all such engagement. By giving us a more conscious mastery over the settings of our practical and passionate relations it can turn us more truly into the architects and critics, rather than the puppets, of the social worlds in which we live. Call the sum of these varieties of empowerment that result from disentrenchment negative capability.

Disentrenchment also matters for another, related reason. We have grown accustomed to thinking that our lives in society are overshadowed by a series of unyielding tensions between, for example, the attractions of the social control of economic activity and the benefits of decentralized markets or, at a still more primitive level, between autonomy and community. But principles like social accountability and economic decentralization or ideals like autonomy and community have little meaning apart from the practical arrangements that are made to represent them in fact. Just as the content of these tensions varies, so does the extent to which they are indeed recalcitrant rather than open to partial resolution. Cumulative disentrenchment, if it can be achieved, may increase the part of these disharmonies that can be reconciled. Thus, for example, a market system based on rotating capital funds rather than absolute property rights may extend the opportunities for *both* the social control of accumulation and the decentralization of economic decisions.

The Theme of Possible Movement Toward Disentrenchment: Cumulative Change Without Evolutionary Compulsion. A thoroughly antinaturalistic social theory takes the final step in the development of the historical point of view. It affirms that we can change not only the content but also the force of our formative contexts: their relative immunity to challenge and their active encouragement to a structure of social division and hierarchy.

Because more disentrenched frameworks make possible a range of forms of empowerment, a cumulative move toward greater revisability is possible. Such a move may occur as a result of intentional action: more disentrenched arrangements may be inaugurated by groups and ruling groups who want to secure the benefits of negative capability for themselves or their countries. Alternatively, the move may result from a social counterpart to natural selection: the more disentrenched contexts outdo the less entrenched in the worldwide rivalry of practical capabilities and ideological seduction. Cumulative emancipation from false necessity may even result from efforts that override the contrast between intentional and unintentional agency. For example, more disentrenched practices and organizations may initially emerge as the unexpected by-products of other endeavors and without benefit of any understanding of the relation between disentrenchment and empowerment. Yet these organizations and practices may seem worth preserving for the sake of the advantages they produce. Moreover, the people who control them may have to develop a conception – of, say, enterprise management or legal doctrine – that requires an implicit, fragmentary understanding of negative capability and its conditions.

The advance toward greater disentrenchment is never more than possible. It can be reversed or overridden by other factors. Above all, it does not preset its own practical forms and implications. We can say that a particular formative context is more disentrenched than another. But we cannot generate prospectively a list of the institutional arrangements or imaginative preconceptions that correspond to different degrees of disentrenchment. In our efforts to build more revisable and hierarchy-subverting frameworks we work with the materials of the institutional and imaginative contexts that we are in or of past or remote sequences of context making that we study and remember. Even our boldest and most original inventions represent penumbral extensions of these legacies.

Each formative context influences its own sequel without determining it. For some parts of such an institutional and imaginative framework are usually less open to change than others: harder to replace without also replacing other arrangements or preconceptions. The biases that a formative context imparts to its own transformation can reinforce one another over time and thereby open up another source of cumulative context change.

In an evolutionary deep-structure theory such as Marxism the sequence of social frameworks can never be more than an outward product of the directing forces in history. But in a theory organized around these themes the pull of negative capability and the push of the sequential effects of formative contexts are independent influences that disturb and reshape each other. On the one hand, an advance in negative capability limits the force of sequential effects: when formative contexts become more disentrenched, their influence over their own sequels also diminishes. On the other hand, when we set out to change the character as well as the content of our frameworks, we have nothing to work with but the outcomes of many loosely connected histories of context change.

The Theme of the Piece-by-Piece Replaceability of Formative Contexts. While positivist social science disregards the distinction between formative contexts and formed routines, deep-structure social theory sees every social framework as an indivisible package. Once we define a formative context with enough detail to show how it shapes routines of social conflict, we see that its components do not in fact develop simultaneously nor come together in a single moment of closure. The major institutional or imaginative components of a formative context are often changed piecemeal. Their replacement reshapes some of the deals and conflicts that reenact a scheme of social division and hierarchy and that determine the uses to which economic capital, governmental power, and scientific knowledge are put. Such revisions typically destabilize some parts of the established framework while strengthening others.

Like the style of social theory it exemplifies, the illusion of the indivisibility of formative contexts has dangerous practical consequences. It suggests that all changes short of total revolution must amount to mere conservative tinkering. It thereby induces in its adepts a fatal oscillation between unjustified confidence and equally unjustified prostration.

A view of the internal constitution of formative contexts is always just the reverse side of an account of context making. Thus, the approach to context change outlined earlier suggests an approach to the composition of social frameworks. This approach allows for a piece-by-piece reconstruction of social frameworks. Yet it also identifies constraints upon the replacement and recombination of the elements that make up such an ordering of social life.

These elements may not be able to coexist for long if they represent widely disparate degrees of emancipation from false necessity. Consider in this light the relation between two major parts of a formative context: the method of capital allocation and the organization of government. The property-based regulated market system of the contemporary North Atlantic countries can coexist with many different styles of democratic or authoritarian polities. But it is hard to see how this property regime can survive side by side with arrangements that closely link caste or class privileges in government and privileged degrees of group control over land and labor. Such arrangements are found in formative contexts more resistant to challenge and more supportive of rigid roles and hierarchies than the democratic or authoritarian regimes that ordinarily accompany economic decentralization based on absolute property rights. Neither is that property regime likely to coexist with polities even less entrenched than the polities that now accompany property-based market systems. Such systems include a mobilizational democracy committed to open up every feature of the social order to collective challenge and revision and to liquefy all rigid roles and hierarchies or a mobilizational dictatorship determined to shift people around according to an artificial plan for economic and military strengthening. For different reasons and with different consequences, these political orders would not tolerate the exercise of private privilege and the restraint on social control that nearly absolute and eternal property rights imply.

Institutional solutions at such different levels of negative capability give irreconcilable messages about the extent to which we can or should remake and reimagine society. More important, they permit and require very different degrees of collective engagement from the bottom up or of reformist initiative from the top down.

Practical Implications

The antinaturalistic social theory whose themes I have just outlined has many implications for transformative practice. The evocation of these practical lessons may help elucidate the character of the theory that inspires them.

A Mission for Programmatic Thought. Programmatic thinking gains a secure place in our ideas only when we believe both that the formative contexts of social life can be remade and reimagined and that the outcome of this reconstructive activity is not foreordained. Positivist social science denies the first of these two conditions by disregarding or downplaying the difficulty of explaining the frameworks of our deals and conflicts in the relatively noncontroversial way in which we justify choices within these frameworks. Deep-structure social theories fail to meet the second condition by imposing predetermined limits on the results of context revision. In a view like Marxism such limits are especially severe. We are told little about the next stage of social evolution (socialism), yet are discouraged from usurping the prerogatives of the dialectic. If a detailed description of the next stage were to fill this gap, we would still be left with no more room for invention than the protagonists of past modes of production enjoyed. Our role would be merely to suit a necessary structure to local variations.

But in an antinaturalistic social theory like the one anticipated here, programmatic thought has its work cut out for it. The formative institutional and imaginative contexts of social life can be remade and reimagined – though rarely all at once. Moreover, the results of this transformative work are not preestablished. For the directional forces invoked by this view do not even select a list of possible frameworks, much less a compulsive sequence of frameworks.

A social theory with the central themes outlined in the preceding subsection does not merely give programmatic thought a mission. It also provides our programmatic efforts with a measure of guidance. It offers us the beginnings of a credible account of context change. It thereby allows us to escape a striking consequence of current views of social reality, which is to equate the realism of a proposal for reconstruction with its proximity to current arrangements. By giving content to a conception of the meaning and conditions of human empowerment, the theory also helps identify a goal for social reconstruction. In particular, it frees the definition of the radical project from unnecessarily restrictive assumptions about the possible forms of social organization and personal experience.

The Search for Alternative Institutional Forms of Market Economies and Representative Democracies. Even those who hold no conscious allegiance to the assumptions of deep-structure social theory and positivist social science habitually treat abstract types of governmental and economic organization such as command and market economies or representative democracies as if they had a detailed, built-in institutional content. Thus, people speak as if they had to choose among different blends of market and planning but not among radically different ways to centralize or decentralize and to combine centralism and decentralization in the economy. They take for granted an identity between the abstract idea of a market – as an order in which many economic agents bargain on their own initiative and for their own account – and a particular system of contract and property rights. They equate the social control of economic activity with familiar methods of nationalization or regulation. They make the idea of representative democracy equal the peculiar combination of eighteenth-century liberal constitutionalism and nineteenth-century party politics that history has bequeathed them.

Liberals and radicals share these prejudices with conservatives. Liberals fail to confront the constraints that inherited institutional forms impose on the realization of their ideals. Radicals take liberals at their word. They seek alternatives to current market economies in an unnecessary rejection of market principle. They often attack bourgeois democracy in a futile quest for direct democracy and permanent civic engagement.

The antinaturalistic view sketched previously liberates us from these prejudices. It turns our attention to the work of imagining alternative forms of market economies and representative democracies. Economic regimes – it suggests – differ in the success with which they resolve the tension between the social control and the decentralization of economic activity; we can achieve more of both. Democratic regimes differ in the seriousness of the explicit or implicit obstacles they set in the way of bold institutional experiments and of attacks on privilege. Systems of legal rights differ in the facility with which the devices established to safeguard the individual against governmental or private oppression lend themselves to the exercise of subjugation over other people and restrict the plasticity of social life. The interest lies in the practical details of these variations. The liberal and the radical do not awaken from their slumber until they seize the opportunities such variations create and set themselves to the work of imagining and establishing less entrenched frameworks of social life.

The Provisional Force of Group Interests. A theory like the view outlined in this section presents an approach to transformative political practice that recognizes the force of established group interests yet treats these interests as no more secure than the institutional arrangements and the imaginative preconceptions that help sustain them. The transformative movement that begins its work in a relatively stable social situation (and no situation can be more than relatively stable) knows that the ranks and communities into which society is divided have recognized interests. The movement must take care to relate its cause to these interests. However, it also needs to think and act with the awareness that these definitions of interest are not for keeps. They rest on assumptions about collective identities and social possibilities. These assumptions in turn depend on the serenity of established institutional arrangements and enacted models of sociability that shape a world of routine deals and quarrels.

Escalating conflict over such arrangements and models shakes assumptions about group membership and transformative possibility, and it reshapes conceptions of group interest. The direction taken by the new views of group interests depends on the precise ways in which formative contexts have been changed. Because there is no closed list of possible frameworks, and no preestablished sequence of formative contexts, there is also no secure limit on the changes that a current system of group interests can undergo. Thus, the transformative movement must take established conceptions of group interest seriously while anticipating how these conceptions may shift as new institutional or imaginative elements enter into the framework of routine conflict and exchange.

This approach has an important corollary. In a stabilized social world some class or communal alliances are easier or harder to establish than others. Some classes or communities are more likely to welcome or to oppose a given transformative program. But there is no permanent logic of group collaboration or hostility and no class or community anointed to serve as the indispensable agent or vanguard of a particular change of the social order.

The Means of Stabilization Generate Opportunities for Destabilization. In the theory whose themes I have sketched, the fighting that goes on within a stabilized social framework is only a more truncated version of broader and more intense struggles about the framework. Formative contexts differ in the extent to which they effect and enforce this truncation. All practical or imaginative conflicts can get out of hand. None need await the cue to play an assigned part in the script. Through the give-and-take of alliance and animosity, of compromise and contradiction, each petty quarrel hints at opportunities of human connection beyond the possibilities countenanced by the established order.

An antinaturalistic social theory formulated on these lines enables us to understand how a formative context gains a semblance of deep necessity after practical and imaginative conflict has been contained or interrupted. But the theory also shows how each of these methods of stabilization creates opportunities for destabilization.

Thus, for example, a pacified formative context is both presupposed and reinforced by a set of explicit or implicit deals among groups and of accommodations between groups and parts of the governmental apparatus So, too, such a context serves as a template for assumptions about collective identities and social possibilities, which in turn help shape conceptions of group interest. Once the deals, the accommodations, and the conceptions of group interest are all in place, the institutional and imaginative order begins to seem almost immutable.

Look closer, though, and you find hidden disharmonies, ready to be seized on and developed. For example, even the most narrowly conceived group interest can always be defended through two different strategies. One strategy clings to the group's present station and prerogatives and defines the closest or the immediately inferior groups as rivals and enemies. The other strategy makes common cause with these groups against higher-ups. These two methods have radically different implications. While the former reaffirms the established order, the latter sooner or later challenges it. For what begins as a transitory tactical partnership often leads to a new collective identity, encourages new views of group interest, and contributes new preconceptions and arrangements.

Thus, too, a stabilized institutional and imaginative order of social life serves as a foundation for the development of a distinctive technological and organizational style. Everything from the way enterprises are managed to the way machines are designed begins to take the basic institutional and imaginative settlements of the society for granted. The overturning of these settlements poses a real threat to a dominant managerial and technological style. The dimension of the threat increases as this style spreads through a system of nation-states at unequal levels of economic and military power. The reforming elites of the more backward countries discover only slowly that they can reach the most advanced levels of productive or destructive capability on the basis of novel social arrangements. Even after they have made this discovery, it takes time to develop an alternative managerial and technological approach.

Nevertheless, practical pressures and rivalries also provide opportunities for destabilization. The development of practical productive or destructive capabilities may require that people and resources be moved around not just once but repeatedly. The arrangements capable of ensuring this greater plasticity can be either coercive or consensual in their temper, and they can either minimize or maximize the break with the preexisting pattern of group interests. A perennial stream of middle-level crises supplies occasions to begin fighting over the future order of society.

If the transformative movement can find opportunities for destabilization in the very methods of stability, it can discover inspiration in the failure of a formative context fully to inform people's practical and passionate dealings or to supersede the residues of past and distant versions of social life. The vestiges, the anomalies, the deviations, the transgressions represent countless small-scale experiments in the making of alternative social orders. Yesterday's defeated alternative, recast in new institutional terms, becomes tomorrow's triumphant solution.

No decisive crisis ever ensures that any particular reconstruction of an institutional and imaginative order will succeed. But with such opportunities and inspirations, no stability is tranquil enough to give the would-be subversive an excuse for prostration.

The Primacy of Revolutionary Reform. A political imagination formed by positivist social science is predisposed to prefer incremental social reform. For this mode of social analysis encourages us to bring the established procedures for problem solving and interest accommodation closer to a supposedly noncontroversial ideal of neutrality and efficiency. It prompts us, for example, to ask how a given market economy can be rid of oligopoly without jeopardizing the ability to take advantage of economies of scale, how the harms that an entrepreneur imposes on other people may be incorporated into his cost of doing business, or how social needs may be protected by administrative regulation that restricts and supplements market allocation. Those who press such questions ordinarily take for granted particular institutional forms of economic decentralization and social control. By contrast, the deep-structure social theorist treats the formative institutional and imaginative frameworks of social life as indivisible units, each of which stands or falls as a piece. As a result he believes that political action always faces a choice between a revolutionary substitution of the entire formative context of social life and a reformist tinkering that merely wards off serious change.

But for a theory built on the themes sketched earlier the normal mode of transformative action is revolutionary reform, defined as the substitution of any one of the loosely and unevenly connected arrangements and beliefs that go into the making of a formative context. The criterion for the occurrence of revolutionary reform is a corollary of the standard for the inclusion of a practice or belief in the definition of a society's formative context. A revolutionary reform changes the institutional and imaginative presuppositions taken for granted in the everyday struggles over the uses and mastery of the resources – of capital, governmental power, technical expertise, or legal and moral justification – that enable the occupants of some social stations to set terms to what the occupants of other social stations do. As a result, such a reform changes the plan of social division and hierarchy in content and even in character. The existing cycles of governmental policy and economic prosperity or decline acquire a new structure and new consequences. And a different set of biases is imparted to the effects that forces exogenous to the formative structure – such as demographic or technological change – will exercise on social life.

Thus, in the circumstances of the contemporary Western democracies it would be a revolutionary reform to impose a version of public control over the basic flows of investment decisions in the economy or, on the contrary, to prevent elected governments from influencing investment decisions through differential fiscal policies; to set up a special branch of government with the mission of reconstructing large-scale organizations and major areas of social practice in conformity with unfulfilled ideals of the legal order such as nondiscrimination among classes, races, and genders or, on the contrary, to prevent current administrative or judicial officials from pursuing any more modest variant of this reconstructive activity; to require the unionization of all labor (e.g., putting a corporatist labor-law regime in place of a contractualist regime), to prohibit unions altogether, or to replace unions as an instrument of labor representation by a system of joint public and workers' control of enterprises.

Revolution becomes the limiting case of transformative action rather than the sole alternative to the statecraft of stability through tinkering. The vulgar idea of revolution includes two elements. The first part is a process: a violent seizure of the central government, with the participation of large masses of ordinary people and the paralysis or active collaboration of the repressive machinery of the state. The second part is an outcome: the comprehensive reconstruction of an entire form of social life, of its distinctive arrangements and its established hierarchies and divisions. But the process often occurs without the outcome, if indeed this outcome ever takes place at all. Moreover, a revolution in the sense defined by violent upheaval is an event so uncertain in its course and so dependent for its occurrence upon government-shattering events like war and occupation that we are fortunate not to depend on it in order to remake our contexts.

TWO WAYS TO DEVELOP THE IDEA THAT EVERYTHING IS POLITICS: SUPER-THEORY AND ULTRA-THEORY

The claim that everything is politics can be developed in two radically different directions. These twin agendas offer alternative responses to the predicament of social thought, alternative ways to go beyond both deep-structure analysis and positivist social science. Let me label them here, ironically, super-theory and ultra-theory.

The response of super-theory is to develop a comprehensive view, rich in explanatory claims about social facts and historical events. Such is the intellectual direction whose major themes and practical implications are outlined in the preceding section and developed by *Politics*. Super-theory rivals deep-logic practice in the scope, generality, and concreteness of its hypotheses and arguments. It preserves the first move of deep-structure analysis – the distinction between formative context and formed routines. But it also replaces the second and third moves – the subsumption of each framework under an indivisible and repeatable type of social organization and the recourse to the lawlike constraints and tendencies that can generate a list or sequence of such types. The view offered shows how general explanations in social and historical study can dispense with the conception of indivisible and repeatable types of social organization while nevertheless specifying constraints on what can be combined with what within a single framework. It offers an account of context making, indeed even of the possibility of cumulative change in the character as well as the content of our frameworks. Yet this antinaturalistic social theory does not rely on the ideas of a world-historical evolutionary logic or of a set of criteria that any possible social world must satisfy. Nor does it imply any qualitative contrast between the social knowledge available to historical agents and the insight of a theorist who describes and explains their actions.

The resulting method of social analysis vindicates the principal intention of deep-structure theory – the understanding of social order as made and imagined rather than as given – against the scientistic baggage that has compromised the realization of this intellectual project. It therefore pushes to the limit the internal criticism of deep-logic work, recognizing the fragments of a constructive view in what may otherwise seem merely a long series of disappointments. Such a response to the problems of social thought shifts the sense we give to our practices of social and historical explanation and to our modal categories of contingency and necessity. But the reformed explanatory style continues to be recognizable as general theory. In some ways it may be even more ambitious in its self-conception than the theory it replaces. It therefore also remains vulnerable to the objection that it merely carries deep-logic analysis to another plane, perpetuating its deficiencies in novel or disguised form.

Politics takes the direction of super-theory. The argument of this book anticipates by diagnosis and criticism the broad outline of the super-theoretical view presented more fully in the constructive work that follows. The merit of the proposed view depends in part on its success at escaping the objections leveled against deep-structure analysis and in part on the comparison of its achievements with the results of alternative ways of dealing with the problems of social thought.

For super-theory is not the sole possible response to these problems. There is at least one other intellectual agenda open to whoever comes to share the critical perspective on the situation of social thought described in the earlier parts of this book. Call this alternative ultra-theory. Let me add immediately that ultra-theory, like super-theory, is a project, not an accomplishment. Nobody has actually developed its program or codified its practice though many fragments of both its practice and its program have long been available.

The key difference between super-theory and ultra-theory is that ultra-theory rejects the attempt to develop a theoretical system. The ultra-theorist believes that the quest for comprehensive and systematic explanations betrays the principle that everything is politics (man as maker, society as artifact, conflict as tool) and leads to another version of the problems of deep-structure thought. He sees the deep-logic endeavor as an example of the quest for foundational ideas: for the big picture, the underlying reasons, the ultimate causes, and the hidden truths. He believes, on the basis of his reading of intellectual history, that, whatever its proclaimed intentions, a systematic and comprehensive theory will compromise with foundationalism. And foundationalism in social thought, he adds, means the appeal to controlling structures or to the laws that govern them. It means hedging on the insight that everything is politics. From this standpoint, the ultra-theorist suspects the super-theorist of falling into a new version of the errors of deep-logic analysis. Even the super-theorist can agree with him that the weak point of super-theory is precisely that it might fail in the end to solve the problems from which deep-structure theory came to grief.

Like super-theory, ultra-theory rejects positivist social science and naive historiography. It therefore makes at least one exception to its habitual theoretical negativism: the exception necessary to affirm the central importance of the difference between formative contexts and formed routines. It therefore also insists on the discontinuity and originality of particular contexts. But it does not seek to develop these insights through more defensible counterparts to the second and third moves of deep-structure analysis.

More generally, the ultra-theorist denies that his negativity produces intellectual paralysis or that it undermines a critical perspective on existing society. On the contrary, he insists that only by following his path can we avoid replacing necessitarian superstitions by ideas that resemble them. Ultra-theory defines itself by its recurrent use of a set of intellectual practices rather than by its adherence to a theoretical system. The ultra-theorist believes not only that these practices require no comprehensive system of explanations but that they cannot be reconciled with any such system. Consider three characteristic practices of the ultra-theorist.

The first activity is a negativistic explanatory therapeutic. Each time the ultra-theorist encounters a deep-logic explanation of a social transformation he shows how the same events can be fully explained without deep-structure arguments. He presents them as the outcomes of a particular history of practical and imaginative conflicts. Each time he finds a conventional social-science treatment of a topic he shows how the explanation has been skewed or trivialized by the failure to understand the controlling influence of a framework. But he rejects the attempt to develop a general theory of frameworks, of their making and their internal constitution. He is much less interested in making abstract points than in puncturing the illusory accounts offered by the deep-structure theoretician and the positivist social scientist. What others may deride as intellectual emptiness he defends as a refusal to be drawn to his adversaries' level of discussion.

A second distinctive practice of ultra-theory is the vindication of repressed solutions, of yesterday's missed opportunities, today's forgotten anomalies, and tomorrow's unsuspected possibilities. The ultra-theorist (and in this, as in so much else, he resembles the super-theorist) sees a connection between insight into social reality and sympathetic interest in the losers. The vindication of defeated or deviant solutions follows directly from the criticism of deep-structure or conventional social-science accounts of what actually happened. To the extent that dominant institutions or ideas cannot be adequately explained as the result of an evolutionary logic or of entrenched economic, organizational, and psychological constraints, to that extent they must be ascribed to particular causes and conflicts. No deep change in human nature or social reality would have been required for the result to have been different. If the triumph of certain institutions and ideas was relatively accidental, their replacement can also more easily be imagined as realistic.

The ultra-theorist denies that he needs any general theory of frameworks and of their making in order to develop these themes of contingency and replaceability. He wants, instead, to nurture an imagination of the particular that does not depend on the pretense of a comprehensive knowledge or of a privileged vantage point. He remembers, he anticipates, and he defies, but he does not claim to disclose secret and fundamental knowledge.

A third practice of ultra-theory is constructive and prescriptive. The ultra-theorist may go beyond criticism and explanation to develop anticipatory visions of more ideal forms of social life. But here too the ultra-theorist avoids first principles or elaborate theories. Rather than relying on a general view of realistic trajectories of transformation, he seeks analogies to the successful changes of the past. Rather than working out the implications of fundamental ideals, he seizes on the deviant elements in our present experience that suggest ways to realize more fully our received ideals and to reevaluate them in the light of these new realizations. If he is pressed to state the standards by which he chooses one such deviant solution as more worthy of extension than another, he denies he has such preestablished standards. He appeals instead to a pretheoretical experience of repressed or disappointed aspirations, and he frankly acknowledges that we have to choose between these aspirations by acts of commitment, choices that are also gambles, gambles that are also experiments.

The weak point of ultra-theory is the difficulty it has in resisting the standpoint of conventional social science without the help of a countervailing theory of formative contexts, of their genesis and internal composition. Though the ultra-theorist claims to acknowledge the influence of institutional and imaginative frameworks and the distinctiveness of the ways of life they shape, he can affirm this acknowledgment only by implication or through narrowly focused acts of criticism, explanation, or utopian vision. Except for a long memory and a vigilant intention, he has no prescription against the danger of taking a particular context for granted. He has no way, at least no general and discursive way, to justify any particular approach to frameworks and their history. He must even deny that he is committed to a particular approach. Nor can he easily explore a theme like the idea that the formative contexts differ, among other things, in their relation to the context-revising freedom of the people who live within them. There is only a tenuous distinction between not having a theory of formative contexts and not having a way to talk about them. When this distinction crumbles, ultra-theory lapses back into positivist social science, like a once militant leftist party that repeats the rhetoric of structure-defying activism while surrendering completely to the politics of structure-respecting redistribution.

When ultra-theory escapes the slide into conventional social science it stands exposed to another peril. It risks expressing a precommitment to a particularly perverse and misleading version of modernism. This version is the existentialist idea that true freedom consists in the perpetual defiance of all settled structure, in the endless flight from one context to another. This existentialist reading of the modernist message fails to take into account both the bad news that we must live and think most of the time in a context and the good news that we can create contexts that more fully respect and encourage our context-revising freedom. Having asserted that all our structures are historical, the existentialist does not see that the relative force with which they imprison us and turn us into the victims of unseen compulsions is itself up for grabs in history.

The project of ultra-theory has a more than superficial affinity with this form of modernism. Both the rejection of explanatory or prescriptive theories about our formative contexts and the commitment to trash every argument for the necessity or authority of a given context suit a view that sees in the "endless labor of negation" the sole true source of authentic humanity. At the same time the absence of a theory of frameworks suggests by default that, as constraints on freedom, frameworks will be frameworks. No wonder many of the most cogent foreshadowings of the program of ultra-theory are found among the defenders of this modernist heresy.

Ultra-theory may seem at least easier to carry out than super-theory. It does not require a big book, only an open collection of particular exercises. It may not make such sudden and comprehensive claims on knowledge and research nor demand so arduous a translation into small-scale explanatory and programmatic discourse. It may therefore also more easily inspire and be inspired by our ordinary experience of social understanding and social criticism. But the impression of relative facility begins to dissipate once you remember how much must be done to keep ultra-theory from degenerating into positivist social science and to either prevent or to justify its alliance with the negativistic, existentialist version of modernism.

There are nevertheless no persuasive a priori reasons to prefer either super-theory or ultra-theory as responses to the contemporary situation of social thought. Each represents a research agenda, and research agendas have to be judged ultimately by what people do with them. Prospectively, each student makes a gamble, informed by guesses about the relative fruitfulness of a line of work and by his assessment of his own strengths and weakness. Retrospectively, we compare results.

Politics pursues the super-theory route unequivocally and unabashedly. The super-theory perspective already overshadows the ideas of this critical introduction. But I hope the ultra-theorists are out there working away.

The Making of Contemporary Formative Contexts

5

The Genesis of Three Complexes: Work-Organization, Government, and Private Rights

A SKEPTICAL PROLOGUE: PRIVATE ENTERPRISE AND GOVERNMENTAL POLICY

BEFORE turning to the genesis of the major institutional complexes described, consider, by way of preliminary example and admonition, the history of a subordinate, derivative, and eclectic institutional practice: the division of decisional responsibilities between central governments and large-scale business enterprises. In one sense this division merely extends the private-rights complex: the corporate institution, relatively insulated from public control and public controversy, takes its place alongside the system of contract and property rights. But it is also closely connected both with a style of governmental politics that limits the assertion of collective control over the basic shape and pace of economic growth and with an approach to the organization of work that mixes technical coordination with a generic disciplinary authority and thereby makes possible a stark contrast between task-defining and task-executing activities.

The massive network of governmentally granted subsidies, incentives, and privileges, the overt partnership between government and business in some sectors, and the domination of public enterprise in others, do not eviscerate the division between government and business of its force. Large concentrations of capital and labor are realized in the form of separate realms governed by managers in the name of the property norm. The mythical history would have us believe that this arrangement is a necessary consequence of the attempt to reconcile economic decentralization with economies of scale. But is it? A little bit of history suffices to make you wonder. Consider how this solution came to prevail in the country with which it is now most closely identified.

In early nineteenth century America, government and business stood in a multiplicity of relations, and many doctrines about the proper association between governmental and corporate power competed with each other. You appreciate this variety best when you focus on policy debates at the state level. The institutional situation was one in which enterprises under mixed public–private control and ownership played an important role; the right of incorporation, often closely guarded, became an instrument for bestowing and receiving illicit favor, and a justification for exercising a potentially high degree of control over the corporation in exchange for those powers of government (like the power of eminent domain) that were delegated to it. Three main doctrines of incorporation struggled for influence; the first, responsive to a populist vision, was hostile to all incorporation, invoking an ideal of individual enterprise; the second proposed to develop those aspects of the current situation that involved a major overlap of governmental and corporate powers and that therefore opened the internal structure and the external activities of the corporation to control by the agencies of government; the third view wanted to make the privilege of incorporation more readily available and to build a thicker wall between corporate discretion and governmental authority. By the start of the Civil War, this third doctrine had triumphed in practice, and its victory was consolidated by the 1880s. In the end, the corporate form became a device that allowed large concentrations of economic power over workers and markets to operate at a crucial remove from the risks of partisan democratic conflict. The reform movements of the late nineteenth and the twentieth century, from Progressivism to the New Deal, took the structure generated by the earlier contest for granted. Whether the theme of restraint upon business or that of administrative organization in the service of business prevailed in these latter-day movements, neither the restraint nor the rationalization ever went so far as to endanger the fundamental screening of business from national politics that had been settled upon at an earlier date.

The facts that converged to this end were of very different kinds. One of them was the division of the forces opposed to autonomous private incorporation between the populist critics of corporate business and the proponents of a broader overlap of the spheres of corporate and governmental power. Another was the economic influence exercised by the businessmen themselves: though cliques of insiders stood to benefit from the favoritism of closely guarded incorporation, a much larger group was anxious both to incorporate more easily and to rid their incorporated businesses of tight governmental interference. More often than not, they had the material means and the personal connections to translate this anxiety into political influence. Moreover, the self-operating, relatively unpoliced corporation might well seem to involve less of a break from established practice than the attempt to deepen the relations between government and business; the latter would force upon state institutions and party politics a mounting burden of responsibility. For that burden to be discharged the forms of political action and organization would, sooner rather than later, have to be transformed.

An additional decisive cause of the outcome, however, had to do with the ascendancy of a doctrine of freedom and efficiency, forged by lawyers and publicists who often regarded themselves, and were regarded in their own time, as hostile to the business interests whose legal and conceptual underpinnings they helped cement. The core of their conception of freedom was the unwarranted identification of the abstract idea of decentralized market decision with a concrete system of contract and property rights organized around spheres of absolute discretion in the control of labor and commodities. The core of the related idea of economic development was belief in the existence of an unbreakable natural link between economic growth – including repeated breakthroughs of the capacity barrier – and the security in vested rights that inheres in the chosen system of contract and property. This belief represented a double mistake: first, by supposing the existence of security *tout court* as distinguished from security for some against others; second, by failing to deal adequately with the constraints that vested rights impose on innovation. What these doctrines of freedom and development had in common was the effort to depoliticize the basic structure of rights and economic policy.

Once the earlier conflicts and uncertainties had been forgotten, their settlement took on a specious semblance of naturalness and necessity. The structure that emerged, however, was no more necessary and natural than the interests and the illusions, the tactical achievements and the tactical failures, that accounted for its initial consolidation and avoided its later disruption. An aspect of that structure was the definition of a tight stranglehold of powers over the flow of basic investment decisions: by the time mass party politics came into its own and the protective shield of sound finance doctrine had been cast aside, a characteristic dilemma of macroeconomic policy emerged: the need not to surrender totally to business interests for fear of losing elections and even of undermining the conditions of prosperity itself; and the contrasting need not to forfeit business confidence entirely in order to avoid disinvestment. The emerging system also existed in the imagination: in the clear-cut separation between all areas of social life, governmental politics, to which democratic principles applied, and a larger world of work and exchange, to which they did not apply. In the end, the weight of these richly textured though largely tacit conceptions of what ideals fitted where turned out to be more important than the naive doctrines of freedom and security that had once been their polemical spearhead.

The full significance of these developments becomes plain when they are placed in a broader comparative historical setting. Western countries, like the United States or Britain, that were to have a relatively ample experience of democratic conflict had chosen a growth path that accepted a strong barrier between business and government, each marked by contrasting principles of organization. On the other hand, later industrializing countries, like Germany and Japan, that experimented with a deeper mutual involvement of government and business did so in the setting of a more authoritarian national politics: for the commitment to economic growth and the chosen route to it were, in both Japan and Germany, part of a conscious strategy of building national power under the aegis of a revamped and reunified elite. The third option was missing: the combination of democratic mass politics with a close and varied net of relations between state and enterprise. The absence of this combination – easier to achieve perhaps in the pioneering instances of industrialization than in the cases when an elite could present itself as the custodian of a collective effort to catch up – was decisive for the whole later course of politics and economy in the West and in the world at large. Yet it never did follow any immanent, unstoppable logic.

This American episode suggests two points of more general interest. First, the controversy over the proper institutional form of economic decentralization may have characterized other aspects of economic history as well. Recovering the structure of this controversy may help us shake loose the misleading identification of the market form of economic order with the particular kinds of markets we know now. Second, as soon as we try to understand in greater detail the emergence of a particular institutional arrangement in a particular place we discover not the smooth operation of developmental compulsions and lawlike constraints but messy struggles, punctuated by surprising turns and conducted by people who often helped to frustrate their own confused objectives. We should think twice before concluding that these events and personalities were just the unwitting agents of objective and inescapable imperatives, such as the imperative that supposedly determines a unique set of market institutions capable of combining economic decentralization with economies of scale. The invocation of such requirements may seem the only alternative to theoretical agnosticism. But we may find a way to save the appearances – the detailed texture of historical life – and to vindicate our reconstructive freedom while nevertheless continuing to explain the facts.

THE GENESIS OF THE WORK-ORGANIZATION COMPLEX

The Mythical History of Work Organization

The dominant form of work organization in the advanced Western societies is characterized by the prevalence of the rigid form of rationalized collective labor in the mainstream of industry and by the confinement of the flexible form to the industrial vanguard. Remember that the rigid form accentuates the contrast between task-defining and task-executing activities while the flexible form softens it. This allocation of approaches to the organization of work depends upon the prevalence of mass-production industry, manufacturing standardized products through rigid production processes, product-specific machines, and large, centralized concentrations of capital and labor. The prevalence of the mass-production style is sustained by favorable institutional conditions and by a particular international division of labor.

The point of much traditional historical, economic, and sociological work, conservative and radical alike, has been to show that this particular compromise of styles of economic organization was necessary whether or not, as the radicals claim, it represented only a necessary stage to something else. This explanatory aim is ordinarily pursued through an argument central to the mythical history of work organization. The argument claims that the English path to industrial growth – or, rather, what is commonly identified as the English path – represented the preferred if not the only road to early industrial development. The stereotype of the English experience includes the replacement of the small family farm and independent peasantry by large-scale agrarian businesses owned by aristocratic magnates or rising peasant proprietors who often produced for a foreign market; the eventual substitution of artisanal guilds by mechanized factories and corporate enterprises as the end result of a passage through ever more centralized versions of the putting-out system; the reorganization of work as a system of well-defined and repetitious tasks within the new large-scale industries and their nonindustrial counterparts, all the way from bureaucracies to hospitals, in other sectors of practical life; and the reorganization of the entire world economy as a machine to reproduce this industrial style on a worldwide scale through the specialization of entire national economies.

This story forms the core of the mythical history of industrialized market societies and of that confused entity, capitalism, at once a historical universal and a historical particular. It is the trajectory of economic development exposed by *Capital* as a diabolical but providential drama and presented in numberless textbooks as the most natural thing in the world. The social counterpart to this path of economic growth has been the continued existence of prosperous families that have a good chance of bequeathing from generation to generation their privileged control over labor, capital, culture, and governmental power. The mythical history is therefore also a story about them and an assurance that their interests were on the right side of social evolution.

Here, as in later sections of this interpreted narrative, I argue that this view of industrial development drastically underestimates the degree of deviation from the mainstream that occurred even in such prize exhibits of the mythical history as the economic and social transformation of England. In fact the deviant forms reveal more of what was distinctive to the West and what made it incomparably revolutionary than do the dominant ones. I also claim that the traditional view gives a mistaken sense of the degree of prevalence that the more rigid type of work organization in fact achieved. According to the mythical history the deviations appeared for special reasons – the idiosyncracies of the regions where they arose – but failed for general ones – the inherent imperatives of industrial development. But there are grounds to conclude that the now dominant institutional form of Western industrial society won and maintained its preeminence over its rivals for reasons that have little to do with its intrinsic productive capabilities. One set of reasons for this conclusion has to do with the many ways in which state power was mobilized against the deviant forms and in support of the hegemonic ones. Another reason is the threshold effect of early and still precarious success. Machine design, organizational practices, and even technical and economic ideas began to consolidate around the emergent style of work organization and to bestow upon it a second-order necessity. Deep-logic social analysis itself and the historical interpretations it has inspired contributed to this fabulous bootstrap. For they helped form a restrictive view of historical possibility that aggravated rather than qualified the sense of naturalness that always surrounds victorious settlements and solutions.

One particular line of deviation from the mainstream of industrial development stands out by its ubiquity. A discussion of it brings into focus the issues at stake in the larger controversy. In every period of modern Western history some controversialists denied that the canonical style of industrialization had to prevail, even as part of the transition to an alternative economic order. They took sides with those who defended an economy of family farms and cottage industry, of technological revolution and cheap production without armylike factories, of market decentralization without the license to concentrate wealth, and of more cooperative forms of labor and exchange. Their advocacy has been traditionally derided as the program of petty bourgeois sentimentalism, engaged in a losing debate with tough-minded radicals and conservatives. Their critics point out that the petty bourgeois alternative would have been both self-destructive and inefficient. It would have been self-destructive because the more successful petty enterprises would soon have expanded into large-scale businesses unless they were constantly restrained and dispossessed by a state that would have then become the real power in the economy. It would have been inefficient because the alternative system could never have accommodated the enormous economies of scale that made continued economic revolution possible.

But these critics turn out to have no larger a share of the truth than their petty bourgeois adversaries. The tough-minded are right in the sense that the alleged alternative would have been both self-destabilizing and inefficient *unless* it built for itself institutional arrangements for markets and democracies different from the arrangements that have in fact come to prevail. Petty commodity production had no long-term future within property-based market economies and American-type democratic institutions. It would have required a different institutional framework. And this framework would have radically altered its social meaning and consequences. But the petty bourgeois romantics are right to insist that their alternative has been repeatedly suppressed rather than defeated in an impartial Darwinian competition. They are also correct in claiming for their program the status of a feasible point of departure toward an alternative industrial society. They even have a point when they argue that in fragmentary form this alternative industrialism has played a much larger role in the actual industrialization of the West than the mythical history acknowledges.

This debate has practical importance because the alternative has never been definitively discarded. Continuously reasserted in the course of modern economic history, it remains today, in altered form, a serious possibility of industrial organization. The case or the alternative is of theoretical and practical interest because it suggests a different approach to modern economic history and prefigures a theory of transformation free from the errors that beset deep-logic social thought.

My discussion advances in three stages. It begins with the early forms of industrial development, then turns to their agrarian counterparts, and finally takes up the latter-day manifestations of the contest between dominant and deviant variants of industrialism.

The Conflict over the Organizational Form of Manufacturing

The most powerful intellectual tool of the mythical history of manufacturing and agriculture in early modern Europe has been the proto-industrialization theory. The most significant polemical result of this theory is to define the petty bourgeois deviation as an unstable transitional form that turns into a blind alley of economic development when it does not quickly give way to the high industrial road. The main elements of the proto-industrialization thesis are the following. Because of the relative poverty of their soil or the pastoral character of their agriculture, certain regions started out with large amounts of underemployed labor. These regions were the star candidates for those early bursts of country-based industrialization whose uses and ultimate failure the proto-industrialization thesis purports to describe. The advance of agricultural techniques in the more fertile regions resulted in still greater underemployment in the poorer ones. The peasant household, like most economic agents in the preindustrial world, was more concerned to preserve a customary way of life than to maximize a rate of return. The peasants of the impoverished and overcrowded regions therefore clung to their land and sought additional employment. They provided the cheap labor that the putting-out system could exploit. Thus there began simultaneously in many regions of Europe a flurry of decentralized manufacturing activity, closely linked with agricultural work and held together by merchants primarily engaged in long-distance trade.

At first the merchant may have served merely as the commercial intermediary and the purveyor of raw materials to a household that continued to own the instruments of its own labor. But the residual independence of domestic industry was eventually doomed by the destruction of its agrarian base. The spread of small-scale rural industry undermined the Malthusian constraints upon early marriage. The resulting abrupt rise in the population of regions that already suffered from an impoverished agricultural base helped fragment peasant landholding. Peasants who had once been both smallholders and independent contractors often found themselves landless wage employees, working for an entrepreneurial landowner or merchant.

The story did not end there. From the standpoint of the merchant, now in charge of the production process, the rusticated industry of the putting-out system suffered from several incurable defects. It confronted the master with formidable problems of control over the efficiency of workers whom he could not directly oversee. It ran into the resistance or unreliability of laborers who would work only the time necessary to safeguard their accustomed standard of living (a backward-bending labor supply curve). And its decentralized character imposed transportation costs that limited the expansion of putting-out networks.

These problems, the proto-industrialization argument continues, could be solved only by the concentration of workers in centralized factories. The factory system therefore preceded and made possible the mechanization of industry and the extreme, technical division of labor. The attempt to prolong the life of decentralized, rural industry either failed or generated satellites to the central form of productive activity. This central form became the mechanized, mass-production industry, operating against the background of a countryside emptied of most of its population and given over to large-scale agricultural business.

It is embarrassing to the broader social and historical ideas supported by the proto-industrialization thesis that many of the features we now regard as intrinsic to the dominant model emerged only recently and ran into trouble only a few generations after their original introduction. The Fordist, assembly line production process and the divisional structure pioneered by some of the large American corporations of the 1920s and 1930s may serve as examples. This belated development suggests that even after the events described by the students of proto-industrialization had run their course, the contemporary form of market organization was very far from being in the cards. For the moment, however, consider only how much the proto-industrialization thesis understates the degree of deviation and conflict in the history of early European industrialization. Most of the anomalous experiments and trajectories that the proto-industrialization argument fails to accommodate illustrate the career of that petty commodity variant of industrialization whose condescending dismissal by mainstream theory and historiography I earlier recalled.

In early modern European history many regions witnessed the development of manufacturing complexes that exemplify this alternative industrial path. These industrial ventures were distinguished by their relative smallness of scale, their resourcefulness in using flexible production processes to satisfy particular, varying needs rather than rigid processes to fulfill standardized needs, and their efforts to organize work in ways that allowed for a closer interplay between supervision and execution. In all these respects, these early industries were forerunners of what has since become the vanguard sector of the advanced Western economies. Indeed, in many cases they survived to become part of the vanguard sector, though in others they either disappeared or assimilated to the dominant industrial model.

Among the instances of deviation were the woolen industry of West Riding, the Birmingham hardware trade, the cutlery industries of Sheffield in England and Solingen in Germany, and the textile industry of Lyon. These and other experiences of industrial development have benefited from an increasing number of studies by both historians and social theorists. A close reading and comparison of these studies suggests an account of the reasons for the failure or success of these experiments that cannot be reconciled with the mythical history. The pattern of success and failure does not support the premise that most sectors of an economy are inherently more suited to what we now consider the mainstream or the vanguardist forms of production: the deviant experiments succeeded and failed in distinct sectors as well as in different regions and at different times. The deviations were more likely to flourish when governmental power was not used exclusively to institute legal rules and economic policies that consolidated the dominant model and when the deviant entrepreneurs themselves responded to periodic economic crisis in ways that exploited the flexibility of their enterprises.

Compare, for this purpose, the experience of the Sheffield cutlery industry with that of the Lyonnaise textile producers. The general line of governmental policy and market organization in England unequivocally favored large-scale merchants and manufacturers in their generations-long struggle against artisans and petty entrepreneurs and helped force these petty producers into the role of economic reactionaries or satellites. Against this already hostile background, the cutlery makers of Sheffield responded to the economic crisis of the 1870s and 1880s, to higher tariffs, and to competition from their more resourceful Solingen counterparts by the classic defensive maneuvers of cottage industry under attack. These maneuvers drastically restricted the potential economic significance of the deviant mode even when they ensured the marginal economic survival of the petty entrepreneurs themselves. A few of the cutlery makers found a niche in the narrow market for custom-made luxury goods. In this way, they gave up the battle to occupy a portion of major productive activity, resigning themselves to economic insignificance. Others switched to the economic, organizational, and technological methods of the dominant model. They began using product-specific machines, rigid production processes, and a more pronounced hierarchy of the supervisors and the supervised in order to make specialty steels. Burdened by the inflexibility of big business without its advantage of scale or governmental favor, they became easy prey to the next changes in market conditions.

Contrast this outcome to the history of Lyonnaise textile manufacturing. There the manufacturing of textiles by artisanal cooperatives and petty entrepreneurs had been pursued, with occasional interruptions, from the seventeenth century onward. After having been disorganized during the years of the revolution, this style of manufacturing was reconstituted at the outset of the Orleanist regime. Its most characteristic organizational device was the subcontracting of weaving to master artisans.

Two successive shifts in taste jeopardized the textile manufacturing of Lyon. The first was the change from more intricate fabrics, prized for the texture and design of their weaving, to the cheaper cloths, admired for the vividness of their colors. This shift in demand resulted in a massive transfer of contract orders to less expensive and less proficient subcontractors, which in turn brought on, in the Lyon uprisings of 1831 and 1834, one of the great artisanal revolts of the nineteenth century. The second such change was the surge, during the 1870s and 1880s, of a taste for still cheaper cotton-and-silk-waste fabrics. This might well have caused the downfall of the Lyonnaise *fabrique* had the manufacturers and artisans not played upon the economic and technological ambiguities of their situation to draw strength out of weakness. The small-scale manufacturers used mixed fabrics and new forms of printing and dyeing. The high instability of demand in the textile markets, the diffusion of electricity as a cheap decentralized power source, and the relatively low wages of rural weavers all favored the *petite fabrique*. Moreover, the larger setting of French national policy had never ceased to be more congenial to the alternative style of manufacturing than its English counterpart. The survival of artisanal or petty entrepreneurial cadres in much of France, as in the other European regions where they flourished, found support in the vitality of independent smallholding agriculture. This vitality in turn reflected the continuing ability of French peasants and petty bourgeoisie, from the consolidation of absolutist government to the successive postrevolutionary regimes, to enlist governmental power in their own favor. At their most successful, the smaller entrepreneurs and proprietors mobilized governmental power not only to obtain narrow material advantages but to safeguard whole ways of life. By the 1960s, the cottage industries dominated the textile manufacturing of Lyon: 55 percent of weaving and 70 percent of spinning were in the hands of the *petite fabrique*. By a continuous series of self-transformations, punctuated by major crises and ingenious responses, petty commodity producers, the ridiculed reactionaries of industrial history, had secured a prominent place in the most advanced sectors of industry.

At a minimum, success stories like this one show that there is no natural allocation of economic activities to the dominant and the deviant types of industry, the rigid and the flexible forms of work organization. The kinds of textiles produced in Lyon by the latter-day version of cottage industry were made in many other parts of the world, from Great Britain to Taiwan, by mass production, with product-specific machines, rigid production processes, and stark contrasts between planning and execution.

The successful alternatives exemplify a continuity between artisanal manufacturing or petty commodity production and vanguardist industry. They suggest how national styles of industrialization, acquired capacities to enlist state power, and collective strategies influenced the boundaries between the two types of industrial organization. They even demonstrate a surprisingly frequent link between the artisanal rearguard and the high-tech vanguard of Western industrialization. But they do not prove that the alternative industrial type could have then, or can now, gain a dominant place in the economy and impart to it a different social character. Even the successful cases were, in another sense, failures: in no instance was the consolidation of the alternative style in one sector of the economy followed by changes in the defining institutional form of markets and polities that might have permitted a more drastic shift in the character of Western industrialism.

The attempt to assess the larger promise of the deviant cases must therefore be indirect. One approach is to study the dependence of the dominant industrial style upon a variety of extraeconomic institutional arrangements that were themselves subject to constant struggle. The study of this dependence could then be complemented by an attempt to imagine the institutional conditions under which the alternative industrialism could have flourished more widely. This is a theme pursued throughout this interpretive history of contemporary formative contexts as well as in later parts of *False Necessity*. Another, much narrower approach is to consider how the rivalry between the dominant and the deviant models relates to early modern struggles over agriculture and to contemporary conflicts about economic organization. In this way what has usually been seen as a highly localized and long-settled quarrel can be shown to be part of a general and continuing dispute.

The Conflict over the Organizational Form of Agriculture

The parallel to the deviant model in the history of manufacturing was a style of agricultural development that gave a preeminent role to the family farm and to cooperative relations among smallholders. The significance of the parallelism is hardly self-evident. Cottage industry sometimes flourished, as in the heyday of the Birmingham and Sheffield metal trades, against a background of land concentration. Conversely, family-scale agriculture was occasionally accompanied by the near absence or the stagnation and involution of manufacturing activities, as in Piedmont, Catalonia, and some parts of the Netherlands. Nevertheless, the deviant agricultural style did have broader economic and social implications. The proto-industrialization thesis, put in its place, shows the economic implication: the destruction of small-scale ownership or tenancy played a decisive part in the particular trajectory of manufacturing history studied by the exponents of that thesis. Their mistake was only to see this trajectory as the preferred or even the necessary route to the maximum development of productive capabilities. The broader social implication becomes clear when you consider that the dominant and deviant models of manufacturing and agriculture favored, or injured, the same social groups. Cottage industry was quickest to escape the role assigned to it by the proto-industrialization thesis wherever there flourished a class of small-scale producers. Yet, factorylike manufacturing and land concentration never abolished this class nor did they create a polarized society of magnates and dependents. The large and rigid enterprises needed the buffer of small-scale production against economic instability. For reasons still to be discussed, the legal arrangements that defined these more concentrated market systems and the polities that protected them never allowed the repetition of the deadliest crisis known to the agrarian-bureaucratic empires of antiquity: the reduction of small-scale producers to servile status and the consequent shrinking of the market in labor and in goods.

Modern Western agricultural history supports two main conclusions about the practicability of relative agrarian decentralization. These conclusions illustrate the elements of falsehood and truth in the polemic against petty commodity production.

The first conclusion is that the family farm turned out to be as efficient, by the measure of acreage and even labor productivity, as the more concentrated forms of agriculture. This style of agricultural development prevailed in many of the regions that proved to be most successful in the earlier phases of the approach toward industrialization. Where ownership was concentrated, the form of agricultural exploitation often continued to resemble that of familial production in most other respects. And in many of the instances in which this productive style gave way to larger-scale units, tilled by laborers under centralized control, the active alliance of national governments with landowning magnates, exerted through law, policy, and calculated omission, was largely responsible for the result.

A second conclusion, however, qualifies this first one. In those instances where small-scale production flourished well into more advanced stages of industrialization and agricultural mechanization, it proved to be unstable or else to depend upon a special deal between government and the family farm. This deal enabled the small producers to resist the risks of agricultural instability while cordoning off the agrarian sector from an economy largely organized on different principles. This second conclusion suggests once again that a more secure and influential place for small-scale agriculture would have required a change in the institutional character of markets and polities. The following paragraphs use a variety of allusions to European history to illustrate the first conclusion and the experience of nineteenth-century France and America to exemplify the second.

A comparison of agricultural regions in sixteenth-, seventeenth-, and eighteenth-century Europe shows that the most flourishing areas were often the ones characterized by family-scale agriculture, whereas the concentration of ownership and management prevailed in many of the more backward regions. Piedmont and Lombardy in contrast to Sicily and Naples; Catalonia in comparison to the rest of Spain; Flanders and Holland as against Germany beyond the Elbe – all tell, in this one respect, the same story, though each brings out a distinct facet of the common problem. Thus, the history of Catalan agriculture clearly shows how access to governmental power (e.g., the Catalan representative assembly) and to a vital urban market benefited family-scale agriculture. And the example of Flanders, where highly specialized, labor-intensive farms coexisted with large grain-producing estates, demonstrates that smallholding could continue to flourish in a milieu of precocious industrialization.

The significance of these early modern European experiences comes out most clearly when they are placed in a world-historical context. The most populous and enduring societies before the revolution of techniques and ideas that radiated out of the North Atlantic were the great agrarian-bureaucratic empires. A characteristic crisis repeatedly jeopardized the prosperity and even the survival of these societies, narrowing markets, sapping the authority of central governments, and cutting off opportunities of advance toward irreversible commercialization and industrialization. Whenever unforeseen economic or military dangers required the central state to demand additional fiscal or military contributions, the landowning magnates, largely thanks to their control of local public administration, managed to shift the brunt of the burden onto the smallholders and other petty producers. These small folk, ruined by exactions they could not meet, then voluntarily sought, or were compelled to accept, a status of personal dependence upon the very potentates who had undone them. This surrender to lordly protection shook the most important support of market activity. The sphere of exchange narrowed to the dealings among larger domains that tended toward economic autarky and hierarchical discipline. The central government, dangerously weakened, found itself even more beholden to the great landholders than it had been before. No wonder the most acute statesmen and reformers in these societies were obsessed with the attempt to preserve the smallholding and petty mercantile sectors as a basis for the government's fiscal and military strength.

Why they repeatedly failed, why Europe, less deliberately, escaped the destructive cycle of those empires, and why both questions can best be answered by an antinecessitarian social theory are issues to be taken up in another part of this volume. What matters for the moment is the suggestion that the most distinctively European form of agricultural development was the supposedly deviant and regressive agriculture of smallholders. The remarkable feature of the standard, "English" model of agrarian concentration – a feature that requires further elucidation – was its ability to move as far toward concentration as it did without provoking the market-destructive crises that had frequently accompanied superficially similar movements in other societies.

But given that the family-run farm represented a practicable alternative to agrarian concentration in the economic circumstances of early modern Europe, could it continue to play a progressive role in the era of industrialization and mechanized agriculture? The answer to this question lies – surprisingly – less in technical-economic considerations than in the uses of governmental power. In France – with its densely settled land and strong traditions of alliance between the state and the peasantry – legal rules and governmental policy helped safeguard the relatively labor-intensive tillage of middle-sized and small-sized farms. The resulting style of agricultural development was almost by definition less labor productive than its more concentrated English counterpart. Yet recent studies have demonstrated that, at least in the nineteenth century, the total economic effect was only negligibly prejudicial if it was prejudicial at all. If output per worker remained lower in French than in British agriculture, it was consistently higher in French than in British industry. And during the entire 1815–1915 period, commodity output increased at the rate of only 1 percent per annum less in France than in Britain. It seem doubtful that any significant portion of this differential could justifiably be attributed to a contrast in the form of agricultural organization. And to the extent that it could, the difference might well be considered a low price to pay for avoiding British extremes in the destruction of peasant-provincial life and in the creation of a desperate urban mass.

By contrast, the nineteenth-century American family farm – located in a land of receding frontiers, less defined social classes, and more meager communal traditions – had to survive in a less protected environment. From the 1830s and 1840s on, the farmer needed constant technical innovation and crop specialization to survive in his struggle to pay off the bank creditor and compensate for the unlucky harvest. The counterpart to a more highly mechanized and relatively larger farm was the emerging division between a successful rural petty bourgeoisie and a mass of landless laborers. The former provided a major market; the latter, the initial work force for the manufacturing sector. Only with the price-support and agricultural-extension programs of New Deal and World War II years was this style of family-run agriculture stabilized at a higher level of productivity than its French counterpart.

The French and American cases present contrasting but complementary examples. In the United States, competition leading toward concentration was allowed to go farther than in France. The American government took longer to settle with the small farmer, the whole period between the relatively ineffective Homestead Act and the much more effective technical and price-support systems. The less successful farmers were weeded out. The American and French experiences show that the critics of petty commodity production are right to this extent: given the general character of the polities and markets in which these farms have existed, competition produces concentration and empties out the land. For it is the large producer who can most readily mobilize capital, secure access to distant markets, and outlast a bad harvest. In both France and the United States, special governmental action was essential to preserve the family farm as the dominant form of agricultural production. And in both countries, this action took a form that drastically curtailed the exemplary significance of decentralized production for the economy as a whole while preserving it in its isolated, agricultural sector.

Governments did not reformulate the legal categories of property and contract in ways that might have ruled out absolute and permanent control over large accumulations of capital. Nor did they reorganize their own constitutional arrangements and methods of party-political rivalry in order to facilitate popular-democratic control over the main lines of investment and accumulation. They merely helped a particular form of productive activity survive despite the institutional conditions that, together with the inherent risks of agriculture, constantly threatened to destabilize it. In manufacturing, petty commodity appeared as either the rear guard or the vanguard of an industrial system organized on alternative principles. In agriculture, it emerged as an anomaly justified by its peculiar social charm and undeniable practical efficacy. In both areas, its potential significance remained fragmented and obscured, and its possibilities of development were sacrificed to a hostile institutional system.

Contemporary Debates

No institutional structure of governmental or economic activity emerged in the West that might have turned petty commodity production into a realistic form of social organization capable of carrying economies to ever higher levels of productive output. Nevertheless, the alternative possibilities signaled by the deviations in the history of early modern European manufacturing and agriculture continued to reappear at later moments in the social and economic history of the West. These later experiments with the basic form of work organization fell into two main clusters. The first group consists in the revolutionary attacks of the nineteenth and the early twentieth centuries, typified by the 1848 revolutions and the years immediately after World War I. The second group comprises the recent forms of vanguardist industry. To understand the relationship between the early and the late deviations is also to take a first step toward seeing how closely connected the two latter-day types of deviations really are, despite the absence of an apparent connection.

There is a continuum between the simple despotism of the early factory and the advanced forms of assembly line organization. In this assembly line approach to work, the supervisors continued to exercise a disciplinary power that far outstripped the functions of technical coordination. This system served accelerated growth by its facility for appropriating surplus and for moving men and machines around. But its basic economic disadvantage – and the disadvantage of the institutional arrangements that sustained it – was to subordinate the opportunities of economic experimentation to the interests of economic privilege. A real relation also exists between the artisanal or family-farm team and the flexible, commando-type organization that characterizes the vanguardist sectors of modern industry, administration, and warfare. The essential shared trait is the fluidity of work plans. If the strength of the commando style lies precisely in its practical opportunism, its weakness is its difficulty in adapting to the requirements of scale and complexity.

In each of these parallel lines of economic and organizational development, the most recent phase – the Fordist plant or the vanguardist work group – represents the more rationalized one. It is more rationalized in the sense that the relations it creates among people at work embody more fully a conception of the interplay between abstract productive tasks and concrete operational acts. Each of the two lines of development – I have already shown – gives a different interpretation to this interplay.

But what of the link between the popular insurrectionary challenges to the dominant form of manufacturing and the axis that leads from artisanal shop to commando-style industry? To be sure, many of the revolutionary movements were often fought out in the name of doctrines that derided these deviations as the sentimental or reactionary commitments of the petty bourgeoisie. Yet such slogans are belied both by the nature of the social forces that sustained many of the radical protests and by the actual content of many of the revolutionary experiments.

Contemporary historians have repeatedly emphasized the key role that skilled workers and sentimental petty bourgeois ideologists played in the insurrectionary movements of the nineteenth and early twentieth century. Not only did these groups resist, more fiercely and consistently than any others, the development of the dominant model of industrialism but they often served as the chief organizers of revolutionary alternatives. Indeed, the classic form of these alternatives in the economy and the polity – the cooperative work group and the soviet or council-type of administrative body – can best be understood as idealized versions of the organizational forms that the petty producers and their sympathizers were trying to defend. This origin explains the striking mixture, in these experiments, of archaic and even neofeudal characteristics with visionary commitments. It also sheds light on the continuing failure of these insurrectionaries and ideologists to come up with schemes of economic and administrative organization capable of reconciling their aspirations with the requirements of large-scale production and administration. Thus, the revolutionary experiments repeatedly failed to bequeath the elements of an institutional scheme that might have provided a realistic alternative to the ruling styles and conceptions of industrialism and democracy. And this failure, with its sequel of smug or embittered disenchantment, contributed further to the entrenchment of the dominant approach to work organization.

To interpret the latter-day manifestations of the deviant style from this perspective is, once again, to deny that their extinction or confinement can be explained by the necessity of the institutional arrangements that they were meant to displace. But it is not, in any simple sense, to disprove that the proposed alternative was incompatible with social requirements for the accelerated development of practical capabilities of production (or of administration and warfare). For the alternative mode of economic organization remained incompatible with those requirements so long as its advocates failed to come up with institutions that would have perpetuated economic decentralization without permitting large and permanent accumulations of private capital and that would have established governments capable of supporting and administering these economic arrangements. Just what such alternative institutions might have looked like in the past or should look like in the future is a subject of Chapters 10 to 14.

You can now put together the elements of a way of accounting for the relative defeat of the deviant mode of work organization that rejects the mythical history and dispenses with the hypothesis of deep-logic social theory and with the prejudices of unreflective conservatism. Though this revised account is constantly strengthened by new historical findings and new social experiments, it expresses less a revolution in ground-level empirical studies than a reinterpretation of familiar but underplayed or misunderstood events.

Proceeding along this route, you would observe that the revolutionary experiments in work organization were all forcibly suppressed before they had been tried out for any extended period or revised in the course of their application. You would then go on to emphasize that the activists and theorists of these deviant movements were consistently misled by prejudices about possible class alliances and possible institutional alternatives to the existing or emergent forms of market and democratic order. These prejudices prevented them from using their brief moments of experimental opportunity to develop the elements of realistic alternatives. In this way, the would-be architects of a reconstructed society were defeated in part by their inability to free themselves sufficiently from the intellectual authority of the world they had set out to destroy. This inability often encouraged them to seek refuge in an ideological fantasy that merely turned upside down a reality it had failed to understand or to escape.

Turning to the exceptional status of the flexible vanguardist form of industrial organization, you would argue, along lines previously suggested, that the predominance of mass production is not the direct result of superior economic efficiency. Rather, this predominance depends upon the institutionally guaranteed ability to ward off instability in the product, labor, and financial markets as well as upon an international division of labor that prevents either cheap-labor or technologically innovative economies from disrupting stable world markets. If these conditions failed to be satisfied, mass-production industry, with its stark contrast of task-defining and task-executing activities, might not suddenly crumble in all sectors of the economy. But it could be expected to lose its secure hold over many areas of production.

Nevertheless, the resulting extension of the flexible, vanguardist type of industry might simply make way for a competition among new economic enterprises. The more concentrated businesses might once again evolve into new versions of the old mass-production industries and use their influence over markets and governments to protect themselves against economic instability and foreign competition. Indeed, such an outcome might be expected to follow as a matter of course unless the most fundamental economic arrangements of the economy had been revised: the arrangements that establish an equivalence between the means for decentralizing economic decisions and the devices for concentrating capital.

Because such changes in the character of economic institutions might involve the overtly political administration of capital (e.g., a national rotating capital fund), they would in turn require changes in the organization of government and of the conflict for governmental power. An authoritarian, revolutionary state would merely create a class of people obsessed with the exercise of social control and with the interests of their own clients and creatures: bureaucrats, managers, and technical personnel. On the other hand, a demobilized liberal democracy would lack both the governmental structures and the civic militancy required to subject the basic form of economic accumulation to effective partisan rivalry.

This counterfactual fable has a double point. It shows how the problems confronted by the initial forms of petty commodity production – the inability to gain a more than peripheral place within the established institutional framework – might reappear as a dilemma faced by the distant but still recognizable counterparts of those early deviations. This lesson suggests another. The availability and the identity of alternative forms of work organization have depended largely upon the prospects for imagining and establishing alternative ways to organize markets and democracies. How should we understand the genesis of the forms of market and democratic organization that have in fact achieved primacy?

Note that the preceding argument against the mythical history of work organization does not deny force to technological and resource constraints. It does invoke and support the assumptions: (a) that at any given time those constraints significantly underdetermine the style of work organization; (b) that technological constraints are as much the result as the cause of social settlements, codified in institutional arrangements such as forms of work organization; and, more surprisingly than (a) or (b), (c), that we cannot comprehend either in advance or in retrospect the range of feasible organizational responses to technological or resource constraints. We do not need to define the range of possible alternatives in order to understand the history of economic organization. So, too, on a larger historical scale, we do not need to predefine branching points in the history of formative institutional contexts in order to understand how contexts get remade.

THE GENESIS OF THE PRIVATE-RIGHTS COMPLEX

Its Elements Reviewed

The private-rights complex consists in the arrangements that define the institutional character of the market. These arrangements are largely sets of legal rights. One of their more striking features is the ability to structure the basic framework for non-economic dealings (other than those of party politics and public administration) in the very course of defining the market. But why should the legal categories that shape the market provide the model for all entitlements? The answer to this question is far from self-evident; it is one of the facts that an account of the emergence of the private-rights complex must explain.

Remember that the central feature of this complex is a system of property rights that ensures economic decentralization by distributing nearly absolute claims to divisible portions of social capital – absolute in scope of exercise and in continuity of temporal succession. The contractual counterpart to this property system is a structure of contract rights that denies legal force to those relationships of personal interdependence and mutual reliance that cannot be characterized either as the fully deliberate undertaking of an obligation by a rightholder or as the unilateral imposition of an obligation by the state.

The spirit animating this private-rights complex – it will be remembered – is the search for a pure, prepolitical logic of free human interaction. To a surprising extent the system of contract and property is presented – and, even when not so presented, it is implicitly understood – as the legal structure inherent in private ordering. Autonomous self-regulation may not, it is conceded, be good for everything. The main points of the private-rights system can be varied in many ways. And some people may be better placed to exercise their rights than others. But such qualifications do not prevent the identification of these private entitlements with the general project of setting up a system for private coordination. This identification is no mere theoretical afterthought. Nor can it even be adequately understood as simply a requirement of legitimation. It orients the understanding and application of private rights. It prevents people from asking anew, at each crucial turn in ideological or legal controversy, what institutional form the market in particular and private ordering generally can and should have.

There is a mythical history of the private-rights complex that seconds, in style and effect, the traditional way of accounting for the development of the work-organization complex. Few would subscribe to this historical approach in its crudest form. But, like the broader habits of social and historical study that it exemplifies, it continues to inform much of our actual thinking about legal entitlements and the institutional arrangements they define. A testimony to the authority of this conception is its influence upon liberals and Marxists alike. The liberals see the gradual development of a market structure – its gradual emergence from the feudal and neo-feudal restrictions that so arbitrarily and expensively restricted the free play of self-interested exchange. As the market order expanded only gradually into wider areas of social life, so too its inherent legal structure was discovered only step by step. This structure was made up in large part by the modern system of contract and property. Thus, liberals and Marxists alike view the private-law arrangements and ideas of early modern Europe as necessary points on the continuum that led to current contract or property law, a law that could in turn be seen as an indispensable prop to the market system. In its conception of the relation between this market order and political freedom, the dominant liberal view has spanned the gamut between the confident conviction that the two cannot be separated (for each is both the condition and the extension of the other) and the more negative and skeptical belief that any attempt to replace this market order entirely will produce arrangements that jeopardize freedom.

Marxists have traditionally dissented less than might have been expected from this additional element in the mythical history. The market economy makes three highly controlled appearances within Marxist-influenced left social theory. First and primarily it is the central institutional device of capitalism – a well-defined stage of world-historical evolution. Second, it supplies the institutional framework for petty commodity production, an unstable social order, destined to pass into capitalism or to perform a subsidiary role within it when it does not disappear altogether. In both these appearances, the basic market structure is assumed to be identical with the familiar contract and property system. Third, the market may reappear under communism, relieved of the burden of oppression and scarcity that has weighed upon it until now. But because communism represents less a well-defined program than the far beckoning culmination of class-ridden history, its institutional arrangements remain in the shadows. Its advocates fail to give practical detail to the idea of an exchange system that presupposes neither the traffic in human work nor a stable social and technical division of labor.

The Marxist ambivalence toward the market carries over into an ambivalence toward private rights, which appear sometimes as an incident in the commodified world of capitalism and, at other times, as a feature of any tolerable social regime. Thus, the Marxists, like the liberals, accept the fundamental tenets of the mythical history of private rights: the certainty that the development of contract and property institutions in modern Europe embodied the emergence of the market order as one of the necessary stages or permanent possibilities of social life. Liberals and Marxists differ only in how they propose to correct the defects of the market system: by combining it with alternative forms of allocation (planned social democracy) or by reducing it to a peripheral role.

The argument of the following pages attacks this mythical history at its root premises, the premises that Marxists and liberals share. It pursues this attack by discussing three seemingly paradoxical features of the private-rights complex and its formation. To set these paradoxes side by side is to underline the specificity of our contract and property system. More particularly, it is to confirm that the dominant system of contract and property rights constantly struggled with alternative principles of social organization and that some of these principles even suggest elements for the successful institutional reshaping of petty commodity production. But the most telling implication of the view able to replace the mythical history is the suggestion that this system of contract and property could inform social life only by combining with arrangements that negated and even reversed the professed aims of the private-law order. Conversely, success in the attempt to bring practical economic life closer to the ideal conception of an exchange of goods and labor among free and deliberate agents would have required a radically different legal basis for economic decentralization.

The Paradox of Origin

The development of private legal entitlements in the specific form in which we have come to know them did not smoothly accompany the gradual formation of a society of free rightholders confronted with a submissive and accountable government. Those entitlements and theories emerged, instead, as part of a particular social settlement that included as one of its incidents or results the formation of an absolutist state. The contract and property rights fashioned and systematized by the jurists of early modern Europe supplied instruments for the familiar process by which the consolidation of absolute rights (especially in land) could advance hand in hand with the strengthening of a unified governmental sovereignty. Tax (as governmental finance) and rent (as the private rightholder's charge for the use of allodial property) became clearly separated. At the same time governments altered what had, up to that point, been their characteristic ways of dealing with gainful economic activity. Sometimes states had treated manufacturers and merchants (especially in long-distance commerce) as pliant victims to be milked for all they were worth. In more settled and ambitious empires, this predatory attitude gave way to the more aggressive tutelage of economic production and exchange with a view to maintaining the conditions of social harmony. This attitude characteristically prevailed in agrarian policy even when not applied to commerce and industry. In early modern Europe the most successful governments pioneered a new approach to economic activity: they deliberately manipulated governmental authority and military force, domestically and internationally, in order to promote economic growth. Thus, the same pattern of retrenchment and partnership that characterized the relationship between government and allodial property in land carried over to public policy toward trade and industry. Ways were thereby found to protect wealth-making activities without stifling or starving them through the very devices of protection.

These institutional innovations were both the products and the instruments of a particular social compromise. In countless variations, a redefined elite of enterprising nobles and successful commoners gained a more unchecked control over land, labor, and movable capital while governments won greater administrative cohesiveness, broadened their area of maneuver, and deliberately subordinated the maintenance of harmony to the acquisition of wealth. Much in this outcome can be understood as the expression of a straightforward deal: the state would grant the elites a more untrammeled control over land, labor, and commercial wealth while the elites would in turn allow the managers of the new state – at once weaker and stronger than many of its counterparts in non-European civilizations – to dispose more freely of taxes and troops, to develop an aggressive administrative apparatus, and even to experiment with different approaches to the relation between the creation and the protection of wealth. The contract and property system represented merely the first half of the exchange, the half that permitted the consolidation of private control at the ground level. To recognize this deal is not to suppose that central governments were staffed by other than members of the elites or were devoted to nonelite objectives. You need only assume that, against the double background of a relative fragmentation of the elites and an irreversible commercialization of the economy, the masters and agents of the new-model state won the power to pursue their narrower aims more freely. They owed part of this freedom to having never had pervasive responsibilities or powers in the management of the national economy.

The uniqueness of this institutional solution can be inferred from a comparison with the experience of the agrarian-bureaucratic empires of antiquity. In those societies, the assumption by elites of a more unchecked control over land, labor, and commercial wealth typically signaled the decommercialization of the economy and the ultimate fragmentation of governmental authority. Thus, a superficially similar tendency possessed in context an entirely different meaning. For in the early modern West, this proprietary victory of the elites took place in a society that had already been transformed by the irreversible commercialization of the economy and the thoroughgoing diversification of the elites, phenomena that in turn reflected the relative success of Western European peasants and artisans in resisting complete subjection to great landholders and local potentates. Although this resistance was less successful in some places than in others (compare again England to France or Catalonia to the rest of France), it was almost uniformly more successful in Europe west of the Elbe than in the great agrarian-bureaucratic empires of premodern and non-European history.

The argument about the paradox of origin permits a tentative conclusion. The contract and property system represented an important element in the emergence of a social order and a social vision radically at odds with the ideas we now attribute to this system. Of course, it might have outgrown these marks of origin. But this preliminary insight already suggests that contract and property rights are not what they seem. The remainder of the discussion shows that they could never close this gap between appearance and reality: the idealized market vision could be more fully realized only by legal arrangements that departed drastically from those that have come to define market regimes in modern Western history.

The Paradox of Specification

A second paradoxical feature of the private-rights complex generalizes and deepens the lesson taught by the first paradox. If we are tempted to dismiss the first paradox as having shown merely that the legal structure of the market has an incongruous origin, we now discover that this legal structure was constantly and mysteriously bound up with alternative principles of social order that altered, and even inverted, its apparent significance. This inversion reflects less an ideologically motivated dissimulation than the inability of the contract and property system to govern crucial features of the practical dealings among people without the help of arrangements antagonistic to the manifest spirit of that system.

The traditional Western form of contract and property has proven unable fully to penetrate at least two aspects of social life – one central and the other tangential to practical economic life. The central aspect is the actual organization of production, in particular the effort to coordinate labor in the pursuit of practical objectives. A practical organization cannot operate effectively if the relations among its members are predetermined by a regime of rigidly defined entitlements and obligations demarcating zones of unchecked discretion. The rationalization of collective labor means precisely that the work team can become a visible embodiment of practical reason, with its relentlessly opportunistic calculation of means to ends and its accelerated interplay between task definitions and operational acts. The strength of the flexible variant of rationalized collective labor is to carry to the extreme this opportunism and this freedom from the constraints imposed by any preexisting plan of social division and hierarchy. Conversely, to bind every practical decision about the organization of production to the absolutes of right and obligation is to ensure practical failure. As soon as you concede the need for discretionary maneuverability, you face the problem of deciding who exercises the discretion and under which restraints. The pure system of contract and property provides no answer to this question because, though it may legitimate certain exercises of power, it remains in its form merely a legal structure of coordinate relationships.

The other aspect of social life that the modern regime of contract and regime cannot fully penetrate may be peripheral to much of productive activity in its most characteristically modern variants. But it has always been vital to our practical experience of society, and it has always persisted as an undercurrent theme in our workaday lives. This is the domain of communal relations where mutual ties are valued as ends in themselves, the effects of action upon one's fellows really matter, and an acceptance of heightened mutual vulnerability overtakes the punctilious reckoning of tit for tat.

Both practical and communal life resist the procrustean limitations of the classical rights-regime. The private-rights complex simply cannot go far enough in specifying these practical or communal arrangements without appealing for help to other methods of social organization. This demand for further specification creates the possibility of something we in fact observe: the private-rights order takes on an entirely different social significance once it operates alongside the ideas and arrangements that provide it with its necessary complement of specification.

Two main sets of complementary principles of social organization have, in succession, given private rights their indispensable wedge into practical social life. The first such body of principles simply generalized and restated the particular social settlement in which the modern system of contract and property originally figured. This was the corporate-estatist society (*Ständestaat*) of early modern Europe. This approach to social organization saw society divided into well-established divisions and hierarchies. A particular group or institution was visibly defined by the place it occupied in this social map, visibly because the communal-hierarchical unit often possessed an explicit corporate identity. The most notorious examples were the Church and the standing army – organizations that, together with many others, were considered to perform natural functions in society and to cement the social order. People had prerogatives – or duties – just by virtue of belonging to one of these corporate entities in their societies.

The mythical history of the private-rights complex would have led you to expect early modern legal doctrine to be overwhelmingly preoccupied with the single-minded defense of the canonical contract and property system. And indeed you may find such a defense in the writings of later publicists like Bentham, Beccaria, von Humboldt, or Stuart Mill. But when you turn instead to the most influential jurists, such as Blackstone or Christian Wolff, concerned to systematize and justify the details of the institutional order, a different and more interesting picture emerges. Their major intellectual ambition was to synthesize or, when synthesis failed, merely to juxtapose the legal arrangements of the *Ständestaat* with those of the liberal contract and property system. Quite correctly, they viewed this reconciliation as a crucial element in the legal description of a defensible social order rather than as a tactical and temporary compromise between the archaic and the modern. The *Ständestaat* was no mere hangover of feudalism; it arose simultaneously with the rudiments of the private-rights complex. Thus, the favored classifications of rights in general and property in particular typically included both the rank-specific prerogatives of an estatist legal order and the formally universalistic rules of contract and property. Jurists repeatedly failed to develop a general conception of right capacious enough to include these two species of entitlement yet sufficiently narrow to exclude all others.

The second set of specifying principles of social order to have complemented the contract system consists in the extralegal techniques of order and control that characterize large-scale organizations in the societies where the private-rights complex continues in force. To a large extent these are the techniques intrinsic to the work-organization complex and supported by the distinctive links between state and society that the governmental-organization helps explain. Take the basic employment relation in the sectors of the economy marked by large-scale organizations. Even in those legal systems that continued to define employment contractually, individual contract was only the beginning in the regulation of labor. The individual agreement was first set in the framework of a system of collective bargaining meant to reestablish the reality of contract on a terrain otherwise marked by a contract-subverting degree of group inequality and personal dependence. The agreements that issued from this special contractual process could set only the most general terms for the exercise of supervisory authority. Even if submission to this authority could be treated as a manifestation of choice (what choice in a worker's world of few and similar jobs?), the actual process of supervising work could not, for the reasons earlier described, be fully turned into material for rigidly defined obligations and entitlements. It therefore became necessary to invoke, explicitly or implicitly, the technical necessity, the practical inevitability, of these work arrangements. And because everything, from the design of machines to the idea of rationality, had been influenced by this approach to the organization of labor, the claim acquired a semblance of plausibility. The mistake was only to credit the claim with an ultimate truth, a truth that transcended the actual sequence of conflicts and truces that had produced these results. The less well founded the appeal to technical necessity and the more the underlying social reality involved outright subjugation, the starker the contrast established between the picture of social life conveyed by the contract and property system and the daily reality of work.

A straightforward example of the conceptual and political embarrassments engendered by this contrast can be found in the legal issue known in American labor law as the problem of retained rights and familiar, under different names, in all modern Western legal systems. To what extent are the matters not covered by prior collective agreements a proper subject for collective bargaining and to what extent, on the contrary, are they properly reserved to managerial discretion (reserved rights of management)? To narrow the scope of retained rights is to enhance the applicability of the revised contract scheme (i.e., the framework of collective bargaining) at the cost of jeopardizing both the necessary practice of managerial discretion and the particular set of institutional arrangements (i.e., the work-organization complex) through which this discretion is currently exercised. Thus, the attack on these arrangements can be parried by the justified but only partly pertinent observation that a margin for discretion must be preserved in the interests of practicality. What routine legal and political thought cannot recognize is the distinction between the undoubted practical imperative and the contingent institutional means for satisfying it.

A great deal of legal-doctrinal argument in the advanced Western countries – perhaps most such argument in the area loosely known as private law – devotes itself to problems of the same order as the question of retained rights. By this I mean problems that arise from the attempt to reconcile the contract and property system with the actual institutional practices of exchange and production, practices perpetuated against the backdrop of highly developed links between social privilege and governmental power. This is Blackstone's and Wolff's task all over again; though the identity of the specifying complement has changed, its subversive force upon the private-rights order it completes remains the same.

The alternative to the mythical history gives rise to a readily testable hypothesis about the history of modern Western law and legal thought. The dominant legal controversies have been about what I have described as the danger of inversion through specification. The primary task the jurists set themselves was to reconcile the content and vision of the legally defined market order with alternative principles of social organization. These alternative principles were needed for the private-rights complex to penetrate production and community and to accommodate the real institutional framework of society. Yet, in each of the major instances, the complement threatened to compromise and even reverse the original liberal message supposedly expressed by the private-rights complex. To manage this irreconcilability became the continuing preoccupation of legal doctrine. If this hypothesis is true we should expect to find the familiar, liberal version of private rights – the one that the mythical history sees as "rising" and "falling" throughout these events – most prominently displayed in the relatively brief interlude when estatist principles were on the wane and contemporary styles of work organization had not yet crystallized. Even then we should expect the liberal ideas and arrangements to be stated more aggressively by propagandists and philosophers than by lawyers who had to make sense of the detailed structure of institutions.

The criticism of the mythical history gives rise to the suspicion that *no* complement of the private-rights system could do other than reverse its supposed significance. This suspicion would turn into a persuasive argument if it could be shown that an alternative legal definition of the market suffers from no such instability, precisely because it departs in certain specified ways from the received institutional definition of a market. To show that some elements of this alternative were prefigured in deviant aspects of past experience and that they escaped the instability is a step toward the explanatory goal and a concern of this institutional genealogy.

The Paradox of Superfluity

There is one final paradox to consider in the history of the private-rights complex: the classical theory of contract and property continues to be upheld although it accounts for increasingly less law. Consider the general theory of contract, the very model of analytic purity in modern Western law, the supreme technical achievement of the nineteenth-century jurists, and the part of legal thought that most perfectly expresses the assumptions of liberal political philosophy. What did classical contract theory still govern by the end of the twentieth century? Some of the limitations upon the applicability of core contract theory had been there from the start.

First, there were the exceptions to the dominant principles. Freedom to choose the contract partners and the contract terms had always been restricted by counterprinciples. The freedom to choose the partners would not always be allowed to operate in ways that undermined the communal aspects of social life. Thus, for example, reliance or enrichment in fact might generate legal obligations that had not been voluntarily assumed and the manipulation of the rules and presumptions governing intent to be legally bound kept intra-familial relations from subjection to the logic of contract theory. The freedom to choose the contract terms hit against the limits imposed by the counterprinciple that unfair bargains would not always be enforced. The unfairness might consist either in a gross disparity of real values (including a disparity that arose from unexpected changes in market conditions) or in a measure of inequality and dependence that effaced the difference between a contract regime and a power order. No higher set of principles governed the relation between principles and counterprinciples. When principles and counterprinciples lost distinct institutional agents, such as courts of law and courts of equity, there ceased to be any simple way to draw the boundaries between the dominant principles and the exceptional counterprinciples; no one could or can say for sure just how far the exceptions reach.

The reach of the ruling contract theory had always been qualified by repressions as well as by exceptions. The categories of this theory were far better suited to one-shot, arm's-length transactions than to continuing business relationships that occupied a position midway between deals among strangers and the internal arrangements of an organization. Despite the importance of these continuing relationships to the real workings of the economies that contract law governed, they were left without adequate legal regulation. Part of the difficulty lay in the assumptions and implications of a contract law centrally addressed to extended and close business dealings. Such a law would have to deny the stark contrasts between contract and organization and between contract and community and to recognize partly articulate relations of interdependence as sources of obligations. This recognition would in turn imply a view of law and obligations dangerous to the idea that absolute property provides the very model of legal right, and incompatible with the view of law and obligations embodied by the private-rights complex.

Over time, the constant repressions and exceptions of classical contract theory were aggravated by outright exclusions. At the zenith of its influence, contract theory had appeared capable of absorbing the better part of the law. But one by one whole bodies of rule and doctrine were removed from its purview and subject to special rules and categories, incompatible with the general theory. These rejects included commercial law, labor law, antitrust, family law, and even international law.

Adding up the exceptions, the repressions, and the exclusions, classical contract theory seemed to have become, more than ever, an irrelevancy. There simply was very little of the law that it still actively informed. Such was in fact the trivializing conclusion drawn by the exponents of the mythical history: freedom of contract had risen and then fallen, a victim to the twofold assault of legal skepticism and social democracy.

But this conventional explanation fails to account for two striking features of modern law and legal history: one explicit, the other subjacent. The subjacent trait supplies the key to an understanding of the former. The explicit feature is the persistent obsession with classical contract law: the excluded bodies of law continue to be worked out by opposition to the supposedly defunct model, without, however, generating any alternative general theory of the sources of obligation and the nature of rights. The subjacent feature is the negative significance of the classical contract theory: any alternative, systematic approach to private rights and obligations, even by judicial extension from the principles implicit in the specialized bodies of law that had been excluded from contract, would have threatened the established form of market organization. Thus, for example, to apply throughout the private-rights system even the limited revisionist methods of labor law would be to ask at every turn just when a given situation resembled a power order more than it did a contract regime. To revise contract bargains too often or too drastically, in response to an inequality of bargaining power, would be to replace contract by a noncontractual method of allocation. But not to revise them frequently or radically enough would be to court the danger that a vast range of contractual transactions represented merely a cover for allocation by command. Nothing guarantees that in any particular institutionalized version of the market the minimum of correction needed to secure the reality of a contract regime falls below the maximum of correction compatible with the decentralized decision making such a regime requires. It might well happen that, over a vast range of economic life, you could never correct enough by one criterion without correcting too little by the other. Even if the solution of labor law – the special framework for collective bargaining – were adequate on its own ground, it could not be generalized to the entire economy without drastically changing the institutional form of the market.

The point of the seemingly irrelevant contract theory was simply to occupy the space that might have been occupied by an alternative scheme of contract and property rights and therefore by an alternative institutional version of the market. In this ghostly and prophylactic role, contract theory did not merely fade away or merge comfortably with more progressive ideas, as the mythical history suggests. It stood there, and would continue to stand there, until a different market order had been developed. The shared assumption of its defenders and critics was that if it failed, nothing that rivaled it in generality could succeed.

Yet here lay one of the unrecognized dilemmas in the history of modern law. The core of contract theory remained defensible only if many areas of law and social practice were excluded from its scope of application, while legal principles that opposed classical theory survived within the central body of contract as exceptional or repressed elements. But each of the exclusions, exceptions, and repressions showed in its own way that exchange and production might be set within a different institutional framework and conducted under different rules. Some of these deviant possibilities, once generalized, recombined, and reformulated in the course of the revision, might significantly diminish the degree of revisionary intervention needed to preserve the distinction between contract regimes and power orders. Contract law included deviant elements that pointed toward a private-rights order that gave legal force to relations of reciprocal dependence and confined both the fully articulated act of will and the unilateral imposition of a duty by the state to anomalous roles as sources of obligations. Other deviant tendencies changed the institutional identity of the bargaining partners or revised actual markets by reference to the operations of a preferred, imaginary market. But a real turning point would come if these particular deviations could be overtaken by a restructuring of the basic legal form and setting of decentralized economic decisions: a restructuring that could replace the absolute control of divisible portions of social capital with a mechanism of rotating, divided, or otherwise conditional access to capital. Without such a redirection the fundamental relation between the need to correct transactions and the need not to correct them could not be changed. Nor could there be hope of building an institutional framework that would interpret and develop the major alternative to the dominant form of work organization. Such an alternative would create the practical means with which to distinguish more effectively the conditions for scale and continuity in production from the circumstances that starkly contrast task executors and task definers, mass-production and vanguardist industry, the prerogatives of concentrated, self-reproducing capital and the claims of innovation and experiment.

THE GENESIS OF THE GOVERNMENTAL-ORGANIZATION COMPLEX

Its Elements Reviewed

Arrangements for the organization of government and for the conflict over governmental power make up a third part of the formative institutional context.

The chief feature of the constitutional structure of the state in this institutional order is its combination of popular sovereignty, through representative democracy and universal suffrage, with devices that disperse power among different agencies of the state and different arenas of constitutional conflict. These devices limit governmental power and render it accountable only by subjecting it to constant deadlock. The opportunity for deadlock increases, under this constitutional regime, in direct proportion to the disturbances in the settled pattern of institutional arrangements and group deals that a proposed use of state power threatens to effect.

The central trait of this style of conflict over governmental organization is the method of competition among political parties or among factions of a dominant party. These partisan conflicts sometimes map and at other times disregard the major communal and hierarchical divisions of the society. From this ambivalent relation of partisan strife to social order – the mark of a society whose categories of division and hierarchy have been weakened, fragmented, and yet preserved – all other leading characteristics of modern party politics follow. The conflicts of party politics remain only tenuously related to the quarrels dividing people in everyday life. The issues on which these partisan conflicts get fought out are characteristically a hodgepodge of vague ideological commitments and cynical, mercenary promises to organized interests. Because these two components are only rarely connected by coherent and developed programs, it is often hard to tell to what extent a party platform requires or even intends a change in the formative institutional context. In the ensuing confusion the individual elector or politician may find it hard to know when his ideological slogans are serving to mask cruder and more immediate interests and when, on the contrary, these interests have been irretrievably confused by an ideological haze.

The confusion is no mere fault of insight or skill; it is rather the sign of a society whose experience of governmental politics is at odds with important features of its social order. Politics, in the narrow and traditional sense, have become largely a matter of shifting alliances among vaguely defined groups with crisscrossing memberships. But social life continues to be marked by a relatively stable and historically unique division of labor that resists disturbance and helps reproduce a scheme of social division and hierarchy.

These styles of constitutional organization and partisan rivalry produce a regime whose commitment to the free combination of free wills, though supposedly limited only in the interests of its own continuing freedom, is in fact powerfully restricted. Major areas of social practice and organizational life – including the basic form of the division of labor – remain secluded against the disturbances of party politics and reformist ambition. Meanwhile, a civically inactive populace, divided into stabilized classes and communities, expects from governmental politics little but occasional threats or sops to its habitual standard of living or its received moral ideas. The skeptic will say that this circumstance is the best that can reasonably be hoped for and that it is far better than the most probable alternatives. Though historical understanding cannot refute him it may help shake some of the assumptions that make his view plausible.

Two Chronologies

The governmental-organization complex is the element of the formative context of contemporary North Atlantic societies with the longest unbroken history. The style of constitutional organization just recalled, if not the method of partisan rivalry with which it was eventually combined, had been developing continuously since the late Middle Ages. The formation of central chancelleries, the emerging contrast between territorial and administrative specialization, the relation of central governments to a fundamental law they could adjust but not radically disturb or disrespect, and even the distinctive characterization of the administrative, judicial, and legislative bodies – all this formed part of an institutional tradition that new doctrines of popular sovereignty took as an unavoidable starting point.

In another sense, however, the governmental-organization complex has the shortest history of any component of the formative context. It developed in brief and distinct spurts from the late eighteenth century to the late nineteenth century. The first spurt was the development of liberal constitutionalism in the late eighteenth and early nineteenth centuries. These constitutional schemes sought to grant rule to a cadre of politically educated and financially secure notables, free from both clientalistic dependence and untrammeled factionalism and fully able to safeguard the polities they governed against mob rule and seduction by demagogues. Thus, this early liberal constitutionalism added to its techniques for the dispersal of power and the fragmentation of conflict, methods for filtering out unwanted or excessive popular or demagogic influences. These methods, often justified by the desire to keep civil life in the hands of independent people, included restrictive suffrage, a prodigal use of intermediate levels of representation, and a variety of precautions and prejudices directed against the emergence of popular factions capable of disrupting local notable leadership.

The second major spurt of institutional inventions occurred in the second and third quarters of the nineteenth century in leading Western countries – notably Britain, France, and the United States. Its distinctive feature was the replacement of the filtering-out techniques by universal suffrage and by a new practice of mass-based political parties. These parties rarely approached the condition of mass movements. But neither were they merely electoral syndicates, enlisting popular support opportunistically the better to succeed in a fight for access to privilege-sustaining governmental power. They were simultaneously fragile alliances of office seekers and spokesmen for the recognized interests and ideals of particular classes and communities, simultaneously such spokesmen and advocates of causes that joined people across class or communal lines. No institutional artifact expresses as perfectly as the modern political party the paradoxes of a partial freeing of social life from rigid division and hierarchy.

Among the decisive events in this second spurt were the realignment of voting rules and party organization in the period of the two English reform bills, the development by Martin van Buren and his contemporaries of a doctrine and practice of party politics, and the change in the character of national and local contests for governmental power brought about by such associates of Napoleon III as Persigny, Ollivier, and Morny. The special interest of the late nineteenth century German experience is to show how extensively the new party-political practice could be realized even though the first moment of liberal constitutionalism had remained drastically truncated.

Why did this remarkable shift take place? Credit must be given to the continual demoralization of overt hierarchical exclusions in societies that had already tasted a relative disengagement of governmental power from a hierarchy of social ranks and that had experimented, in all the ways described by other parts of this institutional genealogy, with the partial emancipation of society from false necessity. Against this background the normal temptation of an elite faction to promise more power to the people in exchange for greater popular support became harder to resist. An additional cause of the shift toward a new style of party politics was the pressure to secure mass loyalty and to transcend regional rivalries in a period of national conflict, a pressure that increased dramatically when the system of limited wars began to break down. But it is hard to think these causes could have produced such rapid and decisive effects if the ruling and possessing classes had not discovered that the filtering-out techniques and the prerogatives of notables could be abolished without giving way to all-out social agitation and to the radical redistribution of wealth and power. This discovery was surprising, in fact the single biggest surprise in nineteenth-century political history. What we still mean by representative democracy is the outcome of this unforeseen merger of an earlier constitutional scheme with a set of mid-nineteenth century innovations. Like all the other achievements with which this institutional history deals, this merger may seem the uncontroversial outcome of an irresistible progression. Yet it was a cut-and-paste job if there ever was one.

The products of these two quickly paced moments of institutional invention, and the dogmas that made them intelligible and authoritative, eventually spread throughout the rich Western world. The consolidation of these institutional arrangements and imaginative preconceptions greatly altered the terms of conflict over the other aspects of the emerging formative context. Before this change, the work-organization and the private-rights complexes had been far more effectively up for grabs than they became after it. The new way of arranging governmental power and partisan conflict effectively channeled institutionalized disputes away from more radical threats to the institutional framework and to the plan of social division and hierarchy that this framework helped reproduce. It lent a semblance of authority to the most influential half-truth of modern politics: the need to choose between reformist tinkering and all-out revolution. A successful attack against other parts of the formative institutional context now came to require a prior reckoning with the governmental-organization complex: if not its all-out replacement at least its partial displacement by unorthodox styles of collective organization and collective conflict. It is on this shorter and more dramatic, rather than on the longer and more subtle, chronology of the government-organization complex that the following sections concentrate.

The Mythical History of Democracy

A mythical history of modern representative democracy goes side by side with the mythical histories of industrial organization and private rights. Once again, liberals and Marxists share its key elements though giving them very different senses. The view of the outcome colors the understanding of the process. The exponents of the mythical history combine curious anecdotes and allegedly unavoidable developments to tell how the masses were gradually incorporated into polities and how freedom-guaranteeing constraints came to be imposed upon governmental power. The actual forms of constitutional organization and party conflict that made this result possible had a tangled and often surprising history. But, according to this mythical history, the trials and errors of modern political experience, and the undoubted failure of many proposed alternatives, have confirmed that the emergent institutional solutions were much more than flukes. They represented the strongly determined and perhaps even necessary compromise among the main constraints of size, complexity, administrative efficacy, legal restraint, and popular accountability that a contemporary democracy must satisfy. For all practical purposes, they are the real meaning of democracy.

The ideal outcome of this democratization is the circumstance in which all major social arrangements fall under the control of simple or qualified majorities acting through elected representatives and competitive political parties. Though some minorities may be effectively excluded from the political nation, their apprenticeship in familiar methods of group organization and group pressure may suffice to draw them in. At a minimum, in this view, the contest among elites and parties for control of the state must be crucially influenced by the relative success with which each group elicits mass support. Of course, if the majorities use their power to undermine the system for combining free and equal wills – by destroying, for example, the method of rotation in office – democracy ceases to exist; the democratic republic is a definite structure, not just the popular verdict.

Why, if social life under democracy tends toward such an outcome, do we so often find stability and even stagnation in democratic politics? Why does governmental policy characteristically revolve in such a narrow circle through all the reversals of electoral politics? Why, in particular, do relatively deprived majorities not use the suffrage to award themselves the wealth and the power that remain so unequally divided in their societies? To these questions, the mythical history and the view of democracy it supports give one of two answers. The first answer claims that the live options of current policy represent, in fact, the solutions with the best chance of commanding majority preference, albeit a preference formed reluctantly, in the light of disappointment with many unrealistic and dangerous alternatives. The second available answer is that, though these active options would not head any particular faction's list of preferred policies, they describe the resultants of many vectors of deliberate group or individual choice, the unintended, movable compromise among many group interests coexisting in tension with one another.

A view of the relation between democracies and markets completes the mythical history. This view recognizes that market economies and the richly defined systems of private right that accompany them can develop outside a democratic framework. They have often been reconciled with limited authoritarian regimes that respect the contract and property rights of the citizenry. But the mythical history tells us that the reverse does not hold. Democracies have never survived and cannot persist without markets. For the allocation of goods and services by central authorities or princely overlords would undermine the independence indispensable to the authentic exercise of democratic citizenship. Nothing in the standard versions of this thesis is necessarily incompatible with a recognition that markets and the entitlement systems that define them might assume forms entirely different from the forms that have in fact come to prevail. But the practical force of the argument depends on the assumption that the market system that democracy requires is the same market system that has in fact prevailed in the course of modern Western history. The thesis that democracy depends upon markets, like so much else in the mythical history and in the broader social ideas this history exemplifies, turns out to be true only in senses very different from those in which it is usually intended. The emergent style of democratic politics did and does depend upon the existence of some kinds of market organization just as it was and is incompatible with other market systems. A more radical democracy – one that carries to a further extreme the authority of combinations of will over social arrangements – would also have to give a large role to decentralized economic decision. But it would do so under different institutional auspices.

One approach to the criticism of the mythical history is to attack the mythical characterization of the outcome: the idea that current forms of democracy approximate the ideal of government by free combinations of free wills, or, at least, that they offer no insuperable obstacle to an approach toward that ideal. The discussion of the reform cycles that set the stage for the present analysis has already explored this task. Another approach is to dispute the actual picture of the genesis of democracy that the mythical history paints. This is what I now do by examining two aspects of the developments of modern representative democracies that the traditional historical account cannot adequately explain.

Objections to the Mythical History: The Surprise of Universal Suffrage

The mythical history fails to accommodate the surprising effect of universal suffrage. The central assumptions underlying the mythical history might lead you to sympathize with the view, common to most nineteenth-century conservatives and radicals, that universal suffrage would revolutionize society. The vote, it was feared or hoped, would give the mob and its leaders the means with which to wreak havoc with the established structure of authority and advantage in social life. Both the moderates (classical liberals, modernized conservatives, and outright cynics) and the radicals came up with explanations for why this expected result did not in fact occur. These explanations made only minimal dents on the mythical history, and they revealed just how many assumptions the radicals share with the moderates. But the explanations do not work. Their failure indicts the ideas they were meant to save.

Thus, the moderates emphasized that, with the economic success of the advanced countries, increasingly large sectors of the population had won a stake in the preservation of the established order. The moderates underlined the fragmentation of estates and classes into countless factions composed of overlapping and incompatible memberships. They reasserted the nonexistence of realistic alternatives to existing institutional arrangements. The primary test of realism here became simply the interaction between constant human desires and the inherent organizational requirements for satisfying and reconciling these desires at given levels of scientific knowledge and technical capability.

Before examining the merits of these attempts to deal with the consequences of electoral democracy, remember that the early radicals and conservatives were not entirely wrong about the vote. They were at least more right than our anachronistic sense of the inevitability of present forms of democracy can readily acknowledge. In many of the advanced countries, the incorporation of the masses did turn out to be full of danger: it often seemed that deprived or resentful electorates, entranced by right-wing or left-wing demagogues, would use the party pluralism of liberal democracy to advance partisan causes and popular leaders subversive of the liberal-democratic system. The ultimate defeat of these threats was due less to the foreordained triumph of democracy than to the forcible defeat of these rightist and leftist alternatives, a defeat imposed in the course of the civil wars and the world wars of the nineteenth and twentieth centuries.

But, though the remembrance of these events serves as an important corrective to a contrived sense of natural progression, it is neither here nor there on the basic theoretical issues at stake in the present controversy. The moderates will still want to claim that once these perils are met, democratic republics have an inherent institutional structure, although one that only collective trial and error can reveal. And they will still insist on explaining the relative tranquillity of these democratic republics in ways compatible with the basic conception that such an inherent structure exists and that it ensures to the extent possible (even if it is a modest extent) the government of society by free combinations of free wills.

The traditional explanations for the surprise about universal suffrage run up against two objections – one, crude and seemingly straightforward; the other, more subtle and controversial. The force of the former, however, depends on the truth of the latter. The crude objection begins by conceding that the lower orders may be satisfied by the gradual rise of their material standard of living and that each individual hopes to escape, through himself or his children, from his place in the social hierarchy. But the objection states that even these admissions fail to explain why electoral majorities continue to tolerate the extremes of inequality in wealth, income, and power that have persisted through the age of mass politics. This passive majoritarian response would begin to appear reasonable or natural only when the hope for material advancement is combined with the disillusionment with the practicability and the benefits of alternative forms of social organization.

The more subtle and controversial objection to the traditional attempts to reconcile the surprises of the suffrage with the mythical history of democracy addresses precisely this experience of disillusionment. It is one thing to accept a series of options as the only ones readily available in a historical situation. It is another, entirely different matter to attribute to these options a deep practical necessity and to treat them as the sole possibilities that economic, organizational, or psychological imperatives make practicable. On the first of these two interpretations the task becomes to explain how these limiting options acquired and maintained their force, an inquiry that proceeds from assumptions already antagonistic to those of the mythical history. But the second interpretation, with its invocation of unyielding practical necessities, implies a thesis that much of this interpreted narrative and indeed much of this book has been meant to criticize.

Marxist and non-Marxist radicals alike have often shared much more than might be expected of this mythical-historical gloss on the tamed suffrage. They have often attributed the stability of partisan conflict to "false consciousness." In this view, people live under the spell of ideas that make the established institutional order intelligible and authoritative; they mistake the regularities of a pacified social order for the eternal laws of society and human nature. But perception and sensibility are never as completely at the mercy of established preconception and power as they would have to be for the false consciousness argument to explain the taming of universal suffrage.

Once open conflict over any element of a formative context has been contained or interrupted the pacified order begins to win a second-order necessity; the routines that it shapes influence people's assumptions about the possible and the real. To this extent the false consciousness thesis is correct. But the proponents of the thesis go wrong whenever they forget that this influence over people's assumptions is never stronger than the framework of institutions, practices, and preconceptions on whose continued stability it depends. The order, I have argued, is subject to an endless stream of petty disruptions that can escalate at any moment into more subversive conflicts. Indeed, as soon as this escalation begins, people may abandon with surprising alacrity the pieties that until then had seemed to bewitch them. This observation applies with redoubled force to the disturbed and only half-trusted formative contexts that can subsist in the age of mass politics, world politics, and enlarged economic rationality. We therefore need to explain why the sense of possibility in modern democracies continues to be so narrowly constrained and why the context-preserving quarrels so rarely grow into context-disturbing struggles. If the general argument of this essay is correct, a satisfactory account must not rely on the notion that the context resists transformation because it embodies built-in necessities of social organization or historical evolution.

The more extreme the false consciousness thesis, the harder it becomes to distinguish it from the liberal approach to the surprises of universal suffrage. These extreme views still see the live options that dominate political experience as direct expressions of individual or group preferences rather than as the unintended consequence of the reciprocal interferences among organized group interests. Only the choices are now thought to be made under the influence of compulsions the agents themselves barely grasp. These compulsions supposedly establish a sharp contrast between the illusions of the participants in historical struggles and the insight of theoretical observers.

The radical steeped in Marxism, in the tradition of deep-structure social analysis, and in the habitual practice of the European left will characteristically assert that only a very different institutional system could truly embody the free combination of free wills. But the idea that social systems are inseparable wholes, the belief that each of these wholes represents a moment in a foreordained sequence, and the polemical opposition of true and false consciousness – the paralyzing legacies of deep-logic social theory – collaborate to deny constructive programmatic thought the resources it needs. On these inherited radical assumptions, the inauguration of an authentic democracy appears to require an all-or-nothing, cataclysmic regeneration of society, perhaps even of all societies throughout the world. The actual institutional proposals, though laying claim to "scientific" foundations, often turn out to be little more than an imaginative reversal of existing institutional arrangements. This reversal puts direct democracy in the place of parliamentary representation, and a strenuous all-encompassing political life in the place of the reluctant and episodic activity of the modern citizen. Its characteristic product is the soviet or conciliar style of organization that has been constantly re-created, and just as constantly abandoned, in the course of modern insurrections. This attempt to construct through mere inversion is less an exercise of programmatic thought than a manifestation of despair at the ability to think programmatically. It remains overawed by the very social reality that it pretends to escape. Its implicit intellectual conservatism is the reverse side of a disengagement from a social reality whose transformative opportunities are mixed together with resistances to transformation.

Objections to the Mythical History: Parties and the Conditions of Stability

Another embarrassment to the mythical history refers to the relation among the assumptions that normative democratic theory makes about the conditions of governmental stability. This argument against the mythical history connects with the earlier argument focusing on the failure to explain the domestication of the vote. For both objections develop the implications of the divergence between actual social life and the promised subjection of social arrangements to the will. Moreover, a crucial part of this second line of criticism builds upon the conclusions of the earlier line.

Throughout the early modern period, as indeed in much of earlier Western political history, the organizations and movements most closely resembling modern political parties remained objects of intense suspicion. This suspicion went beyond the residual but vague belief that partial interests were inherently dangerous and illicit. It expressed the belief that all such factions would be nefarious in one of two ways. On the one hand, these factions might be no more than predatory syndicates of office holders, of seekers after office, and of hangers-on, organized to pillage the state or to prostitute its authority to the syndicate's private interests. On the other hand, the faction might participate in an all-out struggle between large social classes or confessional groups. Such a struggle would inevitably prove incompatible with the minimal conditions for stability in society as well as in government. Though Machiavelli had seen the running quarrel between patricians and plebeians as a source of strength in the Roman Republic, his view remained more persuasive as a criticism of the simpleminded equation of communal cohesion and social strength than as an analysis of the relation between partisan conflict and institutional continuity.

In the liberal democracies of the modern West both popular sovereignty and the restraints upon it worked through the rotation of political parties. A major task of the fabulous history of democracy therefore became the attempt to show how political parties had ceased to be mere predatory syndicates without becoming the instruments of ferocious social or religious warfare. It was also important to show that this result had come about in a manner compatible with the government of society by the free combination of free wills – or at least that it had come as close to this ideal goal as could reasonably be hoped for.

To these ends, three conditions had to be satisfied. First, the parties had to adopt programs for the exercise of governmental power. These programs had to be animated by ideal conceptions of public policy, social welfare, or the content of rights as well as by promises to accommodate the narrowly selfish interests of particular groups. The programmatic element distinguishes the modern party from a gang of pillagers. The second condition to be satisfied was the privatization of religion. Religious differences had to become matters for the intimate forum. Confined there, they had to lose some of their intense and immediate relevance to secular conflicts over the structure of society. The third condition was the creation of a more fluid and fragmented society, made up of groups who select their membership on criteria that overlap at some times and are incompatible at others. Each group – a segment of the work force, ethnic or national collectivities, regional cultures – influences only a limited part of the lives of its members. And the total array of groups fails to generate any cohesive system of social divisions and hierarchies.

The third condition, operating in conjunction with the first, does for class differences what the second condition is meant to do for confessional antagonisms. Religious antagonisms cannot be murderous because they have been privatized. Secular ideological contests cannot be destructive because the stark class oppositions that might make them dangerous have been defused by a far-reaching change in the character of society.

But suppose that the account of this change – that is, of the events alleged to satisfy the third condition – is so exaggerated as to be largely false. Suppose, more specifically, that this account confuses the quality of party politics in modern democracies with the characteristics of actual social life. A truth that radical social theorists influenced by the idea of the epiphenomenal character of "politics" have always had trouble acknowledging, but that ordinary experience and empirical study have regularly confirmed, is that electoral behavior, party affiliation, and professional-political divisions very often defy any obvious logic of social order. To study an election in, say, the America of Jackson or the America of the late twentieth century is to discover the severe limits of the attempt to understand partisan differences as the predictable results of particular social stations. Even when you move beyond class analysis to include considerations of ethnic origin, religious persuasion, and regional milieu, the explanations characteristically suffer from a retrospective, makeshift quality; the next coalition at the next election discredits it. And this shifting and unreliable quality of divisions in the electorate is usually accentuated in the realignments of the parties or party factions and of the professional politicians who lead them. Only the idea of politics as epiphenomenal could explain the facility with which these familiar characteristics of party-political rivalry are attributed to society itself.

But the actual divisions and hierarchies of contemporary Western societies are hardly the mirror of liberal party politics. Class positions, ethnic identities, and segmentations of the work force are often a great deal more stable than the electoral antagonisms and alliances of liberal-democratic politics. To take seriously the idea that liberal society is like liberal politics we would have to see existing social life as marked by an easy freedom of movement among social stations that were themselves subject to constant revision. But though such a view may occasionally be implied by the self-congratulatory rhetoric of conservative politicians, it accords neither with ordinary experience nor with the common assumptions and conclusions of empirical social study.

The argument of this book suggests an explanation of the disparity between the quality of politics and the character of social life. The practices of party politics in the advanced Western democracies belong to a distinctive style of governmental organization and partisan rivalry. Rather than embodying, together with the market, a pure method for the free combination of free wills, this style helps reproduce a distinctive organization of society, rich in particular divisions and hierarchies and committed to a particular scheme of possible and desirable association. Parts of the explanatory argument in *False Necessity* are designed to show this constraining influence at work, while other parts emphasize the relatively accidental character of the underlying institutional settlements. The programmatic arguments complete the attack by presenting an alternative better suited than existing liberal institutions to traditional liberal ideals. Thus, liberal society differs from liberal politics (in the narrow and traditional sense of the term politics) precisely because liberal politics are what they are. To recast society in the image of liberal politics, we would have to change political life; liberal-democratic society can become what it is supposed to be only if liberal-democratic politics become different from what they currently are.

This argument requires no radical revision in our ordinary observation of social life. Apart from its closeness to a social theory free from the assumptions of deep-structure theory and positivist social science, its strength is simply to account for a disparity between the acknowledged qualities of partisan conflict and social life. The major available liberal and Marxist approaches to politics deny this disparity by reducing one of its terms to the other.

In the light of these considerations the reconciliation of partisan conflict with indispensable stability becomes an embarrassment to the mythical history of democracy and to liberal-democratic theory. The contest among parties of opinion that share an ambivalent relation to the system of social divisions and hierarchies works both to open society up to democratic politics and to put society beyond the reach of democratic politics. Many of the fundamentals of the social order remain relatively immune to the types of conflict and controversy that this established regime permits.

The skeptical, minimalist liberal may acknowledge these points while trying to avoid their force. He may claim that the partial deflection of conflict from basic arrangements and preconceptions, even from those generating social divisions and hierarchies, is necessary to secure the degree of individual freedom and economic efficiency that is realistically possible. A satisfactory response of this defense ultimately requires a discussion of the possible alternative forms of economic and governmental organization. The institutional program presented in Chapters 10 to 14 promises to secure individual liberties and civic peace through a style of governmental organization and party strife that helps weaken both the hold of rigid hierarchies or roles and the contrast between context-respecting routine and context-transforming conflict.

But there is one aspect of this debate with the skeptical democrat that can be separated out for early, tentative treatment. This aspect is the problem presented by the idea of stability, which from the outset has been the guiding theme in the debates about party politics. One of the assumptions of the original hostility to parties was that fundamental disagreements about society destroy the indispensable minimum of civic peace because such disagreements cannot be compromised. The latter-day defenses of party politics have drawn novel conclusions from this premise only because they have seen practical possibilities for the reorganization of state and society that had previously gone unrecognized. Thus, the optimists who view society in the mirror of liberal politics claim that with the privatization of religion and the supersession of entrenched hierarchies and divisions fundamental disagreements have been made superfluous. The skeptics are content to observe that to design politics for more fundamental disagreements would be to court an intolerable level of strife.

But the underlying equation of the nonnegotiable with the fundamental (which we can now interpret as all those matters that have to do with the formative institutional or imaginative context of social life) gains its plausibility from a further, untenable assumption. This assumption is the idea, characteristic of deep-structure social theory, that social systems (restrictively interpreted, once again, as formative contexts) represent indissoluble wholes. They stand or fall as a piece. Moreover, the identification of the fundamental with the nonnegotiable conflicts with an ordinary political experience. Comprehensive approaches to social reconstruction are a great deal harder to combine or compromise when stated as abstract doctrines than when translated into concrete strategies of transition or detailed social practices. The very same institutional devices that might make the dispute over fundamentals more readily available in the course of ordinary life might also root that dispute more firmly in the immediate concerns of ordinary life. Such devices might therefore weaken the conditions that leave fundamentals resistant to compromise and recombination. The programmatic argument of the next chapter follows up on these suggestions. The final vindication of a different view of stability and conflict would be actually to relate stability and conflict in ways that current democratic theory and practice rule out.

6

The Genesis of Another Formative Context: The Communist Alternative

Applying the Spirit of the Institutional Genealogy to the Non-Western World: Two Examples

The institutional genealogy shows that what at first seem to be governmental, economic, and legal arrangements strongly determined by a combination of inexorable technical requirements and irresistible social influences turn out, on closer inspection, to have been a series of complicated and precarious settlements, the outcomes of many loosely connected lines of invention and habit, compromise and coercion, insight and illusion. As soon as we shake loose the dogmas of liberals, Marxists, and modernization theorists, we begin to recognize the astonishing variety of forgotten, suppressed, or subordinated institutional notes silenced under the din of the triumphal march toward the contemporary mixed economy and parliamentary democracy. The din, like the triumph, was always greater in the books than in real life. One cluster of institutional alternatives – labeled here petty bourgeois – reappeared insistently in a wide variety of forms and settings. In a radically revised institutional translation it holds special promise today.

The historical polemic of this chapter closes with a discussion of two episodes in the making of, and in the failure to remake, certain Soviet-style institutions: the decisive events of the late 1920s and the early 1930s in the Soviet Union and the Chinese Cultural Revolution of the late 1960s. This close to my admonitory narrative serves both a general and a particular purpose. The general aim is to show how the same haphazard and hodge-podge processes that provided Western industrial democracies with their distinctive institutions also worked elsewhere in the world to produce radically different institutional systems. An antinecessitarian approach does not apply merely to the details of an institutional tradition; it also illuminates the fashioning of new traditions.

The special purpose of this final twist on the institutional genealogy is to suggest the significance of a revised version of petty commodity production for conflicts and controversies far removed from the North Atlantic world. No party ever actually proposed such an alternative in Russia. Yet the alternative could have done – and can yet do – justice to much in the defeated Bukharinist and Trotskyist causes, revealing their hidden common ground and the changes they would have needed to undergo to ensure rapid economic growth and strengthen mass participation in government.

No faction of Chinese cultural revolutionaries ever advocated such proposals. Indeed, the failure of the cultural revolutionaries, from above or below, to come up with any detailed program of institutional reform helped abandon that mass conflict to violent and sterile frustration. Yet if the militants had freed themselves from their initial sponsors and translated their antibureaucratic intentions into plans with a wider appeal, they might well have moved in the direction of something like the institutional program insinuated earlier and discussed more fully in Chapters 10 to 14.

There may at first seem to be inconsistency in a way of thinking that emphasizes how much institutions are mired in unique histories of conflict and compromise, ungoverned by any master plan, and yet sees similar institutional arrangements as relevant to the problems of widely different societies. Why are the solutions not as particularistic as the histories, each unique and uniquely suited to a particular situation? The answer, in a nutshell, has two parts: our concerns are not as unique as our situations, and our situations, in an age of partial emancipation from false necessity, enable us to treat anything proposed or tried out in one place as potentially applicable, with adjustments, everywhere else.

Institutional histories are accidental and idiosyncratic in the sense that they obey no ready-made or universal script. Each such history is a record of missed opportunities, including opportunities to realize the radical ideas, now circulating all over the world, that invite societies both to seek wealth and might and to empower the individual by smashing the roles and ranks that belittle and enslave him. The more we manage to weaken the influence formative institutions and beliefs exercise over their own remaking, the freer we become to take our cues from wherever we like and to respond in similar ways to similar ambitions and anxieties.

Understanding the Soviet Alternative Without the Help of Deep-Structure Social Theory

Elsewhere I have described a formative institutional context of late twentieth-century communist countries that both differs from the basic institutional order of contemporary Western industrial democracies and resembles it. The Soviet institutional system appeared when its Western counterpart had not yet assumed its contemporary form: each suffered, if only by reaction, the influence of the other. The immediate ideological origins of the Soviet alternative lay, after all, in two reactions to an earlier version of the same Western institutional system whose consolidation my schematic narrative has tried to analyze. One reaction was proudly professed: the commitment to overthrow the economic and political subordination of the working classes. A Western-style institutional system seemed capable of being realized in the conditions of economically and culturally more backward countries only in a form that would perpetuate indefinitely the oppression of the masses. The other reaction remained largely unacknowledged though it was no less powerful: the attempt to achieve Western levels of national prosperity and power in countries traditionally burdened by the intimate partnership between a repressive bureaucracy and a predatory oligarchy.

It was crucial that both these objectives were in the end carried out by a centralized state whose power found no counterbalance in an alternative system of economic decentralization or popular sovereignty. The soviet or conciliar style of organization was the only alternative of which the Soviet revolutionaries and their followers in other countries were aware. And it represented less a serious attempt to establish government and the economy on a new basis than a utopian inversion of established institutions and an escape from the task of dealing with the problems of the large scale. The repeated failure of this stubborn revolutionary dream left in place only the cold reality of a central government concerned to survive domestically and internationally, at any cost. Access to this new source of power came to mean everything. The contrast between task definers and task executors had never been starker, though the former lorded it over the latter in the name of governmental authority rather than the property norm. And the familiar system of Western property and contract was maintained for small-scale property, especially in the agrarian sector, while the centralized and unaccountable government exercised undivided economic sovereignty over the major forms of productive and financial capital. The communist reform cycle assumed its characteristic structure: its recurrent moments of decentralization came to mean merely increased opportunities of initiative on the part of lower-level bureaucrats and managers. So long as this reform cycle kept its distinctive shape, decentralization never produced a genuinely new way of allocating access to capital. Nor did it undermine the contrast between task-defining and task-executing activities or threaten the oligarchic control of governmental power.

How did this institutional system emerge? The methods and ideas that inspire the mythical history of the Western institutional order have a comforting answer: it says that the Soviet model represents, in broad outline, the only possible alternative to the triumphant Western solution open to industrialized or industrializing societies in the circumstances of modern life. If the analyst is out to be sympathetic, or to express a pessimistic and worldly realism, he may go on to observe that only some combination of bureaucratic and entrepreneurial dictatorship – the forcible exaction and reinvestment of a surplus – can lift today's poor countries out of their poverty. This interpretation of the Soviet model draws an additional halo of justification around Western institutional arrangements. For who could want the alternative unless driven to it by desperate circumstances?

The polemic against the mythical history should therefore include a reinterpretation of the genesis of the Soviet model. This restatement makes two central claims. Its first thesis is that we can account for the emergence, diffusion, and tenacity of the Soviet-style formative context in ways that dispense with the appeal to deep-logic constraints of organizational, psychological, or economic necessity. We do not have to suppose that the Soviet system is one of the few options among which humanity must choose at its present level of wealth and knowledge. In fact, a convincing analysis of the origins of the Soviet model must emphasize factors that cannot be connected with the types of causes dear to deep-logic social theory, not at least without postulating a long and fabulous series of intermediate links between these causes and the actual events.

A second thesis of this reinterpretation is that we can identify at least one major realistic alternative to the institutional system that triumphed in the modern West. This alternative represents a counterpart to the institutionally revised system of petty commodity production discussed in earlier sections of this chapter, a counterpart specifically suited to the circumstances of a backward country. Such a solution would have required yet more audacious institutional inventions than its successful rival. But it would also have had many practical advantages further down the line: all the benefits that can result from institutions carrying forward the task of emancipation from false necessity.

The argument develops in two phases. The first discusses the most important turning point in the development of the Soviet-style system. The second phase analyzes the failure to break out of the Soviet model during the Chinese Cultural Revolution, an episode in which the communist reform cycle got out of hand.

The Origins of the Soviet Model

The war between the Soviet state and the Russian peasantry that began in the winter of 1930–31 exercised a decisive influence on the making of the Soviet model. This war, with its immediate antecedents and sequels, was the occasion for the final defeat of both the Bukharinist "right" and the Trotskyist "left" within the party. It gave determinate form to a relationship between state and society that had been left open by the November revolution. It settled for a long time to come what large numbers of people could expect in their material lives and what government could demand from them. The terms of accumulation and collaboration that grew out of this series of encounters were changed only slowly and marginally in later periods of Soviet history. They became the practical groundwork for a communist regime that would be reproduced elsewhere and that elsewhere, as in the Soviet Union itself, would scarcely change for several generations.

In the late 1920s the Soviet government faced an unmistakably difficult situation To stay in power and accomplish its minimal programmatic objectives, it had to achieve rapid economic growth. It could not rely on foreign capital: met by the hostility of the Western industrial powers, it could not avoid a high degree of economic autarky even if it had wanted to. Nor could it readily obtain capital by a sharp and lasting depression of industrial wages. Such a policy would have alienated a social group whose active support or grudging acceptance was crucial to the leadership for reasons that were as much doctrinaire as practical. These considerations accentuated what would in any event have been true for any economy with the relative backwardness and dimensions of the Soviet economy in the 1930s: a major part of the capital for stepped-up accumulation would have to come from the transfer of agricultural surplus in the form of cheap food goods for urban populations and industrial workers, and of agrarian exports that could be used as payment for needed machine tools and industrial inputs.

The severity of the situation was masked during the early years of the New Economic Policy by the existence of a large margin of underutilized capacity in the Soviet economy's productive stock and especially in its industrial plant. As long as this margin continued to exist, the pressure on the agrarian sector remained relatively moderate: manipulation of the terms of trade between agrarian and industrial goods might be enough to effect a transfer of value from agriculture to industry without disrupting the agrarian economy or provoking violent resistance by the peasantry. Such manipulation had proved able to overcome the "scissors crisis" of 1923–24. The result of this temporary success was to lend a semblance of plausibility to the Bukharinist slogans of the NEP period: the ideas that the terms of commodity circulation were enough to determine value and value transfers and that economic growth could be spontaneously assured by the reciprocally reinforcing influence of agrarian and industrial accumulation within a structure of limited market freedom.

But the policies that worked when there was underemployed capacity could not and did not work as the capacity barrier was approached and broken. The squeeze on the agrarian economy became stronger. Other devices had to be found to supplement pricing policy. In this sense NEP policy resembled Keynesianism, and it shared some of Keynesianism's limitations. A doctrine relevant to particular conditions of underemployed capacity broke down when carried over to the task of achieving repeated breakthroughs in productive capacity.

To be sure, confused, widely fluctuating price policy helped disorganize the agrarian economy. But a system of stable, intelligible administered prices would almost certainly not have been enough to avoid the problems that had surfaced by the time of the procurements crisis of 1927–28. If the state wanted to avoid dependence on the kulaks (the larger farmers) and to expand agricultural production rapidly, it needed to pursue an alternative agrarian policy.

One such alternative would have required the Soviet government to gain a foothold in cooperative farming by millions of smallholders. It would have had to create marketing and procurement structures that would make these farming cooperatives dependent upon the state while giving them priority in technical and financial assistance. Such a program, however, could not be easily carried out by a rigid, authoritarian government. It called for a government that would be willing and able to promote grassroots collective organization on the part of a large segment of its citizenry and that would open itself to the deals, pressures, and risks such organization would inevitably spawn. Such an alternative would have represented something like the reconstructed version of petty commodity production outlined earlier.

The policy of coerced collectivization and violent dekulakization that was in fact pursued involved the Soviet state in an unprecedented revolutionary campaign against a peasant society of twenty-five million households. This campaign, for all its fits and starts, did in fact achieve an increased and prolonged transfer from the agrarian to the industrial sector, and generated rapid though discontinuous growth. But it did so at many costs. Soviet agriculture was left scarred for an indefinite time to come: the autonomy that peasants and agricultural laborers had failed to achieve in the form of significant collective organization reappeared in the multiple stratagems of a rearguard struggle against coerced collectivization and the forced appropriation of the agricultural surplus.

Besides, the decision to disrupt millions of households called for a state and a leadership that would stop at nothing in the techniques of revolutionary despotism. The alternative conceptions of communist democracy represented, halfheartedly, by the right and left factions in the party were among the victims of the struggle. Thus, there was a tight connection between the way the problem of economic growth was solved and the development of the state. The whole period from the November revolution to the war against the peasantry could be seen as a time when both the mechanism of accumulation and the organization of government had been left undefined. The counterpart to the economic reprieve of underemployed capacity was the political limbo of unresolved factional rivalry.

Both the Bukharinist right and the Trotskyist left had failed to understand what was happening and what was needed. The Bukharinists did not understand the extent of the accumulation problem until the procurements crisis of the late 1920s was already in fill swing. The Preobrazhensky leftists allowed themselves to be pushed into a mock Faustian language of heroic industrialization without specifying the concrete institutional forms for enlisting the collaboration of the working masses with the economic plans. Both sides raised the issue of democracy within the party and the state only when driven from power, and therefore they did so alone and at different times rather than in concert. Neither faction had grasped the extent to which the forms of accumulation and of government were bound up with each other. Each faction consistently mistook the other for its most dangerous adversary when in fact they had many aims and ideas in common. Among these shared concerns was the central issue of how to structure collaborative economic arrangements in such a way that a market mechanism (in the sense of some system of economic decentralization) could be combined with central political control over the direction and rate of accumulation. An emerging alliance of agrarian or industrial entrepreneurs and party bureaucrats had to be dismantled without precipitating the state into a revolutionary war against society. In the event, the Bukharinists joined with Stalin against the supporters of Trotsky. The remaining leftists had failed to join hands at the right time and to translate their democratic slogans into the organization of mass constituencies.

To understand the outcome, we have to take into account the severity of the available options and the strategic errors of the right and left factions. But, even then, the events lack any irresistible logic of their own. The personalities of the leaders – Trotsky's and Bukharin's vanities and illusions, Stalin's mastery of the bureaucratic apparatus, his surefire instinct for the kill, his genius for dosage, and his luck – played an immeasurable part. The turning points in the history of stabilization policy represent an encounter with the impersonal, intractable forces of material life. Yet even there, the full range of contingencies comes into play, as if to remind us that history never stops being political in either the largest or the smallest ways.

The elements of the outcome determined what the Soviet system would be like in the immediate future. They therefore also established the starting point for other communist regimes. The solution that emerged had two decisive features. Whereas one aspect followed directly from the strategy of coerced collectivization, the other was more obliquely linked with it.

The decision to wage war on the peasantry and to crush the right and left factions within the party meant that the preferred structure of accumulation would minimize the role of cooperation and autonomous organization from the bottom up. Instead, it would emphasize the imposition, verging on systematic state terrorism, of a coercive order. The government and leadership that could manage to do this with the vast millions of peasants would be likely to do it with the industrial work force as well, no matter what the ruling ideological preconceptions might be. The combination of remorseless centralism with the violent shattering of the way of life of a large part of the people and the destruction of almost every remnant of the agrarian populations' independent associative life meant the triumph of a kind of state and leader that would see in every sign of communal autonomy and resistance an indication of conspiracy and breakdown. These were institutions and attitudes that could not be easily turned on and off to deal with different parts of the population. Thus, the Soviet experience confirmed, once again, the fateful importance of the relationship between the presence or absence of collective mobilization and the particular ways in which governmental power is used.

The oblique counterpart to this system of accumulation without mobilization was the emerging partnership between the ruling elites in party and bureaucracy and the technical intelligentsia of managers and professional or scientific personnel. The process of mutual though unequal acceptance (the technical intelligentsia was never coequal with the top cadres) had begun even before the start of the NEP. It had been deepened during the NEP years. Despite the traumatic effect of the purges, it survived Stalinism. Its survival reflected a straightforward fact of reciprocal advantage and dependence. As the regime became increasingly committed to imposition of an order in town and country, it could not afford to fight simultaneously, on a second front, against the technical intelligentsia. The technicians, after all, had the power to disrupt the existing production system until another system could be devised and other technical cadres could be trained.

The regime had something to offer the technical intelligentsia in exchange for its collective support. Though Bukharinist ideas might be rife among the managers, engineers, and other professionals and though the terroristic aspects of revolutionary despotism might be especially hated, there was a basis for minimal agreement. That basis included the desire to preserve a style of work organization distinguishing between the people who formulated general productive tasks, or controlled their execution, and the people who did the routine work. The technical intelligentsia might not rule in the state, but at least it ruled (under watchful eyes) in the bureaus, factories, collective farms, army, schools, and hospitals.

The ruling elites and the technical intelligentsia had in common more than a crude interest in power and its perquisites. They also shared, with increasing clarity, a conception of efficiency and rationality and of the style of organization that would embody them. This conception minimized the break with the style of organization prevalent in the Western industrialized powers of the time (e.g, Lenin's celebrated interest in Taylorism). It also presupposed the foreclosure of widening collective conflict and escalating collective mobilization in every major sector of the economy. Thus, the two elements of the Soviet solution – accumulation without independent collective association, and accommodation with the technical intelligentsia by maintaining the sharpest contrast between task makers and task appliers – were implicated in each other.

The result of this crucial episode in Soviet history was related to the suppression of the soviets after the November revolution. The relationship brings out a special connection between the Western and the communist experiences. It also illuminates the general link between radical conflicts over the mastery of the state and the structure of society and the more subtle or detailed settling of accounts that takes place when new terms are laid down for economic growth and stability.

The soviets were put down almost immediately after the November revolution. They were deprived of their original role as devices of collective mobilization and became, instead, mere instruments of governmental control. In this respect, their history resembled that of peasant communes that had been transformed into passive tools of some agrarian empire's fiscal policy. The suppression of the soviets had created the opportunity to orient the state and the economy in a way that would restrict all independent collective organizations. But the destruction of the soviets did not make this result inevitable, nor did it tell on just what terms accumulation would go forward. Only the conflicts of the late 1920s and their sequels set these terms. In a similar way, the defeat of radical movements in Western Europe after World War I had created an opportunity to minimize the changes in the established forms of power and production that would be necessary for lasting civil peace as well as economic stability and growth. That opportunity was later realized by the forms of economic policy developed during World War II and by the domestic and international economic arrangements and governmental alliances of the postwar era.

In fact, there was more than a generic parallel between the events in Western Europe (or more generally, in the Atlantic zone) and those in the Soviet Union; there was a direct mutual influence. The failure to create an alternative style of work organization and of democracy in one area of the world made the failure in the other area seem that much more unavoidable. The development of organizational structures (e.g., the multidivisional firm structure) was going on in the advanced Western countries after the soviets had already been untoothed, and each refinement of those structures suggested to the masters of Soviet Russia the need to find the closest counterpart compatible with their own forms of rule and property. The war effort added to the plausibility of this selective emulation by making it important to achieve the most rapid possible mobilization of resources and labor with the fewest risks and discontinuities.

The settlement of the late 1920s and early 1930s determined the ground on which later conflicts would be fought in the Soviet Union and other communist countries. There were an outer circle and an inner circle of struggle.

The outer circle presented occasional flare-ups of the defeated "right" and "left" tendencies. An example of the rightist resurgence would be the rebellious movements in Eastern Europe; an example of the leftist, the Chinese Cultural Revolution. They had in common the impulse to reverse the strategy of accumulating without allowing independent collective mobilization. They represented, and were understood to represent, an assault upon this strategy that threatened to upset the established forms of power and production. They jeopardized the prerogatives of the ruling groups and (at least in the case of resurgent leftism) of the technical intelligentsia. They were repeatedly crushed thanks to the reactions of the endangered governmental apparatus, the hesitations of their own leaders, and the military intervention of other communist powers.

The inner circle of conflict was represented by struggles that went on chronically because they arose out of a congenital weakness in the stabilization settlement. There was a limit to the state's use of terroristic violence against society in the effort to impose a growth path upon a passive and frightened citizenry. Terrorism would have its own costs in the breakdown of communication and of simple truth-telling, in the government's need to keep up the remorseless pressure, and in everyone's obsession with survival and self-defense. Once there was a letup in state terrorism, the rulers and planners would have to win a greater measure of active collaboration by the working population at every level of hierarchy. To enlist this collaboration and to compensate for their own relative ignorance of difficulties and opportunities, the central planners periodically felt pressed to allow for greater decentralization in the production system. The loosening of central control, however, could not be permitted to fall into open-ended collective conflict or grassroots mobilization. It could not be allowed to threaten the basic hierarchy of rule within the society at large or the large-scale enterprise. It could not be set free to undermine the barrier between the task makers and the task appliers. Decentralization within these limits invariably meant a greater concentration of power in the hands of managers, technicians, and local authorities. They would in turn make such concessions to their own underlings as were needed to keep things going.

But the decentralizing movement brought dangers of its own. Low-level authorities used every additional amount of discretion to build up more autonomy from dependence upon their rivals or their masters. They tried to turn the advantages they had gained for their enterprises and for themselves into vested rights. The whole economy would then start to sink into a welter of factional privileges and self-defensive actions within the cumbersome and resented framework of the central plan. This was a dreamless apparatchik's version of the ancient regime: freedom through privilege. Correctives milder than revolutionary despotism sufficed to stop it.

No point along these epicycles was satisfactory from even the narrowest perspective of accumulation. At each point, muddling through seemed the best that could be hoped for. Nevertheless, there was no way to avoid the turns and about-turns. They arose from the difficulty of satisfying the practical need for cooperation within an order of the kind that had emerged in the Soviet Union at the decisive point of the late 1920s.

To see what is most revealing about these events, we need to push the comparison between the twentieth-century Soviet and the Western settlements to a more general level. In both cases, the accepted solution resulted in a persistent limit to the government's capacity to push the economy repeatedly into the high gear of accelerated innovation. This is just a particular way of saying that neither settlement did justice to the exigencies of the modern formula for worldly success.

In both instances, the limitation had the same fundamental structure. The dominant stabilization policies, and the formative contexts of power and production these policies helped sustain, enabled a more or less closed and privileged group to exercise a stranglehold over the conditions of collective prosperity. In one case, this group was the party and bureaucratic elite with its allies in the upper rungs of the technical intelligentsia. In the other case, it was the managers and officials who controlled the crucial flows of investment decisions. In both cases, the other groups dug in their heels. They attempted to organize themselves for self-defense and advancement. They tried to turn every new advantage into a vested right. More often than not, they hardened the criteria of group membership and alliance rather than effacing these lines by a strategy of expanding alliances. They sought and received benefits according to their power to disrupt: whether by the slowing down of the production system in a narrower sense or by the withholding of partisan support in a larger sense. There was certainly no general proportion between each group's ability to blackmail and its actual productive contributions to the economy.

The basic obstacle to ever renewed innovation was then the constraining interplay between an elite certain to confuse social opportunity with factional interest and a larger world of groups armed with uneven degrees of collective organization and devoted to the stratagems of preemptive security. Here was an example of the way the same forces that go into the remaking of a social world – the interplay between collective mobilization and the transformative uses of governmental power – turn into the protective shell that helps defend this world against attack.

The outcome of these constraints upon collective material progress was not definitive economic crises. It was an endless stream of squabbles and a recurrent entropic movement toward hardened factional privilege. Most worldly people thought that things had always been and would always be this way.

A Failed Attempt to Break Out from the Soviet Model: The Chinese Cultural Revolution

The Chinese Cultural Revolution offers a contrasting case: the failure to achieve in fact what at one point had looked like a possible breakthrough into a different style of industrial society strengthened by the very forms of production and control that were initially jeopardized. For a while at least, reconstruction for the sake of economic growth – an objective whose relative importance had been one of the very subjects of the contest – was achieved as inconclusive rivalry among proposals gave way to the reassertion of preexisting institutions, with a familiar decentralizing twist. The events by which an entrenched system temporarily rids itself of its domestic challengers and emerges with new strength from a battle for survival are among the most important and the most common ways in which the relation between institutional forms and practical needs gets played out: reaction, like revolution, is not easily separable from reform.

The experience of the Chinese Cultural Revolution also holds a more specific interest for an institutional genealogy that anticipates both a theory of context making and a program for social reconstruction. I have suggested that the "right-wing" Soviet deviationists of the 1920s raised once again the problems posed by the institutional arrangements that eventually became dominant in the West. The fulfillment of what was most original in their program would ultimately have required the realization of the reconstructed, economically dynamic and internally stable form of petty commodity production: hence a novel institutional ordering of market economies and democratic regimes. The Chinese Cultural Revolution highlights the difficulties encountered in the course of an equally confused and halfhearted attempt to establish a stabilized order capable of perpetuating a higher measure of collective mobilization and context-challenging conflict in the midst of everyday social life. The petty commodity and mobilizational ideals may seem only loosely connected. Yet they are indeed linked through the requirements that must be satisfied in order to rescue a radically decentralized economy from instability, perversion, and regressiveness. This argument, first advanced during the discussion of certain turning points in European institutional history, becomes clearer in Chapters 10 to 14, which develops a program for institutional reconstruction responsive to both the mobilizational and the decentralizing ideal.

Consider the basic march of events. The first stage was one in which Mao and his faction attempted to execute an internal coup within the elites. Their initial motives for stepping up the controversies that led to the Cultural Revolution were surely complex: they included, in some blend the participants themselves could hardly have decomposed, an unvarnished power interest – the desire to humble rival centers of power in the state apparatus and the party – and a visionary commitment – the will to escape from the consolidation of bureaucratic power in the manner already perceived as indicative of the Soviet vice. Even at its most radical, however, this commitment seems never to have allowed for the possibility of reorganizing power on a radically new basis and institutionalizing popular participation on an unprecedented scale.

The second stage of the events started when the faction that had begun the quarrel within the elites attempted to enlist broader mass support in order to do its will – a variation on the characteristic mechanism by which the recruitment of mass constituencies shakes up an oligarchy's inward-turning squabbles. The call for mass agitation became progressively more shrill, as befitted the confused, halfhearted assault upon bureaucratic power. The popular response, however, soon began to exceed the expectations of its architects. Its major source of support lay in the dispossessed (such as the temporary and contract workers – the Chinese underclass) and in the youth that had not yet acquired the knack of discounting the value of words. Its centers were a few cities. Its major forms of action were the mass demonstration and the transformation of self-criticism techniques. Self-criticism had been a subtle method for reasserting consensus and control through contained conflict – the very image of routine politics, drawn into the microcosm of the enterprise, the work gang, or the neighborhood and supplemented with a subtle psychology of the way an individual can be made to render himself transparent to his fellows. The fundamentals of power at every level would remain out of bounds to conflict and complaint. In the hands of the practicing cultural revolutionaries, however, self-criticism became a device for humiliating alleged enemies and bureaucratic superiors; the boundaries of what could be done to people, who could be reached, and what could be attacked, began to fall apart. This evolution, a paradigm of the way the very instruments of routine politics may turn into the agencies of political intensification, was symbolized by the assault on Liu Shao-chi, at once leader of the party elites and consummate theorist of the mainstream tradition of self-criticism. The widening conflict forced the politicians behind the Cultural Revolution and their allies in the army to choose between two options, which presented themselves in ever starker and more dangerous contrast as agitation grew. One option was to support the insurrectional movement unequivocally, attempting to lead its temper. The other was to reassert control so that the basic structure of party leadership at the top levels and managerial authority at the lower ones would not be destroyed; the popular tumults would then not depart too far from the purpose originally meant for them: that they should serve as a weapon of intimidation in an elite conflict. Not all surprises would be allowed to happen.

The definitive choice of the latter option inaugurated a third stage: the effort to bring events under control once again started with the "seizure of power" movement of early 1969. The new "revolutionary committees" installed in the enterprises, with the participation of local workers, party cadres, and army representatives, served as the crucial device by which mass participation was whittled down to the point of harmlessness. In this way, too, the more radical factions among the political elites lost any independent channel by which to communicate with their potential supporters below. The extent of the loss became clear only later. The non-army radicals found themselves reduced to the condition of favorites at court with a tenure dependent upon the survival of their master.

The fourth stage of the conflict was the period of settling scores among the erstwhile radical allies in light of the largely successful decision to reestablish control. It was also the phase in which the relationship between the domestic and the foreign policy aspects of these conflicts became clear. The two issues came together in the Lushan Plenum of 1970, when Lin Piao and the radical army faction were attacked for failing to swallow the new line of antagonism to the Soviet Union. The main points of the deal were the acceptance by the party and state bureaucracies of the emerging program of international realpolitik in exchange for a guarantee of minimal security made all the more credible by the annihilation of the radical army faction. Yet it would be a mistake to see in the quest for this reorientation to world politics a cause of the earlier reassertion of control. The masses might also have been mobilized for the new foreign policy, but once they had been demobilized, the issue of the terms on which the reinstated elites would agree to the desired international aims became pressing.

The fifth stage of events was the aftermath of restoration, reaction, and reform: after Mao's death even the appearance that his line was the predominant one could be denied and his favorites could be discarded.

The ending of the story suggests the paradox whose resolution in turn uncovers the deeper meaning of the plot. Mao and his immediate friends and supporters seemed to be in charge of events from the start: they began the agitation; they succeeded in controlling it; and they set the terms on which compromise would be struck after rebellion had been put on a leash. Yet in the end their initial enemies sat in the seats of power and judgment. A program of economic growth was organized around a more clear-cut chain of managerial and party hierarchy than had existed before. Concessions to "socialist legality" left little real substance to popular participation. Decentralizing reform respected the limits of the communist reform cycle.

The explanation of the paradox lies in the choice between the two options of continuing mobilization or demobilization. The unequivocal choice in favor of the latter had taken place before any real alternatives in the organization of production or power had had a chance to consolidate. Indeed by its very nature, the success of such a reassertion depended upon its anticipating the emergence of any alternative logic of power and production capable of making an economy run and a polity stick together. In the end, the alternative modes of organization remained, at best, half-baked compromises or growths upon a body constituted on different principles. None of the participatory schemes had passed the threshold points at which they might have started to pay off and surmount the opposition. In the absence of a developed alternative scheme of enterprise organization and coordination, the equivocal participatory concessions, such as the "revolutionary committees," became at most an annoying and costly though ineffective hindrance to restrengthened managerial authority; a similar problem arises in the Western economies when efforts are made to push through redistributive or regulatory programs without changing the fundamental pattern of powers over investment. So too, as long as no novel system for governmental decision, control, and communication has begun to appear, departures from established practice in the name of the mass line – or any other line, for that matter – will appear as gestures toward chaos. Their fate will depend upon an unequal battle in which well-organized powers are pitted against sinking enthusiasms.

So, once the reassertion of control had taken place, the Cultural Revolution as a mass movement was lost. But so were the elite factions responsible for its beginning and its later paralysis. To survive as a power bloc they would not only have had to dissociate themselves from the personality of the leader: they would also have had to define themselves in terms other than the ones that had set them on course. Their erstwhile enemies, the governmental and party bureaucracies, found themselves in charge of the real machines of administration and production and discovered as well that, in the newly clarified circumstance, their own power interests coincided with the practical needs to get things done and deliver the goods. To admit this much, you do not have to believe that anyone in the Cultural Revolution – elites or masses – was close to coming up with workable alternatives, or even that such plans of association as they might have found would have represented a change for the better. The point is that no alternatives were really put to the test and that the collective process of searching for them was paralyzed close to the start.

Here, then, is a case of failure in breakthrough toward an alternative mode of socialism and industrialism, unless the breakthrough is defined as a return to a clearer version of preexisting institutions, a return permitting limited decentralizing experiments and achieved at the cost of a protracted ordeal of provoked, uncontrolled, and suppressed insurrection.

7

Stability and Destabilization in the Working of Formative Contexts

The Core Conception

The first set of ideas in this view of context change deals with the normal life of an institutional and imaginative framework, the life that goes on in the interludes of revolutionary reform. The point is to understand how the ordinary workings of a formative context make context change possible. This initial group of conjectures represents, then, something like a statics of the minute structure of social life. But it is a statics of a peculiarly antistatic type. For its central themes are the dependence of stability upon artifice and illusion rather than necessity, and the constant reemergence of the opportunities to remake a social world that result from the very means used to defend this world.

Here, by anticipation, are the major claims and assumptions of this part of the argument. There are two moments to distinguish in the stabilization of a formative context. The season of heightened and intensified conflict over some part of the framework must be brought to an end and conflict contained or interrupted. This social peace may be achieved either through an acceptance of the preexisting institutional arrangements and imaginative preconceptions or through their partial replacement. (The total substitution of the framework is the unrealistic, limiting case.)

This peace must be imposed. It must result from a series of violent or nonviolent, practical or imaginative struggles, fought out against the background of antecedent arrangements and preconceptions biasing the result of the struggles without determining it. There must be a victory and a defeat, however modest its dimensions and imperceptible its forms. Only then can the second moment of context stabilization begin. The imposed contexts become the beneficiaries of the stabilizing forces this section of the argument examines.

Consider three sources of the second-order necessity of formative contexts. One is the consolidation of an organizational and technological style of economic activity. Especially when it is realized within a system of nation-states at uneven levels of wealth and power, such a style reinforces the institutional settlement on which it was originally superimposed. A second source is the hardening of assumptions about collective identities, group interests, and social possibilities and of correspondences between the privileges each group enjoys and its relative access to governmental power. A third source of derivative necessity is the transformation of the imposed or accepted institutional order into a set of authoritative models of human association meant to be realized in different areas of social existence. Such an imaginative scheme lives both in the more pliant and organized form of official legal and moral dogma and in the more elusive and ambivalent form of implicit, widely shared assumptions about what the relations among people should be like in the different domains of social existence.

The forces operating at this second moment of stabilization presuppose the interruption or containment of fighting over fundamentals. The stabilizing mechanisms cannot account for the distinctive content of a formative context; they operate whatever this content may be. Their work is not to steer institutions and beliefs in any particular direction but rather to give them a degree of stability that they would otherwise lack. They alter the subjective quality of people's experience of formative contexts. This shift in turn has practical consequences.

The stabilizing forces can therefore be said to lend a second-order necessity to the social orders on which they exercise their influence. The term second-order necessity should be understood by analogy to the traditional idea of custom as a second nature, a distinctive and compulsive nature superimposed upon our indeterminate species nature. The forces of stabilization produce the tropisms in which a routinized form of social life so largely consists. Each force generates opportunities to destabilize the formative context in the very course of bestowing upon it an additional level of stability. It thereby also provides an opportunity for the operation of forces, discussed in later parts of this theory, that make possible long-run cumulative changes in the constraining power as well as in the distinctive content of formative contexts.

The transformative opportunities resulting from the operation of the context-stabilizing opportunities are just that: opportunities. They may or may not be turned to advantage. Each one takes the form of a series of petty disturbances. To be put to transformative use these disturbances must be made to escalate into broader and more intense conflict. We can describe circumstances that usually encourage or discourage this escalation, that make it harder or easier. But we cannot draw up a list of the necessary and sufficient conditions under which such escalation occurs. The obstacle to making such a list does not arise from a mere localized, remediable defect in our understanding of society. Rather, the search for necessary and sufficient conditions rests on mistaken assumptions about what social life is like: the assumptions common to deep-structure social theory and positivist social science.

This part of the view of context change develops through an analysis of the three forces contributing to the second-order necessity of formative contexts. The point is to show how each stabilizing influence regularly produces opportunities for destabilization.* There is no magic to these three. Others may be added, and even these may be divided up or combined in other ways.

The Second-Order Necessity of Formative Contexts: The Organizational and Technological Style

A stabilized set of formative institutional arrangements becomes the basis for an organizational and technological style of economic activity. This style then exerts a retrospective stabilizing influence upon the arrangements it has taken for granted and upon the group divisions and hierarchies these arrangements support. The adversaries of the newly established institutional settlement find they cannot go far in challenging this settlement without jeopardizing the dominant approach to technological design and the ways of organizing production and exchange that have been superimposed upon this approach.

The genealogy of current forms of work organization presented earlier in this chapter provides an extended example. The events that led up to the consolidation of the forms of economic organization characterizing contemporary formative contexts included a vast range of group conflicts, fought out in changing circumstances and with unexpected outcomes. Elites were redefined and their relation to the central and local powers of government was reshaped. Governmental authority was actively enlisted against alternative lines of development in ways that spanned the distance between the most violent methods of repression and the slow, subtle accumulation of legal rules and economic policies. The results of these conflicts favored the rigid form of rationalized collective labor, with its sharp contrast between task-executing and task-defining activities. Varieties of work organization that softened this contrast were relegated to the commercial and technological rearguard and vanguard of the economy. The dominant style of work organization in turn became the basis for distinctive approaches to industrial organization and machine design, closely adapted to each other. Mass-production industry conflated disciplinary and efficiency aims. It developed a panoply of defenses against market instability. And it adopted purpose-specific machines, meant to function in a rigidly organized production process. General-purpose or metamachines were confined to the industrial vanguard, and became for a long time the exceptional rather than the standard form of machine design. Thus, in the end, the institutional arrangements and the group hierarchies became the basis for complex managerial and technological conventions. All but the most discerning identified these conventions with economic rationality.

* In *Social Theory: Its Situation and Its Task*, the idea of the link between stability and destabilization was presented through the discussion of the survival, identity, and oligarchy effects. Now, however, I need categories that can serve the aims of a more detailed analysis, specifically concerned with context change.

The climb to a higher order of stability did not happen all at once: no clear break or time lag separated the crystallization of institutional arrangements and of group divisions and hierarchies from the development of this organizational and technological complex. But once the complex had formed, it offered an additional layer of protection to the underlying institutional order. A different order would require different organizational and machine-design techniques. For example, a reconstructed, practicable version of the petty bourgeois alternative to the dominant industrial style must break down the stark contrast between task-defining and task-executing activities. Such an alternative cannot accept a tradition of machine design presupposing a passive worker, pegged to an isolated, discretionless role. The practicality of the proposals will be disputed, all the more so because adversaries of the established order must often appeal to little more than a speculative possibility of practical organization. Thus, for example, the idea of a metamachine long remained a purely speculative conception, suggested by the theory of machine design, before it became actualized in the vanguard sector of industry.

But even if the ultimate practicality of an alternative style were beyond dispute, its development must still overcome formidable difficulties of transition. One technological and organizational order must be disrupted before another can be established. The disruption exacts a real economic toll. Moreover, the established technological and organizational style ends up influencing people's intangible assumptions about social possibility and, through them, about group interests.

The preceding discussion of this stabilizing mechanism presupposes a hypothesis developed later in this chapter. Functionalist social theories are right to see connections between the forms of social organization and the ability to exploit technological opportunities for productive or destructive, economic or military purposes. The organization of teamwork imposes constraints upon the ability to develop and deploy practical techniques and machines. The larger institutional environment (and, specifically, the part of it I call the formative context) in turn shapes the forms of teamwork. We must recognize these constraints. But we must also understand that there is no one-to-one relation between arrangements at these different levels of technological capability, work organization, and institutional arrangements, and no list of solutions at one level that are required by a particular solution at another level.

An organizational and technological style acquires an additional stabilizing power when it begins to spread throughout a system of interdependent states at unequal levels of economic growth and military strength. (It does not matter for the present purpose whether such a state system actually includes the whole world. But assume that if it occupies a lesser portion of the globe, it is both economically and militarily autarkic.) The state enjoying the greatest economic and military capabilities may be able to impose upon weaker or more backward countries many of its favorite arrangements and dogmas. It may indulge the most primitive of ideological impulses, which is the desire for self-reproduction.

But imposition is hardly necessary. Success remains the best persuasion. It takes time for the ruling or possessing elites of the more backward powers to discover that the practical capabilities achieved by the more advanced countries can be developed through methods of work organization different from the methods prevailing in the pioneering nations of the state system. Only slowly do the relatively backward nations find out that they can combine the same imported ways of organizing work with governmental or economic arrangements completely unknown in the dominant countries. At first, the practical capabilities seem inseparable from their organizational and institutional setting. The setting in turn seems available on a take-it-or-leave-it basis.

The persuasive authority of the organizational and institutional solutions that have achieved preeminence in the dominant powers often gets reinforced by the most influential ideas about practical progress and its enabling circumstances. Cultural ascendancy habitually accompanies practical triumph: the ruling doctrines of statecraft and economic management in the dominant countries represent the established amalgam of a technological and organizational style with a formative institutional and imaginative context as if this amalgam were a prerequisite of worldly success. Thus, for example, many of the ideas about economic policy and management emanating from the universities of the rich North Atlantic countries in the years after World War II presented mass-production industry and its technological complement as the condition of industrial development. Those prestigious theories also treated the contemporary Western forms of regulated market economies and representative democracies as the sole possible institutional basis for industrial mass production outside a modernizing fascist or communist dictatorship. The same gospel, with a slightly different message, had been preached by the liberal political economists and publicists of the early nineteenth century. At that time, the institutional genealogy I labeled the mythical history was already beginning to dominate our understanding of how we came to be what we are.

Illusion, however, is not the necessary basis for the added stabilizing force a technological and organizational style achieves when it begins to spread throughout a state system. Even if the rulers of the more backward nations understand the looseness of the connections between industrial or military capabilities and ways of organizing work, or between such organizational styles and the larger institutional environment, they may well feel they lack the time to develop an alternative. For in the course of the attempt, they might be overcome from abroad or overthrown from within. Given these many inducements to imitation, it is no wonder the follow-the-leader sequence within a state system can so easily be mistaken for a spontaneous convergence, driven forward by the universal influence of the same objective constraints.

Thus far I have described how an organizational and technological style gives a second-order necessity to the institutional settlements on which it is superimposed. Let me now turn the argument around and show how this same stabilizing force creates opportunities for destabilization. To this end I begin with the international twist just discussed and then return to the core phenomenon.

The more widely diffused an organizational or technological style becomes, the greater the variety it is likely to encounter in the social and cultural environments in which it must function. The differences are bound to make the mechanical imitation of the imported technological and organizational style impractical. The institutional order and the methods of work organization in the backward country may be incapable of supporting the technological, economic, or military developments that would allow the country to catch up. Failure to promote revolutionary reform consigns the latecoming country to an ever more dependent position within the state system to which it belongs. But the effort merely to reproduce, lock, stock, and barrel, both the foreign organizational and technological style and its whole institutional setting is equally unrealistic. A practical and imaginative ordering of social life cannot be replaced, and certainly not suddenly, just because a revolutionary leadership wants to replace it in order to revise the position its country occupies within a world order. Successful imitation requires reinvention.

Consider the very common situation in which an elite of renovating reformers and discerning conservatives wants to introduce the changes needed to permit the economic development and military strengthening of their country while minimizing the disturbance to established institutions and to the group divisions or hierarchies these institutions support. This is the situation in which we would expect the stabilizing effect of the proliferation of an organizational and technological style within a state system to be at its strongest. It is therefore also the best circumstance in which to put to the test the hypothesis that this stabilizing force has destabilizing implications.

The renovating elite must identify the connections between the desired practical capabilities and their immediate setting in a form of work organization and machine design. It must also establish that accommodation between this managerial and technological style and the country's basic institutions which requires the least possible deviation from the current arrangements of the backward country. The reformers must invent the counterpart to the foreign organizational and technological style that will bring their country up to the level of the leading nations while minimizing disruption at home.

The most ingenious solutions capitalize on the distinctive characteristics of the backward country and turn what appeared to be archaic obstacles to practical use. But remember the looseness of the connection between an industrial style and an institutional order and the difficulty of developing from scratch a new approach to technology and work organization. Given this looseness and difficulty, renovating reform commonly produces two-sided results. Its managerial and technological approach may remain relatively close to the solutions favored in the original leading powers of the state system while its broader institutional settlements may be far more distinctive. The renovated formative context differs both from the old order of the reformed society and from the alien order of the foreign rivals. It represents an original creation.

The age of world history offers many examples of such national experiments in economic and military strengthening through stabilizing invention. The agent has often been a faction or a coalition of factions within the elite that identifies its own interests with the affirmation of national power and prosperity. Such reforms have continuously occurred both within and outside the West and with varying degrees of deliberation and central guidance. Thus, Wilhelmine Germany developed an organizational and technological style that differed only modestly, though tellingly, from the English original. The German economy followed the broad lines of the rigid variant of rationalized collective labor and embraced the new style of mass production. However, it also incorporated a relatively greater element of artisanal practices into industrial organization itself. It softened the contrast between task-defining and task-executing activities and multiplied intermediate work roles. At the same time the continuous processing industries in which the Germans soon came to specialize encouraged the development and deployment of less purpose-specific machines. Together with this subtle and modest originality in technological and industrial style went governmental institutions and practices that differed far more sharply from the English route to wealth and power. In Germany a more authoritarian constitution came to coexist with practices more conducive to mass mobilization to a greater extent than anything seen in nineteenth-century Britain after Chartism.

Japan provides the most notoriously successful example of conservative reform outside the West. There, the policies of the postrestoration regime were far more deliberate, and the deviations, when contrasted to the English original, far more extensive. The preexisting devices of communal organization and patron–client relations were reconstructed and superimposed upon the rigid variant of rationalized collective labor. At the same time the institutional reorganization of government assured a position of privilege to a reconstituted elite.

The German and Japanese developments exemplify the conservative absorption of a technological and organizational style by latecoming countries within a state system. Yet even this conservative style of diffusion constantly generates transformative opportunities. The successful conservative reform requires changes in the organization of labor. It even alters the basic institutions and beliefs that constrain the forms of practical collaboration in work or warfare. Shifts like these in turn suppose and produce a realignment in the definition and ranking of interests, in the character and composition of the ruling and possessing elites, and in the access of rulers and ruled, possessors and dispossessed, to governmental power. Such a realignment can never be wholly predesigned. It creates uncertainty. It generates conflict. Some groups within the elites or the working masses resist the change. Other groups quarrel over place within the new order. Such transitional disputes can easily grow in intensity and scope, and turn the conservative episode in more radical directions. The conservative reformer reckons with the existence of such struggles. Because he cannot prevent them, he must try to contain them.

It is easy to forget how conflictual even the most successful instances of conservative absorption really were. Thus, for example, the violent mass strikes and social conflicts that shook Japan in the first two decades of the twentieth century are submerged under the retrospective gloss of an institutional outcome supposedly predetermined by the cultural peculiarities and psychological predispositions of the Japanese people. In Japan, as everywhere else, the relatively conservative outcome had to be fought for long and hard before it could assume its deceptive patina of naturalness and necessity. So, too, the cases of national economic and military regression, sometimes labeled "failed modernization" (e.g., mid-twentieth century Argentina), may often best be understood as instances in which the conflict over the institutional and distributive equation of the national catching-up failed to be resolved decisively one way or another.

Pass now from the international dimension of the stabilizing aspect of the organizational and technological style to the core phenomenon itself. Even apart from its diffusion through a variety of social and cultural circumstances, the consolidation of an organizational and technological style produces opportunities for context change. An approach to management and machines never arrests completely the perception of practical productive opportunities, any more than an established scientific theory can fully block out perceptions and discoveries that threaten it. The designers of machines, the managers of work teams, and the heads of businesses have reasons of their own to seize on some of these opportunities and to begin innovating at the boundary of the current managerial and technological tradition. The significance of small-scale, opportunistic experimentation becomes clear when connected with a central hypothesis of this argument. According to the hypothesis a formative context constrains – loosely but significantly – ways of organizing work. Forms of work organization in turn limit people's ability to seize practical productive opportunities. If this hypothesis is correct, the experiments performed on the technological and organizational style must, as they accumulate, put pressure on aspects of the established institutional and imaginative framework of social life. The experiments invite yet larger experiments and, in so doing, they also create opportunities for conflict over basics.

A subsequent part of the theory of context making offers another reason to link such conflict with the progress of industrial or military capabilities. The next section of this chapter argues that under certain conditions the pressure of practical opportunity has a cumulative, directional quality. The constraints that preestablished social roles and hierarchies impose upon the forms of production and exchange must occasionally be lifted if particular classes or whole nations are to avoid defeat or eclipse at the hands of their rivals. Consequently, we must invent institutional arrangements that weaken the hold of social division and hierarchy upon our experience of sociability and soften the contrast between context-preserving routine and context-transforming conflict. The internal development of technological and organizational insight may itself make a modest but real contribution to the recognition of these larger possibilities and connections. It may therefore also help destabilize the very order that it once reinforced.

Later sections of this transformative argument play a series of variations on a practical example that illuminates the case for linking practical opportunity with institutional destabilization. This example looks to the future rather than to the past of the transformations covered by the institutional genealogy.

The changing international division of labor, with the industrialization of the top tier of third world countries, threatens the emphasis on mass-production industry and on the rigid form of rationalized collective labor in the more advanced economies. A similar effect results in the gradual change of consumption expectations and worker attitudes within the richer nations. Finally, the independent development of technology, with the invention of (computerized) general-purpose machines, both relatively cheap and able to make relatively cheap goods, pushes in the same direction. These pressures suggest the need for a greater emphasis on a type of production, work organization, and machine design hitherto largely confined to both the most advanced (capital-intensive and technologically sophisticated) and the least advanced sectors of the economy. The alternative organizational and technological style more nearly approaches the description of the flexible form of rationalized collective labor, softening the contrast between task-defining and task-executing activities.

We can imagine this shift in style accomplished under the aegis of conservative intentions, with a minimum of disruption of established institutions, just as the approach this new style is meant to displace was once absorbed, conservatively, by the elites of relatively backward countries. But the lesson remains the same. No matter how successful the conservative brand of industrial reconstruction, it requires institutional readjustments. Such readjustments disturb the established pattern of implicit accommodation among classes, communities, or segments of the work force and between these groups and national governments.

Consider an example. The erosion of traditional mass-production industry threatens the position of organized labor, entrenched in that sector of the economy. It therefore poses the issue of whether unionized labor is to continue to rely on unionization or whether labor is to be represented and empowered in an entirely different way. The conflicts invariably ignited over the forms and effects of such adjustments can be seized on and broadened by movements with more radically transformative aims. Or they can simply get out of hand and produce institutional results that none of the contenders foresaw.

The Second-Order Necessity of Formative Contexts: The Logic of Group Interests

A formative institutional and imaginative framework produces and supports a set of roles and ranks. The people who inhabit it settle down not just to particular social stations but to an order of stations, daily reaffirmed in the routines of practical collaboration and passionate attachment. These stations and routines cannot be reenacted without also being imagined. The resulting assumptions help close a social world in upon itself.

Some of the assumptions address the boundaries of collective identities. They tell each individual what groups he should consider himself a member of – what *we's* he should identify with – on the basis of his practical roles and life history. They conjure up a series of incomplete and partly contradictory but nevertheless connected and mutually reinforcing pictures of what the relevant *we's* in society are. They define and elucidate the relative authority and necessity of the many ways in which people are divided up into groups and in which groups are ranked.

Other assumptions deal with social possibilities. Such assumptions teach the individual what he may reasonably expect for himself and his family. They describe the live options among which society and therefore the groups within it must choose. They separate the practicable from the utopian, thereby also demarcating the social terrain on which – barring the unforeseeable or catastrophic – the individual knows he must move.

Yet other premises describe the content of group interests. These preconceptions define what each group's interests are and how they clash with the interests of other groups. Different groups need not – they generally do not – agree on how to define clashes of interest. But, once again, for this higher-order stability to be achieved, the disagreement must not be too radical or pervasive. It must not prevent different classes and communities from sharing the sense that they can fight for their interests without quarreling over the reconstruction of basic institutional arrangements or over the distinction between the practicable and the utopian.

The logic of group interests is the most ostentatious and operative part of these assumptions. Yet it depends for its semblance of clarity upon the other premises about social possibilities and collective identities. Only when such beliefs about possibilities and identities have begun to harden can the routinized push and shove about group interests take place.

Once assumptions about collective identities, social possibilities, and group interests have begun to form, they lend a new measure of necessity to the stabilized formative context. A world is constituted in which people know what their interests are because they take for granted all the things that make interest analysis possible. Each person becomes an informal version of the positivist social scientist, speaking the prose of a routinized social world while both invoking and concealing the institutional and imaginative framework he has come to accept unquestioningly.

An example drawn from the earlier historical narrative may help make the point. The narrative repeatedly used the pejorative label petty bourgeois to describe the single most significant set of alternatives to the institutional order that eventually became dominant in the North Atlantic countries. But this label has to be applied with many reservations. Old craft groups, new skilled workers, and small-scale proprietors, tradesmen, and farmers figured prominently in these movements. Yet the dominant self-images of these continuing insurgencies portrayed a resistance of the people against their bosses and rulers that overrode distinctions among corporate estates, classes, or segments of the work force. The subjective acceptance and construction of the gross divisions among petty bourgeois and workers did not fully take hold until the most serious early nineteenth century challenges to the ascendant institutional order had long been crushed. An additional wave of social agitation and institutional invention during the years immediately following World War I saw the development of both collective-bargaining and corporatist labor regimes. Only after these further agitations and inventions occurred did the distinction between the organized working class and the precarious or disenfranchised underclass become part of the way people understood the conflict of group interests.

An alternative approach to the hardening of group interests has to do with tangible compromises rather than intangible assumptions. It describes the development of a detailed set of explicit or implicit accommodations among social groups and of the habits and expectations, privileges and duties, that give each group a distinctive measure of access to the exercise and use of governmental power. The forging of deals among groups and between groups and governments may be no more than parallel refinements of the initial moment of context stabilization, when institutional arrangements cease to be challenged and rough compromises are worked out. But the involvement of the two refinements in each other makes a distinctive contribution to the second-order necessity of a system of group interests.

Public power becomes private privilege: governmental authority is actively enlisted in the defense of a particular allocation to groups of positions within and outside the social division of labor. At the same time, each group uses its overt or covert transactions with other groups – classes, communities, segments of the work force – to maintain a lien upon a parcel of governmental power. Neither the group bargains nor the correspondences between governmental access and factional privilege develop smoothly, free of reversals or ambiguities. Their effects cannot be counted on to harmonize. After a while, however, the two processes become entwined; each compensates for the fragility of the other. Jointly, they help shape both the concerns and the weapons of collective rivalry. The petty fears and ambitions they encourage help keep other aspirations at bay.

So long as the social peace fails to be absolute – and it never really is absolute – people continue to fight both about their perceived interests and about the institutional and imaginative framework within which those interests acquire meaning. Groups join together in ways not determined by the preexisting context, and pass from the normal struggle over interests within a structure to fighting over an aspect of the structure itself. This circumstance represents the prototype of collective mobilization.

The relation of governmental power to private interests always remains at least partly up for grabs. In all but stateless societies the disturbance of the relation between governmental power, on one side, and the system of social roles and ranks, on the other, is an indispensable part of context-transforming conflict. In collective mobilization the controversy over interests extends into conflict over the institutional and imaginative framework for interest accommodation. Similarly, in this framework-disturbing struggle over the state, the effort to harness governmental power to different factional objectives merges into a quarrel over the precise way in which governmental power should be connected or opposed to a differential ordering of group privileges.

When, at the initial moment of stabilization, context-transforming conflict is contained or interrupted, collective mobilization turns into collective contractualism: the practice of partly bargained-out and partly imposed deals between groups. These deals soon begin to seem only marginally revisable. The broadest contest over the state changes into the politics of privilege: the jockeying to move slightly up or down the ladder of access to governmental favor. The key moment of second-order stabilization takes place when the politics of privilege and the politics of collective contractualism begin to fit tightly together and thereby acquire a steadying influence that either would lack if deprived of support by the other.

Thus, for example, the position the unionized and relatively privileged sector of the labor force has come to occupy in contemporary Western democracies depends upon a long series of events that combined deals with governments and accommodations with other groups. These events include: the defeat of the more radical segments of the labor movement, sometimes by violent military action; the self-definition of the labor movement as a defense of factional interests rather than as a campaign for the general reorganization of society; the emergence of a precarious understanding between union leaders and the owners or managers of large-scale enterprise; the acceptance by organized workers of basic distinctions among job categories, each category defined by relative reward and status as well as by the content of work duties; the development of a negative solidarity against both the manager-owners and the excluded, unorganized, less advantaged segments of the work force; and active governmental involvement in the making of laws and policies that fostered the uneven organization of the working class and allowed the better organized segments of the labor force to inflate their organizational advantage by translating it into additional claims upon state power and public largesse. The key point is that from the content of the emergent institutional arrangements you could never have inferred the content of these deals and accommodations. They added something else: a new measure of naturalness and constraint.

Consider now how the hardening of a logic of group interests may generate opportunities for destabilization even as it helps stabilize a formative context. The basic reason why a logic of group interests creates transformative opportunities is that even the most routinized and closely defined assumptions about such interests suffers from persistent substantive and strategic ambiguities. These may be used to put recognized interests at odds with the established institutional and imaginative framework of social life.

The interests discriminated by such a set of assumptions are substantively ambiguous in the sense that they are never unified or detailed enough to provide the occupants of any given social station with a single uncontroversial view of their interests. Thus, similarly situated individuals and groups, or the same groups and individuals at different times, may act on distinct views of their interests. Together with the ordinary clash of interests, these uncertainties fill society with an endless petty agitation. Some conceptions of interest asserted in the midst of this Brownian motion of social life are harder to satisfy completely within the existing institutional and imaginative frameworks than others. Some therefore go farther than others in redefining current arrangements as constraints upon the fulfillment of recognized interests. There are, for example, any number of intermediate beliefs between the idea that industrial workers' sole interests are to secure their jobs, earn more money, and work less and the contrasting view that these and other interests can be fully assured only by a far-reaching reorganization of government and the economy.

Interests are ambiguous strategically as well as substantively. Alternative strategies, with very different implications for the wider social peace, promote even the most precisely defined group interest. Thus, for example, a group may pursue a narrowing tactic of preemptive security that treats all groups one rung down the ladder as rivals and adversaries. As a result, the prerogatives of the better placed group become hostage to the continued impoverishment of its immediate subordinates. Alternatively, the group may adopt a policy of broadening alliances that enlists immediate subordinates and potential rivals in the common struggle against the higher-ups. The broadening and narrowing strategies may be relatively more or less feasible and relatively harder or easier to reconcile with the received view of group interests. But there is no general reason to believe that one of the two strategies will always be more effective than the other.

Yet the strategies have radically different implications for the perpetuation of interest conflict within a social framework as opposed to conflict about the framework itself. The narrowing strategy encourages each group to cling to its established position. It thereby reinstates the received premises about identities, possibilities, and interests, and leaves unchallenged the institutional and imaginative framework on which these assumptions have been overlaid. But the broadening strategy leads back from collective contractualism to collective mobilization. What begins as a tactical alliance ends up as an enlarged collective identity. What starts as a purely instrumental effort ultimately broadens the sense of possibility. For as conflict widens and intensifies, the militants awake to the constraints that current arrangements of power and production impose upon the fulfillment of their objectives. They may even begin to experiment with small-scale versions of alternative arrangements, established by their own initiative or by the parcels of governmental power they and their allies manage to win. The fusion of collective identities and the enlargement of the sense of social possibility in turn change the preexisting definitions of group interests. The new definitions of interests encourage new conflicts and new challenges to the established context. Thus, the strategic ambiguities of interests clarify, extend, and dramatize the substantive ambiguities discussed earlier.

Consider now the promise of destabilization as it appears from the perspective of the alternative description of this source of second-order necessity: the description that emphasizes the hardened merger of governmentally supported privilege with collective contractualism. Implicit or explicit group deals and privileged liens upon governmental power are no more precise in form and unequivocal in implication than are the more intangible assumptions about identities, possibilities, and interests. They will be resisted at the margin, and what is marginally contentious can soon become more fundamentally controversial. The attempt to revise the deals and redesign the liens shades into the defiance of the formative context. If institutional changes occur, they in turn may shake up the bargains and the privileges.

The arrow of destabilization can also move in the reverse direction, from localized institutional change to fighting over the translation of institutional reform into particular deals. The readjustment of a formative context need not come from escalating conflict. It often results from more or less deliberate responses to an internal or foreign crisis. These changes from on top may be modest; but they are also common if only because formative contexts impose constraints upon the ability to seize practical productive opportunities. Thus, modest institutional reform, introduced reluctantly and belatedly to support a shift in the dominant organizational and technological style, shakes up the pattern of state-supported privilege and collective contractualism. It adds uncertainties and sparks conflicts that may be redirected to more transformative goals.

My earlier example of industrial reorganization also illustrates this form of reverse destabilization. The shift from mass production to a greater emphasis on the organizational and technological methods of vanguardist industry threatens the traditional form of unionization. It raises the question of how labor is to be empowered, whether by unionization or by alternative devices, and whether in ways that reaffirm the traditional contrasts between independent, skilled, organized workers, and underclass laborers, or in ways that override these contrasts. The new relations that need to be established among governments, business, and labor may ultimately be accomplished with a minimum of disturbance to established institutions and to the deals and privileges, the roles and hierarchies, these institutions support. But this triumph of conservative statecraft will nevertheless be conflict-ridden. The resulting disputes may serve as points of departure for wider struggles that can help change the basic forms of market economies and representative democracies.

The Second-Order Necessity of Formative Contexts: The Imagination of an Intelligible and Defensible Scheme of Human Association

Still another source of second-order necessity is the reinterpretation of a stabilized formative context as an articulate plan for human coexistence. Because the same theme is taken up again by the programmatic argument of Chapters 10 to 14, discussion of this additional link between stability and destabilization can be brief.

People come to define the restabilized arrangements and the rough compromises distinguishing the initial moment of context stabilization as a plan for coexistence in society. The plan exchanges the abstract and indeterminate idea of society for a particular model or set of models of human association. It establishes what relations among individuals can and should be like in different areas of social life.

The imaginative scheme bestows moral authority on a corrected or idealized version of current arrangements, justifying the strong in the enjoyment of power and privilege and excusing the weak from the continuation of struggle. But its contribution to the intelligibility of a pacified social order is even more basic than its support for the moral authority of this order. The imaginative scheme does not merely tell the occupants of different social stations what to expect from one another. It also provides them with an elementary grammar of social action. It enables them to participate in complicated interdependencies, practices, and institutions without having to spell out all the assumptions about the ways people are expected to act, and the meanings that actions carry, in a particular domain of social existence. The imaginative plan of social life thereby keeps people from having to deal with one another as contract partners who share little common experience or allegiance and therefore try to regulate their dealings with as much prospective detail as possible. To make a social world in this way both authoritative and intelligible is part of what is implied in giving up the fight over the further reconstruction of a formative context.

The acceptance of this intelligibility and authority comes easily. For one thing, the disturbance that precedes the initial moment of stabilization is usually localized. Many practices and preconceptions remain unchallenged. Rather than inventing a new normative practice or even an entirely new imaginative scheme, people need only continue an old practice and revise an old scheme. For another thing, the reigning view of the realistic and desirable forms of human association does not merely redescribe brutal impositions and accidental compromises. It promises to hold up an improved standard of what things should be like, a standard that can be used to criticize as well as to justify, to soften as well as to strengthen. Though the inhabitants of a stabilized social world have surrendered, even their surrender is halfhearted. Onto the revised arrangements and beliefs that emerge from the new settlement they project all their vague, confused longings for happiness and empowerment. The authoritative image of civilization into which the truce lines and trophies of conflict have been recast becomes the vehicle for aspirations left unexamined, undeveloped, and unfulfilled.

The imaginative plan may take the form of a single, exemplary model of human association, meant to be realized with suitable adjustments throughout all areas of social practice. We usually find such a unitary, recurrent standard of sociability accepted in societies with very entrenched frameworks and in cultures that enshrine highly restrictive assumptions about the possible forms of personal and social experience. The characteristic content of this one-model scheme is the patron–client ideal that seeks to combine, in the same relations, practical exchange, communal loyalty, and outright subjugation.

In societies less submissive to the constraints of false necessity the dominant ways of imagining the possible and desirable forms of human association characteristically assign different models of human coexistence to distinct realms of social practice. Thus, in the late twentieth century North Atlantic countries whose formative contexts I have earlier studied, people thought of practical exchange, communal loyalties, and nonreciprocal power as mutually repellent forms of experience. They credited an ideal of private community, meant to be realized in the life of family and friendship; an ideal of democratic participation and accountability, addressed to the organization of government and the exercise of citizenship; and an amalgam of voluntary contract and impersonal technical hierarchy or coordination, suited to the practical world of work and exchange. Moreover, they implicitly identified each of these ideals with particular practices and institutions. Thus, people meant by democracy not only the ill-defined aspirations that their slogans and speculative theories proclaimed but a historically unique way of organizing governments and partisan conflict.

The relation of legal doctrine to beliefs about the possible and desirable forms of human association is instructive. In societies less cracked open to politics legal doctrine can openly refer to a background scheme of models of human association, which are alleged to be inscribed in the permanent requirements of human nature and social order when they are not also mandated by divine authority. But in societies that have moved farther toward disentrenchment and antinaturalistic skepticism, such a style of legal doctrine becomes unacceptable. For the explicit invocation of such overarching standards of possible and desirable human association is now feared to embroil the legal analyst in the open-ended controversies of the ideologue or the propagandist. It therefore threatens to reopen the conflict over the basic terms of social life. Under these circumstances, legal analysis can neither avow nor avoid relying upon such assumptions about the possible and desirable forms of human association. For lawyers cannot relinquish such assumptions without either presenting the law as merely an expression of interest-group or class conflict or attempting to keep legal reasoning very close to narrow precedent and narrow construction. Those who would use legal doctrine to give the social order the gloss of a higher-order rationality now face a more formidable obstacle.*

The imaginative scheme of models of possible and desirable association also lives, in a looser and messier form, in popular consciousness. The classes and communities that make up society give their own distinctive twists to the dominant vision of possible and desirable human association. Much in their professed ideas or implicit assumptions about what relations among people should be like in different realms of social existence may be incompatible with the beliefs of other groups or with the legal, moral, and partisan discourse of the wealthy and the powerful. But unless the country is ruled by a conquest elite alien to the native inhabitants, or unless insulated and antagonistic groups coexist with an imposed structure, we can expect to find a more subtle and contradictory imaginative scheme – or rather a series of overlapping and analogous schemes. The difference between the informal vision of authoritative models of human coexistence and the vision presupposed by elite discourses such as legal doctrine usually resembles the relation of a natural language to an impoverished computer language. Yet the substantive themes of the richer language will carry over, truncated and biased, into the poorer counterpart.

Whether the imaginative scheme is unitary or pluralistic and whether it takes its more elitist and systematic or more popular and contradictory

* See *The Critical Legal Studies Movement*, Harvard University Press, Cambridge, 1986.

forms, it exercises a retrospective stabilizing influence upon a social order. Any marked deviation by an individual from social norms begins to appear selfish and antisocial whatever its actual motives. Any conflict that defies the scheme seems to threaten civilization itself, if not in the large then in the small, in the detailed pieties by which people evaluate one another and in the implicit assumptions that sustain trust and permit communication.

But, like its counterparts, such a stabilizing force generates destabilizing opportunities. To show how these opportunities arise, take an imaginative ordering of social life at its clearest and most coherent, as it can be found in the elite discourses of legal doctrine or speculative moral and programmatic controversy. Ideal images of human association can always be plausibly interpreted in different ways. These ambiguities remain concealed and contained so long as each such image is represented by distinctive practices or institutions in well-defined areas of social life. The amalgam of ideal understandings, representative practices, and domains of application supports the sense of assurance.

But there is always at least a residual uncertainty about the practical forms that properly represent a model of association and the exact domain of social practice in which it can realistically and suitably be applied. Moreover, different classes, communities, and movements of opinion believe themselves to have an interest in seeing these marginal uncertainties resolved in some ways rather than others. Thus, people quarrel about the resolution of the ambiguities. They quarrel by the crude and open methods of factional or class rivalry and in the refined, secluded forms of legal and philosophical controversy.

This small-time bickering can escalate, either because it simply gets out of hand or because a transformative movement deliberately exploits and aggravates it. The result is to disturb the apparent fit among the authoritative images of coexistence, their practical representations, and their areas of application. Such disturbances force people to choose among different interpretations of the antecedent, largely implicit ideals of human association. Some interpretations fit with the current institutional order and reaffirm the dominant models of human coexistence; but others can inspire challenges to the institutional order and begin to unravel the imaginative scheme. For the meanings we confer on these received and enacted conceptions of sociability are never fully exhausted by the practices and institutions that stand for them in particular compartments of social life. Beliefs about how people ought to deal with one another in particular areas of society are more than readily applicable dogmas. They also serve as bearers of ill-defined aspirations for empowerment and mutual acceptance. They are therefore instruments of a mental reservation by which people who seem to have surrendered unreservedly to a particular institutional and imaginative framework continue to nurture a measure of secret independence and unfulfilled yearning. Two analytically distinct but ordinarily overlapping processes can play out this potential ambivalence in the relation of a scheme of authoritative models of association to a stabilized formative context.

First, there are horizontal conflicts. Uncertainty and disagreements always persist about the exact range of social practice to which different models of human coexistence should apply. The great amount of practical and imaginative material resisting assimilation to the formative context adds to the confusion. The resulting border disputes – conflicts over where to draw the line between different ideals and between the domains of social life to which they apply – become topics of speculative moral and ideological debates or of factional conflicts and social experiments. Such border disputes produce a constant pushing and shoving of familiar ideals onto slightly unfamiliar social territory. As such projections or displacements multiply, people begin to disagree about the practical forms that a given image of human association should assume when enacted in an area of social practice from which it has hitherto been excluded. This disagreement exposes the hidden ambiguities of the traditional models and the multiplicity of framework-preserving and framework-transforming uses to which they may be put.

Consider, for example, the implications of attempting to extend the democratic ideal into industrial organization. Whatever democracy may mean in this setting it cannot mean carrying on with the traditional forms of the tripartite state or with the current mechanisms of democratic representation and accountability. If industrial democracy is interpreted to mean a limited level of worker participation in business decisions it may be accommodated without major disturbance to the established institutional and imaginative framework. Suppose, however, it is understood to require a shift in the basic form of capital allocation and of control over investment decisions. It will then also shake up the imaginative vision that contrasts an area reserved for democratic principles with a realm governed by voluntary contract and technical hierarchy. This imaginative disturbance may radiate outward, challenging every part of the dominant vision of social proprieties and possibilities.

There are vertical as well as horizontal conflicts. Even within the core area of social practice traditionally assigned to a particular model of human association, discrepancies and doubts will arise about its appropriate practical form. The marginal conflicts that seize on these disharmonies may be further aggravated by the sense that all the established practical realizations of the ideal fail to do it justice, that they betray its promise. There is always an indefinite penumbra of aspiration that intimates more – more by way of empowerment or solidarity – than can be found in public dogma and established practice. Such variations and tensions feed conflict. And the conflict once again reveals the ambiguities of the received models of sociability and demonstrates their ambivalent relation to the institutional arrangements they ordinarily help justify.

Thus, in the contemporary industrial democracies the blend of technical hierarchy and voluntary contract takes different forms in sectors of the economy that either strengthen or soften the contrast between task-defining and task-executing activities. Widely recognized moral assumptions identify personal subjugation as the exemplary social evil. Neither individual and collective contract nor alleged technical necessity suffice to lift the experienced burden of subjugation from the experience of work in the areas of the economy that most starkly contrast task definers and task executors. Workers continue to suffer strongly felt experiences of powerlessness and humiliation. The vanguard sectors of the economy offer a visible though limited example of an alternative style of work organization. Radical critics have argued that this alternative can be extended and generalized through much of the economy. But extension and generalization cannot ultimately succeed without a series of cumulative changes in the organization of power and production. Nor, once realized, can they be reconciled with ruling beliefs about the proper contrast between the domain of representative democracy and the realm of contract and technical hierarchy.

The Escalation of Conflict: The Unavailability of Necessary and Sufficient Conditions

The main theme of the preceding discussion has been the tightness of the link between stabilization and destabilization, the transformative opportunities generated by the very forces that impart a retrospective, second-order necessity to a stabilized context. An endless series of petty quarrels, a permanent Brownian motion, keep even the most pacified social world in contained but irrepressible agitation. The deep-structure social theorist dismisses these low-level disturbances as trivial, identifying in them either a random and unproductive strife or a confirmation of the lawlike routines of an established social order. He sees a basic discontinuity between these controversies and the conflicts that accompany the replacement of one order by another. The positivist social scientist, on the contrary, exalts this constant bickering as the true stuff of social life: the exercise of problem solving and interest accommodation that plays so large a role in his understanding of society. But because he systematically disregards or avoids the distinction between routines and frameworks and the influence of frameworks and framework revision on the problems that chiefly concern him, he cannot see the Brownian motion for what it is. He cannot recognize the nature and extent of its transformative promise or achieve a comprehensive and unified view of its many forms.

The small-scale, contained fighting engendered by each form of second-order necessity may escalate at any time. The subjective sign of escalation is the growing intensity of the fighting. The more tangible, external sign is the widening scope of the conflict: both by the involvement of more groups in the struggle and by the concern with an ever broader range of issues.

The special meaning of escalation, however, is the step-by-step passage from context-preserving to context-transforming conflicts. The quarrels about practical adjustments, collective identities, and moral ideals that take the framework for granted pass into struggles that bring the framework into question.

The escalation may be the work of a movement that sees its opportunity in the extension of petty bickering. Or it may be the involuntary consequence of conflicts getting out of hand. In this event, the expanded struggle shows its transformative significance only retrospectively. Much more often, foresight and accident combine to cause escalation.

A critic may object that we have explained little until we have established the necessary and sufficient conditions for escalation. But a corollary of one major thesis of this book is that we cannot draw up such a list of necessary and sufficient conditions. The problem does not result merely from a limited and remediable defect in our knowledge, as if we could approach the desired outcome by thinking a little harder or discovering a little more. The facts about social reality and social change condemn this search to disappointment. To believe in the existence of such a list, or in the possibility of gradually revealing it, we have to believe in something that at least resembles deep-structure social theory. We have to believe that context change, and therefore also context selection, are governed by lawlike constraints or developmental tendencies. (The polemic against the style of explanation by necessary and sufficient conditions continues, in different form, later in this account of society making.)

Instead of necessary and sufficient conditions, the view presented here recognizes that some circumstances regularly encourage escalation while others discourage it. Prominent among the escalation-favoring circumstances are middle-level crises, such as those provoked by the need to reform basic institutional arrangements in response to military and economic rivalry from abroad or to shifts in the relative size and wealth of different sectors of the population. A skillful and lucky transformative practice, however, may cause escalation to take place even in the absence of such favoring conditions. Conversely, the most favorable opportunity may be squandered. Most importantly, the antecedent institutions and preconceptions and the schemes of social division and hierarchy they support never predetermine the outcome of escalating conflict, any more than they predetermine its occurrence or scope. The underdetermined choice of trajectories by different groups and governments and the relative insight or illusion, skill or ineptitude, with which people pursue these chosen trajectories help shape the final result. (The programmatic argument of Chapters 10 to 14 considers the favoring and disfavoring circumstances of escalation. This consideration establishes one of many links between the explanatory and programmatic ideas of *False Necessity*.)

Convinced determinists may resist this defense of the refusal to describe the necessary and sufficient conditions for the extension of conflict and the transformative use of the Brownian motion. They may argue that when we look more closely we always find causes that explain the occurrence, scope, and outcome of escalation, causes that range from the momentary situation of a society to the details of individual biography. They may even insist that all these causes connect, at least from the idealized standpoint of a Laplacean mind. Nothing in this or any other part of the explanatory argument of *False Necessity* depends on the refutation of such determinists. It is unnecessary to take a position with respect to their claims. The narrower aim of the approach to context change taken here is to free social explanation from the assumptions of both deep-structure analysis and conventional social science: to respect the distinction between structure and routine while denying that the identity, actualization, or succession of formative contexts is governed by higher-order laws or by deep-seated economic, psychological, and organizational constraints.

Of course, this view of context change would lose much of its authority if our subjective experience of reconstructive freedom were illusory (though remember that there is always the habitual hedge of the speculative monist, who holds that phenomenal distinctions are only *ultimately* illusory). But it is no part of this argument to deal with the metaphysical conundrums of free will and determinism and to show in precisely what sense the experience of freedom harmonizes with the practice of causal explanation. We already do something to vindicate our reconstructive powers when we loosen the link between our interest in the generality of our social explanations and the habit of portraying ourselves as the passive objects of social worlds. We do even better when we are able to show that such worlds differ radically in the constraints they impose upon their own remaking.

The Brownian motion of social life – the emergence of destabilizing opportunity out of stabilizing methods – provides the occasion for influences that may shape long-term context change. These influences, working in concert or in opposition, account for a remarkable possibility. Contexts may change in quality as well as content. They vary in the force with which they imprison the people who move within them. The discussion now turns to the sources of possible long-term, directional change.

8

Negative Capability and Plasticity into Power

The Core Idea

THE very devices that stabilize formative contexts endlessly produce the occasions and instruments of destabilization. The escalation of framework-preserving routines into framework-transforming conflicts creates an opportunity for two great influences upon context making. These influences differ from the mechanisms of stability and destabilization just discussed in that they account for the *possibility* of cumulative context change in a certain direction, not just for the precariousness of every established order. In particular, they give us the prospect of changing over time the quality as well as the content of our formative institutional and imaginative structures: the relation of these structures to our structure-revising capabilities. These long-term influences upon context change share with the mechanisms of stability and destabilization the power to present the transformative will with opportunities as much as with constraints. They certify that no ultimate incompatibility holds between the radical project and the nature of social reality.

Consider what would happen if such long-term influences did not exist and if we were left with only the mechanisms of stability and destabilization and with an open list of circumstances that either favor or discourage the escalation of framework-preserving conflict. We would have trouble explaining how or why the component elements of each formative context stick together and reinforce one another. For our ideas about the internal constitution of social orders are always just the reverse side of our beliefs about how such orders change. We might even find it hard to resist the slide into positivist social science, with its disregard for the significance of the distinction between framework and routine and its picture of social life as a series of exercises in interest accommodation and problem solving.

If we nevertheless managed to rescue the distinction between the forming structure and the formed routines, we would have no basis for believing in selective constraints upon the replacement or recombination of the elements composing a formative context. Thus, we might be drawn to a truncated version of deep-structure social theory, seeing the institutional and imaginative frameworks of social life as indivisible but ultimately arbitrary – there, but there for no good reason. If in turn we succeeded in avoiding this conclusion we would still have no reason to hope to become more fully the masters of the social orders that we construct. History would be a procession of conditional social worlds: each a law unto itself, each conditional in the same sense as the others. The radical project would therefore be based upon an illusion, at least if it is true that the disengagement of social life from structures of dependence and domination requires that no major aspect of social organization remain shielded against challenge and conflict.

This section is devoted to the most controversial of the two long-run influences upon context change, which is also the influence most directly relevant to the attempt to change the relation between freedom and structure. Formative contexts and the extended sets of arrangements and preconceptions that constitute them vary with respect to the quality I called disentrenchment, denaturalization, or emancipation from false necessity. This quality has two aspects; that these aspects are connected is an empirical claim.

One aspect of disentrenchment is the degree to which a formative context can be challenged in the midst of ordinary social life. A structure is entrenched or naturalized to the extent that it prevents such challenge, and it is disentrenched or denaturalized insofar as it facilitates the challenge. On an equivalent definition, disentrenchment implies a shortening of the distance to traverse before our context-preserving activities can become context-transforming activities. It is the relative facility with which we can interrupt the oscillation between the narcoleptic routines and the revolutionary interludes of history and achieve conscious mastery in the midst of civic peace. Moreover, a more disentrenched structure designs this greater opportunity for revision into the very activities on which its reproduction depends.

The other aspect of disentrenchment is the relative disengagement of our practical and passionate dealings from a preexisting structure of roles and hierarchies. In this sense, disentrenchment is the diminishment of the influence that the social station of the individual – of the place he occupies in the contrast of categories, classes, communities, and genders – exercises over his life chances and experiences. It is the lifting of the grid of social division and ranking from our practical and passionate relations to one another.

The connection between the two sides of denaturalization is far from self-evident. There are no scripts for particular social roles and ranks until the institutional and imaginative assumptions that define a particular version of social life become secure. Such assumptions cannot in turn become secure unless they provide for their own relative immunity to attack. They do so by forming routines – of economic exchange, factional conflict, and normative controversy – that take established institutions and preconceptions for granted. Earlier discussion has emphasized that the contrast between stabilizing and destabilizing activities can never be absolute. The concept of disentrenchment implies that the contrast is variable as well as relative.

These clarifications help introduce the main thesis of this part of the view of context making. Disentrenchment of formative contexts provides societies with a range of material and intangible advantages, all the way from the encouragement of the development of productive capabilities to the exercise of a more conscious mastery over social circumstance. In fact, all the varieties of individual and collective empowerment seem to be connected in one way or another with the mastery the concept of disentrenchment or denaturalization describes. I call these varieties of empowerment "negative capability" when considering them in relation to the context change that makes them possible. Thus, we may use the poet's turn of phrase to label the empowerment that arises from the denial of whatever in our contexts delivers us over to a fixed scheme of division and hierarchy and to an enforced choice between routine and rebellion.

It should already be clear from the definition of disentrenchment that the route to negative capability is not a leap into anarchy, permanent flux, or mere indefinition. The institutional and imaginative frameworks that strengthen our negative capability are no less particular and no less capable of being described than frameworks relatively lower on the scale of disentrenchment. Thus, for example, the actual institutions and guiding doctrines of the liberal bourgeois democracies are less entrenched and more favorable to negative capability than the arrangements and dogmas of the European absolutist monarchies they succeeded. The hypothetical institutions and doctrines of the empowered democracy described by the later programmatic arguments of this book are in turn just as distinctive as the versions of representative democracy and market economy they are intended to replace.

To be sure, the less entrenched structures are by definition more open to revision in the midst of ordinary social life. But they are not therefore more unstable, except in the very special sense in which a circumstance of frequent, partial adjustments can be said to be more unstable than a situation of rigid structures, periodically disrupted by sudden, major transformations. Rigidity is not stability, nor does the increased transparency and revisability of our practices mean we will want constantly to revise them. The liberal bourgeois democracies have been no less stable – though stable in a different sense – than the absolutist monarchies before them. Moreover, because disentrenchment involves a weakening of the mechanisms of dependence and domination, ordinary working men and women have been more rather than less secure in these democracies.

The attractions of negative capability account for the possibility of a cumulative movement toward greater disentrenchment. In some instances this movement may result from a more or less deliberate striving for the advantages of denaturalization. In other instances the movement may be explained by a social counterpart to Darwinian natural selection: societies achieving the advantages of greater disentrenchment are that much more likely to survive in the economic and ideological struggle with their rivals, and their styles of organization and vision are therefore also that much more likely to proliferate. But by far the most common way in which the advantages of disentrenchment account for the emergence and persistence of more denaturalized formative contexts does not fit into either the intentionalist or the Darwinian mold. This most common and distinctive form of agency requires special analysis.

The idea of negative capability as an influence represents a frankly functionalist or ideological element in the theory of context making. The appearance and propagation of less entrenched institutional and imaginative orders is explained by the consequences they may produce – the development of negative capability. But qualifications, soon to be discussed, diminish the functionalist character of this idea. For one thing, countervailing forces may override the attractions of negative capability. The most important of these is the ability of coercive surplus extraction, based on relatively more entrenched orders and on the hierarchies they sustain, to serve as a rival basis – and in certain circumstances even a stronger basis – for the development of productive or destructive capabilities. Moreover, the forms of empowerment summarized under the heading "negative capability" can advance through alternative packages of institutional arrangements. Some alternatives jeopardize other non-economic varieties of empowerment. The most important consequence of such qualifications is that every advance toward greater negative capability is precarious and reversible, not just susceptible to being deflected into a minor and temporary epicycle.

The influence of negative capability operates on the institutional and imaginative materials generated by particular historical sequences of context making. These sequences in turn constrain only loosely and fitfully our capacities of resistance and invention. Thus, there is no limited list of institutional systems that consitute the necessary vehicles of any given level of negative capability. To speak of an advance in negative capability is not to specify the particular institutional and imaginative forms the advance must take. Nor does a cumulative movement toward less naturalistic orders imply any preestablished evolutionary sequence of institutional systems and social dogmas awaiting a chance to advance to the next step.

When you add up all these qualifications, the result is not to take back the thesis about negative capability but, rather, to detach the thesis from the prejudices of evolutionary, deep-structure social analysis. What emerges is the conception of a possible progression, which presents the radical project with its chance. The ideas that make sense of the notion of a possible move toward more revisable and hierarchy-subverting structures run together with the ideas that justify a commitment to the radical project. For the thesis of negative capability has a prominent role in a view of the conditions of human empowerment and of the means by which we may limit more successfully the part played by dependence and depersonalization in our dealings with one another.

From the vantage point of this preliminary statement, look back once again to the polemical genealogy in the first part of this chapter. Emerging economic, legal, and governmental institutions were all less naturalistic than the arrangements they replaced. The advantages they made available may help explain their appearance and success. Further analysis must specify the mechanisms by which these advantageous consequences helped bring more denaturalized contexts into being.

The institutional and imaginative materials with which such transformations worked were unique to European history. But the solutions developed out of such materials proved exemplary. The dominant institutional and imaginative orders of the world-conquering Western powers appeared as the setting for a quantum leap in the development of economic and military capabilities. They also provided a basis for a relatively greater emancipation of communal life and individual self-expression from pre-existing roles and hierarchies. No wonder that conquest often proved unnecessary to spread European arrangements. Reforming elites anxious to secure similar benefits for themselves and their countries accomplished what conquerors did not. It took time to discover that such benefits could be given institutional and imaginative foundations radically different from the formative contexts of the pioneering Western countries. But the classic European social theorists wrote at a time when these alternative possibilities had not yet become apparent. They were therefore tempted to misunderstand the triumphant European settlements as the necessary form of a stage in world history.

Remember also that these prevalent European solutions were far from secure or self-evident within the European world itself. Throughout the history of their development they had to accommodate to rival institutional ideas. In fact, the most significant rival – the alternative whose economic aspect I have been calling petty commodity production – might well have gone farther than the now dominant economic and governmental arrangements in promoting negative capability. But to make their cause practicable, the advocates of the petty bourgeois alternative would have had to find new ways to organize representative democracies and market economies.

From this initial exposition it should already be clear that the thesis about negative capability requires two key analytical refinements. The first is to distinguish the varieties of empowerment the idea of negative capability encompasses and to show how each aspect of empowerment depends on the invention of more disentrenched, revisable institutions. The second refinement is to solve the problem of agency. We must describe how the ability of certain arrangements to encourage an advance in negative capability helps cause their emergence and persistence. We need to understand the mechanisms by which the functional consequence or advantage becomes an explanatory cause.

The Practical Advantages of Disentrenchnent

The most tangible instance of negative capability is the development of the productive and destructive powers of society. The idea of a connection between institutional disentrenchment and practical empowerment merely appropriates and generalizes a familiar belief about requirements of practical progress. The narrower and relatively precise version of this idea is the thesis that economic rationality or efficiency requires the freedom to combine and substitute to best advantage the factors of production. The relatively broader and vaguer form of the notion is the idea that maximum flexibility serves practical success.

Our practical activities are opportunistic. They require the constant substitution of resources and the revision of technical and organizational means in the light of changing circumstances. To be sure, they also demand a framework of shared understandings and practices so that not everything has to be constantly reinvented or fought over. But to ensure worldly success we must be able to revise this framework in the light of emergent practical opportunities. We must not allow it to predetermine the way we combine with one another and with machines in our joint practical endeavors. More specifically, the keynote of practical reason and of rationalized collective labor is the continuous interplay between the definition of ends and the choice of means, the setting of tasks and the operational activities designed to carry them out. The organization of human labor and its coordination with the material and technical resources at its disposal should become a visible image of practical reason. Conversely, the idea of practical reason translates a view of flexible, self-correcting teamwork into a conception of individual mental activity. In order to make our practical collaborative ventures a more faithful image of practical reason, we must weaken the influence of preestablished social roles and hierarchies upon the relations among co-workers. We must not allow fixed rules to predetermine the ways in which the holders of particular jobs, or the members of particular communities or ranks, may deal with one another. We must crack the routines of practical life open to the recombinational activity of practical reason. The same changes that enable a formative institutional and imaginative context to loosen the hold of social roles and hierarchies also diminish the contrast between context-preserving routine and context-transforming conflict.

Consider from another angle the link between disentrenchment and the development of practical productive and destructive capabilities. The organizational style of economic or military teams limits the full development and exploitation of a technological capability. The broader institutional setting of governments and economies in turn constrains the organization of the work group. The work team cannot be flexible unless its internal life comes partly out from under the influence of a scheme of social stations. Practical empowerment requires institutions and preconceptions that permanently weaken social divisions and diminish the arbitrary, recalcitrant just-thereness of our social orders.

Here is a typical, narrowly focused example. The decades preceding the French Revolution saw the development of lighter and more accurate artillery pieces. The armies of revolutionary France were able to take the fullest advantage of these new weapons by innovating in battle tactics and troop deployment. The dense military formations then in use favored rigid forward marching procedures. Such units could not deploy on the field with the flexibility needed to take maximum advantage of potential combinations of infantry and light artillery. At the same time traditional military formations offered an easy target for the more accurate guns, manned by more flexible adversaries.

The prerevolutionary social situation influenced the preferred tactics and deployments of the prerevolutionary armies. In an army like the German one, of sullen serfs and near serfs, pressed into dynastic wars whose aims they did not share or even understand and lacking nationalist ardor, officers feared their men would break and run away as the moment of battle approached. Often, a row of special soldiers with stretched bayonets had to walk at the back of each unit, literally propping forward the reluctant warriors. The armies of revolutionary France found it relatively easy to adopt thinner formations and more supple tactical procedures. They had better reason to count on the discretion and loyalty of soldiers who were called to defend a national and popular revolution beleaguered by absolutist monarchies.

Thus, successful use of the new technological opportunity required a new organizational style. The institutional and spiritual inventions on which the style depended convinced the soldiery that the army belonged to the nation and that the nation did not just belong to privileged elites. Multiply this particular example many times over, to cover other aspects of military technology, organization, and strategy, and you can begin to see that the armies of revolutionary and Napoleonic France had at least one major advantage in their wars with their Continental adversaries.

The story does not end here. The enemies of France could not exploit the new technological and tactical opportunities presented by such developments as the improved artillery pieces without changing the institutional form of the state and the relation of the ruling and possessing elites to the working people. But France's rivals did not need to change the ancien régime as much or as violently as the French revolutionists had set out to do. They required only the measure of popular reform needed to justify a sense of national community (even right-wing nationalism had to make concessions to egalitarianism) and to enlarge the influence of merit-based recruitment and promotion in military and governmental organization. In the age of Stein and Hardenberg, the Prussian military reformers demonstrated what successful conservative reformers rediscover: that they can have their cake and eat it too. They can reconcile the measure of institutional disentrenchment needed to take advantage of current technological and organizational opportunities with a suitable version of the present plan of social division and hierarchy. The jeopardized elites fail when they feel compelled to choose between trying to reproduce a foreign institutional example and rejecting reform outright, for fear it may inevitably shake the established social order to the ground. Thus, for example, the Mamluk state in Egypt lost its ability to resist Ottoman attack when it refused to shift its military emphasis from cavalry to armed infantry. As an alien, corporately organized ruling class, the Mamluks (or, rather, the Mamluk leaders) felt unable to disengage their apparatus of rule and their collective identity from a cavalry-based military organization.

Some may object that the example of the light artillery pieces lacks broader significance. Other productive or destructive faculties might not make any demands on the broader institutional and social environment. Such powers might even require more rigidity and hierarchy rather than more flexibility and equality. The thesis of negative capability in the practical domain does indeed presuppose a belief in the possible pre-eminence of cumulative disentrenchment as an enabling social condition of the development of practical capabilities. A defensible version of the thesis of negative capability must recognize that the coercive extraction of resources and manpower, supported by more entrenched contexts and more rigid roles and hierarchies, can provide an alternative basis for the development of productive or destructive forces. The question is whether this entrenchment-based alternative can be given its due weight within a theory that nevertheless continues to see in cumulative disentrenchment at least a possible axis of practical progress.

Institutional arrangements that help reproduce rigid roles and hierarchies can certainly serve as a basis for coercive surplus extraction. Hierarchical duties, enforced and sanctified by challenge-resistant institutions and arrangements, encourage the near automatic transfer of material and manpower resources to limited elites. This device has the formidable practical advantage of making the confiscation of resources appear to be the unavoidable implication of a moral or natural order rather than a result of will and conflict. After all, the human sense of institutional entrenchment is to make the order of social life appear more like a natural fact than like a political artifact. In the relatively more entrenched order the concentration of claims to capital and labor is that much more likely to be taken for granted and that much less likely to be disturbed by threats, deals, and challenges. But the cost is to limit the capacity of experimenting with combinations of resources, machines, and labor and with alternative forms of exchange and production.

Surely in certain historical situations the practical advantages of disentrenchment fall below the practical benefits of coercive surplus extraction. But what are these situations? They seem to be ones in which the creation of a surplus of labor and capital over current consumption remains the overriding practical problem of society, towering over the problems of technological innovation and organizational flexibility.

You may be tempted to say that such is precisely the condition of all societies, at least until they achieve prodigious wealth and come close to eliminating economic scarcity. But in fact it seems to be the circumstance only of very poor countries – of countries poorer than the more prosperous agrarian-bureaucratic empires of world history or than early modern European nations before the onset of the industrial revolution. Economists and historians have repeatedly shown how hard it is to explain sudden surges in productive output and productivity – such as the series of events we call the industrial revolution – by reference to differences in social-savings rates. Often, both the general rate of saving and the amount of surplus coercively appropriated by economic or governmental elites seem to have been even higher in economically stagnant societies than in countries making a quantum leap in their productive capabilities. The main point about nineteenth-century England in contrast to, say, Ch'ing China, is not that the English saved or skimmed off more than the Chinese but that they used resources, performed activities, ran organizations, and recombined factors of production in different ways. The need for surplus extraction does not disappear but becomes subsidiary to the manner of use.

We have an additional reason to think that the practical advantages of entrenchment are more limited than they may at first appear. Not all coercive surplus extraction depends upon rigid social roles and hierarchies, nor is the route to emancipation from false necessity always uncoercive. The opening of social life to practical experimentation may occur through consensual, decentralized, and participatory methods or through centralized command and coercion. The institutions that make this opening possible may advance toward a radical democracy that destroys privileged holds upon the resources for society making. But such institutions may also move toward a mobilizational dictatorship that relentlessly subjects social life to plans imposed by a central authority, willing and able to recombine people and resources. From the narrow standpoint of encouraging the development of practical capabilities, the risk of the consensual path is that decentralized, participatory claims will harden into a system of vested rights that narrows the area of social life open to practical innovation. From the same limited perspective the risk of the dictatorial route is that the willingness to exploit practical productive opportunities will be sacrificed to the power interests of the central authorities.

A mobilizational despotism should not be mistaken for an entrenched order of division and hierarchy, although each of the two may serve as a basis for the development of practical capabilities and although many societies in the age of mass politics have regularly combined aspects of both. The mobilizational dictatorship reaches for negative capability through coercive means. It therefore attempts to crush all intermediate corporate bodies, all independently organized social ranks, communities, and local governments. Its distinctive economic ambition is not merely to extract a surplus but to recombine and reorganize and to keep reorganizing and recombining. Long ago social theorists such as Tocqueville understood that a new breed of democracies and despotisms shared both a hostility to stable orders of social division and hierarchy and a willingness to treat social relations as subjects for practical experiment. Modern planning dictatorships characteristically engage in a quest for greater negative capability. Forced recombination rather than naturalistic entrenchment is their thing. Once we understand their distinctiveness the historical role of the search for practical progress through entrenchment begins to look much more limited.

Compare the thesis of negative capability to the Marxist thesis about class society and the development of the productive forces. The sequence of modes of production depicted by Marxism portrays all historical societies as driven forward by the logic of coercive surplus extraction based upon class hierarchies and upon the institutionally defined relations of production that such hierarchies require. Primitive communism is egalitarian. But under primitive communism people remain enslaved to both material scarcity and unreflective tradition. Mankind must undergo the immense, painful detour of class society and class conflict before it can attain through communism a higher because freer form of the equality it possessed under primitive communism.

Yet the evolutionary scheme of historical materialism includes a significant minor theme that we can reinterpret as a special case of the thesis of negative capability. The sequence of modes of production is also a series of steps toward the assertion of the free-floating, unitary, universal quality of labor. The divisions and hierarchies of class society mask and constrain this quality. Thus, though capitalism may aggravate many aspects of class oppression and working-class misery, it also reveals more clearly than its predecessor modes of production the interchangeable character of all human labor power. The despotism of capital may take charge of the modern factory. But this despotism tears down barriers to the free recombination of men and machines. At the same time the primacy of exchange values over use values in the sphere of circulation, combined with the relentless treatment of labor as a commodity, emphasizes the convertibility of all forms of productive activity into all other forms.

In Marx's writings these ideas, so close to the thesis of negative capability, remain imprisoned within an evolutionary variant of deep-structure social theory. Moreover, Marx fails to draw the distinction between coercive surplus extraction, based upon entrenched hierarchies, and experimental recombination, premised on institutional disentrenchment. The absence of any counterpart to this distinction is, to use the language of his followers, no accident. For historical materialism sacrifices the insight into negative capability to the belief that the emergence of communism represents the single decisive and definitive turn from necessity to freedom.

A Comparative Historical Perspective on the Thesis of Negative Capability

Consider how this discussion of the development of the economic aspects of negative capability relates to the character of the institutional arrangements whose emergence the earlier schematic narrative studied. The new forms of agrarian and industrial organization exhibited aspects of coercive surplus extraction. The legal rights and governmental institutions sustaining them made possible a basic continuity of the elites. In their historical setting, the engrossment of leaseholds and the factory system represented advances in the degree of command over large pools of land, capital, and labor that could be exercised by large-scale enterprises.

However, once you locate these organizational shifts in a broader comparative-historical background it becomes clear that the refinement of coercive command was only part of the story. The new coercive arrangements did not merely embody new forms of entrenchment. They also reflected more disentrenched arrangements. Agrarian concentration was a qualitative as well as a quantitative process: the single, consolidated right to a piece of land replaced the coexistence of many claims, vested in different rightholders. If the quantitative side of this shift contributed to the development of the factory system by making more labor available, the qualitative side contributed by helping destroy the constraints of clientalistic relations between social superiors and subalterns. The qualitative shift took place even where the quantitative change remained modest: in the regions where smallholding and small-scale manufacturing achieved their greatest vitality.

I have emphasized that the new system of contract and property rights coexisted first with estatist prerogatives, specific to a particular social rank or corporate body, and then, increasingly, with methods of organizational discipline and surveillance that were justified in the name of technical necessity. The classical system of private rights allowed the persistence of entrenchment-based coercive surplus extraction. The latter-day disciplinary techniques, on the contrary, stood for coercive forms of practical experiment and disentrenchment. The universalistic system of property and contract rights provided a legal structure for recombining resources, people, and practices, even though it was worked out and compromised in ways that remained biased toward an authoritarian contrast between task definers and task executors. The early liberal and utilitarian propagandists of the new order were correct to see a promise of free social experimentation in the ascendancy of the new system of universalistic rights. Their mistake was to sanctify the particular form and content of these rights and to misunderstand the compromises that qualified and even inverted the real social meaning of the entitlements.

Every major aspect of early modern European society confirms the reality of this heightened availability of social life to willful experimentation.

The early factory was not only an organization for controlling workers; it was also a method for rearranging people and machines in ways not predetermined by any social script. You can say the same, on a larger scale, when you look beyond the early factory to the society in which it appeared. The absolutist monarchies of the period, and the people who staffed the emerging central governments, may seem to have been only barely capable of acting with a measure of independence from landowning or mercantile elites. Yet when you compare these states to the central governments of the major agrarian-bureaucratic states of past history, you see that the new Western regimes had become immensely less vulnerable to the crises that periodically fragmented the agrarian bureaucratic empires and delivered disintegrated polities and economies into the hands of warlords and magnates. The new Western states were better able to maintain a direct fiscal and military link to smallholders and small-scale traders and manufacturers. These low-level producers preserved their independence more successfully. The commercialized agrarian economy became less prone to the recurrent catastrophe of decommercialization. Such changes laid the institutional and economic basis for persistent group conflict. The possessing and ruling elites never became so united that they were able to close off institutional experimentation from the bottom up or from the top down, not at least to the extent that experimentation had been regularly closed off in the agrarian-bureaucratic states.

Remember that before the new European arrangements could exist as a stable order, they had to live as a fluid series of conflicts. The circumstances in which the Roman order in the West broke up allowed collectively organized peasants to fight it out with local landowners and overlords on more equal terms, for there was no governmental apparatus to tilt the scales in favor of the nobles. The "crisis of feudalism" merely sealed a result that had been achieved through continuing group struggle. Where grassroots collective organization was weakest and centralized noble reaction strongest – as in Eastern Europe – the same demographic crisis led to enserfment rather than to a freer peasantry. As centralized governments emerged they usually strengthened the hands of local elites. But they did so more in some countries and regions than in others. A few states approached the antimagnate alliance between smallholders and central governments that had eluded even the most successful and determined reformers in the agrarian–bureaucratic empires. Even where the alliance between central governments and landowning or mercantile elites proved strongest in Western Europe, it respected a measure of free movement by the working mass, of decisional autonomy by the governmental apparatus, and of elite conflict and fragmentation. No great agrarian and bureaucratic state of the past had done as well.

PLASTICITY AND COMPROMISE: EUROPEAN EXAMPLES

My examples from European history are drawn from episodes bounded chronologically, on one side, by the disintegration of the medieval style of fighting and, on the other side, by the rise of mass mechanized armies, supported by industrial economies, in the nineteenth and twentieth centuries.[1] Despite the broad sweep of time during which they took place, these events show an amazing unity of persistent themes and reciprocal effects. They represent turning points in warfare under the double pressure of expanding scope and developing weaponry. At each crucial juncture, the major attempts made to seize on the technological or mobilizational opportunity directly influenced one another. They also helped shape the social terms on which industrialization and quickened economic innovation would occur in its initial European or North Atlantic versions.

The dominant style of warfare of medieval Europe, as most characteristically developed in the core areas of feudalism, was the horde of ever more heavily armed mounted knights, fighting individually, with the support of foot soldiers and archers. The major military technology had, for many centuries, been the shock of the cavalry charge with piercing iron weapons. Improved stirrups and saddles had given this shock its force. The manpower and resources for fighting were not continuously available to any central authority. The knights, with their own arms and auxiliaries, were bound by ties of loyalty and exchange to come together under specified conditions for bouts of fighting that were rarely more than sporadic.

This combat unit fought with a minimum of tactical flexibility and coordination. Its fighting style oscillated typically between two modes: the compact mass of the cavalry charge, usually followed by individual hand-to-hand combat. From the start, both variants of this approach suffered from a lack of operational adaptability. As the mounted knight began to confront improved weapons – steel-tipped pikes and primitive firearms used by foot soldiers – he responded with heavier armor. As a result, he became increasingly immobile. He exemplified the futile search for isolated invulnerability at the cost of maneuver and teamwork. Thus, the overall effect of the attempt to achieve protection against new weapons was the further degeneration of a mode of combat already deeply flawed.

Clearly, this was an approach to warfare inseparable from a highly restricted stock of weapons and a sharply limited way of mobilizing men and resources for battle. It allowed for little organizational depth or tactical subtlety. It could not be expected to survive beyond the circumstance of

[1] Like all who write on military history, I owe much to Hans Delbrück's *Geschichte der Kriegskunst, im Rahmen der politischen Geschichte*, Berlin, G. Stilke, 1900–1936, especially part 3, "Neuzeit." Another major source of help and inspiration is William H. McNeill, *The Pursuit of Power: Technology, Armed Force, and Society since A.D. 1000*, Chicago, 1982, especially chaps. 3 and 4.

disintegrated governments and disordered markets that had encouraged its original development.

There was, however, no single way of waging war that was sure to displace the cohort of armed knights. From the very start, there were alternative emergent lines of development, even in the preference for different kinds of weapons. At least two distinct routes were taken, over the same period of European history, in the struggle against the high medieval style of warfare. Each route exploited technological and mobilizational opportunities that lay beyond the reach of an army of mounted knights bound together by feudal ties. Each was therefore sufficient to deal a knockout blow to the armored knight of the High Middle Ages. Yet neither route proved capable of meeting the next round of technological and mobilizational opportunities without undergoing a radical transformation of its own.

The first line of antifeudal military developments could be called the standing army approach, although I use the term more broadly and loosely than its conventional application would warrant. It was characterized by a regular army of foot soldiers drawn from the peasantry of an emerging territorial state, placed under the supreme command of a monarch–warlord, and provided with improved weapons. At its most solid, such an army consisted of wage-earning soldiers drawn from an independent yeomanry and capable of combining for battle and maneuvering on the field in a way that allowed sudden concentrations of force and enabled different weapons to reinforce one another. In particular, the more powerful missile weapons, longbow – or muskets – could be allied with the shock of the infantry. This combination in turn permitted the development of defensive-offensive tactics in place of the wild attack that a feudal army had to undertake in order to engage at all.

One early example of this challenge to the high medieval style of warfare came at Crécy in 1346, where the tactical and organizational superiority of Edward III's army seems to have been at least as important to the outcome as the effectiveness of the Welsh longbow.[2] Another instance came a century later at Formigny, where the French were this time the victors and the culverin, a medieval fieldpiece, replaced the longbow as the missile that softened up the enemy for the annihilating strike. Charles VII's army was, in fact, among the earliest prototypes of the standing army. It deployed resources and manpower on a vastly enlarged scale, and it united missile weapons with concentrated infantry and cavalry shocks.

Despite its initial successes, however, this fighting style could not easily absorb the impact of a widening mobilizational scope of warfare. The gathering of manpower and resources for the war effort remained open to one of two threats. Oligarchies, entrenched in landowning, trade, or government, might starve emerging central governments of funds and

2 See Herbert James Hewitt, *The Organization of War under Edward III, 1338–1362*, Manchester Univ., Manchester, 1962, pp. 28–49.

recruits or set the terms on which material and human resources were available. This tendency repeatedly reasserted itself throughout European history. It was superseded only when politics became mass politics and wars became people's wars – from the campaigns of revolutionary France to the world wars of the twentieth century. When the central monarchs, who were also the commanders and creators of the new standing armies, attacked their oligarchic adversaries, they risked being crushed by aristocratic reaction or overtaken by the popular agitation they themselves had incited. The danger of runaway popular rebellion was almost always more remote than the risk of oligarchic domination, given the typical accommodation between sovereigns and oligarchies in absolutist states. It could nevertheless materialize wherever the rural and urban masses had managed to keep a vibrant communal independence and the ruler was determined to make common cause with them against the magnates of the realm. The struggles of Erik XIV of Sweden supply an example.[3] Despite its extraordinary escape from the periodic governmental and economic collapse that another part of this book describes as reversion to natural economy, Europe had not broken completely free of the ancient quandaries of statecraft in the agrarian empires.

The technological opportunity generated by the continuous development of firearms could also not be easily absorbed by the early examples of standing armies. Effective handling and evasion of firepower and its coordination with shock tactics required skill and subtlety. An army adept at such practices could not be organized internally as a microcosm of the surrounding society, with its set hierarchies and divisions, nor could it operate effectively by the same crude juxtaposition of personal or family initiative and coerced obedience that characterized most of the society's productive activity. It was not enough to get your hands directly on soldiers and funds without having to rely on the good offices of independent oligarchs. It might also become necessary to inaugurate a form of organization that would stand as a disturbing countermodel to the most common forms of coordination and subordination in society at large. The earliest successful versions of standing armies arose in circumstances in which the level of technical development of firearms had not yet made acute these organizational, operational, and tactical demands of more advanced weaponry, while an exceptional domestic and foreign situation had allowed a truce in the struggles among state-building monarchies, realigned aristocracies, and working masses.

Call the other route to the subversion of high feudal warfare communal resistance. Its distinctive characteristic was the deployment of massed square formations of free peasants or town dwellers, bound together by communal ties and by a shared commitment to resist foreign overlords, and

[3] See Ingvar Andersson, *A History of Sweden*, Weidenfeld, London, 1955, pp. 147–149.

armed with clubs and poles (first pikes, then halberds) that could be used to unseat the charging knights. An early crude variant can be seen in the mauling that Flemish burghers gave to French knights at the Battle of Courtrai in 1302, where the people's weapon was a club more primitive than its Aztec counterpart and the tactical exploitation of the marshy ground proved essential to victory. The more advanced version of the same approach was the sixteenth-century Swiss phalanx, deployed triumphantly against Austrian knights.[4]

Defense combined with offense, and anticavalry shock weapons, like the spear and the halberd, with missiles, ranging from the crossbow to the handgun. The resisting popular communes of town or country provided the manpower for combat. The approach to army organization and operation that put these technological and mobilizational opportunities into effect drew on a preexisting experience of communal life. The need to give combat on this new basis in turn strengthened and diversified the forms of collaborative organization in Flemish and Swiss popular life.

But the armies of communal resistance, and the societies that established them, could not readily meet the tests of expanding mobilizational and technological opportunities in warfare any more than the early versions of the standing army. To compete with the resources and manpower available to the emergent large territorial states, the zones of popular resistance would themselves have had to create central state institutions, capable of ruling over large territories and populations and of acting decisively in the struggle against foreign powers. Such an experiment in state building could hardly have been achieved without bold institutional reforms that would have amounted to a major collective self-transformation. Even the access to technological development in weaponry was not easily open to the warfare of communal resistance.

There needed to be a developed state structure able to sponsor firearms production in partnership with manufacturing and technical cadres. Once the weapons were available, there had to be an organizational, operational, and tactical style capable of exploiting them fully. The fierce collective loyalties of massed formations were no substitute for specialization, coordination, and supervised discretion. But the countries that supported the communal armies were often mountainous or peripheral areas, where feudal institutions had never fully developed or had broken down. Often – although this could not be said of Flanders, Bohemia, or northern Italy – they were also lands that had failed to develop a more varied commercialized agrarian and manufacturing economy. Thus, the communal-resistance approach offered few pointers for an army able to translate weapons breakthroughs into operational inventions.

4 See the detailed discussion of the *Landesknechte* in Eugen von Frauenholz, *Das Heereswesen in der Zeit des freien Söldnertums*, 2 vols., Beck, Munich, 1936.

Not every obstacle to increasing levels of military capability applied in every instance of communal resistance. But the difficulties were usually serious enough to require a major change in the organizational and social bases of communal resistance. The sustaining institutions of the early forms of popular warfare needed to be combined, one way or another, with some of the strengths exhibited by the new standing armies of the large territorial states.

You can detect a movement toward such a combination among the Hussites of the early fifteenth century. The armies of Jan Žižka repeatedly showed an ability to fight at the mobilizational and technological vanguard of warfare although Tschernembl's call in the Bohemian War Council for mass recruitment remained largely unheeded.[5] No fighting force of the Europe of that time was more subtle in its organization and tactics. None could count on more varied and vital economic support. Yet the Hussite state gave a vastly larger role to independent popular organization than did the territorial monarchies. Its destruction was brought about by its own internal dissensions against the background of unified foreign opposition and of the difficulties attending experiments "in one country." The most farsighted military reformers and political propagandists in the north Italian city-state republics also understood that radical changes in the organizational and social bases of the popular militia were necessary to resist French, Spanish, and papal armies. These changes had to go all the way from the establishment of an Italian confederation to the bold coordination of small combat units, armed with varying styles of weapons.

The internal transformation of the standing army approach might produce a similar outcome. The territorial monarch might carry his struggle against the magnates to the point of transforming his whole national standing army into a popular militia based on grassroots collective organization by independent rural and urban proprietors. Erik XIV of Sweden came close to forming such a militia, and similar tendencies recurred throughout sixteenth- and seventeenth-century Swedish history. Alternatively, the state structure might begin to fall apart as oligarchic struggle escalated. The more broadly based armies called into existence by the civil strife might then gain a popular momentum of their own and threaten to bring down the country's whole structure of ordered hierarchy. Thus, in the course of the English Civil War, the New Model Army almost got out of hand and jeopardized the country's basic institutions.

At the start of the seventeenth century, then, both major modes of antifeudal warfare – the standing army and the communal militia – faced obstacles in creating and exploiting technological and mobilizational opportunities for greater destructive capability. But there was a significant difference of timing in the major difficulties faced by each of these modes

[5] See J.V. Polišenský, *War and Society in Europe, 1618–1648*, Cambridge, Cambridge, 1978, p. 64.

and in the practical benefits each might bring. In the long run the communal resistance solution might prove more responsive to a total war that engaged resources and manpower on a vast scale and extended the vanguardist style of operations to ever wider segments of the fighting forces. But in the short run the communal resistance approach required the invention of institutions and beliefs that would allow strong, stable states to be directly and willingly sustained by large numbers of more or less organized smallscale proprietors. The development of the standing army solution, in absolutist and aristocratic Europe, might fail to cut through the constraints of oligarchic privilege and mass coercion, constraints that, in the long view, could prove fatal at still higher levels of technological and mobilizational intensity in warfare. But in the short run a standing army was likely to require less redefinition and dispossession for already entrenched powers than a popular militia, wherever kings, landowning aristocracies, and big time merchants already held sway. Any attempt to compensate for its short-run disadvantage as an overall European solution would have required the defenders of the communal resistance direction to translate as quickly as possible their long-run advantages into short-term gains in mobilizational and technological capacity. The path-breaking quality of the Hussite forces suggests the feasibility of such a translation.

In any contest between alternative organizational and social bases for a similar level of practical capability in production or destruction, victory depends partly on the ability to appropriate aspects of the rival solution and to make them subordinate parts of one's own approach, thereby changing or even inverting their entire political sense. To succeed, small republics and peasant or urban collectivities committed to the path of communal resistance needed to develop large confederations, technical or managerial cadres, and permanent specialized forces. The monarchic creators of standing armies did the opposite. Faced with the difficulty of recruiting and funding such armies without an all-out struggle against the national aristocracies, they tried to turn the strengths of the communal armies to their own benefit. They attempted this reversal by transforming the popular armies into mercenary units in their own service.

The mercenary corps recruited by military entrepreneurs served as a way to incorporate the new popular formations, with all their strengths of operational style and combined weaponry, into the national army. Yet because these units were in every sense an alien corps grafted onto the social body, they posed little threat as a countermodel of association. It is a stratagem that has been employed throughout history, often in areas of statecraft far removed from military reform. During the Köprülü reform period, for example, in the late seventeenth-century Ottoman Empire, Albanians played a major role as staffers in state administration. Because of the sanctity they attached to the oath of friendship, or *besa*, they could be counted on at a time when most patron-client relationships in high administrative circles had dissolved without giving way to an alternative organizational structure.[6]

At the outset of the Thirty Years' War, the dominant mode of warfare in Western and Central Europe had become a restricted version of the standing army pioneered by war leaders like Charles VII of France or Edward III of England. Precisely because of the difficulty of maintaining the precarious conditions that would allow direct access to a broad, popular base of manpower and capital, most large territorial states had to make heavy use of mercenary armies combined with coerced levies of peasants. These were initially temporary fighting units hired or raised for limited periods of time. The extraordinary, one-shot financial burden drastically limited the possibilities of manpower and resource mobilization for warfare and delivered would-be warlords into the hands of cagey bankers.

Moreover, the nature of these armies had a constraining influence on their ability to exploit the technical advances in firearms and to coordinate firepower with shock. This point is borne out by the compulsion to deploy rigid mass formations in order to guarantee discipline on the part of coerced peasants or short-term hirelings. The result was to undermine offensive and defensive mobility in the field and to prevent surprising, concentrated blows with missile and shock tactics.[7]

Consider the widespread popularity of two ineffective firearm maneuvers. One of them was the use of the cavalry charge with a wheellock pistol. The firing of the shot into a compact mass of enemy pikemen and musketeers often became the end rather than the beginning of the cavalry charge, whose value as a shock instrument was thereby entirely lost. In the infantry battalions, a parallel development took place: the musket was used less as the preliminary to a shock attack with pikes than as the main instrument of battle. Infantry combat degenerated into inconclusive encounters between opposing musketeers. Siege warfare became the best proving ground for the newer weapons.

There is a recurrent tendency in the history of warfare to see in a technical advance an alternative to maneuver and engagement rather than an occasion for them. Thus, the Ottomans in the eighteenth century looked for safety to enormous, unwieldy artillery pieces whose imprecision made their paralyzing tactical effects all the more unjustifiable. During the Vietnam War of 1960–1973, the Americans habitually used the helicopter as a weapon with which to land an overpowering number of troops directly into a combat theater.[8] They disregarded what the British had already

[6] See William H. McNeill, *Europe's Steppe Frontier, 1500–1800*, Chicago, Chicago, 1964, pp. 134–135.

[7] See Gustav Droysen, *Beiträge zur Geschichte des Militarwesens im Deutschland während der Epoche des Dreissigjährigen Krieges*, Shlüter, Hannover, 1875, especially pp. 10–11.

[8] See Robert B. Asprey, *War in the Shadows: The Guerrilla in History*, Doubleday Garden City, N.Y., 1975, vol. 2, pp. 1412–1414.

discovered during their counterinsurgency operations in Borneo:[9] that a transport vehicle must not be made into an excuse to lose the advantages of tactical surprise in a futile quest for instantaneous, unbeatable concentrations of force. Although such operational mistakes are understandable, given the horror of combat and the fascination of invulnerability, they were greatly aggravated in early modern European armies of brutalized peasants and lackadaisical mercenaries.

The circumstances surveyed in the preceding pages suggest a context for understanding seventeenth-century military advances. In essence, these advances consisted in the attempt to develop the standing-army route in a way that came closer to its earliest bold prototypes than to its more recent degenerate forms.[10] The aim, in the minds of the most innovative leaders, was to exploit technological and mobilizational opportunities for warfare through reforms in the organizational and social bases of the war effort. But it was essential that such reforms stop short of a radical transformation of state and society. The armies produced by these changes were the most effective fighting forces in Europe until the day of the national levy, the people's war, and the industrialized war machine. Yet they, too, had severe limits, and during the eighteenth-century era of limited dynastic wars they too underwent a degeneration encouraged by the intricate series of compromises on which they had originally depended. The boldest architect of this new military style was Gustavus Adolphus of Sweden. Its earliest fragmentary models were the Spanish tercio and the infantry battalions organized, at the turn of the century, by Maurice of Nassau.

My account of these changes begins by focusing on reforms in the nature of armies: their innovations in structure and recruitment, operations and tactics. Then it suggests how these developments in the organizational basis of warfare enabled the innovators to enlarge and exploit technological and mobilizational opportunities. These advances in destructive capability could not be initiated or maintained without deliberate reforms and unintended shifts in other aspects of state and society. The compromises struck in the course of making or tolerating these changes in turn imposed limits on the capacity to develop and deploy military power. The particular accommodations at each point along the way were not predetermined by basic institutional arrangements of power and production or by the class relations these arrangements helped sustain. Yet such settlements, together with many other compromises in many other theaters of practical or visionary conflict, exercised a formative influence on whole societies. They influenced the social terms on which economic progress would take place.

9 See Walter Walker, "How Borneo Was Won," *The Round Table* (Jan. 1969).

10 See Michael Roberts, "The Military Revolution, 1560–1660," in *Essays in Swedish History*, Univ. of Minnesota, Minneapolis, 1967, pp. 195–225; Geoffrey Parker, "The Military 'Revolution' 1550–1660 – A Myth?" *Journal of Modern History*, vol. 48 (1976), pp. 195–214.

Wherever possible, the army became a permanent organization. If it was staffed by mercenaries, they were to be hired without limit of time. If it was raised by conscription, the landowning oligarchies were to be given special responsibilities for enlistment in their own areas (e.g., the Prussian cantonal system) and special rights to monopolize the officer corps. The Swedish method of direct recruitment from a class of independent smallholders with state-protected farms remained an exceptional solution: it most closely approached a revolutionary partnership between sovereign and people.

Whatever the manner of enlistment, war finance became more secure. The most common institutional background to this development was a bargain that included at least three terms: the corporate representation of the tax-paying estates; the active commitment of state power to defending their preferential access to governmental office, land control, and commercial advantage; and agreement by the estates to help provide the money and manpower for war. A similar deal brought central governments and oligarchies together in the financing of armaments production.

Within this context of support, the operational style of armies could be more readily reformed. More effective central command combined with increased discretion and flexibility. On the one hand, drill, marching in step, and uniforms created the background of common discipline. On the other hand, the ordinary soldier was turned into something of a technician and a tactician. Infantry formations were progressively divided into smaller groups, able to disperse and converge rapidly in the field and to take advantage of the mutually reinforcing effects of different kinds of weapons. Thus, in Gustavus Adolphus's new army the operational unit was the battalion, a mobile combat group of pikemen and musketeers, with their own light artillery. Firepower could be used as a prelude to shock by light cavalry and pikemen, and maneuver could regain its prime strengths of concentration and surprise.[11]

These advances were not achieved at a single leap. The Spanish tercio remained an unwieldy and relatively inflexible formation, while the much smaller combat units inaugurated by Maurice of Nassau and his mercenaries habitually preferred evasion to engagement.[12] There were many occasions and pathways to reach the similar tactical results. The tactics that Cortés used to such stunning advantage against the Aztecs were essentially a commando variation on the procedures of the tercio. Yet they progressed in the same general direction as the Swedish operational innovations, tested almost a century later at Breitenfeld.

These developments in the support and conduct of warfare made it possible both to foment the production of new weapons and to work out their tactical implications. The lighter and faster-loading muskets and the

[11] See Michael Roberts, "Gustav Adolph and The Art of War," in *Essays in Swedish History*, pp. 56–81.

[12] See Werner Hahlweg, *Die Heeresreform der Oranier und die Antike*, Junker, Berlin, 1941, pp. 33–38.

more mobile field artillery introduced in the course of the Thirty Years' War were the products of tenacious partnerships between governments and manufacturers. They were also among the first results of a process of accelerated technical innovation in which cadres of tinkerers and practical scientists learned to understand machines: to establish a limited catalog of machine parts and principles of construction. The parts could be placed in divergent combinations and the principles be given analogous uses across a broad range of contexts, from docks and church bells to handguns and field artillery.[13] But these technical breakthroughs would have been squandered for military purposes in an army incapable of rapid maneuver, interlocking specialization, and the simultaneous development of both command discipline and on-the-field discretion. The same set of improvements in the army's recruitment, structure, and fighting style enabled its masters to use more heavily and effectively the resources and manpower of large territorial states in a period of brutal state struggle.

The essential social basis of these military achievements was the type of accommodation with domestic elites described earlier. Its most developed form appeared in the armies of Brandenburg-Prussia, given the more exceptional character of the Swedish state at the zenith of its military power. The example of Prussian military organization is striking as a source of insight into the constraints that respect for oligarchic interests imposed on military capability, for Prussia was the most successful military power in prerevolutionary Europe.

Without compromises similar to those made in Brandenburg-Prussia – or still more radical departures, like those tested in Sweden and Bohemia – the organizational basis of warfare, with its corresponding operational implications, could not have been transformed, as it was, in seventeenth-century Europe. European armies would have remained temporary collections of resentful peasants and floating mercenaries, incapable of being trusted with greater tactical discretion and technical responsibility. War finance and recruitment would have continued hostage to unreconciled oligarchs. Armaments production would have lacked sustained support and guidance. Yet such deals had limiting effects on the long-range maintenance and development of military capability.

Some of these effects were exercised directly on the opening and exploitation of technological or mobilizational opportunities. Governmental sponsorship of weapons research and manufacture was rarely more than episodic. Despite examples as precocious as the Venetian Arsenal and rope factory and the manipulation of the Venetian funded debt, these reformed European states lacked the institutional means with which to maintain a steady level of investment flow into weapons making. Any attempt to forge these means might quickly draw states into the management of economy-

13 See Carlo M. Cipolla, *Clocks and Culture, 1300–1700*, Norton, New York, 1977, pp. 39–40, 50–51.

wide investment decisions and into clashes with the commercial oligarchies. Thus, in his navy-building efforts a reformer like Colbert could easily get caught in a position that fell between the stools of independent governmental responsibility for production and effective governmental partnership with willing investors.

The danger of strangulation that beset the armaments industry held more generally for war finance. The funded debt and the organized representation of estates in local and national assemblies certainly helped turn public finance into an ally rather than an enemy of private banking and entrepreneurship, but these mechanisms were quickly overstrained in periods of intensified warfare. Any fragility in the financial system might turn marginal stress into major crisis. Thus, the relatively modest French involvement in the American War of Independence became part of the sequence of events that laid the ancien régime open to violent destruction. Again, the effort to widen the sources and methods of finance might require a more far-reaching change in the structure of the state and the character of its relations with particular social classes.

Similar compromises had a constraining influence on manpower mobilization. Here the effects were even more complex and subtle than in the instances of arms manufacture and war finance. The mere effort to guarantee a steady flow of recruits presented the state with unpalatable dilemmas. Take the experience of Brandenburg-Prussia itself. In its early phases, the canton system multiplied reasons for grassroots conflict and corruption. To satisfy their recruitment obligations, military captains and estate owners would try to conscript peasants exempt under the law, who would in turn defend themselves by resistance, bribery, and desertion.

On the other hand, if the central government intervened to fix clearly the rights and responsibilities of each estate, as it did under Frederick the Great, the result was to freeze the entire social order in a manner reminiscent of the regime of Diocletian in the late Roman empire. This solution had its own disadvantages. The hardening of the relationship of each social rank to the state and, through the state, to every other rank diminished the room for conflict and innovation in every area of social life. It also kept the peasantry in a condition of institutionalized subordination that made it a permanent internal enemy of the government and a sullen, resentful participant in the state's military endeavors.

This last point brings out the more intangible aspect of the constraint on manpower mobilization implicit in the seventeenth- and eighteenth-century strategies of compromise. Rulers could hardly count on a populace that felt no commitment to the military fortunes of the state. Popular commitment would have required popular trust, and such a trust would not easily flourish unless overweening oligarchies assumed a more limited and, above all, a more self-effacing role. A change so fundamental could be imagined and achieved only in a circumstance of protracted struggle over governmental power and private privilege.

During the latter part of the seventeenth century and most of the eighteenth century, the advances in military structure and method that had been achieved during the Thirty Years' War suffered a characteristic involution on several fronts. Each aspect of this decline was decisively encouraged by the compromises underlying most of the innovations in the first place. One sign of this fallback was the triumph of rigid, linear field tactics. This development is particularly revealing because it shows the wastage and perversion of technological breakthroughs achieved after the operational reforms of the early and mid-seventeenth century. The invention of the socket bayonet made it possible to dispense with the protective pike, making the effective combat units shallower and more flexible. The production of lighter, more mobile field artillery enabled supporting firepower to advance more rapidly in pace with the infantry line and to combine the missile with the shock. The development of the more rapidly reloading flintlock musket gave the infantryman greater autonomy and made him less dependent on protective fire during reloading. Such changes reestablished the tactical advantages of the shallow line. Yet these advantages were almost lost by the rigid, mechanical formations favored by the tacticians of the late seventeenth and the eighteenth centuries.[14]

The soldier, however, could not easily be made into a more autonomous technician and tactician when he still remained a mercenary or a conscript without any vital commitment to the state, when he still took every opportunity to break ranks, hide, or desert, when his relations to his own officers were still modeled on those of the peasant to the landlord and the lackey to the master, and when he still lacked exposure to organizational responsibility and mechanical dexterity.[15]

Another aspect of the setback was the strangulation of tactics by logistics. Armies easily became tied down to fixed supply centers and vulnerable to the capture of such bases. There was more to this dependence than limitations in the technology of transport. There was the difficulty of establishing a broad enough base of financial support to fund multiple supply points during intense or protracted warfare, and to do so without entering into destructive conflict or deadlock with the tax-voting oligarchies. The supply story had another side as well. A people's army, like the French revolutionary force, might turn its logistic weakness to tactical advantage by commandeering resources on the spot. But the armies

[14] On the tactical and operational implications of the weapons mentioned here, see David G. Chandler, *The Art of Warfare in the Age of Marlborough*, Hippocrene, New York, 1976, especially pp. 28, 75–78.

[15] Compare the description of the peasant-soldier situation in Otto Busch, *Militärsystem und Sozialleben im Alten Preussen*, Ullstein, Frankfurt, 1981, pp. 21–50, with the tactical and operational ideals advanced by a military reformer like Scharnhorst in his "Three Essays on Light Troops and Infantry Tactics" (1811), a translation of which is published as an appendix to Peter Paret, *Yorck and the Era of Prussian Reform, 1807–1815*, Princeton, Princeton, 1966, pp. 249–262.

of the eighteenth-century European monarchies could not easily make such a move without seeing their soldiers become pillagers and thus turning the civilian populace into an indignant adversary.

The direct and indirect constraints imposed on the development of military capability by compromise strategies were far less influential in naval power. The navy remained what the mercenary army had once been: an alien body, separated from the main life of society, which might serve as a field for organizational experimentation without jeopardizing the central institutions of power and production. Its needs for manpower were relatively limited, and its advantage for commerce was obvious (though not obvious enough to Dutch and French commercial elites). Naval tactics, which could not easily fall into the rigidities of lockstep land warfare, provided an early model for that more subtle relation between command and discretion that was to be so spectacularly developed in twentieth-century armored combat. All these factors encouraged development of naval technology. And the Western naval advantage was crucial in determining the precise terms of the initial encounters with non-Western powers in the Orient. The whole course of events in Japan, for example, might have been different either if the Western invaders had lacked their naval edge or if the Japanese had proved capable of an early and decisive land invasion.

The next rounds in European military history confirm the points that have already been made. The armies of revolutionary France compelled the European powers to enter the next great wave of military innovations. The appeal to the people permitted a degree of operational flexibility that made it possible to capitalize on the most recent developments in armaments and to broaden the resources and manpower actively engaged in warfare.

Once again, there was a wave of relatively successful accommodations. No simple contrast holds between pioneering countries and reluctant latecomers. For example, conscription in revolutionary and Napoleonic France was limited by the conscript's option of buying himself out, a sop to the propertied classes that Prussia did not allow. Once again, compromises exacted a price in military capability at every level. Once again, the particular series of concessions and advances helped shape the formative contexts of power and production in Western societies. Within the West, the pattern of compromise was an element in setting the social terms of industrialization and the outer limits to mass politics. Outside the West, it laid the basis for the fateful Western advantage in destructive force and for the brand of state and economy to which elites and peoples in other parts of the world were forced to respond. These other nations, I have repeatedly argued, would be faced with the imperative of dissociation: the need to disengage practical capabilities from the institutional foundations on which these capabilities had originally rested in the core Western countries. But the point of departure – the reality offered up for dissociation – was the outcome of particular struggles in several realms. The quest for military power was simply one such domain. These struggles, fought out in different settings over different issues, were not the same fight in different disguises, nor can they be understood as episodes in a relentlessly unfolding transformative sequence. Nevertheless, they had similar features that reveal a general characteristic of society making: what we learn from them connects the analysis of practical capabilities and of their enabling circumstances to a general political understanding of society. Before these lessons can be worked out, however, the analysis of the European examples must be pushed a few steps further.

In the total wars of the twentieth century, the technological and mobilizational intensity of warfare repeatedly threatened to churn up the social order. For the defeated, it did so by shattering the state and discrediting its most visible masters. For all belligerents, it delivered this threat through a complicated series of wartime pressures: the need to assume an increasing measure of control over investment and manpower policy, the maintenance of full employment with its attendant risks to workplace discipline, the introduction of new forms of joint decisional responsibility by workers, managers, and officials and, most notably, the universal sense that so incalculable a horror as total war would have to be compensated for by creating a society that, in every respect, belonged more fully to its ordinary workers and soldiers.

The technological and mobilizational demands of intensified warfare also made demands on the organizational practice of armies. Wherever the innovations in decisional structure and operational style went furthest, they offered a countermodel to the organizational style prevailing in most of the production system. The most telling of these departures from organizational orthodoxy occurred in the development of tank warfare.

When the tank was first put to use during World War I, most official military thinking confined it to a subsidiary role. Some thought of the tank as no more than a trench-crossing vehicle, an additional siege weapon. Others went further. The tank would provide firepower to support infantry advances in the face of enemy barrages with automatic weapons; it was, once again, the missile supporting the shock. Lighter and faster tanks would serve as the mechanical counterparts to cavalry: they would protect exposed infantry flanks and undertake scouting missions. These conceptions of tank warfare required few radical changes in the relations among the army's branches, in its command structure, or in its operational style. The technological development was, on the contrary, used to preserve arrangements and procedures (like the infantry charge) that had been jeopardized by other technical inventions (such as the machine gun).[16]

16 See Field Marshal Lord Carver, *The Apostles of Mobility: The Theory and Practice of Armoured Warfare*, Weidenfeld, London, 1979; Edward N. Luttwak, "The Strategy of the Tank," in *Strategy and Politics*, ed. Edward N. Luttwak, Transaction, New Brunswick, New Jersey, 1980, pp. 295–304.

The more insightful understood that the tank might mean much more. It could become the weapon of an entirely distinct branch. The establishment of tank units, however, was just a beginning. The capabilities of the tank division could be fully exploited only by a new structure of communication and control. Even some of the most famous tank commanders of World War II failed to grasp this requirement. The junior officer in charge of each tank crew had to be able to exploit sudden opportunities for rapid and deep penetration or envelopment. He could not be held to a fixed, preconceived plan nor reduced to the role of intermediary between the men who gave orders and the men who carried them out. If, however, central guidance failed to counterbalance this discretion, the tank force would disintegrate and lose its power of concentration. There had to be a voice to say where to concentrate and how to coordinate the armored attack with covering air support. (Airplanes could do for tanks what a more retrograde military mind had expected tanks to do for infantry.) Nevertheless, the commander had to move around in the midst of battle, and his plan had to be constantly revised in the light of the opportunities seized and the obstacles encountered by individual tank crews.

At its best, this approach to tank warfare illustrates the vanguardist style of production and warfare. It is a way of waging war that weakens the distinctions between task and execution, and between taskmasters and executors. The self-revising plan in the protracted battle became the heart of operations. If all branches of the army had adopted similar procedures, the entire war machine would have provided a countermodel to the organizational and operational approach that continued to prevail in industry. Given the overwhelming convergence of interests, preconceptions, and habits threatened by any such extension, this countermodel was likely to take hold only where its practical advantages were immediate, unmistakable, and indispensable. The economic and governmental arrangements of the rich Western democracies in the latter half of the twentieth century would have been fundamentally different if such vanguardist forms of collective effort had been allowed to penetrate the mainstream of industrial and military organization.

PROVISIONAL CONCLUSIONS

The episodes from European history discussed in the preceding pages already suggest some provisional conclusions about the enabling circumstances of destructive capability. These conclusions in turn serve as a partial model for an understanding of the general relation between practical capacities and their organizational and social bases. Thus, these claims must be read twice: first, as an account of linkages within the military setting; and second, as the outline of a view of the relation between the transformation of society and the development of productive or destructive powers. Each of these conclusions, however, is so hedged in by qualifications and ambiguities that its value can be determined only by casting still more widely the net of analysis and comparison.

As armed conflict reached greater degrees of intensity in the course of European history, the effort to develop or exploit technological and mobilizational opportunities generated pressures for a change in the organizational and social basis of warfare. When you consider these pressures and the responses to them in a broad historical sweep, you discover that, despite many setbacks and diversions, they seem, on the whole, to have moved in an identifiable direction.

In the social basis of warfare, the movement of change was toward the subversion of all predetermined social hierarchies and divisions that would constrain the ability of government to mobilize resources and manpower for war and to lay claim to the loyalty of its citizens. This movement did not spell egalitarianism or democracy in the state and the economy. But it did mean that no independent oligarchies could be allowed for long to interpose themselves squarely between the heights of governmental power and the access to men and capital. Even rights and privileges that helped define the formative contexts of power and production might have to be shifted around quite radically, at least during the high points of the war effort. As the age of total people's wars dawned, these subversive pressures increased. The society and its government had to be so ordered that some semblance of truth could be given to the pretense that the state's violent struggles were everybody's business.

In the organizational basis of warfare the direction of movement ran toward the development of a command structure and an operational practice that did not merely reproduce the relationships of clientage and coerced dependence in the surrounding society. In structure and style, the fighting force would have to be a cyst of organized collective effort that defined specialized responsibilities and methods of coordination capable of resisting the test of battle. As the violence and the technical subtlety of warfare mounted, the most advanced branches were pressed to adopt an approach that sacrificed all fixed distinctions between task making and task following at the same time that it preserved a structure of control and coordination.

The social and organizational movements reinforced each other in message and effect. Without some disruption of the surrounding social hierarchies, the crucial organizational reforms could not be introduced. The established structure of privilege sharply constrained governmental access to recruits and funds. It also limited the schemes of collaborative effort readily available in the society and ultimately transferable to warfare. In its own organizational structure and operational procedures, an army could not easily remain an inverted picture of society. Either the familiar routines of everyday life would end up penetrating and deforming the military organization, or the army's own underlying principles would invade other areas of collective effort. The influence ran in the opposite direction as well. Without organizational reforms the increased engagement of resources and manpower made possible by a shake-up of entrenched privilege was likely to be wasted.

The direct causal links between organizational and social transformation were accompanied by a more inclusive parallelism. The maximum readiness for war would presumably be achieved in a society in which the entire social order was infused by the spirit and habits of flexible, rationalized collective labor. In civilian settings, you might have much more popular accountability and institutionalized conflict than could be tolerated in a tank battalion. But you would have the same constant availability for the recombination of units, the joinder of supervision, coordination, and discretion, the merger of task making and task following.

Many of the decisive military reforms taken here as examples anteceded their civilian counterparts, and were explicitly understood as responses to technological and mobilizational opportunities in warfare. An important methodological conclusion follows. The formative institutional arrangements of the emergent industrial economies resulted either from conflicts that occurred in nonindustrial and even noneconomic settings or from disputes about the core zone of industrial organization and investment. The struggles that took place in these distinct areas obeyed no master plan. But our chances of giving any general explanation of events like the North Atlantic industrial breakthrough depend on the discovery of significant analogies of structure and theme and ties of reciprocal influence among the different military, economic, and administrative realms of social life.

At each major turning point in military history there were alternative organizational and social routes to the development of destructive capability. Some of these alternatives – like the communal resistance and the standing army options at the time of the disintegration of high medieval warfare – were unequally subversive in their organizational and social implications. Moreover, every time a country faced a military force based on a complex of organizational and social reforms that seemed to require a radical reordering of society, its rulers could discover a less radical way to achieve a similar level of military capability.

At first, these alternative accommodating solutions appear to be no more than stopgap measures. They place a heavy mortgage on the future by restricting a country's responsiveness to the next round of mobilizational and technological opportunities. But this view is too simple. The successful compromise is not just a way to hold off the next steps in some already preestablished long-run sequence, based on necessary relationships between practical capabilities and their enabling circumstances. It is the point of departure for a somewhat different long-run sequence. How different is not something that can be said beforehand or in the abstract, but only piecemeal and provisionally. Thus, the conflicts over the organizational and social bases of practical capability – military or not – are much more than accelerations or delays in travel along a mapped route. They both open up unsuspected paths and relocate the points of arrival.

The periods of most rapid innovation in the organizational and social bases of armed conflict were all eras of intensifying warfare. They culminated in the idea and the practice of the total people's war. The characteristic moments of involution were those, like the latter half of the seventeenth century and the greater part of the eighteenth, when absolutist rulers waged wars for limited aims and in cold blood.

The goals for which these limited wars were waged had no ultimate, self-evident importance. There is no determinate logic of state interests that transcends the conflict of interests and visions within rival countries. Every appeal to such a logic serves, in context, a particular set of social alliances and visions. The logic of state interests may be understood in varying ways. Even on the same understanding, it may be compatible with different solutions.

It is also true that the social climate of limited wars favored costly rigidities and illusions in the concrete operational aspects of warfare. My eighteenth-century examples were the inflexibility of linear infantry tactics, the logistic strangulation of maneuver, and the consistent avoidance of combat. But when all is said and done, limited war encouraged economy in the use of means, clarity in the definition of ends, and careful control over the proportion of means to ends.

The same points hold in reverse for the total people's wars of the twentieth century. The aims of such conflicts must at least appear to bear some relation to collective goals whose authority ordinary workers and soldiers acknowledge. Entire organizational and social systems of warfare are thrown into the furnace of relentless reordering. Anything for success. But the dynamic of violence and hatred gains a life of its own. It disorients the calculus of means and ends. Ultimately, it threatens to interrupt any intelligent process of organizational or social innovations and to confuse any notion of why the war was waged in the first place. It creates circumstances in which the desperate gambles of all-out battle and domestic dissension overtake the sequence of deliberate experiments.

Here, then, in summary are the conclusions to be drawn from this discussion of European military history. A state, in order to survive in the struggle against its deadly enemies, must succeed in loosening up and reordering the two crucial linkages in the relation of destructive capabilities to their enabling conditions: the linkage between technological and mobilizational opportunities and the immediate organizational, operational, or tactical setting of warfare and the linkage between this setting and the broader institutional framework of economic and political life. Over the long sweep of modern European history, the successive rearrangements of both connections appear to have a powerful directional thrust. Throughout much of modern experience rearrangements of the first link have moved toward reconstructing practical activity as teamwork among task definers and task executors. At the extreme, in the vanguardist sectors of warfare and production, these rearrangements have even undercut the contrast between task-defining and task-executing jobs. The readjustments of the second linkage have helped weaken rigid social roles and hierarchies; at a minimum, they have loosened the stranglehold of privilege over governmental power and enlarged the areas of social life open to organizational experiments.

Several considerations, however, counterbalance the sense of a directional movement. For one thing, this apparent evolutionary march does not coincide with any particular vision of democratic accountability, egalitarian redistribution, and individual emancipation. Its content is almost entirely negative. The axis of movement points toward an increased social plasticity whose true nature and implications should be defined more precisely. Successive approaches to this goal can take concrete social forms utterly opposed to our ideals. But these anti-ideal outcomes may still share a common basis with ideal goals that we do entertain: a greater loosening of the constraints imposed by a rigid order of social division and hierarchy on collaborative effort for practical ends, whether in war or peace, whether in large organizations or outside them. This possible, cumulative movement allows at every point along the way for alternative realizations of the new order and for successful compromises with the old one. It flourishes in situations of aggravated conflict whose special characteristics, however, give the achievements of military reform a quality of randomness, precariousness, and obscurity. Heightened social and organizational revisability may also take utterly different institutional forms. Although any particular set of constraints on this revisability will prove dangerous sooner or later, we cannot expect any particular group of institutions or even of procedures to be the perpetual motion machine of social innovation. Moreover, we can rarely dismiss renovating reforms and the clever compromises they enshrine as no more than doomed efforts to delay an inevitable progression; they create an alternative future.

These qualifications to simple progressivism shade into one another. The overabundance of paths to increased destructive (or productive) power shows that no ideal program can be sure to be on the winning side. Nevertheless, programs for social reconstruction that do hold fast to a particular fixed scheme of hierarchy and division are sooner or later cast off indignantly as both practical embarrassments and moral outrages.

We achieve the deepest insights into the connection between military power – or, more generally, any practical capability – and its favoring social conditions when we put the progressivist view in its place without rejecting it altogether. (By progressivist view I mean the thesis that the demands of material progress point in the same direction as liberal or socialist ideals of freedom and equality.) The progressivist view is at once true and not true. An adequate account of the enabling conditions of practical capabilities identifies the precise relation between its truth and its falsehood.

These conclusions help us understand how an economic order capable of being pulled apart and recombined with other institutional arrangements could have been put together in the first place. As the whole world began to industrialize, the initial Western versions of an industrial economy and an industrialized war machine were placed on organizational and social bases different from the ones that continued to sustain them in the West. And even in European and American history itself, there were significant though limited variations in the institutional context of industrialization. The form taken by the production system resulted from conflicts in a series of theaters only loosely strung together, some of them remote from disputes over the style and consequences of industrial organization. Military history gives us the example of one such theater, somewhat removed from the core area of economic organization.

Once industrial economies had appeared, the power to destroy became ever more closely bound up with the capacity to produce. Yet the capabilities of production and destruction were never the same. Separate organizations wielded them. They had distinct if connected histories. The military compromises influence, and are influenced by, the economic solutions. If, for example, the flexible, vanguardist style of organization remains confined to a restricted region of one of these two fields – the industrial and the military – then it is that much more likely to be restricted in the other.

There is another and more general way in which the inferences this study draws from military history fit into an argument about the institutional conditions of military and economic success. We come out better able to see and to describe how limiting influences coexist with a potential for variation. We begin to enlist the imagination of what did not happen in the understanding of what did.

Each of the points made here about the history of destruction translates into a thesis about the history of production. The analogy holds for the analytic scheme of relations among practical capacities and institutional arrangements, for the theme of a directional thrust to military and economic history, and even for the qualifications that make this theme more limited, more precise, and more truthful.

Consider, for example, one of the many qualifications to the directionality thesis: the ambiguous effects of all-out war on the development of destructive powers. One requirement of quickened economic or military advance is a periodic shaking up of vested rights. This upheaval characteristically requires that government-promoted reform from the top down converge with some form of mass mobilization from the bottom up. If this twofold assault on established arrangements is too violent – if, for example, it depends on war and revolution – it will be very rare, very chancy, and very destructive. Society will oscillate between long periods of relative stagnation in which state-protected privileges and collective deals crowd out experiments in the organization of production and brief interludes in which much is destroyed before anything can be created. To perpetuate the practice of innovation, societies must replace such drastic and violent swings with a more constant liquefaction of deals and privileges. They must invent the structures that make structures easier to change.

THE LIMITS OF COMPROMISE: CHINESE AND JAPANESE EXAMPLES

The themes discussed up to this point in the context of European conflicts can now be reexamined in the larger setting of world history. This new stage in the analysis focuses on the problem posed by the confrontation of an already industrialized and militarily powerful West with non-Western peoples. The examples I use to explore this issue are the different responses of nineteenth-century China and Japan to the Western military threat.

The European episodes provided an occasion on which to understand how something capable of disaggregation could have been assembled in the first place. The combination of productive capabilities, forms of work organization, and larger aspects of state and society that seemed so naturally stuck together in early Western industrialism could nevertheless come apart. The account of their initial combination must therefore be compatible with the later discovery of their separability. The mode of analysis that is brought to bear must show how limitation combined with variability in the making of the initial Western versions of industrialism; the necessitarian connotations of explanation must be weeded out.

To this end, it is useful to analyze developments in an area somewhat distinct from the core zone of the production system. We can then understand the profile of Western industrialism as the result of conflicts that not only had uncertain outcomes but that took place in somewhat different areas of social life, over somewhat different issues, and therefore ran a somewhat different course. The histories of productive and destructive capabilities are, for each other, the most important neighboring regions.

The series of examples I am about to discuss pose the same problems in reverse. In the typical situation, a non-Western country faces a Western power's destructive capability already combined in certain ways with a productive power and with certain organizational and social conditions of both production and destruction. The question for the threatened country then and for the student of society now is: How can we understand the reconstructibility of such a system once it has already been constructed? If reconstruction is possible at all, it has to begin somewhere. One of the most likely places is military organization and production for war. The reason for this likelihood is simple. The military threat cannot easily be disregarded: it is urgent and it is brutal. But the rulers and elites faced by such a threat do not want to recast their entire society in the image of the foreign intruders. They lack the capacity, the time, and the will for such faithful emulation. Count on them to dissociate if they know how.

A purpose of the earlier European discussion was to suggest a more general understanding of relations between practical capabilities and their enabling conditions. The job was made easier and the conceptual scheme simpler by taking examples from a period in which military capability remained more tenuously tied to military power than it became after the emergence of industrialized economies. Now, in the next series of examples, when the military threat is posed by industrial war machines, the organizational and social bases of productive and destructive power begin to merge more fully into each other. As a result, the view of the conditions favorable to the development of productive and destructive capabilities begins to lose its distinctiveness from the ideas used earlier to explain the European escape from the closed circles of an agrarian society. This convergence prepares the way for a more general account of the institutional conditions of collective worldly success.

My primary aim in comparing the Chinese and Japanese responses to the military threat from the West is not to examine why, in the short run, Japan was more successful than China. The criteria of success are, in any event, elusive even when they are confined to the realm of worldly wealth and power. If you compare China to India during the nineteenth century, you find that, despite military and diplomatic humiliation, China remained relatively impervious to foreign governmental and commercial penetration. The treaty port cities in China failed to become, as they had throughout much of India and Southeast Asia, the bases of countrywide military domination and economic disruption. If you extend the comparison with Japan a half-century ahead, the inferences of Japanese success no longer seem as striking. Although the material standard of living in Japan continued to be much higher, the Chinese failure, in the earlier period, to come up with a workable accommodation to Western military and productive techniques set the stage for a more drastic Chinese transformation of Western industrial models. Not worldly success as a whole but the enabling circumstances of military prowess lie at the forefront of my comparison. But because the armed confrontations already take place against the background of industrialized economies, the conditions of military power can no longer be kept even provisionally and relatively separate from those of economic capability. Thus, the Chinese and Japanese examples extend our vision and deepen our insight into the two linkages that stand at the center of this stage of my argument: the connection between practical productive or destructive capacity and the marshaling of its technical and organizational instruments and the connection between these instruments and the larger reshaping of state and society.

Consider first the situation of Chinese military capacity as it stood at the time of the 1910 revolution or, for that matter, of the disastrous 1895 encounter with Japan in the Korean theater. There were formidable constraints on every significant aspect of Chinese military force: the production of firearms and warships, the mobilization of resources and manpower for warfare and weapons making, and the actual operational capacity and organizational strength of the armed forces.

China had pioneered in the early development of firearms. The gunpowder invented in the tenth century was already propelling explosive projectiles in the thirteenth century. But the monopoly controls over armaments production established by the Chinese state since the time of the Han Dynasty, the characteristic concerns of the Confucianized officials in a self-centered agrarian empire, and the existence of long periods of relative peace all worked against the rapid development of firearms. So, in a more far-reaching way, did the absence of an industrialized economy and of a continuous interaction between experimental science and mechanical technology. During Ming rule (1368–1644), the inferiority of Chinese firearms to European ordnance became unmistakable, and the Chinese themselves recognized it as soon as they saw the first Portuguese weapons, in 1520. They bought these arms and, with foreign help, tried making them on their own. They used them to stave off the Manchus. The Manchus in power used them successfully against the Russians in 1685 and 1686. But by the time of the first Opium War (1839–1842), the Chinese guns and artillery were fatally inferior to their British counterparts, and Chinese naval power remained insubstantial.

The immediate background to the establishment of arsenals and rapid development of armament production in the period after the Opium War was twofold: the suppression of the dangerous popular rebellions of the Taiping and the Nien and the threatened intrusion of foreign military power, whether from Europe and the United States or from Japan. The response to the Western threats interfered with the reaction against the Japanese. The degree of reliance on foreign financial and technical help accepted for the sake of crushing the popular rebellion proved to undercut Chinese military independence in any confrontation with Western powers.

The reforming statesmen, lower officials, and comprador intellectuals who took the initiative in arsenal making and military reform were realistic. They understood that rapid firearms and naval development were vital to the security of the state, that the steam-powered machinery, the techniques, and the organizations employed in the arsenals would have transformative implications for the entire Chinese economy, that the necessary productive initiatives and military policies would require wider administrative, fiscal, and social reforms, and that it was impossible to foresee the outer limits of the impact. Many of the reformers nevertheless seem to have expected and hoped that the "self-strengthening" reforms would leave the basic hierarchical order of state and society untouched.[17]

[17] For an analysis of the initial phase of the late Ch'ing military reform efforts, see Mary Wright, *The Last Stand of Chinese Conservatism: The T'ung-Chih Restoration, 1862–1874*, Stanford, Stanford, 1957, pp. 196–221.

By 1875, the major arsenals at Shanghai, Tientsin, and Nanking were producing at full capacity and a national maritime defense policy had begun to emerge. Administrators and industrialists soon carried over to other fields of manufacturing the forms of governmental sponsorship and merchant management in enterprises pioneered in armaments production.[18] The arsenals, and their periphery of related industries, represented a real beginning in military power backed by industrialization. But they suffered from the limitations imposed by the wider social and governmental context. The major responsibility for these constraints lay in the failure of a weakened government to cut through the costly bickering among different categories of managers, merchants, and officials; to assemble the needed workers and funds; to suppress the privileges of some and grab the money of others; to identify the dissident, ambitious, and enterprising elements of the elite that might serve as the instruments and beneficiaries of such a policy; and to keep out of foreign adventures until the Chinese state was ready for them. Certainly the conflict with Japan put more of a strain on the arsenals than their managers were prepared to handle.

The arsenals themselves were a promising although abortive start. But the larger financial and manpower basis of military force and industrial experimentation remained entirely inadequate. One sign of this inadequacy was the weakness of central control over local military power. In the course of the desperate struggle against the popular rebellions of the mid-nineteenth century, the local elites, already well encased in the apparatus of the state, had come to lead and master the militias that were the country's major source of military manpower. This stranglehold on manpower that might have been used by central reformers for military or productive purposes was closely allied to the fiscal starvation of government. Although the total burden of the land tax was relatively high, an extraordinary amount of it stuck to the fingers of local officials and oligarchs or got spent for relatively unproductive uses. The burden fell most heavily on the minor tenants and proprietors who had become the mainstay of the agrarian economy. Yet the funds were largely unavailable for investment in military or civilian industrial plant and in the recruitment and provision of centrally controlled armies.

Late imperial China lacked a numerous, self-confident cadre of entrepreneurs, institutionalized opportunities for industrial and military innovation, and rulers committed to elicit mass support for reform efforts. In such a circumstance, neither military forces nor industrial enterprises could easily become areas where soldiers or workers dealt with one another and with their superiors in untried ways. The characteristic development was not the emergence in the internal life of the military or industrial

18 See Thomas L. Kennedy, *The Arms of Kiangnan: Modernization in the Chinese Ordnance Industry, 1860–1895*, Westview, Boulder, Colo., 1978, especially pp. 152–154.

organization of a counter-model to the surrounding society. It was instead an unguided mixture of residual forms of peasant solidarity and deference with the rough-and-ready discipline of trying to get a strange new job done, one way or another. Much later, the Communists would self-consciously exploit the self-defensive organization of the peasantry as a basis for military organization while gradually drawing peasants into a different structure of hierarchy and belief. The failure to produce a similar organizational experiment at the earlier moment of military and industrial reform exacted a high price. It resulted in armies that could not be counted on to fight in small units with high measures of operational discretion, coordination, and flexibility and in an industrial labor force that worked most effectively when it was allowed to remain a collection of ingenious, self-taught artisans operating newfangled machines under a single roof.

The constraints and the opportunities of Chinese military development in the closing decades of the empire were part of a larger struggle over the control and uses of governmental power. The late Ch'ing state emerged with few advantages from its bout with the mass insurrections and the foreign intrusions of the mid-nineteenth century. The relationship of the landowning, mercantile, and official cadres to one another and to governmental power was an especially important element in the story. By the late Ch'ing, the Chinese elite of landowners, officials, and merchants was sufficiently unified in its perceived interests and active beliefs to monopolize in its own favor the powers of the state and to unite aggressively against any force that might threaten its privileged access to central and local government. But it was also diverse enough to deny broad-based support to any reforming clique that proposed bold realignments for the sake of essential continuity and national salvation. The pressure to defeat the popular rebels had led high officials to deliver effective authority over local military forces into the hands of local gentry leaders. The decadent corporate forms of village life had been largely replaced by these new, militarized and gentry-controlled forms of local organization. And the reformist movement toward local self-government had itself become something of a cover-up for the manipulation of local administration by landlords and merchants and for the further blurring of the lines between grassroots government and grassroots oligarchy. The state was cannibalized in its foundations.

Other aspects of the situation come to light when the focus shifts to the dealings of this oligarchy with the rural masses – smallholders, petty tenants, and agricultural laborers – and with the dissident intellectualized elites that flourished in the country's larger cities. In both instances, the early years of the republic clarified the facts and their implications.

When you consider the extent to which ground-level administration had been captured by a relatively unified ruling and possessing class with deep local roots, it seems surprising that the late Ch'ing saw so little of what I earlier described as reversion to natural economy. In fact, petty tenancy and proprietorship continued to account for a major and even increasing part of agrarian production. All sectors of the population participated heavily in market activities.[19]

The explanation lies in the consequences of the earlier interplay between the reform of governmental structures and the deepening commercialization of the economy. The state, under the impact of successive encounters with the steppe peoples, had gained the institutional means with which to guarantee a minimal local presence and to save itself from fiscal starvation and administrative impotence. At the same time, the elites had been progressively redefined in ways requiring their active participation in both markets and administration. Their characteristic forms of dominion over the rural masses worked through, rather than around or against, governmental and market institutions. This fact illuminates the importance of various forms of "parasitic landlordism" and manipulations of the tax burden.

Although this was not a formula for full-fledged economic and governmental collapse, it did mean that the masses of town and country were robbed of the legal facilities and economic occasions for recurrent self-organization. Nothing is more telling in this respect than the functional replacement of the corporate forms of village organization by gentry-controlled local militia.[20] If the communal structure of local popular life survived, it did so because the gentry leader was also a lineage head or because in moments of economic and military crisis, the village continued to close ranks self-defensively. In such a circumstance, collective popular organization, when it could emerge at all, readily took covert or adversarial forms. This underground, oppositional militancy encouraged secret societies and inspired countermodels of community and hierarchy during its periods of successful resistance. The breathing space in which working people could organize collectively had always been some partial distinction between state administration and local elites. Whenever this distinction vanished, the laborers and petty proprietors and tenants were in trouble. Their chances for nonviolent organized militancy diminished.

Another aspect of the situation was the relation between the dominant, locally based, economic and governmental oligarchy and the more Westernized and footloose elites that sprang up in the larger cities. Because these dissident elites had no deep link with the bases of power in the

19 For an analysis of the final state of the money-based agrarian economy in China before the establishment of communist rule, see Ramon H. Myers, *The Chinese Peasant Economy: Agricultural Development in Hopei and Shantung, 1890–1949*, Harvard, Cambridge, 1970, especially pp. 288–291. Studies like Myers's confirm the vitality of a broad range of large-scale and small-scale holdings. But they also depict the technological stagnation that usually attends the gradualistic, nonconflictual escape from reversion cycles.

20 See Philip A. Kuhn, *Rebellion and Its Enemies in Late Imperial China: Militarization and Social Structure*, Harvard, Cambridge, 1970, pp. 211–223.

countryside and the smaller cities, they had little commitment to the preservation of the established social order. Their vague nationalism and leftism became the crucible for republican agitation and national resistance. This activism played a major role in the Communist advance at a time when the peasantry had shown itself unresponsive, when leftist putschism had been undercut by Soviet vacillation, and when the politics of national unity against the invader provided an invaluable shield for building revolutionary armies and popular support.

Thus, China witnessed a far-reaching paralysis of state power and the denial of opportunities for recurrent popular mobilization. All the particular aspects of constraint on the development of military capabilities can be traced back to this more fundamental circumstance. Like every real situation, however, it was full of dimly perceived and barely missed opportunities. There were any number of moments at which an alliance of reforming statesmen and discontented gentry, officials, and intellectuals might have seized the state and disentangled some of its powers from the hold of locally based oligarchies. The most striking of these occasions during the late Chi'ng was the Hundred Days reform of 1898. It was not written in the stars that the young Kuang Hsu emperor and his reforming coterie would be defeated and destroyed by the reaction organized around the Dowager Empress. Reformist takeovers might in turn have been combined with different measures of appeal to mass organization. The wave to the masses might have failed to initiate an outright plan of radical reform, but it could easily have become an incident in the effort of besieged reformers and putschists to stay in power by hook or by crook.

During the same period, Japan provides an example of far more successful development of military power than China. The analysis of the contrast helps illuminate the enabling conditions of force and wealth in a period when the means of both production and destruction have already become industrialized. At the outset of this second pendant in the comparative analysis, however, it is illuminating to see how much each country's experience was shaped by the other's.

One of the most important causes of Japan's ability to hold off direct Western domination was China's failure to do so. The Western imperial powers were tied up in their Chinese adventures as well as in a spate of largely unrelated internecine struggles, from the Franco-Prussian War to the American Civil War. The Opium Wars (1839–1842, 1856–1860) in China gave warning to the most farsighted Japanese leaders of what awaited countries that failed to submit to the ordeal of transformation for the sake of wealth and power.

Later, Japan's worldly success, translated into imperialist attacks, became decisive for the form of China's own transformation. The national resistance to Japanese occupation became the arena for the struggle between Communist and Nationalist forces and the school for a new relationship between the working masses and the political nation. The resistance period therefore left its mark for all time to come on Chinese society. It became the occasion for China's fitful reach toward a disaggregation of the North Atlantic models of industrialism far more drastic than any yet realized in Japan.

The reciprocal interferences between the histories of these two peoples at the moment of their encounter with Western might serves as an initial admonition about anything that can be said in a comparative analysis. Whatever larger truth we may infer from a comparative analysis of these Chinese and Japanese experiences depends for its force on such seemingly extraneous circumstances as the physical proximity of the two lands: the particular way in which the land masses happen to have been disposed on the surface of the planet at the time these historical collisions were occurring. One of the tests of historical realism must be the ability to acknowledge the disorder introduced by all such random connections and to recognize that this disorder is not confined to some limited aspect of experience but penetrates every aspect in different ways. Any insight with a true claim to generality must reconcile its vision of emergent reality and possibility with its understanding of the relentless and fateful accumulation of loosely related circumstances and choices.

Consider, to begin with, the defining elements of Japan's military capability at the times of the Sino-Japanese War of 1895 and of the Russo-Japanese War a decade later.

The initial basis of this capability was the armaments industry. Even more than in any Western country, industrialization in Japan was spearheaded by mechanized, factory-based arms manufacture. During the closing years of the Tokugawa regime, initiatives had already begun to proliferate in the crucial vanguard areas of foundries, weapons production, and shipbuilding. The actual or anticipated pressure of Western encroachments was by far the most far-reaching motive for these efforts. The first reverberatory furnaces built for iron processing were set up by the Tokugawa government and by the powerful domain governments of Satsuma, Mito, and Saga. A still greater number of domains (*han*) participated actively in the construction of shipyards.[21] After 1868 the Meiji government dramatically expanded its industrial initiatives in all these areas.[22] Even the textile industry – the first large industrial sector not directly related to military aims – began under governmental auspices. Only later were the industries sold into private hands. Although the immediate occasion for their sale was fiscal pressure on the state, the decision also reflected the crystallization of an alliance and a program. Reactionary and popular forces had been put down, and enough

21 See W.G. Beasley, *The Meiji Restoration*, Stanford, Stanford, 1972, pp. 123–124.

22 See Kajinishi Mitsuhaya, "The Birth of Heavy Industry in Japan: With Reference to a Re-Examination of the Meiji Restoration," summarized in *An Outline of Japanese Economic History, 1603–1940*, eds. Mikio Sumiya and Koji Taira, Univ. of Tokyo, 1979, pp. 201–203.

of a consensus among realigned bureaucratic and business groups had been established to make direct governmental management of industry dispensable and embarrassing.

Many of these late nineteenth century industries ran at a loss when first established. The major source of investment funds came from the land tax, which underwent a significant change in definition and allocation through the reforms of 1873–1874. The use of this source of finance, together with the obsessive study of Western engineering and science, gave the Japanese armaments industry a degree of independence from Western capital and assistance entirely lacking in China.

Certainly the existence of a large agrarian surplus was vital to this policy. In this sense, the military buildup reaped the benefits of the earlier escape from periodic reversion to natural economy that had taken place during the early Tokugawa. Nevertheless, the total tax–rent burden on the actual cultivators – petty tenants or proprietors and agricultural laborers – seems to have been, on the whole, higher in both Meiji and Tokugawa Japan than in late Ch'ing China. The Meiji seizure of central government, the further advance of local landlords, and the repressive demobilization of the peasantry were all crucial to the investment strategy that prevailed.

The second foundation of Japanese military power, alongside the armaments industry, was the establishment of a mass conscript army. Again, the breakthrough depended on a definition of the state's basic character and supporting alliances. It was necessary to defeat the strong samurai groups who resisted the conscript army as a threat to their power interests and self-definition. The resistance of these groups sparked confrontations that mixed the recruitment issue with the struggle over the abolition of samurai stipends and the debate over the invasion of Korea.[23] Again, the danger of popular rebellion had to be quashed. The raising of a conscript army presupposed a minimal degree of control over insurrectionary movements. Once such an army had been raised, it could in turn be used to terrorize the people. But the threat of rebellion within the ranks persisted, as shown by episodes like the 1878 mutiny of the Imperial Guard. The new masters of the state owed their success in transforming the military structure of power to not having had to face all these dangers simultaneously. For this reprieve they could thank their luck as much as their cunning.

A third and more intangible boost to Japanese military capability was the gradual development of an organizational structure, in the military, industrial, and administrative enterprises, that reconciled the achievement of high degrees of effectiveness with two other aims in apparent tension with each other.

[23] See E. Herbert Norman, *Soldier and Peasant in Japan: The Origins of Conscription*, Univ. of British Columbia, Vancouver, 1965, especially pp. 43–47.

One of these goals was to minimize the disruptive impact of the new organizational arrangements on the hierarchies and habits of the reordered society and the reformed state while exploiting the opportunities that Japanese forms of corporate solidarity and hierarchical deference might create for industrial discipline. The protracted though declining vitality of corporate village institutions through the Tokugawa period provided an initial apprenticeship in joint, supervised activities within large organizations. The system of commercialized agriculture combined with petty handicraft provided large numbers of people with an experience of skilled labor in primitive manufacturing. It also deepened an agrarian economy that helped finance industrialization.

The other, contrasting purpose in the development of organizational life was to minimize the need to invent structures radically different from those that were emerging in the West. Few leaders of the governing classes were willing to take chances with an organized complex of men and machines radically different from the military and economic enterprises that had already broken in upon the country; any drastic redesign of organizations or technologies would take time, entail risks, and require imagination. The contrast between the desire to avoid social disruption and the uninterest in bold organizational invention was diminished by the sharp divisions between task-defining and task-executing jobs within the Western models. It was also moderated by the way in which Japanese dispositions could be used to deal with the weak points in the Western schemes, and most especially with confrontation and resistance inside the enterprise. The equivocal fusion of contract, community, and domination could be extended more readily because it did not have to pass directly from the agrarian to the industrial setting. The many corporate bodies that flourished in an increasingly commercialized economy allying agriculture to petty manufacture supplied facilitating links.

Such circumstances, however, failed to produce an easy marriage of Japanese and Western styles of organization. There were brutal struggles whose outcome long remained uncertain, as evidenced by the conflicts surrounding the Factory Act of 1911 and other waves of violent labor unrest.[24] For the new rulers of the country and their allies in business and bureaucracy, success in these struggles was unthinkable without a minimum of consensus among themselves and a willingness to use every repressive and financial weapon at the disposal of government. The outcome, which came to look so natural in retrospect, was in fact constantly jeopardized by the dissensions of the leading circles in Japanese society and the desperate attempts of workers and agitators to find an alternative future.

24 See Stephen S. Large, *Organized Workers and Socialist Politics in Interwar Japan*, Cambridge, Cambridge, 1981, pp. 40–50; Andrew Gordon, *The Evolution of Labor Relations in Japan: Heavy Industry, 1835–1955*, Harvard Univ. Press, Cambridge, 1985, pp. 116—121, 211–235.

The military capability whose elements I have just described resulted from two interwoven lines of development. One of them was the association established among the restored state, the realigned elites, and the working people. The other was the relation of the empire to foreign powers.

To understand the first of these two sequences, you need to distinguish the ambitions and alliances that produced the Meiji Restoration from the content of governmental policy in the aftermath of the Restoration. There is no direct inference from the former to the latter. Many of the groups most important to the overthrow of the Tokugawa regime suffered defeat and disappointment in the factional struggles that took place from the very moment of the *bakufu*'s downfall. No one could safely predict the identities of the winners and losers in this contest from the events that had led up to the Restoration or for that matter from any deep-seated features of Japanese society.

In the late Tokugawa, at least two major social groups remained only very imperfectly integrated into the structure of the state: the middle-level or village samurai and the more enterprising landlord–entrepreneurs of the commercialized agrarian and handicraft economy, who were largely excluded from the immediate benefits of participation in state power. The entrepreneurs were harassed by governmental regulation without being broken or tamed by it. The samurai were cut off from the *bakufu* structure without being systematically deprived of the means for doing violence. Both these groups provided vital support to the Restorationist movement. Neither had any ready counterpart in China, where the relatively tight entente of officials, landlords, and merchants had ensconced itself more deeply and uniformly in the structure of local administration and military force. Besides, the domain governments had a greater autonomy as bases of power than the regional Chinese authorities. The Japanese elites, as a whole, had a keener awareness of national distinctiveness and vulnerability than their Chinese counterparts.

But the content of the crucial reforms in the first decade of the new regime was another matter. That the reshaping and administration of the land tax would favor landlords over small tenants might have been expected from the forces at work before and during the Restoration. But the destruction or redefinition of samurai privileges was the work of men anxious to keep the financial and military resources of the state from being immobilized by a stipendiary caste. These men expected and got from their victories in the quarrels of the early Meiji era (1868–1912) a wider margin of maneuver to revise the organizational settings for production, administration, and warfare in ways that wedded national and oligarchic interests.

The seizure of the state, the use of the agrarian surplus to finance militarily oriented industry, and the careful avoidance of premature military adventures permitted a growing measure of independence from foreign control. Each such advance in national autonomy in turn enlarged the state's options in redefining the country's relationship to world alliances and the world economy.

By all these means, governmental power was disengaged from an order of privilege so confining that it would have blocked any sequence of trials and errors in the search for the enabling conditions of military and economic power. Yet the wealthy and powerful retained a continuing identity; the defeated in the internecine quarrels of the new regime won a chance to survive and prosper under a new identity. The realignment of the elites, the redefinition of land-tenure and land-tax arrangements, and the halting, precarious creation of a semi-constitutional regime of government and industrial relations all created a structure within which groups could redefine and reorganize themselves. This limited opportunity for recurrent collective militancy, however, was not allowed to escalate into the style of mass mobilization and institutional invention that might have produced a more path-breaking industrialized success. Power at the center, resolute, relatively available for transformative use, and capable of supporting an atmosphere of differential and limited but real opportunities for collective redefinition and self-organization – this was the essential achievement of the Meiji state, the source of its superiority over late Ch'ing China, and its primary contribution to Japan's military and industrial success.

The comparative study of these Chinese and Japanese experiences suggests two related conclusions. One of them has to do with the nature of freedom and constraint in the relation between enabling circumstances and practical capacity. The other conclusion deals with the connection between the bases of military and of productive capability and between the line of argument developed in this chapter and the view of the North Atlantic breakthrough suggested by the earlier chapters.

Do not misread this comparative discussion as an analysis of the reasons why late nineteenth-century China was doomed to fail and late nineteenth-century Japan guaranteed to succeed in their respective efforts to match the Western threat. Remember the relativity of success and failure that becomes apparent as soon as you take a longer temporal view. Consider the enormous importance of the effect that each of these countries had on the other in the course of their contrasting response to the Western powers. Bear in mind the barely lost opportunities at every crucial juncture in the events.

It is true that every measure of success served as a platform from which to launch further advances. In the Japanese experience, the mutual reinforcement of domestic reform and foreign autonomy had enormous importance. More generally, every step toward the disengagement of governmental power from a tightly defined structure of privilege and collective alliances, from a fixed scheme of hierarchy and divisions, multiplies options at the next round. It loosens the connection between military, productive, or administrative activities and their organizational bases and between these bases and the larger ordering of state and society. It allows a reformist or revolutionary leadership to cast about for a redefinition of these linkages that will be both effective and (to their eyes) justifiable.

But the drawing of success out of success and of failure out of failure is easily exaggerated. For one of the striking facts about any real historical situation is the frequent inversion of hierarchies of apparent achievement. Power is paralyzed by privilege and collective organization by the hardened deals and hierarchies that emerge when people think they have averted such threats to worldly success. The opportunities for transformative politics – reformist or revolutionary – suddenly reappear when government seems helpless and any major restructuring of collective alliances and identities appears out of the question.

Again, you might reasonably infer from the comparative discussion that, on several counts, Japan in 1860 was in a better position than China to achieve a limited, reformist accommodation to Western military and industrial power. The single most important Japanese advantage may have been the existence in Japan of significant, locally based elites who were imperfectly incorporated into the structure of central government and in whose eyes, society – the society that counted – was already at war with the state. China, it seems, would have been forced from the start to stage a far more radical break with its established social and governmental order if it was to have a chance at success.

Nevertheless, this judgment of relative advantage for a politics of protective reform is much more tentative than it seems at first. The more closely you study the sequence of events in China, the more you are impressed by the number of occasions on which a reformist clique came close to seizing the state. The most you can plausibly say is that, in China, such a clique would soon have been forced to appeal to a larger mass constituency than proved necessary to the founders of the Meiji state. The Chinese reformers would have confronted an elite more uniformly and deeply ensconced in the privileges of local governmental power, a more immediate foreign threat, and a more formidable task of communication and control. In this view, the Chinese reformers would have been driven to more radical expedients or else would have forfeited their chances of survival. Comparative analysis is on safer ground when it suggests that, at any level of radicalism and accommodation, the Chinese and Japanese solutions would have had to differ in the particular content of their sustaining alliances and transformative programs.

Yet vulgar historiography and social science, deep-logic social theories, and common prejudice, all join in giving a semblance of retrospective necessity to the different outcomes. We ridicule the court historians of the ancient agrarian monarchies for their kowtowing. At least they professed to find moral insight in accomplished fact. Some even used the lessons of history to urge restraint on the powerful. Latter-day necessitarians have no such excuse.

UNDERSTANDING AND HARNESSING THE IMPERATIVE OF SOCIAL PLASTICITY

The European experiences discussed earlier in this essay focus attention on the dissociations and recombinations of institutional arrangements that allowed certain countries to exploit new organizational and technological opportunities in warfare. The later, Asian examples present the same problem from a slightly different angle. They draw our attention to efforts to dissociate some of the traits of the Western industrialized, imperialist societies from other traits: to combine Western levels of productive or destructive capability with indigenous or newly invented ways of coordinating work or, more commonly, of combining imported Western styles of work organization with non-Western governmental and economic institutions.

In both the European preindustrial and the Asian postindustrial situations, success, even survival, required the practice of an art of institutional dismemberment and recombination. This art constantly rearranges the two linkages repeatedly considered in this essay. One link joins a practical capability to the immediate organizational setting of that capability – a style of coordination in production or warfare. The other link connects a way of organizing work to a more comprehensive set of governmental and economic arrangements. The practice of institutional dissociation and recombination shakes up and wears down a society's plan of social division and social ranking. Roles and hierarchies depend for their perpetuation on the stability of particular institutions. This shaking up and wearing down represents one of the major forms taken by the imperative of self-transformation in history.

The experiences of military success and failure traced here highlight a series of puzzles and paradoxes in the practice of institutional dissociation and recombination. To consider these puzzles and paradoxes is to begin the work of generalizing the argument of this chapter into a thesis about the institutional conditions of worldly success. It is to turn from the mirror of destruction to the productive activities this mirror imperfectly reflects.

The military examples suggest that the repeated practice of institutional dissociation and recombination is not a random walk. It has – at least, it has often had – a direction. Practiced long and often enough, it moves societies toward greater plasticity. Again and again, the changes that prove most congenial to the development and the exploitation of technological and organizational opportunities in warfare or production unite two sets of characteristics.

The superior solutions turn the relations among soldiers or workers into a visible social image of experimental, practical reason. The workers or soldiers do not remain the passive executants of a rigid predefined plan. They vary the plan – and yet maintain overall coordination – in the course of executing it. As a result, they do not stay pegged in immutable roles.

The fluidity of the contrast between task-defining and task-executing acts coincides with the softening of the distinctions among task-executing acts themselves. Today, the vanguardist forms of warfare (commandos, tanks, air power) and production (high-technology industry operating with flexible production processes and nonspecific "meta-machines") represent the practical activities that have moved furthest toward this fluidity. But even if we go back to periods long before the emergence of these modern varieties of production and warfare we can distinguish among military or productive styles by their relative closeness to the same practical ideal embodied in contemporary vanguardist warfare or production. Movement toward this ideal has generally brought success to the individuals, groups, and countries that have achieved it.

The persistent practice of institutional dissociation and recombination also favors social arrangements with a second set of characteristics. This second group of traits has to do not with the immediate organizational setting of production or warfare – the style of work organization – but with the larger framework of governmental and economic institutions within which these forms of work organization exist. If we can discern a cumulative movement in the institutional frameworks of our practical activities of warfare and production, it is a movement toward solutions that do not allow a rigid set of social roles and hierarchies to predefine the practical relations among people. The waning of the influence that any such plan of social division and hierarchy exercises on the ways in which workers or soldiers collaborate keeps the organization of work and exchange open to opportunistic experiment and to the social imitation of practical reason.

Beyond a point, the weakening of the influence of social roles and hierarchies on jobs or exchange relations implies the weakening of the social roles and hierarchies themselves. For the strength of a system of social stations consists in the extent to which it imposes a ready-made script on people's practical or passionate dealings. The Prussian military reformers of the early nineteenth century – like all perceptive reformers before or after them – knew that they could not expect soldiers who were hardly more than reluctant serfs to enact the new, more mobile tactical and operational techniques Something had to be done to change German society.

Notice that this cumulative change in the broader institutional setting of economic or military activity requires the occasional invention of new institutions, even different kinds of institutions. It does not require fewer, less definite, or less stable institutional arrangements. It does not mean anarchy or even permanent flux. Some institutions and practices are better than others at keeping open the area of practical experimentation. In fact, the solutions that diminish the practical influence of rigid roles and hierarchies are likely to be more explicit if not more elaborate than the institutions they replace. For such hierarchy-subverting and role-loosening arrangements represent an artifact of the will imposed on inherited, half-articulate routines.

These two sets of characteristics give precision to the idea of social plasticity. Their description elucidates the thesis that the quest for collective wealth and power requires a cumulative movement toward greater plasticity in the organizational and institutional setting of production, exchange, and warfare. The imperative of plasticity requires that advances in productive or destructive powers be achieved through the subversion of fixed plans of social division and hierarchy and of stark contrasts between task setting and task following. All possible combinations have to be tried out, as quickly and as freely as possible. The only structure that can be allowed to subsist is one that offers the fewest obstacles to this principle of pitiless recombination.

No sooner do we state the thesis of plasticity with greater richness and precision than we see that it must be qualified in several ways. The preceding discussion of episodes in military history illustrates these qualifications and suggests their force. The question is: What remains of the initial thesis once we have done full justice to these reservations?

The first qualification concerns the multiplicity of relatively conservative responses that are always available. An elite can use such responses in its efforts to reconcile the imperative of greater plasticity with the preservation of the vested interests and the traditional pieties supported by the established institutional order. It is not enough for an alternative style of work organization and an alternative set of governmental and economic institutions to outdistance its rivals in the degree of plasticity it embodies. The reform program must be accepted and implemented. Besides, the struggle over alternative responses to practical challenge takes place amid institutional arrangements and widely shared preconceptions that bias the outcome of the conflict. They bias it not only by placing certain groups in a better position to dictate the solution but also by discouraging solutions that require too violent a break with inherited ways.

Moreover, the test of success that counts is the comparison of one war machine or industrial economy with its closest and most threatening adversaries. In the long run, we all die. In the short run, we die differentially. A competent conservative elite always finds that it can catch up to a rival country, or simply meet its own people's expectations, on the basis of organizations and institutions that preserve a great deal of the preexisting social order, with its roles and hierarchies and its enacted dogmas about the possible and desirable forms of human association. Thus, those same Prussian military reformers of the Napoleonic era correctly understood that they did not have to make Hohenzollern Germany into revolutionary France in order to lay the social and institutional basis on which Germany could meet the French threat. With luck and ingenuity, reformers like these can even find ways to turn to competitive advantage what seemed archaic features of their societies.

The availability of the intelligent conservative response to the imperative of plasticity reminds us of another qualification to the thesis that the search for wealth and strength has a particular institutional direction. We seem unable to discover any limited list of necessary institutional vehicles for any given measure of social plasticity. We can compare alternative sets of practices or institutions as more or less responsive to the twin aspects of plasticity distinguished earlier. But we cannot say that a given level of plasticity – or of the practical capabilities that plasticity permits – must be realized through particular institutional arrangements. We know that we cannot because every attempt to specify such necessary correspondences has been foiled by the next episode of institutional dissociation and recombination in the present or by the next discovery about institutional dissociation and recombination in the past. Thus, the successful institutional responses to the military challenges discussed in this essay simply fail to fit the patterns favored by theories that relate levels of practical capability to particular institutional systems. The most influential doctrines in the history of modern social thought have been just such theories; Marxism provides the exemplary instance.

The art of institutional dissociation and recombination does not work by selecting the best solutions from a closed list of alternative arrangements. For even if such a list exists, we do not know what it is, and our ideas about its nature and content have been repeatedly discredited. Institutional reinvention operates, instead, with the practical and conceptual materials handed down by the traditions people are in or by the traditions they can remember, recover, and study.

The influence of sequence, which so often serves the cause of the conservative reformer, also helps explain why we find less variety in the history of institutional forms than a justified skepticism about the deep-seated necessity of past or present institutions might lead us to expect. The record of experiments with the organization of military and economic activity is too messy to exemplify a table of correspondences between particular levels of capability and particular institutional systems. But it is also too tainted by narrowing obsessions and imitations and by privileged strangleholds on social resources to demonstrate the untrammeled freedom of invention that in our most optimistic moments we may be tempted to claim. It is because of the influence of what comes before on what comes after that our institutional settlements and inventions can have both an ad hoc, pasted-together quality and a surprising repetitiveness.

The significance of sequence can be generalized in a way that both qualifies further the thesis of plasticity and connects it more intimately to the experiences analyzed in this book. The general point is quite simply that the practice of institutional dissociation and recombination has a history. This history is, and increasingly becomes, worldwide.

In the course of their domestic and international conflicts the Western powers created a version of an industrialized war machine and production system that settled accounts with the mobilizational and technological requirements of warfare in a particular way. There are no deep-seated reasons why the vanguardist style of warfare could not have emerged more quickly and taken over a broader range of military activities than it did. But it seems that in prerevolutionary Europe a faster pace of radical organizational innovation would have required a lasting alliance between the people in charge of central governments and the ordinary working people. The results of a large number of conflicts, in different areas of social life, would have had to converge toward unprecedented forms of popular self-organization or revolutionary despotism.

Such innovations might have required a higher measure of institutional invention than the solutions that in fact prevailed. They might have also demanded a larger number of failures on the part of conservative statesmen, anxious to discover practical compromises between higher levels of capability and the maintenance of established orders of privilege. Nevertheless, breakthroughs of comparable magnitude had occurred before. Without them, the European escape from the closed circles of the agrarian societies would not have been possible.

Alternatively, you can easily imagine that the settling of accounts with the pressures of intensified conflict would have allowed an even smaller place to vanguardist warfare and to the subversion of established forms of hierarchy and division. The European oligarchies, relatively successful as they were, might have proved even better at accommodating a more flexible style in the war machine and production system with the maintenance of their inherited privileges. They would have had to have been bolder in turning patrons and clients, masters and servants, into managerial task definers and skilled but obedient task executors. Later, the Japanese came somewhat closer to doing precisely this.

Once the initial Western version of an industrialized economy and war machine had been set up, it influenced the immediate options available to the non-Western peoples as responses to this Western threat. Had the triumphant Western model of industrialism and warfare gone further toward the vanguardist, flexible styles of production and of fighting, the effort of the Japanese elites to disaggregate this model in order to preserve the essentials of their own privileges and their own identities would have been that much more difficult. The art of dissociation and recombination would have demanded a still greater virtuosity from conservative reformers and it would have offered still more opportunities to their adversaries among the masses or the elites. On the other hand, had the dominant Western model of industrialized armies and economies been less hierarchy-subverting and role-loosening than it was, the Chinese reformers would have had a shorter distance to go, and a greater chance of success. Reforming elites around the world would have had reason for even more confidence in the possibility of achieving even greater productive and destructive power with a minimum of disturbance to established social orders.

Thus, when we place institutional experimentation on a worldwide scale and examine its workings over long stretches of time we discover that its earlier and later moments have a relation we cannot adequately understand as the outward effect of lawlike forces. Each move in this sequence represents a transaction between the aims of people who have gained control of central governments and who are trying to impress their will on events for conservative or revolutionary purposes and the versions of workable production systems or war machines currently available in the world as models. The current forms of industrial and military organization may be ill suited to the aims of the rulers. Then, the work of dismemberment and rearrangement becomes that much harder. The people in charge, or their would-be successors, have to go further in the invention of an alternative organizational and social context for practical capabilities. This more ambitious practice may fail. It may fail because its practitioners choose unworkable solutions or because the inventors invent too slowly. Foreign and domestic enemies may do their will while the innovators try to come up with new ways of conducting production and warfare.

To appreciate the complex relation between the pull of plasticity and the push of sequence in the history of the institutional forms of warfare and production is to grasp a central, unresolved ambiguity in our collective drive for practical empowerment. Does the movement toward plasticity converge toward particular ways of organizing work and of arranging the broader institutional framework of productive and destructive activity? Or does it, on the contrary, leave us free to choose among an indefinitely large number of forms of social organization? Is it a particular fate or only the fate of a radical contingency?

We do not know the answers to these questions. We cannot tell how much built-in content the requirement of plasticity will prove to have. Nor can we console ourselves with the idea that it would be paradoxical for it to have any content at all. There is nothing paradoxical about the idea that a machine – or an institutional system – capable of accelerated self-revision may have to be designed according to precise specifications. It would not be surprising to find that people may revise such a machine or such a system in ways that make it either less open or more open to further revisions. The appearance of paradox dissipates further once we replace the vague ideas of indefinition or revisability with the more precise conception of plasticity on which the argument of this book draws.

Whatever the extent of our freedom to determine the practical forms of social plasticity, our task remains the same. The influence of sequence and the requirements of flexibility allow many different institutional combinations to emerge and to survive. We must choose the variants that also serve a more inclusive conception of human empowerment. For even if plasticity turns out to make many particular demands on us, we are still likely to have room for maneuver in choosing how and how much to satisfy these demands. A mobilizational despotism may be able to meet them. But so may a more radical democracy that fragments and liquefies claims on the resources – economic capital, governmental power, or technical expertise – by which we create the social future within the social present.

We can harness the requirement of plasticity to a higher social ideal. We can respond to it in ways that continue to lift from social life the taint of dependence and depersonalization – of servitude to rigid hierarchies and prostration to inherited roles. We can satisfy it by means that enable us to assert, as individuals and as groups, a more deliberate mastery over the terms of our practical, emotional, and cognitive access to one another. We can turn it into a foothold for our attempts to make our social contexts nourish our context-revising powers and respect our context-transcending vocation. We can give the imperative of plasticity the focus and the authority it lacks.

The Institutional Program of Empowered Democracy

9

A Proto-Theory

EXPLANATORY AND PROGRAMMATIC THEMES

False Necessity presents an explanatory theory of society and a program for social reconstruction. The theory works toward a radical alternative to Marxism. The program suggests a radical alternative to social democracy.

As an explanatory theory of society, *False Necessity* seeks to free social explanation from its dependence upon the denial of our freedom to resist and to remake our forms of social life. It offers a relentlessly anti-necessitarian view that nevertheless generates a broad range of social and historical explanations: some comprehensive and abstract, others focused and concrete. It carries to extremes the thesis that everything in society is politics, mere politics, and then draws out of this seemingly negativistic and paradoxical idea a detailed understanding of social life.

As a program for social reconstruction, *False Necessity* shows how we may carry forward the radical project of freeing our practical and passionate dealings from the constraints imposed upon them by entrenched social roles and hierarchies. It argues that the best hope for the advancement of this radical cause – the cause that leftists share with liberals – lies in a series of revolutionary reforms in the organization of governments and economies and in the character of our personal relations. The explanatory and programmatic ideas of the book are closely connected: each supports the other, and each expresses an aspect of the vision that both share.

This vision takes the last and most surprising step in the itinerary of modern historicism. For it recognizes that the quality of our relation, as context-revising agents, to the institutional and imaginative contexts we establish and inhabit is itself up for grabs in history. We can construct not just new and different social worlds but social worlds that more fully embody and respect the creative power whose suppression or containment all societies and cultures seem to require. In this way we can break a little farther out of the tedious, degrading rhythm of history – with its long lulls of collective narcolepsy punctuated by violent revolutionary seizures. We can lift a little higher the burden of social division and hierarchy that weighs upon our efforts to gain practical, emotional, and cognitive access to one another. And we can do a little better at finding the limited circumstances that somehow express our inconformity with limited circumstances.

Explanatory Themes

The guiding concern of the explanatory theory can be described in several equivalent ways. Most of the comprehensive and influential social theories advanced in the last two centuries suffer from an internal tension. The tension is especially noticeable in the doctrines – Marxism preeminent among them – that have provided the left with its intellectual tools. All these theories, whether or not radical in their intentions, see society as an artifact. They treat every organization of social life as made and imagined rather than as given in an eternal pattern by human nature or social harmony. They therefore also emphasize the stark discontinuities among forms of social life, recognizing each such form as the expression of a different way of being human.

Yet these theories repeatedly betrayed their understanding of society as artifact by the fashion in which they turned this understanding into a concrete practice of social explanation. They pinned their theoretical ambitions to the development of a supposed science of history and society. This science presents man as the product of an evolutionary logic, or of deep-seated economic, organizational, or psychological constraints, that he is unable to alter. The weakening of the intention in the execution may be justified by the sense that without this hedging, we would fall into theoretical agnosticism, and transformative politics would lose intellectual guidance. As a result, we would become all the more subject to the influence of the social worlds we inhabit.

But the explanatory theory of *False Necessity* is meant to show that we can resolve this apparent dilemma. We can carry to its ultimate conclusion the view of society as artifact. Moreover, we can do so without abandoning ourselves to theoretical nihilism and without weakening our ability to resist the established social order. Thus, one way to describe the explanatory theory of this book is to say that it pushes to extremes the idea of society as made and imagined. It argues that when we go to these extremes we find theory rather than no theory.

On a second interpretation the book represents an attempt both to take sides in a dominant though largely implicit debate in modern social thought and to change the terms of this controversy. On one side of this controversy stand people – conservatives, leftists, or centrists – who claim that the currently available forms of social organization reflect deeply rooted constraints or a logic of social development. Alternatively, these people explain the institutions of each society as the cumulative outcomes of many episodes of interest accommodation or problem solving. Such outcomes, they hold, are shaped by objective facts about actual interests and possible accommodations, actual problems and possible solutions.

What do the opponents of these people mean when they claim that everything is politics? At a minimum, they mean to deny that the established forms of social organization reflect such impersonal and irresistible forces. Instead, these critics direct our attention to the particular sequence of practical or imaginative conflicts from which, they claim, established arrangements have emerged. The conflicts they have in mind are first and foremost the struggles over the uses and mastery of governmental power (politics in the narrow sense). But these conflicts also include the disputes over all the other material or intangible resources with which we make the social future within the social present. By denying that current social arrangements reflect a higher rational or practical necessity, the critics mean to argue that these arrangements can be reimagined and remade.

The slogan that everything is politics is nothing if not deflationary of the traditional claims of social theory: the received style of generalization in social thought and historical writing explains conflict by reference to institutional or imaginative structures, the fighting that goes on in all societies by reference to the framework within which it takes place. Thus, the adversaries of the people who say that everything is politics can plausibly claim that the endeavor of those whom they criticize is self-defeating. For we cannot act to change society in radical ways unless we have ideas that lay bare the pattern of constraint and opportunity in our historical situation and that illuminate the probable effects of our actions.

The explanatory theory of *False Necessity* takes sides decisively with those who say it is all politics. But in taking sides the argument of the book asserts that we can develop the everything-is-politics idea into a comprehensive set of explanatory conjectures and explanatory practices. The resulting theory remains faithful to everything the critics want, except perhaps to their characteristic hostility to comprehensive theories. But this hostility, I argue, is misplaced. Social theory can be cleansed of the qualities these antitheorists find so objectionable, so long as we are willing to accept a fundamental shift in our sense of what it means to explain a state of affairs. Indeed, the attack on the equation of prevailing social arrangements with practical necessities must be armed with a theory if it is to avoid trivialization and paradox.

There is yet a third way to define the main point of the explanatory theory of *False Necessity*. It may be the most telling of all these statements because it addresses permanent puzzles and concerns rather than the development of a specific theoretical tradition or the resolution of a particular contemporary controversy. The explanatory view of *False Necessity* tries to give its due to two aspects of our experience of social life that seem hard to reconcile.

In every social circumstance much of what takes place can be explained as the product of the institutional and imaginative context (order, structure, or framework) within which routine activities and conflicts occur. Wherever we look in history, we can identify a small number of basic arrangements and preconceptions that mesh together to exercise an overwhelming influence over social life. Often, we seem to be mere puppets of these frameworks or of the forces that generate and sustain them.

But our social experience also shows another face. We sometimes put these frameworks aside. We think and act, incongruously and surprisingly, as if they were not for real, as if we had merely pretended to obey them while awaiting an opportunity to defy them. We cannot live without a set of formative institutional arrangements and enacted ideals of human association, nor can we ever completely override the contrast between the things that are up for grabs in our ordinary conflicts and activities and the things that are not. But we can disrupt these established structures. We can replace them if not all at once, then piece by piece. We can even diminish the force with which they constrain and imprison us. Most importantly, this structure-disturbing and structure-inventing activity is not itself governed by a system of lawlike constraints and tendencies, certainly not by the evolutionary logic or relentless practical imperatives that the most ambitious modern social theories have traditionally invoked.

The explanatory practice developed in *False Necessity* suggests a way of imagining ourselves in society and history that does justice to these two contrasting aspects of our experience. We cannot accomplish the task merely by juxtaposing the two sets of observations – the constraints of structure and our powers of structure-disturbance – for we do not know how much credit to give each of them in any particular instance. We need a developed and supported view. A sign of the power of such a view is that it can criticize and help change both the structure-obeying and the structure-defying sides of particular societies.

The explanatory social theory developed in this book takes no stand on ultimate controversies about free will and determinism. So long as we treat all issues in social theory as reducible either to the most general problems about knowledge, reality, and value or to narrow factual and normative disputes, we cannot hope to reorient our approaches to society and history in any but the most haphazard and unselfconscious way. For we cannot resolve the metaphysical conundrums. We must try instead to factor out from the traditional metaphysical agenda the most tractable and urgent problems. Nowhere is this maxim more imperative than in the discussion of free will and determinism.

The framework-revising freedom that occupies so central a place in the social theory of *False Necessity* may be illusory from certain physicalist or theological perspectives. But it is one thing to deny this freedom in the name of forces internal to our social descriptions or explanations, and another thing to concede that these descriptions and explanations may be misleading or illusory in a view remote from our everyday experience. Our freedom remains in jeopardy until we have a normal discourse that both respects it and clarifies its sense.

False Necessity develops an antinecessitarian approach to social and historical explanation through an attempt to solve a particular explanatory problem. This problem is the origin and basis of the cycles of reform and retrenchment that characterize both the Western industrial democracies and the communist countries of the present day. Again and again, we find that partisan conflicts and attitudes about the uses of governmental power with respect to major issues, such as the direction of economic policy, move among a small number of familiar options. Thus, national governments in the industrial West oscillate between bouts of halfhearted redistribution and attempts to rekindle economic growth by concessions to big business and organized labor. Similarly, communist regimes regularly alternate between periods of economic centralism and decentralization, each swing of the pendulum complete with a detailed set of well-tried techniques and recurrent difficulties. Each traditional option is generally conceded to be a second-best solution by all the major contenders in the dispute. Only rarely is an option added to the list or subtracted from it. Why should policy keep returning to proposals that inspire so little hope? Some attribute the compulsive rounds of governmental politics to the mutual resistance of organized interests in highly fragmented societies that lack any single coherent plan of social division and hierarchy. Others emphasize the inescapable psychological, organizational, and economic imperatives that doom all imaginary alternatives to impracticality. But these comforting explanations do not work, and their failure reinstates and deepens the initial puzzle. The stubborn, mysterious cycles represent a permanent insult to societies whose official culture claims to base fundamental social arrangements upon the wills of free and relatively equal citizens and rightholders rather than upon blind drift or coercive authority.

The riddle presented by these contemporary cycles of reform and retrenchment in contemporary societies is only a special case of a far more pervasive characteristic of our social and historical experience. Wherever we look in history we see that the conflict over the use of the resources that determine the future shape of society has always moved within a narrow ambit. Prominent among the subjects of such conflict is the ongoing controversy over the relation of governmental power to social privilege and over the nature of the reforms needed to protect the established social order against its foreign and domestic enemies. But these routines of social reproduction also include all the other collective activities by which the economic or cognitive resources of society are mobilized to perpetuate or transform current social arrangements: the range of available forms of work organization or economic exchange and of acceptable moves within moral, political, or legal argument. When, for example, we consider the scope of live options in the high governmental politics of institutional reform, we find even the most powerful, determined, and clairvoyant rulers and politicians insistently returning to a small set of unpromising strategies, always unable to accomplish what they themselves consider necessary.

They act as if they were in the thrall of unseen and irresistible compulsions. (An example discussed in detail in another part of this book is the repeated but futile attempts by the leaders of the agrarian-bureaucratic empires to preserve an independent class of smallholders, capable of providing the central government with a direct source of taxes and soldiers and therefore also of diminishing the government's financial and military dependence upon great landowners and warlords.)

Why should the scope of active and recognized possibility be so narrowly defined in all these theaters of conflict and choice? Explanations that appeal to the constraints of practical necessity or the balance of interests and opinions characteristically prove both too little and too much. They prove too little because the social arrangements that might satisfy basic practical needs always seem far more numerous than the institutional solutions that are actively considered; a persuasive social theory must show how and why the subset of live options gets selected. They prove too much because the range of options is sometimes abruptly enlarged, and the enlargement retrospectively deepens the puzzling quality of the previous narrowness. The attempt to understand the forces holding the cycles of reform and retrenchment in place can serve as a vehicle for the theoretical enterprise described at the outset of this chapter. For these cycles merely exemplify the more general experience of arrested and diminished possibility: the fabulously compulsive and somnambulent character of history, the long narcoleptic seizures of routine and repetition, punctuated by interludes of surprising social invention.

As the argument of *False Necessity* advances, the explanation of these narrowly defined options resolves itself into a study of the influence and the character of what I shall call the formative contexts, structures, or frameworks of social life: the basic institutional arrangements and imaginative preconceptions that circumscribe our routine practical or discursive activities and conflicts and that resist their destabilizing effects. A successful social theory must recognize the influence of these contexts. Yet it must also account for our ability not only to rebel against them but to diminish or intensify the force by which they constrain us. It must do justice to the mutual reinforcement of the institutions and beliefs that compose them. Yet it must also testify to the looseness of their internal relations. It must provide us with a way of understanding how such contexts get made. Yet it must acknowledge our inability to discover nontrivial laws, constraints, or tendencies that can explain their actual content and history.

The explanatory strategy of this book is therefore essentially simple. To explain the cycles of reform and retrenchment – and, more generally, the repetitious quality of ordinary social conflict – we need a theory of formative contexts, of how they are composed and made. An adequate theory of formative contexts, a theory capable of explaining experiences such as our experience of these reform cycles, turns out to be the theoretical enterprise I earlier described in three equivalent forms.

Given its scope, the explanatory argument of this book is largely speculative. The main purpose is to suggest a way of understanding society rather than to uncover particular facts or to test isolated conjectures. Inevitably, the discussion relies heavily on empirical work influenced by the very traditions of thought that it seeks to revise. The main test of such an explanatory argument is ultimately its ability to inspire detailed explanations more successful than the explanations made possible by current forms of social analysis.

The standards for what constitutes a successful explanation are neither unchanging nor easily malleable. They are neither an Archimedean vantage point towering above particular theories nor a subject for arbitrary stipulation by each theory. Our ideas about what constitutes a successful explanation change, slowly but significantly, as the substance of our explanatory ideas shifts. The explanatory argument of this book proposes a change in our received beliefs about what adequate social and historical explanations should be like.

It would be misleading, however, to suggest that the descriptions and explanations of this book are open to verification or falsification only at a second remove. The argument cuts across many problems and many disciplines. It advances conjectures about particular situations, processes, and events. It invokes facts, enlists familiar and less familiar learning, and proposes changes of emphasis and of approach in the understanding of many detailed affairs. Along this extended periphery of empirical implication, it remains open to more direct empirical assessment. The cumulative evaluation of these numerous and connected hypotheses casts light on the explanatory promise of the core theoretical project. Throughout, I reject any stark contrast between formulating a view and confirming it, or between considerations of theoretical coherence and appeals to scholarly research or to common experience.

Those who are wary of ambitious theories in social and historical study may feel their fears confirmed by this admission of the speculative character of the argument. But there are no uncontroversial alternatives. *Social Theory: Its Situation and Its Task* – the critical volume that introduces the present constructive work – argues that the seemingly modest practice of cumulative induction preached by much of contemporary social science cannot give its due to the central distinction between the formative institutional and imaginative contexts and the formed routines of social life. It cannot help us understand how these contexts are internally constituted, how they get remade, and how they inform a richly textured life of practical and argumentative routines. This explanatory failure has practical consequences. It disarms us before our social contexts by blinding us to their influence, their specificity, and their revisability. It tricks even the skeptical, the learned, and the disillusioned into not recognizing the makeshift, pasted-together, and alterable character of the social worlds in which they live.

The sole real alternative to the kind of comprehensive view developed here would be what the introductory volume labeled ultra-theory: a set of critical and constructive practices carefully crafted and militantly wielded to preserve their antinecessitarian power.This alternative intellectual style is not inherently better or worse than the theoretically aggressive strategy that *False Necessity* adopts. It merely presents a different mix of difficulties, dangers, and opportunities. Moreover, if this ultra-theoretical practice is to remain truly distinct from the prostrate, falsely modest versions of social science, and if it is to deal with the central distinction between formative contexts and formed routines, it must be just as bold and controversial as the unabashed theorizing practiced in this book.

Programmatic Themes

A program of social reconstruction accompanies the explanatory theory of *False Necessity.* The program addresses both the major institutions of social life – the large-scale organization of governments, economies, and workplaces – and the fine texture of personal encounters and social roles. The programmatic argument deals most directly with the practices and circumstances of the same contemporary countries that provide the explanatory theory with its focus. Yet that argument develops an ideal and a method that may take forms very different from the proposals advanced here.

The guiding theme of the program of social reconstruction is the attempt to imagine institutional arrangements and social practices that can advance the radical project beyond the point to which contemporary forms of governmental and economic organization have carried it. By the radical project or the project of the modernist visionary I mean the attempt to realize the many forms of individual or collective empowerment that result from our relative success in disengaging our practical and passionate dealings from the restrictive influence of entrenched social roles and hierarchies. The influence of such schemes of social division and ranking depends – as the explanatory theory seeks to show – upon institutional and imaginative contexts that remain unavailable for revision in the course of ordinary social life. The program suggests how our contemporary formative contexts might be disentrenched, that is to say, how they might be more fully opened to challenge in the midst of our routine conflicts and therefore also how they might undermine or prevent rigid forms of social division and hierarchy. Against the background of almost universal disappointment with the communist revolutions of the twentieth century, the program suggests that current institutional arrangements represent merely an imperfect, initial step in the attempt to weaken the extent to which an established scheme of class, communal, gender, and national distinctions constrains our experiments in practical collaboration or passionate attachment. The weakening of the influence of this prewritten social script is to be valued not only negatively, as an occasion for a broader range of choice, but affirmatively for the forms of empowerment it makes possible. Moreover, the disruption of the script implies no lack of formed institutions or practices; it requires the invention of practices and institutions that possess certain qualities.

The empowerment that the program is meant to foster is in part the development of our practical productive capabilities. But it is also the freedom resulting from what we most prize even in current versions of democracy and community: the promise of forms of social engagement that save us from having to choose between isolation from other people and surrender to them and that describe modes of attachment that are also exercises in self-assertion. Finally, it is the empowerment that consists of conscious mastery over the institutional and imaginative contexts of our activities. The programmatic argument shows how these varieties of empowerment connect, and it explores their implications for the detailed reorganization of social life.

The commitment to advance human empowerment through institutions and practices that loosen the stranglehold of fixed schemes of social division and hierarchy over our practical and spiritual access to one another is hardly idiosyncratic. It has supplied the unifying element in the great secular modern doctrines of emancipation: liberalism, socialism, and communism. But in all these doctrines the pursuit of this aim suffers the effect of unjustifiably restrictive premises about social possibility. Just as I want to free the central insight of classical social theory – the insight into the artifactual character of social life – from its scientistic incubus, so too I want to detach the radical project from the dogmatic assumptions about possibility that represent the counterpart to this incubus. The most important of these confining assumptions are those that impoverish our sense of the alternative concrete institutional forms democracies and markets can take. Much of the programmatic argument in *False Necessity* describes ways of organizing markets and democracies that can be more useful to the radical project, and even more responsive to our received ideals, than current modes of economic and governmental organization.

The real meaning of our social ideals is largely defined by our often implicit assumptions about the institutional arrangements and social practices that realize these ideals. When, for example, we speak about democracy or community, our abstract principles and fighting words may be less telling guides to what we mean than the practical forms that realize these ideals. If someone proposes to us, or if we discover on our own, an alternative version of democratic institutions or communal life, we may be forced to confront a previously unsuspected ambiguity in our received ideal conceptions. In choosing between the alternative versions of democracy and community, we shall in effect be deciding what really matters most to us in our democratic and communal aspirations. And what holds for the understanding of ideals such as democracy or community applies to whole movements of political thought and sensibility. For the meaning of these movements also depends on the practical arrangements they are assumed to require.

The forms of governmental and economic organization proposed and defended in this book emphasize the development of practices and institutions that prevent factions, classes, or any other specially placed groups from gaining control over the key resources of a society (wealth, power, and knowledge). These same institutions and practices diminish the gap between routine conflicts within a framework of social life and revolutionary struggles about that framework. The explanatory theory of *False Necessity* explores the connections between the disruption of the mechanisms of social subjugation and the development of social arrangements that lay themselves more effectively open to challenge. The institutional proposals make good on these connections. Only from the perspective offered by these theoretical and practical ideas can we arrive at the broader understanding of the radical project that I earlier mentioned. From the vantage point of this understanding, the struggle for social equality – the most familiar aspect of radical concerns – can be seen as a fragment of a more inclusive and complex endeavor.

The modernist criticism of personal relations and the leftist criticism of collective institutions have remained only fitfully and obscurely connected. This parting of the ways in the cultures of leftism and modernism has been amplified in political experience. The attack on stereotyped roles in personal relations has often proved strongest where the politics of institutional reinvention are weakest. The separation between these two cultures and these two transformative movements – the most powerful of all found in the modern world – has been destructive to both. It has helped deprive leftist practice of its ability to reach direct social relations and to change their fine texture. It has also threatened to degrade the politics of personal relations into a desperate search for gratification.

The generalized understanding of the radical project presented in this book both incorporates and criticizes the personalist politics of modernism. This understanding recognizes the attack on stereotyped social roles as yet another facet of the attempt to achieve empowerment by subverting entrenched social division and hierarchy. And it finds in the commitment to imagine a freer and richly detailed form of social life an antidote to solipsism and selfishness.

The Explanatory and Programmatic Themes Related

The explanatory and programmatic ideas of this book connect at many different levels. The most superficial link is the historical circumstance that both arguments address. The explanatory view develops a theory of social transformation in the course of attempting to answer a particular question: Why do the cycles of reform and retrenchment in contemporary societies have the shape and the tenacity they do? This question quickly turns into one of how to represent the formative institutional and imaginative contexts that keep these cycles going. To understand the influence of such contexts and to discover how it may be resisted we must understand how such contexts are made and what holds together their component elements. The programmatic parts of the book advance proposals designed to replace the same institutions and practices that account for the contemporary reform cycles.

There is also a more general and significant relation between the explanatory and programmatic arguments of *False Necessity*. The prevailing forms of social analysis leave no room for programmatic thought. Consider the comprehensive social theories, like hardcore Marxism, that draw on an evolutionary and functionalist determinism. Such theories distinguish a small number of possible frameworks of social life, often ordered sequentially in a few possible trajectories of social evolution. They appeal to an inexorable logic of social transformation or to economic, organizational, and psychological constraints that are supposed to underlie this logic. For such systems of thought, programmatic argument can at best anticipate the line of historical evolution or compare the benefits and dangers of the few possible futures that lie before us. Alternatively, many forms of conventional social science deprive programmatic argument of its mission by failing to focus on the discontinuities among the institutional and imaginative frameworks that circumscribe our routine activities. Programs of social reconstruction amount to more than exercises in routine problem solving or interest accommodation, for they deal with the structures within which such exercises take place. Programmatic thought can be secure only against the background of a style of social and historical analysis that does not treat the institutional and imaginative molds of social life as inevitable or as determined by an irresistible dynamic of change.

We must develop such a style of analysis in order to possess a credible view of transformation. Until we formulate such a view, programmatic argument has no role. It is also deprived of the sense of reality that might enable it to distinguish feasible and utopian endeavors. The lack of such a sense shows in the bastardized and paralyzing criterion of political realism dominating so much contemporary ideological debate. People treat a plan as realistic when it approximates what already exists and as utopian when it departs from current arrangements. Only proposals that are hardly worth fighting for – reformist tinkering – seem practicable.

There is yet another and deeper link between the explanatory and programmatic ideas of this book. Both sets of proposals present mutually reinforcing variations on an old and central theme of our civilization: that we are an infinite caught within the finite. The finite, in this instance, is the open series of social worlds – the formative institutional and imaginative contexts – that we construct and inhabit. The infinite is the personality. It is also an inchoate open-ended fund of the forms of practical collaboration or passionate attachment that may bind people together. Central to the whole argument of *Politics* is the notion that no one context can be our permanent home: the place where we can institute all the varieties of practical or passionate connection that we have reason to want.

The explanatory theory of society making presented here develops this theme by suggesting how we can imagine ourselves as both controlled and not controlled by our institutional and imaginative frameworks. The programmatic argument elaborates the theme by asking how we can make these finite worlds a more suitable habitation for context-revising and context-transcending agents. The explanatory theory shows how the institutional and imaginative frameworks of social life differ in the extent to which they aggravate the distinction between framework-transforming conflict and framework-respecting routine that perpetuates schemes of social division and hierarchy. Contexts may be increasingly designed to soften this distinction and undermine such schemes. The view of transformation concluding the explanatory part of the book describes the influence of such a change upon a range of forms of human empowerment. It also probes the conditions under which such a progression can occur. The programmatic argument takes up these suggestions by detailing a set of institutional arrangements and social practices that take this shift further than it has yet been carried, and do so for the sake of the many forms of empowerment that may result.

The critic may always object that he does not sympathize with this generalized version of the radical project and does not desire the varieties of empowerment it seeks. However, he must then possess either an alternative vision of social reality or a different approach to the relation between factual and normative judgments. Taken together, the programmatic and explanatory arguments of *False Necessity* illustrate the view that the relation between factual and normative issues is far more intimate than any relation the mainstream of modern philosophy since Kant and Hume has been inclined to allow. Consider the results such a view may achieve by both incorporating and changing familiar modes of prescriptive argument.

The visionary element in our ideas about self and society must ultimately always take one of two directions. It may invoke a single, authoritative arrangement of social life and human emotions. This is the direction followed by the most influential social doctrines in world history. It usually culminates in a system of sanctified social roles and ranks, echoed and sustained by a conception of hierarchical order among our faculties and dispositions. Alternatively, the visionary drive may appeal to the transcendent personality or to the opportunities of human connection that are constrained and betrayed by fixed divisions and hierarchies within humanity and by rigid rankings of subjective experience. The modernist radical or visionary prefers this second path. From this path one route leads to the "endless labor of negation": the creed of those who believe that contexts will be contexts and that true freedom lies solely in perpetual defiance to all stable institutions and conventions and in perpetual flight from one context to another. The other route, on this fork of the modernist visionary road, is the one traveled by those who argue that some contexts improve upon others in their ability to respect and to encourage the context-making and the context-transcending qualities of the self. This is the direction of *False Necessity*.

Such an intellectual enterprise must deliberately transgress the boundaries traditionally separating the intimate, the evocative, and the prophetic from the prosaic concerns of detailed explanatory conjectures and programmatic proposals. The task of making discourses that more fully combine realism, practicality, and detail with visionary fire, the moves inside the context with the moves about the context, is an integral part of the radical project. We have to strive for this confusion of discourses at every opportunity: in our most ambitious efforts at social understanding as well as in our particular practices of legal, moral, and party-political controversy.

The Explanatory Themes in Their Implicit Polemical Setting

The introductory volume (*Social Theory: Its Situation and Its Task*) presented the critical diagnosis that constitutes the point of departure for the explanatory and programmatic theory of *Politics*. In *False Necessity*, the first part of the work, this polemical setting remains almost entirely implicit; I offer here an affirmative view. In order, however, to fix more clearly the scope and the intentions of this constructive argument, it may help to make some aspects of the concealed controversial setting explicit, highlighting ideas the preliminary book left undeveloped.

Social Theory: Its Situation and Its Task distinguished two types of social analysis that jointly define the current predicament of social and historical studies: deep-structure theory and positivist (or empiricist or conventional) social science. Let me recall briefly the characteristics of each.

Deep-structure analysis represents the major though by no means the exclusive element in many of the comprehensive social theories that come down to us from the nineteenth and early twentieth centuries – the theories that contemporary social scientists often deride as "grand theory." Marxism is the most coherent and influential statement of the deep-logic style, although we can easily find in the works of Marx and his followers many ideas that not only resist assimilation to deep-structure thought but contribute to its reconstruction. Three recurrent explanatory practices distinguish this tradition of social thought.

The first characteristic operation of deep-structure analysis is the effort to distinguish in every historical situation the routines of practical and imaginative conflict from the basic framework, structure, or context that shapes these ordinary disputes while resisting their subversive effects. Deep-logic theories define such frameworks to include institutional arrangements, imaginative preconceptions, or some combination of both. The second defining operation is the identification of this framework as an example of an indivisible and repeatable type of social organization: indivisible because its elements stand or fall as a single piece and repeatable because it can emerge at different times in different societies (even if it always occurs at the same point in a sequence of stages of organization). The third typical move of deep-structure analysis is the effort to explain the identity and the realization of these indivisible and repeatable types on the basis of lawlike tendencies or deep-seated economic, organizational, and psychological constraints. These constraints or tendencies yield a list of possible social worlds or a compulsive sequence of stages of social organization. Notice, then, that this threefold description of deep-structure analysis embraces both evolutionary and nonevolutionary styles of theorizing. Marxism stands preeminent among the former. The latter has never had an elaborate statement, although economics (which has since become the model for chief variants of positivist social science) once promised to supply it.

The later history of deep-structure theories is one of attempts to deal with the difficulties of reenacting these three key mental operations in the face of inconvenient facts and resistant experience. Two related difficulties stand out; they refer to the second and third deep-structure moves. On the one hand, there does not seem to be a finite list of possible types of organization or a small number of possible trajectories of social evolution. On the other hand, the alleged lawlike tendencies or determining constraints fail to explain the actual identity and sequence of frameworks for social life. The explanatory failure of the would-be laws is obscured only when they are left so vague that they can be made, retrospectively, to explain anything.

The proponents of deep-structure social analysis deal with these difficulties by diluting their original claims. They may, for example, replace a unilinear evolution with the idea of a small number of alternative trajectories of social change. But each such loosening turns out to be both too much and not enough. It is too much to safeguard the earlier, stronger theory against a slide into vacuity. It is not enough to meet the initial objections or other objections in their spirit. The theorist finds himself driven to ever greater concessions. He holds on for fear that if he did not he would fall into theoretical nihilism and lose the intellectual basis for a critical perspective on society. The leftist experiences an additional reason for reluctance: the canonical status to which socialist movements raised Marxism often makes a repudiation of Marxist premises seem like a betrayal of the leftist cause.

The other major component of the contemporary situation of social thought is positivist, empiricist, or conventional social science. This mode of analysis sees social life as an interminable series of episodes of interest accommodation and problem solving. It denies the primacy of the contrast between the shaping context and the shaped routines and therefore also slights the discontinuities among contexts. The practical consequence of this denial is the weakening of our ability to see a whole institutional and imaginative ordering of social life as something connected, distinctive, and replaceable.

But the problem of social frameworks and of their influence upon the routine conflicts that take place within them cannot easily be avoided. Even the most prosaic activities of collective problem solving or interest balancing assume limits on acceptable solutions or compromises and procedures for identifying and ranking problems or interests. In short, they assume, under other names, the existence of a framework. The main variants of positivist social science can therefore be distinguished by the explanatory practices that enable them both to acknowledge the problem of the framework and to confine the implications of this acknowledgment.

The strategy of agnosticism (evident, for example, in the most austere branches of microeconomics) is to offer an analytic apparatus, free of independent causal content, and designed to serve disciplines expected to possess their own, independently justified explanatory conjectures. But the responsibility to come up with a view of contexts, of their genesis and internal constitution, does not go away; it merely shifts to another discipline.

The strategy of idealization treats the choice of a framework by analogy to the choice of optimal solutions or accommodations within a framework. Thus, the more propagandistic, overtly ideological forms of right-wing economics identify particular economic institutions with the free market and treat this particular version of the market as the device that makes efficient resource allocation possible. But the pure logic of maximizing choice can apply to all market or nonmarket orders, and market systems can take any number of concrete institutional forms, some of them far removed from the arrangements the conservative economists have in mind. The point can be generalized: we can never explain the making and transformation of contexts by the same relatively straightforward and uncontroversial means with which we explain decisions and outcomes within these contexts.

The strategy of hollow concession recognizes this last point in principle but fails to draw out the consequences of this recognition for the actual practice of explanation. Thus, the neo-Keynesian macroeconomists may concede as trivial that relations among aggregate economic phenomena such as inflation and unemployment depend upon particular institutional arrangements: say, the form and depth of trade unionism or the relation of national governments to organized labor and central banks. Yet the content of their discipline continues to be an analysis of economic movements against an institutional background taken as given rather than an inquiry into the interplay between economic facts and institutional constraints. Protracted stagnation in institutional reform may perpetuate certain relations among economic phenomena. It may therefore also invite the misleading conclusion that these relations are lawlike constraints, inherent in very general and vaguely defined types of economic organization, such as a regulated market economy. In fact these apparent laws depend upon very detailed and relatively ad hoc institutional configurations. As soon as any element of this institutional framework begins to change, the supposed laws start to break down.

The explanatory theory of *False Necessity* represents the constructive sequel to a polemic against both deep-structure social analysis and positivist social science. But the methods and insights available for the execution of this task come chiefly from the self-criticism and self-correction of these same two traditions of social thought. The materials and even the principles of a more tenable view are already at hand.

Neither deep-structure social analysis nor positivist social science can solve the problem that provides the point of departure for the explanatory argument of this book: the problem of explaining the content and the persistence of the cycles of reform and retrenchment in contemporary societies. Positivist social science cannot do it because the force of practical constraints and the tension among organized interests fail to explain the tenacity and the substance of these cycles until we also take into account the restrictive influence of the framework of institutions and ideas within which those interests and constraints operate. But positivist social science denies us a way to understand such frameworks: their internal composition, their genesis, and their influence upon the routines that they shape.

Deep-structure social analysis is equally powerless to elucidate the cycles of reform and retrenchment. As soon as we define the formative institutional and imaginative contexts with enough detail to explain the routines of conflict and policy that take place within them we discover that these contexts are too detailed – too mired in historical particulars – to exemplify plausibly an indivisible and repeatable type of social organization. The inability of deep-logic social theory to come to terms with the problem of the reform cycles is merely a symptom of its difficulty in squaring historical research and practical experience with belief in a list of types of social organization, ruled by an evolutionary dynamic or by deep-seated economic, organizational, or psychological imperatives.

The explanatory theory worked out in this book recognizes the shaped or structured quality of social life: the distinction between the routine moves within an institutional and imaginative context of social life and the more radical conflicts about this context. Because it takes this distinction seriously it also emphasizes the distinctiveness of the forms of social life these contexts support. But it describes and explains these contexts without resort to the ideas of a list of possible social worlds or of possible pathways of social evolution. Nor does it invoke the tendencies or constraints that might generate such a list. Though acknowledging the power that connected sets of institutional arrangements and imaginative preconceptions exercise over us, it does not turn this acknowledgment into an occasion to treat history as the enactment of a prewritten script and to treat society as a product of unmade laws. Thus, this theory accepts the first characteristic move of deep-structure analysis while rejecting the other two moves: the subsumption of the framework under an indivisible and repeatable type and the search for general laws governing the identity, the actualization, and the succession of such types. The outcome is not to abandon generalizing social and historical explanations but to transform them in content and character. The proposed view is at least as comprehensive and aggressive in its claims as the original, hardcore version of a deep-logic system such as Marxism.

Unlike positivist social science this theory recognizes the ubiquity of the contrast between transformative and routine activity. But unlike deep-structure analysis it also affirms that we can diminish the force of this contrast and enlarge the sense in which an institutional and imaginative order of social life stands open to revision. We can efface this contrast by the right social inventions. Unlike positivist social science this theory insists upon the connectedness of the elements that make up a formative context of social life. But unlike deep-structure thought it does so without falling into the prejudice that each framework exemplifies one of a series of possible social worlds or of necessary evolutionary stages. Unlike positivist social science it gives weight to the influence that entrenched institutional and imaginative contexts exert upon ordinary action and petty conflict. But unlike deep-logic theories it also does justice to our astonishing ability to act at times as if these contexts were powerless and our allegiance to them a mere ploy we were waiting to cast aside. Like deep-logic analysis it proposes a way of representing and explaining the transformation of routine-shaping or rule-producing frameworks. But unlike deep-logic argument it does not portray such changes as if they were themselves governed by a rule-bound structure. In all these ways the theory does more than offer a different explanation; it revises our received sense of what explaining a state of affairs means.

Only a theory that satisfies these demanding criteria can draw a detailed understanding of society out of a view of human activity that emphasizes our ability to revise our imaginative and institutional contexts. Only such a theory can allow us to integrate theory and historiography without forever diluting the former and distorting the latter. Only such a theory can overcome the illusory contrast between the perspective of the theorist or the historian and the quality of lived experience, a quality that includes both an awareness of messy constraints reflecting no higher rational order and a constant rediscovery of the surprising transformative opportunities that emerge in the very midst of these same constraints. Only such a theory can teach us how we may empower ourselves, and cleanse social life of some of its taint of domination and depersonalization, by gaining greater mastery over the contexts of our activity. Only such a theory can avoid the betrayal of this teaching that occurs whenever we present empowerment or equality as the predetermined outcome of a relentless historical progression.

The Programmatic Themes in Their Implicit Polemical Setting

The explanatory theory presented in *False Necessity* stands in close connection with a program for social reconstruction. The argument of the book should therefore also be read against the background of an implicit programmatic controversy. It is customary to criticize normative political theories from the angle of the substantive ideals that they enshrine and of the justificatory arguments that support these ideals. One of the many reasons why such debates are so often frustrating, and the claims of the contending doctrines so unpersuasive, is the lack of clarity about the translation of these commitments into particular institutional arrangements and social practices. We hear an ideal attractively though vaguely described. We wonder what it will actually be like when realized in a going form of social life. We hear another ideal disparaged as unrealistic because it falsely promises to reconcile all good things and fails to acknowledge the tensions between, say, freedom and paternalism, or autonomy and community, or heartfelt engagement and critical self reflection. We wonder to what extent these tensions are indeed intractable and to what extent they may respond to changes in the practical arrangements of social life. There is good reason for our doubts.

Our accepted rhetoric tells us less about the content of such ideal visions than does the background of institutions and practices we implicitly imagine to realize these visions in practice. So long as we traffic in the ruling dogmas of society our doubts are kept to a minimum. If someone talks about political democracy we *know* what he means even if his litany of slogans and theories leaves us unenlightened. We can refer to a specific tradition of constitutional arrangements and of party-political rivalry that is visible in the world we inhabit. But the more ambitious the ideal vision, the farther it departs from current solutions, the less self-evident the relation between the proposed model of social life and its practical form becomes. A theoretical understanding must then supply what established reality fails to provide. This understanding belongs at the center of normative debates and cannot be relegated to a subsidiary, informative role.

The implicit programmatic polemic of this book deals with the major modern political doctrines from the underemphasized but crucial perspective of their institutional assumptions. The conservative and centrist political movements in the Western industrial democracies usually take for granted inherited ways of organizing democracies and markets. Yet these current forms of market and democratic organization *can* be replaced. In their present forms they vitiate the very aspects of the conservative or centrist message that carry the widest and most powerful appeal.

The leftist criticism of contemporary societies, and especially of bourgeois democratic and market regimes, fails to appreciate the extent to which both markets and democracies can be radically reorganized. Preoccupied with the hierarchy-producing effects of inherited institutional arrangements, the leftist reaches for distant and vague solutions that cannot withstand the urgent pressures of statecraft and quickly give way to approaches betraying his initial aims.

The main point of the polemic may be restated in a way much more fully developed in Chapters 10 to 14 of this book. Sooner or later the conservative, centrist, and leftist parties that now exist in the prosperous democracies must resolve the tension between their programmatic commitments and the governmental and economic arrangements they normally take for granted. If the right-wing free marketeer, or the centrist communitarian, or the left-leaning redistributivist accept the established institutional order they find themselves repeatedly frustrated in the accomplishment of their professed goals. They can realize these goals only in compromised forms, and they are reduced to claiming that their proposals have never been given a fair chance. But if, on the other hand, the proponents of these movements of opinion do opt for an institutional reconstruction they tread a path for which their previous habits of thought, bolstered by the dominant styles of social analysis, have left them unprepared. They must develop elaborate institutional alternatives, a strategy for putting them into effect, and a view of social transformation to inform both their programmatic and their strategic ideas. They must also redefine their guiding ideals and their conceptions of the relation of these ideals to the aims of their political opponents. For if the real meaning of an ideal depends upon its tacit institutional background, a shift in the latter is sure to disturb the former.

These general points can now be made more concrete. The following remarks compare and contrast the programmatic orientation of the argument in *False Necessity* to some of the major familiar positions in the conflict of modern political opinions. Throughout, the central idea remains the subversive effect a disabled institutional imagination exercises upon our normative political ideas. Only a credible account of social transformation – that is, of how the formative institutional and imaginative contexts of social life are made and reconstructed – can free us from this disablement. Assumptions about the relation between our explanatory and our programmatic ideas envelop the controversy over substantive social ideals.

Consider first the classical liberal doctrine, in the form it took during its nineteenth-century heyday. The program set out in *False Necessity* shares with classical liberalism a belief in the connection between economic decentralization and political democracy. The ceaseless recombination of workers, machines, and organizational forms of production and exchange may be achieved by a centralized authority. It is certainly possible to design arrangements that render this authority accountable. But if the central power is to make and enforce allocative and recombinatory decisions, and to resist the pressures to maintain established jobs and firms and to make consumption increase faster than output, it must enjoy a considerable measure of autonomy. The combination of this discretionary authority with the direct control of matters vital to the security of the entire population makes it likely that economic centralism will first overshadow and finally undermine political pluralism.

But the program worked out in this book differs from classic liberalism by its refusal to equate political democracy and market organization with the institutional tradition of the contemporary North Atlantic countries. The traditional version of democracy combines distinctive constitutional techniques, characterized by a devotion to the dispersal of power and the distancing of mob influence, with a style of partisan conflict and organization that came into its own only several generations later. The traditional version of the market economy relies upon the more or less absolute property right – absolute in permitted usage and absolute in its temporal duration – as the primary device of economic decentralization. But I argue here that though these governmental and economic arrangements influence our whole understanding of the liberal ideal they also frustrate its realization. They help prevent a more thoroughgoing fragmentation of social divisions, hierarchies, and roles. They contribute to a social circumstance in which the principles of a liberal vision are more fully expressed in the practice of partisan politics – with its crosscutting coalitions of relatively ill defined and transitory interests – than in the quality of ordinary social life. Each person's opportunities and experiences continue to be powerfully influenced by his place in a resilient scheme of social stations.

There is a different institutional ordering of markets and democracies that further weakens the hold of collective categories over individual experience. The conflict over the mastery and uses of governmental power may be so arranged that it provides an occasion to subject every feature of the established order of division, hierarchy, and roles to the pressure of challenge. Once these alternative arrangements are worked out, in practice or in imagination, they in turn suggest a broadening of the original liberal vision. The goal of freeing men and women from subjugation can be reinterpreted as a particular aspect of what I earlier described as the project of the modernist visionary: the search for individual and collective empowerment through the dissolution of the prewritten social script. It hardly matters whether we describe the result as an extension of the liberal doctrine or as a replacement of it. The point is that we have disengaged the inherited message from its implied institutional setting and transformed its content in the process. You can already see how a similar analysis might be applied to the other familiar options of contemporary political thought.

Consider the extreme variant of classical liberalism sometimes known as libertarianism. The libertarian seeks to re-create society as a world of maximally independent agents whose collaborative relations all arise from freely bargained contracts. He wants to see government reduced to a residual role as a mutual-protection association. The program of empowered democracy defended in *False Necessity* shares with the libertarian the aim of freeing individual experience to the greatest possible extent from the overbearing influence of predetermined collective categories of class, community, or gender. But the programmatic argument of this book also reflects the belief that the way in which the libertarian proposes to accomplish this objective is misguided in two crucial respects.

For one thing, no neutral uncontroversial system of private rights is capable of defining the pure case of a market, maximally free from interference. We must choose among an indefinitely wide range of alternative sets of rules and rights, of alternative arrangements for decentralized production and exchange. Which of them are most decentralized, or most conducive to political pluralism, or even most likely to promote economic growth – these represent empirical questions that cannot be answered by the mere analysis of the concepts of a market economy or of a private order.

For another thing, the libertarian errs in his attempt to solve the problem of social coordination by in effect bombing out the state and all other large-scale or inclusive institutions. In order to increase dramatically both the decentralization of economic decisions and our freedom to experiment with the institutional arrangements for production and exchange we must devise institutions that subject capital allocation to more explicit collective deliberation and control. We can achieve this accountability of capital without abandoning the principle of market decentralization. Thus, for example, absolute property rights, still the primary device of economic decentralization, may be replaced by a rotating capital fund from which conditional and temporary disbursements or loans might be made to teams of worker-technicians and entrepreneurs. Then, government and the conflict over governmental policy would have to be arranged in ways that prevented this more deliberate method of capital allocation from serving as a tool for oppression, clientalism, or the perpetuation of vested interests. The key idea here is that we cannot come closer to the libertarian's dream of a less oppressive form of social coordination by allowing an allegedly natural private order to emerge as social interference recedes. We can more fully realize that dream only by inventing ever more ingenious institutional instruments for our objectives. There is no escape from artifice. New artifice must cure the defects of past artifice. We pursue a mirage when we seek the pure, undistorted system of free interaction. This pursuit must end either in an embittered disillusionment or in the apologetic identification of a particular market system with the abstract idea of a market.

The program advanced in *False Necessity* can also be compared and contrasted to a view that has traditionally had a more modest presence in the English-speaking countries than in other parts of the Western world. This view identifies the great wound of modern societies as the disruption of communal bonds that place each individual securely within a network of reciprocities. The wound is to be healed by the development of organizations intermediate between the individual and the state, organizations that can serve as a basis for communal life. This program is centrist in that it characteristically emphasizes the improvement of hierarchy through loyalty and self-restraint rather than through the radical subversion of hierarchical bonds. It is sometimes corporatist because the intermediate bodies, which may be productive enterprises as well as territorial entities, are to occupy a recognized place in the organization of the society. This place allows them to operate as veritable extensions of government.

The program of *Politics* shares several aspects of the centrist communitarian vision. It imagines a set of social arrangements that promise to help us reconcile more fully the enabling conditions of self-assertion: the need for engagement in group life and the effort to avoid the dangers of dependence and depersonalization that attend such engagement. Indeed, the whole program can be read as a vision of the forms and conditions of human community.

The centrist and corporatist program, however, remains ambivalent toward current institutional arrangements when it does not wholeheartedly accept them. Its proponents speak as if the existing productive and bureaucratic organizations could serve as the suitable vehicles for the communal ideal, with only minor adjustments. Workers, for example, should be given job tenure, they should participate in enterprise policymaking, and they should deal cooperatively with their employers. But the result of this acceptance of the underlying institutional framework is to both jeopardize and impoverish the communal ideal. The jeopardy consists in the intertwining of community and subjugation: so that the struggle against dominion, or even the imperative of practical innovation, is made to require the betrayal of present communal bonds. The impoverishment lies in the representation of community as a protected haven from which conflict is banished rather than as a zone of heightened mutual vulnerability in which people may entrust themselves more fully to one another, whether they conflict or agree.

A version of community less susceptible to the apology of dominion or the superstition of false necessity in social life can flourish only in an institutional framework that disrupts more effectively than current institutions the mechanisms of dependence and subjugation in social life. Such a framework must invite conflict rather than suppress it. It must weaken all the stable forms of social division and hierarchy and all the canonical sets of social roles that support community in its old, restrictive sense of a nonconflictual sharing of purposes and values. In preferring this revised institutional structure the programmatic argument of this book therefore also opts for a conception of what really matters most about community. The argument identifies this element as our ability to experiment, in a climate of equalized trust, with varieties of practical collaboration and passionate attachment that more fully reconcile the enabling conditions of self-assertion. The communitarian who begins by attempting to construct a more suitable institutional vessel for his commitments discovers that he has pushed the received communitarian ideal in a particular direction or resolved its internal ambiguities in a certain way.

Consider finally the relation of the programmatic vision of this book to the institutional program of the left. The radical left has generally found in the assumptions of deep-structure social analysis an excuse for the poverty of its institutional ideas. With few exceptions (such as the Yugoslav innovations) it has produced only one innovative institutional conception, the idea of the soviet or conciliar type of organization: that is to say, direct territorial and enterprise democracy. But this conception has never been and probably never can be worked into detailed institutional arrangements capable of solving the practical problems of administrative and economic management in large countries, torn by internal divisions, beleaguered by foreign enemies, and excited by rising expectations. Thus, the conciliar model of popular organization has quickly given way to forms of despotic government that seem the sole feasible alternatives to the overthrown bourgeois regimes.

The program of this book is a leftist program. It seeks the individual and collective empowerment that can result from the creation of institutional arrangements that undermine the forms of dependence and domination, and that do so in part by effacing the contrast between routine and revolution. Like all leftist views, it holds that only such an institutional transformation can realize in practice our ideals of freedom and community. But it differs from the mainstream of radical leftist programmatic ideas, so influenced by Marxist social theory, in several important respects. First, it assumes a background of explanatory ideas that makes the development of detailed programmatic proposals possible, legitimate, and significant. Second, it refuses to equate the market economy and the representative democracy with the particular institutional forms these principles have hitherto assumed. On the contrary, it sees in the development of alternative forms of democracies and markets the best hope for the accomplishment of leftist as well as liberal aims. Third, it draws heavily upon a tradition of institutional thought and experimentation to which the main current of leftist theory and practice has been implacably hostile: the tradition of petty bourgeois radicalism.

Thus far I have compared and contrasted the programmatic directions taken in *Politics* to a few of the major familiar positions in modern political thought. But the most significant implicit normative polemic in this book addresses an actual tendency of social transformation rather than the doctrines of a political movement. The single most attractive emergent model of social organization in the world today – least oppressive, most respectful of felt human needs, and therefore also most likely to attract the most diverse support of the most thoughtful citizens – is social democracy. The supporters of social democracy do not paint it as utopia, nor do they claim that all countries are equally ready for it. They recognize how hard it may be to achieve amid the extremes of poverty and ignorance when its achievement remains precarious in even the most favorable circumstances. They merely affirm that social democracy is the best that mankind can hope for, for an indefinite time to come. The great political issue before us is whether they are right.

As both an emergent institutional system and a familiar institutional proposal social democracy combines the following characteristics. The social democrat accepts the particular institutional versions of market economies and representative democracies that have come to prevail in the course of modern Western history. He pursues his ideals of redistribution or participation within the broad outlines established by this framework. He favors the welfare state. He wants to see the satisfaction of basic material needs guaranteed. He supports redistributive policies designed to redress gross inequalities of wealth and income. He is committed to see people more actively engaged in self-government in the places where they live and work.

But when you view social democracy as a practical experience rather than a programmatic commitment you see that these redistributive and participatory goals characteristically get realized within very narrow limits: the limits imposed by the economic and governmental arrangements that the social democrat accepts, if only because he views them as superior to all feasible alternatives. Thus, for example, the control that relatively small groups of investment managers continue to exercise over the crucial flows of investment decisions may require welfare-state programs to be repeatedly sacrificed to the demands of business confidence.

Finally, the social democrat sees the weakening of inclusive ideological struggle over the basic structure of society as something between an inevitable outcome and a desirable goal. The world of social democracy is a world where people can at last devote themselves to their practical concerns, by which the social democrat means, again, the form that people's perceived practical interests assume within the established institutional order of social life. Demobilization becomes, in this vision, the counterpart to realism and decency. Once the great ideological fevers have been spent, people can settle down to the prosaic but primary task of taking care of one another and making a practical success of their life in common.

This book can be read as an argument that social democracy is not enough and that we can establish something better than social democracy. The explanatory ideas of *False Necessity* provide an understanding of society that presents the institutional arrangements on which the social democrat relies as the relatively contingent and revisable outcome of a particular sequence of practical and imaginative conflicts. More generally, these explanatory arguments support a view of social reality within which the rejection of social democracy seems reasonable. The programmatic ideas propose an alternative to social democracy that realizes more fully the ideals that the social democrat can only imperfectly achieve and radically redefines these ideals in the course of realizing them.

But what is wrong with social democracy? The narrowest objection is that the social democrat cannot go beyond a certain point in making good on his promises of redistribution, participation, and mutual caring. He cannot go beyond the point set by his institutional assumptions and in particular by his assumptions about how market economies and representative democracies can be organized. His project, like those of the centrist communitarian or the conservative free marketeer, suffers from an incurable internal instability. The perpetuation of its institutional premises restrains the realization of its defining ideals while the reconstruction of the institutional framework invites a radical redefinition of these ideal aims.

When we view social democracy from the vantage point provided by the explanatory and programmatic ideas of this book, we can identify its key defect as the constraint it imposes upon the means of emancipation and empowerment. Once again, the constraint results from the forms of economic and governmental organization that social democracy presupposes and perpetuates. These organizational forms circumscribe our opportunities for practical innovation by limiting economic decentralization and economic plasticity. They prevent us from devising institutional means to free the practices of practical collaboration or passionate attachment more completely from the structures of dependence and domination in which these practices so easily become entangled. They keep us from affirming a more deliberate mastery over the institutional and imaginative contexts of our collective existence. We are too little under social democracy.

The force of these criticisms depends on the availability of alternative institutional arrangements that do indeed more effectively promote these connected dynamics of emancipation, arrangements described in *False Necessity* under the name empowered democracy. The objections all come down to the thesis that social democracy makes the liberal project of the enlightenment – the cause of liberty, equality, and fraternity – unnecessarily hostage to a transitory and replaceable institutional order. Once the liberal cause enlarges its sense of institutional possibility it merges into a revised and generalized version of the project of the modernist visionary and the leftist radical.

You may protest that it is perverse to hold up the image of empowered democracy when social democracy already seems a distant dream for much of mankind, abandoned to poverty and despotism. The program of empowered democracy may seem an open invitation to repeat with even more disastrous consequences the old leftist temptation to pass from a crude stage theory of social transformation to a disregard for the consequences of backwardness. But remember that many third world countries seem likely to achieve a measure of economic equality and political freedom only through the organized militancy of masses of semi-employed workers, agrarian laborers, smallholders, and radicalized petty bourgeois. Not only must they organize but they must stay organized. They and their leaders must forge institutions that sustain in the midst of routine social life a degree of civic engagement and grassroots activism that the existing democracies witness only at times of war and national crisis. The forms of economic and governmental organization developed by the Western industrial democracies do not lend themselves to this task. Designed to sustain only relatively modest levels of mobilization and conflict, they usually meet one of two fates in a third world setting. On the one hand, they may provide new ways in which to carry on the ancient game of patronage and clientalism. On the other hand, they may be used as the basis for a style of radical partisan conflict whose intensity and scope they cannot accommodate. Then, in the language of American political science, participation outruns institutionalization, and the society falls into a dissension that can end only in dictatorship or in a burst of institutional invention. Thus, the argument from backwardness may be turned on its head. For many contemporary nations social democracy may be the unrealistic choice. These countries may be able to escape governmental and social oppression only by catapulting beyond the social-democratic heritage to a style of democratic politics and of economic organization that more successfully effaces the contrast between structure-preserving routine and structure-transforming conflict.

The world looks different if you believe in the existence of an attractive and realistic alternative to social democracy. For our understanding of every historical situation expresses our tacit conception of possibility: our view of what things might become when subjected to varying degrees and forms of pressure. The explanatory alternative to deep-structure social analysis and positivist social science informs the programmatic alternative to social democracy. The ideas that inform and support the program of empowered democracy in turn advance our insight into the arrangements this program is meant to replace.

In developing the program of empowered democracy I seek inspiration in an aspect of modern Western political practice that until very recently has met with derision from centrists and leftists alike: the tradition of petty bourgeois radicalism. Historical research has produced mounting evidence of how much of the radical challenge to the emerging dominant forms of governmental and economic organization, throughout nineteenth-century Western history, came from skilled workers and artisans, technicians and professionals, shopkeepers and even petty manufacturers rather than from the proletariat or the lumpen that have played so prominent a role in traditional leftist historiography. The program of this petty bourgeois radicalism was chiefly articulated by publicists who earned the pejorative label "utopian socialists." These publicists championed one or another version of what Marx called petty commodity production: the coexistence of a large number of relatively equal small-scale producers or productive enterprises as the mainstay of economic organization. The petty bourgeois radicals concerned themselves with the methods of cooperative production or distribution that might sustain such a system. And they sought to extend to the organization of government the same principles they applied to work and exchange.

Though the radical petty bourgeois alternative was everywhere defeated and repressed, its defeat and repression were both less complete and less directly attributable to inherent practical deficiencies than historians, entranced with a stereotype of modernization, industrialization, or capitalism, have generally supposed. Many of its proposals were in fact realized as deviant or subsidiary arrangements within economies mainly organized on different lines. These arrangements continued and continue to exercise an important economic role in the most innovative as well as the most retrograde sectors of industry. Moreover, these bids to establish a different form of industrial society were rarely put to a test that would make it possible to assess their advantages and drawbacks. Their proponents lost a long series of political and ideological wars; they did not fail at an impartial economic examination.

The practical objections to petty commodity production, shared by hard-headed centrists and radical Marxists alike, can be reduced to three main criticisms. First, petty commodity production is economically regressive. It does not permit the economies of scale and the market organization that encourage technological dynamism. Second, petty commodity production is economically unstable. The more successful petty entrepreneurs would soon drive the less successful out of business and reduce them to the condition of wage laborers. Only a corrective system of redistribution can prevent such an outcome. But such a system would then become the real economic order, and it would disrupt or dwarf the economic calculations of small-scale producers. Third, petty commodity production is politically unstable. The national governments capable of supporting such an economic regime would always be either too weak or too strong. The government, resting on a population of independent proprietors obsessed with their little worlds of property and family, might be starved of the resources that would enable it to administer and defend the society. On the other hand, if the government did obtain these resources it would soon overpower a social order bereft of large-scale organizations capable of counterbalancing its own authority. To these considerations, and to others like them, we may attribute Marx's confidence that petty commodity production is at best a transitional or a satellite mode of production.

These objections do indeed weigh against the unreconstructed version of petty commodity production: the version that presupposes economic decentralization through absolute property rights and representative democracy through the constitutionalism of checks and balances, the institutional solutions that in fact came to prevail in the course of Western history. The advocates of petty bourgeois radicalism can be faulted for having failed to appreciate the destructive implications of the emergent or established institutional order for their programmatic aims. They never entirely escaped the obsession with the thinglike image of independent, small, absolute, and permanent property, which was the downfall of petty bourgeois radicalism as of so many earlier dreams of yeoman commonwealths.

Imagine a form of economic and governmental organization that attempts to relocate a program of radical economic decentralization, social solidarity, party-political pluralism, and civic engagement within an alternative institutional framework. Such a framework might, for example, put a system of conditional and temporary claims upon a social capital fund in place of absolute property rights (the same solution anticipated in another passage of this chapter). But then to prevent the administration of this fund from serving as a means for bureaucratic domination or social conservatism, this new institutional structure would provide a far broader range of forms of accountability and participation, and of opportunities to try out radical social experiments on a large scale, than are permitted or encouraged by the inherited constitutional forms of representative democracy.

Such an institutional program might well be repudiated by the champions of petty bourgeois radicalism for giving up on the essentials of independent and eternal property. In assessing the program they would be in the same situation as all who ask themselves whether the proposed translation of an old ideal into a novel institutional form preserves what ultimately attracts them to that ideal. The program of empowered democracy can justly claim to respect the more intangible and enduring aspect of the radical, petty bourgeois cause, the aspect less tainted by the transitory experience of a particular class. For it combines respect for a sphere of vital individualized security and immunity with a promise of opening society more fully to unplanned experimentation.

The pressure under which the advanced industrial nations now find themselves to shift from an emphasis on the traditional mass-production industries to the development of more flexible and innovative enterprises, with their characteristically closer association of task-executing and task-defining activities, can provide one of many occasions to work out this alternative institutional framework. For like all shifts in organizational and technological style, this change can be accomplished in ways that either minimize or maximize the reform of established arrangements and of the vested interests they support.

The reconstructed version of petty commodity production, newly suited to the concerns of the day, can now be recognized as an inspiration to the invention of institutions that carry the radical project, the project of the modernist visionary, beyond the limit of social democracy. And the mechanism of the change – the recasting of deviant and repressed solutions as new, dominant principles of organization – is one that *False Necessity* presents as typical of the way in which we remake our contexts.

A PROTO-THEORY

The Sense of a Proto-Theory

The whole social theory worked out in this book may well be seen as a development of the conception of human activity outlined at the beginning of *Social Theory: Its Situation and Its Task*. The following pages restate this conception briefly.

We must always settle down to particular social or mental worlds, the collective settings of discourse and human association. We cannot forever act as if everything were up for grabs. But neither are we justified in treating any particular mental or social world as the definitive, uncontroversial face of reason or civilization. No context can accommodate all the discoveries about the world that we might make or all the practical and passionate relations we might have reasons to establish. We can never resolve the tension between the need to accept a context and the inadequacy of all particular contexts. We can nevertheless diminish this tension by our success at inventing contexts that give us the instruments and opportunities of their own revision and that thereby help us diminish the contrast between context-preserving routine and context-transforming struggle.

This diminishment of the imprisoning quality of our contexts not only offers a partial solution to the problem of contexts but also enables us to deal with the other basic difficulty of our predicament: the conflict between the enabling conditions of self-assertion. To sustain and develop ourselves we must participate in shared forms of life. Yet all such engagement constantly threatens us with subjugation to other people and with the impersonal constraints of a social role or station. The creed of the visionary modernist is that the same practical and imaginative devices that strengthen our mastery over the established frameworks of social life also help us deal with the problem of human solidarity by purging group life of some of its evils of dependence and depersonalization.

I have shown in another book (*Passion: An Essay on Personality*) how this conception of our relation to our contexts can serve as a point of departure for a study of our intimate life of encounter and how this study can in turn inform a distinctive moral ideal or existential project. *False Necessity* develops the same basic conception in the direction of an explanatory social theory and of a program of social reconstruction.

Before the detailed explanatory and programmatic argument of *False*

Necessity begins, it may help to suggest the elements of a rudimentary approach that links this abstract conception of our relation to our contexts to the social theory advanced in this book. This connecting set of notions amounts to a proto-theory: less the outline of a single, coherent theoretical system than the description of ideas that can supply a basis for many different theories. This proto-theory (i.e., not quite a theory) in turn represents but one controversial direction among the many directions that the basic view of human activity mentioned earlier can follow when applied to the explanation and criticism of social experience. Yet the proto-theory really does link the particular proposals and explanations of this book to a general view of human activity: the conception of our relation to our contexts can inspire a basic understanding of society, and this understanding can inform a social theory. The final, detailed results are what matter most.

The statement of this proto-theory serves two independent purposes. First, it elaborates the thematic and polemical introduction set out in the earlier parts of this chapter, suggesting how these ideas can begin to take shape as a coherent view. Second, it provides one way to distinguish the intention from its execution. You may reject much of the actual explanatory and programmatic argument of this book while continuing to sympathize with the rudimentary ideas sketched in the next few pages. Then, all you need do is turn the proto-theory into a theory better than the one offered in *False Necessity*.

Theses of the Proto-Theory

The initial idea of the proto-theory that anticipates the argument of this book is the existence, in every social situation, of a distinction between a set of formative institutional arrangements and imaginative preconceptions, on one side, and the routines that this formative context helps shape, on the other side. Once the elements of this institutional and imaginative context are in place, they reinforce one another. Most importantly, they bias the forms and the outcomes of the ordinary practical and imaginative conflicts through which we determine the social future within the social present. They do so in the first instance by giving different groups – classes and communities – a privileged measure of control over the means of society making: mastery over capital and productive labor, access to governmental power, and familiarity with the discourses by which we reimagine society and govern nature.

None of the routines perpetuated by a framework of social life are more striking or puzzling than the stubborn cycles of reform and retrenchment, the hapless, bungling alternation among recognizably second-best solutions to the absorbing practical problems of the day. Again and again, we find rulers and governments resorting to policy options in whose adequacy they themselves disbelieve. Practical constraints are rarely enough to account for these disheartening compulsions until their effects combine with the restrictive force of an entrenched institutional and imaginative order.

The most formidable statecraft is therefore always the one that can enlarge the range of possible solutions by changing this context. At its most ambitious, this transformative political art does not merely replace one set of institutional and ideological assumptions with another system of the same kind. It inaugurates a framework that is permanently more hospitable to the reconstructive freedom of the people who work within its limits.

Every formative context of habitual social life arises from the containment of conflict. It results from a particular, unique history of practical and imaginative struggles. It becomes entrenched, indeed it exists, only to the extent that it gains immunity to disturbance from the rivalries and challenges of day-to-day social activity. These frameworks of social life do not exist in the manner of the atomic structure of a natural object, open to observation and measurement. Nor do they merely depend upon beliefs that a changed understanding might dispel. They subsist in a practical sense, through the resistance that they oppose to a transformative will or to the back-and-forth of our petty group rivalries.

A framework of social life becomes stable only when it is reimagined as an intelligible and defensible scheme of human association: a set of models of practical or passionate human connection that are meant to be realized in the different areas of social existence. Until society has been thus reimagined, people cannot settle down to a definite context. They cannot even understand one another except as the exhausted veterans of a perennial war.

The stabilized social world that results from a containment or interruption of conflict depends for its continuance upon certain practical or conceptual activities. These activities – which go all the way from group rivalry and party politics to moral and legal controversy – constitute the most important of the routines shaped by a formative context; they renew its life and connect it with the concerns of everyday life. Yet each of these context-reproducing activities can escalate under favorable circumstances into context-disturbing conflicts. No stable, clear-cut, and rigid line separates the routine from the subversive. The basic reason why escalation cannot be precluded is the inability of any institutional and imaginative structure of social life, or even of a closed list of such structures, fully to inform our practical and passionate dealings with one another. Nothing can entirely reduce us to the condition of puppets of a formative context or of the laws and constraints that might generate a limited set or a compulsive sequence of such contexts.

One of the most important differences among formative contexts lies in the extent of their immunity to disturbance. Some formative institutional and imaginative orders make themselves relatively more open to revision than others. Some strengthen while others weaken the force of the distinction, which never entirely disappears, between the conflicts that they shape and the conflicts that shape them. Some therefore also broaden and others narrow the distance that must be traversed before a context-preserving activity turns into a context-subverting one.

The variation of formative contexts on this scale of revisability or disentrenchment appears unmistakably in the character of social hierarchies. For example, hereditary castes, corporately organized estates, and social classes mark the presence of institutional and imaginative frameworks increasingly open to challenge and revision. Beyond the social class lies the movement of opinion, organized or not as a political party. In societies distinguished by class hierarchies and by unorganized communal (i.e., ethnic) divisions, the political party has a double nature. It is both the voice of particular classes or communities and an alliance of people whose shared commitments cannot be adequately explained on the basis of their membership in particular classes or communities. In a society placed yet farther along the spectrum of disentrenchment, the party of opinion might become, in its own right, the primary form of social division. That is just what it temporarily does become whenever escalating conflict disrupts people's assumptions about collective identities and social possibilities and therefore also about their individual and group interests.

This distinction among frameworks of social life with respect to their availability to transformation accounts for only a small part of the qualities that may otherwise distinguish them. But the distinction nevertheless holds extraordinary interest for us because of its close connection with a host of ways in which we empower ourselves and make ourselves more fully available to one another. As a formative context of social life becomes more revisable or disentrenched the range of experience open to the recombining activity of practical reason broadens. The resulting development of our productive capabilities represents one sense of empowerment. Moreover, the disentrenchment of formative contexts undermines any stable plan of social division and hierarchy or any rigid system of social roles. It thereby enables us to reconcile more fully the conflicting conditions of self-assertion: the need to participate in group life and the effort to avoid the dangers of subjugation and depersonalization that attend such engagement. This more successful reconciliation of the enabling conditions of self-assertion represents another side of empowerment. But the most straightforward sense in which the disentrenchment of formative contexts empowers people lies in the greater individual and collective mastery it grants them over the shared terms of their activity. Because this range of forms of empowerment is achieved by creating formative contexts that soften the contrast between context-preserving routine and context-transforming challenge, it might be called negative capability.

People can act as more or less intentional developers of negative capability. One reason they can do so is that the achievement of a greater measure of negative capability may be implicit in the satisfaction of more particular material or ideal interests, interests more closely connected with other varieties of empowerment. Moreover, the intentional pursuit of negative capability does not imply the invention of formative institutional and imaginative contexts with fewer or less determinate characteristics, hence a leap into anarchy or pure negativity, but rather requires the creation of formative contexts with certain specifiable features. Some ways of organizing governments, economies, and families – to mention only the most obvious concerns of a formative context – lie farther along the spectrum of disentrenchment, and succeed better at producing negative capability, than others.

The advance toward negative capability can be cumulative, either because its fruits of empowerment are intentionally sought or because the social orders that favor it are more likely to survive and triumph in the competition with their rivals. However, this advance is neither irreversible in its continuance nor determinate in its implications. It is at most a possible progression, and at any given level of its development it may take an indefinite number of institutional forms. Moreover, it always interacts with another, very different type of cumulative, long-term historical causation. Each formative context not only reproduces certain routines but also makes certain trajectories of context change more accessible than others. Much happens just because of what happened before, and the more or less intentional pursuit of negative capability has to share its influence with the power of mere sequence.

A view of context making represents always just the reverse side of a conception of the internal relations among the elements that make up a context. A theory of long-term change that focuses upon the interplay between the influence of sequence and the attractions of negative capability implies a particular approach to the internal constitution of social frameworks. These frameworks are not indivisible packages that stand or fall as a single piece. They cannot be placed on a predetermined list of possible types of social organization or assigned to a stage in a master process of historical evolution. But neither are these formative contexts random juxtapositions of freely recombinable or replaceable elements. The arrangements and preconceptions that constitute them can coexist stably only when they represent similar levels of negative capability. Moreover, the institutional or imaginative materials that compose these frameworks can be harder to combine when they are drawn from very different historical sequences of context making.

Programmatic Implications of the Proto-Theory

Though the theses that define this proto-theory are extremely abstract, they have far-reaching implications for social explanation, social reconstruction, and even party-political strategy. The proto-theory suggests a way to break once and for all the link between our ability to understand ourselves and our denial of our freedom to smash and remake our contexts. This theory gives a central explanatory and programmatic role to the very fact that seems to represent the chief source of difficulty in our efforts to develop a general understanding of social life. We often seem to be helpless puppets of the institutional and imaginative worlds we inhabit. The social theorist is tempted to see in this diminishment of our freedom the condition of explanation. But the proto-theorist introduced in the preceding pages recognizes that we can always act in ways that violate the rules and assumptions of our established settings. Though some circumstances are certainly more favorable to these transgressions than others, no statable list of structures or of underlying laws and constraints can fully govern our structure-revising and structure-transcending activities. The proto-theorist invites us to take these activities as a topic for speculation and as a source of insight rather than as a limit to our explanation. The theorist who follows in his steps shows that the relation between the freedom of the agent and the constraints of structure is not a constant but itself a subject of conflict and change in history. He even argues that our ability to form contexts more congenial to our freedom is involved in all our particular efforts to empower ourselves individually and collectively and to cleanse social life of some of its evils of subjugation and depersonalization.

Such a social theory incorporates the first characteristic operation of deep-structure social analysis: the identification of a difference between the routines of conflict, exchange, or communication and the structures that shape these routines. But the significance of this operation undergoes a drastic shift when combined with the rejection of the other two characteristic moves of deep-structure thinking about society. The proto-theory points to a social theory that does not try to present each structure, framework, or context as an example of a general type: as a member of a closed list of possible social worlds or as a distinctive stage in a worldwide process of social evolution. Nor does the proto-theory invoke the kinds of developmental laws and hidden economic, organizational, or psychological constraints that could yield such a list or such a process.

The aggressive methods of deep-structure social theory have often seemed an unavoidable basis for social and historical generalization. The sole alternative has appeared to be the framework-denying practice of positivist social science, with its failure to acknowledge the importance of the contrast between routine and structure and the discontinuities among structures. The fact-battered skeptic is inclined to think that the errors of deep-structure social theory can be cured only by diluting its claims or by retreating to a posture of modest theoretical agnosticism. But the strategy of theoretical modesty turns out to be both incoherent and unnecessary. The proto-theory suggests an explanatory practice no less general in its scope and no less rich in its implications than the deep-structure theorizing it rejects.

This approach to the contemporary predicament of social thought has a special meaning for the leftist. Marxism has served the left as its main tool of explanation and criticism. And Marxism is also the clearest example of deep-structure social theory, though many of the devices that help us escape that theoretical tradition can be found in Marx's own writings. All too often, radicals have felt able to overcome the procrusteanism of a theoretically rigorous but very restrictive version of Marxism only by watering it down into a loose series of concerns, categories, and attitudes.

The argument of *False Necessity* follows a different tack. The aim here is to carry the self-transformation and dissolution of Marxism all the way, in the conviction that the outcome will be another and more defensible theory rather than a theoretical collapse. The result bears a complicated relation to Marx's own ideas, as well as to the teachings of other classic social theorists. In some ways, the view developed in this book represents an effort to vindicate the original spirit of Marxism and, indeed, of all classical European social theory – the effort to see society as made and imagined rather than as given in the nature of things – against the letter in the scientistic, necessitarian apparatus that betrayed the radical intention in the name of carrying it out. In yet other ways the theory of *False Necessity* salvages and reinterprets a wide range of Marxist ideas by taking Marxism as a special case of a more general and tenable account of social experience.

The explanatory aims of *False Necessity* are linked to its proposals for social reconstruction and political practice. The approach anticipated by the proto-theory gives programmatic thought a secure place. If our ability to explain social and historical facts depended upon the moves of deep-structure social analysis, proposals for social reconstruction would be both misguided and superfluous. History could be counted on to take care of itself; its protagonists could do little but recognize more quickly or slowly where things were heading. On the other hand, by denying us any credible view of long-term trajectories of transformation, the conventional social-science alternatives to deep-structure social theory fail to provide programmatic thought with the sense of realistic transformative possibility it requires. As a result, we are led to a bastardized and paralyzing conception of political realism: a conception that dismisses far-reaching reconstructive ideas as utopian fantasies and immediate, partial reconstructions as reformist tinkering.

The social theory developed here has a more intimate relation to programmatic thinking about social institutions than the preceding remarks may have suggested. This theory affirms that the cause of our empowerment requires us to devise institutional arrangements that advance our negative capability and that further rid social life of its mechanisms of domination and depersonalization. And it denies that current forms of social organization can be adequately understood and justified as an unavoidable stage on the road to greater negativity and empowerment.

The argument of *False Necessity* supports and develops these suggestions, drawing out their significance for the reconstruction of society. The radical project, the project of the enlightenment, the project of empowerment through the making of institutions that encourage and perpetuate the breakdown of social divisions and hierarchies, has bogged down in the face of many disappointments. The most important of these disappointments has been the failure of the twentieth-century communist revolutions to offer an attractive alternative to the institutional solutions that happen to have triumphed in the course of modern Western history. And the stultifying effects of this disappointment have been aggravated by the lack of a believable view of social transformation. Such a view is needed to account for the resiliency of contemporary forms of social organization and to supply a perspective from which to assess the realism of programmatic proposals.

We can reimagine present governmental and economic regimes, and the forms of social organization they help support, as incomplete realizations of the radical project. We can explain their stability without treating them as the necessary expressions of deep-seated economic, organizational, or psychological constraints. We can acknowledge the replaceability of inherited institutions without giving credence to the idea of a foreordained sequence that predetermines what can or must come next. Most importantly, we can formulate programs of social reconstruction that push farther the effort to achieve empowerment through the weakening of social division and hierarchy. These programs include ideas about the reorganization of governments and economies and even of our intimate life of personal encounter. They provide a basis on which to connect the leftist criticism of institutional arrangements with the modernist criticism of personal relations.

The programmatic ideas indicate an approach to political action. This approach seeks to identify opportunities for a style of political practice committed to generating small-scale or transitional versions of its more comprehensive goals. The ends must be prefigured in the means for their achievement. Nevertheless, in conformity with its rejection of deep-structure social theory, this approach denies that any one social group bears primary responsibility for the advancement of the radical endeavor. It rejects the belief that any particular class alliances or antagonisms are inherently necessary or impossible. It proposes a way to take an established logic of group interests seriously while recognizing that escalating practical and imaginative conflict weakens and shifts the influence of preexisting group interests.

The argument of *False Necessity* is doubly hopeful. It sees a hope of surprising insight in what appears to be a situation of intellectual entropy or confusion. It discovers a hope of social reconstruction in what seems to be a circumstance of blockage and disappointment. These two hopes connect. To follow this connection through its many vicissitudes in the stuff of our social experience and visionary aspirations is the central concern of this book.

10

The Practice: In Quest of Power and In Power

THE PROBLEMS OF TRANSFORMATIVE PRACTICE

The Task of a View of Transformative Practice

The institutional ideas presented in this chapter have two sources: one is intellectual; the other, practical. The intellectual source is a practice of normative criticism and construction: exceptionally as visionary thought but more often as normative argument from within a tradition. In the sequence of exposition such visionary conceptions and internal criticisms anticipate the outline of the program they help to justify. But, in the actual psychological experience of formulating programmatic ideas, institutional proposals and ideal commitments develop simultaneously. Surprising turns in internal normative argument – our ever-present ability to deduce controversial conclusions from relatively uncontroversial premises – may suggest departures from current institutional arrangements. And the fragmentary description of these institutional proposals, together with our ideas about realistic trajectories of transformation, may in turn awaken us to unsuspected tensions between our ideal models of human association and the institutional arrangements that realize these models in fact.

The institutional program has a basis in political practice as well as in normative argument. The institutional ideas have to be realized by collective action. They remain unpersuasive and dreamlike until we have complemented them with a view of the social activities that might establish them. Our ideas about transformative practice and our programmatic commitments exhibit the two-way relation we find in our experience of the interplay between justificatory argument and institutional invention. Program and practice form a single vision; each can be inferred from the other, given a certain background view about the remaking of formative contexts. (The background view invoked here is the explanatory theory presented in earlier parts of this book.) The correspondence between practice and program comes out even more clearly in the small-scale politics of personal relations than in the large-scale politics of institutional arrangements.

By imagining a style of practice that prefigures a desired programmatic outcome we deal with the demonic problem of politics: the tendency of means to create their own ends, or the difficulty of realizing our chosen ends except through means that bring about results we do not want. A programmatic vision that cannot rely on a corresponding style of practice remains unstable: its proponents must choose at every turn between inaction and betrayal. The indispensable prefigurement of the ends within the means may refer to the social character of the transformative movement. The movement may embody a living, fragmentary compromised image of the future it advocates for society as a whole. Alternatively, the prefigurement may take the form of localized experiments in novel styles of social organization, experiments that the transformative movement helps stage in the surrounding society. The practical solutions and the enacted ideals that distinguish these small-scale foreshadowings must be revised when those ideals and solutions extend to broader areas of social life. But the revised forms may still be recognized as transformations of the early, anticipatory experiments.

The following pages present a view of the style of transformative practice that can establish and reproduce the programmatic arrangements discussed later in the chapter. The ideas about justification and those about practice converge to support the institutional proposals. And the view of transformative practice establishes yet another link between the explanatory and the programmatic themes of *False Necessity.*

It may seem that nothing that is not trivial could possibly be said about the generalities of transformative practice. For the realm of practice is the domain of the constraints imposed by each unique context. Nevertheless, the theory of social change and the program for social reconstruction presented in this book help support an approach to problems of transformative practice. Indeed, if they did not, we could hardly hope to establish the necessary correspondence between program and practice. For the program itself is pitched at a level of generality beyond the distinctive problems of individual nation states. Success at speaking cogently about practice even at this transnational level lends support to a central thesis of this book: that we not only can break out of particular formative contexts or sequences of formative contexts but can also change the character of the relation of these frameworks to our freedom as agents. The generality of the programmatic and practical ideas is more than a convenience of exposition; it is a corollary of a whole view that refuses to give the constraining influence of context the last word and that promises to alter the sense in which our societies imprison us.

Two great problems must be confronted by the transformative practice described here. The portrayal of the practice begins with a discussion of these problems and an anticipation of the way the following argument resolves them.

Reconstructing Institutional Arrangements and Revising Personal Relations

The first major problem of transformative politics has to do with the relation between the effort to reconstruct social arrangements and the attempt to change the character of the direct practical or personal dealings among individuals. Neither endeavor can prosper without the other. Yet they cannot easily be integrated into a single undertaking.

The ultimate stakes in politics are the qualities of the direct relations among people. As the practical and visionary fighting over the content of social life gets contained or interrupted, as a formative context of power and production settles into place, as the routines of work and domesticity grind on in the protective climate of the social peace, as men and women learn to give to their abstract moral slogans a meaning compatible with the recurrent experiences of their everyday lives, the styles of personal relations harden. Among these habits of personal dealings are the available forms of friendship and marriage, the things that people expect from one another's company, and the methods they use to cope with conflict and disappointment and to express their wants and feelings in the conventions of society. These habits also include the manner and degree in which, in the different circumstances of social life, people reconcile self-assertion and attachment and deal with the significance of hierarchy for community. In all these ways, men and women show how they hope to achieve a measure of redemption through their dealings with one another. This fine texture of routinized human relations is the primary social reality. Even the boldest transformative efforts often take it for granted or, having acknowledged its importance, fail to alter it.

People understand differences in material standards of living, they care about them, and accept or reject them, largely for what these differences reveal about the ordering of human relations and the place each person occupies within it. To be sure, an individual may desire more material goods simply as a means to realizing his independently chosen ends. Short of the most basic needs for security and survival, however, the ends people entertain are commonly shaped by a background scheme of images of feasible and justified human association and by the desire to hold a certain place within this scheme. Even when, through exceptional insight, faith, and courage, an individual defines and pursues goals that seem to contradict the ruling vision of collective life, his aims make sense only in relation to some other view of human association, whose sovereignty he recognizes or desires to establish. The chief objects of human longing are other people and the character of dealings with them. The whole world of material things is like a stack of poker chips that people use to signify the ups and downs in the great game they play about the nature of their relations to one another.

For all its importance, however, the politics of personal relations cannot advance unless it is accompanied by the reconstruction of the formative context of power and production. This institutional framework helps shape the routinized dealings and preconceptions that constitute the fine texture of social life. It defines the occasions, and tilts the scales, of the ordinary individual and collective conflicts that take place just because people want to remain who they are and to keep what they have. It enables some people to set terms to other people's activities.

This pinning down of the collective power to remake social life affects, more or less obliquely, every aspect of people's relationships to one another. Even the seemingly most private aspects of love and marriage, of religious devotion and intimate ambition, bear the marks of the experience of each individual's power or powerlessness in the face of the circumstances of social life. The available forms of practical collaboration or passionate attachment hit against the limits of preconceptions and institutions that, in turn, obey and sustain the larger order of the society. By these means, both the powerful and the powerless are denied opportunities to discover the indefinition of self and society. Each institutional order denies these opportunities in a different fashion and to a different degree.

The formative context of power and production influences people's elementary dealings with one another in another, more subtle way. The stabilization of a social world requires the spiritualization of violence. The haphazard sequence of truce lines in the ongoing group struggle must be reinterpreted as an intelligible and defensible scheme of human association: a canon of the possible and desirable models of human association to be realized in different areas of social life. The ability to assign relatively stable meanings to a system of legal rights requires at least a tacit reference to such a scheme. Even people's effort to make sense of everything in society, from the appropriate use of different buildings to the expectations that attach to different roles, must appeal to another, vaguer version of this imaginative scheme of social life.

Our immediate experience of practical and passionate attachments always includes more than is dreamt of within this implicit map of possible and desirable forms of human association. The exorbitant elements in our experience, the elements that fail to fit the established context, provide us with an endless flow of incitements to reimagine and remake society. But this reconstructive opportunity can be taken advantage of only to the extent that people manage to redefine their enacted ideals and establish a new relation between actual social practices and the assumptions about possible and desirable association that support and authorize these practices. Until the marriage of presupposed meaning and realized institutionalized practice has been achieved, our incongruous experiences remain anxieties without a message and rebellions without a legacy. Transformative struggle must then proceed without the incalculable prestige and credibility that a model of human association acquires just by being realized in a routinized practice.

The history of the world religions has repeatedly shown the price of the failure to embody a novel vision of personal interaction in a changed institutional ordering of practical life. The religious movement submits to the state. Often this submission takes place under the delusive appearance of a religious conversion of the power holders. The votaries of the religion limit rather than push the struggle over the formative institutional context and over the routinized personal dealings and preconceptions that take place within it. The iconoclastic spiritual vision strikes a compromise with the established forms of behavior and perception: not just the deal inherent in the slow process of changing people's most elementary habits and ideas but the additional accommodation that arises from the willingness to take a large portion of social life more or less for granted. Then, the thing the religion forgets perverts the thing it remembers. The untransformed social order ends up taking its revenge against the vision of transformed personal relations.

Just as the attempt to change the character of direct personal relations soon requires a transformation of fundamental institutional arrangements, so the enterprise of institutional reconstruction calls for a vision of the transformed personal relations that the new institutional arrangements are meant to sustain. It even demands anticipatory examples of the realization of this vision.

For one thing both the persuasiveness and the realism of an institutional program require that gross institutional arrangements be changed into the small coin of personal relations. The human sense of institutional proposals depends in the end on their implication for the social microcosm. Only when we reach in thought and practice this level of personalized detail can we see a radically reconstructive program chastened by its confrontation with the stubborn, daily cares of ordinary people.

For another thing the vision and anticipatory experience of transformed personal relations encourage the self-restraint vital to successful institutional reconstruction. When the government's active engagement in the defense of established institutional arrangements has been shaken by violent or peaceful means and when settled assumptions about collective identities, interests, and opportunities have come partly unstuck, institutional reinvention enjoys its favored moment. This opportunity can, nevertheless, be squandered if redistribution of material advantages takes priority over institutional reconstruction. Redistribution may exercise a mobilizing effect by granting larger numbers of people the security that enables them to give themselves more wholeheartedly to escalating conflict. But both rapid redistributive and institutional change disrupt routines of production, exchange, and administration. The need to contain the disruptions of the transition period often requires that institutional aims be given priority over redistributive goals, except to the extent that these goals result immediately from those aims. When the tide of enthusiasm recedes and the opportunities for revolutionary reform shrink, a changed formative context must already be in place. The ability to see institutional transformation as part of an attempt to change the character of our most elementary personal interactions pushes conflict over the form of society beyond the instrumental struggle over material advantages. It extends strategic prudence into visionary ardor, thereby offering the incitement to sacrifice and self-restraint that cold calculation is rarely enough to ensure.

But though the transformation of personal relations and the reconstruction of institutional arrangements depend upon each other in all the ways described, they cannot easily be combined. The two undertakings seem to require devotion to divergent and partly conflicting aims. The effort to reorder institutional arrangements demands the churning up of the social practices in which personal attachments are embedded, and it turns the imagination away from the delicate and intricate texture of personal interdependencies. The dangers appear vastly to increase when the reconstructive program aims to carry society to a circumstance of heightened plasticity. Moreover, efforts to combine, in a single programmatic vision, proposals for institutional change and ideas about the transformation of personal relations have traditionally been associated with a naturalistic view of society and personality.

The intellectual solution to this first overriding problem of transformative practice is given by the many links of thematic analogy and mutual dependence that the programmatic argument of this chapter establishes between the reform of institutional arrangements and of personal relations. The argument integrates the two concerns on the basis of a radically antinecessitarian view of society and of a corresponding commitment to reduce the extent to which society is just there, as a set of entrenched roles or stations, beyond the reach of the will. The two practices of revolutionary institutional reform and of transformation in personal relations can reinforce each other despite the conflicts sure to arise between them.

Transformative Practice from the Top Down and from the Bottom Up

A second great problem of transformative political practice is internal to the attempt to reconstruct the formative institutional structure of power and production. Stated in the most general terms and with respect to the broadest range of projects of social reconstruction, the problem is the tension between the importance and the dangers of using governmental power in order to transform society in the image of a programmatic vision.

The use of centralized, coercive state power to impose a plan of social life is likely to be both futile and dangerous unless it is prepared by a less willful change of habits and sentiments. The masters of the state will soon find themselves waging war against a resistant society. The results of the interplay between the transforming will and the social resistance may bear little relation to the initial program. The commitment to carry this program out may soon take second place to the struggle to hold on to an isolated and rebuffed authority.

The attempt to gain control over an aspect of governmental power and use it for transformative purposes cannot, however, be left to take care of itself. For the control of governmental power exercises an overwhelming influence upon the course of conflict over the basic form of society. Those who postpone to the end the bid for governmental power may find their enemies holding the cards.

Like the first great problem of transformative practice, this second is a special case of the conflict and mutual dependence between means and ends. Like the earlier problem, it takes on a peculiar intensity because of the distinctive goals the program outlined here assigns to transformative action. In one description, the program of empowered democracy seeks to diminish the gap between framework-preserving routine and framework-transforming conflict. It does so by increasing the mastery we exercise over our contexts in the midst of our normal activities. Our practical and passionate dealings and our relations to the social worlds we inhabit are to be improved by our success in putting the basic arrangements of society within reach of ordinary collective conflict and decision and thereby breaking the hold of factional privilege over the resources needed to remake society. The style of transformative effort most closely anticipating this programmatic goal is the same style earlier labeled as collective mobilization. The second problem of transformative practice is therefore the tension between the strategy of changing social life through the capture and use of governmental power and the attempt to change society by gradually heightening collective mobilization. Governmental power may indeed be used both to enlarge opportunities for grassroots collective militancy and to consolidate its achievements. Nevertheless, the imposition of a reconstructive plan from the top down seems to be the very opposite of what a practice emphasizing collective self-mobilization and self-organization requires.

Before developing in detail this program-specific formulation of the second problem of transformative practice, remember the defining characteristics of collective mobilization. It is the coming together of people in ways that already differ from the kinds of relations that exist in the surrounding society and for the purpose of changing aspects of these relations. At first, the aims may be narrow and the innovations modest. But as the mobilizational movement presses forward, with its mixture of disciplined organization and organization-denying militancy, the goals become bolder. The gap between society as currently established and as recast within the movement widens. People broaden their sense of the groups to which they belong and of the possibilities of social experimentation. Their conception of the interests worth fighting for change accordingly. At every stage of its progress collective mobilization offers people an experience of reinventing the terms of their social existence. It undermines the clarity of the distinction between the aspects of life surrendered to a prosaic calculus and the areas in which personal relations matter for their own sake. It draws defined impersonal institutions back into the undefined personal realities from which they arise. It may do all these things faintly or strongly. But it does them always. Collective mobilization is thus more than a weapon for the remaking of social life; it is the living image of society dissolved, transformed, and revealed, in the course of the fights that take place over what society should become. Mass mobilization occurs when collective mobilization turns into the experience of large numbers of ordinary men and women.

Ideally, the capture and use of governmental power would be the last step in the gradual transformation of society. Mastery of the state would represent only the final consolidation of a victory achieved by other means; governmental power would be like ripe fruit falling from the trees. One domain of institutional life after another – connected areas of social practice and the internal arrangements of largescale organizations – would be transformed by an exercise of collective mobilization inspired by a programmatic vision such as the one later sections of this chapter discuss in abstract and systematic terms. A shared feature of the new arrangements would be to preserve more fully in routinized social practice some of the qualities social experience assumes in the moment of collective mobilization.

It is not absurd to think that these many moves of collective mobilization might take a predominant programmatic direction, even though no one has written this program down and no one has orchestrated in detail these many experiments in social change from the bottom up. To admit this possibility of shared direction you have only to accept a number of assumptions that have already been presented and will be further justified. You must believe that this trajectory of transformation can be imagined and justified in bits and pieces, through the interplay between received social ideals and more inclusive understandings of social possibility. You must think that the normative doctrine of the program is not radically different from the ideal conceptions to which we already resort in our fragmentary attempts to criticize or justify particular institutions. You must concede that the connected reforms advocated by the program represent at least one possible route to the varieties of empowerment earlier discussed. And you must recognize that the logic of group interests, and of group alliances and antagonisms, begins to lose its clarity and its determining influence as soon as conflict starts to escalate.

Consider the dangers of the attempt to reverse the sequence that puts escalating grassroots mobilization first and the use of centralized governmental authority last. For the sake of clarifying the stakes, focus initially on the extreme case. A revolutionary vanguard seizes the central government and the military apparatus through force, guile, or luck, and attempts to impose its program by coercive means. We may even assume their take-over has been facilitated by mass agitation. Yet nothing but the experience of agitation itself has established anticipatory, fragmentary versions of the programmatic aims. In such a circumstance, two forces may easily converge to foreclose opportunities to realize any program resembling empowered democracy. These forces show two ways in which means may overtake ends.

On the one hand, the rulers may commit themselves to a project that finds little echo in the vague discontents and tangible wants of the populace. They rightly feel themselves threatened by rejection from within if not by invasion from abroad. To hold on to power becomes, in this precarious situation, their paramount concern. The obsession with the maintenance of power at any cost gains a semblance of justification from the need to keep custody of the supposed means of transformation. The effort to hold on to power in the circumstance of isolated and rebuffed authority is itself an all-consuming project. It requires the containment of conflict, the exaction of obedience, and the exercise of a vigilant distrust. It tempts its votaries to violence and rhetoric – those "two ways of denying reality." And it brings to the fore men skilled at perpetuating and strengthening an apparatus of control. Those rulers who take the prophetic dogmas at the heaviest discount will rise most quickly. The moment to carry out the program of empowered democracy will never come. Alternatively, the program will be carried out with so many concessions to the imperatives of the apparatus and to the power interests of those who staff it that little of its original content will remain.

On the other hand, plain people will fail to see in the professed aims of the revolutionary regime the elements of an alternative order of life. Once secure in power, the willful regime may succeed in promoting economic growth and material welfare. But it cannot credibly stand for the ideal of a society broken open to everyone's will or for the varieties of individual and collective empowerment permitted by the opening of privileged holds on the resources of society making. Faced with a mixture of unbelievable slogans and unmistakable coercion, ordinary men and women will withdraw into their families and careers in search of whatever tangible advantages they can secure. From these havens, they will emerge, because they must, only to engage in a sullen wrangling with their bosses and rulers.

These dangers stand out most clearly in the extreme instance of a revolutionary vanguard that attempts to impose a radical plan upon a resistant populace. But the same perils reappear, on a more moderate scale, whenever the struggle over governmental power as the master tool of social reconstruction takes precedence over the reform of one domain of institutional practice after another through escalating collective mobilization. The struggle for governmental power imposes a relentless discipline of its own. Militants and supporters must be converted through a language they can understand. Battles must be fought in circumstances where they can be won. Such tactical imperatives may require compromises and self-restraints incompatible with the conflictual style of a mobilizational strategy. In all these ways the effect of focusing on the struggle to win governmental power is to tempt partisans of the transformative movement to take for granted current assumptions about collective interests, identities and possibilities.

The effort to cling at any cost to whatever measure of governmental power has been won presses the would-be reformers to depart farther and farther from their initial aims. Thus, for example, institutional reforms may be subordinated to immediate redistributive goals, and the reformers' time in office may come and go before they have had a chance to alter the formative institutional context of power and production. First the cause of partisan victory and finally the concern with partisan survival may prompt the sacrifice of one programmatic aim after another. The growing disparity between the slogans and the achievements of the reformers may provoke their disappointed supporters into ever greater degrees of withdrawal from militancy at the grass roots.

Despite all the dangers of anticipating the attempt to gain governmental power and use it for transformative ends, state power cannot in the end be treated as the final, spontaneous trophy of collective mobilization and institutional reform. The risks of leaving the take-over of governmental power to the end are even greater than the perils of using public office to reconstruct society. To begin with, governmental power may decisively influence the opportunities and obstacles of an organized, structure-revising militancy. It may do so through all the ways the state reproduces society. Government may enlarge or constrict the freedom to organize and proselytize. By redistributing wealth, it may free people from the extremes of a demobilizing poverty. It may counterbalance factional privileges even before it has abolished them.

Moreover, although a programmatic vision and a distinctive trajectory of transformation may emerge from the dispersed activities of many movements, this activity is unlikely to maintain a minimal cohesion and continuity of direction unless the grassroots efforts interact with at least occasional help from those who determine the most important rules and policies. The institutional reforms must enjoy sustenance in law and economic policy. The policy and legal obstacles to their further expansion must be overcome. And in all these ways tentative experiments and visionary routine must find an anchor in alternative, emergent structures.

The very attempt to win governmental office may prove almost as important as its exercise. The electoral or extra-electoral contest to gain position in government shakes the many links that connect access to the power of the state and entrenched privilege in society. The pattern of public intervention in favor of factional prerogatives gets disturbed. This disturbance in turn helps put the established definitions of collective identities, group interests, and human possibility up for grabs.

Even if your party were to arm you with an endless patience and propose to wait many generations for a slow but solid victory, you would find opportunities lost and lost forever. You would watch your enemies renew the life of institutional arrangements that would help shape future wants and self-descriptions. You would see people give to your party's slogans a meaning in accord with practical experiences you were powerless to influence. You would stand by while the aspirations of your movement withered in isolation. Why would these results surprise you if you had truly abandoned faith in the dialectic of history and learned to recognize how closely the dealings among groups connect with their relation to government?

The second key problem of transformative political practice may now be restated in formulaic terms. Collective contractualism (the explicit or implicit bargains among groups entrenched in the division of labor) changes into collective mobilization. This change encourages and depends upon the process by which the hardened links between private privilege and governmental power turn into a more intense and less defined struggle over the state. Yet each process makes voracious demands of its own. Each, followed to the end, threatens to disrupt and displace the other.

The ready antidote to this danger may seem to be an interplay between the pursuit of governmental power and the propagation of self-guided collective mobilization. Each move forward in the capture of parcels of state power can be used to improve the conditions for autonomous grass-roots militancy. Each successful change of stabilized deals into an open-ended fight over the redefinition of ideas about collective identities, interests, and possibilities can help prevent the power of the government, and the quest for governmental office, from becoming an instrument of demobilization.

The allusion to this interplay, however, represents the name of a solution rather than its description. The description comes in the form of a view of transformative practice or, rather, of the limited insight into the problems of such a practice that can be achieved outside a particular setting of conflict. The ideas and maxims constituting this view are formulated here at two hypothetical moments of transformative practice: a moment when the movement, still far from the heights of governmental power, has only just begun to take root in society and a moment when it wins the highest offices. This view of practice should be general enough to apply to transformative movements that culminate in either the peaceful or the violent seizure of state power. The wager is that even at this level of generality, so remote from the problems of any individual circumstance, we can discover principles of action that illuminate the task of transformative practice.

Who are the agents of this program? They are the people whom I sometimes call the radicals, the transformers, or the transformative movement and, at other times, the defenders of empowered democracy. By radicals I mean the adherents to the radical project as previously defined: the men and women who seek to promote specific varieties of human empowerment by developing economic and governmental institutions that both diminish the conflict between framework-preserving routine and framework-transforming struggle and loosen the constraints of established social hierarchies and roles upon the forms of production, exchange, and personal attachment. The program of empowered democracy represents a proposal, informed by a view of social reality and social transformation, to develop the radical project in a certain direction. As a version of that project, it addresses a distinctive historical circumstance (the circumstance of contemporary industrial democracies and their rivals). But like any other social vision of comparable generality it embodies ideals, methods, and assumptions intended to have a broader reach.

This preliminary loose identification of the transformative agents should be read against the background of a refusal to treat any particular class, community, or nation as the natural proponent of this or any other program, even though it is possible to identify the strata, parties, and even countries most likely to be receptive to it. The explanatory theory of *False Necessity* has already justified this refusal. The programmatic argument justifies it further. The relation of the transformative movement to existing parties and classes and the relation within the movement among cadres, rank and file, and potential supporters are taken up in the course of the following discussion of transformative practice.

THE TRANSFORMATIVE MOVEMENT IN QUEST OF POWER

The First Task: Linking Grassroots Mobilization with the Contest for Governmental Power

The first and most persistent task of the transformative movement is to maintain the connection between grassroots mobilization and the contest over governmental power. The allusion to the importance of maintaining this link merely restates the basic problem of transformative practice discussed in the preceding pages. But the first principle of practice describes the organizational basis for a successful solution to the problem.

The point of departure for this strategic approach is a recognition that neither the effort to capture parcels of governmental power nor the attempt to develop collective mobilization must be allowed to crowd the other out. Each must be practiced with an eye to the requirements of the other. At every juncture of activity the participants in the movement ask: Which grassroots organizations are most likely to be useful in the contest for governmental power and what style of engagement in this contest can encourage militant collective self-organization? Nevertheless, the two contending goals of transformative practice are characteristically served by two different types of organizations. To insist on an immediate synthesis of the two types is to risk creating a political enterprise unable to perform either role effectively. The conditions that would allow for the organizational synthesis cannot be assumed; they must be created.

In the contemporary Western democracies the primary tool for the conquest of governmental power is the political party, often little more than an electoral syndicate held together by a strange combination of transitory interest-group alliances, vague but powerful affinities of vision and sensibility, and career ambitions of professional politicians. The poverty of the institutional imagination regularly makes for an incongruous, shaky fit between tangible promises to particular groups and ideal commitments to social reconstruction. The same lack of clarity about the relation of formative contexts to routine policy options helps prevent the parties from breaking or even understanding the cycles of reform and retrenchment that so greatly influence their electoral fortunes. Such an electoral syndicate ordinarily takes for granted current definitions of group interest, collective identities, and social possibilities. It is tempted to seek the broadest possible alliance of interests and opinions it can achieve consistently with these assumptions and with its sense of its historical identity. It understandably resists challenges to such assumptions, which risk sacrificing its chances for high office. It tends to defer to organizations, like labor unions or ethnic associations, that claim to represent its prospective constituents. And it usually confines its activities out of power to planning for future electoral campaigns or to the ritual reassertion of its distinctive identity. All these proclivities make it ill-suited to the work of grassroots collective mobilization. The available experience of partisan struggle, directed to central power, may bring people together. But it is much less likely to bring them together in ways that already begin to defy this context and to step beyond the assumptions about the interests, identities, and possibilities the context helps sustain.

To the extent that the work of collective mobilization is carried on at all in the contemporary industrial democracies it is undertaken by a medley of nonparty organizations: the more militant and less economistic labor unions, social activists committed to organize as well as to defend the unorganized poor or oppressed minorities, and citizens' movements devoted to social interests perceived to fare poorly in mainstream governmental politics. Each variety of popular extrapartisan militancy can remain detached from any general program for social reconstruction, or it can make common cause with the social-democratic parties and reinterpret its commitments from a social-democratic perspective. But if its participants accept the internal criticism of the social-democratic program outlined earlier, they will come to believe that their objectives cannot adequately be accomplished within the institutional frameworks to which social democracy remains committed. They will also be more ready to see the campaign for empowered democracy as a fulfillment of their own efforts.

This shift in the self-definition of extrapartisan grassroots activity may be paralleled by a reorientation of any of the existing political parties or by the creation of a new party committed to empowered democracy. The internal criticism of contemporary party-political programs has shown how the established institutional forms of market economies and representative democracies frustrate the realization of the classical liberal, the centrist communitarian, and the social-democratic programs. The program of empowered democracy can persuasively claim to realize the part of existing party-political platforms the established institutional framework excludes. But, of course, abstract commitments are one thing, and represented interests are another. The program of empowered democracy has a far better chance of taking root in the reform, labor, socialist, and communist parties of the industrial democracies than in the centrist and conservative parties.

The initial concern of the defenders of empowered democracy, then, must be to work loosely within the political parties and the extrapartisan grassroots movements most open to their vision. Success in influencing the programmatic orientation of these movements and parties can in turn be expected to bring about a shift in the conception of the relation between partisan politics and social activism. The convert to the program of empowered democracy wants to develop the style of political practice whose character I am now beginning to describe. Because he seeks to tighten the link between collective mobilization and the quest for governmental power, he also desires to bring together the grassroots organizations and the political parties that most fully represent each side of the transformative effort. But it does not follow that he should try to abolish the contrast between the political party and the extraparty organization as quickly as possible. For the result might be to harness the grassroots social activism to the short-run perspective and the consensus-building concerns of the electoral syndicate while exposing this syndicate to the risky, long-term experiments and aggravated factionalism of the grassroots activities.

So you can imagine the friends of empowered democracy working, at first, with a loose sense of their shared identity, within political parties and nonparty social movements. They work both to change the direction of the party or movements to which they belong and to prepare the day when party and movements can safely unite. The picture here is not one of a conspiratorial organization that sends its militants out as secret agents and partners. It is rather an image of people who from several points of departure and in different theaters of activity gradually converge toward the sense of sharing in a common undertaking.

The interplay between social activism and party campaigns can be vastly reinforced by the presence of a third element, distinct from both traditional partisan rivalry and collective mobilization. The task of this third element is to detach a parcel of governmental, economic, or technical authority from service to the reproduction of the existing formative context and to turn this fragment of power, instead, into a floating resource – a resource that can be fought over and converted to transformative uses.

In countries with a strong statist tradition the lower rungs of the governmental bureaucracy constitute the most likely agents for the development of such floating resources. For example, in many Latin American nations whole sectors of the economy (e.g., agriculture) are closely supervised and co-ordinated by economic bureaucrats: public-credit officers and agronomists. Such countries often provide for corporatist union systems that compulsorily include most of the labor force. The unions may be staffed, guided, or manipulated by public lawyers and agents of the Ministry of Labor. Normally these forms of state activity seek social harmony in the form of submission to economic and bureaucratic elites. But the bureaucracies are typically mined by a multitude of more or less well-intentioned, confused, unheroic crypto-leftists – middle-class, university-trained youth, filled with the vague leftist ideas afloat in the world. The ambiguities of established rules and policies and the failures of bureaucratic control can supply these people with excuses to deny a fragment of governmental protection to its usual beneficiaries and make it available to other people, in new proportions or new ways. A tiny flaw is then introduced into the manner in which the state apparatus fits into the social order. The result is to create a floating resource – one the transformers can appropriate or fight about.

In countries with a weak statist tradition (such as the English-speaking democracies) reliance on state-provided resources is dangerous. For the welfare-state programs that enable social workers or public-interest lawyers to carry on their organizing efforts tend to be precisely the programs sacrificed first during the retrenchment phases of the reform cycle. In these countries, however, the learned professions are often proportionately stronger than in the societies with a more marked statist heritage. A vast area of social practice is effectively withdrawn from the scope of party-political conflict and treated as a subject for the application of professional expertise, when in another country some of the same subjects might be handed over to bureaucratic supervision. The outcomes of fighting and of the containment and interruption of fighting reappear as, say, the structure of legal rights inherent to a democratic market system or the style of work organization necessary to the management of an advanced industrial enterprise. The rights-defining practice of lawyers and the efficiency-defining practice of managers and engineers represent the two most prominent professional methods for the depoliticization of social decisions. But such depoliticization invariably depends on violent truncations of analysis: on the creation of a fictive sense of determinate rational constraint at the cost of arbitrariness in defining the methodological and institutional assumptions that make this determinacy possible. As a result, the depoliticization can be reversed. The domain of professional expertise can be turned into one more arena for carrying on, under special though contestable constraints and with special though revisable tools, the struggle over the formative institutional and imaginative assumptions of social life.

A fragment of the power exercised by the efficiency experts and rights specialists becomes a floating resource: a society-making capability whose uses and beneficiaries are not predefined.

Whether the floating resource results from a bureaucratic betrayal or from a politicization of professional discourse, it serves the alliance of grass-roots mobilization and state-oriented party politics. It turns the attention of both party and extraparty activists toward the immense depoliticized area of social practice that stands between them. It also provides those who begin to agitate and organize in this area with an opportunity to enlist resources, previously devoted to the reproduction of the existing social world, in the construction of enclaves and countermodels: enclaves for further experiments in the blend of grassroots mobilization and party politics; countermodels to a portion of the current formative context of social life. The point of the next principle of transformative practice is to explore the relation between enclaves and countermodels.

The Second Task: The Experimental Anticipation of Empowered Democracy

The need to prefigure the goals of empowered democracy in the means for its attainment does not merely require that collective mobilization and the struggle for governmental power be allowed to reinforce each other. It also demands that the transformative movement succeed in establishing small-scale, fragmentary versions of the future it advocates for society. Without these experimental anticipations of the program, there would be no way to bridge the gap between reformist tinkering and wholesale revolution and no way to pass from one set of assumptions about group interests, collective identities, and social possibilities to another.

Several features of the explanatory theory of this book suggest the characteristics of social reality that make such experimental anticipations possible. One characteristic is the looseness of the relations among the constituent elements of a formative context: despite the existence of constraints upon the institutional or imaginative elements that can be successfully combined, formative contexts can be changed piecemeal. Another enabling feature of social reality is the relativity of the distinction between the practical or imaginative activities that respect and reproduce a formative context and the activities that challenge and transform it.

Each fragmentary anticipation must satisfy two basic requirements. First and fundamentally, it must represent a step on a possible passage from the present formative order to the desired order. Like the situations it connects, and despite its limited scope, this step always has a double significance. It involves institutional changes. It also requires a shift in the assumptions about group interests, collective identities, and social possibility that help sustain, and receive sustenance from, current institutional arrangements. The correspondence between institutional order and the logic of group interests holds good for parts of a formative context, not just for a formative context as a whole. An act of experimental anticipation should satisfy another requirement: it should contribute to the solution of the overriding problem of means and ends by serving both as an anticipatory image of broader transformations and as a strategic tool.

As an anticipatory image the experiment embodies a partial, tentative, transitional version of part of the program. As a strategic tool it constitutes an enclave within which people may collect forces in order to engage in further episodes of grassroots mobilization and further efforts to win parcels of governmental power. When the anticipatory experiment goes well, its instrumental and expressive uses cannot be clearly distinguished. It then resembles the type of artwork (say, a late romance of Shakespeare's) that invokes a higher, renewed order of human life and demands an assent which is also a redemptive complicity. It gives people a more tangible and therefore more persuasive sense of what the desired transformation of social life would be like. As a result, the vision that inspires the transformers stands a better chance of enticing the will and the imagination to collaborate in making it come true.

No anticipatory experiment can maintain its content unchanged when extended to another area or transposed to another scale. The fragmentary version of the program is never just the program in microcosm. It is a transaction between an established and imagined reality and an effort to work out the implications of a complex program for particular problems.

One form the anticipatory experiment can assume might be called the movement as model. The movement as an organized political party or as a loose confederation of grassroots activities seeks to be an image of the future it advocates for the society as a whole, a picture of the true republic within the false republic. The relations between superior and subalterns, or between centralized collective decision and individual or factional initiative, the merger of democratic and communal ideals with each other, and their extension to ordinary practical dealings, must all turn the movement into a living icon of its program. To be sure, the fidelity of this image to the societywide program is limited both by the constraints of current institutional arrangements and current perceptions of group interest and by the distinctive problems of a political party or a grassroots organization. The opportunity nevertheless exists because it arises from the very nature of collective mobilization. For remember that collective mobilization occurs when people come together for transformative aims in ways that defy, however modestly, established hierarchies and roles. Collective mobilization can hope to change the formative context of social life only because it already escapes the pattern this context prescribes.

The success of the method of movement as model depends in part on an ability to capture some of the legal and financial support that normally goes to organizations with no transformative aims. To this end, it helps to exploit the structural similarities between the passive and the militant organization and to take advantage of the difficulty of distinguishing them in the eyes of the law. For example, a unitary, all-inclusive, corporatist union structure, such as can be found throughout much of Latin America, may have originally been designed by pseudopopulist authoritarian regimes as a device of controlled mobilization. Yet once the union structure is established it may be susceptible to gradual, piecemeal take-over from within. The "liberated" parts of the union system may become just such fragmentary models of the desired society. And the work of liberation may be facilitated by the failure of existing labor-law rules (if not of the people who administer them) to discriminate clearly enough between passive and radical unions or union militants.

The other factor on which the success of the movement as model chiefly depends is its ability to break down the distinction between the work of organization and agitation and the ordinary responsibilities of practical life. The prospects for prefiguring a reordered formative context increase as the activity of the movement goes beyond a narrow focus on conflict with bosses or bureaucrats and turns into a setting where people can go about their ordinary activities. At that point, engagement in the work of the movement ceases to compete with practical concerns or to be the special province of professional agitators and politicians. Clearly, this objective can be far more easily attained by the movement as a loose confederation of social activities and organizations, conducted both within and outside established institutions, than by the movement as a political party. The importance of this goal suffices to ensure the inadequacy of a party model of transformative practice.

The movement as model is not the sole form of the anticipatory experiment. Its other, even more important method can be labeled the exemplary conflict. Every society plays host to an endless series of petty practical conflicts, constantly renewed by the ambiguities in the accommodations struck between different groups or between these groups and governmental policy. The transformative movement must seek out the more promising of these disputes and intervene in them on the side of its present or potential allies. It must attempt to solve the disputes in ways that foreshadow a portion of its broader program. A sign of success in this work is that the intermediate solution provides a link between current assumptions about group interests, collective identities, and social possibilities and the form these assumptions would take if the program of empowered democracy were to be fully accepted and established. Such conflicts are thus doubly exemplary. They exemplify the ordinary controversies that proliferate throughout the society. And they can be met with solutions that prefigure, on a modest dimension, alternative institutional arrangements.

Once again, an example may help bring the method into focus. The example is all the more revealing because of its distance from the conventional picture of social agitation. Consider the economic tensions between small-scale and large-scale producers. At one extreme of contemporary economic and technological sophistication the small-scale producers may be peasants working at the periphery of capitalized agribusinesses or on relatively unmechanized plantations. At the other extreme, they may be high-tech "cottage" manufacturers, working for and against mass-production industry, as a permanent vanguard and an occasional rival. As rearguard or as vanguard, the petty producers work in an economic and institutional environment that disfavors them, if only by forcing them to do business in markets mainly organized by the large-scale producers. The small-scale producers may embrace the subaltern and dangerous role and accept whatever work the large-scale producers allot to them. They may press for governmental support in the form of fiscal policy or financial, commercial, and technological assistance. Alternatively, they may couple this pressure upon government with cooperative organization among themselves. Cooperative financial, marketing, and machine-sharing arrangements may help them capture economies of scale, diminish their vulnerability to market fluctuations, and escape the role to which the large producers want to confine them. Thus, some form of competitive partnership among the smaller and more flexible firms may emerge from an implicit or explicit contest with the dominant businesses. As the small-scale enterprises expand their experiments in resource-pooling they begin to develop a version of the rotating capital fund – a major principle in the economic organization of empowered democracy. As they combine this flexible pooling arrangement with various forms of state support they establish a preliminary model for dealings among many tiers of governmental capital givers and private capital takers. They pioneer in methods for using governmental assistance to change the character of markets rather than to supplant the market principle. In all these ways they give a little object lesson in the establishment of a reconstructed, dynamic version of petty commodity production. By participating in the problems of petty producers and by promoting the types of solutions just described, the transformative movement practices the method of exemplary conflict. The sense of incongruity this example may cause reflects the influence of unjustifiably restrictive views of what context-transforming conflict may be like and of who may serve as its executors.

The practice of exemplary conflicts may become more powerful when the radicals learn to connect the practical solutions they advocate with the ideals implicit in the most morally ambitious models of human association: the models that promise to reconcile more fully the enabling conditions of self-assertion. Representative democracy and private community are the most important of these models in the societies the program of empowered democracy most directly addresses. The exemplary solutions to exemplary conflicts – the solutions that most faithfully anticipate the transformative program – are also characteristically the ones that extend democratic or communal ideals and practices to areas of social life from which they had previously been absent and that reconstruct these ideals in the course of extending them. By such means the practice of exemplary conflict gains the element of visionary intensity it might otherwise lack.

The Third Task: Recruiting and Managing the Cadres

No problem of transformative practice is more important, or less studied, than the recruitment and management of cadres. The inequalities in existing societies combine with differences of temperament to maintain the distinction between the cadres and the rank and file. The cadres, activists, or militants are the people whose relatively privileged social circumstances and intimate psychological identification with the movement enable them to devote themselves to its work. Distinct from the ordinary supporters or sympathizers of the movement, they are also not its leaders although the leaders are usually recruited from their midst. These militants make the movement, and they can break it.

The further the movement goes along the spectrum of escalating mobilization, the more its fate depends on the cadres. For the sporadic exchange of favors or the occasional show of support must then be increasingly replaced by experimental deviations from existing arrangements, with or without the use of governmental authority. The militants supply the personnel to staff the experiments and keep them faithful to the program.

A politician who is good at everything in practical politics may find himself frustrated and defeated by the problem of the cadres. With luck, it is even possible to go a long way by being good at cadre management though bad at almost everything else. (Remember Mussolini.) The visionary leader and the egalitarian participatory movement are especially apt to be undone by trouble with the cadres. For the visionary leader who begins by fearing that too close an association with the recruitment and management of activists will compromise his moral authority may end up transformed into a symbol, manipulated by other, more astute politicians. (Contrast Gandhi's failures to Saint Paul's achievements.) And the radical movement, embarrassed by the social and psychological realities of leadership, may find itself destroyed or perverted by the very tensions among leaders, militants, and supporters it has failed to acknowledge and control.

In the practice of the movements that can serve as vehicles of a fuller democratization of social life the problem of the cadres comes to a focus on a single issue. Although no aspect of the techniques of radical politics has greater practical importance, none is more consistently disregarded in the literature of social activism. The problem consists in the range of difficulties presented by two types of cadres that, coexisting in very different proportions, tend to dominate the political movements that have arisen from the radical traditions of modern politics. Each major type of agitator and organizer suffers from deficiencies of vision directly reflected in failures of action. Such defects have been the ruin of many a radical campaign.

They must be corrected or contained by something other than the good intentions of the militants themselves or the restraining influence each type exercises upon the other. For the coexistence of the two kinds of activists is just as likely to aggravate the dangers of each as to balance them out.

Consider first the sectarian cadre. He is obsessively concerned with the fidelity of the movement to the right line: to just the right programmatic objectives and social alliances. Although he may speak incessantly of the corrective value of practice, his tendency is to refer every major controversy about practice to a preestablished scheme and, particularly, to the kind of scheme congenial to deep-logic social theory. He treats a specific set of group (i.e., class or community) alliances as given in a predefined type or stage of social organization. If hard-core Marxism did not exist, he would need to invent it; the pompous subtleties of a hairsplitting scholasticism provide his natural element.

The truths he fails to appreciate are the insights the criticism of deep-structure social theory makes explicit. He does not understand the extent to which the reconstructive program can and must be chosen rather than found in a preexisting list of options. Nor does he recognize how much the apparent clarity of a calculus of class interests, class alliances, and class antagonisms depends on the very stagnation his movement seeks to interrupt.

The illusions of the sectarian result in two related habits of action and thought. On the one hand, he stands ever ready to split the movement for the sake of the line. He delights in internal antagonism, seeing in it the confirmation of his political seriousness. His energies are consumed in an endless and unproductive infighting rather than in a cumulative, outward-turning struggle. On the other hand, the divisions he provokes, expressed as they are in an idiom of manipulable political rhetoric and superstition, easily become the vehicles of personal or factional rivalries that are driven by baser motives. The very starkness of the gap between the categories to which the sectarian appeals and the content of practical politics makes the confusion between correctness and malevolence all but inevitable. Indeed, the sectarian may switch lines sharply and frequently, and change them all the more abruptly because the ideological contrasts that absorb his attention have so tenuous a foothold in practical experience.

The typical rival of the sectarian is the consensualist, coalition-building cadre. He nurtures a moralistic, antistrategic view of politics. He envisions a struggle between the rich and the poor or, more simply, between the good and the bad. He stands ready to fight in the battle of the little people against their masters. He therefore exudes confidence in his ability to tell who his allies and adversaries are and what must be done in the given situation. But this confidence rests on a naive and sanctimonious moralization of the social order rather than on an allegiance to the dogmatic prejudices of deep-logic social theory. He repeats, in modernized form, the oldest and most universal pattern of social criticism, for he imagines politics as the reenactment of a drama, outside historical time, that tries to preserve or restore the rightful order of society. He is an inveterate goody-goody.

What the consensualist cadre fails to grasp is the controversial and conflictual character of social life. He does not appreciate that the cause of the little people can reasonably be understood in different and incompatible ways, and that these alternative interpretations imply, and are implied by, divergent trajectories of institutional reform and coalition building. He does not recognize the need for fundamental choices that are also gambles. He does not admit that these choices entail and legitimate a large measure of internal factionalism.

These illusory assumptions also take their toll in a misguided strategy. The consensualist cadre often imposes a particular line under the mistaken impression that there is nothing particular about it. He thereby barricades himself against the lessons of experience. Because he thinks he knows who the friends and enemies of the movement are, he fails to manage existing divisions or to exploit potential alliances that are not self-evident. Because he believes that the demands of his cause are clear he fails to develop arrangements capable of replacing established practices. And because his naivete is supported by a sanctimonious disposition he can be as repulsive to the outsider as the most bigoted sectarian.

Theoretical enlightenment would seem to be the necessary and sufficient cure for the inadequacies of the two types of cadres. Have the right ideas about politics, and you are on the way to being the right kind of cadre. But, in the short run, theoretical criticism is not enough. For the perversities of the sectarian and the consensualist result from a circumstance of divided loyalties as well as from a legacy of mistaken ideas. The consensualist and the sectarian alike are caught between the leaders and the rank and file. Both kinds of cadres accept leadership and in turn perform a custodial role that cannot easily be acknowledged and legitimated within the tradition of radical politics. Moreover, sectarian and consensualist cadres alike can exercise power and submit to it in the name of impersonal ideological rectitude or uncontroversial popular solidarity. Neither type of activist has to confront the discretionary, controversial character of the choices he makes or has made for him. For it is discretion that gives power its most painful edge.

There is a realistic, second-best solution to the problem of the cadres, an alternative to full theoretical enlightenment. The first step of the solution is to create another manner of cadre, one who does not share the complementary illusions and defects of the consensualist and the sectarian and who is animated by the view of transformative practice these pages describe. This better cadre is able to play the other two against each other. The creation of a third style of cadre represents a far more modest accomplishment than the total renovation of the corps of activists. For this achievement not only dispenses with the total substitution of the cadres but can also draw on the reinforcement of insight by ambition. The third type of cadre can turn to his own advantage the resistance that the consensualist and the sectarian are almost sure to provoke in the rank and file and in the populace among which the movement does its proselytizing work.

The next stage of the second-best solution plays out the rivalry among the sectarian, the consensualist, and the "enlightened" cadres for the favor of the rank and file. The leaders who emerge from this new group of militants or who have helped create them provoke the rebellion of the ordinary activists against the ideological purists and the goody-goodies. They hardly need to fabricate occasions for this rebellion; it is enough for them to await the frequent occasions when the beliefs of the consensualists or sectarians suggest strategic decisions that endanger the movement.

The final stage of the next-best solution is to complete the rebellion both by propagating a more defensible understanding of transformative practice and by effacing the starkness of the contrast between who is and who is not a cadre. The situation in which all members of the movement are simultaneously cadres and noncadres will be realized more fully and easily when the ideas animating practice no longer resemble an esoteric science or a sacred creed and when they develop rather than deny the uncertainties and opportunities that inform ordinary political life. (Remember that the social theory underlying this conception of practice rejects any sharp contrast between the subjective experience of the agent and the insight of the theorist.) The ideal of maximum possible overlapping between cadres and noncadres can also be approached more easily when the dogmas of a mistaken style of practice do not defeat at every turn efforts to carry forward the work of emancipating society from false necessity and entrenched order.

The three-step solution to the problem of the cadres can never be easy. It must contend with limitations of insight and generosity against which no theoretical rectification can guarantee us. It must be performed again and again, rather than once and for all; the three steps must be made to overlap and to recur. At least, however, this approach to the problem of the cadres remains in close touch with the ideas that inspire this whole view of transformative practice and the program of social reconstruction this view anticipates and confirms. Moreover, it makes no demand of extraordinary selflessness or privileged knowledge.

The Fourth Task: Recognizing and Devaluing the Logic of Group Interests

The theory of society that underlies the view of transformative practice presented in this section implies a certain view of the agent's relation to the logic of group interests. By the logic of group interests I mean the overall constellation of positive and negative aims that seem to inhere in the distinct places that every system of social division and hierarchy generates.

Both deep-structure social theory and conventional, empiricist social science encourage belief in the clear and determining influence the logic of group interests exercises over the course of conflict in social life. The deep-structure theorist in his hard-core Marxist guise believes a system of class interests to be implied by the structure of a mode of production and by the forces commanding the succession of modes of production. He believes, as confidently as he believes anything, that escalating conflict reveals the system of underlying class interests and that those who persist in making or disregarding the class alliances this system requires will be destroyed. Hence, he enters political practice with a clear sense of the alliances that are necessary and of the antagonisms that are unavoidable.

The positivist social scientist or the routine politician (remember the affinity between routine politics and positivist social science) gives a different sense to similar conclusions. He may concede a significant element of give and ambiguity in the established logic of group interests. He may even acknowledge that the clarity of this system of alliances and animosities depends entirely on the persistence of institutional arrangements that can be challenged and replaced. But, having made this acknowledgment of principle, he then wants to get back to ordinary politics and ordinary thought. He has no way to represent to himself the transformation of group interests that is brought about by a change in their institutional framework. The moment of rupture is, for him, a limit to thought and action rather than a central problem to be explained or an objective to be achieved.

The activist who has understood the problems of transformative practice in the light of the social theory developed in this book must respect the constraints that group interests impose upon collective action. Yet from the outset he must also act in the spirit of one who sees these collective interests as dependent upon institutional frameworks that are not themselves guided by higher-order laws. This determination to recognize the immediate realities of class or communal interest while denying that they are for keeps is no ad hoc reconciliation of clashing attitudes toward the force of class and communal interests. It is, rather, the direct expression in practice of a certain theoretical understanding of society. And this understanding turns what would otherwise be a vague prudential formula into an approach to the problems of political practice.

The narrower the range and the dimmer the intensity of conflict over the institutional and imaginative framework of routinized social life, the more transparent, rigid, and influential the system of class and communal interests will appear. This clarity of the system of collective interests will grow stronger when the institutional framework provides for its own insulation from destabilizing strife. For a system of group divisions becomes secure when it is constantly regenerated by the institutional arrangements that shape our routine activity and that allot the economic and cultural resources for society making. These arrangements in turn achieve safety when they stand protected against the disturbing effects of ordinary conflict.

If the transformative militant finds himself in such a situation, he must strive to understand it and to mold his actions according to its dictates. He must identify the groups that will most easily support his cause given their preexisting view of their own interests. He must not pursue group alliances or antagonisms that frontally disregard the constraints that currently perceived group interests impose. Nor must he propose objectives that cannot readily be translated into the language of such interests. (Even the political prophet, who ostentatiously breaks with the system of group interests, must appeal to the anomalies of current personal experience.)

But the subversive activist entertains a mental reservation even when he seems to be bending to the stabilized social world and its active repertory of interests and possibilities. He sees its stability as predicated upon the temporary interruption and containment of broader conflict and the partial realization of negative capability. He is committed to an alternative institutional order he sees as capable of pushing farther the emancipation of social life from false necessity. Moreover, as the next maxim of this view of transformative practice emphasizes, he understands that even the most rigidified social situation is rich in ambiguities that can be exploited by the resolute transformer.

At moments of quiesence the whole art of the transformer consists in the attempt to find in the modest opportunities that never entirely disappear a foothold for larger conflict. He must take everything *almost* as given: *almost*, because the relation between the uncertainty about just what is given and the vision of something beyond the given create the possibility of movement.

As conflict escalates, the institutional niches and collective identities that lend a real but superficial clarity to group interests begin to fade. It now becomes clear that choices must be made among alternative routes along which each preexisting group interest may be both fulfilled and redefined. Each path involves a commitment to a set of institutional arrangements – or, rather, to a sequence of institutional reforms – that is just the reverse side of a group of social alliances. Each sequence ends up changing how people see their interests. The possibility was always there. But now it can begin to be lived out. And this living out gives the thesis of the provisional, redefinable quality of group interests a credibility it would otherwise lack

Consider, for example, the situation of the labor or socialist parties in the industrial democracies of the late twentieth century. They might continue to define themselves as spokesmen for the organized work force, entrenched in the mass-production sector of the economy, while speaking with another voice to a larger, indistinct constituency outside the traditional working class. Following this strategy, they would seek no drastic alteration of the established institutional arrangements for government and production: only the incremental redistribution of wealth and income, the gradual development of social assurance schemes, the extension of nationalized industry, and the occasional experiments with more participatory methods of decision in workplaces and neighborhoods. But these parties might also well conclude that there was no future in the privileged commitment to a shrinking part of the work force (i.e., the unionized workers of the mass-production industries), anchored in a declining sector of national industry. Prudence alone might lead them to cast about for an alternative program that could turn them into representatives of a larger coalition: an alliance of people committed to novel or archaic forms of small-scale entrepreneurship and professional independence as well as of the unemployed, the unorganized, and the poor. One candidate for such a program would be the reconstructed version of the suppressed alternative in Western history: revised petty commodity production, with its many consequences for the regimes of governmental organization and capital allocation, consequences the program of empowered democracy spells out.

As the execution of this program advanced, the distinctions among the underclass, the skilled workers, the old and the new petty bourgeoisie, and the independent technical or professional cadres would weaken, not because a single homogeneous work force would emerge but because the surviving distinctions within the labor force would be numerous, fragmentary, and volatile. Each stage in the trajectory of institutional reconstruction would be both preceded and followed by a shift in the way people imagined the groups they belonged to and the interests that were theirs.

At the extreme of escalation of conflict all rigid social relations collapse into the twofold circumstance earlier described. On the one hand, society passes into the Hobbesian conflict of all against all. Each person grabs whatever he can and gives himself to the relentless search for preemptive security. On the other hand, the contest of class and communal interests dissolves into a struggle of parties of opinion, animated by alternative programmatic visions. On the one hand, the man in tooth and claw steps outside the social station: all are equalized by the brutal struggle for defense and self-defense. On the other hand, the successor to the interest-determined agent is the individual as a context-transcendent being whose commitment to certain ideals and opinions is not determined by his membership in particular classes and communities. The strongest assertions of spiritual independence resemble the most brutish contests for material advantage in their power to weaken the constraints that social stations impose upon the will and imagination of the individual. In this circumstance of maximum conflict the perspective of the transformative militant becomes, in part, the standpoint of the theorist and the prophet.

Thus, at each stage of escalation, the transformative activist must change his attitude toward the established system of group interests: first finding his allies within the constraints this system imposes and then helping to overthrow such constraints. His apparently incompatible attitudes, however, are motivated by the same theoretical conception; what seems to be a shift in assumptions turns out to be faithfulness to the same ideas. At the beginning of the process the enlightened militant may easily be mistaken for the traditional leftist, content with deep-structure social analysis, or for the conventional, interest-group politician, who shares the premises of conventional social science. But from the outset he recognizes that moral and political intelligence requires you to see in real people more than examples of a social category and in social categories *no more* than the expression of a conditional social world, with its definitions of interest and identity, of associative reality and possibility.

His ultimate aim is not merely to replace one set of collective interests by another but to change the sense in which society making remains at the mercy of a preexisting system of group interests. The program of empowered democracy that this view of transformative politics anticipates and supports seeks to undermine the basis of fixed social stations in a formative institutional order effectively protected against recurrent challenge. The normal experience of politics (both in the narrower sense of conflict over the mastery and uses of governmental power and in the broader sense of struggle over the remaking of society) must more fully embody the dissolution of classes and communities into parties of opinion. The attitude toward group interests that characterizes the moment of escalation must become the normal attitude. But the further dissolution of social classes into parties of opinion must be achieved without the Hobbesian search for preemptive security. For the dissolution that is sought results from the adoption of particular institutional arrangements rather than from a violent anarchy, and these arrangements ensure the vital security of the individual. However, the institutional means for ensuring this security must not, like consolidated property, allow any one group to gain a privileged hold on the resources for society making. They must minimize the rigidifying implications of individual security upon the surrounding social order. (See the later discussion of immunity rights.)

The Fifth Task: Identifying and Exploiting Transformative Opportunity in the Midst of Stability

The transformative movement must learn to identify and exploit opportunities for practical and imaginative destabilization even when the current formative context seems most stable and entrenched. (Remember that entrenchment designates the extent to which the formative institutions and preconceptions make themselves unavailable to challenge and revision in the midst of routine social activity. Stability, on the other hand, is about resilience to pressure or danger, such as economic or military crisis, at any given level of entrenchment. To adopt a contrast beloved of leftists whose minds have been formed by deep-structure analysis: entrenchment is an attribute of structure, whereas stability describes a conjuncture.)

The fifth task is merely an extension or a special case of the fourth task. The preceding principle of transformative practice describes an approach to prevailing assumptions about group interests, collective identities, and social possibilities. It teaches a way to take these assumptions seriously while denying them the last word. I now consider the circumstance in which this approach is hardest to apply and easiest to forget.

The discussion focuses on three characteristic instances of transformative opportunity that persist in even the most stable moments of societies like the contemporary North Atlantic democracies. For this purpose I choose examples of practical collective conflict, although I might just as well have selected situations drawn from the routines of, say, legal controversy. The analysis of these transformative opportunities draws upon several basic themes of the social theory worked out in this volume: the close connection between perceived group interests or identities and institutional arrangements, the failure of any institutional or imaginative framework to accommodate all emerging opportunities for practical or passionate human connection, and the irrepressible ability of context-preserving activities to escalate into context-transforming struggle. In each instance the analysis of transformative opportunity shows how the response to a relatively minor crisis or disharmony may be achieved in contrasting ways. These responses may either maximize or minimize the disturbance to formative institutional arrangements, or to formative ideas about possible and desirable human association and to the assumptions about interests, identities, and possibilities that these ideas or arrangements help support. The transformers must recognize the initial opportunity. They must master the practice of the disturbance-maximizing response. They must turn each success in the pursuit of this response into an example of the fragmentary anticipation of their program.

One irrepressible source of transformative opportunity arises from the relation between the enlistment of governmental power in the service of private privilege and the more or less negotiated or coercive accommodations private groups make to one another. The place that each class, community, or segment of the labor force occupies in the scheme of social division and hierarchy depends in large part upon its relative success at securing direct or indirect governmental protection for its interests. The protection may take the form of legal rules, of economic policies, or even merely of a refusal to upset an established pattern of group advantage or compromise. The influence thus gained and secured can in turn be used to renew a measure of privileged access to governmental power: if not through hereditary claims upon office then through economic and cultural influence upon elections, policies, or even assumptions about the appropriate and inappropriate uses of public authority. Every group must engage in this struggle unless it resigns itself to the lowest social positions. Every group must fight to stay ahead in order not to fall behind.

But the translation of governmental power into group advantage and of group advantage into governmental power is a trick that must be constantly repeated. The less immediate the connection between the power and the advantage, the greater becomes the attention that must be devoted to it and the less predictable the results it may produce. While government personnel and policies shift, the relative economic, organizational, or demographic strength of different groups also changes. The structure of government-supported prerogatives and disabilities within which groups must operate is therefore incurably unstable. This low-level, contained instability results in an endless series of petty conflicts and anxieties that the transformers must learn to recognize and exploit. For what may seem from one standpoint an annoyance without a message may be reconceived from another perspective as a revelation. If the boundaries of recognized group interests and identities can be shaken by conflicts over the mastery and uses of governmental power, then perhaps everything in the current logic of group interests and identities may be changed by this or some other type of conflict. The transformative agents must do all they can to carry this insight into the subjective experience of the fighting over group advantage and governmental privilege. To this end they must play upon two other major transformative opportunities that persist in the presence of stability.

One such opportunity arises from the existence of an irreducible strategic ambiguity in the requirements for the defense of group interests. Suppose that the formative institutional and imaginative context of society is very clearly defined and largely uncontested. Each segment of the work force occupies a well-marked place in the social division of labor: characteristic jobs, complete with a distinct relative level of wages and discretion, a shared style of life, and many shared attitudes, ambitions, and apprehensions. (The segmentation of parts of the labor force is only one aspect of the logic of group interests. But it suffices to illustrate the point now under discussion.) Each segment of the work force may pursue either of two strategies in the defense of its interests. It may adopt a narrowing strategy. It then seeks to hold on to its current position and prerogatives strictly conceived. It defines the groups just below it or most similar to it as its rivals and adversaries. The resistance it opposes to its superiors is tempered by the fear that they might make common cause with its inferiors to prejudice its interests and its place. This strategy has the advantage of minimizing short-run uncertainties and risks. But aside from making it difficult for a group to achieve a significant improvement on its current position, it also makes each group hostage to the continuing inferiority of its immediate subordinates. The group will hesitate to engage in acts of defiance for fear that such acts might incite its own inferiors to rebellion.

The alternative is an expanding strategy. The group and its leaders seek to ally themselves with the closest coordinate or inferior groups against their common superiors. They may do so at first in a spirit of mere tactical alliance. But what begins as a tactical partnership may slowly turn into a broadened definition of collective interests and identities, a definition cemented by alternative institutional arrangements or by the experiments that prefigure them.

Even if you suppose that the logic of group interests, collective identities, and social possibilities is both well defined and unchallenged, this logic provides no general reason to prefer either the narrowing or the expanding strategy. Each has its advantages and its risks. The relative persuasive force of each depends on specific traditions and circumstances of collective action. Although both strategies may be equally compatible with such rigid assumptions they have radically different implications for the future of those assumptions. The narrowing strategy encourages the perpetuation of assumed interests, identities, and constraints on possibility. The expanding strategy leads directly to their subversion. The militants of the transformative movement must seize on this strategic ambiguity. They need to argue and act whenever possible in favor of the expanding strategy, even if they have to begin by doing so on the basis of received views about interests, identities, and possibilities. In so arguing and acting they await the first chance to show how the enlargement of alliances for the sake of currently perceived group interests may help bring about a redefinition of these interests.

The coexistence between a more conservative and a more radical response to the same problem reappears in another situation, the most promising of the transformative opportunities likely to appear in a circumstance of seemingly unshakable stability. Societies and their governments regularly face middle-level crises brought on by the need to adapt their institutional arrangements to unexpected economic or military challenges. To exploit an opportunity for the development of practical productive or destructive capabilities they must revise an aspect of their current formative context. If they fail to execute this revision they risk economic decline or diplomatic and military defeat. Either is likely to spark conflict over current institutions. But if they go ahead and execute the reforms, they must face the prospect of conflict nevertheless. The institutional arrangements to be changed or preserved support complex accommodations among groups or between groups and governments. The practical objectives may be satisfied with minor institutional adjustments. But it is important to understand that these goals can invariably be realized through alternative institutional adjustments, each with its distinctive effects upon the relative positions of contending groups or their relation to the state. The crisis-diverting reforms are unavoidably productive of conflict both because they disturb existing deals and because, depending on their content, they can upset these deals in very different ways. Once the conflict arises, it can widen in scope and intensity. The aim of conservative crisis-managers is to seek the reforms that meet the immediate practical danger while minimizing the disturbance to established institutions and recognized interests. The goal of the transformative movement is just as clearly to exploit the controversies that will inevitably take place: to expand and intensify them and to meet them in ways that also represent steps in the direction of the transformative program.

By way of example, consider again the rich industrial countries who now find themselves under pressure to adapt to changes in the international division of labor by changing their style of industrial organization. They must move from an emphasis on traditional mass production industries (the favored ground of the rigid variant of rationalized collective labor) to greater strength in the more flexible, vanguardist forms of high-tech manufacturing and provision of services. This shift can be staged in forms that scrupulously avoid challenge to the current institutional forms of capital allocation and representative democracy. But even in this modest version they require new arrangements and new deals. They therefore also produce new conflicts. Thus, for example, a labor movement traditionally entrenched in the mass-production industries may find its inherited forms of representation threatened. It may then seek alternatives that redefine the relation of organized labor both to governments and to the previously unorganized sectors of the labor force. Such alternatives may also change the balance between union militancy and participatory representation in enterprise decision making. Managers and bureaucrats may find that a haphazard pattern of covert subsidies and transfers has to be replaced by a more organized relation between public policy and entrepreneurial decision. Large-scale enterprises may come under pressure to reconstruct their internal divisions in the image of the smaller businesses that had previously flourished as their junior trading partners, subcontractors, or unofficial research departments. All these changes are compatible with what can be broadly described as a conservative route to industrial reconstruction. Yet none of them can be accomplished without offering alternatives and generating conflicts.

The advocates of the program of empowered democracy may seize upon these conflicts. They may do so all the more easily because they can justifiably claim to favor institutional arrangements that push the same shift farther. The system of capital allocation they support deprives the mass-production industries of the devices by which these industries have traditionally protected themselves against instability in the product, labor, and capital markets. It also gives the more flexible vanguardist enterprises the institutional advantage previously reserved to their mass-production rivals.

Middle-level crises like these provide the standard occasion for revolutionary reform and are the stuff with which conservatives and radicals alike must chiefly work. No wonder the frequency and the importance of such crises have been dramatically understated by both positivist social science and deep-structure social analysis: the former insensitive to the distinction between solving problems and changing frameworks, the latter obsessed with the idea of total and sudden framework change.

The ideas implicit in the discussion of this final source of transformative opportunity become both more general and more precise when they are related to three theses of the explanatory social theory developed earlier in this book.

The first relevant thesis is the existence of a relation between the development of practical capabilities and the making of institutional arrangements that loosen the constraints imposed by a preestablished scheme of social division or hierarchy upon the organization of work. (Remember that at certain levels of resource availability and technological development this relation may be temporarily overridden by the service that entrenched hierarchies and roles render to coercive surplus extraction.) The thesis shows why a series of middle-level crises and of responses to them may result in a cumulative creation of institutional arrangements that weaken rigid social roles and hierarchies while narrowing the gap between context-transforming and context-preserving activities. Thus, the thesis draws attention to the special interest such crises hold for a political practice committed to the program of empowered democracy.

A second pertinent thesis of the social theory advanced here is that any move toward greater negative capability can be accomplished through alternative sets of institutional arrangements and therefore also through alternative effects upon the wealth, power, and prestige of different groups. The particular content of existing institutions, available ideas, and traditions of group action may limit the range of existing solutions. No solution is likely to succeed if it requires too sudden an advance in negative capability or if it draws upon materials too far removed from the unique history that produced a formative context. But such limits remain loose and ambiguous; they fail to specify a unique solution to any given middle-level crisis or even a well-defined set of possible solutions. Because such a crisis can always be met by alternative institutional reforms and because any such reform disturbs vested group interests, conflict is sure to result. The conservative must try to contain it. The radical must attempt to turn it to his purposes.

A third implicated thesis of the social theory is the frequent existence of an inverse relation between the contribution an institutional reform makes to the development of negative capability and the ease with which it fits into a received history of institutional reinvention. The radical (by whom, remember, I mean the champion of the radical project as earlier defined, not just the person who wants more change) has the strategic disadvantage of demanding – at least ultimately – a bigger break with current assumptions about group interests, collective identities, and social possibilities. But if he thinks and acts correctly, he may gain the countervailing advantage of plausibly claiming to make the organization of social life more hospitable to the further development of practical capabilities and the further management of middle-level crisis. He even promises to turn this speculative future benefit to present use. By understanding and respecting the affinity of the radical cause to the practical interest in social plasticity, he helps to even the odds in his contest with the conservative.

The Sixth Task: Formulating a Visionary Language

Success in executing all the tasks of transformative practice previously discussed will not ensure the availability of a language in which to discuss practices and programs. The forms of discourse now available to radical transformative movements are largely unsuited to the program of empowered democracy. Some represent the sloganlike versions of deep-structure social theory. Others merely appeal to established conceptions of group interest. Some have a utopian content almost entirely devoid of institutional specificity. Others describe institutional reforms without making explicit their connection to any general program of human empowerment or emancipation. In a very real sense the movement must talk itself into power, and its talk, like its more worldly stratagems, must be both a tool of persuasion and a device of discovery.

The first standard an appropriate mode of discourse must satisfy is the ability to combine an appeal to recognized group interests (i.e., the recognized interests of the groups composing the initial coalition of program supporters) with a reference to a sequence of institutional reforms that move in the desired direction. A suitable discourse enables people to reflect upon the interplay between definitions of group interests and successive adjustments of the institutional framework within which these interests get defined and satisfied.

Consider the habits of thought and expression on which such an interaction depends. In order to prefer the forms of satisfying preexisting groups that require institutional reconstruction to those that do not, it will be necessary to anticipate in the earliest and most prosaic discussions something of the visionary impulse that underlies the program. Strategic calculation alone never suffices to tilt the scales in favor of an unmistakably risky course of action.

The institutional proposals, for their part, must be stated in terms that are modest and concrete enough to allow for linkage with current debates and concerns. But they must also be sufficiently far-reaching to exercise a visionary pull. The solution to this apparently intractable dilemma is to focus on a whole sequence of cumulative institutional changes going from minor reforms to major reconstruction. It is the trajectory that matters rather than any single place along it. Thus, the language of the movement must speak of right and wrong routes, of realistic and unrealistic paths. It must repudiate the exclusive contrast between reformist tinkering and all-out revolution. It must bring to bear on the identification of realistic paths of change the applied version of an entire understanding of social transformation. In these, as in so many other ways, the discourse of the movement should represent the practical extension of the style of social theory for which this book argues.

The preceding considerations already suggest that the language of the reconstructive movement must be prophetic as well as institutional. It must achieve a visionary freshness and immediacy to enlist energies on the side of the institution-challenging forms of interest satisfaction and to maintain the instructive and encouraging connection between present experiences and ultimate programmatic aims. These aims are the subject of political prophecy because they promise a better solution to the problems of solidarity and contextuality: a better opportunity to diminish the conflict between the enabling conditions of self-assertion and to make our social contexts less arbitrary and imprisoning.

Thus, the language may play on aspects of our current ideals and practices of democracy or private community that, however flawed, offer a more complete experience of self-assertion through attachment than we can find in the everyday world of work and exchange. The talk of the transformer then suggests how these higher experiences of solidarity may be extended to broader areas of social life and how they would be revised in the course of this extension. Alternatively, the discourse of the transformer may make use of whatever in pop culture emphasizes the idea of the adventurer, at once ordinary and extraordinary, who is able to fight back against his context and to triumph over the belittling routines of humdrum practical life. The purpose is to show how this fantasy can be made real, which is to say how it can be actualized in a form that is both collective and institutionalized.

But whatever the rhetorical strategy pursued, the emphasis of language must always fall on the subtleties of personal experience rather than on the more impersonal aspects of dogma and practice. For one thing, only the reference to detailed, person-to-person relations can give the discourse of the movement an intelligible and persuasive immediacy. For another thing, only the test of personal experience, as shaped by changing institutional context and as interpreted by theoretical analysis, can ultimately validate our ideas about possibility and empowerment. There can be no real conflict between the rhetorical uses and the intellectual value of the appeal to personal experience. The exercise of political prophecy presupposes the failure of established dogmas and institutions fully to inform our direct practical or passionate dealing. The prophetic vision takes the anomalies resulting from this failure as points of departure for the regeneration of social life.

A political language couched in this spirit will not easily be produced or accepted by militants formed in the tradition of deep-structure social theory. Until the cadres are transformed and the theory is replaced, many compromises may have to be made with theoretical prejudice. It may take time before what seems merely a concession to the demands of popular understanding can be accepted as a requirement of true insight.

THE TRANSFORMATIVE MOVEMENT IN POWER

A Second Moment of Transformative Practice

The preceding discussion deals with the problems faced by a transformative movement when it remains distant from governmental power and struggles to gain a foothold in social life. Consider now the problems faced by that same movement when it comes to exercise a fragment of central state authority, that great and perilous lever of transformation.

Once again, the analysis treats simultaneously the peaceful winning of power by electoral and parliamentary processes and the violent seizure of the state against a background of revolutionary action. Here, even more than at the earlier moment of practice, the analogy may seem misleading. Yet here, even more than previously, it pays off. Although it presents distinctive problems the revolutionary situation also simplifies and dramatizes the difficulties transformative practice must confront in the evolutionary circumstance.

The following discussion of practice at the moment of governmental power makes explicit a pattern only implicitly present in the analysis of the moment of relatively powerless agitation. Once again, the overriding goal is to use methods that both anticipate and produce, both express and serve, the desired outcome. Once again, the aim requires that centralized collective decision combine, in both its practical methods and its transitional results, with decentralized, grassroots engagement and decision. The program of empowered democracy, which this style of transformative practice is meant to suit, rejects the one-way imposition of institutional solutions from the heights of state power. But it also repudiates, as misguided and self-defeating, any attempt to do without large-scale governmental and economic institutions and to replace institutional arrangements with an uncontroversial system of pure, uncoercive human coordination. A premise of the program is that no such system exists and that the development of less coercive systems of coordination is bound up with the transformation – not the abolition – of governmental institutions.

The Primacy of Institutional Reconstruction over Economic Redistribution

The transformative movement in office must affirm the primacy of institutional reform over the redistribution of wealth and income. It must also prefer the forms of economic distribution that result from institutional reconstruction to those that leave basic institutional arrangements unchanged.

Both major redistribution (meaning, in this setting, economic redistribution) and institutional reform have disruptive effects. They provoke resistance and dislocation and do so in the parliamentary as well as the revolutionary situation. Both redistribution and institutional change must go forward in the face of opposition from those whose advantages they threaten and whose beliefs they insult. Moreover, both can disorganize practical activities of production, exchange, or administration and cause an opposition that arises from the fear of disorder and jeopardy. The resistance-provoking effects of redistribution may be even stronger than those of institutional reforms whose redistributive effects are delayed or unclear. They may take the form of disinvestment and capital flight as well as of overt antagonism to the party in office. But these "non-political" consequences may soon produce "political" results; if they are allowed to persist too long they will quickly erode any government's base of popular support or tolerance. On the other hand, institutional reform is sure to provoke major disruption even if its redistributive consequences are not overt and immediate. A transitional period exists during which part of the established formative context ceases to operate – a series of arrangements for production, exchange, or administration – before the intended replacement is secure. The transitional difficulties may well be further aggravated and prolonged by the need to make the new institutions fit with the arrangements that are left unchanged, and to reconstruct them so they can fit.

The transformative movement in office inevitably runs a race against time. No matter how successful it may be in its policies, it must count with disappointment on the part of many of its supporters. This disappointment is in part psychological. The hot moment of social life – the moment of escalating collective mobilization and public enthusiasm – cannot be permanently sustained. To recognize that it cannot is not to introduce an ad hoc claim about motivations but merely to emphasize the subjective side of the whole view of human activity that animates the explanatory and programmatic argument of this book. Although we can transcend our contexts, we cannot pursue any of our ordinary human concerns outside a context.

The radicals want something of the quality of the hot moments of social life – the periods of accelerated collective mobilization – to pass into the cold moments – the ordinary experience of institutionalized social existence. Thus, the whole program of empowered democracy can be seen, from a limited but nevertheless illuminating perspective, as an effort to capture in a stable context part of the heightened freedom from false necessity that is discovered in the course of our activities of context making.

The uncertainties and resistances of the transition increase the pressure to establish the alternative arrangements as quickly as possible. Here the relative priority given to redistributive and institutional aims becomes crucial. If the transformative movement attempts to pursue all its redistributive and institutional aims simultaneously, it aggravates the disruptions and antagonisms and increases the likelihood of being voted out of office, overthrown, or perverted from within before it has had a chance to carry out its plans for institutional reconstruction.

Suppose, however, that the movement decides to give priority to noninstitutional redistribution. The difficulties of transition will still occur, and though disruption may be less than it would be if the focus remained fixed upon institutional reforms with delayed or implicit redistributive effects, resistance may be even greater. The people threatened in their most tangible interests will organize to agitate against the party in power. Even if they remain entirely passive, the nearly automatic response of investment capital to heightened risk will ensure the occurrence of economic difficulties that will jeopardize support for the government. If it has come to power by democratic parliamentary means, the transformative movement in office will soon find itself under pressure to abandon its more ambitious redistributive goals, to content itself with a program of economic growth and restabilization, and to assuage the very business groups it previously assaulted. If the radicals in power fail to retrench, their tenure in office may well be shortened. But whether they retrench or not they risk leaving office without having executed any part of their institutional program. Redistributive tax-and-transfer measures, which require the constant correction of outcomes generated by the ordinary arrangements for production and exchange, can more easily be reversed. Even when they prove lasting, they may turn out in retrospect to have at best redistributed a little for the sake of not reconstructing much. The radicals would have unwittingly contributed to keeping politics at the limit of marginal redistribution within an unchallenged institutional framework.

When the transformative movement holds power by revolutionary means, the danger of giving priority to redistribution presents itself in a different way. The quickened resistance excited by the redistributive plans may tempt the regime to retrench or drive it out of power. But resistance may also provoke the radicals into the relentless centralization of authority. The redistributivist emphasis then becomes an episode in a series of events culminating in the dictatorial perversion of the movement and its program.

These arguments suggest the importance of emphasizing the primacy of institutional reconstruction over redistribution. Whether their situation is parliamentary or revolutionary, the transformers generally come to power on a wave of urgent redistributive demands. To resist these expectations the transformative movement must rely on many sources of help: the preference for redistributive policies resulting from institutional reforms rather than for those supplanting these reforms; the long-term development of insight into transformative practice; the careful sustenance of the ardor attending the experience of collective mobilization; the concern with the personalist, noninstitutional parts of the program, which help inspire this ardor; and the active engagement of ordinary men and women in the emergent economic and governmental arrangements.

In the most extreme revolutionary situations the primacy of institutional reform over noninstitutional redistribution may hardly be a matter of choice. An institutional order has already been disrupted. No distribution or redistribution can take place until an institutional framework for production, exchange, and administration gets consolidated. The only question is, which framework? The revolutionary government must do its best to resist the tendency of some of its peasant, worker, or petty bourgeois constituents to demand redistribution according to notions of fairness and right embedded in the prerevolutionary order.

In parliamentary circumstances these distinctive reasons to assert the priority of institutional reform over economistic redistribution no longer hold. But the government has a countervailing reason to struggle against the tendency of some of its constituents to adopt a clientalistic attitude to the state: to await passively the benefits it may shower upon them. By engaging people in the conflicts and experiments required for the development of new institutions, the movement gives them a focus of concern other than immediate redistribution. It thereby establishes a bond with ordinary working men and women stronger than the gratitude or love that people may be expected to show a paternalist welfare state. It also keeps alive the type of relation between central government and decentralized social action that the whole program of empowered democracy is designed to encourage.

The principle of the primacy of institutional change must be qualified in several ways. Some forms of economic redistribution are needed to tear people out of the misery and fear that effectively prevent them from mobilizing. Such situations – pervasive in third world countries and common to the underclass in even the richer Western nations – trump institutional goals. But it may still be possible to pursue these goals in ways that combine institutional and redistributivist effects.

The significance of this qualification becomes clearer in the light of another qualification, already present in the initial statement of the principle. Almost all forms of institutional reconstruction produce long-run redistributive effects. Some institutional reforms, however have dramatic consequences for the redistribution of wealth and income, while some forms of redistribution presuppose no change in the society's institutional arrangements. Consider the difference between a mere tax-and-transfer mechanism, on one side, and, on the other side, the broader involvement of workers' delegates in salary-setting and investment-making decisions or a change in the terms on which capital is made available to workers and small-scale entrepreneurs.

A particularly favorable and instructive case for early redistribution is presented by agrarian reform, especially when it seeks to replace the large, relatively unmechanized, plantation-style estates that still flourish in many third world countries with family-style farms, organized in a cooperative financial, marketing, and technological network, with governmental support. Such an agrarian reform illustrates the qualifications to the principle of priority of institutional change over economic redistribution, while also serving as the exception that proves – or, rather, elucidates – the rule. It alleviates the single most important source of extreme poverty and clientalistic subjugation in the countries to which it is suited: the condition of the landless agrarian laborers and of migrants and marginal smallholders. At the same time it provides an occasion to anticipate a major theme of the program for economic reorganization. The collaboration among small-scale and medium-scale farmers on the basis of government-supported arrangements for the pooling of financial, marketing, and technological resources modestly prefigures the multitiered system of rotating capital allocation the program of empowered democracy embraces.

Notice, however, that agrarian reform is the easiest case in which anticipatory institutional experimentation combines with economic redistribution and long-run programmatic commitments converge with short-run practical needs. It is, in the terms of earlier arguments, a relatively unreconstructed form of petty commodity production. The industrial counterparts to such agrarian solutions require more far-reaching institutional changes and therefore demand from the radicals in power a more careful balancing of redistributive and institutional methods. It is then all the more deplorable when the special opportunity offered by this style of agrarian reform is sacrificed either to the dogma of agricultural collectivization or to a strictly privatistic and proprietary form of smallholding.

The Combination of Central Decision with Popular Engagement

In both the revolutionary and the parliamentary situation the transformative movement needs to combine a change in the methods, forms, and uses of central governmental power with a heightened degree of popular engagement in ground-level economic and administrative institutions. In its most general form the commitment to achieve such a recombination simply restates the basic principle of prefiguring the ends in the means. But here this commitment takes a specific form, suited to the moment of achievement of central power, when the passage from means to ends is most visible and the tension between means and ends most dramatic.

The need to combine a reorientation of central power with an increased popular involvement in the organization of production, exchange, and local government and administration breaks down into two tasks: one governmental, the other economic. The two problems often come to a head at different moments: the governmental first, the economic later. A common but fatal error of transformative movements is to suppose that they have solved the latter when they have disposed of the former. Then, the failure to understand and to accomplish the economic task quickly undoes the governmental achievement.

The governmental task is to work toward a mutually reinforcing relation between effective use of the central governmental apparatus and popular participation in local government and administration. By effective use of the central governmental apparatus I mean in part the ability to press forward toward the reconstruction of governmental institutions the program of empowered democracy advocates (see the discussion in later sections of the chapter). Top priority must be given to replacing the traditional constitutional techniques that guarantee freedom and pluralism only by preventing bold transformative projects. A later part of the programmatic argument describes how full-blown empowered democracy accomplishes this objective.

Effective use also means that the radicals in high office do whatever possible to act within present governmental institutions as they would act if their desired governmental reforms had been achieved. This attempted conversion of established institutions to a new style and new uses is not an exercise in political bad faith or a mere tactical gamble, though its use must be tempered by an awareness that it may be seen as both of these. It is, on the contrary, a consequence of the perspective of internal normative argument, which sees the constitutional and legal order as a disharmonious conversation between controverted ideals of human association and the practical arrangements supposed to embody them in different domains of social existence. Theories of the constraints appropriate to different institutional roles – including the roles of such officeholders as cabinet ministers, parliamentary representatives, and judges – are not self-evident parts of present arrangements; they presuppose a view of the ideals that present institutional arrangements should be considered to serve. Many views may be excluded as plausible candidates. But the closure comes from the rough, loose continuum of a constitutional and legal tradition and the larger climate of opinion within which it developed, not from the practical arrangements standing alone. Thus, for example, ideas about the proper limits of the judicial role are likely to depend upon a conception of the kind of democracy the constitution establishes. Though the choice of this conception is not a free-for-all, neither can it be kept entirely separate from the question of what kind of constitution people now living would like to have. The separation becomes harder to establish when (as in the United States) the constitution is treated less as an easily replaceable artifact than as a structure within which the nation, with the help of occasional amendments, can endlessly renew itself.

The incongruous use of existing institutions grows in importance relative to the development of new institutions when the setting is parliamentary rather than revolutionary. In parliamentary situations incongruous use is most important when the inherited constitutional structure of the state possesses a special sanctity. But it is never an adequate substitute for reconstruction, only a diminished though real possibility of action. If there is enough popular support to prevent a putschist vanguardism, there must also be enough support to change the constitutional arrangements.

There is one aspect of the effective use of central government that no movement can avoid, whether it comes into power by peaceful elections or by violent revolution: the effort to prevent the permanent bureaucracy from silently undermining its plans. In the revolutionary situation the inherited bureaucratic and military structure must be replaced. The failure to do so with sufficient relentlessness has been the bane of many a revolutionary experiment. (Consider the experience of some of the revolutions in Central Europe immediately following World War I.) In the parliamentary circumstance the need is just as great though both opportunities and risks are more modest. The movement in power must discipline its inherited bureaucrats – if it cannot rid itself of them – by a combination of political will from the top and popular engagement at the grass roots. The preservation of a nonpolitical civil service is compatible with such an approach so long as technocratic authority is not allowed to masquerade as administrative neutrality and civil servants continue to be pressed by resolute politicians and an engaged populace.

The principle of transformative practice now under discussion requires the reorientation of central government combined with the active engagement of ordinary men and women in ground-level government and administration. In both revolutionary and parliamentary situations the achievement of this objective may require the widespread use of rotation as well as party-political pluralism and the partial deprofessionalization of lower administrative positions. Popular engagement succeeds best in its purpose when it can seize on the opportunities created by the central government for decentralized collective decision-making. The mass of actively engaged citizens must in turn press the central reformers not only to decentralize power but to decentralize it in ways that prevent its devolution to inherited oligarchies.

The primacy of institutional reform over economic redistribution and the preference for redistributive measures that presuppose institutional reconstruction are vital to the successful interplay between grassroots engagement and the reorientation of governmental policy. The preferred policy must make the redistributive program depend upon the activities of local governments and the internal transformation of large-scale productive enterprises. The byword "No redistribution without militancy" must be incorporated into the design and work of institutions.

Notice that the combination of a reoriented central policy with intensified grassroots engagement has both a programmatic sense and a strategic use. The combination is successful to the extent that the tension between the sense and the use disappears. A basic premise of the program of empowered democracy is that the diminishment of the contrast between context-preserving routine and context-transforming conflict cannot be achieved either by bombing out the state and putting a pure system of human coordination in its place or by submerging fixed institutional arrangements in personal charisma. Nor, on the other hand, can it result from solutions imposed by a self-appointed vanguard upon a recalcitrant and sullen populace. Empowered democracy attempts instead to change the relation between large-scale, inclusive institutions and noninstitutionalized collective action, to make the former into a more congenial home for the latter. The closer the movement comes to its moment of power – and therefore also to its hour of institutional definition – the less room there is for discrepancy between means and ends. The key themes of the program must be directly and faithfully represented in the relation between what the movement does with central power and what it does with local or nongovernmental organizations.

A government committed to revolutionary reform needs active grassroots engagement to stand strong against its foreign and domestic enemies, to replace untrustworthy bureaucrats, and to prevent the disruption of essential services. To the objection that a major part of the population may be hostile to the government's intentions, the answer must be that plans without broad support are bad plans to execute; at least they are not plans that can produce the institutions of an empowered democracy. The government must retrench to whatever extent necessary to maintain broad support at the ground level, so long as it continues to respect, in its retreat, the principle of the primacy of institutional change over economic redistribution. A parliamentary government stands less in need of active popular support than does a revolutionary regime under siege. But the importance of preventing an attitude of passive clientalistic dependence upon a redistributive state becomes correspondingly greater.

An economic as well as a governmental task must be accomplished to secure the interplay between the reorientation of central policy and grassroots popular involvement. This economic mission can be dealt with summarily, in part because its difficulties are similar to those of the governmental task and in part because such difficulties can be better understood in the context of specific proposals for the reorganization of the economy. The reformers in power must attempt to combine a measure of political control over the basic flows of investment decisions with the active engagement of the working population in the basic activities of production and exchange.

The central government should try to consolidate as soon as it call the degree of control over investment decisions that is necessary to prevent the destabilizing trauma of economic crisis. It should prefer the forms of control that foreshadow the system of capital allocation defended by the program of empowered democracy. The nationalization of a range of large-scale enterprises may represent in many countries the easiest way to secure a public nucleus of capital accumulation that provides the minimal conditions for economic stability and growth at a time of heightened social and ideological conflict. But nationalization is far less promising as a transitional experiment than any number of ways in which central governments may begin to explore procedures for allocating capital, conditionally and temporarily, to smaller and more flexible enterprises while preserving, through pooling devices, the economic advantages of scale. (A number of such transitional forms of reconstructed capital allocation are discussed later, in a section on transitions, alliances, and opportunities.)

Just as the emergency form of central political guidance of the economy is nationalization, so the corresponding emergency method at the grass roots is the actual occupation by workers of factories, shops, and farms. In such a revolutionary circumstance the alternative market order – with its several tiers of capital givers and capital takers – must ordinarily be built within a dominant, semiautarkic state sector. But reform governments that come to power by parliamentary means in a contemporary mixed economy must employ a more subtle and varied range of techniques. Instead of the actual occupation of the productive stock by workers, they must press for checks upon private investment policy – and in particular upon the power to invest or to disinvest in ways that maximize financial return rather than productive advantage. They must link these checks from the top down with a cumulative transfer of parcels of capital access and decision-making power not only to the labor force of existing enterprises (many of which would eventually be broken up into smaller, more flexible units) but also to teams of workers, technicians, and entrepreneurs who want to go into business. The objective is to come closer to a situation that is neither that of an economically sovereign government facing powerless workers nor that of tenured workers who have succeeded private capitalists as the joint holders of absolute property rights. It is to approach a circumstance in which economic access, decentralization, and flexibility advance through the disassociation of consolidated property into several different faculties, allocated to different types of capital givers and capital takers, rather than through the transfer of consolidated property to a new absolute and permanent rightholder – the central government or the enterprise labor force.

The programmatic sense and the strategic use of the combination of central control and grassroots engagement run closely parallel to the sense and use of the governmental counterpart to this economic task. The economic program of empowered democracy must be prefigured in the early, partial realization of its key commitment: the social control of economic accumulation must be achieved in ways that promote rather than supplant decentralized economic access, discretion, and organizational flexibility. The revolutionary regime must guarantee production and distribution lest a disappointed populace seek protection from old elites or new rulers. But it must do so in ways that do not tempt it to denature its program on the pretext of carrying it out. The parliamentary reform government must break out of the cycle of reform and retrenchment by preventing the capital strike while engaging working men and women in an active, nonclientalistic relation to its economic proposals.

11
Constitutional Reorganization

AN EXPERIMENT IN CONSTITUTIONAL REORGANIZATION: THE EXAMPLE OF THE DUALISTIC SYSTEM

The program begins with a discussion of the constitutional structure of central government. In no area of the institutional order is our dependence upon a unique tradition more striking. For our views about the organization of democratic governments are very largely beholden to a small stock of ideas that come to us from the end of the eighteenth century and the beginning of the nineteenth. We have long ceased to appreciate that those ideas were once regarded as rivals for a primacy that seemed anything but certain and as instruments of specific social goals that would now be regarded as suspect and even shameful. This protracted exercise in forgetting, buttressed by the stabilization of the social world we inhabit, has persuaded us that these techniques of governmental organization represent the very nature of liberal democracy. The act of persuasion has been all the easier because of the inability of the recurrent socialist dream of worker-council government ever to outlast the briefest revolutionary interludes and the failure of the communist-style popular democracies to provide a respectable alternative to the liberal-democratic institutions that we have.

So complete has been the suppression of historical experience, we seem hardly to remember that these same liberal institutions of government changed their real social meaning, while maintaining their outward forms, at least once in the course of their history. In the pioneering democracies, this change took place during the mid-nineteenth century, when the system of universal suffrage and mass-based political parties first took its modern form. Until then, liberal constitutionalism seemed to be the instrument of a republic of notables that carefully filtered out the fickle mob and the dangerous demagogue. And the sole alternative to such an overtly elitist polity seemed to be the peril and chaos of a radical democracy. Few, if any, foresaw that the same liberal constitutionalism would, in conjunction with the emergent style of partisan conflict, shape the mass democracies we now know.

Given our delusive tendency to equate representative democracy with a very distinctive constitutional tradition, it may be helpful to consider the one significant wave of constitutional reforms this tradition has in fact witnessed. At a minimum these reforms remind us of the artifactual and revisable character of our ways of organizing central democratic governments. But I have another, stronger reason to discuss them. They prefigure, in a limited setting, many of the concerns and techniques of the parts of the program defended here that deal with the organization of the state, just as the vanguard sector of contemporary industry anticipates much of what the program advocates for the reorganization of work and industry.

I have in mind the series of constitutional innovations introduced by the post-World War I constitutions in Europe and developed further by some of the post-World War II ones. You have to distinguish two aspects of this wave of constitutional innovations: the ideas and practices originally championed by the theoreticians of the constitutions adopted in the immediate aftermath of World War I and the quite different set of constitutional conceptions and arrangements that emerged, piecemeal, when those earlier approaches were abandoned or revised.

Many of the constitutions promulgated in the wake of World War I – like the German, the Austrian, and the Polish, or, for that matter, the constitutional program of the Russian provisional government – arose from the reciprocal effect of two forces: the predominance of a hesitant, embarrassed left in the constitutional conventions or cabinets of that almost revolutionary era, and the teachings of the legal theorists who identified themselves, more or less explicitly, with this political faction, men like Hugo Preuss or Hans Kelsen. The social-democratic majorities had even less of a conception of a radically new governmental structure than they had of an alternative industrial organization. To their left, they saw only the revolutionary tradition of conciliar-type government (the commune, the soviet) constantly revamped and reabandoned in the history of popular insurrections. Their main concern was simply to react against the immediate past. As their characteristic political experience had been the struggle against an authoritarian executive, their primary constitutional objective became to ensure the obedience of the executive to the parliament. The legal theorists added the goal of "rationalizing" government: of identifying every aspect of governmental power and creating the legal form that would shape and discipline it. In pursuing this aim they continued to be guided by the implicit equation of accountability with the techniques of dispersion of power and distancing among branches and levels of government. The force of their commitment to these techniques seemed to be undercut by the theoretical concentration of almost unbounded power in the parliament and by the use of the popular initiative and the referendum alongside electoral representation. The commitment was nevertheless reaffirmed by the weight of the constraints upon the governing ministry that actually had to carry out legislative policy.

The collapse of many of the European democracies of the interwar period cannot be attributed primarily to defects in their constitutional structures. It took place in the setting of the unresolved challenges to the emergent formative context of power and production, the very same setting that, at an earlier moment, had allowed the new constitutionalism to take hold. Nevertheless, the relative immobility to which those constitutional arrangements often condemned the government sometimes helped hasten the downfall of republican institutions.

The new constitutions, however, did not stay put. They were revised. Most of these revisions had two immediate causes: the change in the balance of political forces, from left to right, and the desire to give the executive decisional mobility in a domestic and international circumstance of perpetual insecurity. Some revisions, like the amendments to the 1921 Polish constitution, almost completely reversed the original spirit of the constitutional plan and established a plebiscitarian presidency with all-inclusive powers. Other shifts, however, like the Austrian reforms of 1929, the Portuguese constitution of 1933, or even the changing constitutional practice of the Weimar Republic, contained the elements of an alternative, though highly limited, constitutional program. This program proved insufficient to rescue states that had already been caught up in the deadly struggles of the interwar period. But it did contain the elements of the dualistic structure developed later, more explicitly, by constitutions like the Icelandic of 1944, more lopsidedly by the French of 1958 and 1962, and most fully by the Portuguese of 1978.

Two closely connected arrangements distinguished this emergent constitutional scheme. One was the establishment of two governmental powers elected by direct universal suffrage – the parliament and the presidency, whence the core meaning of the term "dualism." The other was the decision to make the active government – the parliamentary cabinet – dependent upon both those powers, yet for that very reason not entirely dependent upon any one of them. Three leading institutional ideas worked in this dualistic system.

One was the effort to maximize the popular aspects of indirect democracy. The plebiscitarian features of the presidential regime, subversive of party oligarchies, would be joined to the vital partisan conflicts of a parliament elected under proportional representation.

The second idea was the attempt to give the acting government decisional initiative by allowing it to lean on either the president or the parliament and not to fall automatically or immediately because it had lost the support of either. The goal therefore became to permit the rapidity and continuity of governmental action by making the ability to act effectively independent of a consensus among all the powers of the state. (Think, for example, of the impact in a presidential regime of the antagonism between president and legislature; in a parliamentary one, of the effect of fragile party coalitions in a wider social context of frantic but petty collective bickering.)

The third institutional idea put limits on the second one and allowed it to operate without jeopardizing the primacy of the appeal to the mass electorate recognized by the first idea. It consisted in the use of devices that allowed different powers in the state to resolve deadlocks by provoking immediate general elections at which they themselves would be at risk. This technique had already been used in some of the European constitutions of the immediate post-World War I years. For example, the parliament might be able to remove the president on purely political grounds, dissolving itself by that very act. The president might simultaneously be allowed to bring about an electoral confrontation with a hostile parliamentary majority.

The significance of these parallel rights of appeal to the mass electorate increased when combined with a more general duplication of functions among branches of government. More than one power might be allowed to perform the same acts: to propose or even provisionally pass certain laws. If one of the duplicated powers in the state failed to obtain some required agreement on the part of its twin, there would be a deadlock that justified new elections.

These devices had an ambiguous relation to the mainstream constitutional tradition. On the one hand, they might be seen as minor adjustments to practices they did not displace. Examples of the dualistic revision coexisted with the older constitutional arrangements, and most had been initiated by moderate reformers or even by Conservatives, uninterested in any radical reconstruction of state and society. On the other hand, the shift in the constitutional tradition could also be seen as the small-scale, limited version of a more drastic change. This alternative interpretation seemed to be supported by the internal analysis of some of the professed or tacit goals that motivated the dualistic experiments. Instead of disciplining power through the perpetuation of impasse, constitutional dualism disciplined it by the rapid resolution of deadlock. In the place of the techniques of distancing and dispersion, it put devices that replicated functions, focused conflicts, and broke up political oligarchies. No wonder the Portuguese constitution of 1978 – the only one of the late twentieth-century constitutions to show an explicit commitment to aspects of institutionalized collective mobilization – was also the one to adopt most unreservedly the institutional ideas worked out through the dualistic experiments. In fact, the alternative constitutional structure presented in the next section of this chapter generalizes the principles already exhibited by the dualistic reforms.

There is no cause for surprise at the ambiguous relation of the dualistic system to the earlier constitutionalism: such an ambiguity marks all significant reforms. More specifically, dualism resembled those changes in industrial organization that, in the course of the twentieth century, introduced aspects of the flexible form of rationalized collective labor into sectors once dominated by the traditional assembly line and the other trappings of the rigid approach to industrial organization. Constitutional dualism shared with these industrial innovations its substance and historical circumstance as well as the ambiguity of its relating to the tradition within which it arose. Constitutional and industrial reforms could either remain minor variations on the established formative context of power and production or become steps toward the inauguration not just of another context but of a new measure of freedom over contexts.

THE ORGANIZATION OF GOVERNMENT: THE MULTIPLICATION OF OVERLAPPING POWERS AND FUNCTIONS

The attempt to emancipate social life more fully from false necessity can succeed only if our ordinary social experience gives us the occasions and the means to challenge and revise every aspect of the basic institutional structure of society. To every major feature of this structure there must correspond a practical or imaginative activity that puts it up for grabs, and this activity must be available to us in the midst of our routine conflicts and concerns. Among these routines none are more important, as a domain for context-challenging activities, than those that respect the struggle over the mastery and uses of governmental power. For this struggle directly influences the terms on which we conduct all our other disputes. A main point in my earlier criticism of the established version of democracy was precisely that by placing much of the established institutional order effectively beyond the reach of democratic politics, that mode of democracy fails to give adequate application to even the most modest conception of inherited democratic ideals.

Viewed from this standpoint, the classical liberal technique of dividing central government into a small number of well-defined branches – executive, legislature, and judiciary – is dangerous. It generates a stifling and perverse institutional logic, and it does so whether the division of powers takes the rigid, tripartite form of presidential systems or assumes the more flexible style of parliamentary regimes. The effort to put every aspect of the social order on the line will characteristically require many ways of using governmental power – or of fighting over its use – that find no suitable setting in the existing order. Would-be reformers may be told, for example, that the reconstructive activity they have in mind does not quite fit either the legislature or the judiciary. So it should not be done at all, for fear of distorting the system of institutional roles that supposedly helps define the inherent constitutional structure of democracy. But the result of abstaining is typically to leave a faction of society with an inordinate measure of control over the human and material resources by which we create the future society within the present one: money, expertise, and governmental authority itself.

The program that seeks to empower democracy in order to empower people must therefore multiply the number of branches in governments while attributing overlapping functions to agencies of the state. The multiplication of powers in the state should obey two overlapping criteria: first, that when the total system of powers and functions has been established, it will work to prevent any section of society from gaining a lasting stranglehold over the material or human resources that can be used to generate the future form of society; second, that the same system provide an opportunity for the exercise of every major variety of transformative activity, practical or imaginative. The first criterion looks to the result; the second, to the means. Each may predominate in the design of a particular power.

Another reason to multiply the number of powers in the state with overlapping functions is the usefulness of increasing the number of governmental authorities that are chosen, one way or another, by a general electorate. The point is to transfer to the relations among governmental institutions the same device by which mass politics loosen the oligarchy effect: the effort to enlist increasing mass support in the course of rivalries over the mastery and use of state power. One of the many reasons why this loosening of the oligarchy effect remained so imperfect had to do with the defects of the institutional means by which the loosening was achieved. The fewer the lines of access to the grass roots of popular involvement, the greater the likelihood that oligarchic tendencies will assert themselves within the institutional order and thereby constrain or defeat the wider intentions of the constitutional plan.

Consider two examples of the creation of new powers in the state. Each illustrates one of the two criteria cited earlier. And each displays, in a more focused setting, a more general concern of the whole constitutional scheme. The commitment to avoid a monopoly over the resources of society creation may justify the establishment of a branch or agency of government especially charged with enlarging access to the means of communication, information, and expertise, all the way from the heights of governmental power to the internal arrangements of the workplace. The effort to control the sources of technical knowledge and expertise is the natural ambition of unresponsive power. It becomes all the more attractive as wealth comes to consist, in ever increasing measure, in the capacity to undertake instrumental activities on the basis of specialized knowledge, routinized at its core and flexible in its applications. It is vital to the enlarged democracy that the tendency, at every level of social life, to gain an entrenched, uneven access to this capacity be constantly resisted. The power able to resist this tendency cannot be a mere instrumentality of any other power or a limited governmental organization. For the struggle about what exactly it should do would be a major form of conflict over the uses of governmental power and a chief determinant of the terms on which people can collaborate practically.

Such a branch of government must be legally and financially qualified to oversee the basic arrangements separating technical coordination and managerial advice from a generic disciplinary authority in the workplace. (See the later discussion of the regime of capital.) It must be able to make know-how available to those who, under the conditions I shall describe, set up new productive enterprises. It must be able to intervene in all other social institutions and change their operations, by veto or affirmative initiative. Its power to intervene must be directly related to the task of securing the conditions that would maximize information about affairs of state and achieve the maximum subordination of expert cadres to collective conflicts and deliberations. The officers of such a branch would be selected by joint suffrage of the other powers in the state, the parties of opinion, and the universal electorate.

Now take an example of the prevalence of the other criterion by which to multiply branches of government: the commitment to give every transformative practice a chance. The order of right – the laws generated by the joint, constitutionally regulated collaboration of all the other powers of government – constitutes a repository of social ideals. Though these ideals never form a cohesive whole or justify a single imaginative scheme of right and possible association, they stand in greater or lesser tension toward the internal life of particular institutions.

There is a practical and imaginative activity that works out the implications of such prescriptive models of association for the remaking of institutional life. Its imaginative aspect consists in understanding and elaborating a large body of law as a project to advance a certain vision of life in common. Its practical aspect lies in the series of procedural devices that involve some far-reaching intervention in an area of social practice. These devices aim to strike down obstacles to the advancement of the ideal, to prevent such obstacles from arising in the first place, and affirmatively to reconstruct the chosen area of social life in conformity to the guiding vision. Such interventions may involve the branch or agency that undertakes them in the ongoing administration of major institutions: productive enterprises, schools, hospitals, asylums. (Think of the complex, collective injunctions afforded by American law in the late twentieth century, and imagine their radical extension.)

As the governmental power moves forward in its attempt to reconstruct a body of social practice, it finds inducements to go still farther. First, the partial execution of the reconstructive effort reveals new causal connections: more or less remote social forces that prevent the fuller realization of the ideal pursued. These causal links extend, continuously, in all directions. Only standards of institutional limitation and reservations of institutional prudence, or the qualifying force of other powers in the state, could keep every instance of this procedural intervention from expanding, bit by bit, into a complete remaking of society. Second, each step forward in the application of an ideal to social life reveals new ambiguities in its content and new disharmonies between it and established social practice. Even a well-defined and seemingly limited reconstructive project never ends: each new occasion for its realization reveals both new ambiguities in its meaning and new requirements.

The imaginative aspect of the activity I have described – the understanding of bodies of rule and principle as expressive of ideals of human association – is universal to all forms of legal doctrine. Indeed, I shall argue later that any extended practice of legal doctrine failing to render explicit this reference to ideals of common life degenerates, by virtue of this truncation, into a pseudorationality, an arbitrary choice of results that the ambiguous body of law cannot support and that only a broader exercise of social criticism could justify. But the practical aspect of this activity is another story. When the implementation of the broadened conception of doctrine involves a systematic intervention in large areas of social practice and the consequent disruption of major institutions, it does not seem to lend itself easily to any of the branches of government admitted by the received constitutional traditions of democracy.

The characteristics of the traditional judiciary – devoted, as it primarily is, to the settling of more or less focused rights and wrongs under the law – make it a less than ideal instrument for far-reaching and systematic intervention in social practice. The adjudication of localized disputes over the boundaries of rights may best be conducted by officals removed from the pressures of conflict over the uses of governmental power and expert in the entire body of law, or else by ordinary laymen involved in the life of a community (popular tribunals). Neither type of adjudicative corps may be well suited to conduct a radical extension of complex procedural intervention. The expert judges, with their vaunted immunity from direct influence by the other powers in the state, or even by the general electorate, would, with such procedural weapons in hand, turn into a nearly absolute censorial authority. They would hover over the republic like a Lycurgus who had forgotten to go away after completing his work of state building. The popular tribunals of ordinary laymen are equally disabled from the performance of this task because both their inexpertise and their fragmentation prevent them from acting effectively as the agents of a systemic reconstructive intervention in social life.

If the traditional judiciary seems ill-qualified for the purpose so does the conventionally understood legislative body. Preoccupied as it is with the struggle over more or less marginal adjustments to the existing law and with the support or subversion of the party in power, it cannot be easily expected to undertake the ideal, long-range, and systematic interventionism that would provide such a power with its mandate. There would always be the danger that a legislature's attempts at such an engagement would become subordinate to short-term partisan rivalries, and the reasonable suspicion that it had been so tainted would, even if unjustified, rob it of authority. The point is not that the activity of such a power should be or seem unpolitical, but that it should represent politics carried on by somewhat other means and to a somewhat different end. The conventional legislature is defective in another way as well. Though its members may be expected to be proficient in the more general styles of political persuasion, most may lack firsthand familiarity with the more specialized forms of normative argument – religious, moral, and technically legal – that flourish in the society. An enlarged conception of legal doctrine weakens these distinctions but does not abolish them.

These arguments suggest that the power responsible for systematic interventions should be a branch apart, staffed and organized according to the principles most suitable to its overriding task. Like the power responsible for rescuing know-how from privilege, its members may be selected by the other powers, the parties of opinion, and the universal electorate. They should be drawn from activities that have acquainted them with the different modes of normative thought important in the society. They should have at their disposal the technical, financial, and human resources required by any effort to reorganize major institutions and to pursue the reconstructive effort over time.

Such a branch of government must have a wide latitude for intervention. Its activities embrace, potentially, every aspect of social life and every function of all the other powers in the state. If the other powers could not resist and invade the jurisdiction of this corrective agency, it would become the overriding authority in the state. The broad-based selection of its members would not compensate for this evil: the control of a primary access to the general citizenry, the very circumstance the technique of overlapping powers and functions wants to avoid, would have reappeared under the new constitution. The resistance the other powers impose must not, however, exemplify the rigid distribution of functional competences, the checks and balances, of the tradition inherited from the eighteenth century. The paralyzing impasses such devices favor, hostile to the aims of a constitutionalism of decisive experiments and broadened participation, would become all the more deadly when many more branches of government coexisted and collided. Thus, the effort to describe the appropriate workings of this reconstructive power nicely illustrates the problem addressed by the constitutional technique of multiple and overlapping branches of government.

THE ORGANIZATION OF GOVERNMENT: SHAPING AND RESOLVING THE CONFLICT OF POWERS

A main way in which the received constitutionalism tried to discipline power was its appeal to an automatic mechanism of containment: any branch that went beyond its proper sphere would be automatically stopped by all the other branches. This banal system of checks and balances has a meaning that does not become apparent until you understand both the problems that it was originally designed to solve and the effects it continues to produce long after those problems have changed beyond recognition.

In the prerevolutionary Europe of corporatist and estatist politics the different powers in the state were often identified as representing particular segments of a hierarchically ordered society. The attempt to create a state set up without regard to the internal divisions of society, in a society whose disorganized classes replaced corporately organized estates, meant that the powers of the state had to be defined by reference to one another. And as the division of government into different departments (branches) with specialized functions achieved greater fixate, it also became more important to establish a mechanism that would hold these departments to their assigned tasks and keep them from invading one another's domains. One device would be appeal to an outside umpire. If this umpire were an unaccountable sovereign claiming to stand for the collective good (such as a monarch), he would pose a serious threat to the form and spirit of a republican constitution. But neither could a universal electorate serve as the arbiter every time power clashed. For such a procedure would be dangerous as well as cumbersome. It would run counter to the liberal aim of establishing a representative regime that would minimize the opportunities for popular agitation and for the scheming of demagogic agitators. Thus, it became important to invent a built-in method of mutual restraint that would avoid the need to turn to the outside umpire.

It is remarkable that as the republican order became more democratic, the constraining effect of the system of "checks and balances" continued to operate. When first devised, the system was subsidiary to another, more ostentatious method of restraint: a filtering-out technique that both restricted the suffrage and established many levels of intermediate representation between grassroots electorates and central governments. In time this technique – once justified by the commitment to ensure that electors be independent and informed – proved both an intolerable insult to popular sovereignty and a superfluous guarantee of social stability.

The founding liberal myth of a constitutional mechanism and a system of rights that tower above the hierarchical and communal divisions of society has since become true in an unacknowledged and embarrassing sense. Liberal-democratic politics and the society in which it is practiced have indeed become separate: a social order that consists largely of groups entrenched in fixed niches within the division of labor and occupying stable places in the established scheme of social hierarchy coexists with a political practice that plays up to shifting coalitions of interest formed by groups with crisscrossing and unstable membership. A major thesis of my explanatory and programmatic arguments has been that liberal politics – and its defining institutional framework – help perpetuate a form of social order that can be remade in their image only by a transformation of the liberal conception and practice of political life. To make society resemble what liberal politics to a considerable extent are already like, we would have to change the institutional form of the state and of the conflict over governmental power and push the liberal vision beyond the point to which its creators have up to now been willing to take it.

The classical technique of checks and balances is only a small part of the structure that would have to be changed. But it exemplifies in a particularly heavy-handed way the constraints imposed by the larger structure to which it belongs, just as the arguments deployed in its favor illustrate with peculiar clarity the vision we must replace.

Because of the system of checks and balances, a faction bent on an ambitious program must capture more or less simultaneously the different departments of government. And the leaders of each branch of government can usually be counted on to be so jealous of the prerogatives of their offices that pride of place becomes identical with resistance to every bold plan. Indeed, the most noticeable feature of the system is to establish a rough equivalence between the transformative reach of a political project and the obstacles that the constitutional machinery sets in its way.

Some say this method of mutual restraint and deliberate deadlock serves as a necessary defense of freedom. But a program that proposes ways to extend the enjoyment and meaning of public freedoms while avoiding the paralysis of experimental capability in politics helps discredit belief in this necessity. Others say the pattern of stalemate is an unavoidable consequence of the conflict among narrow organized interests in societies in which most people remain reasonably satisfied most of the time. But this view is a principal target of a theory that wants to show all the ways in which a contingent, revisable institutional order forms the occasions and instruments of conflict and shapes assumptions about identities, interests, and possibilities.

A constitutional program committed to the empowerment of democracy therefore has many reasons to replace the inherited strategies of automatic and reciprocal institutional constraint. The multiplication of overlapping governmental powers and functions lends added urgency to such an innovation.

Three principles may concurrently govern the conflict of powers under the reformed constitution. The first – and the only one of the three widely used in the established liberal bourgeois democracies – is the absolute restraint one power may impose upon another. This restraint can be overcome only by the reciprocal influence the different branches may exercise upon one another's composition. Suppose that a party succeeds to office on a platform of far-reaching distribution of wealth and power, reforms directed against the institutional framework of the economy. Imagine, further, that the new rulers keep the support of the highest representative assemblies, which also form part of the decisional center of government. (See the next section, on the organization of the center.) Some of the innovations may involve an attack upon the basic rights guaranteeing the individual's security and his access to conflict over the mastery and uses of governmental power. An agency in the state, isolated from the immediate effects of the struggle over governmental power, must be able to hold back such assaults. It hardly matters whether it is the same judiciary that settles particular controversies or some distinct constitutional authority. What does matter is that the nature and basis of this individual immunity change. (See the later discussion of immunity rights.)

The second principle to govern the conflict of powers is one of priority among the different branches. The third is the use of the immediate or delayed devolution of constitutional impasses to the general electorate. These two principles qualify each other. When the branches of government are few and the constitution limits power by perpetuating impasses, it is natural to treat the branches as equal. The force of this conclusion vanishes together with its premises. The test of a power's relative hierarchical position lies precisely in its right to impose its will upon other powers. The two most important justifications of higher hierarchical place are the breadth of the composition of the branch or agency (the extent to which its members are chosen by an organized societywide struggle) and the scope of its responsibilities (how far into the social order its central constitutional responsibilities allow it to reach). By these criteria, for example, the interventionist power responsible for vindicating the ideals that underlie the entire legal system is more important than the power charged with maintaining the integrity of access to information. The decisional center of government is more important than both.

The constitution may establish circumstances in which a conflict between powers justifies an immediate devolution to the general electorate. This will be peculiarly appropriate to circumstances in which the contest arises within the decisional center and indicates a failure of popular support for the party program. A prodigal use of this technique, however, would paralyze the state's capacity for action just as surely as a commitment to the method of restraining power by perpetuating impasses. Thus, the normal method for resolving conflicts between unequal powers will be delayed devolution (referendum) to the electorate. Suppose, for example, that the party in office enters into conflict with the power responsible for disrupting established institutions in the name of the systematic ideals attributed to the legal order. If the party is acting in the execution of its program, and if it has not been stopped in this course by the judicial protection of individual security, it would be allowed to proceed. But the dispute would be set for debate and resolution at the next general election.

No one of these constitutional procedures is essential to the constitutional scheme. The particular institutional proposals represent no more than a plausible interpretation of the project of an empowered democracy. Which of these interpretations works best, in the spirit of that project, cannot be inferred conclusively from general arguments. The same loose connection between the details and their reasons holds for the relationship between the entire institutional plan and the conception that underlies it.

THE ORGANIZATION OF GOVERNMENT: THE DECISIONAL CENTER

Just as the multiplication of overlapping powers and functions threatens to worsen the paralytic effect of the system of checks and balances, so too it threatens to submerge the decisional center of government under a confusion of clashing agencies. This result would be fatal to the aims of the revised constitutional order, which must give a party of opinion, supported by a broadly based social movement, a chance to try its program out. The instruments at its disposal for doing this must be even more effective than those available to the ruling parties of the established style of democracy. They must be able to reach the sources of private power this style ordinarily leaves untouched. They must be proportionate to the intentions of collective movements capable of linking struggles at the heights of state power to the rivalries of everyday life. They must be able to deal with the complexities introduced by the presence of many branches of government. Moreover, so long as the state exists in a world of rival states, it must have at its head an authority capable of decisive diplomatic and military action.

The decisional center of government includes the executive and the legislature foreseen by received constitutional doctrine. It hardly matters whether these are conceived as two distinct branches of government, in the context of a presidential regime, or as something close to a single power, under a parliamentary system. For the new-model constitution may either include an elected president or dispense with him. The powers forming this decisional center are those most immediately responsible for the implementation of a partisan program that may address the overall structure of society and for the ultimate control over the state's dealings, in peace and war, with other states. It may not seem self-evident that these two concerns should be joined in the hands of the same public agencies. But those governmental institutions that stand closest to the citizenry and that provide the broadest scope for popular decision must also be the ones to make the choices that involve most dramatically the lives and fortunes of the people. The powers that stand outside this decisional center are the ones charged with a more focused responsibility and removed, to a relatively greater degree, from immediate partisan rivalry.

In order to understand the place of the decisional headquarters within the constitution of the empowered democracy, it helps to consider its nature and responsibilities in earlier constitutional schemes. In these schemes, it often amounted to almost the entire constitutional system.

Start with a simplified version of the medieval European constitution. The central constitutional task – usually performed by a king in parliament – was the occasional declaration or restatement of the law, conceived as a body of sanctified custom that determined the rights and obligations of each estate in the realm. For this conception to become dominant, the origin of these customary arrangements in a history of particular conflicts had to be forgotten or denied, and the conflicts themselves interrupted or contained. The other, subsidiary constitutional function was the power of the prince to deal with the unexpected by taking emergency measures that might involve some ad hoc revision of the customary order. Without this power of princely correction the stability and survival of custom might be jeopardized by every significant change in circumstance. The corrective function – the *gubernatio* by contrast to the *jurisdictio* – could not easily be assimilated to the system of thought that informed the central vision of right. To exercise or to accept it was to acknowledge, even if only marginally and implicitly, the failure of the established order to exhaust the possible forms of social life. Whether the prince claimed to act by divine inspiration or secular wisdom, he, his advisers, and his critics made use of a faculty of inventing measures that might endure, turning into custom.

The liberal-democratic states of the modern West did not alter this picture as much as at first appeared. The nostrums of the dominant political rhetoric might proclaim a popular sovereignty limited only by the sanctity of individual and minority rights. Under a presidential regime, the president and the legislature were able, in conflict or cooperation, to work out the implications of party programs for existing social arrangements. Under a parliamentary regime, this conception of a sovereign decisional center stood out even more clearly. The occupants of the highest executive offices became the instruments by which an electorally successful party could act upon the principles for which it had stood in the elections. The head of state turned, at most, into an official responsible for overseeing the mechanism by which rival parties fought for power.

Even with the reforms introduced by the dualistic system, the reality of constitutional practice qualified the idea of programmatic initiative to the point of radically changing its understood meaning. All the traits of a demobilizing constitutionalism made it hard for a victorious party to seize the state or, having seized it, to execute its program rapidly and decisively. The link made by the legal system between the means of immunity against government and the forms of control over individuals meant that the attempts to carry a partisan program into the reconstruction of the private order appeared as more or less direct threats to individual or minority freedom. Reigning opinion and constitutional principle conspired to ward off these threats. Thus, even under the most flexible parliamentary regime, with the greatest measure of unity between cabinet and parliament, policy making and legislation by the decisional center rarely amounted to more than marginal and fragmentary interventions in a social and legal order with a tenacious structure of its own. Thus persisted the older constitutional idea of a legislature that debates and enacts occasional changes in the laws. Despite its seeming archaism and unsuitability to the structure of a dynamized parliamentary regime, it expressed the reality of constitutional practice. For just as the larger attempt to realize the idea of a state hostage to no faction would require a major change in the organization of government and in its relation to society, so too, on a smaller scale, the idea of government organized to make and implement a coherent party program would demand a change in the conception of the decisional center, in its structure, and its relation to the other agencies of the state.

Suppose, for the sake of simplicity, that the new constitution includes a qualified parliamentary regime (which provides for a popularly elected president, independent of the parliament, with significant powers of his own, as in the dualistic system). The supreme representative assembly must carry out two tasks, neither of which can be easily assimilated to the traditional idea of legislation. On the one hand, it must supervise and ensure the fidelity of the party or parties in office to the program to which they committed or came to commit themselves in the course of their campaign or of their tenure in office. On the other hand, the assembly should serve as the maximum level of a series of forms of popular representation that spread out through society. In this second role, it may work, in an interlocutory capacity, as the agency responsible for settling conflicts among the other branches of government. Its task will be most important in those cases of lesser importance when the solution is not immediately entrusted to the universal electorate. It must also provide the vehicle by which these lower-level representative bodies can stop the ruling government in its tracks and go to the country.

These two tasks – the supervision of the party in office and the interlocutory representation of the larger electorate – need not be performed by the same representative body. A smaller council within the larger one may represent the parties in office and supervise the execution of the program. This program-supervising work may seem like a job done anyway under existing democratic institutions. But its delicacy and importance increase dramatically when the partisan conflicts at the summit of governmental power extend down to the disputes that occur on the familiar ground of work and leisure and when the entire structure of society is at stake in this struggle.

Under such a scheme, the whole idea of legislation undergoes a change. The laws and directives embodying the program are worked out together by the cabinet and the smaller supervisory council. No hard-and-fast distinctions exist between the different kinds of norms that result from the process. The supervisory partisan council performs a role that could be called jurisdictional as much as legislative: it judges in each instance the conformity of enactment to program. The large representative body, to which this smaller council may belong, serves to stop rather than to initiate or enact measures of state. At the same time, thanks to its size, the multiplicity of the forms of election and representation that generate it, and the closeness of its ties to lower-order representative assemblies, this more inclusive body provides a running preview of the broader electoral struggle.

The cabinet and council govern subject to the restrictions imposed by this greater assembly and the other powers in the state. Thus, there will be conditions under which the power designed to preserve the integrity of communication, or to vindicate by interventionist procedures the imputed ideals of the legal order, or to adjudicate individual disputes and safeguards, can impede the exercise of governmental power in a particular instance, or reserve a matter for later electoral decision, or even provoke an impasse requiring immediate devolution to the electorate. But the cabinet need not necessarily count on a majority in the larger organization. In circumstances of party fragmentation and intense partisan rivalry, a method may be devised that allows a minority force to rule so long as it can win compensatory support from other powers in the state or from lower-level representative bodies.

THE ORGANIZATION OF GOVERNMENT: MAKING MINICONSTITUTIONS

There are limits to the extent to which any particular set of institutional arrangements can embody a principle of permanent self-revision. By its very existence in a particular form, it excludes other constitutional arrangements. By excluding other such schemes, it also rules out certain modes of practical or passionate association that people may come to want. No constitutional system can be perfectly elastic in relation to all possible instances of collective life. Nor can this limitation be adequately remedied by a conventional power of constitutional amendment. For the exercise of such a power can rarely change more than an isolated fragment of the established constitutional order.

The normal constitutional system must include among its own precepts the opportunity to establish special constitutional regimes for limited contexts and aims. These special regimes amount to miniconstitutions. At the most modest level, the party in office may have as part of its program to set up institutions able to act in anomalous ways, with exceptional degrees of power, in particular sectors of the society. (See, for example, the later discussion of a regime of extreme entrepreneurial freedom within an economy whose main lines remain subject to direct political control.) At the highest level, the leaders of a party may appear before the universal electorate requesting some special regime of power – a temporary change in the arrangements and prerogatives of the decisional center – that can be reconciled with the crucial constitutional safeguards for individuals, minorities, and oppositions. In this event, the election becomes, simultaneously, a conflict over the form of the state and the identity of the highest officeholders.

Whatever the scope of the miniconstitution, its use always requires a specific precautionary method. To each special venture in the establishment of an extraordinary power there should correspond a special venture in control. Thus, the higher power that institutes an anomalous lower power must provide for the special independent board that will supervise the anomalous agency's actions and regulate its connections to the other, normal parts of government. The party that appears before the electorate in search of special arrangements and prerogatives must at the same time come with a proposal for the institution of a special supervisory authority, an ad hoc branch of government. Thus, every special power, under the exceptional constitutional regime, has a shadow power in its pursuit. The shadow grows longer in proportion to the dimensions of the special power it follows.

THE ORGANIZATION OF PARTISAN CONFLICT: POLITICAL STABILITY IN AN EMPOWERED DEMOCRACY

The most obvious objection to the constitutionalism of permanent mobilization defined by the preceding techniques is its apparent inability to guarantee a minimum of stability. Everything in such a constitution might seem explicitly designed to reduce state and society alike to bitter strife and paralyzing confusion. Carried to the extreme, such an instability would deny people the practical and moral benefits of all lasting, secure forms of association. It would disrupt the social basis for the development of productive or destructive capabilities just as much as if it had allowed a principle of vested rights to preclude all innovation in social life. In the end, a regime of extreme instability would turn out to destabilize itself and to give way, at whatever cost, to a stabilized order. People would cry out for firm leaders and peacemaking institutions. Their freedom would seem intolerably burdensome to them if they could keep it only by accepting an uncertainty that disturbed every aspect of life and an antagonism that always stood ready to turn from programmatic disagreement to bitter quarreling and from quarreling to violence.

The attempt to explain the nature and bases of stability under the transformed constitutional regime requires us to consider the role to be played by organized parties of opinion under such a regime. More generally, it serves as an invitation to imagine the actual dynamic of central political struggle that would characterize such a reordered society. Once again, our ability to make reasonable conjectures about the workings of adjusted social practices puts to the test our understanding of the practices we actually have. For once this understanding goes beyond the most external and mechanical descriptions, or the most ambiguous correlations, it requires ideas about the difference it would make to change particular arrangements or enacted beliefs.

Remember first that the emancipation of society from false necessity takes in part the form of a dissolution of social classes into parties of opinion. To some extent, this dissolution has already taken place: it is always reemerging through history, and the liberal-democratic polities of the present day have carried it to an unprecedented point. The classical liberals who have betrayed their early radical vocation claim society has already reached this condition. But if the early analysis is correct the relatively rigid quality of social life differs fundamentally from the comparatively fluid organization of politics, and our political ideas and institutional arrangements are partly responsible for the results. The institutional program outlined here seems calculated not only to propose carrying this dissolution of social classes into parties of opinion still further but to aggravate its destabilizing effects. The problem of instability has its focus in the relation between an extended partisan strife and the constitutional and social conditions that seem to turn this strife in a dangerous direction.

The ancient hostility to factional struggle always had a double foundation. One basis was the conviction that factions would be inherently selfish and thus subversive of the common good. The other was the fear that contending parties would destroy the civic peace.

Factional struggle seemed incompatible with the stability of any polity so long as it cut to the most basic matters of life. Chief among these, in an age of belief, were the terms of salvation. Thus, parties of religious opinion seemed to be the exemplary case of factions that would tear a commonwealth apart. Their differences could not be compromised, and their partisans would rest only with the complete defeat of their adversaries. At least, this uncompromising demand would persist so long as the religious principle demanded a privileged if not universal community of belief.

The closest secular equivalent to religious controversy was all-out ideological disagreement. When the major factions defined themselves by sharply opposing secular visions of what society should become, or pitted the tangible interests of one large class against those of another, the republic would be equally in trouble. The normal conflicts for and over governmental power might quickly slide into a social warfare that put everything up for grabs. For the sake of realizing nonnegotiable goods, all restraint in the use of means would soon be forgotten.

Partisan rivalry became safe, in this view, when it came to be characterized by two related features. The principles and interests to which each major party was committed no longer fitted into a single cohesive vision, sharply and clearly contrasted to the visions championed by the other leading factions. At the same time and for the same reasons, a multiplicity of crosscutting factions – if not parties, then segments of parties and other collective bodies – would organize for the prosecution of particular goals. The citizens would find themselves divided in many contradictory ways rather than enlisted into two or three civic armies ready to do battle, first figuratively and then literally, over the organization of society. In such a circumstance, partisan conflict would rarely seem to be about society's formative institutional context or its enacted imaginative scheme of association. It would be largely about the marginal advances of certain groups within that context. Any change in the defining institutional arrangements or the embodied vision of social life would normally come about as a by-product of the struggle over fragmentary goals and interests. It is precisely because of this relative deflection from the fundamentals that, on this view of minimal stability, partisan rivalry appears compatible with republican life.

Notice that this received conception of the sources of stability and instability depends upon two crucial identifications. The first is the equation of instability, understood as a heightening of the intensity and a broadening of the scope of conflict over the uses of governmental policy, with instability, interpreted as a resurgent threat to the individual's most vital interests in material security and welfare. This link presents instability in the image of Hobbesian civil strife, as the nightmare from which people must and will escape at any cost. My later argument about the reorganization of the system of legal rights suggests how to uncouple these two types of jeopardy so that the basic security of the individual is guaranteed and even strengthened in a mobilizational democracy.

There is another identification at least as central to the received view of stability: the equivalence established between fundamental conflicts and non-negotiable disputes. The concept of a formative institutional and imaginative context provides a more precise interpretation of what is fundamental and permits restating the classical approach to stability in the following terms: an institutional order deliberately designed to favor repeated controversy over the formative context will, if it succeeds in its objectives, inevitably result in an escalation of nonnegotiable demands that will tear the civil peace apart. It will create precisely the style of partisan strife that the mainstream of Western political thought has always considered intolerable.

It is tempting to see a refutation of the equivalence between fundamental conflict and nonnegotiable practice in the partisan rivalries of many Western European democracies in the two or three generations since World War II. There you found major parties committed to radically different programs for the organization of society and of its relation to the state. Large numbers of partisan cadres treated this program as the articles of an intransigent faith and managed with varying degrees of success, to draw the larger electorate into their own vision of fundamental differences. Yet these states remained stable by any plausible test of stability you might care to propose.

The actual practice of party politics and administration, however, told a different story from the programs and the speeches. For the most part, this party-political activity continued to revolve in the toils of reform cycles. No matter how bold their intentions upon arriving in office, reformers typically found themselves dragged down by the cumulative force of resistances that undermined their hold on the state before allowing them to establish the basis for an alternative organization of power and production. Thus, in practice, the system of partisan rivalry departed much less from the conventional model of stability-preserving partisanship than the contenders' rhetoric seemed to indicate. For the rhetoric came from periods, such as the aftermath of World War I, when a formative context had been in jeopardy or had failed to achieve a determinate form. But the reality was that of a stabilized social world where wide swings in governmental policy were much more likely to end as costly disturbances than as lasting innovations. In all the ways described, the very structure of institutions had been, more or less intentionally, rigged against too many surprises.

The real trouble with the traditional identification of conflicts over fundamentals with conflicts not lending themselves to compromise is its failure to appreciate that the relation between what is negotiable and what is fundamental changes according to the beliefs people entertain about society and the institutional structure of party conflict. As a result, the classical approach to stability in politics disregards the possibility of a circumstance distinct from both marginal, peace-preserving and basic, peace-destroying disputes: a style of factional rivalry that regularly questions the practical and imaginative foundations to the established social order.

The feature of the conflict over the basic arrangements of society that most directly makes it resistant to compromise is, paradoxically, its characteristic vagueness, its elusive and almost dreamlike quality. The less the abstract vision championed by the contending parties is worked into a texture scheme of social life, the flimsier the basis for any compromise. In the absence of a detailed plan for a reordered society, the only sure sign of victory becomes the triumph of an exclusive allegiance: the defeat of the disbelievers and the rise of the orthodox. At the same time, whenever a factional program combines vagueness of definition with intensity of feeling, it easily becomes hostage to whatever interpretations of its airy, murky promises may, for wholly secondary reasons, come to prevail. The temporary circumstances of a movement, the choices made by a leadership, or the mere desire to contradict an adversary lead the faction to embrace one particular version of its commitments over others. This almost accidental preference is then invested with all the devotion that had been reserved to the abstract conception. It is as if these details, rather than counting for their own sake, represented surrogates for the faction's image of its own identity and fortunes. In this substitute capacity, they again refuse compromise: there are no standards, other than the crassest material ones, by which to judge the cost of concessions, and any concession may seem to jeopardize the faction's essential identity.

Even the feared quarrels of confessional parties confirm this idea. These disputes become uniquely venomous in one of two circumstances. In the absence of any worked-out view of the implications of religious truth for the secular life of society, the relative preponderance of competing allegiances may be all there is left to fight about. Or the religion may include a detailed program of social life that pretends to prescribe almost every important feature of collective existence down to the last detail. The personal quality of the relation to God – the deepening in the relation to Him of all the claims and emotions that may exist among individuals – is falsified by the arbitrary, inscrutable character of the link between the central points of revelation and the unrevisable details of sacred laws. The detailed plan begins to look untouchable precisely because it is arbitrary. People lack the criteria by which to judge whether a similar vision could be realized, more perfectly, by different arrangements. There is, in this view, no underlying vision to be discovered and stated apart from the details of sacred law.

The more the conflicting partisan visions get translated into detailed schemes of collective life, down to the lowest levels of work and leisure, the less likely it becomes that these visions will seem impenetrable to one another. The force of concreteness changes the relation between the depth and the deadly intransigence of a partisan struggle. The deeper a programmatic position, the closer it comes to offering a revision of society's basic institutional arrangements and, even, of the fine structure of elementary personal relations. Take, then, a number of practical ways of doing things: of getting work done and assigning incomes and jobs, or organizing exchange and distribution; of living in families and dealing with superiors, subordinates, and equals. Impose the sole restriction that each competing scheme have the qualities allowing it to carry conviction for its specificity rather than for its vagueness (and consequent openness to the free play of connotation). Within its circumstance, it must seem practicable. It must appeal to an established, though inchoate, sense of personal realities, needs, and longings. Views with such characteristics are likely to be, and to appear, deconstructible and recombinable in many different ways. They will have the same features that theory shows societies themselves to possess, for they are nothing but social worlds, or variants of the existing social world, prefigured in the imagination. Moreover, the requirements of practicability and of responsiveness to personal aspiration impose constraints upon the extent of the divergence of the proposals from actualities.

That these views must seem practicable in the near future, or that they must be capable of immediate though partial realization, makes persuasion depend if not upon insight then upon the appearance of insight. Despite the inexistence of any metascheme that sets limits to possible societies or determines their unique sequence, the actual experience of transformative effort shows that some features of the existing order resist pressure more than others. The persuasive force of a program depends in part upon its success in incorporating into the definition of its aims and strategies a view of these differential pressures that ongoing events continue to confirm. Fidelity to personal experience exerts a similarly restraining influence. For the prophetic dogmas of politics, like the images of the self in world literature, differ more than do the actual wants of people.

The argument of the social theory developed in this book offers a justification for these common observations. It does so by working out the idea that each imaginative and institutional form of society represents an attempt to freeze, into a particular mold, the more fluid experiences of practical and passionate relationship characterizing the immediate, relatively unreflective, uninterpreted, and undisciplined life of personality. The dogmas and arrangements inform this life and alter it. But they do not completely overcome its recalcitrance or determine its inner nature. The visionary impulse in politics draws much of its persuasive force from the appeal to this defiant experience. The competing programmatic visions that, by dint of both their depth and their concreteness, touch people's ordinary concerns and inward longings do not thereby set themselves on the track to some ultimate convergence, any more than do whole societies under the negative impact of the dissolution of their rigid schemes of hierarchy, division, and associational possibility. But they do find the lines of divergence blurred by the presence of overlapping themes.

Both the political ideas and the actual institutional organization of the conflict for power in present-day liberal democracies discourage the alliance of scope and specificity. They do so, most directly, by denying opportunities for a continuous connection between the disputes of official politics and the quarrels of everyday life. They do so, more generally, by adopting institutional arrangements that make the choice between reform cycles and revolutions seem the normal condition of civic life. Thus, every radical vision has to be imagined as an abrupt and total deviation from existing society and nurtured without the chastening influence of practical experience and responsibility.

This circumstance does not merely enforce a constrained view of stability and reassert the dilemma of routine and revolution. It also accounts, in significant measure, for the strange, dreamlike quality of a politics that serves, at the same time, to accommodate the crassest interests and to express a struggle among abstract opinions. The experiences defining the situation of mass politics, world history, and enlarged economic rationality deprive all but the crudest interests of their appearance of self-evidence and make explicit their dependence upon opinion. Were it not for this disturbance of concreteness, party politics in the modern sense could never have emerged, for one of its crucial elements, from the start, was the commitment to speculative principles. These principles, however, remain, for the most part, both fragmentary and abstract, or they become only sporadically concrete. Thus, even in the circumstance of routine and reform cycles people act as if dazed by abstraction. Their political conduct has something of the arbitrariness of confessional factions clinging all the more woodenly to literal prescriptions, or lurching all the more haphazardly among conceptions of the ideal, because people lack any developed vision of a transfigured human reality.

To organize the conflict for and over state power in a way that encourages the combination of depth and concreteness, you need both ideas and institutions. Without the institutions, the ideas would lack transformative influence. You could expose the arbitrarily narrow assumptions of the received account of social peace and invoke the possibility of another style of stability. But you would be unable to deny the reality of the dilemma posed by this account within the institutional framework it took for granted. Your proposals would seem like proposals for another time. Without the ideas, however, the reformed institutional arrangements would lack a vision that made them intelligible and linked them, by a series of mediating connections, to an understanding of social reality and social transformation. The fuller and truer account of the varieties and conditions of stability must do the same work for the revised constitution that the more truncated and misleading view of tolerable strife did for the earlier democracies.

The ideas necessary to inform such a revised style of partisan conflict can be developed and supported by a social theory freed from the preconceptions of naive social science and deep-logic thinking. The two most important contributions such a theory can make to the intellectual climate of this practice of fundamental but negotiable disputes are the view that formative contexts can be replaced piecemeal and the thesis that the deviant elements in any social order have a subversive and reconstructive potential. Because revolutionary reform – defined as the substitution of any element in a formative context – is possible, a conflict can deal with fundamentals while stopping short of a confrontation of ultimate views. Not only can schemes of social life – proposals for alternative formative contexts – be recombined, but they can be recombined in different ways. Because new dominant solutions must typically begin as attempts to extend an already existing deviant principle of organization or imagination, we can usually translate even the boldest vision into proposals that work with familiar and intelligible materials.

The ideas that inspire this approach to social stability and invention gain practical influence upon the style of partisan rivalry only when combined with a change in the institutional setting of party conflict. Such changes proceed outward in a net of mutually reinforcing measures revealing the connections between the narrowly constitutional proposals discussed in earlier sections and the ideas about economic organization and legal rights put forward in later pages.

The most significant practical reform addresses the relation of political parties to the organizations that absorb everyday life. In the midst of daily experience, the forms of practical or passionate association must be subject to methods of collective deliberation and conflict that connect with the most general issues of national politics. People must be able to see the positions they take within this more intimate circle as partial but recognizable extensions of their stand in the largest national sphere and vice versa. To this end, the partisan conflict needs to be fought in terms of programs combining breadth of scope with concreteness of intention: these programs should address structures of authority and advantage within and outside large-scale organizations.

The other institutional changes are the enabling conditions of this shift. They contribute to the connection between central political conflict and everyday concern. They keep this connection from taking the spurious form of the reduction of the societywide parties of opinion into the weapons of social classes or of segments of the work force rigidly defined by the niche they occupy in the division of labor. Frequent devolution to the universal electorate and the maximization of opportunities for factional propaganda and agitation at all levels of society bring many major conflicts before the citizen in a manner that penetrates his awareness of the immediate concerns of life even when it occupies only a modest portion of his time. The guarantee of welfare rights enables the individual to accept these conflicts without feeling they jeopardize his basic safety. His conception of minimum stability shrinks to the extent that his most intimate interests in material and moral security for himself and his family get disentangled from a system of vested proprietary rights that turns the forms of immunity from governmental power into the means of control over other people. (See the later discussion of the system of rights.)

The single most important condition to the linkage between conflict at the grass roots of social life and conflict at the heights of governmental power is the reform of the reigning practical institutions that allow small groups of people to exercise a general disciplinary power over everybody else in the name of the property norm, of the state's control over the economy, or of the inherent imperatives of organizational life. The arrangements and preconceptions of these institutions systematically confuse technical or managerial expertise with a more indiscriminate capacity for ultimate decision and command. To the extent that collective conflict and choice gain a significant role within major organizations and that expertise and coordination are distinguished from the ultimate choice of goals and methods, to that extent the opportunity arises for partisanship in the midst of humdrum practical activities. (See the later discussion of the regime of capital for an analysis of how, concretely, to create this opportunity while maintaining both the primacy of national politics over the national economy and the chances for bold entrepreneurial innovation.)

These practical institutions, broken open to collective conflict and deliberation, would also have to take on many of the tasks and characteristics previously attributed to the state. Thus, they should be drawn into the forms of popular representation and administrative responsibility. They should not become exclusive channels for the distribution of essential welfare benefits, for such a role would give them a formidable power of intimidation over their members and jeopardize the integrity of welfare rights. Law and policy, for their part, should give priority to the varieties of distribution and redistribution that strengthen militant collective organizations rather than replacing them: that prefer, for example, the cooperative, public–private offer of services to lump-sum transfers.

The institutional arrangements outlined in the preceding pages remain dangerously compatible with an outcome inimical to the aims of empowered democracy. The national political parties get entrenched in the organizational settings of everyday life. There, at the grass roots, people divide up in ways that help constitute and reflect their divisions at the societywide level. But each party of opinion merely serves in the end as the instrument of a large social group or class or work force segment defined by a relatively stable place in the division of labor. In such a circumstance, a politics of preemptive security, petty bickering, and marginal adjustment would again be likely to dominate the greater part of civic life. The logic of fixed collective interests, rigid definitions of collective identity, and arbitrarily narrow assumptions about historical possibility would again gain an independent force that, though ultimately false, was true relative to its circumstance. Programmatic specificity would turn out to be the enemy of depth and scope in political struggle.

The entire constitution, rather than any one of its features, is designed to prevent such an outcome. By relativizing, through all its provisions, the contrast between an original formative struggle over the basic order of society and the routine contests that go on within this order, the empowered democracy would counteract emergent schemes of rigidly defined interests, identities, and ideas of possibility. Insofar as the attempt to extend the vulnerability of structure to conflict and choice succeeds, the source of partisan division among people becomes to an ever greater degree the diversity of their opinions rather than the nature of their stations. This diversity will be to an ever lesser extent the mere surface expression of some underlying scheme of independently defined collective interests. Opinion will instead be nothing but each individual's partly corrigible interpretation of the meaning of his experience: of what he needs and wants and thinks possible for himself and for other people.

It is important to understand just how this condition compares with the conventional idealized picture of the social basis of the "liberal-bourgeois" democracies: the existence of crosscutting groups that never agglutinate into coherent, long-lasting, and potentially dangerous factions. For one thing, the reformed constitution wants to realize in fact the circumstance described by this picture and, indeed, to carry it to extremes rather than to reverse it in favor of a fantasizing, sentimental, archaic, tyrannical prospect of devotion to a shared vision of the common good. The point is not just that groupings on the basis of collective interest will be fuzzy and unstable but that they will constantly be exploded as soon as they begin to harden.

For another thing, precisely because the destabilization of the collective positions gets pushed so far, the individual's commitment to a party of opinion cannot be based primarily upon the material advantages of groups defined by a stable niche within the social division of labor. It must depend, increasingly, upon a combination of immediate, tangible personal interests and personal vision or conversion. The citizen becomes more and more an individual rather than a puppet of collective categories of class, community, or gender, or a player in a historical drama he can neither understand nor escape.

Suppose all these changes in ideas and institutions were realized. Minimal stability might still seem threatened in another way. A society organized under a regime such as this would appear peculiarly subject to a virulent form of the invidious comparison that already characterizes the established democracies. Because mass politics denies people the experience of a more or less naturally assigned and stable place in the division of labor, everyone compares his advantages to those of everyone else. To this degree, almost everybody has to judge himself a relative loser. The reformed and empowered democracy seems to aggravate the situation by undermining still further the sense of natural social place and hierarchy. Thus, the citizenry of such a republic would be thrown into an endless anguish of envy and longing. This anguish might itself be a source of radical instability in the life of the republic. The citizens might always alternate between a paralyzing self-contempt, when they felt they had failed and deserved to fail, and a resentful hatred of the constitution, when they blamed their institutions for their discontent. Their minds might be totally absorbed in petty deals and comparisons of advantage. They would find themselves unable ever to accept any collective provision for the distribution of jobs, opportunities, and material benefits, unable to accept it, at least, as anything more than the transitory triumph of some factions over others.

The way the constitution avoids this instability is basically the same as the way it prevents the entrenchment of partisan divergence in everyday life from turning into the mere self-defensive jousting of groups defined by relatively fixed places in the division of labor The social conditions that generate the dynamic of invidious comparison in the existing democracies must be radicalized. Three connected reforms fix the meaning of this radicalization.

First, all the institutional arrangements that sustain a high level of collective mobilization in normal social life prevent the dynamic of invidious comparison from focusing upon the differential relations among relatively fixed social places. They dull and disorient indignation. They help liberate the contest of opinions from obsessional concern with disparities of advantage.

Second, the disconnection of the forms of immunity against the state from means of control over other people – a disconnection carried out primarily by the regime of capital outlined in the following pages – presupposes and makes possible a major equalization in the material circumstances of life. It opens up ultimate issues of income differentials, job access, and educational opportunity to the centers of national decision. At the same time, however, it enables ground-level organizations to provide a series of variations on the minimal levels of equality mandated from above. This second series of institutional revisions does not necessarily moderate the experience of invidious comparison. Such a comparison may seize all the more fiercely upon the most modest material inequalities or upon the more intangible but ultimately more important differences of honor and achievement. But it helps separate out from this experience of invidious comparison the distinct element of class struggle over the organization of material life. By so doing, it draws attention to the more general problems of envy, equality, and the acceptance of differences. Here, as elsewhere, the aim is less to suppress fighting than to liberate it from the exclusive and bitter obsession with confined aspects of the structure of society.

Yet a third effect of these constitutional changes upon the dynamic of invidious comparison has to do with the power of the reformed constitution to increase the importance of aims to which that dynamic simply fails to apply. For the force of such comparative judgments depends in part upon the exclusivity of the struggle for relative advantage within an order taken as given. But the more the duel over relative place within the order gets mixed up with a conflict over the order itself, the more the dynamic of invidious comparison is likely to be overshadowed and transformed from within by other motivations. (A later section comes to terms with the relation between institutions and motivations.)

Consider, by way of example, the likely effect of such changes upon what was known in the North Atlantic democracies of the late twentieth century as the problem of incomes policies. To ensure economic stabilization through continued economic growth and the control of inflation, governments needed a minimum of broadly based acquiescence in the distribution of the benefits and burdens imposed by any coherent recovery program. From the pure standpoint of economic growth, it often seemed less important to decide which of several possible recovery paths would be taken than to settle on one path in particular and to remain on it for some time. One aspect of the ability to stay the course was the capacity to secure some basic agreement to the established distribution of income shares among segments of the work force and, more generally, of the entire population. Without such a minimal consensus, the better-organized or more protected segments of labor and business constantly tried to cash their organizational advantage into additional income. Everyone else attempted to catch up. Those who lost out (unorganized workers, independent professionals, proprietors, and rentiers) sought, one way or another, for compensatory help from government (through manipulation of the tax burden or of welfare rights). In such an atmosphere, enterprise investment strategies were skewed by the overwhelming concern to maintain a stable, core labor force. The downward rigidity of the wage structure helped keep markets from clearing and inflation from correcting itself. Group wage and income differentials were unstable both because groups remained unevenly organized and because their power to defend themselves in the marketplace did not coincide with their ability to pressure governments. This disparity perpetuated an inconclusive, paralyzing bickering among social ranks or work force segments with fixed niches in the division of labor.

The deeper historical situation that underlay these tendencies reflected the coexistence of two facts. The first was that the hierarchy of collective positions in the division of labor had been shaken to the point of undermining its appearance of naturalness and its claim to moral authority. The idea that customary wage differentials were fair just because they were customary coincided with an active sense of the arbitrariness of the entire scheme – of its vulnerability, in the large and in the small, to renewed collective conflict. No group had any reason to accept the place assigned to it within the job and income hierarchy if it could hope, by rebeginning the fight, to do better. At the same time – here entered the other defining fact – the hierarchy of collective places had been only partly disturbed. Though too weak and fragmented to guarantee acquiescence in a particular pattern of distribution, it was strong and unified enough to regenerate the system of collective stations people would fight over.

The reformed constitution acts upon this circumstance by altering the second of these two facts. The system of stations is more thoroughly fragmented. This fragmentation occurs less by a once-and-for-all redistributive fix than by the deepening and enlargement of the conditions that make the passage of collective contractualism into collective mobilization an ongoing rather than a sporadic and anomalous feature of social life. The result should be not to guarantee spontaneous consensus over income shares but to strike at the basis of the resentful collectivism and unbroken, grubby impasse that the failure of income policies exemplified.

BREAKING THE RULES: THE FORMS OF DECENTRALIZATION

The program of empowered democracy requires that power be decentralized in a way that resolves a familiar dilemma. Central governmental power is the greatest lever for the transformation of social life. But to put all hope in central power holders and in the forms of accountability that may be imposed upon them is to sacrifice social experimentation to a single-minded plan. It is to focus civic engagement on a distant, barely visible point and to concentrate in the hands of the few the short-term authority taken away from the many. Empowered democracy would be an illusory, self-contradictory program if this dilemma were indeed intractable.

But the dilemma need be no more insoluble than any other tension between abstract institutional commitments. The tension is real enough. What is illusory is the fixity of the antagonism between the two aims. Both centralism and decentralization can assume an indefinitely wide range of institutional forms. Some forms aggravate the tension, whereas others mollify it.

The traditional program of decentralization relies upon the two basic principles of subsidiarity and functional specialization. The principle of subsidiarity requires that power to set rules and policies be transferred from a lower and closer authority to a higher and more distant one only when the former cannot adequately perform the particular responsibility in question. Of course, everything depends upon the standard of adequacy. Nevertheless, against the background of a view that sees established institutions as uncontroversial, the principle works to justify the maximum possible decentralization. It draws force from the commonsense notion that the authority or group closest to the individual ought to be the most involved in the resolution of his problems. And it merges into the liberal conviction that the ultimate residual authority is the individual himself. Functional specialization, the other plank in the traditional platform of decentralization, requires that the same task not be performed by two competing or overlapping authorities. It is the logic of entrepreneurial efficiency extended to the organization of the governmental hierarchy in both unitary and federal states.

The program of subsidiarity and functional specialization is what contemporary right-wing and centrist parties have in mind when they defend the decentralization of governmental power. But this style of decentralization merely disarms central governments before an untransformed society. It hands decision over to local elites. It respects entrenched privilege. For all these reasons, it aggravates the dilemma mentioned earlier.

An alternative road to decentralization should leave room for major swings in the emphasis different political parties may give to either greater centralized authority or more decentralized experiment. But it should also place these swings within a framework that upholds the broader commitments of empowered democracy. Such a framework must prefer the forms of centralization and decentralization that are less likely to immunize privilege against effective challenge. Imagine, then, a constitutional order that provides for two complementary methods of decentralization. The relative weight to be given each method depends upon the programs of the political parties in office. The system composed by the two strategies applies to both federal and unitary states, and it changes the relation of legal rules to individual conduct.

The first method is the conditional right to opt out of the norms established by higher authorities. Under this approach, the central representative agencies lay down rules governing a broad range of social situations.

But a minimum of two individuals, or a larger group of people, can opt out of these rules and establish an alternative charter. The opting parties must satisfy two key conditions. First, when they set up the alternative structure they must stand in a relation of relative equality, whether as individuals or as enterprises. Second, the optional charter must not have the effect of casting one of the parties into a relation of enduring subjugation. The first condition is primary. The criteria that give it content can take current private-law doctrines of economic duress as their point of departure.

Such an approach may still rule out certain innovations simply because they conflict with the minimal standards of conventional morality. Nevertheless, the spirit of this form of decentralization is to permit a much broader range of deviation from public rules than we are now accustomed to: a range broad enough to include both economic and family matters.

The other method of decentralization, the qualified devolution of power, reallocates power among the levels of the governmental hierarchy rather than between government and people. The qualified devolution of power seeks to transfer power from higher to lower governmental authorities in just the way the traditional principle of subsidiarity recommends. But it differs from the traditional, right–center style of decentralization by attaching to every episode of devolution a corresponding guarantee.

The point of the guarantee is to prevent the devolution from helping to entrench old or emergent privileges. More specifically, the transfer of authority and resources must be prevented from serving to build up a local citadel of hierarchy, strengthened against both internal challenge from the disfavored and external challenge from the broader politics of the republic.

The form of the safeguard is proportional to the extent and duration of the transfer of authority. An example at the highest level of government is the special branch, described earlier, that would disrupt and reconstruct whatever organizations and practices condemned people to a circumstance of subjugation subversive of their role as citizens of the empowered democracy. Many other safeguards may apply to more local or transitory forms of devolution. Among these mechanisms, the empowered democracy may use ad hoc supervisory boards, special rights of challenge and appeal, and the practice of transferring authority or resources to overlapping and competing bodies.

THE ORGANIZATION OF ANTIGOVERNMENT: THE STRUCTURE OF VOLUNTARY ASSOCIATION

The program of empowered democracy for the reorganization of government has its counterpart in a scheme to facilitate the self-organization of society outside government. The point of this plan is twofold. The negative aim is to organize a parallel state or even an antistate. It is to form a set of institutions that, without canceling the opportunities for government-sponsored social experiments, diminishes the risk of despotic perversion: the danger that the governmental arrangements of the new-model democracy may be used to initiate a concentration of power unrestrained by independent social organizations.

An analogy and a distinction may help bring out what is at stake. According to a familiar theme in modern political thought, predemocratic anciens régimes enjoyed a complex, differentiated structure of privileges and power. This scheme of group prerogatives and disabilities limited both popular sovereignty and centralizing despotism. The destruction of the tissue of intermediate association in the name of democracy creates opportunities for a more thoroughgoing despotism than any practiced under the ancien régime. If the contemporary liberal democracies have stood fast against this danger – so the conservative-liberal argument goes – they have done so by incorporating more of a system of differentiated collective prerogatives and immunities than the more naive apologists of liberal democracy like to acknowledge.

The negative work of this part of the program of the empowered democracy can be redescribed, with the help of this skeptical argument, as the attempt to establish a style of restraining social counterweights. These brakes, however, no longer take the form dear to conservative–liberal propagandists and aristocratic–corporate polities. They cease to be anchored in institutions that help establish privileged strangleholds on society-making resources and that reproduce a scheme of fixed social roles and ranks.

The affirmative point is to turn the organizational instruments of nongovernmental association into better means of discovering, questioning, and revising each formative institutional and imaginative context of social life. The ways people have of coming together to pursue individual and group interests within a framework left both undisturbed and unremarked should draw closer to the ways they can challenge such frameworks. We should abandon the futile or self-defeating attempt to superimpose upon the factional pursuit of private interests an activity of selfless or enlightened devotion to the common good. Instead we can create practical institutional conditions that enlarge the scope and the sense of our prosaic, self-regarding efforts. The conflict over interests can always escalate into struggles over the preconceptions and arrangements that help define the interests. Let us institutionalize the escalation, depriving it of its supposed terrors. And let us do so for the sake of the forms of empowerment served by the whole program of institutional reconstruction outlined here.

Consider the issue of union organization as a setting in which to formulate ideas that can later be generalized. The legal setting of union organization in the advanced Western democracies follows, more or less resolutely, a contractarian approach. This approach seeks to reestablish in the employment relation the minimal degree of freedom from economic duress required to make of labor contracts between employers and employees something more than a cover for outright subjugation. The remedy against such duress is to ensure an opportunity for collective organization and collective bargaining. This opportunity enables workers to counterbalance the overweening pressure employers might be able to exercise if they could deal with the workers on an individual basis. The law must make an exception to contractual forms the better to uphold the essentials of contract. What counts is not that most workers in fact unionize and avail themselves of collective bargaining – individual labor bargains may continue to preponderate – but that workers can unionize if they find themselves under contract-subverting duress.

Two master principles work out this idea. A principle of freedom from government requires that unions remain under only the minimal form of public control inherent in the establishment, elaboration, and application of the labor laws. A principle of structural pluralism commands that the law impose no unitary scheme of union classification: no system for determining which unions are to represent which workers or how the labor force is to be divided up for the purpose of union representation. Certain dominant principles of classification may emerge. But the union structure looks like a collection of fragmentary pieces of different puzzles, with the fragments forming no single, coherent picture.

Only in a few countries, and often due to fascist influence, do we find elements of a corporatist model of labor relations. Under this contrasting approach, unions represent an extended part of the structure of government. By their power to establish and tutor labor organizations central governments gain a chance to practice controlled mobilization. Governmental control replaces autonomy from the state. At the same time, the corporatist labor regime follows a principle of unitary classification. This principle affirms that the entire work force should be divided up into a single, coherent classificatory scheme: all the fragments should in fact be pieces of the same puzzle.

Any democrat must oppose the governmental-control aspect of the corporatist model. But the principle of pluralistic classification, characteristic of the contractarian approach, has defects of its own. It forces union organizers and militants to expend much of their efforts in the attempt to unionize. It absorbs them in the peculiarly inconclusive factional struggles a pluralistic union system encourages. The struggles remain indecisive because the contenders need not fight for place and join issue within a single structure. They can simply inhabit different, hostile but noncommunicating union hierarchies. Moreover, both the dispersive pluralism of the contract regime and its treatment of collective organization as a mere surrogate and safeguard of private bargaining encourage a sharp contrast between worker-employer and worker-government relations. The result is to discourage workers from treating workplace disputes and conflicts in national politics as parts of the same continuum.

No wonder the quasi-contractual organization of labor seems to favor a purely economistic style of militancy, relatively unconcerned with the organization of the work force, even less interested in the larger institutional structure of the economy and the polity. When the core economic basis of the unions in the mass-production industries declines, the union movement formed under the contract model comes to be perceived, and to perceive itself, as just one more interest group. It ceases to speak as the voice of all working people and as the bearer of a message for the whole society.

By contrast, the corporatist approach may better serve the extremes of repression and mobilization. When administered by a strong, authoritarian government, it represents – just as its authors intended – a formidable tool of industrial discipline. But against the background of governmental weakness or openness, its unitary organization facilitates an institutionally committed militancy. The work force is already unionized and unionized in a single framework. This structure need not be created from scratch. It can be taken over by those who see the conflict over interest-defining structures as the continuation of fights over structure-defining interests. Their work is made easier by an institutional and imaginative tradition that dramatizes rather than conceals the links between the domains of government–worker and worker–employer relations.

Why not then join together, in the interest of empowered democracy, the contractarian principle of autonomy from governmental control and the corporatist principle of unitary classification? Different currents of opinion – linking the organized political parties to the distinctive problems of the workplace – would contend for place in this unified structure of labor organization, just as the political parties themselves compete for position in the unified structure of government. And the workers in the labor movement as a whole or in particular job categories may even initiate changes in the classification scheme, subject to veto by the national legislature.

The familiar role of unions will change as the style of industrial organization shifts. It would change all the more under the economic program of empowered democracy, outlined later in this chapter. But a role for the organization and representation of people on the basis of job categories will remain long after workers cease to confront managers imposed upon them by an alien and unaccountable authority.

The same combination of autonomy and unity that applies to unions can also extend to territorial organization. A unitary system of neighborhood associations may also be established, at least at the local level, as a stimulus to popular engagement in local government and as an independent control upon local authorities.

On the solid ground of this organization of people in the places where they work and live, a host of other forms of association may flourish, pluralistic and fragmentary in structure as well as free from governmental control. Legal opportunities, public resources, and free access to the means of communication support these additional groupings. But such open-ended associational experiments complement rather than replace an associative structure established by law and made, by law, independent from government. This antistate helps keep the state humble and the people proud, inquisitive, and restless.

12

Economic Reorganization

THE ORGANIZATION OF THE ECONOMY: THE CURRENT MARKET REGIME AND ITS COSTS

A second domain for reconstruction is the institutional framework of economic life. The major theme of this part of the program is the attempt to imagine an alternative institutional definition of the market just as the major theme of earlier parts of the program lies in the proposal of an alternative institutional setting for democracy. This part of the institutional scheme anticipates the outline of a theory of the enabling conditions of material progress that extends the central social theory of this book into an area of life that may seem peculiarly resistant to its intentions.

In any society the organization of government and of the economy depend upon each other. But the character of the institutions, and of the forms of thought that explain and justify them, often make the connection both indirect and obscure. In the constitution outlined here, the link becomes, instead, direct and transparent. This shift represents far more than an accidental and minor feature of the institutional proposal; it exemplifies a general truth about society, a truth to which the social theory underlying the proposal attaches great importance.

Collective mobilization is the exemplary form of the collective creation of society, of society making conceived as an ongoing and deliberate event, intentionally undertaken by particular people rather than as a definitive foundational act or a permanent, unknowing drift. A constitutional order that tries to multiply the occasions for collective mobilization gives immediate practical effect to the hidden truth that any given institutional and imaginative order both arises out of practical or visionary fighting and depends upon its partial and provisional containment. The segments of social life that appear to operate by some distinct logic of their own do so only on sufferance from a peace whose continuation they can never themselves guarantee. To the extent the peace gets broken, it becomes evident that what seemed to be distinct spheres of social life governed by laws of their own are in fact only temporary versions of some larger, inchoate realm of practical or passionate association whose unity is more important than its temporary internal differentiations. A constitution that perpetuates mobilization in the moment of normalcy brings this unity out;

the distinctive self-operating laws of different spheres of social life begin to lose their appearance of even relative autonomy. Contemporary cosmologists have pointed out that a universe approaching its higher-energy moment of maximum collapse and density would exhibit directly the symmetries and connections that, in the cooler stages of its history, had to be discovered scientifically and represented mathematically. The constitution of the empowered democracy produces in the social world the effect of that moment of greatest transparency.

This section prepares the description of an alternative institutional framework for economic life through a criticism of existing economic arrangements. The criticism emphasizes the unity of the explanatory and normative ideas that can help guide a constructive effort. The immediate target of the criticism is the private-rights complex of the advanced Western countries, especially insofar as it influences the organization of production and exchange.

The private-rights system establishes a practical and imaginative equation between the abstract idea of a market and a historically unique group of institutional arrangements. The abstract concept of a market means no more than the existence of a large number of economic agents able to bargain on their own initiative and for their own account. The historically specific arrangements with which this abstract market idea gets improperly identified have as their core the consolidated property right: a more or less absolute entitlement to a divisible portion of social capital – more or less absolute both in its discretionary use and in the chain of voluntary transfers by successive property owners. Once this initial identification has been established, the market economy is often further assumed to imply a particular style of industrial organization: the style that puts standardized mass production in the mainstream of industry and flexible production in its vanguard. Indeed, if we accept the identification of the market with the system of relatively decentralized consolidated property, we also have some reason to further assume that an industrialized market economy will favor this method of industrial organization. For the system of consolidated property does contribute to the conditions that allow mass-production industries to arrange markets and to counteract what might otherwise be instabilities in the product, labor, and financial markets. Rigid, highly capitalized enterprises could not hope to survive such oscillations.

It may seem surprising that the consolidated property system and the mass-production style of industrial organization also characterize the major contemporary alternatives to the economic systems of the advanced Western countries. Yet consolidated property and mass production are also at home in the distinctive business cycles of socialist-bureaucratic and workers' ownership models. In one case the consolidated property rights are transferred to a central government; in the other case, to the workers who have secure jobs within a given enterprise when the transfer takes place. Though the immediate target of my critical arguments is the economic regime of the advanced Western countries, many of these arguments carry over, with only slight adjustments, to the main rival economic systems. The present section suggests this carry-over. To deny that the available alternatives are the necessary options among which we must choose, to show what these alternatives have in common, and to suggest how this common element might be replaced all form part of the view.

Consider first a series of criticisms of the established forms of democracies and markets. These criticisms fall into two main categories, anticipated by the earlier discussion of reform cycles. Some are arguments about the effect of established economic arrangements upon freedom. Others address the influence of existing or alternative institutional arrangements upon economic efficiency and growth. I do not assume that what contributes to material progress always enhances freedom. There is nevertheless an element of truth in the superstitious belief that the two go together. Liberation from poverty and drudgery is one of the chief forms of empowerment. Moreover, it depends as much as the other forms on a partial lifting of the constraints an entrenched plan of social division and hierarchy imposes upon our collective experiments in the organization of exchange and production.

Our current version of market institutions jeopardizes freedom on both a large and a small scale. On a large scale it leaves a restricted number of people with a disproportionate influence over the basic flows of investment decisions. It thereby withdraws the basic terms of collective prosperity from effective democratic choice and control. As a result, the plans of reform governments are easily frustrated in precisely those areas that so often matter most to the reformers. Any attempt to assert governmental control over the main line of economic accumulation seems both to undermine the effective decentralization of economic decisions and to enhance the authority of bureaucratic officials. The difficulty of imagining an alternative governmental structure both more capable and more democratic makes all the more fearsome such a strengthening of central authority.

At the same time the current market form undermines freedom on a small scale. It does so, diffusely, by generating and permitting inequalities of wealth that reduce some people to effective economic dependence upon others – those who occupy the supervisory positions. It does so, more precisely, by helping to prop up a style of industrial organization that thrives on the relatively rigid contrast of task definers and task executors.

The earlier stages of the programmatic argument suggest yet another sense in which our present mode of economic organization limits freedom. The empowered democracy outlined in earlier parts of this program represents a requirement of freedom. Yet such a democracy cannot flourish if the everyday world of work and exchange is organized in ways that not only differ from the principles of democratic government but limit their scope, undermine their influence, and disrupt their workings. If markets cannot be given a different institutional form, if the only practical alternatives to the established economic regimes are the socialist-bureaucratic and the worker-ownership models, the program of empowered democracy is doomed from the start, and with it our hope of extending the meaning of freedom.

Take now a series of arguments about the constraints the established market system imposes upon economic progress – that is upon the ability to sustain repeated breakthroughs in productive capacity and productivity. (Remember that these same criticisms apply in a different sense, but with redoubled force, to the major acknowledged alternatives.) After enumerating these critical arguments, I make explicit the basic view of the enabling conditions of economic progress that underlies them.

The first criticism focuses upon the absolute degree of economic decentralization. Within the established regime of capital, economies of scale seem to require almost by definition the consolidation of property rights over large amounts of capital in a single decisional center, even if – as in many large stock corporations – shares of ownership are widely distributed. A centralized management acting in the name of fragmentary shareholders supervises the large-scale pooling of manpower and capital resources. These managers can then act almost as if they held their power by the accumulation of personal wealth. An apparent fragmentation of the consolidated property system may thus end up preserving the essential features of this system. The most important of these traits is precisely the legally protected faculty to organize production and exchange in the name of a more or less absolute claim to a divisible portion of social capital.

Without an extreme dispersion of business power, the breakup of trade unions in turn appears intolerable, at least in the absence of an alternative way of asserting the power of the labor force to resist business authority. But the alternative devices that respect the principle of consolidated property while changing its locus – greater central governmental control over economic accumulation or outright workers' ownership of enterprises – seem to aggravate the threat to efficiency and freedom, or both. Conversely, the unacceptability of breaking up the trade unions provides an additional excuse to accept as inevitable the current degree of economic concentration. Attempts to encourage economic decentralization can therefore be derided by tough-minded publicists as sentimental reveries.

A second economic criticism addresses the plasticity of the current market economy rather than the absolute degree of decentralization it permits. Plasticity is the generalized form of economic rationality: the ease of recombining the components of the institutional context of production and exchange as well as of combining factors of production within a given context. The point of plasticity, broadly speaking, is to increase the opportunity for experiment and innovation in social life. The move toward more plastic economic arrangements loosens the predetermination of exchange and production relations by rules and regularities that remain unavailable for revision in the light of emergent practical opportunities.

The economic value of this loosening may seem uncontroversial when the constraints to be weakened are those of a social order that arranges production and exchange according to noneconomic standards and subordinates the logic of restless practical reason to respect for entrenched social divisions and hierarchies. But the case for plasticity may seem a great deal less persuasive when the constraints to be loosened are universal rules that seem to cast everyone in the same position of formal equality. For, it may be objected, the interest in experimentation must stop at the limit dictated by the even more fundamental need for a stable and generally understood framework for practical dealings. To this objection there are two answers. One response, implicit in a general thesis of the social theory developed in this book, is that the only assurance that fixed arrangements will not generate new systems of entrenched social division and hierarchy is precisely that they be open to challenge and revision at all levels of activity. The other answer, specific to the present economic arguments, is that alternative economic regimes and indeed alternative market systems, though equally stable, may differ in the extent to which they permit variation in the social forms of exchange and production. Relative openness to organizational innovation, like relative conduciveness to economic decentralization, is a feature of discrete institutional systems, not a characteristic of economies or markets in the abstract. The idea that the functioning of a competitive price will automatically ensure that over time the most efficient innovations prevail has been traditionally criticized for not taking account of market failure. But this criticism misses the more fundamental point that a competitive price system is institutionally indeterminate. Precisely because of its indeterminancy, no automatic identification exists between allocative efficiency relative to a particular price system and the encouragement of continued breakthroughs in productivity and productive output – all facts that would be too trivial to mention were not their implications almost universally disregarded.

A third economic objection to the present market system, seen in its broader governmental and social setting, has to do with the constraints it imposes upon a growth-oriented macroeconomic policy. A strategy for economic growth may be realized through any number of alternative patterns of distribution: differential wage, tax, or subsidy levels. It is vital, however, that one such distribution be made to stick, at least to the extent necessary to avoid an inconclusive conflict over the proper distribution. For even when such conflict fails to cause major disruption, it prevents governmental policy from being decisively marshaled in favor of any given strategy of economic growth.

In the rich North Atlantic democracies we find two correlations of forces in two relatively distinct domains. In the market arena, big business and organized labor, both entrenched in the rigid, mass-production sector of industry, exercise a disproportionate influence over the organization of markets and production. Through investment and disinvestment policies, through the disruption of the core productive system, and through their influence upon the means of mass communication or the financing of politics, they can strike back against any distributive deal that fails to respect their position of strength. On the other hand, the groups relatively weak in the economic arena – petty proprietors, independent professionals, and the unorganized underclass – will seek to overturn through the vote, through social agitation, and even through appeals to conscience and prudence the distributive bargains that do them in. No distributive bargain can respect both correlations of forces and none can preserve itself against the destabilizing effect of the powers it devalues.

To be sure, this inconclusiveness might be avoided by many possible institutional changes: if, for example, the government had dictatorial powers ("authoritarian capitalism"), thereby enabling it to impose a solution, or if unionization extended to the entire labor force, thereby bringing the two correlations closer, except insofar as big business retained a broad measure of independent decisional authority. But each institutional change would produce more far reaching and disturbing consequences for society. Thus, if an authoritarian, nonrevolutionary state is not the relatively passive instrument of a particular class, it must reach a modus vivendi with different classes. It will find itself continually pulled among conflicting claims: the desire to pander to established elites, the effort to win wider popular support, and the attempt to assert an independent power interest, justified in turn by the strengthening of the nation-state. The competing claims may maintain the effect of deadlock while drastically changing its causes and content. On the other hand, the general unionization of the labor force and the overcoming of the distinction between the working class and the underclass would, at a minimum, put pressure on the established style of industrial organization by denying the rigid, mass-production industries one of their instruments of defense against oscillations in demand: subcontracting work or hiring temporary workers. To the extent the unionization was militant and led the unions to define themselves as the people rather than as an interest group, the resulting mass mobilization would be far more consequential. For either it would be suppressed or it would lead to yet more drastic changes in the basic institutions and enacted beliefs of society.

Consider now the general view of the enabling conditions of economic progress that underlies such criticisms. The statement of this view suggests the broader range of ideas within which the critical arguments would have a secure place. It reveals the basic unity of those arguments. It provides a perspective from which to criticize the major available alternatives to economic regimes of the contemporary Western democracies. It supplies a basis on which to imagine the reconciliation between enlarged political freedom and accelerated economic growth.

Economic progress occurs through the acceleration and deliberateness of leaps in productivity and productive output. To this end, the relations among people at work must become as much as possible an embodiment of practical reason: they must give expression to the free interplay between problem definitions and problem solving. In this interplay, new definitions suggest new solutions; and new solutions, new problems. Presuppositions – such as the rules governing inference and the idea of what counts as a solution or as the instrument of a solution – are gradually dragged into the interplay. As a result, the boundary becomes increasingly fluid between what is treated as a problem and what is accepted as a presupposition. In the organization of production and exchange these presuppositions may be the limited stock of associative and technical ideas that people bring to economic activity, the practices that compose the institutional setting of production and exchange, or the social divisions and hierarchies generated by an entrenched formative context of social life, predetermining how people can deal with one another at work or in trade. The last point is especially important: economic relations cannot become practical reason on the march so long as they remain subject to a closed logic of the social stations that are possible and the activities that occupants of these stations may undertake.

How does this view of a basic condition of economic progress relate to the familiar idea that economic growth requires that particular groups combine innovative capability with access to capital? So long as we continue to accept the naive view of the market as possessed of an inherent institutional structure, we can count on the price system to channel capital automatically to those best able to use it. But once we abandon the idea of inherent institutional structure of the market, the identification of the most productive users becomes, like everything else about an economy, a matter of experimental fact. The institutions and the people responsible for setting the ultimate framework of economic life must compare the results of different institutional arrangements. Such a comparison becomes more valuable as the experiments compared become more numerous; and they become more numerous as the framework itself becomes more flexible, enabling economic agents to renew and recombine the arrangements making up the institutional context of production and exchange. The transformation of economic life into an embodiment of practical reason describes both the expected outcome of this ongoing experiment and the means for carrying it out.

Such a transformation of economic organization may take two main directions. One direction is coercive. A commanding will, ordinarily ensconced in the central government, repeatedly shatters the constraints that old or reemergent routines and privileges impose upon the dynamic of problem solving and the renewal of institutional arrangements. In particular, it disrupts social divisions and hierarchies and the institutional arrangements that give life to them, at least to the extent necessary to prevent these institutionalized roles and ranks from closing down the range of social life left open to economic experimentation. The basic problem with the coercive approach is the tendency of the institutional center that exercises this directing function to subordinate the practice of the problem-solving dynamic to the power interests of those who hold this power or serve as the agents of the powerholders farther down the command ladder. The crucial practical difference among institutional versions of the coercive approach is, therefore, the relative facility with which they lend themselves to such abuse.

The alternative direction is consensual. The economic order takes the form of a decentralized framework for interaction by parties able to bargain on their own initiative and for their own account. The characteristic problem of such market solutions is their tendency to define economic positions or the claims upon capital and labor that make them possible, as vested rights. Interest in the perpetuation of these claims, sanctioned by law and keyed into current styles of economic organization, takes precedence over the seizure of emergent productive opportunities, and the resulting price system confirms a rationality that remains only loosely connected with its productive economic uses. Market systems differ in the extent to which they avoid this difficulty and encourage both absolute decentralization and institutional plasticity. These decisive differences are rooted in the institutional arrangements defining the context of production and exchange, including the detailed texture of contract and property law. The crucial point is the legal–institutional device for decentralizing claims of access to capital. The belief that this device must always amount to a variation on the consolidated, relatively absolute property right represents a groundless prejudice, but one from which even the most subtle forms of political economy have only partly freed themselves.

Neither the coercive nor the consensual realization of the problem-solving dynamic can ever prevail to the complete exclusion of the alternative. Even the most coercive system must count on voluntary collaboration, on pain of resorting to a runaway governmental terrorism that both disrupts the production system and overtaxes the capabilities of the state. Every working collaboration in turn implies settled expectations and partial reciprocities that imply a significant measure of de facto consensual decentralization. Conversely, every consensual market system requires the degree of centralized direction needed to establish basic guidelines and other rules governing the power to vary those fundamental norms of exchange.

From the pitiless standpoint of developing practical capabilities to produce or to destroy, the problem is not to choose between coercion and consensus. It is rather to invent the consensual or coercive solutions that go farther than do existing economic regimes toward freeing economic initiative from the constraints of administrative or proprietary privilege.

Many nineteenth-century utilitarians and liberals thought they had solved this problem once and for all by discovering the pure system of market coordination, just as they also claimed to have expounded the built-in institutional structure of a democracy. But they were mistaken, having drastically understated the ambiguity of the institutional arrangements that might both realize and redefine market economies and democratic governments.

Notice also that although the coercive and consensual realizations of problem solving and plasticity may be equally promising or troublesome when viewed in the narrowest practical terms, an important difference between them emerges as soon as they are placed in a broader setting. The consensual emphasis in economic life fits with the broader program of an empowered democracy, whereas the coercive one does not. The objection to be made against current market systems from this wider perspective is the same one they deserve on narrower economic grounds: their failure to move far enough along the consensual path and to heighten the plasticity of economic life.

This sketch of a general approach to the enabling conditions of material progress suggests why the available alternatives to the mixed economies of the rich North Atlantic countries of the present day are inadequate, both as machines for accelerated economic growth and as integral parts of an empowered democracy. Each alternative system establishes a balance or an oscillation between the prerogatives of those who exercise a directing will and the vested rights of those who represent the lowest significant rung of effective decentralization. In the Soviet-type model, the prerogatives of the central rulers and bureaucrats are balanced against the settled positions of the managers in charge of economic enterprises. In the Yugoslav "worker-control" model, they are balanced against the vested rights of the workers who occupy an entrenched position within an enterprise. (Even this distinction loses its force to the extent that effective job security becomes an accepted constraint within the Soviet model.) The reform cycles characterizing each system show the outer limits within which both the most coercive and the most consensual moments of these economic systems remain, limits that prevent either the coercive or the consensual approaches from achieving a form more congenial to the ceaseless renewal and recombination required by accelerated economic progress.

An alternative economic order must minimize the constraints current economic systems impose upon the free interplay of problem definition and problem solving. It must do so both to make a practical success out of the experiment in a more empowered democracy and to create a form of economic life that extends and sustains the social ideal underlying the whole constitution. The scheme of economic life must emphasize the consensual interpretation of organizational experimentation over the coercive one. This emphasis requires an attempt to imagine a mechanism of economic decentralization more radical in its bias toward decentralization and plasticity than the classical property right. Nor should we imagine that transferring economic sovereignty to a central state apparatus or to the enterprise work force represents the sole alternative to the familiar version of a market system. But what then might a better market structure be like? And how would it connect with the exercise of effective democratic conflict and control over social resources?

Before considering an answer to these questions, reflect on two clues for construction implied by the preceding critical arguments.

The first hint has to do with the shape of the property right. The economic systems discussed in the preceding pages all maintain consolidated property: they keep together the many heterogeneous powers that compose this right, and they assign all these powers to the same rightholder. The systems differ solely in the way they define the identity of this major rightholder: the freely accumulating individual and the beneficiaries of his inheritance, the state and its delegates and favorites, or the work force of each enterprise. The consolidated property entitlement serves as the most striking instrument of the privileged control over capital. The reason why it does so is not self-evident: it appears, after all, to be compatible with substantial equality. Nevertheless, the attempt to combine substantial equality with the consolidated property right turns out to be both paradoxical and impractical. It is paradoxical because it can be achieved only through some independent institutional mechanism that eviscerates the significance of the consolidated property right by drastically limiting its exercise and its accumulation by the rightholders. It is impractical because the immediate effect of such limitations is to undermine the market principle in the legitimate abstract sense of economic decentralization and to impede the mobility of capital. The severance of the link between politics as organized group conflict and politics as privilege or stalemate seems to require a systematic breaking up of the property right.

The other clue in the criticism of existing economic systems refers to the relation between the regime of capital and the organization of government. The critical discussion suggests that the idea of a connection between the market and freedom holds good, although not in the sense in which it has been ordinarily understood. We find the legal tools of privileged hold over capital reciprocally linked, through a series of mediating institutions and preconceptions, to the forms of privileged access to state power. The trouble comes from mistaking democracy and the market with some marginally adjusted version of the institutional arrangements already established in the advanced Western countries. I have shown how, in the Soviet-style economies, even the most technical microeconomic constraints on the operation of a market mechanism related, directly or indirectly, to the failure to bring the control of state power into question. Thus, to take one of the more oblique examples, you could not understand the force of the nearly absolute job security constraint without taking into account the implications of the attempt to uphold the pretense of a workers' state in a society where workers had few powers. Such powers as they might have – like the claim to job security (by no means acknowledged in all communist economies) – depended upon their ability to play on the unintended consequences of existing institutional arrangements (such as the tightness of the labor market, under conditions of severe wage control, a situation giving the workers shop-floor power while also helping establish job security). In the Western-style economies, the analogous connections were more subtle.The microeconomic constraints in markets connected to macroeconomic constraints that included the need of elected governments to accommodate to the relatively small groups controlling the major flows of investment decisions. Conversely, the stability of the established institutional arrangements, including the arrangements that defined markets, depended upon a long-lasting social demobilization that had in turn been encouraged – and at one time deliberately sought – by the constitutional organization of government.

THE ORGANIZATION OF THE ECONOMY: THE ROTATING CAPITAL FUND AND ITS DEMOCRATIC CONTROL

The Core Conception

A regime capable of working out the implications of the clues described in the preceding section brings the structure and direction of economic life into the domain of central conflicts over society's alternative futures, a domain in which no segment of society and no cadre of experts can easily gain the upper hand. Such a regime constantly resists and reverses the subjection of capital to the more or less permanent and unrestricted dominion of particular rightholders. It pushes the economy farther into becoming a perpetual innovation machine and increases the freedom of economic relations from predetermination by a challenge-resistant scheme of social life.

The key idea of the institutional proposal is the breakup of control over capital into several tiers of capital takers and capital givers. The ultimate capital giver is a social capital fund controlled by the decisional center of the empowered democracy: the party in office and the supporting representative assemblies. The ultimate capital takers are teams of workers, technicians, and entrepreneurs, who make temporary and conditional claims upon divisible portions of this social capital fund. The central capital fund does not lend money out directly to the primary capital users. Instead, it allocates resources to a variety of semi-independent investment funds. Each investment fund specializes in a sector of the economy and in a type of investment. The central democratic institutions exercise their ultimate control over the forms and rates of economic accumulation and income distribution by establishing these funds or by closing them out, by assigning them new infusions of capital or by taking capital away from them, by charging them interest (whose payment represents the major source of governmental finance), and, most importantly, by setting the outer limits of variation in the terms on which the competing investment funds may allocate capital to the ultimate capital takers. The investment funds may take resources away from one another, thus forming in effect a competitive capital market, whose operations are also overseen by the central representative bodies of the democracy. The investment funds in turn allocate resources to the primary capital takers – teams of entrepreneurs, technicians, and workers – under two different regimes. The funds set the terms on which financial and technological resources may be obtained. The capital users pay an interest charge to their investment fund just as the latter pays a charge to the central social fund. Within the limits laid down by both the central governmental bodies and the competing investment funds, these direct capital takers buy and sell. Within those limits they, too, may bid resources away from one another. They profit from successful enterprise and suffer from business failure. But they never acquire permanent individual or group rights to the capital they receive. Nor does success entitle them to expand continuously, to buy out other enterprises, or to introduce into their own business a special category of relatively disadvantaged and voiceless workers. Success merely increases their income.

Thus the proposed regime provides for three tiers of capital givers and capital takers, the second tier being both a taker and a giver. The precise balance of economic power among these levels represents a major topic of political conflict under the empowered democracy. The discussion of the following pages strikes a particular balance only in order to clothe the central intuitive idea in more tangible dress.

The basic legal principle of this alternative economic order is the disintegration of property: its breakup into distinct powers, vested in different agents. To be sure, much in the design of this alternative may already be recognized in germ in the interplay between consolidated property and relatively haphazard governmental regulation as well as in the subtleties of contemporary capital markets. You can hardly expect otherwise from a programmatic argument that draws on internal criticism, addresses a particular historical circumstance, and eschews a millennarian utopianism while nevertheless claiming to express a visionary impulse. Yet the proposed regime offers an institutional framework within which the principle of deliberate social control over the forms and consequences of economic accumulation can be more fully reconciled with decentralized economic decision making than it can be within a market order using consolidated property as its device of decentralization and occasional administrative regulation as its means of control. The economic order of the empowered democracy is both more a socially responsible economy and more a market economy than the system it is meant to replace; the impression of paradox results from a failure to grasp the effect of institutional variation upon the tensions between general principles. It is more of a socially responsible economy because the means for collective review of the arrangements and results of economic life are deeply integrated into the institutional order rather than dependent upon a relatively haphazard pattern of governmental intervention. It is more of a market economy because it promises to increase both the absolute degree of economic decentralization and the revisability of the organizational settings of production and exchange, although, admittedly, it does so at the cost of circumscribing both the duration and the absoluteness of individual capital claims. Consider now, in greater detail, each of the three major tiers of capital givers and takers.

The Central Capital Fund

The first tier, the social investment fund, falls under the control of the central executive and representative bodies of the empowered democracy. The central social fund establishes the competing investment funds, which form the second tier of the system. It occasionally opens new funds or closes old ones and shifts resources from some to others. But its single most important task is to draw the limits of variation within which the competing investment funds must operate. Some limits are institutional; others, parametric. The institutional decisions set boundaries to the permissible organizational forms of production and exchange. The parametric decisions influence the employment and cost of capital, most notably through the interest charged for its use. Rules and policies that restrict either wage and authority disparities or the right of enterprise personnel to distribute business gains as current income share institutional and parametric characteristics.

Among the key parametric or institutional decisions to be made by the fund are: the basic underlying rate of interest to be charged to all specialized investment funds; the choice between forced reassignments of capital and variable rates of interest as alternative ways to control the relative size of the specialized funds and the relations among gross sectors of the economy; the alternative regimes or terms under which the second-tier, specialized funds may give out capital; the minimal restraints upon accumulation, reinvestment, investment in other enterprises, distribution of profits as income, preference for capital-intensive technology, and exclusion of outside workers that must be respected either in the economy as a whole or by particular funds and sectors; the extent to which the specialized funds may allow the enterprises they deal with to insulate managerial and technical prerogatives from the collective decisions of its members and thereby establish a hierarchy of privilege among segments of its labor force; and the outer limits to wage (or other income) inequality that must be respected by enterprises in the economy as a whole or in particular sectors.

Some decisions may take the form of economywide rules and policies, others may be written into the charters of particular investment funds, and still others may be left entirely open to the discretion of these funds or of the enterprises and teams that receive capital from them. The correct balance among these options, as more generally the relative power of the three tiers of capital givers and capital takers, constitutes a major concern of governmental party-politics under the empowered democracy. The evisceration of the second and third tiers of the system, through the making of increasingly detailed and intrusive decisions, would destroy the distinctive character of this economic regime. The disintegration of property would give way to the transfer of property to the central government. But the abdication of decisional responsibility by the central democratic institutions, and its resulting concentration in the specialized funds and the primary capital takers, would be equally subversive of the regime. For one thing, the democracy would lack effective means to assert ultimate collective control over the two aspects of economic life that are crucial to the character of a society: first, the direction and rate of economic growth, and the consequent balancing of economic and noneconomic goals and of the claims of different generations; and, second, the relations of equality and inequality, of joint responsibility and mutual distancing, allowed to exist in the organization of production and exchange as well as in the distribution of their benefits. For another thing, the division of property rights between the specialized investment funds and the primary capital takers would not long survive if these two levels of the regime were left on their own. A new system of consolidated property rights, in the service of a new plan of entrenched social division and hierarchy, would emerge from an economy reorganized by the more successful funds or enterprises.

The Investment Funds: Capital Auctioning and Capital Rationing

The second tier of the capital regime consists of investment funds established by the national government or the social fund through which government sets economic policy. The investment funds hold capital from the social fund and give it out to the primary capital takers, who represent the third tier of the economic system. Without this intermediate level – at once capital taker and capital giver – the central democratic entities would be forever tempted to exercise a roving, ad hoc economic clientalism, and the prospects for extreme decentralization and organizational diversity would greatly diminish. The investment funds, chartered by the central government, specialize in a sector of the economy or a type of investment (short-term or long-term, low-risk or high-risk, oriented to small ventures or large ventures). But these specialities are not meant to peg the funds at fixed positions in the economic order. Their areas of operation intersect; many funds may compete within the same sectoral or functional area. In fact, within the limits established by the top tier of the system, they may even bid away one another's assets on an investment-fund capital market placed under the control of the central social fund.

The special funds are semi-independent bodies, much like contemporary central banks or even philanthropic foundations in contemporary Western societies, with their technical personnel chosen by a combination of appointment from above and election from the sectors in which they operate. The method of appointment should vary, as later discussion suggests, with the specific aims of each fund and the nature of the system by which it allocates capital. The definition of this system is by far the most important issue to be faced in designing the second tier of the capital order.

In their capital-allotment policies the funds operate with a mixture of general rules and discretionary judgments. The danger that a promising entrepreneur may be turned away is diminished by the existence of numerous overlapping and competing funds. And if this opportunity seems insufficient remember that even under the regime of consolidated property an entrepreneur must either already be rich or succeed in convincing others to give him money.

Each fund conducts its activities under one of two regimes: capital auction and capital rationing or rotation. The choice between them, set by the fund charter, has far-reaching consequences for the role of the fund in the economy and for the structure of its dealings with other funds and with the primary capital takers. The interaction between the two regimes influences the whole character of the economic order of an empowered democracy.

The key feature of the capital-auction system is that, within certain gross limits, the primary capital takers can buy one another's resources by offering to pay the capital-auctioning fund more for the employment of these resources than their current users. If the value of the resources has been run up, part of this added value may be paid to the current users as a reward, though it may then be subject to capital, income, and consumption taxes designed to restrain the resulting economic inequality. (Notice that the tax system, which becomes subsidiary to state-charged interest as a source of governmental finance under empowered democracy, must reappear as a constraint on inequality in the capital-auctioning area of the economy.) To guard against the continued depletion of assets, on the other hand, the capital-auctioning fund must use a blend of screening guarantees, penalties, limits on the distribution of profits, and provisions for repossession.

The capital-rationing or rotation system, by contrast to the capital-auction system, largely avoids the buying-out of some capital takers by others. Instead, it emphasizes the conditional and temporal limits to the capital taker's employment of the resources placed at his disposal. It demands a much heavier use of parametric constraints than can be reconciled with the capital-auction regime: the setting of standards about the minimal levels of permissible reinvestment and maximum levels of allowable profit distribution. The capital-rationing fund must be ready to take the initiative in pooling financial and capital resources, in bringing teams of worker-technicians and entrepreneurs together for large-scale, durable enterprises, in redistributing capital from time to time to new teams, and in designing incentives and disincentives.

As under the capital-auction system, successful enterprises cannot be allowed to build industrial or financial empires. Once certain limits of personal enrichment and enterprise investment are reached, the additional capital goes back to the original capital fund for reassignment. But much more clearly than under the capital-auction system, continuing enterprise decline must be met by fund intervention, followed by the recovery and reassignment of the residual capital and the reentry of a retrained enterprise work force into the labor market, a blow softened though not annulled by the welfare rights described later in this chapter.

The advantage of the capital-auction system is that it maximizes opportunities for the trial and error of entrepreneurial decisions. Its danger, for the program of empowered democracy, is that it jeopardizes social control over economic accumulation and economic inequality. The advantages and disadvantages of capital rationing are just the reverse.

To identify this dilemma may seem tantamount to recognizing the persistence of the tension between social control and market decentralization under the economic regime of empowered democracy. But remember that the point of this whole programmatic argument is less to abolish the basic tensions familiar to our vocabulary of ideological controversy than to change their sense and moderate their force. Both capital auctioning and capital rationing reconcile market decentralization and social control more fully than the inherited combination of property-based markets and administrative regulation, although they do so by different means and in different proportions. The auction and rationing regimes encourage this reconciliation more effectively through their combination than either could alone.

Some capital funds, possibly in the more standardized sectors of the economy, would operate primarily on the model of rationing, whereas others, possibly in the more experimental areas of manufacturing and services, would follow the capital-auction model. In this way the whole economy would benefit from an ongoing experiment with these alternative styles of market organization.

Because a rationing fund exercises a much stronger influence over the economic fortunes of its capital takers than does a capital auctioning fund, it should give them a major role in its decision making. The fund and its recipients may form a veritable industrial confederation, subject to both the pressure of conflicting interests within the confederation and the demands of the central democratic agencies. By contrast, an auctioning fund may be expected to keep more clearly apart from its capital takers. It stands in some ways in the position of an investment bank dealing with its clients and in other ways in that of a governmental agency supervising a capital market, except that here no one exercises absolute and permanent control over any portion of capital. These last remarks carry the discussion from the second to the third tier of the system: the primary capital takers with whom both auctioning and rationing funds deal.

The Primary Capital Takers: Problems of Scale and Incentives

Within limits set by the capital-giving fund, the capital users transact freely with one another. Theirs is a market system, though the specific quality of their decision-making autonomy depends upon the extent to which they operate under the auction or the rationing regimes. Either regime, however, provides the enterprise work force with the conditions for exercising a crucial say about the organization of work and about the range of income and power disparities. It is only required that these decisions remain within the ample boundaries established by the higher tiers of the economic order.

Under the auction regime the power to organize production is evident: the auctioning fund can more easily leave its users to their own devices. It is more concerned with long-term rates of return and organizational or technological breakthrough and experiments than with the maintenance of any particular system of work organization. Under the rationing regime the independence of capital takers is more restricted. But the counterpart to these restrictions becomes greater engagement of the capital takers in the governance of their fund.

Under both regimes the capital-taking unit is a team that, as a whole, receives capital grants or bids capital away from other users. Within ample bounds it remains free to govern its internal relations. Moreover, the entire economic order of dissociated property deprives the mass-production industries of the instruments with which they protect themselves against instability in their product, capital, and labor markets. It thereby favors extending into the mainstream of the economy a style of organization previously confined to the economy's experimental vanguard and distinguished by a closer and more continuous interplay between task-defining and task-executing activities.

Neither the auction nor the rationing regime, however, turns its clients into new individual or collective property owners. The economic system of empowered democracy is not worker corporatism. The individual worker does not even have an absolute or permanent right to job tenure within his enterprise or team, and the enterprise or team has no absolute or permanent right to the resources temporarily put at its disposal or to the wealth it accumulates through their use. But every citizen does have an unconditional right to the satisfaction of his legally defined minimal welfare needs (see the later discussion of immunity rights), qualified only by the size of the welfare fund available to government, which is in turn influenced by the price charged for the use of capital and by the decisions made about the basic desired rate of economic growth.

The discussion of the third tier of the reformed economy raises two problems deserving more detailed analysis and influencing the operation of the economy as a whole. One problem is the compatibility of the proposed system with economies of scale. The other is its probable effect upon the motivation to work.

Many forms of economic activity will always require the pooling of large-scale resources in manpower, technology, and financial capital and the continuity of enterprises over long periods. But the resulting concentration of workers, capital, and machines need not have the familiar characteristics of contemporary mass-production industry, operating under a system of absolute property rights.

Large-scale enterprises may be relatively loose confederations of teams or units that move in and out of a particular enterprise, just as an entire capital-rationing fund may be a loose confederation of these enterprises. Such an organizational scheme would combine flexibility with pooling to an extent still uncommon in the contemporary practice of mass-production industry. Yet it would merely exaggerate an already discernible tendency in some of the more innovative large-scale businesses. Many such enterprises have organized themselves into small-scale, tenuously integrated units, each emulating the organizational style of the smaller, more flexible, vanguardist enterprises that proliferate in the high-technology and service sectors. The influence of technological evolution favors this tendency while the managerial and financial interests generated by property-based market and work-organization systems continue to frustrate it. We cannot reasonably expect to tell in advance exactly which current characteristics of large-scale and continuous enterprise would change under an institutional reform like the one proposed here, and which would prove to result from more intractable economic, organizational, or psychological constraints.

There is at least one other foreseeable effect of the dissociation of property rights for the conduct of large-scale business. Such a system prevents managers from exercising a broad-ranging discretionary authority over their workers that confuses the requirements of technical coordination with the right to act in the name of property (whether the private property of stockholders or the public property of an economically sovereign state), a right fitfully restrained by explicit or implicit collective bargaining. Nor may the enterprise work force under the proposed system entrench itself against disadvantaged or jobless workers from outside or hire them to occupy a subordinate status. The common association of mass-production industry with a distinction between a core, almost tenured work force and a variable periphery of unstable workers or subcontractors violates the spirit of the economic system described here. Such a distinction would quickly generate a hierarchy of vested interests, benefiting workers entrenched in the more successful sectors and enterprises. And it would constrain the opportunities for organizational innovation and ceaseless recombination.

There is indeed a price to pay for avoiding such privileges and constraints. Neither individuals nor groups would be able to nurture distinctive forms of life that are based upon the permanent occupancy of stereotyped positions in the social division of labor. But there are compensations. The attempt to develop varieties of practical collaboration less dependent upon a preestablished set of social roles, hierarchies, and divisions is more than a practical goal; it is a major aspect of the ideal underlying this entire argument for empowered democracy. It would not be a powerful ideal if it did not also promise a special sort of happiness. I explore the character of this happiness when dealing, in the final part of this chapter, with the spirit that inspires this whole institutional program.

Consider, finally, the effect of these economic institutions upon the motivation to work. The economic system outlined in the preceding pages allows for a large range of variation in the income rewards to particular capital takers. Under both the auction and the rationing regimes the individual prospers with the economic success of his team and suffers with its economic failure. Moreover, within the limits established by the central and specialized funds each team is free to establish economic rewards and penalties.

The conflict between incentives to diligence, on one side, and egalitarian or welfare goals, on the other, is not abolished. At the very least, however, it becomes a subject of explicit collective experiment and discussion at each tier of the capital-allocation system. The reformers may even hope to moderate the conflict by diminishing the dependence of work incentives upon stark inequalities of wealth and income. For many aspects of the proposed regime are calculated to universalize within society the conditions encouraging people to shift the focus of their ambitions from the accumulation of a patrimony to the shape of a career and to the slightest nuances in the semblance of worldly success. The result is not spiritual redemption. But it does help push motivations beyond the obsessions peculiar to a society in which people feel unable to distinguish their most vital interests from their continued hold upon a particular type of job.

This eclectic and open-minded approach to the problem of incentives and inequality illustrates the general attitude of the whole programmatic argument toward the mutability of human nature. The view of society and personality that informs this argument refuses the consistently disappointing and misleading attempt to distinguish a permanent core and a variable periphery of human nature. It takes into account the loose, contradictory, and complex set of motivations and aspirations that people demonstrate in the societies it wants to reform. It recognizes that even the most intimate and seemingly unyielding of these propensities are influenced and cumulatively remade by the institutional and imaginative context in which they exist. But it rejects as unrealistic any institutional scheme whose success requires a sudden and drastic shift in what people are like here and now.

Contrast with an Inheritance-Free Property System

The whole character of the democratized economy stands out by comparison to a system that preserves the traditional mix of property-based markets and ad hoc regulation but that limits private fortunes by abolishing inheritance and levying a heavy capital tax. The economic program of empowered democracy also abolishes the hereditary transmission of substantial assets. Each individual would be given instead a wide range of minimal welfare guarantees, including support during job transfers and opportunities for ongoing reeducation and retraining. What the mere abolition of inheritance cannot do, however, is to develop an economic order congenial to the spirit of empowered democracy. It cannot open ordinary social life to the same practice of collective conflict and deliberation that people experience in the exercise of citizenship. It cannot turn the arrangements of production and exchange into subjects of deliberate social experimentation and thereby give a practical as well as an ideal sense to the conception of a formative context more freely open to revision in the midst of ordinary social life. It cannot knock the institutional props out from under a style of industrial organization that continues to emphasize the discontinuity between task-defining and task-executing activities. It cannot cleanly sever the link between the ability to take advantage of economies of scale and the opportunity to command large numbers of workers in the name of property: for while an inheritance-free system does away with magnates, the managers of great businesses may have all the freer a hand as the fictive delegates of countless petty holders of equity. It cannot overcome, though it may diminish, the conflict between the rewards for economic achievement and the methods for ensuring basic social equality. The redistributive state would still have to intervene through tax-and-transfer policies. Thus, the logic of rough equality and the flow of actual market outcomes would remain far more starkly opposed than the need for incentives to work requires or than the economic order of a radical democracy permits.

Supplementary Ideas

A number of subsidiary or qualifying ideas help fill out this institutional picture. Remember first that the proposed regime should not be misunderstood as a compromise between a centralized ("command") and decentralized ("market") economy. It should be taken instead as a proposal to provide both the market economy and the social control of economic forces with alternative institutional definitions. From the mere fact that this alternative system provides for the central institutional and parametric decisions I have described, you cannot legitimately infer it would result in markets less decentralized (i. e., with fewer and less independent decision-making agents) than the Western-style economies of the late twentieth century. Such central institutional and parametric decisions are also made in those economies, only in a fashion more fragmentary, invisible, and invidious because susceptible to being either manipulated or overridden by privileged social groups. The forms of this decision making range from the unstable conduct of discretionary economic policy within the institutional limits described to the marginal legislation of a system of contract and property falsely equated with the very nature of a market. Such choices are also made within a constitutional structure that disempowers collective action and deliberation in the many ways pointed out by the internal arguments explored at the beginning of this chapter. Moreover, by their selective character, their underlying vision of what a market has to be, and their mistaken assumptions about the requirements of industrial efficiency, these decisions permit the emergence of vast centers of private power that also represent constraints upon decentralization.

But once you set aside the polemical comparison between the Western-type economies and the alternative system, you still have to acknowledge the presence of powerful centralizing tendencies within the economic regime of empowered democracy. Unless compensated, such tendencies can pervert the democratizing program. (The next section discusses both these tendencies and their antidotes.)

A second clarifying idea is that the fidelity of the regime of capital to its goals depends closely upon the implementation of the other, more narrowly constitutional part of the republican program. Only such a reformed government can be technically capable of performing these enlarged responsibilities. Only such a government can resist more effectively the risk of becoming the instrument by which particular groups transform temporary advantage into lasting privilege.

The third auxiliary idea is that the realization of such a regime of capital presupposes a different background order of right. In particular, it presupposes the disaggregation of the consolidated property right. This disaggregation takes place in two related ways. First, the different powers that appear merged within the consolidated property right get pulled apart. To take the single most obvious and important point, the employment of large amounts of capital is always conditional and temporary and the recipients' powers of use always coexist with the powers of the administrators of the social capital fund and of the competing investment funds.

The other aspect of the disaggregation of property is therefore the assignment of these separated powers to different entities: the three tiers of capital givers and capital takers. There is nothing novel about disaggregation in either of these senses; the consolidated property right, after all, represents an artifact of particular traditions. In most legal orders, in most historical periods, property always has been disaggregated in both these senses. What matters for the program, however, is that the disaggregation takes the particular form that suits a democratised economy.

THE ORGANIZATION OF THE ECONOMY: THE DANGER OF CENTRALIZATION AND ITS ANTIDOTES

The capital regime just outlined has certain centralizing tendencies that, if left unchecked, would pervert the whole system. The presence and peril of these tendencies become the more obvious once you enlarge the ideas of centralization and decentralization. Decentralization refers, at a minimum, both to the number of agents who are able to trade and produce on their initiative and for their own account and to the extent of their independence. This second element may be expanded to include the extent of variety in the conduct of economic affairs: variety in the ways of doing business, organizing work, variety even in the results of labor, variety measured chiefly by the margin of departure from what most other economic agents do. This is the sort of decentralization that the normal regime of capital chiefly endangers.

It does not help to say that this recentralizing impulse is no more hostile to economic pluralism than are contemporary economic systems. Whatever comparison may show, the centralist tendencies are noxious in themselves. They undermine the economy's capacity to achieve repeated breakthroughs in output and productivity, a capacity that depends largely upon the persistent exercise of an almost frenzied inventiveness applied to the very context and structure of productive activity. The centralizing tendencies also threaten the basic aims of the constitution. Once the internal arrangements and external strategies of economic organizations stabilize into a single dominant mode, they favor the emergence of well-defined groups, formed on the basis of rigid conceptions of collective interest, identity, and opportunity. Each organization, each segment of economic life, becomes a little world whose structure mirrors the arrangements of all the little worlds with which it coexists and collides. That repeated pattern, supported by central power, supplies the mold in which the group divisions and hierarchies can form.

Apart from any genuine technical constraints of economy by scale and repetition, two main centralizing forces operate within the normal regime of capital. One centralizing dynamic merely works out the implications of the threat that the reemergence of well-defined groups poses to the constitution.

The normal regime of capital applies in principle throughout the economy. It establishes a distinctive style of control and decentralization. However indeterminate the institutional implications of this style may be and however significant the margin of autonomy allowed to the individual enterprises, this approach to the relation between central economic authorities and decentralized economic agents may become the basis for a dominant type of enterprise organization and enterprise dealing. A casual combination of biases and transitory market circumstances may turn into an enduring mode of industrial organization. The parties elected to office may then adjust the parametric and institutional decisions so as to favor this dominant type and thereby further consolidate its ascendancy. With this, a renewed, subtle version of the politics of privilege emerges. The dominant enterprise type readily becomes a system of niches in which economic groups can form. The most favored and the most numerous, if they are also most numerous or most favored in the society at large, can then attempt to use governmental power to entrench their advantages. Thus, the state would become an enemy to deviant types of business organization and once again help turn the occasional disadvantages of some segments of the work force into continuing subordination. This outcome would jeopardize both the specific goal of avoiding unconditional claims upon capital and the general commitment to avoid the reappearance of a stabilized plan of social division and hierarchy.

The other dynamic of centralization is internal to the government itself. The governmental bodies that make the institutional and parametric decisions belong to a scheme designed to perpetuate, multiply, and extend collective mobilization. This mobilizational context, however, may be insufficient to prevent the assertion of a bureaucratic interest in the transparency and stability of the economic order. Once the basic decisions about the parametric and institutional bases of economic activity stop being fragmentary and implicit, they become all the more subject to a characteristic bias. The administrative foundation of this bias is everyone's desire to cover his tracks in a realm where public scrutiny and controversy are intense. Its general form is the tendency to treat variation first as folly and then as an immoral assault upon the collective interest. Its economic manifestation is the intolerance toward radical disagreements about the risks that are reasonable for a business to take, disagreements whose very occurrence represents one of the conditions of continued economic progress. The chosen institutions and parameters may be more or less deliberately rigged against deviant risk schedules and systematically increase the dimension of risk relative to the margin of deviation. Many kinds of risk taking may even be intentionally prohibited as irresponsible or indirectly excluded by their incompatibility with the institutional or parametric requirements imposed from on high.

No constitutional scheme can guarantee itself, once and for all, against the renascence of a politics of privilege. Conflict produces winners and losers. The winners will try to keep their own prizes and abolish their own example, and so long as a central state exists, they will find ready at hand an instrument with which to do so. It would be unwise, even if it were possible, to destroy a central government if you understand such a government simply as the terrain on which people can fight about the basic terms of collective life and carry their opinions into practice. For the risk of a mutual reinforcement between privileged access to the state and privileged advantage in society is overshadowed by the danger that a structure of social life may emerge that cannot be revised by any readily available means at all: the naturalization of society is the peculiar risk of statelessness. To justify the destruction of a distant central government, a circumstance would have to arise in which people's material and moral connections to one another were so completely contained in a narrow social and geographical area that the structure of their social existence would be wholly determined by what went on within this circle. But this reduction of the polity to a metaphorical if not a literal village would mean the naturalization of society with a vengeance: the turning away from the larger clash of alternative visions and versions of society, the eternal dream of those who want to get off the roller coaster of history.

Short of statelessness, no society can protect itself against the reappearance of the politics of privilege. So, too, as institutions become the explicit contexts and instruments for revising the basic terms of social life, the reorganized economy confronts the other centralizing danger: that parties and governments, armed with new opportunities to try out their proposals, may exclude too much random or dissident variation. The result may be to impoverish the practical and imaginative resources available to the programs of another day. The generic antidote the constitution of the reformed republic gives to these perils is the twofold effort to achieve the maximum incitement to conflictual collective mobilization outside governmental institutions while obtaining the greatest permeability of governmental institutions to the results of this mobilization. An approach to voluntary association that draws its strength from mere opposition to the state cannot be secure – for it lives under threat from rulers at home and powers abroad. Nor can it freely transform social life in its own image – for it comes up against institutional limits it can overcome only by perennially defeating or neutralizing the state. Thus, the need to imagine a state with a built-in bias toward the self-organization of society.

The preceding discussion has shown that the generic risks of the appeal to an empowered democratic state take distinctive forms in the economic domain. The compensations must be correspondingly specific. One such compensation is the provision for an extraordinary regime of capital, to exist alongside the ordinary one. The most basic antidote, however, is the existence of the intermediate tier of the capital-allotment system: the specialized competitive investment funds, which shield the primary capital takers from ad hoc or detailed governmental control. They operate with a vast array of different sets of investment policies and different combinations of institutional and parametric constraints. They span the distance from maximal guidance to minimal checks. Moreover, the auction or rationing regimes they follow represent two radically different versions of market organization.

THE ORGANIZATION OF THE ECONOMY: THE DESIGN OF WORK

There is another compensation to the perils of centralism and monotony: the effect of the constitution upon the organization of work. The importance of such an effect goes far beyond the problem of decentralization. The organization of the workplace represents the area in which the striving for social control of economic activity and permanent collective mobilization most clearly confronts the demands of practical effectiveness in a highly mechanized and industrialised economy. The character of ordinary work experience also either strengthens or undermines the psychological dispositions on which the constitution depends; more than any other aspect of social existence, except the family, it serves as the school of everyday life and teaches the only lessons that ordinary people in ordinary times cannot easily forget.

The proliferation of the flexible version of rationalized collective labor matters to this enriched idea of decentralization in several ways. The flexible style of work organization, with its softening of the contrast between supervisors and supervised, can flourish in large enterprises and plants (offices, stores, outlets) or small ones. But the rigid type favors the large enterprise and the large plant or office: large enterprises, to permit and justify successive infusions of capital; large plants or offices, to organize the work force in the fashion of a conventional army. Moreover, the flexible mode encourages the proliferation of divergent forms of production by making it unnecessary to subordinate experiments in the organization of work to the maintenance of a fixed structure of control. In this sense, it does for the organization of work what the breakup of oligarchic control of government does for the society as a whole.

Each economic system criticized in the preceding section enshrines the rigid variant of rationalized collective labor as the mainstream form of work organization and relegates the flexible variant to the vanguard of industry, administration, and warfare. Elsewhere I have argued that the overwhelming predominance of the rigid variant cannot plausibly be understood as a consequence of the inherent organizational requirements of technologically advanced, large-scale industry and warfare. It depends, on the contrary, upon the fulfillment of certain social and technical-economic conditions. It may help to recall briefly what these conditions, in the industrial sphere, are, and how they came to be satisfied by the Western-style economies of the post-World War II period.

The social conditions include both a negative and a positive element. The negative element was the defeat of the social movements that threatened to overturn, at a single stroke, the constitutionalism of permanent demobilization, the quasi-oligarchic control of basic investment decisions, and the rigid contrast between task definers and task executors at work. The positive element was the development of an order of right that – in the name of both property and technical necessity (each covering for the other) – distinguished the task definers from everybody else. In so doing, this order also conflated technical coordination with a broad disciplinary authority, limited only by the collective contracts struck by an unevenly organized work force. The technical-economic condition was the avoidance of the various forms of economic instability that would jeopardize the large-scale, mass-production industries operating largely with product-specific machines and relatively inflexible production processes. In these industries, the rigid variant of rationalized collective labor prevailed. They sank successive amounts of capital into product lines, production processes, and even work arrangements that could not easily be altered. The combination of deepening capital investment with structural inflexibility made these enterprises all too vulnerable to the disruptive effects of instability in the financial, product, and labor markets. Against the instability of financial markets they employed the generation of internal investment funds. Against the convergent effect of instability in labor and product markets, they developed ways to reconcile the maintenance of a relatively privileged and pacified labor force (working to produce for the unstable part of demand) with the deployment of outside subcontractors or occasional, unorganized laborers, who absorbed, on the front line, the shock of downturn and helped fill burgeoning orders during booms.

The economic order of the reformed republic knocks the props out from under each of these social or technical-economic encouragements to the prevalence of the rigid variant of rationalized collective labor. It does so as an automatic consequence of the institutional arrangements it establishes. The attack upon the stabilizing conditions of the established style of work organization does not guarantee that the flexible variant will prevail throughout the economy. It merely destroys the bias in favor of the rigid mode and facilitates different versions of the continuous interplay between task definition and task execution to take hold in many sectors of the economy. Consider just how the proposed economic system subverts each of the conditions mentioned; the argument moves in the reverse order of the earlier enumeration.

Take the technical-economic conditions first. The recourse to internally generated investment funds is drastically curtailed by the overall method of assigning capital conditionally as well as by the limits on enterprise accumulation. In fact, the assignment of capital will even be subject to terms that affirmatively require efforts to moderate the contrasts between task-defining and task-executing activities and among job categories in general. The interconnected defenses against instability in the labor and products markets cannot survive the measures designed to limit job exclusivity within the enterprise, the shift in the fundamental status of workers, and the open-minded favor to all manner of small and medium-size enterprises.

Consider now the affirmative element in the social conditions for the predominance of the rigid style of work organization. The whole constitutional scheme takes away the legal basis for concentrating in a few hands the power to direct other people's labor: its goals, forms, and rewards. To prevent the emergence of economic entitlements that enable individuals to control large amounts of labor, property must be disaggregated in the sense defined earlier: not handed over lock, stock, and barrel to the capitalist, the government, or the enterprise work force. Disaggregate property (rather than transfer it) is what the reformed regime of capital does.

Finally, take the negative aspect of the social conditions of contrasting styles of work organization. The inauguration of such a radical democratic program would mean reversing the defeat of the revolutionary movements and leftist experiments that took place throughout Europe in the aftermath of World War I. Despite the relative crudity of their programmatic ideas, these experiments and movements came closer than any other episode of collective conflict to articulating the very vision this transformative program develops. The program represents, in a sense, the development of what they left vague and confused. Its implementation presupposes the victory of which they were robbed. The previous discussion of transformative practice and the later analysis of transitional institutional arrangements suggest how this victory may be won.

13

The System of Rights: Four Rights

THE SYSTEM OF RIGHTS

Redefining Rights

The system of rights represents a distinctive domain for institutional reconstruction. By a system of rights I mean simply an institutionalized version of society, which is to say, a form of social life acquiring a relatively stable and delineated form and generating a complicated set of expectations. The stability and the expectations are not merely those of the prison camp: a system of rights defines arrangements that many people (how many?) treat as the expression of a defensible scheme of human association. The organized social world that a system of rights describes is not presented and understood primarily as a collection of mere truce lines or trophies in ongoing social and party warfare. Each such social world seeks to provide the exclusive setting of human life and, though it invariably fails in its attempt at exclusivity, it succeeds enough, while it survives, to shape beliefs and motivations as well as opportunities and practices.

We have come to think of the vocabulary of rights as ordinarily limited to the legal definition of institutions and practices and therefore to state-described and state-enforced law. The following discussion presupposes this narrower conception of right while effacing the clarity of its boundaries. For the system of rights described here is meant to transcribe an institutional structure that weakens the contrast between state and civil society just as it softens the opposition between devotion to the common good and the pursuit of private interests.

The remaking of the system of rights is not a separate task of institutional reconstruction, as if we could change the constitutional form of government, the style of conflict over the control and uses of governmental power, the regime of capital, the organization of work, and *then* the content and form of legal entitlements. It is rather the indispensable expression of all those other changes. But this expression is not transparent or automatic. It poses specific problems and clarifies hidden connections.

Consider two objections radicals frequently make to any program for the redefinition of legal entitlements. To anticipate a response to these objections is to indicate the direction taken by this stage of the programmatic argument.

One source of hostility to theories of legal rights is the belief that rights, any rights, are inseparable from a particular type of social and economic organization – such as "capitalism" – that can and should be overcome. In a more inclusive variant of the argument, legal rights become a form of social regulation inherently suited to a particular social practice – such as the market exchange of commodities and of labor. Though the critic acknowledges that this law-sustaining practice may exist in a broad range of societies, he insists it cannot be reconciled with other types of social organization and especially not with the type (e.g., communism) to which he is committed. All versions of this objection rely upon the idea of a limited and well-defined list of possible types of social organization, a characteristic theme of deep-logic social theory. They depend even more directly on the unjustified identification of rights with a particular style of entitlement, with what I earlier called the consolidated property right.

These critics know perfectly well that every body of law includes entitlements that differ in content from consolidated property rights. They may even acknowledge that differences in the content of rights and in the character of the social activity to which rights apply influence the ways in which entitlements are created and interpreted. But they drastically underestimate the extent to which legal entitlements may differ, in form and content, in different legal systems. Like their conservative adversaries, they allow themselves to be beguiled by the imaginative dominance of the consolidated property right as a model to which all entitlements in all legal systems must conform. The programmatic argument about rights developed here claims that the construction of an empowered democracy requires the elaboration of types of legal entitlements differing, in form as well as content, both from one another and from the consolidated property right, that there are no obvious insuperable conceptual or practical obstacles to development of these alternative models of rights, and that the rudiments of such alternatives can already be found in current legal thought and practice.

If this first objection to rights theories reflects a sociological radicalism preoccupied with the built-in constraints of social types, a second objection arises from a modernist or existentialist radicalism. It denounces rights not for serving a particular institutional order but simply for establishing any institutional order. The radicalism that underlies this objection believes we achieve freedom only by a ceaseless struggle against all institutional routines. Such a vision recognizes the disproportion between our capabilities and the limited social or mental contexts in which we attempt to exercise them. But its great weakness is its failure to come to terms with the imperative of contextuality. We must in the end inhabit a particular social world, and we can never perform the act of denial often or quickly enough to prevent individual and social experience from being largely, though not entirely or ultimately, governed by the practices and assumptions of the world we live in. Nevertheless, the argument for the empowered democracy and for its system of rights rescues something from the wreck of this self-defeating ideal. It preserves the conception that formative contexts of power and production vary in the extent to which they respect and encourage our context-smashing abilities and enable us to exercise a vigilant and self-conscious mastery over the collective settings of individual activity. The system of legal rights outlined here defines a society that diminishes the dazed, narcoleptic quality of routinized social life and does so for the sake of a vision of individual and collective empowerment. Each detail of this set of legal entitlements connects back to this seemingly empty but in fact inspiring ideal.

The Trouble with the Established System of Legal Rights

What is the trouble with the established system of legal rights? From the standpoint of the criticism and the vision that underlie this whole institutional program, the trouble can be summarized by a single fact: the practical and imaginative ascendancy of the consolidated property right. The consolidated property right that exercises this overwhelming influence can be defined by both its content and its form. In content it is the principle of economic decentralization that consists in the allocation of more or less unrestricted claims to divisible portions of social capital: unrestricted both in the chain of temporal succession and in the scope of permitted usage. To be sure, the law has always recognized limits to this absolute discretion, just as in the counterpart area of contract it has always tried to restrain the dominant principles of freedom to choose the partner and the contract terms. But these qualifications remain anomalies. They acknowledge the existence in current society of forms of human association irreducible to the central categories of property and contract. They show that the co-existence of absolute property rights generates practical problems that cannot be solved by more absolute property rights. But they do not present alternative, developed models of entitlement.

Consolidated property right works its restrictive influence most directly through its relation to a version of the market economy that stands in the way of an advance toward greater economic plasticity and even toward greater degrees of economic decentralization. The result is not only to circumscribe unnecessarily the opportunity for permanent economic innovation but also to reproduce an ongoing conflict between the practice of democracy and the organization of the economy. Democratic control over the forms, pace, and result of economic accumulation is undercut while the contrast between task-defining and task-executing jobs turns the workplace into a permanent countermodel to the exercise of democratic citizenship.

The continuing authority of consolidated property also exercises a more indirect influence. By identifying the abstract principle of economic decentralization with a particular version of market institutions, it drastically restricts our vision of the possible alternatives to current market systems.

The imagined alternatives – the transfer of undivided economic sovereignty to central governments or the attempt to cast the workers in each enterprise as the holders of consolidated property in their own business – jeopardize public freedoms and economic dynamism in all the ways previously discussed. And the basic institutional choice seems to be the selection of a mix of economic centralism and decentralization. But the radical who has freed himself from the vestiges of deep-logic social theory and the spell of a particular theory of rights knows that any given mix of centralism and decentralization can assume different institutional forms. Thus, the functional and imaginative centrality of consolidated property within the system of rights contributes to the negative prejudice that underlies some of the paradoxes discussed in my earlier account of the genesis of the private-rights complex. Though the received system of private rights provides some people with the instruments with which to reduce other people to dependence, though it coexists with other rights that pose no such threat (welfare and civic entitlements), and though it needs to be combined with methods of organizational surveillance and hierarchy that nullify or reverse its overt meaning, it may nevertheless seem indispensable. Any attempt to replace it may seem bound to cause tyranny and inefficiency. The polemic against this negative prejudice can be completed only by a proposed system of rights that defies the negative prejudice on which the "realistic" defense of current institutions depends.

The prejudicial effect of the influence exercised by the consolidated property right does not stop at the direct and indirect contributions of consolidated property to a certain organization of the economy. It also exercises a broader, more intangible influence because it readily becomes a model for rights dealing with matters far removed from the methods for economic decentralization. It provides a form that, once abstracted from its specific content, is reproduced in almost every area of thinking about rights. The absolute portion of capital delineates a zone within which the property owner may act as he pleases, no matter what the consequences of his actions, and outside of which he may expect no protection, no matter how appealing his claim. The boundaries of such a right are primarily defined, at the moment of its creation, by law or contract; the relational setting in which the right is to be exercised remains largely irrelevant to its definition; thus, the discretionary action constituting the heart of this model of entitlement may be circumscribed but cannot be eviscerated. The definition of the right must be connected to its application by a rulelike or principled method of adjudication that can keep under control both open-ended normative controversy and complex causal analysis. The source of the right must be suited to the decontextualization that characterizes its later life: the unilateral imposition of a duty by the state, the fully articulated act of will, or some combination of the two.

The effect of attempting to cast all rights in this mold is to force large areas of existing social practice into incongruous legal forms. Thus, the obligations arising from relations of mutual interdependence are governed by contractual and delictual incrustations upon a body of law obsessed with instantaneous contracts and confrontations between hypothetical strangers. The organization of work in large-scale institutions is treated either as the beneficiary of a paternalist police power or as the parallel to a regime of free contract. The need to combine widespread supervisory discretion with at least the facade of a regime of contract is in turn justified as a requirement of impersonal technical necessity.

Why does the legal form of the consolidated property right exercise the influence I have just described? You need not conjecture that this influence betrays a conspiracy of judges and jurists to maintain the property regime or that it demonstrates the unconscious subjection of motives and beliefs to the functional requirements for the reproduction of an established social order. Each type of legal right represents, even in its most formal aspects, the incomplete but significant picture of a certain model of human association. The stubborn understatement of existing, much less possible, diversity in the form and substance of legal rights is a version of the idolatry of the actual. It shows a failure to grasp the extent to which the models of human association already accepted in the less practical parts of social life (the exercise of democratic citizenship and the life of family and friendship) offer imaginative points of departure for the remaking of practical institutions.

The Generative Principles of a Reconstructed System of Rights

Two basic constructive principles inform a system of rights that gives legal form to the governmental and economic institutions of an empowered democracy and escapes, once and for all, the confining example of consolidated property.

The first and basic constructive principle is that the security of the individual should be established in ways that minimize both the immunity of institutional arrangements to challenge and conflict and the ease with which some individuals can reduce others to dependence. The meaning of this principle can be brought out by a brief discussion of its elements: the security of the individual, the avoidance of social petrification, and the antidote to dependence.

The security of the individual is his justified confidence that the conflicts of the republic will not put at risk his most intimate concerns with physical security, minimal material welfare, and protection against subjugation by any public or private power. The individual remains secure only if he enjoys basic freedoms to express himself and to combine with other people, most especially to combine with them for the purpose of influencing the future form of society. Security requires that the individual feel assured that overwhelming practical need will not periodically threaten him with poverty or force him to submit to a superior power.

The commitment of empowered democracy to expand the scope of context-revising conflict makes it all the more important to assure the individual that his basic security, and the security of those closest to him, will be protected. If he lacks this assurance, the institutionalized controversies and reinventions of social life will quickly become intolerable to him and he will see each as a threat to himself. Of course, nothing can ensure that the institutions guaranteeing the immunity of the individual will not be undermined, but only in the trivial sense that nothing can entirely prevent any institutional arrangement from being changed.

If the attempt to give the constitution a transcendent basis may prove temporarily useful, it may also turn out to be dangerous once transcendent justifications go out of fashion. If an antimobilizational style of politics seems to diminish the risk that any arrangements, including those that guarantee immunity, will be altered, it does so only by producing dangers of its own. No contribution to public freedoms is more important than the attempt to make them rest on a basis that puts the fewest possible constraints upon experimentation with the institutional forms of social life. In this way, they need not be jeopardized every time conflict produces change. And because the entrenchment of practices and arrangements that cannot easily be challenged and altered usually goes hand in hand with the development of structures of dependence and domination, the rebellion against these structures can easily turn into an attack upon the protections of immunity.

Though the constitution of the empowered democracy requires an effective defense of immunity, it is not compatible with all possible views of security. The individual may, for example, feel that his vital sense of protection requires that he live in a quiescent polity and that he have at his disposal private wealth in the form of consolidated property rights. He may even feel he is secure only if he has a lifelong guarantee to occupy a particular job or to live in the manner customary to a certain caste. The constitution of the empowered democracy expresses a social and personal ideal incompatible with this version of the ideal of security. Like all our other ideas about ourselves, subjective conceptions of security are stubbornly held, and no single set of facts serves to disprove them. But if the ideals and understanding underlying this institutional program hold up, people will have reason to change their views of what essential security consists in. They and, if not they, their children will discover that the security that matters does not require the maintenance of a narrowly defined mode of life. They reach this conclusion in part by finding senses and varieties of security compatible with an ever greater jumbling up of distinct styles of life and in part by awakening to a conception of the personality as both dependent upon context and strengthened through context smashing.

It may be objected that any arrangement for securing immunity, must be, by definition, an institutional practice not open to revision. But this objection misses the key point. The institutional interpretations and foundations of security differ in the measure of their abstractability: that is to say, in the extent to which they can be disengaged from a complex texture of social life. At one extreme, the safeguard of individual immunity may consist in the intangibility of a particular way of life, defined by the position a group occupies within a well-defined communal and hierarchical order. At the other extreme, it may consist in a set of rights whose main demand upon the other parts of the social order is that they lay themselves open to challenge and revision and that they contribute to the overcoming of the gap between contextualized routine and context revision. Along the spectrum defined by these two poles, the rights afforded by empowered democracy have the same relation to a property-based rights system that absolute property has to inherited ranks. The point is to diminish the extent that safeguarding security rigidifies social life and thereby helps reproduce inflexible roles and ranks. A major theme of the programmatic argument developed here is that, in a particular circumstance, with its available stock of available institutional practices and models of human association, this seemingly vague ideal can be made to yield affirmative proposals. And so, too, one task of the system of rights is to give a distinct content to the seemingly empty idea of a more abstractable immunity right.

From even the little that has been said it should be clear that differences in the abstractability of the institutions that establish the immunity of the individual are not just isolated technical features of certain arrangements. They represent both rival interpretations of the meaning of security and causal conjectures about the most effective way to realize in fact this particular ideal of security. In both guises they exemplify the general views of society and personality they help sustain.

Just as the forms of immunity differ in the extent to which they bar social life against transformative pressure, so too they differ in the ease with which they lend themselves to use as instruments of domination. To recognize this difference, it is enough to recall an earlier comparison between two kinds of rights within existing legal systems. The property owner can use consolidated property rights, freely accumulated and transferred by inheritance, to diminish his dependence upon other people (or rather upon their discretionary decisions) while increasing their dependence upon him. But welfare entitlements and civic or public rights do not lend themselves to this use except through a far more indirect chain of deliberate manipulations or unintended effects. This imbalance between the subjugation-producing effects of the legal forms of immunity within a legal system can extend into differences between entire legal systems, according to the way each legal order goes about protecting individual security.

Immunity guarantees in the reformed constitution should satisfy two negative standards: they should not supply instruments of subjugation and they should not help protect the social order against effective challenge and revision. A major theme of this book has been that a necessary condition for maintaining a system of communal and hierarchical divisions is that these divisions be generated and regenerated by institutional arrangements protected against the risks of the routine practical and imaginative conflicts of social life. Precisely this seclusion from conflict represents the surest sign of triumph in the social warfare. It would also be a sufficient condition of structures of dependence and domination, were it not for the following qualification: society may be highly routinized in a fashion that gives communal division primacy over social hierarchy. The social order may then appear as a confederation of relatively equal and rigidly separate communities, although foreshortened hierarchies may appear within each community or group. In such a circumstance institutional arrangements, sanctified by slowly changing custom, may aggravate the contrast between context-preserving routine and context-transforming conflict. Something like this situation is said to exist in many tribal societies. Moreover, the longing for such a circumstance marks a long succession of political utopias from the idea of a republic of relatively equal yeoman farmers to the unreconstructed versions of petty commodity production. But even when such a rigidified system of communal divisions (sometimes called a segmented society) can be realized in fact, it suffers from a peculiar instability. If the view of the enabling conditions of material progress presented in earlier parts of this book is correct, the development of productive or destructive capabilities requires a shifting around of people, jobs, and institutional arrangements. It even demands that the organization of work represent a visible embodiment of practical reason, understood as a method for the continuous interplay between task definitions and operational acts. Whenever the rigidified society as a whole or a group within it faces a practical emergency (or an exceptional opportunity), its leaders must mobilize resources and manpower in ways not predetermined or even tolerated by the established institutional order. Those who take the lead in this extra-constitutional mobilization find themselves with a floating quantum of power in their hands: the power represented by the emergency resources. They may then fashion arrangements that transform this exceptional control over free-floating capital and manpower into an institutionalized part of the social order. Notice how this line of argument suggests a speculative conjecture about the genesis of social hierarchies out of relatively egalitarian tribal societies. The larger view of the enabling conditions of material progress that this hypothesis presupposes explains why the combination of rigidity with equality fails to recur at higher levels of the development of productive capability. The segmented tribal society is a historical fact, whereas the idea of the yeoman republic is an archaizing fantasy.

The first generative principle of a system of rights for the empowered democracy is the commitment to establish the individual's position of immunity in a way that minimizes both the rigidification of the institutional order and the risks of personal subjugation. But though this principle represents the most important constructive idea of a system of rights suitable to the empowered democracy, it can generate this system only when complemented by a few subsidiary principles. One of these auxiliary ideas is that the legal devices for granting access to divisible portions of social capital should contribute to the making of a decentralized economic order; which is to say, of an economic order that privileges the consensual route to the development of negative capability. The legal form of economic decentralization, however, must carry negative capability beyond the point it can reach under a regime of consolidated property rights and mass-production industry. Market rights must therefore be created that combine certain features of consolidated property with other traits that consolidated property lacks. Thus, under the reformed constitution, the terms of access to capital emphasize the provisional and conditional character of all proprietary control. But within these terms and for this period, the discretionary use and transfer of the resources may be nearly absolute and may resemble, to that extent, consolidated property. Indeed, the clearer the assertion of ultimate collective control over the forms, rate, and fruits of accumulation, the stronger the justification for property and contract rights similar to the most unforgiving versions of nineteenth-century private law. This subsidiary principle requires no further discussion here; the arguments that support and elaborate it have already been worked out in the course of discussing the proposals for economic reorganization.

Another subsidiary idea does require more extended analysis because its foundations and aims outreach those of the institutional program. This principle is the effort to affirm legal rights that, by their form and content, suit the obligations of interdependence that characterize communal life. And these rights, when viewed in their interaction with the other types of entitlements constituting the system of rights, should embody and promote a certain prescriptive vision of communal relations.

The program for institutional reconstruction worked out here does not exhaust the reach of the vision that inspires it. The ultimate stakes in politics are the fine texture of personal relations. The institutions of the empowered democracy matter not only for the heightened freedom, prosperity, and self-consciousness they promise but also as the framework for a style of personal attachments. At the center of this revised approach to direct personal relations stands a conception of community as a zone in which the increased acceptance of mutual vulnerability makes it possible to multiply ways of diminishing the conflict between attachment to other people and the claims of self-consciousness and self-possession. Overcoming this conflict represents but another facet of the project of human empowerment.

Traditional legal thought has accustomed us to think of communal life as almost beyond the proper scope of legal rights. If the jurists are to be believed, legal regulation appears in the domain of intimate and communal relations as the hand of Midas, threatening to destroy whatever it touches. But this supposed antipathy between rights and community reflects both a rigid view of rights and an impoverished conception of community. Its actual effect is often to leave communal life all the more subject to the forms of self-interested exchange and domination from which the policy of legal abstention is expected to protect it.

A legal theory under the spell of consolidated property imagines rights to establish sharply demarcated areas of discretionary action. But the rigid related contrast of right and no-right, the refusal to take into account the effect that an exercise of right has upon the associates of the rightholder, and the insistence upon explicit bargain or unilateral state imposition as sources of obligation are all inappropriate to communal life. In fact, they are even unsuitable to continuing business dealings that involve significant collaboration between business partners. Communal and collaborative relationships demand that the scope of a right be contextually defined in the light of standards and judgments about the effect the exercise of the right might have upon other people. The legal penetration of community and collaboration also requires the legal acknowledgment of obligations that arise from half-articulate and half-deliberate relations of interdependence rather than from either completed bargains or unilateral impositions of duty. Though current law occasionally protects such interdependencies, it characteristically does so through a haphazard sequence of subordinate principles and exceptional bodies of doctrine. The effect is to make the protection depend upon mechanical distinctions.

The policy of legal abstention reveals an inadequate view of community as well as a single-track conception of rights. It sees community as the exclusion of conflict or the restraint on self-interest and, in either instance, as a contrast to the quality of workaday life. Because the received vocabulary of legal rights is associated with both conflict and self-interest, it appears here as an alien and subversive presence. But the imagined contrast between a communal idyll and the everyday world of work and exchange is both unrealistic and corrupting. It fails to recognize the element of conflict that inevitably arises from the development of independent subjectivity. It does not see that the restraint on self-interest retains its vital connection to the communal ideal only to the extent that it remains subordinate to a principle of radical mutual acceptance. However, the strongest argument against the stark contrast of communal harmony and practical activity is that this antithesis forms part of a scheme of social life that harms both the elements it so rigidly opposes. It abandons practical life to unrestrained self-interest and technically justified hierarchy and reduces private community to a futile refuge against the brutality of the outside world. To the extent that the forms of dependence and domination remain undisturbed, the communal ideal becomes the softening mantle of a power order. Every attempt to assert equality in the distribution of trust requires a betrayal of existing communal attachments.

The generative principles discussed in the preceding pages connect the other parts of the institutional program to the reconstruction of the system of rights. They suggest the creation of distinct types of entitlements, distinguished along lines that, in fainter and more tortuous outline, can already be discerned in modern law. These types of rights differ both by their operational characteristics and by the particular areas of the institutional program to which they give legal form. The distinguishing operational features concern the relation between the right at the moment of its initial formulation and the right at the moment of its legitimate exercise. They also include the modes of argument and analysis most relevant to the passage from formulation to exercise. The aspect of the institutional program to which each type of right refers presents less a distinct model of human association than part of a scheme designed to prevent such rigid distinctions from taking hold. Within such a view, the operational characteristics of entitlements cease to be seen as the inherent features of rights, just as rights themselves are no longer thought to mark the built-in structure of an institutional type of governmental, economic, or communal organization. Now the form of a right can be made to reflect, deliberately and directly, its programmatic role.

Market Rights

Market rights are the rights employed for economic exchange in the trading sector of the society. They come into their own within a fully realized version of the reconstructed economy: the economy that allows teams of workers, technicians, and entrepreneurs to gain conditional and temporary access to portions of social capital and that thereby develops both the absolute degree of economic decentralization and the extent of economic plasticity.

Market rights show two different faces, according to whether we focus on the relation between the capital takers and the capital fund or on the dealings among the capital takers themselves. In the relation to the capital fund, what stands out, by contrast to the existing market systems, are both the general commitment to a scheme of conditional and provisional rights of access to capital and the turn to explicit collective decision making to set the precise terms of use. These terms may fix the time for which capital may be available, the interest charged by the fund for its resources, the uses to which capital may be put (e.g., the extent to which it may be employed to expand the enterprise), and the outer limits that must be observed in experiments with the form of work organization. They may leave a broad and nearly unlimited scope for entrepreneurial discretion in certain sectors of the economy while circumscribing this discretion severely in other sectors.

The key legal significance of the new relation between the capital fund and the capital takers is brought out by its impact on the traditional contrast between private and regulatory law. This contrast typically combines and confuses two ideas that should be kept distinct. First, there is the opposition between the rules and practices defining a particular type of market and those correcting its results in particular transactions. This distinction, though never entirely clear-cut, has its justifications. The reformed market and the revised theory of market rights would not abolish the difference between market definition and contract correction. It would simply make this difference less important by weakening, for reasons soon to be remembered, the felt moral and social need to correct particular deals.

But implied in the contrast of private and regulatory law there is another, indefensible idea. This idea, rarely confessed but even more rarely abandoned, is the distinction between the rules and practices establishing a market (the content of private law) and those correcting the operations of the market economy as a whole, or of broad sectors of this economy, rather than the results of particular transactions. This supposed general correction may be motivated by social policies, such as distributional fairness, that market institutions are supposedly unable to accomplish (the task of regulatory law). The contrast between market definition and general market correction makes no sense as a distinction between two inherently different activities or topics. The market may indeed substitute nonmarket for market forms of organization. But nonmarket forms are just as likely to represent fragments of a different style of market organization – one at odds with the style enshrined in the established rules of private law. Received economic and legal thought has trouble recognizing these exemplary deviations because of its habitual confusion of the market with one particular version of market institutions. Under the reformed economic system, however, such confusion would lose its props; the basic norms of contract and property would be seen to be no less "political" than the distributional issues fought out in the categories of regulatory law. The resulting advance in intellectual clarity would also be a gain in our effective mastery over the terms of practical social life.

Consider now the second side of market rights: the side that refers to the dealings among the economic enterprises themselves. Here firms are free to transact with one another within the limits of time and use prescribed by the central political decisions. The constraints on entrepreneurial discretion are certainly more overt than in the current style of market institutions. But I have already suggested several reasons to expect that the overall workings of such a system would actually broaden the opportunities for the exercise of entrepreneurial initiative. One such line of reasoning deserves further development here because of its close bearing on the form and effect of economic rights.

A transactional system retains its character only so long as it can be distinguished from a power order in which some people make decisions at the behest of others. Yet market transactions constantly produce inequalities of wealth, and they commonly presuppose inequalities of information. Success in the market appears, first and foremost, as the acquisition of advantages that can be used to secure further advantages in subsequent rounds of market transactions. If all such inequalities are canceled out as soon as they have been gained, the market is reduced to little more than the facade to an overriding method of redistributive allocation. But if these inequalities are allowed to accumulate too much, the market is gradually replaced by a power order. We cannot deduce from the abstract idea of the market an ideal reconciliation between the imperatives to correct and not to correct. We cannot even expect that there will be such a reconciliation for all possible versions of market institutions. For a given economy, or sector of the economy, the minimum of correction needed to prevent it from collapsing into a power order may be greater than the maximum of correction compatible with the autonomy of market decisions. Market systems, and the broader formative institutional contexts of power and production to which they belong, differ crucially in the extent to which they realize the idea of a structure of decentralized bargaining, without having constantly to correct or compensate the outcomes of particular transactions.

Legal systems often appeal to a stratagem that moderates or obfuscates, rather than solves, the problem of overcorrection and under-correction. This stratagem replaces outright redistributive correction by rules and standards that distinguish between contractual situations according to the degree to which the parties are allowed to treat one another as unrestricted gamblers. The antigambling theme includes the notion that the parties had in mind a rough equivalence of performances. It also incorporates the idea that they are engaged in something of a collaborative venture and may not exploit to the hilt one another's unexpected misfortunes or guileless mistakes. Both because it characteristically works through presumptions of intent and because it singles out only certain transactions, the antigambling impulse softens and conceals the subversive force of redistributive correction. Yet it does in effect circumscribe the scope of decentralized economic decision. The frequency with which it appears in the setting of significant disparities of power between the contract partners suggests that one of its major, half-conscious uses is to protect the weak from the strong.

An economic system that dispenses with consolidated property as the principal mechanism of economic decentralization may increase the constraints of time and usage on the employment of capital, although even these constraints may be set very differently in different sectors of the economy. Within these limits, however, it lessens the need for ad hoc redistributive corrections. In the core area of the dealings among takers of capital from the rotating capital fund, it diminishes the pressure to restrict initiative in all the ways suggested by the antigambling impulse. For this reconstructed system is designed precisely to encourage decentralization and plasticity and to undercut all the devices enabling entrenched economic organizations and accumulators of capital to protect themselves against the effects of market instabilities. The provisional teams of capital takers, secure in their basic welfare entitlements, can be treated to a very large extent as unrestricted gamblers.

What follows for the operational characteristics of market rights? Such rights would have the basic operational features of contract and property entitlements in current private law. In fact, for the reasons previously considered, these characteristics may be realized in an even more untrammeled form. Property, to be sure, would be disaggregated, as it has been in so many periods of its history, into a series of distinct powers assigned to different entities or rightholders: central representative bodies of the democracy, the competing investment funds, and the capital takers who have access to the fund on explicitly temporary and limited terms. But within these limits the capital takers would benefit from market rights with all the formal characteristics of current contract entitlements. The limitations of time and use could be absorbed, as conditional terms or public policy prohibitions, without damage to the three basic operational traits of the consolidated property right itself.

First, the source of obligation must be either the unilateral imposition of a duty by the state or a fully articulated agreement. The half-deliberate relations of interdependence and reliance that occupy so prominent a place in our ordinary views of moral obligation have no force here.

Second, the boundaries of the entitlement are primarily defined at the moment of its initial formulation. The specific relational context in which a market right may be exercised has only a limited bearing on the definition of how the rightholder may or may not use his right. To be sure, the commitment to demarcate the scope of the right at the moment of its birth must inevitably be fudged in a system of judge-made law, just as it unavoidably weakens even in a system of legislated law that has cast doctrinal conceptualism aside. But there a distinction must be drawn between the reinterpretation of entitlements in the light of general purposes, policies, and principles and the willingness to make this reinterpretation depend upon the detailed relational setting in which the right is exercised.

From this second characteristic there follows a third: a bright line separates the areas of entitlement and nonentitlement. Within the boundaries of the entitlement, the rightholder may act as he pleases, deaf to the effect that the exercise of the right may have upon other people. Outside those boundaries, however, he cannot expect to be protected, no matter how appealing his claim may seem morally. This bright line between the zones of right and nonright keeps the rightholder in the circumstance of a gambler.

The market rights of the reformed constitution do not bring about any major change in these operational characteristics, which already apply to the consolidated property rights of existing economies. The number of legally imposed conditions and prohibitions increases while the direct or indirect correction of transaction outcomes diminishes. Yet the practical effects and the imaginative message of the rights that possess these familiar structural features are radically transformed by the institutional reconstruction of the economy.

Immunity Rights

Immunity rights protect the individual against oppression by concentrations of public or private power, against exclusion from the important collective decisions that influence his life, and against the extremes of economic and cultural deprivation. They give him the justified confidence of not being fundamentally endangered by the expanded conflicts of an empowered democracy. This confidence encourages him to participate fearlessly and actively in making collective decisions about the organization of society. This initial definition of immunity rights requires several clarifications.

The interests to be protected by such entitlements may not always be identical to the ones people may themselves define as crucial to their security. But neither are these interests the expression of an independently defined and externally imposed view of what vital security requires. The theory of immunity rights rests, in part, on the empirical hypothesis that freedom from violence, coercion, subjugation, and poverty (defined in both absolute and relative terms) enters into people's ordinary conception of essential security. These goods are rivaled in importance only by the more intangible sense of being accepted by other people as a person, with a place in the world. But, to a varying extent, people have also always put their sense of basic security in the maintenance of particular social roles, jobs, and ways of life. Any attempt to indulge this conception of security would prove incompatible with the institutions of the empowered democracy and with the personal and social ideals that inspire them. The case for the reformed constitution draws heavily on the argument that people can and should wean themselves away from a restrictive, rigidifying view of where they should place their sense of protection.

Modern history has abundantly showed that motivations can be changed in just this way. The triumph of liberal or authoritarian mass politics has weakened the system of fixed social stations that might enable people to seek their essential safety in the performance of a precise social role and in the claims upon resources and support that may accompany these roles. The experience of world history, with its headlong recombination of institutional practices and ways of life, has forced whole peoples increasingly to disengage their abstract sense of collective identity from their faithfulness to particular customs. The play of economic rationality has taught everyone that an insistence upon the perpetuation of rigid social stations and ways of life exacts a formidable cost in economic sluggishness. The constitution of an empowered democracy merely carries these tendencies farther while harnessing them to a liberalizing rather than a despotic cause.

The chief goal of the system of immunity rights is to afford the citizen a safety that encourages him to participate actively and independently in collective decision making. The point is not to favor public engagements by contrast to the pursuit of private interests, a choice that would confront the individual with real dangers and unattractive options. The institutional arrangements and the animating ideas of an empowered democracy progressively weaken the antithesis between civic participation and the pursuit of private interests. Immunity rights encourage the citizen to share in an activity combining features of both, within a more integrated experience of mastery over the social contexts of activity.

The idea that individual security must be strengthened if individual involvement in expanded collective conflicts is to be encouraged also rests on straightforward empirical assumptions. Unless the citizen feels secure in the most vital matters, he will live in constant fear of the controversies in which the life of an empowered democracy abounds. He will soon try to escape from what will appear to him an intolerably perilous situation. He may try to flee the anxieties of this free-for-all by throwing himself under the protection of whatever aspiring strongman may offer to shield him. The republic would soon degenerate into a battle of demagogues or warlords in command of frightened retinues.

Freedom as participation presupposes freedom as immunity. The critics of traditional democratic theory go wrong when they polemically contrast positive and negative freedom to the advantage of the former and treat participatory opportunities as a more than satisfactory substitute for immunity guarantees. But the defenders of conventional liberal democracy are mistaken to treat the narrow forms of participation available in a demobilized democracy as an adequate complement to the safeguards of immunity. They also err in viewing consolidated property rights (which they mistakenly identify with the market form of economic organization) as an indispensable condition of freedom, indispensable if only because their replacement would destroy liberty.

Note that the suggested relation between immunity and participation merely appropriates and develops a familiar theme of classical republican thought. Thus, one traditional justification of the property qualification to the suffrage was the conviction that the poor elector would become dependent upon patrons for physical protection and economic support. This traditional fear has in fact been borne out by the perversions of universal suffrage in contemporary third world countries.

We are accustomed to think that the legal means for assuring individuals a sphere of inviolable security necessarily impose a measure of rigidity on social life. Thus, there may arise the false belief – so characteristic of the diluted, modern versions of social necessitarianism – in an inevitable tension between the desire to secure an area of protected individual safety and the commitment to leave the shape of social relations open to experimental innovation, especially when innovation comes through governmental policy.

A minimum of tension is unavoidable; here as elsewhere we do not have to become perfectionists when we stop being fatalists. Any solution to the problem of immunity requires that some rules remain stable and some resources be set aside. But there is no fixed inverse relation between individual security and social rigidity. You can have more, or you can have less, of both at the same time. A caste system affords individuals a mode and a measure of security, in a fashion bound up with the entrenchment of dependence and dominion and at the cost of an extreme rigidification of social life. Absolute property rights give security too: a protection that leaves more room for movement, and condemns fewer people to gross oppression, than does caste. The immunity rights of an empowered democracy have the same relation to consolidated property that property has to caste.

Immunity rights safeguard two main sets of vital interests. They secure against governmental or private oppression especially insofar as such oppression may threaten or circumscribe the opportunity to participate, actively and equally, in major decisions about the organization of society and the disposition of social resources. They protect against economic or cultural deprivation, especially insofar as it makes the individual dependent upon governmental officials or private patrons. Each major direction of the immunity right requires further discussion.

The narrowly political and civic freedoms that a more democratic constitution must protect do not differ in kind from the freedoms already upheld by conventional democratic practice. They include freedom of expression and association and freedom from arbitrary imprisonment or imprisonment for subversive activity. If the wealth of society permits, these liberties may well incorporate a freedom to opt out of ordinary, gainful social activity and to lead, with a minimum guaranteed income, what many may view as a self-absorbed and parasitic existence. Society stands to benefit from the alternative social visions that may be dreamt up and enacted by these internal exiles or by the countercommunities they form. And the individual's awareness that he may at any time withdraw from society into a proud independence may make it easier for him to display this self-possession within society. But the special quality of political and civic freedoms under an empowered democracy depends less on such additional entitlements than on the enlarged opportunity to exercise the ordinary freedoms and on the many features of the institutional plan that contribute to protect these liberties.

Under this institutional proposal, the exercise of public freedoms ceases to be either a last-ditch defense against despotic governments or an ecstatic deviation from the tenor of ordinary social life. For example, the freedom to associate politically gains new force when institutional arrangements make it easier to establish a connection between disputes at the center of governmental power and debates inside the grassroots organizations that absorb much of people's everyday lives. Even the vote for the central representative bodies and higher offices of the state takes on a greater authority when constitutional arrangements no longer deliberately link the safeguards of freedom to the obstacles that stand in the way of institutional experimentation.

The constitutional scheme contributes to the stability of these essential freedoms by the beliefs that it exemplifies and confirms, by the motivations it reinforces, and by the methods of institutional design it deploys. These contributions help define the distinctive quality of the traditional political and civic freedoms under an empowered democracy.

Remember, first, that these immunity rights do not lend themselves to the exercise of domination and that they impose a minimal rigidity upon the organization of society. For these reasons, no part of the essential security of the individual is made to rest upon the exercise of consolidated property rights. Thus, the rebellion against domination and the attempt to experiment need not endanger – as they so often have – the indispensable safeguards of liberty.

Consider also that the institutional structure of the empowered democracy shares with the traditional version of democracy a commitment to avoid the concentration of governmental power into a small number of offices. Indeed, the proposed constitution multiplies the spheres of institutionalized conflict over the resources for society making. The aim is to avoid associating this multiplication of independent parts of government with constitutional techniques that encourage and perpetuate deadlock and thereby help insulate social arrangements against effective challenge. But because there are many arenas of conflict, the take-over of the state by a faction determined to pervert the constitution, or the withdrawal of the citizenry into a dangerous passivity, cannot be sudden or invisible. Such events would result in the derangement of the relations among governmental institutions and in the stultification of these many, independent centers of institutional experimentation. No constitutional plan can save citizens who have lost the desire for self-direction. It is nevertheless possible to devise institutions that give us many chances to discover the perversion of our political ideals.

Other psychological and intellectual forces complement the stabilizing effect of these methods of institutional design upon the arrangements that secure the immunity of the individual. The institutions of radical democracy increase opportunities of empowerment that merge the sense of satisfying a private interest into the experience of mastery over the social contexts of individual action. Such experiences of empowerment have an addictive force, and the longing for self-assertion becomes attached to the complex of institutions that presuppose and guarantee the security of the individual.

Just as the motivations encouraged by a more democratized constitution are tenacious, the insights on which this constitution draws are irreversible. The programmatic vision defended and developed here has many connections to descriptive and explanatory ideas. But it is important to distinguish the more affirmative and contentious aspects of these ideas – such as the particular theory of transformation presented earlier – from the initial negative conceptions of which the affirmative ideas try to make good – such as the theses that institutional systems do not fall into a predefined list or sequence and that they differ in the extent to which they aggravate or efface the contrast between context-preserving routine and context-transforming conflict. These more elementary and largely negative ideas form a proto-theory: a body of ideas that can serve as point of departure for different views of social reality and possibility. They represent an advanced form of skeptical disenchantment with attempts to present particular social orders as either holy or necessary. From the perspective of this proto-theory, deep-logic social thought can be recognized as only a halfhearted version of the experience of seeing through false necessity. The conventional democratic creed of the present day can be seen to continue the superstitious and unargued identification of markets and democracies with the forms of democracies and markets that happen to exist. Freedom is intangibly but immeasurably strengthened when its safeguards no longer depend on such superstitions and when seemingly nihilistic insights can be enlisted in the cause of a liberalizing program.

Freedom against governmental or private oppression represents only one of two major sets of immunity rights. The other set consists in welfare entitlements: guarantees of access to the material and cultural resources needed to make a life. These include provision for nourishment, housing, health care, and education, with absolute standards proportional to the wealth of society. The right to opt out of gainful social activity can be viewed as an extension of these welfare entitlements rather than as a development of the traditional civic liberties.

The key point is that under the proposed regime welfare entitlements must provide a minimal, equal amount of resources, whether as money or as services in kind, rather than respect a claim to keep particular jobs or positions. The enforcement of such claims to specific social places would undermine a program of democratization that puts its hope, and the hope for developing the productive capabilities of society, in the cumulative opening of social life to revision and recombination. The rejection of job tenure as a major direction for welfare entitlements highlights the contrast between the program of empowered democracy and traditional proposals for recommunalizing social life.

The economic institutions of an empowered democracy help generate the resources to fund the welfare entitlements and encourages individuals to make their conceptions of material welfare more independent of tenure in particular jobs. The arrangements of an empowered democracy contribute to the development of productive capabilities and thus promise to increase the absolute amount of wealth available to finance welfare rights. Those arrangements also diminish the familiar conflict between the bias toward economic growth and the commitment to satisfy welfare needs. Collective and individual choices – between consumption and saving, and between short-term and long-term or safe and risky investments – must still be made. But the basic flows of investment decisions are no longer critically influenced by relatively small numbers of investors, managers, and entrepreneurs who may be frightened into disinvestment by every concession to the poor or every advance toward greater equality of circumstance. Moreover, together with the sharp curtailment of inheritance, the rejection of consolidated property rights as the chief vehicle of market decentralization makes it unnecessary for the welfare system to serve as a relatively futile and disruptive means to moderate inequalities that the operation of the economy constantly re-creates and sharpens.

At the same time, the institutions of the empowered democracy weaken the fixity of special social roles, or stations in the social division of labor, and restrain the allegiances that attach people to these fixed places. In this way, the institutions help stabilize a type of welfare entitlement that minimizes the creation of vested rights in particular jobs.

Welfare entitlements and civic freedoms have the same operational features, readily inferred from the preceding discussion of the social ideals and empirical assumptions underlying the theory of immunity rights. Discussion of these structural characteristics can be summary, because in all but minor respects they coincide with the formal traits of consolidated property. But the social significance of the structural features changes radically with the shift in their institutional setting.

First the source of the immunity right is the situation of ongoing connection to the society – the mere circumstance of continuing involvement in its institutional arrangements. The importance of a clear-cut dichotomy between citizenship and residency diminishes when decisional processes within grassroots or productive organizations resemble and amplify decision making in the central representative bodies of government. Note that the source of the immunity right is a situation – and, indeed, a situation that transcends all particular engagements. Yet the specificity of this source does not make the other structural features of immunity rights any different from the operational characteristics of traditional rights of contract or property, whose sources are articulated agreements or state-imposed duties.

The immunity rights are defined as rigidly as possible at the time of their initial formulation. There is no more latitude for their redefinition at the moment of exercise than inheres, inevitably, in the interpretive freedom of the law applier. The particular relational circumstance in which the right is to be exercised is largely irrelevant. For the immunity rights define the safeguards – the minimal defenses – with which the individual enters all the dealings in which he does participate.

Consequently, a bright line circumscribes the boundaries of each immunity right. The rightholder can expect to distinguish confidently between the factual circumstances in which the law protects him in the asserted exercise of such an entitlement and those in which it does not. He need not subject the use of his right to a calculus of its effects upon other people. All the entitlements that make up the system of rights must be developed and enforced without prejudice to these safeguards, which secure each individual in a proud and jealous independence and enable him to experiment with contract and community without the fear that he may become another person's dependent.

Destabilization Rights

Destabilization rights protect the citizen's interest in breaking open the large-scale organizations or the extended areas of social practice that remain closed to the destabilizing effects of ordinary conflict and thereby sustain insulated hierarchies of power and advantage. The combination of immunity rights with destabilization rights gives legal expression to the central institutional mechanism of the whole constitutional plan. The destabilization entitlement ties the collective interest in ensuring that all institutions and practices can be criticized and revised to the individual interest in avoiding oppression. The empirical basis for this connection is the role that closure to effective challenge plays in the entrenchment of factional privilege.

The primary respondents to the citizens who claim a right to have an organization or an area of social practice destabilized are the nongovernmental organizations or the actual individuals who are legally competent, or actually able, to reconstruct the objectionable arrangements. The subsidiary respondent is the state, perhaps even a special branch of government. Governmental action to disrupt and reconstruct the overprotected and subjugation-producing arrangements may be needed not only because the people in charge of the organizations or practices at issue may be the biggest beneficiaries of the insulated hierarchies but because there may be no people visibly in charge. Such a situation is especially likely to occur when the claimant seeks to disrupt an area of social practice rather than a discrete organization.

Consider now in greater detail the content of destabilization rights. They encompass both a negative and a positive use. Their negative aim has already been described as the attempt to deny protection against destabilizing conflict to either institutions or noninstitutional arrangements whenever this immunity to conflict seems to generate stable ties of domination and dependence. The destabilizing conflict that must be kept open may come from within a particular institution, if such an institution is the target of the right. It may result from the ordinary activities of a sector of the society or the economy. Or it may even take place in the central deliberative processes of the republic. What matters is that the arrangements in question be available to some mode of attack. When the focus falls on the evil to be remedied rather than on its cause, the destabilization entitlement can be redescribed as the citizen's right to prevent any faction of the society from gaining a privileged hold upon any of the means for creating the social future within the social present. The destabilization right can also be depicted in a way that draws attention to the process by which immunity to conflict arises and gives rise to power and privilege. The two descriptions overlap because the exercise of a privileged hold over the resources for society making allows those who exercise the hold to subjugate those who do not.

The voluntary passivity of potentially affected publics may be the original cause of an entrenchment of prerogative. But the turning point that justifies the exercise of a destabilization right takes place only when a new burst of collective activity by the immediate victims of the newly entrenched prerogatives can no longer easily overcome the entrenchment-producing effects of this political withdrawal.

Destabilization is not enough; intervention provoked by the exercise of a destabilization right must change the disrupted practice or institution. The entire argument of this book supports the idea that susceptibility to revision is not a merely negative characteristic. Some sets of institutional arrangements go farther than others toward overcoming the contrast between context-preserving routine and context-transforming struggle. What is true of large constellations of practices must also hold, though less clearly, for particular, relatively isolated practices. But the search for the affirmative content of the seemingly negative idea of a structure-revising structure must be tempered here by a concern not to circumscribe unnecessarily the freedom to experiment either with the content of the general laws or with the design of particular institutions. The reconstructive activity unleashed by the exercise of a destabilization right must therefore obey a negative presumption. It should aim at the minimum of reconstruction required to satisfy the negative aims of the entitlement rather than at the form an institution or practice would take if it were to make the greatest possible contribution to the development of negative capability. Instead of being used to force men and women to be free, it should give them a second chance before they decide to enslave themselves.

The destabilization right whose negative and affirmative content I have just described has counterparts in variants of the complex injunctive relief found in contemporary law. Such relief frequently has courts intervening in important institutions, such as schools and mental asylums, or in major areas of social practice, such as electoral organization, and reconstructing them in the name of democratic ideals said to inspire complex bodies of law. The character of the relief afforded by destabilization rights can be brought out all the more clearly by contrast to these established remedies. On the one hand, the destabilization entitlements go farther than anything available in current law. Freed once and for all from the restrictive model of consolidated property, they can develop unashamedly as devices of institutional disruption and reconstruction. The exercise of these rights brings into question a part of the collective structure of society rather than serving merely as a means to vindicate a transitory interest within that structure. Because they do not suit standard judicial or legislative settings they may even have to be elaborated and enforced by a special branch of government. (Recall the suggestion, in the section on the organization of government, as to how such a branch might work.) On the other hand, however, the destabilization rights have a more precise focus than the complex injunctions of present law. They serve not to embody specific ideals of human association but to ensure that, whatever the enacted forms of human association may be, they will preserve certain minimal qualities: above all, the quality of being readily replaceable.

The whole theory of destabilization rights outlined in this section rests on a key empirical hypothesis: the belief that treats insulation against destabilizing conflict as a necessary condition for the entrenchment of structures of domination and dependence. The explanatory social theory helping sustain this program of empowered democracy emphasizes the connection between freedom from subjugation and freedom as mastery over context. The legal practice of destabilization rights must itself become one of the principal ways of testing and developing this hypothesis experimentally.

To gain a sense of the practical settings in which to deploy the abstract ideas discussed up to now, consider an example of a situation calling for the exercise of destabilization rights under a fully mature version of the proposed constitution. Suppose some of the enterprises trading under the capital fund are unusually successful, thanks to a combination of exceptional diligence or skill and unforeseen market conditions. They succeed in using economic influence, electoral pressure, and policy persuasion to change the terms on which capital is made available. Under the new terms they are allowed to gain control of other, subordinate enterprises and to hire workers for temporary, dead-end, and underpaid jobs shunned by the stable, relatively privileged labor force of the enterprise. Once established in this new situation, they can extend their wealth and influence still farther. They increase the autonomy of the capital fund from the central deliberative processes of the democracy, leaving technocrats, beholden to the favored enterprises and groups, in effective charge of crucial financial decisions. The subversion of the nascent privileges now requires something between a mere shift in policy and a constitutional revolution.

In such a circumstance, the agency of government responsible for developing destabilization rights may move to rob the nascent prerogatives of their defenses. The law may provide that some of these interventions take effect unless and until reversed by a combination of other branches of government. Thus, the enforcing authority may order the enterprises in question to moderate their internal hierarchy or relinquish some of the devices by which they exclude new workers or relegate them to a permanently inferior status. Other destabilizing interventions may come closer to jeopardizing the democracy's freedom to experiment. Although taking effect immediately, they may need to be reconfirmed, within a short time, by other branches of government or by the general electorate. Such a procedure might be suitable, for example, when the responsible agency of government intervened to prevent the bodies directly responsible for administering the rotating capital fund from using their discretion in a systematically biased fashion to favor a certain group of enterprises in ways not adequately justified by the importance of support for up-and-coming innovators. Other types of intervention would not take effect at all until confirmed by the electorate or by a broad range of intermediate representative bodies. This suspended application might be called for whenever the asserted destabilization right came into conflict with decisions of the democracy's major representative assemblies: the privilege-entrenching measures might, for example, have been laid down by the national parliament.

The example of the perverted capital fund already suggests the importance of developing standards that give specificity to the abstract ideal inspiring the theory of destabilization rights. There are two ways in which the ideals underlying the theory of destabilization rights gain the concreteness that enables them to produce practical consequences. Analyzing these processes serves to link the basic conception of destabilization rights with the distinctive operational characteristics of such rights. Each form of specification affects the other types of entitlement, and each has an established place within the reigning styles of legal doctrine. Yet their importance undergoes here a hypertrophy that imprints special features on the right.

The first method of specification is the advance of the abstract idea of availability to criticism and challenge toward increasing concreteness. The subsidiary standards required by the march toward particularity may be drawn to some extent from the developing body of explanatory and normative ideas that lends sense and justification to the entire constitutional plan. But because a constitution must gain a life independent of the doctrines that may have originally inspired it, the criteria must also rely upon the laws and arrangements of the society. For the bulk of the arrangements and laws of an empowered democracy must give a range of concrete expressions to the vague notion of a structure-revising structure. No legal theory or legal practice can keep this ideal alive once it has lost its hold on the conscience of the citizenry and has ceased to be realized, however imperfectly, in the actual organization of social life. Experience, recorded in a tradition of institutional practice, must show how far the quest for negative capability has gone, what distinctive problems it must face in different areas of society, and which of its varied social meanings it takes at each moment of its history and in each area of its application.

The other, complementary method of specification consists in treating self-revision not as an abstract ideal to be made more concrete by a series of contextual definitions but as a goal to be advanced by suitable causal means. Empirical questions must be asked and answered with respect to each major area of application of the destabilization rights. Which institutional practices are in fact most immunized against challenge and revision? When is this immunity to attack most likely to generate stable relations of dominion and dependence? And when does it in fact generate them? Which forms of disruption and reconstruction will promote most effectively and economically the goal of openness to revision? And which will minimize the danger of continuing intervention by external authorities? The empirical difficulty of answering these questions and the administrative difficulty of acting upon the answers are two reasons why traditional court institutions may be unsuitable to develop and enforce the entitlements.

The operational characteristics of destabilization rights result directly from the two modes of specification just discussed. First, the immediate source of the right is neither a fully articulated agreement nor the unilateral imposition of a duty by the state but the interplay between a basic commitment of the constitutional plan and the emergent practices that place the commitment in jeopardy. Second, the initial, legislative definition of the entitlement must always be complemented by an important element of specification at the moment and in the circumstance of the claimed exercise of the right. Legislation may go some way toward codifying the two processes of specification: it may distinguish situations and remedies in ways that implicitly answer the relevant causal questions and that implicitly provide contextual definitions of the abstract ideal of freedom from subjugation through availability to revision. Both sets of issues, however, must be reopened at the moment of the asserted exercise of the right if contextual definition and causal investigation are to do the work required by the theory of destabilization rights. A third operational characteristic follows from the second. Because the redefinition of the entitlement must pass through the surprises of causal investigation and the shifts of contextual analysis, no bright line surrounds the area of the protected legal claim. The point of destabilization rights is not to demarcate a fixed zone of discretionary action, within which an individual rightholder may do whatever he pleases, but to prevent recurrent, institutionalized relationships among groups from falling into certain prohibited routines of closure and subjugation. So the controlling image is the mandated, context-specific disruption of complex collective arrangements rather than the vigilant defense of a zone of untrammeled individual discretion.

Solidarity Rights

Solidarity rights give legal form to social relations of reliance and trust. The aims of the theory of solidarity rights extend beyond the limited goals of the institutional program to the transformed communal and personal relations an empowered democracy may help generate and sustain. The establishment of a system of entitlements that gives an explicit place to solidarity rights represents part of a plan of institutional transformation. But it also serves the cultural-revolutionary transformation of personal relations that goes hand in hand with the plan to empower democracy.

Solidarity rights form part of a set of social relations enabling people to enact a more defensible version of the communal ideal than any version currently available to them. This reconstruction of the idea of community does not rest content with either the commitment to exclude conflict from a charmed circle of group harmony or with the willingness to limit the play of self-interest. Both altruism and harmony are deemphasized in this reconstructed image of community. Insofar as they continue to play a role, they do so for the sake of their contribution to the view of community as a zone of heightened mutual vulnerability. In this zone people may experiment more freely with ways to achieve self-assertion through passionate attachments.

A later section develops this communal ideal and argues its superiority over altruism and harmony as the nub of the communal ideal. This revised conception of community relates the communal ideal to the central concern with empowerment instead of relegating it to the role of refuge against the brutality of workaday life. It encourages people to recognize and use the element of conflict that marks even the closest personal connections.

This changed understanding of community helps resolve an apparent paradox: an institutional program that seems to exalt collective militancy, with all its conflictual consequences, is claimed to support a communal ideal. But the paradox fades once each of its supposed elements is put in its place. For one thing, the ideal of community invoked here is no longer defined by contrast to conflict. For another thing, the institutional program is oriented less to the perpetuation of struggle than to the emancipation of social life from the automatisms and hierarchies with which the rigid contrast of conflict and community is invariably associated. Only through the softening of the opposition between context-preserving routine and context-transforming conflict can the mechanisms of domination and dependence be subverted. Only through this subversion can communal attachments be rescued from their traditional status as mere reprieves from the brutality of everyday life or mere restraints upon the untrammeled exercise of privilege.

Solidarity rights apply to relations within distinct communities and to relations of trust and reliance that take hold outside a well-defined communal setting. (Compare to destabilization rights, which encompass relations within and outside an organization.) The domain of solidarity rights is the field of the half-articulate relations of trusting interdependence that absorb so much of ordinary social life but remain troublesome aberrations for a legal theory devoted to the model of consolidated property. The situations calling for the exercise of such entitlements include family life, continuing business relationships (as distinguished from one-shot transactions), and the varied range of circumstances falling under fiduciary principles in contemporary law. The trust such relations require may be voluntary and reciprocal or half-deliberate and unequal, usually in the setting of disparities of power or advantage.

The chief practical legal expression of the refined view of community underlying the theory of solidarity rights is the legal protection of claims to abide by implicit obligations to take other people's situations and expectations into account. By contrast to traditional contract law, the obligations are only partly explicit and the expectations refer to detailed, continuing relational positions rather than to instantaneous arm's-length transactions. The restraints these entitlements impose on individual self-interest matter solely as a by-product of the effort to vindicate a delicate texture of interdependencies and representations. It is through an analysis of this texture that the central categories of the law of solidarity rights must be developed.

It follows that solidarity rights should not be misunderstood as claims to a subjective state of mind on the part of the person who owes the rightholder a duty. The point is not to ensure that the owner of the duty has a benevolent and concerned frame of mind. Pursued to its ultimate conclusions, such a subjectivist goal would result in a stifling and hypocritical despotism of virtue, obsessed with invasive yet futile methods. The immediate aim, instead, is to accomplish just the reverse of what consolidated property offers the rightholder. People bound by solidarity rights are prevented from taking refuge in an area of absolute discretion within which they can remain deaf to the claims others make upon them. Thus solidarity rights deny the discretionary action both immunity rights and market rights seek to protect. Wherever such entitlements apply, people must answer to the claims arising from the usual blend of reliance-in-fact, half-made promises, and customary role-dependent standards of obligations. Subjective motives are to be influenced, if at all, only in the long run: the theory and practice of solidarity rights represent but a small part of an institutional program that enacts certain ideas about society and personality and favors some impulses over others.

The operational characteristics of solidarity rights can be inferred from the theory and practice of their more limited counterparts in contemporary law. These counterparts include the law of fiduciary relationships, the contractual and delictual protection of reliance, the doctrines of good faith and of abuse of rights, and the many doctrinal devices by which private law supports communal relations while continuing to represent society as a world of strangers.

The first structural feature has to do with the sources of the obligations protected by solidarity rights. Such obligations arise from partly articulate relations of interdependence rather than from either fully bargained agreements or the unilateral imposition of a duty by the state. The obligations covered by solidarity rights resemble the vast majority of the duties people have traditionally recognized in the most diverse societies, even in the few societies refusing to give such duties substantial legal protection. But the characteristic quality of these obligations is transformed by an institutional order that encourages the jumbling up of fixed social roles and the disruption of systematic hierarchical and communal contrasts.

The second operational trait of solidarity rights refers to the relation between the entitlement as initially defined and the entitlement as redefined at the moment of a claimed exercise. General principles and discriminating standards must be developed, along the lines previously suggested, to single out the recurrent situations suitable for the enforcement of these entitlements. And other, complementary standards and principles must distinguish between such situations in order to determine the legal consequences of recognizing a particular solidarity right. For example, an unequal relation may require the imposition of a greater duty of self-restraint on the advantaged party, whereas a more equal common endeavor may justify reciprocity in the allocation of duties. But the very standards deployed in this initial definition of the right invoke an additional definition in context. For only the specific relational context, analyzed in detail, can reveal a structure of interdependence and show its complex blend of reliance-in-fact, semiexplicit representation, and equality or dependence. The program of empowered democracy increases the particularity of relations of interdependence because it undermines rigid role systems and the moral expectations such systems produce. It therefore also makes the contextual redefinition of solidarity entitlements all the more important.

The third operational trait of solidarity rights follows directly from the second characteristic. No bright line divides the area of conduct in which the holder of a solidarity right may claim protection and the area in which he may not. Instead of contrasting a zone of unquestioned discretion to an area of no protection, this class of entitlements favors a nuanced grading of degrees of legal support for the rightholder. The determination of where the rightholder stands along this spectrum of legal protection depends in every instance upon an analysis of his prelegal relation to the person against whom he wants to assert the right.

It does not follow from the establishment of solidarity rights that they ought to be coercively enforced nor from the commitment to enforce them that they should be overseen by the same judicial bodies responsible for administering, in last resort, immunity and market rights. I have argued that destabilization rights should be applied by a distinctive branch of government. Similarly, many of the solidarity rights may best be enforced, when they are enforced at all, by more informal means of mediation, with more ample participation from parties, families, communities, or work teams, depending on the subject matter of the dispute.

But many solidarity rights may best remain unenforceable, as a statement of an ideal. The mere threat to let black-robed officials or officious companions enforce them might fatally injure the quality of reciprocal trust they require. The most serious candidates for exclusion from coercive enforcement are the relations in which a rough equality of power coincides with the central importance of trust to the success of the association.

It may be objected that an unenforceable right is no right at all and that merely to speak of such entitlements is to disinter the illogical language of natural rights with its implicit but halfhearted allusion to a natural, absolute context of social life. But it is a mistake to identify the positivism of governmental enforcement and the idea of innate and eternal entitlements as the only two senses that rights language may bear. A system of rights, in the sense employed by this discussion of all rights, is fundamentally the institutionalized part of social life, backed up by a vision of possible and desirable human association. The limits to rights are the limits to institutionalization itself. Not everything in a system of rights need be enforceable, on pain of being treated, if it is unenforceable, as either a natural right or a meaningless gesture. The rights that governmental or other institutions may not enforce remain a public declaration of a public vision, extending, qualifying, and clarifying the ideals embodied in other, enforceable parts of the system of rights.

To be sure, the refusal to enforce certain rights weakens the sense in which the part of social life those rights address is institutionalized at all. But such a weakening fits well with the idea of solidarity rights as a point of passage from the institutionalized to the personal, noninstitutionalized aspects of social life. The vision underlying these rights, and inspiring the system of rights as a whole, is partly a conception of how the institutional and the noninstitutional realms should connect.

The Cultural Program of Empowered Democracy

14

The Cultural-Revolutionary Counterpart to the Institutional Program

The Idea of a Personalist Program

The institutional program of empowered democracy has its counterpart in a program for the transformation of personal relations. Call this program cultural revolution. There are both causal and justificatory links between the institutional proposals and their personalist extension. Like any institutional order the institutions of empowered democracy encourage certain changes in the character of the direct practical or passionate relations among individuals, and they depend for their vitality upon the perpetuation of these qualities. At the same time the ideals inspiring the cause of empowered democracy also support a criticism of the fine texture of social life.

The correspondence of institutional and personalist proposals should not, on reflection, prove surprising. The qualities of our direct practical or passionate dealings always represent the ultimate object of our conflicts over the organization of society. No institutional structure or system of social dogma informs these dealings completely; the inability to do so guarantees in even the most entrenched and coherent frameworks the possibility of anomaly and rebellion. But only insofar as a formative structure does influence these subtle personal relations can it show its mettle. All the routines of practical and imaginative conflict that every such framework helps perpetuate must ultimately take the form of person-to-person encounters, even though they may be encounters in which practical aims and institutionally defined roles prevail. But although institutional arrangements matter because of their influence upon personal interaction, the task of presenting a view of transformed personal relations cannot be accomplished by the mere statement of an institutional program. The links between institutional order and personal behavior are – though real – loose, complex, and obscure. Moreover, influences upon the character of our encounters with one another go far beyond the institutional framework of social life; they include not only biological or technological constraints but also ideas, habits, and attitudes that never quite crystallize into institutions. The institutional agenda must be complemented by a personalist program.

There is also a narrower, tactical reason for the need to make this addition. Successful institutional transformation requires a willingness to subordinate redistributive aims to institutional goals. The subordination implies a sacrifice; the sacrifice must be inspired by a vision; and the vision must address the thing people care about most – their immediate experience of practical collaboration and passionate encounter, of self-assertion and solidarity. A visionary ideal must draw much of its force from its personalist immediacy, whether or not the ideal takes the form this book advocates.

Just as the institutional program needs a personalist vision, so the latter cannot dispense with the former. Personal relations must move within a context that is, to a large extent, institutionally defined. If this framework is not brought into closer accord with the spirit of the personalist vision, it will exact a price in the frustration or perversion of the ideal.

The effort to combine the institutional and the personal was known at earlier moments in the history of Western political thought as the attempt to unite the political and religious, a union Tocqueville recognized as the hallmark of the greatest revolutions. For religious creeds enter this secular realm largely as articulations of a prescriptive phenomenology of subjective experience and personal encounter and as bearers of existential projects containing a social message. The revolutionary need not, indeed he should not, put his faith in the total transformation of an established formative context, recognizing instead that these contexts can be and ordinarily are changed bit by bit. But even revolutionary reform must manage over time to link transformation in the domain of institutions with change in the "pianissimo" of the personal in order to attain its objectives.

The classical liberal would nevertheless object to this personalist extension of the institutional program. You can imagine him reasoning in the following way. An explicit aim of the project of empowered democracy is to deny authority to any entrenched scheme of authoritative models of human association, enacted in the different domains of social life. To advocate a particular style of direct personal interaction, and to support this advocacy with social pressure if not coercive force, is to betray the spirit of the institutional program rather than to extend it. It is also to impose a despotism all the more oppressive because it meddles even with the areas of intimacy that despots are ordinarily content to leave alone. If, however, the program of cultural revolution is not to be backed up by organized or informal coercion, why should it be so closely linked with proposals to reform social institutions?

This objection reflects a double misunderstanding: first about the sense in which institutional orders can be neutral among style of social interaction; second, about the nature of the cultural-revolutionary program itself. The classical liberal is right to object to an institutional program if it embraces a highly defined and restrictive view of what people – and relations among people – should be like. Thus, even the program of empowered democracy would lose much of its persuasive force if its success turned out to depend on the presence of the ever-ready, selfless citizen of classical republican myth.

But the classical liberal is wrong to think – if he does think – that an institutional order can be neutral among all possible styles of personal interaction or to draw a watertight distinction between the public institutions of a people and the forms of close association or intimate experience to which the people are drawn. The futile quest for institutions that are unbiased among all possible manners of association can only impede the search for arrangements that in fact free people more effectively from a closed canon of associative practices and models. The insistence on absolute neutrality can also keep us from appreciating the full extent of what we choose when we choose an institutional program. It can thereby lull us into commitments we might otherwise prefer to avoid.

Once we recognize the impossibility of perfect neutrality we are more likely to acknowledge the inadequacy of the neutrality standard as a guide to the criticism and invention of social forms. The authority of the radical project lies in its vision of the individual and collective empowerment we may achieve by cumulatively loosening the grip of rigid roles, hierarchies, and conventions upon our experiments in practical or passionate association. We can lift the burden of dependence and depersonalization, in part by changing the character of our relations, as individuals and as collectivities, to the institutional and imaginative frameworks of social life.

This conception of empowerment – of its meaning and conditions – incorporates a version of the neutrality ideal both as an end and as a means. It does so in the form of a commitment to free social life from the compulsions of a ready-made script. But it does not claim to be indifferent to the choice among alternative styles of association. Nor does it produce an institutional or moral blank; it is rich with implications for both the design of social institutions and the character of personal dealings.

This two-sided attitude toward the ideal of neutrality stands closely connected with an approach to the vexing question of human nature, its relative determinacy, diversity, and mutability. The institutional and personalist program should not depend upon a narrowly and dogmatically defined account of human nature. The programmatic arguments and proposals must reflect an awareness that in changing our institutions and practices we also change who we are; no motivations and drives are cast in so rigid a mold that their form, intensity, and experienced significance remain uninfluenced by the transformation of the social world. But we also know, as a matter of individual experience and historical memory, that many of our predispositions toward one another resist manipulation. Rather than attempt neatly to separate an unchanging core and a variable periphery of human nature, we can simply impose an ad hoc, loosely defined constraint. The successful realization of the program must not require any abrupt or drastic change in the predispositions we now experience. A programmatic vision could be justly criticized for requiring all-out public-spiritedness or altruism. We can choose who or what to become, but only so long as we go step by step, never expect to move very far at any one time, and resist the temptation to mistake our strongest current desires for a permanent kernel of human nature.

Thus far, I have discussed the part of the classical liberal objection to the idea of a cultural-revolutionary program that rests on a mistake about the sense in which institutional arrangements can and should be neutral. Consider now the part of the objection that reflects a more limited misunderstanding of the nature and scope of the cultural-revolutionary cause. You will soon see that this cause does not specify an inclusive, detailed picture of desirable personal relations and communal forms. It merely indicates certain minimal qualities that such forms and relations should possess. Moreover, by its very nature this personalist program cannot be coercively implemented, either by central governments or by other organizations. What governments and organizations can do to assist the cultural-revolutionary endeavor is to subvert socially enforced roles and hierarchies and to help the individual feel secure in a core of vitally protected interests. The rest depends on the politics of personal relations and decentralized institutions, carried out within these institutions and relations by their participants. Such a politics draws on the devices of fiction and enactment: to tell stories about yourself and others, to represent through these stories untried possibilities of association, and to try these possibilities out.

Despite the many reasons to extend the program of empowered democracy into a vision of transformed personal relations, this book cannot carry the extension out in detail. Both *Social Theory: Its Situation and Its Task* and *False Necessity* have argued that programmatic ideas must be intimately informed by an imagination of reality and possibility. Only then can such ideas suggest credible solutions. Only then can they cut through the false dilemma between the prostrate acceptance of current orderings of social life and the depiction of utopias that merely deny and invert a reality we feel powerless to reimagine and reconstruct.

But the explanatory argument of this book moves at the level of the large-scale institutional structure of society. The understanding it provides is too gross to serve as a capable guide to the formulation of such an intimate personalist program. A successor volume to *False Necessity* will explore the implications of the antinecessitarian thesis for an understanding of the microstructure of social life: the realm of direct practical and passionate relations. The more subtle insight into social and personal possibility to result from that exploration can inform a more persuasive ethic – for an ethic, in an enlarged, loosened, and partial sense of the term, is what the program of cultural revolution ultimately amounts to.

The following pages merely suggest the outline of a vision that needs to be worked out later, with better tools. The argument advances in three steps. First, it suggests a definition of the general theme of the cultural-revolutionary program. Second, it describes two planks in the cultural-revolutionary program: two connecting sets of qualities that this program seeks to impart to our direct dealings. Finally, it lists some of the truncated but rich materials that lie at hand, ready to assist us in our efforts to develop this part of our programmatic ideas and of our transformative practice.

A Unifying Theme of the Cultural-Revolutionary Program: A Transformed Conception of Community

Social theories offering a radical criticism of society have often held out the vision of a regenerate style of personal relations. But all too often the conception of a perfected human community put forward by these doctrines has been literally incredible. The view of the ennobled form of human solidarity has been little more than the reverse image of current experience: the dramatization of a wish to avoid all the dangers of conflict and inaccessibility that result from the independence of our wills and minds. The leftist contribution to this persistent fantasy has often been the hope that the banishment of subjugation from social life would put an end to our self-absorption and our antagonisms.

An impoverished and unbelievable idea of community emphasizes the exclusion of conflict and the sharing of values and opinions. In any society like the societies we know in history this ideal of communal life can gain a semblance of reality only in certain privileged corners of social experience, such as the intimacy of the family. Even then, it often depends for its force upon the polemical and delusive contrast established between this idealized exception to the quotidian and the character of a workaday world surrendered to the heartless exercise of dominion and the unrestrained calculation of advantage. The claim to mark out a privileged circle of communal relations frequently conceals the devolution of these purified areas of private community to the very experiences of oppression and malevolence from which they are supposed to offer a reprieve. When this ideal of community is used to inspire a vision of the transformation of all social life, the opposition between the privileged zone of harmony and the brutal, prosaic world of conflict gets replaced by a contrast between the purgatory of historical experience and the dream of a liberation from history.

The implications of this presumed rupture between history and the escape from history comes out in a comparison with a typical narrative strategy of the early romantic novel. A man and a woman fall in love with a passion whose subjective quality depends upon the vehemence with which it hurls itself against the social obstacles set in its way. Often the lovers spring from different classes, an advance over the romances of an earlier day when a legitimate love and a sound social hierarchy were regarded as inseparable and could diverge only temporarily and thanks to mistaken identities or forgotten origins. The authorities of the family, the church, and the social order are ranged against the lovers' union. The narrative revels in the story of the adventures the lovers undergo as they confront and finally overcome these many resistances. The end is the marriage, the goal and justification of all the preceding struggle and the inauguration of a higher example of human community. The trouble is that the typical romantic novel has nothing to say about what life under the new dispensation is actually like, nothing that would save the ideal of marital felicity from seeming both unrealistic and unattractive. Silence becomes its alibi: let me not bore you, reader, with the indescribable felicities of this happy union. Only in novels that have a more or less deliberately ironic relation to the early romantic ideal of marital community can the marriage be portrayed in credible terms.

A similar narrative structure appears in the radical and millennarian versions of social thought that promise a cleansed community (e.g., communism) as the reward for an immemorial fighting. Mankind, like the romantic lovers, must pass through a many-staged ordeal of class and national conflicts so that it may arrive at a form of life free from at least these forms of conflict. But, like the romantic marriage, this final reconciliation cannot be portrayed in a way that makes it seductive or even believable.

The vision of a perfected community, successful at overcoming the antagonism of its members, would not be so persistent if it did not so often seem the only available alternative to certain familiar doctrines. These doctrines identify the inadequacies of a particular form of social organization with the inherent limitations of social life, or they portray a small number of alternative forms of social organization as the repositories of incompatible sets of ideals among which we must choose. The view of social life that animates the explanatory and programmatic arguments of *Politics* rejects these apologetic doctrines without embracing the millennarian and perfectionist assumption. This view enables us to complement the institutional proposals with an ideal of direct, individual relations that is imaginatively credible. At least, the alternative proposed here does not require a sudden rupture in our prior experience of social life; it merely extends to the domain of the personal the same conception of social reality and the social ideal developed in the parts of *False Necessity* that deal with the institutional structure of society.

The result is a transformed ideal of community. Like any proposal to change an inherited evaluative notion, this revised conception of community draws its tacit meaning from the institutionalized and noninstitutionalized social practices that are meant to realize it. Having revealed, through these novel forms of practical realization, an unsuspected ambiguity in an inherited ideal, it invites us to resolve this ambiguity in a particular direction. It takes a stand on the issue of which aspects of that ideal really do or should matter most to us. (Recall the earlier discussion of the internal, standard mode of normative argument.)

The kernel of this revised ideal of community is the notion of a zone of heightened mutual vulnerability, within which people gain a chance to resolve more fully the conflict between the enabling conditions of self-assertion: between their need for attachment and for participation in group life and their fear of the subjugation and depersonalization with which such engagement may threaten them. Success at these experiments in accepted vulnerability gives us moments of ardor and empowerment, and the quality that life attains at these privileged moments can under favorable circumstances be perpetuated in lasting personal commitments and diffused through a broader social experience. This notion of community shifts the gravitational center of the communal ideal away from the sharing of values and opinions and the exclusion of conflict. Here is a version of community that, although jeopardized by conflict, also thrives on it.

The ideal of community can be most fully realized in the noninstrumental areas of social experience, where constraints imposed by the calculation of practical advantage are relaxed. But it no longer presents itself as the privileged possession of a charmed circle of private existence, contrasted polemically to the rest of social life. It becomes instead a quality that all social relations can enjoy to a greater or lesser extent.

The argument of the following sections suggests that this abstract and seemingly empty conception of community in fact points to a particular line of transformation in the subjective experience of social life. The distinctiveness of this line is brought out by its message about the performance and the betrayal of our received social roles.

A Plank in the Cultural-Revolutionary Platform: Role Defiance and Role Jumbling

A social role is simply a typical place in a recurrent social relation. Roles come in sets, and these sets of roles exist so long as there are recurrent positions some people hold in relation to others and so long as these positions exercise normative authority as well as factual influence upon the practical or passionate relations among the individuals who occupy them. The role requires discrete, repetitious, and normatively charged stations.

Any major change in the formative institutional context of social life has a transformative impact upon established roles. The effect is all the greater when the institutional program aims not merely to replace one set of roles by another but to diminish the force of roles, the influence they exercise over our experience of human connection. The loosening of roles is, in fact, just one more corollary of the softening of the contrast between structure-preserving routine and structure-transforming conflict.

One way to understand the sense of the cultural-revolutionary attack on rigid roles is to ask what it would take for some characteristic ambitions of modern moral thought to be realized. Just as classical liberal theory treats the social world it helps elucidate and support as a fluid mass of free and equal citizens and rightholders, so the dominant styles of moral speculation treat duty and obligation in the language of universalistic, role-neutral precepts. But just as the stuff of social conflict continues to be dominated by the realities of social division and hierarchy, so we expend much of our moral scruple in taking a stand about the obligations, aspirations, and expectations that mark the roles we continue to occupy. We argue about what our role duties are and how we may reconcile them, as well as about the weight we should attach to roles in general and the persistence with which we should rebel against them. Just as the attempt to actualize liberal ideals requires ideas and arrangements unfamiliar to liberals, so the effort to make our moral experience resemble more closely what so much of moral thought already supposes it to be like calls for a practice of role defiance and role jumbling that has little place in traditional moral doctrines.

The cultural revolutionary wants to show how roles can be stretched, pulled apart, combined with other roles, and used incongruously. He acts out a loosened sense of what it means to occupy a role. In this way he helps disrupt frozen connections among social stations, life experiences, and stereotyped forms of insight and sensibility. He thereby carries into the drama of everyday personal relations the effort to free sociability from its script and to make us available to one another more as the originals we all know ourselves to be and less as the placeholders in a system of group contrasts.

The roles that deserve to be targets of this cultural-revolutionary subversion are, above all, those that mark a place within a preestablished scheme of class, communal, or gender divisions: what an older sociological tradition used to call ascriptive roles. Specialized work roles are neither inherently suitable nor intrinsically unsuitable as subjects for role defiance and role jumbling. The more the technical and the social divisions of labor present themselves in everyday life as a rigid grid of functional allocations, the more they deserve to be smashed up at the microlevel of cultural-revolutionary defiance and incongruity as well as at the macrolevel of institutional innovation.

A Plank in the Cultural-Revolutionary Platform: The Confusion of Expressive Means

A striking mutual dependence exists between what people feel about the situations they are in and the means by which they communicate to other people these subjective experiences. There are stock situations and at least so far as these current means of expression go – stock responses to them. A table of correspondences arises between what people feel, or are supposed to be capable of feeling, in the recurrent circumstances of social life and the combined ways of acting, talking, and looking that convey the subjective response. The basis of these correspondences is an accommodation between subjectivity and society.

The differences in the ways that people use these available expressive means are not so great and numerous as to belie the vision of possible and desirable association enacted by society. So long as men and women believe themselves able to communicate to one another what the experiences of social life are like, and to communicate it by some recognizable variation on the repertory of standard expressed response, they continue to accept some of the crucial, realized dogmas of society. The social order may thwart both their ambition and their ideals but it does not leave any part of their subjectivity without a voice. It therefore does not seem to enshrine assumptions about possible experience that they already know to be false.

Far more than a natural language, this social code shapes what it is supposed to convey. By using it faithfully enough, you become a certain kind of person. You fulfill in yourself the implicit prophecy about human possibility the institutions and dogmas of society proclaim. Every naturalistic social doctrine has understood this truth and developed on the basis of this understanding a method of educating the passions through the constant reenactment of the proper social forms and the constant reinstatements of the proper personal responses to the typical situations of social life.

One of the aims and methods of cultural revolution is the disorganization of these codified affinities between subjective experience and expressive means. The cultural revolutionary begins by taking the fullest advantage of the incongruous aspects of all social experience: the fact that people always do feel more than the social code enables them to express. Many of these voiceless experiences may seem to have no bearing on the struggle over the collective structure of society. Yet all represent some opportunity of subjectivity and relationship whose very possibility the available code denies. In following the line of the incongruous, the cultural revolutionary has two aims. When considered in tandem, these goals suggest a method of action.

The cultural revolutionary wants to develop the varieties of relation and subjectivity that a fixed scheme of association denies, subjectivity and relationship being reverse sides of each other. Among these suppressed human opportunities are all the experiences evoked by the other elements in the work of cultural revolution. They, too, must gain vehicles of expression, for, without such vehicles, they cannot develop.

The cultural revolutionary, however, is not content to put one range of expressible subjectivity in place of another. He also wants permanently to loosen the connection between the subjective experience of personal encounters and its symbolic representation. All experience must be capable of expression, and all expression must influence the content of experience. A way must nevertheless be found to keep the life of subjectivity from becoming entirely hostage to a closed list of symbolic forms.

These two aims may seem at first contradictory: the effort to express novel experiences and the struggle to loosen the link between experience and expression. What resolves the apparent paradox is that the experiences to be expressed are primarily those described by the other parts of the program of cultural revolution. All the modes of relationship and subjectivity invoked by this program have in common some incorporation of the indeterminacy of society and personality into the minute episodes of ordinary life. The theoretical affinity between the two seemingly contradictory aims is confirmed by the power of the same practical methods of action to advance both of them.

The most important method is the displacement and combination of expressive forms originally meant to designate supposedly uncombinable subjective responses to the circumstances of social life. There is hardly an alternative: all expression must begin with the stock of available signs. Such mixing does not take place as a mere transitory expedient, to be cast aside once new appropriate symbols emerge. It keeps going on. The continued recourse to it serves to perpetrate the permanent confusion of social or sexual roles and of prescriptive models of association. It carries into the normal course of social life something of the implicit boundlessness of personal subjectivity and relationship. It keeps alive the acknowledged tension between the reach toward the unconditional and the pervasiveness of context.

The disruption of the stock forms of subjective response is accompanied by a particular spiritual anxiety, which reveals yet another side to the ambiguities of cultural revolution. The sense of having enlarged the range of expression and experience alternates with the awareness of speaking a disordered social language and of undergoing incompletely formed and expressible responses to the ordinary incidents of life. The cultural revolutionary drags the element of incongruity between experience and expression from its unmentioned corner into the center of daily existence. The ordinary person becomes to that extent more like the poet, whose visionary heightening of expressed emotion may border on unintelligibility and aphasia.

The Available Points of Departure: Two Truncated Versions of Cultural Revolution

Like the institutional program of empowered democracy that it extends, the personalist program of cultural revolution must start from the arrested and truncated versions already at hand. We need to identify them and to understand the opportunities and dangers they present.

We have witnessed two main movements of practice and sensibility in the twentieth century that approach, by their ideas and their methods, the program of cultural revolution On one side stands the radical experimentation with personal relations that characterizes in varying degrees the industrialized democracies of the North Atlantic world. Its self-reflection is the culture of high and popular modernism. On the other side, you can find in the surrounding poorer and largely non-Western world occasional radical projects for transforming the fine structure of elementary personal relationships and the ideas about self and society that underlie them. But these projects usually remain subsidiary to leftist efforts at institutional reconstruction. In different ways and for different reasons, each of the two movements falls short of the program of cultural revolution. The defects of one provide a reverse image of the flaws of the other. Either form of failure stops cultural revolution dead in its tracks after giving it an initial impulse. But each stops it in a different way.

Consider first the approach to cultural revolution in the advanced Western countries. There, the progress of a cultural-revolutionary politics of personal relations has roughly coincided with the stabilization of the formative institutional structure of society. In fact, this familiar, limited version of cultural-revolutionary practice seems to thrive on passive acquiescence in the established institutional order. Nevertheless, to speak of cultural revolution in this setting is not to grasp at metaphor or to mistake the mere struggle over personal relations for the particular programmatic vision outlined in earlier pages. Each theme in that vision is tenaciously pursued today, not just by small numbers of vanguardist critics but by ever larger multitudes. In fact, by the end of the twentieth century, the program of cultural revolution has seeped into popular culture.

But though all the themes surround us, all appear subject to a characteristic truncation. It is as if cultural revolution had been suddenly arrested in its momentum while continuing to collect details and adherents. With this concealed paralysis comes a distortion of commitment – a distortion, that is, by reference to the personalist program outlined earlier. The most general mark of this mistake lies in the tendency to treat each aspect of cultural revolution as a pretext for endless self-gratification and self-concern. Every part of the cultural-revolutionary program is interpreted negatively as a license to withdraw not only from the particular, rigidified hierarchies of value and power implicit in fixed assignments of role or schemes of association but from the very experience of larger connections and responsibilities, from the possibility of self-transcendence, and from the claims of self-sacrifice. No wonder the emancipation of personal possibility from preexisting institutions and dogmas is so often taken, in the manner of the neoromantic attitude toward love and marriage, as an opportunity to deny the permanence or the exclusivity of any personal relation. For exclusivity and permanence might imply responsibility and renunciation. No wonder the most important attachments begin to seem incompatible with any lasting social form. For a public presence would turn the intimate connection outward toward broader communal engagements. The enemies of this version of cultural revolution are right to denounce such tendencies as a gospel of despairing selfishness, promoted in the disguise of moral enlightenment.

Earlier discussion suggested that the main source of these distortions is the cutting off of radicalism in the sphere of personal relations from any practical experience of struggle over the collective structure of society, from any developed vision of a regenerate life in common. As a result of this severance, people find it hard to recognize, in any but the most abstract sense, the constraints that collective institutions in fact impose upon even the most seemingly radical experiments in personal relations. All the less role-dependent personal relations that require a novel institutional setting or a more generous set of social involvements and responsibilities run up against the limits laid down by the quiescent social world. A failure of vision completes the work of the institutional constraints. Without an active sense of engagement in the remaking and reimagining of society, people feel absolved of responsibility for the larger collective contexts of their existence and irresponsible to any shared enterprise that can precede and outlast them. The illusions of endless gratification and casual intimacy then become less a voluntary choice than an almost irresistible imaginative compulsion.

The poorer and more turbulent countries of the world have witnessed many attempts to alter the basic character of personal relations as part of a larger struggle over the collective structure of society. When these attempts have won a broader popular allegiance, they have in fact established a connection between conflicts in the most intimate and the most public spheres.

Nevertheless, the practice of cultural revolution often emerges in these settings as if distracted and even obsessed by anxieties far narrower and more focused than the concerns embraced by the radicalism about personal relations that has spread throughout the North Atlantic countries. Thus, the link between the remaking of institutions and the transformation of personal relations has been established in a mutilated form that drastically limits and vitiates the significance of the achievement.

This other practice of cultural-revolutionary politics has had two obsessional targets: the contrast between the mass and the elite, and that between the pure and the impure. Sometimes one, sometimes the other, stands at the forefront of concern. The Chinese communist practice of "criticism and self-criticism" and Gandhi's method of pedagogic defilement neatly exemplify each.

The technique of criticism and self-criticism, first conceived by Liu Shao-ch'i and his collaborators, was reinterpreted and revised under the impact of the "mass line." This technique had roots that long predated the communist take-over of state power. It had been a device for reaffirming common purpose, discipline, and hierarchy within an in-group of beleaguered revolutionaries. The victim recanted. The group of cadres readmitted the deviant. All rearticulated and reaffirmed the doctrinal and organizational essentials of their movement. Under the influence of the mass line, pioneered by Mao Tse-tung and his coterie and then accepted and enlarged by zealous agitators, the method changed its form and purpose. In the hands of its most radical practitioners, it became part of an attempt to chasten and, if possible, to destroy the established bureaucracies of party and state and to produce a new man or woman, new above all in their attitude toward authority. The victim now appeared often as the mere pretext for the reenactment of a collective denunciation of every trace that the inherited contrast of masses and elites had imprinted upon the style of direct personal relations. Because that contrast had amounted to a hierarchy of value as well as to a system of control, its subversion had all the seductive and liberating force of an attack upon the distinction between the pure and the impure. The crudest allocations of personal role, or the most rigid conceptions of the style of association suitable to each domain of social life, could be accepted so long as they did not overtly involve the feared contrast between elite and mass.

Recall, by comparison, Gandhi's teaching and agitation in India. Consider the aspect of his activity that comes closest to the status of cultural revolution: not passive disobedience against the imperial master but the attempt to form a man who can be the citizen of a single nation, capable of common allegiance and even compassionate solidarity, across the frontiers traced by the norms of caste and ritual purity. In Gandhi's world, the distance among castes appeared bound up with the ritual contrast of the pure and the impure. To disrespect caste lines was the exemplary form of impurity. The position of each group within the caste hierarchy could be justified, though not explained, by the group's relative closeness to the purest or the most impure activities. The most cultural-revolutionary aspect of Gandhi's politics was his practice of defilement and his recruitment of others to share this practice with him: to reach out to the forbidden person, to undertake the most humiliating work, to touch the dirtiest thing (though exalting cleanliness and continence as high forms of virtue). The empowered person was the person who had emancipated himself, through repeated practice, from the fixed hierarchies of value that stood in the way of mutual responsibility and shared nationhood. Insofar as the caste system represented the chief locus of this ranking of values, the defiance of the values included an attack upon the system. But no more developed vision of cultural-revolutionary practice or program emerges from this relentless, focused concern. Even the longing for a civilization of self-reliant, communal villages represents less a deliberate rejection of the ideals that inspire the program of empowered democracy and cultural revolution than an avoidance of the need to describe in detail the face-to-face relations a suitably empowered individual should hope to experience.

The ideas, attitudes, and power relations implicated in the contrasts between mass and elite or the pure and the impure do indeed act as a bar to the realization of the cultural-revolutionary program. But the single-minded focus on these concerns to the exclusion of others narrows the front on which cultural revolution can be staged and leaves untouched much of the established structure of social life. Stubborn fighting over the mastery of the state and the organization of the economy often occurs side by side with the rebirth of style of personal association characteristic of an earlier, destroyed social order. The radicalism in the sphere of intimacy that has spread throughout the Western industrial democracies and penetrated its world-seducing popular culture combines insight and illusion, both empowering and disabling its practitioners. But it has often been dismissed by the militants and theoreticians of third world cultural revolution, forgetful of their own disabilities, as the autumnal and luxurious self-indulgence of dying classes and civilizations.

In one view, the advanced Western countries represent the privileged terrain for the execution of the cultural-revolutionary program. Their more thoroughgoing supersession of the contrast between masses and elites, and their wider acquaintance with the transvaluation of hierarchies of values, has freed them from constrictive obsessions and enabled them to practice the politics of role defiance and role jumbling on the broadest front. In another view, the poorer and more tumultuous places where the collective structure of society seems more fully up for grabs, represent the favored theater for cultural revolution. There, people fight out the conflict over personal relations, in depth, as part of a questioning of the whole social order. Larger collective involvements and responsibilities sweep aside the corrupting illusions of self-gratification. Both views are one-sided and even impertinent. The point is to connect the revolutionary reform of institutional arrangements with the cultural-revolutionary remaking of personal relations. In this effort there is no uniquely favored terrain and there are no clearly anointed champions of the cause.

15

The Idea of the Transformative Vocation

A First Point of Departure

Three basic ideas about work are now available in the world. These ideas are not just about jobs; seen from a wide enough perspective, they involve people's views of what they can expect to do with their lives, and they put in question the tie between the family and society. The rivalry of these conceptions, as they have been variously developed by different classes and among different peoples, gives rise to an obscure but decisive spiritual struggle. People wage this struggle all over the world, through contrasting visions of society and secret movements of the heart.

Each of these visions of work finds its chief home in the experience and outlook of a part of society. But the groups responsible for developing the idea vary from one moment in history, and even from one society, to another.

Work may be seen as an honorable calling within society. So conceived, labor enables the individual (at first the man but then others as well) to support the family that provides him with his most important sustaining relations. The job as honorable calling helps shape a person's view of his own dignity. He can do something that fulfills one of the natural needs of society. He fulfills it by performing, or preparing for, work that requires proficiency or experience. His job, and the trained and learned capacities with which he performs it, singles him out from the shifting, the dependent, and the useless.

The idea of work as an honorable calling usually accompanies certain preconceptions about society and the family. There exists a catalog of natural needs: social demands that have to be met for a society to go on as it always has. To this catalog of impersonal jobs, there corresponds an equally natural list of occupations, each with its distinctive skills and rewards. The person who occupies one of these positions can expect to live with his family in a certain way. He also has, at work, a distinctive relation to the people who do other jobs. Thus, an idea of natural ranks accompanies the notion of natural social needs and natural jobs.

The social world that these honorable callings keep going knows its share of conflict. But its quarrels – according to this view of social life – deal more with peripheral matters. People may feel that they have been done an injustice. They may try to grab more for themselves and their co-workers than what they are properly entitled to. In either event there will be trouble. But the basic order of needs, jobs, and ranks is not, in its fundamentals, the outcome of such struggles. It is just part of the way things are. You can go a long way toward qualifying this view of social life without giving up its central tenets. For the naturalistic attitude to society seems far more persuasive in the nuance of active belief than in the caricature of exposition.

The image of work as an honorable calling and the larger vision of society that extends and justifies it have often been accompanied by a view of the family. The honorable worker is, above all, the adult man. His performance of the honorable job outside the family lends moral authority as well as economic support to his position within the family. The family itself amounts to a softened, smaller-scale version of the social world. The wife and the children occupy a recognized place within the family. By performing their roles scrupulously, they earn the respect of their wider social milieu. When all goes well, the greater world of society and the smaller realm of the family display a fundamental harmony both in their economic requirements and in their moral principles.

Today, this idea of work flourishes most vigorously among the skilled and semiskilled working classes of the rich Western and the communist societies. It survives better among those who do something with their hands or who apply techniques with tangible results than among the lower ranks of paper pushers and commodity circulators. But until recently in the history of the West, and of many of the civilizations whose life the Western peoples have interrupted, all ranks of society shared this conception of work. Even the most privileged groups embraced it. The gentleman landowner might disclaim anything that looked like a job. But his view of himself included the idea of occupying a natural station that both entitled and obligated him to perform valuable social tasks. He showed he was up to it by exhibiting in his person and his deeds the qualities proper to his caste.

Another, more chastened idea of work is also loose in the world. According to this conception, work lacks any intrinsic authority, any power of its own to confer dignity or direction on a human life. You have to do it to achieve or support the things that count: your family and your community or, if worse comes to worst, your own self. If labor can still be said to be honorable in this instrumental view, the honor lies solely in the activities its earnings support.

The instrumental view of work represents drastically diminished expectations of what a person can make of his life. It is in fact, and is understood to be, an aberration: the stigma of a terrible defeat or the price of a transition to a higher mode of life. In the rich Western countries of the present day, three types of workers seem most often to share this vision of work.

Some are people who have been defeated in their attempt to grow up into the honorable working class or who have been cast out of this class after having gotten into it. They float from one unstable and dead-end job to another, and pine in the suffering underclass.

Others who hold this instrumental view of work also occupy the worst and least secure jobs. They often come from a foreign country or a backward region, to which they hope to return. For them, work is a purgatory governed by rules they can barely understand. They analogize its arrangements as best they can to the ideas of obligation and reward they have brought with them to a new land. Their over-riding goal remains to go back home to a better life that includes the experience of labor as an honorable calling. This hope may eventually be frustrated. It may also be replaced by the desire to stay where they are and there to become the honorable workers they had at first thought of becoming back home. Meanwhile, they live in their communities and find in these communal bonds the consolations and the self-respect their jobs deny them.

Still others who hold the instrumental conception of work are young people or married women willing to take on temporary jobs. For them, too, the immediate conception of work can be unashamedly instrumental because it remains ancillary to their main concern: a future career or the life of the family.

In other parts of the globe – in some of the communist and third world countries – access to the experience of work as an honorable calling remains barred to vast numbers of people. These people may be driven to a purely instrumental vision of labor. But, at every opportunity, they may also put up a rearguard struggle and demand something better.

For to conceive of your workaday activity in this manner is to view the social world as utterly oppressive or alien. If the personality is not discredited and crushed by this world, it is at least (with the exception of the part-time workers) denied any sense of belonging to it. Confidence in a natural order of needs, jobs, and ranks is shaken, though not dissipated. The defeated and the excluded understand more easily what the self-deception of the honorable workers tends to conceal: that the entire order of jobs and ranks – not just its details and adjustments – results from fighting and from the containment of fighting. They have seen the fist without the glove and have looked in through the window, with the undeceived eyes of the outcast, at the indifference of the fortunate. But they would gladly exchange this insight – which is, in part, a discovery of the falsehood of the naturalistic premise – for a reprieve from their defeat or their exclusion.

A third idea of work has appeared in the world, and it is turning things inside out. It connects self-fulfillment and transformation: the change of any aspect of the practical or imaginative setting of the individual's life. To be fully a person, in this conception, you must engage in a struggle against the defects or the limits of existing society or available knowledge. The goals of self-fulfillment and service to society combine with the notion that such service requires you to press against things and conceptions as they are. The quarrel may be pursued in imaginative work rather than out in the open. Even when it involves real-life conflict, it may be moderated and concealed under the appearance of faithful service. But it cannot be abandoned altogether without exacting a price in disappointment and failure. Resistance becomes the price of salvation. Only when you move away from the concern with the terms of collective life toward the more impersonal endeavors of art, philosophy, and science or give yourself over to the immediate care of individuals does the weight of this command diminish.

This idea of work – and of what you can most valuably do with your life – has taken root most strongly among the educated and the privileged, and especially among the young who are educated for privilege. You can find it most unequivocally among intellectuals, agitators, artists, and scientists. But it extends as well into the great professions. Each profession does more than link a privileged exercise of power to a claim of expertise. It also serves as the scene of a conflict between the idea of the honorable calling and the more ambitious standard of the transformative vocation.

The people who have been converted to this view of what they should do with themselves run into trouble in their experience of their own lives and in their relations to all the groups who have stuck with another vision of what work and life are for. Even after you have tried to understand, with a clear mind and a quiet heart, what the trouble means, you cannot easily tell. Is there a flaw in the idea of the transformative vocation that condemns it to futility and self-deception? Is it, in this respect, like a certain romantic view of love with which it has been historically associated? Or are these difficulties and surprises the unavoidable road to higher insight?

A person may come under the influence of the idea of the transformative vocation in his youth. Much may bring him over to it. Even for those who deny that it conveys any ultimate truth about mind and activity, its presence, its omnipresence, in the productions of high culture is hard to miss. The works of literature and social thought, of speculative theory and moral sloganeering, revel in it. The broader popular culture speaks it back in a thousand diluted but still recognizable forms. Both the political heroes and the modernist antiheroes of the age seem to embody one aspect or another of its central concerns.

The more seriously someone takes these ideas, the greater his difficulties are likely to be. As soon as he begins to face the resistances and the entanglements of the social world, the effort to realize the idea of the transformative vocation starts to seem an unrealistic and self-destructive program. It seems to demand both a favorable opportunity and corresponding gifts. If either are absent, what begins in high purpose may end as mere anxiety.

As the obstacles to an actual transformative involvement pile up, the would-be transformer faces ever more clearly a destructive dilemma. He may trim his sails and look for more modest and "realistic" expectations. But it is not easy to pass from the idea of the transformative vocation to the notion of the honorable calling. The former implies an insight into the relation between self and society that strikes at the foundations of the latter. This insight is just too convincing to forget, once the individual has recognized it and acted it out, however incompletely or unsuccessfully.

The assumptions that underlie the idea of the transformative vocation combine an idea about society with an idea about the self. Society lacks natural needs, jobs, and ranks; whatever the social order is, it is as a result of the fights that have taken place and of the fights that have been avoided. Your work may serve a human need whose claim to attention you regard as unquestionable. But what people make of you, your station, and your work is not something that you can take for granted as the natural order of things. This given context may confirm, distort, or defeat your intention.

The idea about self that joins this notion of society is the primacy of transforming denial in all human activities. You satisfy desires by changing something in the world. You understand a portion of reality by passing it, in fact or fantasy, through transformative variations: by imagining it other than what it is or seems to be. All the more complicated enterprises of the personality involve equally complicated revisions of the practical or imaginative setting through which the individual moves. Through such efforts, and through them alone, you discover and make yourself.

These ideas about self and society betray a disbelief in what I earlier called the naturalistic premise as well as revealing a particular view of the purpose of a working life. The notion of an honorable calling cannot easily be made plausible again without resurrecting the vision of self and society implicit in the naturalistic premise.

The person who can neither make good on his commitment to a transformative vocation nor gain faith in the idea of the honorable calling soon finds himself driven down to the instrumental conception of work. He seeks in the family or the spectacles of an ornamental culture compensatory solace for his incompensable loss. He cannot view his own instrumental work as the necessary transition to a higher form of experience.

When the idea of the transformative vocation runs into trouble it can take another direction. It may escalate rather than diminish its ambitions. Beyond the give-and-take of ordinary social life lie the great redemptive exercises of revolutionary thought, practice, and art. The artist sitting in his cork-lined room holds out the only true promise of happiness and salvation (but for himself or for everybody else as well?). Someone grinds away at his desk in the British Museum systematizing views about which most of his informed contemporaries hardly know what to think. A few generations later, people will be slaughtering one another in Manchuria in the name of his doctrines. Someone else arrives suddenly at a train station in the midst of violent civic commotion, seizes the state with the support of a disciplined following and an indignant mass, and inaugurates a new order of social life.

As escape routes for an embattled idea of transformative vocation, these images serve as corrupting delusions. They exclude all but a tiny band of extraordinary people. They cover up the actual texture of compromise, circumstance, resistance, and disappointment, the fantastic incongruity between intention and result, even in these unusual experiences. The heart, in its despair, wants to forget such indignities.

The two directions in which the idea of the transformative calling can move amount to two complementary ways of losing sanity. For the cognitive element in madness is precisely the alternation between two experiences of perception and reasoning. Perceptions and ideas are frozen in place; they cannot be recombined or replaced. At the same time, everything can be effortlessly broken down and combined with everything else. The simultaneous coexistence of these experiences makes all perceptions and thoughts appear arbitrary.

But suppose a person manages to keep the idea of transformative work from falling off in either of these directions. He soon finds himself at odds not only with people who share a different perspective on the aims of transformation but also with people who have a completely different view of work. He then has to recognize that activity inspired by such intentions contains, directly or indirectly, a claim to power that others resist and that he himself may be unable to justify or to confess. He may even try to get them to act in ways justified by his idea of work but opposed by them, in the name of their own ideals of labor and community, as a surrender to selfishness.

For example, a militant in a rich Western country fights to vindicate rights of abortion for unmarried women. He does so in part because he has an idea of personal dignity connected to his own idea of vocation. He wants to imagine, or to make, this idea universal. The working class family fights back not only out of religious belief but out of the desire to preserve, through the repression of occasional sexual unions, its own hierarchic authority, the accompaniment to its own ideas of work as honorable calling. After all, what more inclusive and more perfect form of social solidarity does the self-appointed champion have to put in place of the one he is trying to destroy?

If the would-be transformer is someone who acts in the world, he may fantasize that he belongs to a mass of people who increasingly share his vision of history and work. The existence of factions, the dense confusions of personal animosity and programmatic difference, the struggle for leadership, the elements of self-aggrandizement in his own conception of his calling – each of these amounts to a knock on the door that he would rather not answer. Once he has tasted power, however, he may find such fantasies convenient. He may present himself as the voice of those to whom he gives orders.

The idea of the transformative vocation has begun to influence large numbers of people all over the world. It wages a largely mute spiritual struggle against the other two notions of work. Where did this demanding and even dreamlike view come from? What is its essential human meaning? You would be misguided to see it merely as the result of local episodes in the history of thought. In some parts of the Western world, the idea bears the imprint of a secularized version of Protestant ideas of calling. But it has advanced everywhere, independently as well as by contagion. The conception of an honorable calling has been undermined by the insights into self and society described earlier. Through them, the idea of the transformative vocation connects to everything that shows people the made-up, remakable, and reimaginable quality of social life, to everything that frees the conception and the ordeal of personality from rigid social constraints. People seize on traditional religious, political, and moral doctrines and reinterpret them from the perspective of the new dispensation.

Once you view the idea of the transformative vocation from this more general standpoint you can identify in it a still larger human meaning. This meaning clarifies the hidden ambiguities, aspirations, and dangers of the idea, so carefully concealed in the ordinary thoughts and deeds of its adherents. The less the individual sees himself as occupying a natural position within a society that itself has a natural order, the more acutely he feels a certain aspect of his situation in his world. He feels it, ordinarily, less in its abstract and general statement than in particular and concrete ramifications. The person experiences himself as the center of his own world. He knows himself in a way that he can know no other mind. He feels, in his less guarded moments, a will to self-assertion and to the satisfaction of a desire that knows no fixed boundaries other than the limits imposed by temporary satiation, apathy, or despair. When he imagines the world without himself, after his own death, he still hovers there as a disembodied onlooker. But the individual is also made to confront the world as a subject among many others. He must develop introspection by participating in a practical and discursive give-and-take that constantly denies his claim to be the center of things. He must satisfy his material and spiritual needs by performing activities that force him to deal with people who do not see him as the center and in whose lapses into self-centeredness he sees the barely suppressed traces of his own self-absorption.

But when all the taunting correctives have piled up, the individual's claim to be the center still refuses to go away. How can we even call it a mistake? It is built into the most elementary pretheoretical moments of perception and desire. It belongs to the intimate and ultimate though ill-defined experience of selfhood. Our reflective ideas may refine this experience but they can never repudiate it without ceasing to be persuasive or even intelligible.

That we lay claim to the center while recognizing at the same time that we are not the center is more than a natural fact about us, like our susceptibility to certain optical illusions. It is just as basic to our experience as the structure of conceptual thought whose preconceptions about sameness and difference prohibit us from saying that we both are and are not the center. By what standard can we choose between the conceptual structure and the counterconceptual experience? Though we disbelieve the latter in certain contexts of understanding and action or when certain interests seem paramount, we put aside the former in other settings and for other purposes. A person incapable of making this switch would be judged more insane than many of the madmen we actually meet. For his madness would not be simply the exaggeration of a conflict, a self-division, in ordinary experience. It would be a denial of one of the enabling conditions of our routine perceptions and responsibilities.

The contrast between these two aspects of personality cannot become acute so long as the views of society and self that underlie the idea of work as an honorable calling survive. For these views prevent the experience of subjectivity, and therefore of the self as center, from reaching desperate and anxious lengths. They teach people to understand their internal world of passion and the outward order of society as two complementary realms that display the same principles of order and that, when well ordered, lend each other indispensable support. These naturalistic ideas cannot abolish the contrast in our experience between self-centeredness and the overcoming of self-centeredness. The ideas can, however, deny this experience a voice and make its occasional manifestations look like mere outbreaks of delusory self-regard. When, however, people no longer adhere to the naturalistic view underlying the idea of work as an honorable calling, the conflict between the two poles of experience breaks out into the open.

Personal love and transformative work enable people to escape selfishness and isolation without denying the weight of subjectivity. In love, they find a connection to another person that simultaneously confirms them in their sense of self-possession. Transformative action offers them a way to establish an alternative connection: an engagement with the larger collective context of their lives that gives the acting or imagining self a chance for self-assertion while refusing to sanctify the resistant context. Whichever route of connection you follow, you have surprises in store.

The pursuit of the transformative solution faces two obstacles, which are also riddles. The first embarrassment is the coexistence of constant resistance to all the transforming efforts of the imagination and the will with our failure ever fully to understand the sources of this resistance. This failure plagues us in every area of experience. Some of the reasons for this inability are distinctive to each field of activity; others are common to all fields.

Nonhuman nature remains imperfectly knowable and manageable because of its vast disproportion to our own selves. We know nature only in part, through forms of practice and imagination that, though they imitate transformative variations of the natural world, do so from the limiting perspective of our interests and faculties. One level of insight falls down into another, more basic or universal, without any hope of reaching a place of rest.

Society remains imperfectly intelligible and pliable because it is made up of distinct selves, each with its power to resist submission and disclosure. Moreover, no practical or imaginative ordering of human life represents the definitive, complete form of personality or society, nor do all the orderings that have ever existed, when put together. In every realm of society or non-human nature, our ideas suffer from an incurable instability: we may always discover at the next moment something that is not just novel but incompatible with our assumptions. Not only may we have ignored this truth before, but we may have ignored the whole way of thinking, or seeing, or talking that its full exploration requires.

The recalcitrance of our circumstances to complete mastery by the imagination and the will has an important corollary in political action: the inability fully to comprehend or control the consequences of action. William Morris described the ironic pathos of every transformative conflict over the terms of social life: "Men fight and lose the battle, and the thing they fought for comes about in spite of their defeat, and when it comes turns out to be not what they wanted, and other men must fight for what they wanted under another name."

The other problem with transforming action comes from within. The transformative deed fails completely to bridge the gap between the self as center and the self as one among others. It remains a bid for self-aggrandizement as well as a form of self-renunciation. The vicissitudes of the transformative vocation in society bring out this two-sidedness. The would-be transformer wants to shine and even to rule while portraying himself as the humble and responsive servant of an impersonal good. The self-appointed revolutionary vanguard, lording it over a frightened or passive populace in the name of a doctrine of virtual representation, is simply the extreme case of what appears, less starkly, in countless other disguises.

Most great social theories of the last two centuries accepted and attempted to explicate and develop the ideas underlying this revolutionary conception of work. But they did so in a way that concealed the embarrassments just described. They thereby limited the reach of the idea of the transformative vocation. They viewed the obstacles to transformation as the products of lawlike constraints that a fully informed mind would render fully intelligible. The would-be transformers could present themselves as agents of a historical necessity. The claim to be the unchosen agents of the oppressed and the voiceless remained their characteristic response to the suspicion of self-aggrandizement.

One way to understand the constructive social theory anticipated by this book is to read it as an attempt to carry to the hilt the view of society and personality within which the idea of the transformative vocation makes sense. We must reason about constraints without seeing them as the superficial expression of intelligible, lawlike necessities. We must describe how the antinaturalistic conception of self and society can inform the life projects of an individual. We must even try to show how it can guide these projects in ways that contain and ennoble the self-aggrandizing impulse.

16
The Spirit

THE SPIRIT OF THE CONSTITUTION: EMPOWERMENT IMAGINED AND PERVERTED

In the industrial democracies of the late twentieth century the ideal of empowerment lives a strange double life. This ideal has already been realized in the important but truncated form of an experience of rightholding open to large numbers of ordinary men and women. Here is empowerment as the ability to move within the discretionary zone of entitlements defined on the model of the consolidated property right. The achievements and deficiencies of this version of empowerment, as well as the alternatives to it, have already been discussed.

The felt inadequacy of this experience of rightholding becomes evident in the fantasies of adventure and mastery. These fantasies are not even meant to be lived out. When, in exceptional circumstances, people have taken them seriously and acted upon them, the results have often been disastrous.

The hidden, second life of the empowerment ideal shows the extraordinary force of this longing and the perverse forms it assumes when left unrealized in the ordinary lives of ordinary men and women. Consider a typical example of the aestheticized presentation of empowerment in the twentieth century: Abel Gance's cinematic extravaganza about Napoleon Bonaparte (1934). There he is – the great hero, the man of will, embodying to the highest degree the rage of transcendence and the transformative vocation. He refuses to take the established contexts of action for granted and repeatedly smashes, or threatens to smash, them. He combines an acute insight into the opportunities and dangers of his situation with an ability to imagine possibilities that the logic of this situation excludes. He conducts himself within the established world as if he possessed secret knowledge, and indeed he does.

The context smasher puts himself into situations that others would regard as ridiculous and demeaning (e.g., Napoleon's awkward and self-deceiving pursuit of the philanderer Josephine). He doesn't feel tainted; he just doesn't give a damn. For one thing, his efforts are all turned toward his great enterprise and away from the petty ambitions and fears of ordinary life. For another thing, he transvalues the hierarchies of his contemporaries: his greater freedom from the context enables him to judge by another hierarchy of value. Therefore, he appears to be shameless when he is in fact guided by an alternative moral vision. This vision does not merely replace one hierarchy of values by another; it partly liberates moral judgment from the constraining effect of any clearly defined hierarchy.

The same forces that free him from the fear of being laughed at also emancipate him from small-minded vanities and resentments. (Remember that all this is part of the myth presented in the film rather than of the actual psychological reality of these individuals.) Although he may be ruthless in his treatment of particular individuals and loyalties, he never indulges in revenge for its own sake, nor can he be manipulated through vanity. After all, he is on more important business and has greater pleasures.

Then there are the piercing eyes, the intense, wild expression that the man of will shares with all the secondary characters and even the ordinary mobs drawn into the momentous events he commands. It reminds you of those books of nineteenth- and early twentieth century photographs of Chinese, Japanese, and Russians. The subject looks into the camera with the same crazed expression. Perhaps his disquiet comes from the unfamiliarity of the camera, which seems to puncture the shell of social routine and produce a moment of dazed incongruity in which the familiar limits and aims of action fall away and deeper, wordless concerns rise up. Perhaps the surprise given by the machine serves both to exemplify and to portray the larger shock administered by the Western intrusion. Perhaps, however, these circumstances merely precipitated a distinctive, ambivalent experience of human empowerment. The fierce-eyed subjects, amid their ornate or ragged trivia, look as if they had seen beyond the photographer and their circumstance to a reality previously hidden from their eyes. They had seen something of the God who says, No man sees me and lives. Similarly, in the Gance film, the actors looked at the moving camera as the exotic photography subjects had looked at the still one. The revolutionary interlude replaced with advantage the Western shock. All the way from the transcendent man of will to the agitated crowds, the participants seem in touch with another, higher reality, with the things you see and feel when one conditional world has been destroyed and another not yet emerged, as if this crack in the finite provided a glimpse into the absolute. At any moment, this context-breaking brio might be converted into an idolatrous delusion: people might treat their particular historical endeavors as if these undertakings were themselves the absolute. Such were the risks and complications of a more radiant vitality.

All these aspects of human empowerment – the frenzied pursuit of the transformative vocation; the freedom from the fear of the ridiculous, from the compulsion of mean-minded concerns, and from the "narcissism of petty differences"; the ability to impart to worldly action the ardor that accompanies the loosening of the constraints of context – all this appeared bound up with a special union between leader and followers. At a still more concrete level, it seems inseparable from particular forms of mass organization. The leader achieved empowerment in a basically different fashion from the other people. He alone took events by the hand and thereby realized the transformative vocation in all its purity. He required no teachers or mediators and promised no equality with himself: on the contrary, equality among his followers depended upon their acceptance of his special role. When, for example, he freed himself from the fear of the ridiculous, there was never a suggestion that they could do the same, except perhaps unconsciously as the result of a spell he cast on them and they on one another.

The exceptionalism of the leader was connected, obscurely but significantly, to the form of his historical enterprise. In different degrees and in different ways, pseudorevolutionary nationalism and its surrogates involved the superimposition of a communal ideal upon social hierarchies that this ideal simultaneously adjusted and preserved. Such movements often embraced the cult of warlike force, wielded by the collectivity under the guidance of the leader. Thus, the psychological experience of empowerment was to be realized through social forms that constrained or negated the different aspects of freedom. Yet empowerment meant freedom if it meant anything. Here was a social experience at war with itself: a monstrous equivocation, already prefigured in the circumstance of followers whose access to the sense of empowerment paradoxically depended upon their submission to a leader or upon their absorption in a crowd. Nevertheless, the film presented the experience of empowerment as if it were inseparable from these offensive manifestations.

The audience at the cinema stood at a second, safer remove from the man of will. They responded with barely suppressed fascination to the representation of greatness while ashamed and even repelled by the social forms that greatness took. They got no help in distinguishing the former from the latter, nor could they readily imagine any alternative way by which society might extend the availability of empowerment.

The epic grandeur evoked by such a film did for the audience what the bewitching force of a more or less consciously staged collective drama did for the participant crowds and the secondary characters within the film: it provided their admiration with an alibi. But the apparent alibi ended up calling attention to the crime. The aesthetic of empowerment – the worship of an imaginative power to transform reality unaffected by ordinary human longing, the substitution of art for religion and even for love – ran through much modern art. In the antinovelistic style of works of art like these, it reached its most crudely and overtly political but also most revealing form.

To comprehend what attracted the audience, however ambivalently, to this display of impenitent grandeur, you need to understand some crucial aspects of the circumstance people lived in. The less advantaged ranks of society might be almost entirely preoccupied with the need to find work, to support a family, and maintain a position within a residual local or ethnic community. Many might still adhere to an ideal of the honorable calling that made them relatively immune to larger conceptions of empowerment. But whenever the compulsions of material need loosened, or people's actual or imagined experience of social and personal possibility broadened, the conception of empowerment underwent a corresponding change. All the varieties of happiness that involved the experience of transforming a context emerged alongside the longing to exist safely within a context. There was little chance of a naive return to the mere acceptance of place within an unquestioned world. Return, under these conditions, would produce a sentiment of defeat and self-compromise, poisoning the more limited happiness that people knew and cherished. The extraordinary and lucky individual – the leader, the artist, the thinker, the mover and shaker – might satisfy his aspiration. But he satisfied it in a way that excluded other people and that perpetuated, in some less dramatic form, the paradoxes of empowerment that exclusion produced. Neither the privileged nor the excluded could imagine, much less realize, an alternative social form of empowerment. The character of their fantasies emphasized the nature of their constraint.

A driving force of the constitutional program is the desire to do justice to the human heart, to free it from indignity and satisfy its hidden and insulted longing for greatness in a fashion it need not be fearful or ashamed of. To this end, the experience of empowerment must be made real rather than vicarious. It must be reconciled with the ordinary needs and attachments of ordinary people. And it must be freed from its corrupting association with the cult of leaders and of violence. The program outlined here describes the institutional requirements for achieving these objectives.

THE SPIRIT OF THE CONSTITUTION REDEFINED BY CONTRAST

The spirit of this institutional proposal becomes clearer by contrast to other, familiar doctrines of the present or the past that superficially resemble it.

In the contemporary world, the most persistently attractive program of social reconstruction has often been described as social democracy or as the welfare–corporate state. Its most developed forms have emerged in Western Europe and Japan. To be sure, even in the advanced industrial democracies, it has prospered far more in some places than in others. But its influence, at least among the industrial democracies, is shown by the failure of more left-wing or right-wing political parties to make a major dent on its achievements or to find a political creed of comparable authority.

Recall the major tenets of the social-democratic program. First, it upholds the particular variant of constitutional democracies whose instruments were first perfected in the crucial period from the late eighteenth to the mid-nineteenth century – though its proponents may say this institutional structure is merely the best one around, rather than show much interest in looking for significantly different alternatives. For they believe that the main problems and concerns lie elsewhere. Second, this doctrine holds that government must actively supervise a regulated market economy organized along just the lines of the formative institutional context whose content and genesis have been described earlier. The democratic state must encourage investment in the most promising sectors of industry. It must seek to place the national economy in a favorable place within the international division of labor. And it must broker with big business and organized labor, as well as with other sectors of the population, distributive deals that enable all to turn from disruptive conflict to productive collaboration. Third, people's basic material needs must be taken care of. This objective may be accomplished through either a recognition of universal welfare claims independent of job position, or an emphasis on job security, accompanied by a tie of welfare benefits to job position. Fourth, people should be encouraged to participate in the organization of the workplace and the management of their local areas. These local engagements should help blur the distinction between public and private order and revitalize the sense of citizenship. Fifth, both welfare guarantees and local participation should be achieved in ways minimizing conflict about the social order as a whole. Such conflict gives free reign to ideological posturing, utopian illusions, and selfish defensiveness that draw people away from the collaborative undertakings needed to solve practical problems.

Two mutually reinforcing impulses underlie the social-democratic program and make clear why it is simply the most recent version of the desire to deny or contain the political character of social life. One such impulse is the perennial desire to retreat from the violent connotations of history into a stable life of practical concerns and communal engagement. The other impulse is the effort to discover the objective structure of practical requirements and organizational constraints that the loose talk of the ideologists disguises.

The argument for empowered democracy sees this social democratic program as practically, spiritually, and theoretically inadequate. It is practically inadequate because the development of productive or destructive capabilities requires a more thorough subversion of the hold of privilege over the means of society making than the established institutional versions of markets and democracies allow. It is spiritually inadequate because this same liquefaction of established social structures is needed to develop the richness of our subjective life and to advance our attempts to reconcile more fully the enabling conditions of self-assertion. It is theoretically inadequate because it relies upon yet another diluted residue of the naturalistic idea: it still draws on the idea of a latent structure of flexible coordination and collaboration that is waiting there to be discovered, if only we could get rid of the distractions of ideological conflict.

The program defended here diverges from the social-democratic ideal in its advocacy of radically revised ways of organizing market economies and democratic governments, in its search for the institutional arrangements that further soften the contrast between context-preserving routine and context-revising conflict, in its preference for the styles of welfare guarantees that presuppose these institutional reforms rather than compensating for their absence, and in its effort systematically to connect involvement in local and workplace self-government with conflict over the basic terms of social life.

If social democracy conceived in these ample terms represents the closest counterpart and rival to the program of empowered democracy, civic or classical republicanism may seem to be one of its sources. But the genealogy is no more accurate than the comparison. The civic republicanism to which I refer has been the single most important rhetorical weapon of many who oppose both the selfish privatism and the rampant inequality they see as continuing to vitiate contemporary Western forms of economic and governmental organization. The characteristic republican trope is the need to recapture the selfless devotion to collective ends that supposedly distinguished the ancient republics. Its ambition is to ensure an equality of material circumstance and to enlist a selfless devotion to the common good. Equality is to be ensured by granting each citizen a roughly equal unit of property. Prohibitions of alienation (e.g., of land) and constant redistributions must prevent exchange from undermining this fundamental equality. Devotion to the common good is to be won by requiring the citizens, from childhood on, to participate in public responsibilities and by deploying all the varieties of education and example that may coax them out of their tendency to withdraw into narrow attachments and material pleasures. The tenacity with which some partial version of this doctrine has been upheld under the most diverse historical circumstances is matched only by the regularity of its failure whenever it has been allowed to influence, even obliquely, actual policy.

The material cost of the classical republican doctrine lies in the paralysis of the power to innovate. For, as earlier stages of the argument have repeatedly emphasized, the development of practical capabilities depends upon the ability to recombine and renew, by consensual or coercive means, not only the factors of production but the arrangements that constitute the organizational setting of productive activity. A country nailed to the constraints upon recombination that classical republicanism requires could not survive in the military, economic, and ideological rivalry of nation-states. Nor could it provide its citizens with the many opportunities for individual and collective experimentation that enrichment opens up.

The spiritual cost of the classical republican program is even more terrible. The equal rightholders live in a circumstance of self-conscious austerity. This austerity is not due merely to the constraints such a system of right imposes upon material progress; it results as well from the spiritual incompatibility of this regime with luxury. Luxury means, in part, the surfeit and variety of sensual pleasure particularly insofar as this pleasure is directed away from personal attachment to material things or symbolic representations. The psychology of variation and surfeit cannot easily be reconciled to a circumstance requiring the quiescence of basic social arrangements, a basic sameness in the outward conditions of life, and the comparative isolation of each rightholder within his separate sphere of right. In such a circumstance, the individual readily falls victim to two contrasting sets of emotions, which sometimes coexist and at other times replace each other. He may wallow in a torpor of narrow routine (after all, how much can the yeoman or his latter-day counterpart find to do in his little plot?), while he jealously watches over his shoulder to see that nobody gets ahead of him or trespasses on what is his own. The adherents to this social doctrine have always claimed that the citizen of their desired republic can be expected to put the collective good over private interest. But the content of this collective good is exhausted in the defense of the system of inviolable spheres of right against all domestic or foreign enemies. The sameness of different subjectivities must be ensured by their shared emptiness; any richness of subjective experience creates the danger of cumulative discord or hopeless self-absorption. The citizens may disguise their indignation at any departure from this sameness in the language of a pompous and unforgiving virtue. These emotions will sometimes give way to others: no social order can entirely submerge longing in routine. The individual fantasizes fabulous wants and satisfactions. If his own imagination is inadequate to generate these yearnings, he may receive them from other societies, or from the rebels and deviants he ostentatiously condemns but secretely envies, or even from the mere exaggeration of the satisfactions and desires he already experiences. Such longings can be counted on to be both persistent and forbidden. When openly flaunted, they will antagonize the regime. When denied, they may linger on, as resentment and self-contempt, to poison it.

The program of empowered democracy avoids these material and spiritual costs by redefining both the character and the forms of equality and participation. The rough equality of material circumstance that it seeks is meant to arise as the convergent effect of absolute claims to the satisfaction of minimal material needs (claims that rank among the immunity rights), the temporary and conditional character of access to capital, and the openness of the formative context of power and production to challenge and change. The participation in public life that it proposes is not the cult of altruistic goals rigidly contrasted to private ends, nor is it the fatal mania of meetings that invariably ends in boredom for the many and manipulation by the few. What it wants, instead, is to extend the scope and the clarity of private ambitions by enlarging our sense of the possible forms of association through which they may be realized and redefined. In this way, it seeks to superimpose upon the delights of private enjoyment the pleasures – neither private nor public – of creating, within society, distinctive but shared forms of life that permit shared but distinctive activities.

The radical democratic program outlined here is therefore less a sequel to the classical republican vision than a superliberalism. It pushes the liberal war against privilege and superstition to a point that requires the abandonment of the forms of governmental, economic, and legal organization with which liberalism has traditionally been associated. Having made its peace with modernity, it no longer needs to prepare the future by pretending to restore the past. This superliberalism is also the defensible form of a leftist ideal that breaks the spell of deep-logic social theory, confronts the need to think institutionally, refuses to define itself by reference to class interests shaped by the very institutions it wants to reconstruct, and seeks to further both freedom and equality by turning subversion into a practical way of life.

THE MEANING OF IMPERFECTION

Consider now three apparent dilemmas that, if true, would prove fatal to the programmatic argument. Each is false in its initial form. But each apparent dilemma can be reformulated as the description of a real risk. To acknowledge both the reasonableness and the seriousness of this risk is to emphasize the antiperfectionist character of the program. All that can be claimed for the institutional platform of the empowered democracy is that it represents an advance over the available forms of governmental and economic organization.

Self-Reproduction and Stability

A first apparent dilemma has to do with the self-reproducing quality of the constitution. On the one hand, the constitutional scheme may guarantee its own perpetuation by the success with which it informs motivations and shapes the occasions and instruments of conflict. But such a success at self-defense would discredit the authority of the institutional scheme, for it would show this scheme to be in flagrant violation of the animating ideal of revisability. The formative context of power and production would have become more rather than less entrenched, and the entrenchment would be all the more insidious for being largely automatic and invisible.

Suppose, on the other hand, that the institutional structure could be as easily revised as its claim to legitimacy requires. Imagine that the scope of conflict over the basic terms of social life were as ample as the programmatic argument implies. Then, any political party elevated to office that failed to share the vision underlying the institutional scheme would set out to change it. The decisional mobility the proposed style of governmental organization seeks to strengthen would make such changes all the easier to effect. Only a party that precisely shared the spirit of the constitution could be counted on to develop it according to its ideals.

Clearly, the dilemma draws attention to the relation between disentrenchment and institutional stability. The staying power of a formative context seems to depend to a large extent on its unavailability to revision.

It therefore also depends on the failure of written constitutions or legal rules to make this structure entirely explicit. To explicate the formative context while undermining all other obstacles to its revision seems to be a formula for transience.

The flaw in the description of this dilemma is the assumption that only the entrenchment of an institutional plan – only its protection against the destabilizing effects of ordinary conflict – can ensure its continuity. There is not, nor is there meant to be, any guarantee that this particular institutional plan will, once established, be perpetuated. The plan merely interprets, for a particular historical circumstance, an approach to the project of individual and collective empowerment. The institutional implications of the approach must challenge constantly and unpredictably. These changes will in turn suggest new interpretations of the animating ideas of the institutional plan. Moreover, parties may rise to power that are radically unsympathetic to the spirit of the proposed constitution. They may undo the constitutional plan. And the experiment in empowered democracy, once interrupted, may never be repeated. But do not suppose that an institutional plan can continue, or that its animating ideals can be upheld, only if it remains hard to revise. The argument for the new-model republic includes the hypothesis that once the increased opportunities for individual and collective self-assertion opened up by the empowered democracy are tasted, they will not easily be forgone. The hypothesis may prove wrong. But the spirit of empowered democracy requires us to put it to the test; every obstacle to institutional change takes something away from the distinctive design and ambition of this institutional program. The point is to undertake an experiment, an experiment in whose success we have reason to hope but whose integrity we wish above all to preserve. Here is a style of institution making that presupposes no contrast between an omniscient and benevolent Lycurgus (the founders, the revolutionaries, the fathers of their country) and the ordinary historical agents who live in the world Lycurgus has set up.

Militancy and Empowerment

A second dilemma refers to the psychological attitudes needed to avoid a perversion of the constitutional scheme. The institutional program, it seems, can achieve its desired objectives only if the citizens throw themselves ardently into the organized conflicts of the republic, conflicts whose resolution influences every facet of the institutional order and whose occasions recur in every domain of social life. In the absence of broadly based and wholehearted civic engagement, empowered democracy might suddenly turn from the freest constitution to the most despotic. As the citizens withdrew out of boredom or frustration, into their immediate concerns, the group in power would find in these institutional arrangements an unrivaled opportunity to turn transitory advantages into vested rights. The connections among spheres of social life, the ease with which programmatic experiments could be tried out, at least in the early years of the regime, and the weakening of independent centers of power able to stand up to these initiatives from the center – all this may open the way for the architects of a new order of privilege. The work of entrenchment and enserfment may be all the more dangerous by benefiting from the citizens' impression that they lived under the most free (though, unbeknown to them, also the most fragile) of constitutions.

If, on the other hand, only a constant militancy could prevent these perverse consequences, empowered democracy would depend upon unrealistic and indefensible assumptions about conduct and motivation. The implicit ideal of human existence would be too narrow and biased to carry authority. It would harm or downplay all those forms of subjective experience and practical problem solving that depend upon the containment of civic militancy, which threatens to consume the time of those whom it does not bore, or whom it does not intimidate into privatistic withdrawal.

But we have reason to downplay both horns of this apparent dilemma. The constitution of empowered democracy does not oppose private desires and collective devotions. Instead, it robs this polemical contrast of its force. It does so by enabling people more easily to extend the humdrum practice of pursuing interests within a framework of unquestioned institutional and imaginative assumptions into the extraordinary activity of questioning this framework. Thus, the practice of fantasy and enactment that the institutional program encourages is less a public militancy than an extension of the ordinary activity of defining goals and pursuing them. Its chosen expression is not civic pomp and heroic striving but the activity of a working life. And its favorite devices are conversations rather than meetings, conversations that continue when the meetings end.

On the other side, the constitutional plan eases the formation of a large number of perceived group interests in tension with one another. It multiplies the arenas in which the citizens may engage in organized conflict over the shape of social life. It breaks down the rigid roles and ranks that give stability to conceptions of group interest. It dissolves such conceptions into the more fluid crisscrossing lines of parties of opinion unanchored in social stations. It makes actual social life more closely resemble what, to a considerable extent, democratic party politics are actually like. Moreover, although the program of empowered democracy undermines the independent centers of social authority that a petrified division of labor or a stable corporatist organization of society sustains, it brings into existence other constraints upon central power.

Thus, what initially seemed an intolerable dilemma turns into a calculated risk. There is no assurance that empowered democracy will provide adequate safeguards against the danger that people may withdraw from civic life and through their withdrawal permit a new and more thoroughgoing entrenchment of factional interests. I claim only that the guarantees and benefits of the constitutional plan make it reasonable to run these risks.

Indeed, we must reach toward a regime such as empowered democracy if we are to reconcile freedom as empowerment with the practical drive toward plasticity in social life, the condition of collective wealth and power. Both our happiness and our virtue depend upon the particular institutional forms we give to the search for plasticity. Just as the quest for empowerment through plasticity may enable us to live out more fully our context-transcending identity, so, too, it may subject us to a despotism less messy or violent but more thoroughgoing than any yet known.

Solidarity and Empowerment

A final dilemma refers to the relation between the spirit of the constitution and the social ideals this spirit seems to antagonize. The programmatic argument would make no sense if the spirit of the constitution were neutral among all credible accounts of the meaning and requirements of our project of individual and collective self-assertion. For this argument assumes that neutrality is possible only in the highly limited sense defined earlier. But once we abandon the hope of neutrality we can recognize more frankly the bias and insufficiency of empowered democracy. Of all the values this institutional program downplays, the weightiest is the commitment to communal attachments and to the transforming virtues of personal love and of faith and hope in individual people. To the extent that the ideal of empowerment means something more limited than the general effort to achieve individual and collective self-assertion, it seems to value the development of individual and collective capabilities more than the continuance of particular loyalties to individuals and groups. It slights the customary practices in which such loyalties are inevitably embedded.

Empowered democracy represents only a partial vision of a form of life designed to help us to carry forward our efforts at self-assertion. The details of this vision reflect the legacy and the problems of a particular historical circumstance. The defense of the vision invokes a particular normative and explanatory approach. The content of the vision needs to be complemented by a conception of transformed personal relations.

The ideal of empowerment fails to make up the whole of a defensible social ideal. Taken in isolation, it does indeed threaten to submerge concern with trust under the power-mad or narcissistic flaunting of the will and the heartless cult of magnificent capability.

But the program of empowerment through institutional invention and cultural-revolutionary practice refines as well as threatens our experiences of solidarity. The reinvention and advancement of the radical project, in the form of empowered democracy, make it easier for us to give our attachments the qualities of love: the achievement of a heightened mutual vulnerability; the imaginative acceptance of other individuals that tears through the screen of stereotyped images, roles, and ranks; and the effacement of the conflict between our need for others and our fear of the jeopardy in which they place us. These qualities of love represent the least illusory and most durable aspect of our communal ideals: the part best able to outlast the disappointments of life and the surprises of history.

In many convergent ways the program of empowerment reinforces the ideals of solidarity that it also jeopardizes. The proposals extend a series of social changes that shake up and leave permanently weakened all roles and ranks. The more rigid and influential such divisions and hierarchies are, the more do our attachments and animosities stay entangled in a vitiating dilemma. Every allegiance remains susceptible to confusion with craven role playing or with the exchange of exploitation and servility between oppressors and oppressed. Conversely, every attempt by the subjugated to win more independence seems to require the betrayal of loyalties that represent the strongest available examples of community. The institutionalized destabilization of the hierarchical and divided order of society diminishes the opportunities for this equivocation. It allows us to attach ourselves to others without accepting subservience and to become more free without turning against those to whom we feel closest.

The program of empowerment makes a second contribution to the improvement of solidarity. It strengthens the liberty of the individual to forgive the harms other people do him. The record of these wrongs tempts him to search for preemptive security against other people. It freezes him into strategies of distancing and defense. The empowered are freer to be generous. They can more readily lift the burden of frustration and resentment and imagine themselves related to others in untried ways – especially in ways that diminish the conflict between attachment and independent self-assertion.

The result is a benefit to society, in the form of a boost to collaboration. Above all, however, it is a gain to the individual. For that conflict blocks human capability – to be, to do, to produce, and to connect.

In yet a third and most significant way the program of empowerment helps better our relations to one another. The institutionalized breakdown of rigid ranks and roles continues the work of democracy: it saves us from remaining placeholders in a system of predefined social stations. As the grip of these stations upon individual experience loosens, we become more able to deal with one another, imaginatively and practically, as individuals rather than as stand-ins for collective categories of class, gender, nationality, or race. This opportunity to address the other as a concrete individual never completely defined by the coordinates of his place on a social map is a mark of love. The style of solidarity favored by empowered democracy draws our communal relations closer to love just as it undermines sharp contrasts between the communal and the noncommunal aspects of life in society.

Some may object that they prefer the old version of community, the version based on the opposition of insiders and outsiders, on the intolerance of conflict within the group, on the jealous defense of exclusive communal traditions, on the commitment to outward, even inherited signs of joint identity, and on the insistent sharing of values and preconceptions. But this antique style of solidarity is less capable of reconciliation with other basic goals of ours, less likely to outlast the illusions of false necessity, and therefore also less capable of making us happy. For the happiness it grants us requires special circumstances of social tranquillity and unchallenged prejudice and depends on the maintenance of conditions that hinder the development of our powers.

Considerations like these – informed promises of happiness – rather than assessments of conformity to ready-made standards of right and wrong are what do and should matter to us in the criticism and justification of forms of social life. Such considerations exemplify the methods employed by political argument under the impact of enlightenment about false necessity. They also complement and correct the more closely textured varieties of social criticism that contrast our distinct, received ideals of human association with the practical arrangements supposed to realize these ideals in fact.

Two great constructive forces work upon social life. One force is restless experimentation with institutions, ideas, and techniques for the sake of enhancing our practical capabilities. This search for growth in worldly power shades into the quest for another, less tangible empowerment: the ability to question and revise our shared institutional and imaginative assumptions as we go about the daily business of life. It is the opportunity to join engagement with self-consciousness, and to avoid the choice between alienation and stupefaction, to act confidently within a society or a culture without becoming its puppets. The overlap between the conditions for these two modes of empowerment is a surprising fact rather than a self-evident truth.

The other major constructive force is our acceptance of one another across the barriers of division and hierarchy that keep us apart. We want access to relations and communities that limit the conflict between our need to affirm ourselves in one another's presence and our struggle to escape the incalculable dangers we pose to one another. We want something better than the middle distance, and we know that failure to find it leaves us homeless in the world.

The reformed democracy directly serves the search for empowerment both as practical capability and as mastery over context. Its point is to secure capability to the individual as well as to the society. This aim connects the program to the liberal tradition. But because the commitment to empower individuals – not just societies or groups – sees through the eyes of a theory that looks beyond false necessity, it requires us to break with institutional arrangements that liberals have traditionally identified with their cause. To complete this rupture, we must free ourselves from the received contrast between liberal and socialist programs, which depends upon the same superstitions.

The program of radical democracy has a more troubled relation to the strengthening and cleansing of solidarity. The fulfillment of its proposals does not ensure us of coexisting in peace. It does not take away our hearts of stone and give us hearts of flesh. But it does enable us to live out more fully the tense, ambiguous, ennobling connection between solidarity and empowerment, between the experience of mutual acceptance and the development of our faculties, between our longing for one another and our efforts to find particular expressions for the impulse within us that rebels against all particularity. What more could we ask of society than a better chance to be both great and sweet?

Thematic Index

Proper-Name Index

Printed in the United States
by Baker & Taylor Publisher Services